Joseph Adam Gustav Hergenröther

Catholic Church And Christian State

A Series of Essays on the Relation of the Church to the Civil Power

Joseph Adam Gustav Hergenröther

Catholic Church And Christian State
A Series of Essays on the Relation of the Church to the Civil Power

ISBN/EAN: 9783744725286

Printed in Europe, USA, Canada, Australia, Japan

Cover: Foto ©ninafisch / pixelio.de

More available books at **www.hansebooks.com**

Catholic Church and Christian State.

A SERIES OF ESSAYS

ON THE

RELATION OF THE CHURCH TO THE CIVIL POWER.

TRANSLATED, WITH THE PERMISSION OF THE AUTHOR, FROM THE GERMAN

OF

DR. JOSEPH HERGENRÖTHER,

PROFESSOR OF CANON LAW AND CHURCH HISTORY AT THE UNIVERSITY OF WÜRZBURG.

IN TWO VOLUMES.

VOL. II.

LONDON: BURNS AND OATES,
Portman Street and Paternoster Row.
1876.

CONTENTS.

ESSAY IX.

THE POPE AND THE HOLY ROMAN EMPIRE.

PART I. THE PAPACY AND THE EMPIRE, FROM THE FOUNDATION OF THE EMPIRE TO FREDERICK II.

PART II. CONFLICT OF FREDERICK II. WITH THE CHURCH.

- - - - .

ESSAY X.

THE POPES AND THEIR VASSAL KINGDOMS.

PART I. PAPAL FIEFS IN ITALY.

PART II. PAPAL FIEFS OUT OF ITALY.

ESSAY XI.

BONIFACE VIII. AND PHILIP THE FAIR.

PART I. BONIFACE VIII. AND PHILIP THE FAIR UNTIL THE PUBLICATION OF THE BULL 'UNAM SANCTAM.'

PART II. THE BULL 'UNAM SANCTAM.' CONTINUATION OF THE DISPUTE.

ESSAY XII.

GIFTS OF LAND MADE BY THE POPES AND THE DONATION OF CONSTANTINE.

PART I. GIFTS OF LAND MADE BY THE POPES.

PART II. THE DONATION OF CONSTANTINE.

ESSAY XIII.

THE DOCTRINE OF THE SUPERIORITY OF THE CHURCH AND OF HER AUTHORITY IN MATTERS TEMPORAL.

PART I. THE DOCTRINE OF THE PRE-EMINENCE OF THE CHURCH.

Contents.

ESSAY XIV.

ORIGIN OF THE CIVIL POWER AND THE RIGHT OF RESISTING IT.

PART I. ORIGIN OF THE CIVIL POWER.

ESSAY XV.

ECCLESIASTICAL JURISDICTION.

PART I. ECCLESIASTICAL JURISDICTION BEFORE THE THIRTEENTH AND FOURTEENTH CENTURIES.

PART II. ECCLESIASTICAL JURISDICTION SINCE THE THIRTEENTH AND FOURTEENTH CENTURIES.

Contents.

ESSAY XVI.

THE PUNISHMENT OF HERESY AND THE INQUISITION.

PART I. THE PUNISHMENT OF HERESY.

PART II. THE INQUISITION AND WITCHCRAFT.

ESSAY XVII.

THE CHURCH AND LIBERTY OF CONSCIENCE.

ESSAY XVIII.

CLAIMS OF THE POPE SINCE THE SIXTEENTH CENTURY.

THE

Catholic Church and the Christian State.

———————

ESSAY IX.

THE POPE AND THE HOLY ROMAN EMPIRE.

THE relation of the Pope towards the Holy Roman Empire has been interpreted in various ways, according to the views or prepossessions of the historian. If its origin be ignored, the empire is not seldom confused with the kingdom of Germany, and Popes are charged with having maintained immoderate pretensions against emperors. In the first part of this essay we propose to examine the Papacy and the Empire down to Frederick II.; in the second part, the struggle of Frederick II. with the Church; in the third part, the Empire until its fall.

PART I. THE PAPACY AND THE EMPIRE, FROM THE FOUNDATION OF THE EMPIRE TO FREDERICK II.

§ 1. The empire founded by the Pope. § 2. 3. Under the Carolingian kings. § 4. From Otho I. to Henry III. § 5. From Henry III. to Frederick I. § 6. Schemes of Frederick I. § 7. His conduct towards the Pope. § 8. His excommunication and reconciliation with the Church. § 9. Henry IV. § 10. Conflict between Philip of Swabia and Otho IV. § 11. Otho IV.

§ 1.

It is an historical fact that at Christmas, A.D. 800, Pope Leo III., in the person of Charles the Great, restored the Empire of the West, which included in the ideas of that time the protection

of the Church and the supreme guidance of Christian peoples in
civil affairs.[1]   The See of Rome had perhaps for some time
contemplated this elevation of its powerful protector. Hadrian
I. in 777 said that the world would at some future time see a
new Constantine[2] in Charles the Great, and in 778 expressed
the wish that God would make him victorious over all barbarous
nations.[3]   Still, Leo III. on the day of Charles' coronation
was able, in the face of the whole world, to claim as his own
act the emperor's elevation to the imperial dignity, for the defence and protection of the Church.[4]   He acted in this matter
as head of the Church; not, as many have pretended, merely
as an instrument of Charles' policy. There is no historical foundation for such an assertion. He acted primarily as spiritual
head of the Church, though he was at the same time civil head
of the Romans. The Roman people, who could not have given
a protector to the Universal Church, added to Charles' elevation
those joyful acclamations which were a sign of its completion.[5]
In later times it was universally acknowledged that only a prince
anointed and crowned by the Pope could possess the full imperial
dignity. Even in diplomas the dates of the empire and of the
kingdom were put separate, and the former was often vacant
when the latter was occupied.[6]

Unless Charles the Great had received the title of emperor
from the Pope he must have conferred it on himself. At that
time this could not well have been ; it is supported by no historical witness, and is, on the contrary, disproved by Eginhard's
testimony to the astonishment and reluctance with which Charles
heard of the Pope's intention.[7]   Neither did he receive it by
right of conquest. He came to Rome in 800, not as a conqueror,
but at the prayer of Leo III., to quell a rebellion. He came
as protector of the Holy See, an office held by him as well as by
his father and grandfather, in virtue of the patriarchate conferred
upon them by the Popes. He did not owe his elevation to the
conquest of Rome and Italy.[8]

---

[1] Cf. Niehues, Gesch. des Verhältnisses zwischen Kaiserthum und
Papstthum im M.A. Münster, 1863, vol. i. p. 588 seq.
[2] Ep. ad Carol. Mansi, Conc. xii. 819. Jaffé, Reg. n. 1854, p. 207.

[3] Mansi, l.c. p. 776. Jaffe, n. 1857, pp. 207, 208.

[4] Leo III. Diploma of the 25th Dec. 800. Jaffe, n. 1913, pp. 217, 218: 'Quem (Car.) auctore Deo in defensionem et provectum universalis S. Ecclesiae Augustum hodie sacravimus.'

[5] Natal. Alex. H. E. saec. 9 et 10, dissert. 2, t. vi. p. 397. Bianchi, t. ii. l. v. § 4, n. 1 seq. p. 178 seq. Mamachi, l.c. pp. 242, 243, nota 2. Cf. specially Otto Frising. de Gest. Frid. ii. 22.

[6] Eugen. Lombard. Regale Sacerdot. l. i. § 5, p. 148. Rigantius in Regul. Cancell. Apost. t. ii. p. 226, Reg. 17, n. 9. Muratori, Annali d' Italia, a. 1433, 1493, 1519. Bianchi, l.c. § 3, 4, pp. 164 seq. 177 seq. Phillips, K.R. iii. § 122 seq. p. 92 seq. Cf. also J. N. Neller, Dissert. de Rom. Imp. Idea, in Schmidt, Thes. jur. Eccles. t. iii. pp. 328 seq. 346.

[7] Einhard, Vita Caroli M. (Pertz, Scr. g. ii. 457, 458).

[8] Gosselin, P. ii. pp. 311, 312. Cf. Schrödl, Votum des Katholicismus.

§ 2.

Emperors themselves (for instance, Louis II. in his letter to Basil the Macedonian) have declared it to be beyond doubt that the dignity of emperor was conferred by the Pope's anointing and consecration.[1]

It is certain that in crowning Charles the Great emperor of the West, the Pope had no intention of conferring upon him an hereditary dignity, neither of relinquishing for the future his right of electing the most suitable protector for the Holy See. No historical witness confirms the supposition that the dignity conferred was hereditary; everything speaks to the contrary. No dispositions as to the imperial office were made in the deed of partition at Diedenhofen in 806,[2] although disputes might easily have arisen on this ground. The guardianship and defence of the Holy See were committed to Charles' three sons collectively, after the example of Charles Martel, Pipin, and their father. Italy is apportioned, but only 'to the boundary of St. Peter's territory.' Those who ascribe to the emperor the right of disposing of the imperial title[3] find it difficult to explain the silence concerning it. This is, however, easily understood when the rights of the Pope are given due weight.[4] Charles, no doubt, had associated his son Louis in the empire and called him emperor, but this must have been done with the Pope's consent.[5] The Pope approved also the partition treaty of 806.[6] Louis the Pious was crowned emperor in 816 by Pope Stephen IV. (V.).

Lothair I. informed his father Louis that he had received from Pope
Paschal the blessings, dignity, and title of the imperial office
(April 5, 823).[7] He would not have said this if the empire had
been positively and irrevocably conferred upon him some years
earlier, when his father associated him in the government; in
fact, he only assumed the title after his coronation by the Pope.[8]
Lothair's son, Louis II., was likewise anointed and crowned by
Leo IV.[9]

[1] Baron. a. 871, n. 50 seq. Pertz, v. p. 521 seq. Some critics have
expressed doubts concerning this letter, but for quite insufficient reasons.
It throughout accords with the circumstances of the time. Cf. Annal.
Moissiac. h.a. Anschar. Vita S. Willehadi ap. Mabill. saec. 3, O.S.B. P. ii.
Chron. Ursperg. a. 800; Einhard, Ann.; Pertz, Scr. i. 189; Natal. Alex.
saec. 9, diss. 1.
[2] Pertz, Leg. i. 141. Baluz. Capit. i. 437.
[3] De la Bruère, Hist. de Charlemagne, t. ii. p. 170.
[4] Gosselin, l.c. pp. 312-314.
[5] Ib. p. 319.
[6] Einhard, Ann. a. 806, p. 193. Jaffé, Reg. p. 218.
[7] Mabillon, Acta O.S.B. saec. 4, p. 513.
[8] Bianchi, l.c. § 5, n. 1-3, where also the hypotheses of Bossuet are
refuted. Vide Defens. Decl. Cleri. Gall. P. i. l. ii. c. xxxvii. seq.
[9] Nicol. Ep. 26. Mansi, xv. 288. Jaffé, n. 2104, p. 247. Hefele,
Conc. iv. p. 282 seq.

§ 3.

After the death of Louis II. Pope John VIII. elected Charles
the Bald, in preference to Louis the German, and crowned him
emperor in December 875. All that time the right of the Pope
to confer the imperial crown upon whom he would was undoubted; it was acknowledged even by the Lombard nobles at
the Synod of Pavia in 876.[1] After the death of Charles II. in
877 his nephew, Carloman of Bavaria, applied to the Pope for
the imperial dignity,[2] but his ill-health was an impediment.
John VIII. expressly declared: 'He who is by us anointed for
the empire must first of all by us be called and chosen.'[3]
Shortly afterwards, in 879, Charles the Fat was elected emperor,[4]
and in 881 was anointed and crowned by the same Pope.
During his residence in France, John VIII. had, on September
8, 878, crowned Louis the Stammerer king, but not emperor,
as later we find him giving Louis only the latter title.[5] Stephen

V. (VI.), 21st February 891, conferred the imperial crown upon
Duke Wido, or Guido, of Spoleto, who was only related on the
female side to the family of Charles the Great; and his successor,
Formosus, gave it to Guido's son Lambert on the 27th February
892.[6] But as Lambert disappointed the hopes of the Holy See,
and afforded no protection, the Pope rejected him, and sent for
Arnulf from Germany to raise him to the imperial throne.[7] In
this first age of the renewed life of the Western Roman Empire
we find descendants of Charles the Great, in France, Germany, and
Italy, crowned as emperors by the Popes. Also Louis of Provence,
son of Boso, received the empire from Benedict IV. in 901, and
Berengarius in 916 from John X.[8] Where the Pope was not
influenced by external force he disposed of it as he would.

[1] Mansi, l.c. pp. 303, 304, 308 seq. Hefele, iv. p. 495. It is said in
the synodal decree confirmed at Pontion in June 875 : ' Quia divina pietas
vos beatorum principum Apostolorum Petri et Pauli interventione, per
vicarium ipsorum, D. videl. Joannem, summum pontificem et universalem
Papam, spiritualemque patrem vestrum, ad profectum S. Dei Ecclesiae
nostramque omnium invitavit et ad imperiale culmen Sancti Spiritus
judicio provexit, nos unanimiter vos protectorem, dominum ac defensorem
omnium nostrum eligimus.'
[2] Joh. Ep. 63, 68. Mansi, l.c. pp. 53, 57. Jaffé, n. 2342, 2347, p. 270.
[3] Joh. Ep. 135, ad Anspert. Mediol. p. 108. J. n. 2449, p. 278 seq.
[4] Joh. Ep. 160, 172, pp. 110, 111, 117. J. n. 2453, 2464, p. 279 seq.
[5] Joh. Ep. 125, 128, pp. 95, 97. J. n. 2422, 2421, p. 277. Sirmond.
nota ap. Mansi, l.c. p. 358. Bianchi, l.c. § 5, n. 6. pp. 210, 211.
[6] Jaffé, pp. 298, 299.
[7] The rejection of Lambert can be gathered from (1) the oath sworn
to Arnulf by the Romans (Luitpr. Hist. i. 8); (2) the hatred of the Italian
party against Formosus even after his death; (3) the can. 6 of the Roman
Synod of 898 (Hefele, iv. 543).
[8] Jaffé, pp. 306, 310. Bianchi, l.c. § 5, n. 4 seq. § 6, n. 1-3.

§ 4.

From 924 to 962 the empire of the West was vacant. The
line of German Roman emperors begins, strictly speaking, with
Otho I., who was crowned at Rome in 962.[1] During his own
lifetime, on the 25th December 967, he obtained the empire for
his son and namesake.[2] After the death of Otho II., A.D. 983,
Otho III. was crowned king at Aix-la-Chapelle, but was not
emperor till 996, when he was crowned by Gregory V.[3] The

diploma of Leo VIII., which ascribes to Otho the Great the right
of appointing his successor (not primarily to the empire, but) to
the kingdom of Italy would, as the work of an antipope, have no
weight, even were it not as much a forgery[4] as the false privilege
it cites of Hadrian I. in favour of Charles the Great.[5] Twelve
years after the death of Otho III. St. Henry II. received the imperial crown, after having sworn allegiance to Benedict VIII.
(14th February 1014).[6] Henry II. (as Emperor, Henry I.) had
felt the need of being emperor. Conrad the Salic obtained this
dignity more quickly[7] (26th March 1027); his son Henry III.
(as Emperor, Henry II.)[8] was crowned at Rome by Clement II.
on the 25th December 1046.[9] Henry obtained from Pope
Victor II., who was much attached to him, that he should forbid
Ferdinand, King of Castile, from continuing the title of emperor
under pain of excommunication.[10] No one was surprised at this;
and yet in the ancient Roman Empire powerful captains had
taken the title, and it had met with acknowledgment. At his
death (on the 5th October 1056) Henry placed his son under
the protection of the Pope, to whom also he transferred the administration of the kingdom;[11] but before a twelvemonth had
elapsed Victor had followed him into the grave (on the 28th
July 1057). During its second period, from Otho I. to Henry
III., the empire became too powerful, exercised great authority
over appointments to the Papal See, as formerly had been done by
the Italian nobles, to the injury of the Church. A reaction was imperative, for the vital interests of the Church were at stake. An
arrangement useful during a period of danger and difficulty was
not intended for all time. It was necessary that the Church
should become more free and independent. She became so in
the great struggle about investitures.

    [1] Concerning the coronation of Otho I. we read : ' A Johanne P. ama-
biliter exceptus atque honore imperiali sublimatus est' (Flodoard. Ann.
Rem. 962) ; 'Otto rex consecratione Johannis P. imperator Romae factus
est' (Annal. Ottenburg. h.a.) ; 'Joh. P. (Ottonem) consecratione sua imperatorem fecit' (Lambert). Cf. Luitprand, vi. 6 ; Regin. Contin. a. 962.
    [2] Reginon. Contin. a. 967. Annal. Hildes. h.a. Otto I. Ep. ap. Baron.
a. 968, n. 7.
    [3] Thietmar, Chron. l. iv. c. xviii. Annal. Quedlinburg. h.a. Cf. Phillips,
K.R. iii. § 123, p. 122.

⁴ C. 23, In Synodo, d. 63.   Cf. Baron. Pag. ad a. 964 ; Berardi Gratiani, Can. Gen. ii. ii. p. 307 ; Bianchi, t. ii. l. v. § 6, n. 5 seq. p. 226 seq.; Phillips, l.c. p. 119 ; Floss, Die Papstwahl unter den Ottonen, Freib. 1858, p. 65 seq.
⁵ C. 22, Hadrianus P. d. 63.   Cf. Berardi, l.c. p. 187 ; Phillips, l.c. p. 150.
⁶ Thietmar, Chron. (Pertz, v. 836).   Jaffé, p. 352.
⁷ Wippo, Vita Conradi ap. Pistor. Rer. g. Scr. iii. p. 472. Jaffé, p. 358.
⁸ As the German King Henry I. was not emperor, Henry III. called himself Henricus Secundus, for instance at the Synod at Mainz of October 1049 (Jaffé, n. 3187, p. 370).
⁹ Jaffé, p. 364.
¹⁰ Baron. a. 1055, n. 23.   Will, Victor II. als Papst und deutscher Reichsverweser, pp. 20, 55 seq.
¹¹ Petrus Damiani, l. i. Ep. 5 ; Greg. VII. Reg. l. i. Ep. 19. Will, l.c. pp. 48, 50 seq.

§ 5.

From the death of Henry III. (1056) to the enforced coronation of Henry V. by Paschal II. (1111) there was no lawful emperor.[1] Under Henry V. the same distinction was made between empire and kingdom, for example,[2] at the Concordat of Worms.[3] Lothair did not till the eighth year of his reign as king, on the 4th June 1133, receive the imperial crown from Innocent II.[4] His election as King of Germany, which according to custom gave a right to expect the dignity of emperor, had been confirmed by Honorius II. ;[5] this must have been done with a view to his becoming emperor at some future time, as the election to the kingdom did not require Papal ratification.   Lothair's successor, Conrad III., was never emperor, but was 'King of the Romans,' because he had the expectation of becoming emperor.[6] Only on a few occasions Conrad styled himself, and allowed others to style him, emperor.[7]   He did not comply with the request the Romans made him as their king ; on the contrary, he opened friendly negotiations with the Pope, at that time much oppressed by the mob leaders.[8] Frederick Barbarossa also rejected with scorn the pompous overtures of the republican Romans ;[9] he desired to be crowned by the Pope, like other emperors, treated on the subject with Eugenius III., and was crowned by Hadrian IV. on the 18th July 1155.[10]   Coronation by the Pope was never regarded as an empty ceremony ; it was accounted an all-important and most solemn act, conferring the supreme civil power and the authority of chief protector of Christendom.

[1] Henry V.'s father had only been crowned by the Antipope Guibert, Clement III., in 1084. Jaffé, Reg. p. 444.

[2] Jaffé, n. 5079, p. 540: 'Nihil Henrice, de jure tuo vindicare sibi quaerit Ecclesia; *nec regni nec imperii* gloriam affectamus; obtineat Ecclesia quod Christi est, habeat imperator, quod suum est; si nos audire volueris, cum temporalis *regni et imperii* fastigio etiam aeterni regni gloriàm consequeris.'

[3] Hefele, Conc. v. p. 334. The regnum Teutonicum is quite different from the imperium, as is recognised by Gregory VII. in 1080 (l. viii. Ep. 9, Mansi, xx. 321; Jaffé, n. 3905, p. 436), by Paschal II. in 1105 and 1106 (Mansi, l.c. p. 1209; Jaffé, pp. 490, 492, n. 4515, 4540), by Innocent II. in 1130 (Jaffé, n. 5318, 5321, p. 561), by Eugenius III. in 1148, 1149 (J. n. 6403, 6469, pp. 632, 636), by Alexander III. (Ep. 30, p. 103; Ep. 192, p. 257, ed. Migne), and frequently elsewhere.

[4] Otto Fris. Chron. vii. 18; Suger, in Vita Ludov. vi.; Chron. Maur. a. 1133; Baron. h.a. n. 1-4; Jaffé, p. 571.

[5] Innocent II. on the 20th June 1130 writes to the German bishops (Jaffé, l.c. n. 5321): 'Praedecessor siquidem noster f. m. P. Honorius pro unitate Ecclesiae conservanda et statu imperii in melius reformando, quod a vobis de eo (Loth.) factum fuerit, *auctoritate apostolica confirmavit* ipsumque pro suscipienda imperialis dignitatis plenitudine .... ad Sedem Apostolicam evocavit.' Cf. Ep. ap. Mansi, xxi. 428; J. n. 5320.

[6] 'Rex Romanorum' he is styled by Eugenius III. in the letter of December 11, 1146, as well as in several later ones (J. n. 6273, 6305, 6333, 6343, pp. 624, 626, 628). 'Imperator' is found once, it may be through an error of the copyist or dictating clerk, or possibly because the coronation was shortly expected to take place (Jaffé, n. 6402, p. 632).

[7] Pag. a. 1138, n 3; a. 1149, n. 1. Bianchi, l.c. § 7, n. 8. In the confirmation in 1138 of the privileges granted by Lothair to the monastery of Stablo, the words of the former privilege were repeated according to custom; but instead of 'imperialis sollicitudo' is put 'regia;' instead of 'imperium,' 'regnum.' Cf. the diploma in Migne, clxxxix. pp. 1467, 1471. Canute, King of Denmark, when seeking help from him, called him emperor, and looked upon it as his duty as 'pater justitiae filiusque pacis' to interfere on his behalf. In the same way the other pretender, Swen, placed himself under Conrad's protection.

[8] Otto Frising. de Gest. Frid. I. l. i. c. xxviii. Wibald, Ep. 211, 212.

[9] Otto Frising. l.c. ii. 21. Baron. a. 1155, n. 9 seq. Hefele, Conc. v. p. 475 seq.

[10] Otto Fris. l. ii. c. xxiii. Jaffé, p. 663.

[11] Card. de Arag. in Vita Hadr. Anon. Vat. ap. Baron. a. 1155. Thomassin, P. ii. l. iii. c. lxv. n. 4 seq.

[12] Ep. Conc. Papiens. (Pertz, Leg. ii. 126). Chron. Vinc. Prag. ap. Dobner, Mon. Hist. Boh. i. 68. Jaffé, p. 828.

§ 6.

In spite of Frederick's refusal to receive a democratic sovereignty from the favour of the Roman people, he was by no means disposed to submit to the views of the Pope and the Church concerning the imperial crown, as they had been understood since the time of Charles the Great. His was an imperious spirit, imbued with the notion of Roman law as expounded to him by the jurists of Bologna, especially at the diet held on the fields of Roncaglia (1158). His journey to the East, whither he had accompanied his uncle, Conrad III., had acquainted him with the absolute authority of the Greek emperor and the Saracen sultan. He desired, like a second Justinian, to be an absolute and independent ruler, and to reduce everything to submission to his sway—Pope, princes, and towns, especially the flourishing towns of Italy. He delighted in the phrases, 'I am lord of the world,' 'The will of the ruler is law.'[1] He intended to make the Pope serve his ambitious purpose of universal dominion, and attack with the spiritual sword what Frederick desired to seize with the material sword.[2] It was the same thing as Napoleon's demand on Pius VII.: 'My enemies must be also yours.'[3] Frederick disregarded the whole historical development of the Christian German Empire, and sought to restore the conditions and circumstances of the Roman Empire of old. But the universal feeling of the time was against this. Bishop Arnulf of Lisieux, in his speech at the opening of the Council at Tours[4] in 1163, only confirmed the words spoken by Cardinal Roland at Besançon in 1159, which were ill received at the time : 'From whom has the emperor received his empire (imperium) if not from the Pope ?'[5] The biographer of St. Adalbert writes: 'Rome alone can make kings into emperors.'[6] This condition was at the root of the petition preferred by the Saxons to Gregory VII., as Bossuet has acknowledged.[7] It asserted itself in spite of the many efforts of the Hohenstaufens against it. It was confirmed in the fourteenth century by Ludolf of Bebenberg, one of the most esteemed of jurists ;[8] also by many other writers.[9]

---

[1] L. ix. ff. xiv. 2; l. i. ff. i. 4. Radev. l.c. ii. 4.
[2] Joh. Sar. Ep. 59 (Migne, PP. Lat. cxcix. p. 39): 'Promittebat se

totius orbis reformaturum imperium et urbi subjiciendum orbem eventu-
que facili omnia subacturum, si ci ad hoc solius Romani Pontificis favor
adesset.   Id enim agebat, ut in quemcumque denunciatis inimicitiis
materialem gladium imperator in eumdem Rom. Pontifex spiritualem
gladium exerceret.'
      [3] Letter of the 13th Feb. 1806.   Artaud, Hist. de Pie VII. t. ii. c. xi.
pp. 131-134.
      [4] Mansi, xxi. 1167 seq.   Hefcle, v. 542.
      [5] Radev. l. i. c. x.
      [6] Vita S. Adalb. Prag. ap. Mabillon, saec. 5, O.S.B.   Pertz, M. vi. 590.
      [7] Bruno de Bello Saxon. et Vit. Henr. IV. ap. Urst. p. 382.   Bossuet,
l.c. l. i. sect. 1, c. xii. p. 109. Bossuet remarks on this passage, l. iv. c. ix.
p. 352: 'Quae profecto ostendunt, his jam temporibus in Rom. Pontifice
fuisse notatum peculiare aliquod jus ad constituendum eum regem, qui
postea imperator futurus esset, atque ad eum postea deponendum.'
      [8] De zelo principum Germ. c. 7 seq. ed. Argent. 1609.
      [9] Anon. de potest. Papae ap. Richer, Vindic. doct. maj. schol. Paris.
Colon. 1683, iv. p. 188; Joh. de Parisiis, de pot. reg. et pap. c. xv. xvi.
p. 107, Bossuet, l.c. p. 354.

§ 7.

Frederick Barbarossa was already displeased with Hadrian
IV. for the peace he had concluded with King William III.,
whereby Frederick was deprived of a pretext for making war
on this prince, and thus of conquering Italy.   His displeasure
was fostered by a small party of ambitious cardinals, who were
in close alliance with him.   He also violated in many ways the
Concordat of Worms, and did nothing for the release of the
Archbishop of Lund, who had been taken prisoner in his dominions, although the Pope urged him to this duty.   He wil-
fully misinterpreted Hadrian's complaints on this subject,[1]
poured out volleys of invective against Rome, and asserted that
he had received the kingdom and the empire direct from God
through his election by the princes.[2]   He endeavoured to gain
the bishops of Germany to his side, and many of them wrote to
the Pope from Frederick's point of view.   His sovereign dignity
appeared to him disparaged by an inscription on a painting in
the church of the Lateran ;[3] but later he owned himself satisfied
with the Pope's explanation of the matter.[4]   Their reconciliation
was, however, not complete, and the Pope soon had further
cause to complain of the emperor, for his arbitrary appointments
to bishoprics, and also concerning the decrees of Roncaglia with

regard to the imperial rights of supremacy and the regalia, which were extended so widely. Frederick was ever on the watch for pretexts of complaint against the Pope; he neither listened to the Pope's demands nor gave admittance to his legates.[5] Contrary to custom and respectful observance, he placed his own name in his letters before the name of the Pope.[6] Hadrian IV. a few months before his death, on the 24th June 1159, sent him a solemn admonition,[7] and death alone prevented him from excommunicating the emperor.

¹ Radevic. de Gest. Frid. i. 9. Mansi, xxi. 789. Jaffé, n. 6991, p. 669.

² Radev. i. 10. Pertz, Leg. ii. 105.

³ Radev. i. 15, 16. Würdtwein, Nova subsid. Diplom. xiii. 33. Bossuet, l.c. c. ix. p. 352.

⁴ Radev. i. 22. Mansi, l.c. p. 793. J. n. 7036, p. 672. 'Hoc nomen,' the Pope wrote, 'ex bono et facto est editum et dicitur beneficium apud nos non feudum, sed bonum factum.' The words 'contulimus tibi insigne imperialis coronae' are equal to 'imposuimus coronam.' Even Frederick says of the Pope (Ep. ad Otton. Fris.), 'benedictionem coronae Romani Imperii super caput nostrum effudit,' and quite separates the 'prima unctio regui Teutonici' from the coronation as emperor. Otto of Freising, i. 22, says: 'Imperii coronam accepit anno regni sui quarto.'

⁵ Cf. Döllinger, Lehrbuch der K.G. ii. p. 173 seq. against Bossuet, t. i. l. iii. c. xviii. p. 312 seq. Vide Bianchi, t. ii. l. v. § 13, n. 6 seq. p. 344 seq.

⁶ As early as 865 Nicholas I. blamed a King of Britain for doing this. Mansi, xv. 471. J. n. 2118, p. 248.

⁷ 'Resipisce igitur, resipisce, tibi consulimus quia cum a nobis consecrationem et coronam merueris, dum inconcessa captas, ne concessa perdas tuae nobilitati timemus.' Mansi, xxi. 796. J. n. 7121, p. 677.

§ 8.

Pope Alexander II., elected by a majority of the cardinals, was opposed by Octavian as antipope under the name of Victor IV. Victor was supported by the powerful protection of the emperor, who found in him a willing instrument. In vain did Alexander's electors, whose right had thus been violated, admonish the emperor to return to his duty of protecting the Church.[1] In October 1159, Frederick convoked an 'Ecumenical Council' at Pavia, which was to settle the dispute; but he showed beforehand the bias of his decision by calling the antipope Bishop of Rome, and the lawfully elected Alexander only Cardinal Roland. It was impossible for Alexander III. to submit his just cause to an assembly held under the influence of the emperor. The Council, as Frederick intended, decided in favour of the antipope,[2] invested him with the ring, and clothed him in the Papal robes[3] (Feb. 1160). Alexander complained of Frederick's tyrannical proceedings in the States of the Church, of the illegal imprisonment of prelates returning to Rome, of the favour shown to the schismatic Octavian and his usurpation, and of the unjust decision of the Council of Pavia.[4] At the same time he spared no pains to effect the conversion of the emperor,[5] although after the Council at Pavia he excommunicated him, and, as the real cause of schism and devastator of the Church,[6] released his subjects from their oath of allegiance.[7]

Frederick continued to uphold the schism, persecuted the Pope in Italy so much that he was obliged to seek refuge in France, intrigued against him even there, ill-treated his followers in his dominions, and after the death of the first antipope elected successively two others. Strict Catholics no longer regarded Frederick Barbarossa as emperor,[8] and looked upon Alexander III. as the refuge of the liberties of the Church. The Pope's courageous firmness conquered at length. In November 1165 he returned to Italy, and continued to reside there. Frederick's reverses in the peninsula overthrew his military fame; and, humbled by misfortune, he renounced his schism at the peace of Venice in 1777, and was released from his excommunication. Alexander acted towards him at this time with so much moderation and magnanimity, that until his death, 30th August 1181, Frederick preserved for him esteem and friendship.[9] New discords, however, arose between Frederick and the successors of Alexander, owing to the outrages of Frederick and his son Henry against the liberty of the Church and the Papal States.[10]

[1] 'Qualiter ex imperialis officio dignitatis (S. R. Ecclesiam) protegere debeatis modis omnibus ac tueri.' Radev. ii. 23. Migne, PP. Lat. t. cc. p. 62.

[2] Hefele, Conc. v. p. 509 seq.

[3] Alex. III. Ep. 19 (Migne, l.c. p. 90; Jaffé, n. 7146, p. 681) : ' Ceterum, ut praedictus imperator Ecclesiam Dei suae videretur subjugare et supponere ditioni et eam in supremam redigere servitutem, memorato Apostutico, sicut dictum est, pontificalia insignia reddidit et cum de papatu, quod est a saeculis inauditum, per annulum, prout dicitur, investivit. Sic enim reges et principes diversarum partium sibi intendit tum spirituali

tum materiali gladio subjugare, si in hac parte (quod absit) nefandissimum ejus propositum praevaleret.'

[4] Ep. 20, p. 91 seq. ed. Migne. J. n. 7147.

[5] Ep. 3, p. 73; Ep. 20, p. 90; Ep. 30, p. 101; Ep. 97, p. 169 seq.; Ep. 62, p. 133. J. n. 7188, p. 685. Alexander says : ' Quod si omnipotens Deus ei inspiraverit, quod ad sinum matris vellet Ecclesiae redire, nihil temporale nobis contingere posset in saeculo, quod acceptius et gratius haberemus.'

[6] Joh. Saresb. Ep. 185, p. 194 : ' Quis similis erat Friderico in filiis hominum, antequam in tyrannum [he commonly calls him Teutonicus tyrannus, *e.g.* Ep. 292, ad Bald. p. 337] verteretur ex principe et ex Catholico imperatore *schismaticus et haereticus* fieret? Non dico, quod in articulis fidei, ne recte credatur, inducat errorem, sed quia in sinceritate ecclesiastici ordinis procedere non sinat veritatem. Ille sacerdotium scidit adversus Dominum et a Domino scissuram sentit imperii.'

[7] Card. Aragon. in Vita Alex. p. 451. J. p. 681. Joh. Saresb. Ep. 218, p. 242 : ' Vicarius Petri a Domino constitutus super gentes et regna Italos et omnes, qui ei causa imperii et regni religione jurisjurandi tenebantur astricti, a fidelitate ejus absolvit.'

[8] Acta Alex. III. ap. Baron. a. 1170, n. 54; 1176, n. 15; 1177, n. 13. Joh. Saresb. Ep. 218, ad Subpr. Cant. p. 242. He generally calls Frederick ' ex-Augustus :' vide Ep. 228, ad Joh. Pictav. p. 259 ; Ep. 233, ad Nicol. de Monte, p. 262 ; Ep. 234, ad Bald. Archidiac. p. 263.

[9] Hefele, v. 617 seq. Soon after this Peter of Blois wrote to Cardinal William of Pavia, Ep. 48, p. 142, ed. Migne : ' Ille qui imperat ventis et mari, imperavit imperatori, qui cum nuper in Ecclesiam Dei efferata rabie desaeviret, hodie per gratiam Christi decrudescit in eo severitas et iracundia ejus mansuescit in gratiam. . . . Persecutor Ecclesiae factus est filius, de lupo factus est agnus, de hoste amicus, de superbo devotus.' He then describes the morals and the fall of the antipopes, p. 143 : ' Ecce idolum Dagon, quod juxta arcum Domini fuerat elevatum prius, cecidit prostratum. Erectum secundo corruit, ex magna parte confractum. Erectum vero tertio tandem totum confractum inventum est et toto corpore dissipatum.'

[10] Mansi, xxii. 504, 506, 533 seq. Jaffé, n. 9828, 9947, 10,007-10,099, 10,151.

§ 9.

Henry VI., who was crowned emperor by Celestine III. April 15, 1191, was deeply implicated in the treacherous revenge taken by Leopold of Austria upon Richard Cœur de Lion on his return from the Holy Land, and Henry's conflict with the Holy See began on this account. In 1193, Celestine excommunicated Duke Leopold, and threatened to excommunicate the emperor if he did not release Richard, whose imprisonment was a violation of the law of nations, and who, as a Crusader, was under the protection of the Holy See. The king had to pay a large sum of money for his ransom ; but on his return to England

wrote to the Pope, requesting him to command the restitution
of the ransom money. This Celestine did, to Leopold and the
emperor.[1] Henry wished to enter into negotiations concerning
the indemnification, but he died in 1197, before the return of the
bishops who were his envoys. Celestine forbade Christian burial
to his remains as long as the ransom money was unreturned.[2]
The tyranny of Henry's government had exasperated all parties.
The oppressions and excesses of his officials had given Celestine
much ground for complaint, and he always hoped for their removal. The meek old man endeavoured to soften him by
fatherly admonitions.[3] Henry, by annexing the kingdom of
Sicily, placed the Church in a very dangerous situation.

[1] Jaffé, p. 887. Hefele, v. 666.
[2] Roger de Hoveden, Annal. Angl. P. ii. a. 1191 seq. 1197. Matth.
Paris. a. 1192, 1195. Baron. a. 1191, 1193 seq.
[3] Ep. d.d. 27 Apr. 1195. Jaffé, n. 10,526, p. 900 seq.

§ 10.

Upon Henry's death the majority of the German princes
elected Duke Philip of Swabia, who was the brother of the late
emperor. They passed over his son Frederick, to whom the inheritance had been promised, on the plea that Frederick was a
child, and that the government of the kingdom required a man.[1]
The votes of the minority were given to Otho of Brunswick,
son of Henry the Lion. Otho signified his election to the Pope,
and petitioned for the imperial crown. Pope Innocent III. had
no desire to be engaged in the dispute, and hoped that the princes
would arrive at an amicable arrangement.[2] When he saw that
this hope was vain he wrote to the princes, requiring of them
that concord which was of equal necessity to the empire and
the Church; he also, at the same time, sent legates to Germany.[3]
At length the time came for the Pope to decide in favour of one
or other of the claimants. The points in Philip's favour were
(1) the majority of votes; (2) his superior power; and (3) the
intercession of the King of France. Against him were (1) the
wrongs inflicted upon the Church by his father and brother; (2)
his own hostilities against her dominions; (3) the excommunica-

tion inflicted on him on their account by Celestine III.; (4) the efforts of his family to obtain an hereditary right to the kingdom, as well as to the empire, which, according to the custom of many centuries, went together; (5) his coronation at Mayence by a foreign and unlawful prelate (the Archbishop of Tarantaise), which had preceded Otho's coronation by the proper prelate (the Archbishop of Cologne) in Aix-la-Chapelle, the customary place; (6) his perjury towards Frederick II. of Sicily. For these reasons Innocent acknowledged Otho as Emperor of the Holy Roman Empire on the 1st March 1201, and promised to crown him whenever he wished.[4] Many princes of Germany of Philip's party were offended at this, and complained that the Pope's legate, Cardinal Guido, if he had wished to act as an elector, had encroached on the privileges of the princes; and if he had wished to act as a judge, had violated the law in passing judgment in the absence of one party, and without having invited it to appear. Innocent replied circumstantially to this charge,[5] and declared that he and his legate fully acknowledged the right of the German princes to elect their *king*, but that if the elected king were to become *emperor*, it was the right of the Pope to examine his fitness for the office. This right was shown by (1) the coronation of Charles the Great by Leo III.;[6] (2) by the analogy of consecration, since the right of examining must belong to the consecrator; (3) from the absurd consequences of the contrary doctrine, by which a Pope might be forced to anoint and crown as protector of Christendom any tyrant, madman, heathen, or heretic.

The right of electing the emperor certainly had belonged to the Pope. If the princes now possessed it, they must have acquired it lawfully from its former possessors, the Popes.[7] The Popes make an accurate distinction:[8] the German princes have an undoubted right, confirmed by long usage, of electing *their king*; but that in electing their king they elect at the same time *the future emperor*, is only a privilege from the Holy See. The German king is called by the existing law King of the Romans, in view of his promotion to the dignity of emperor.[9] But it belongs to the Pope to decide upon the question of his promotion; for as it is at the same time an ecclesiastical office, the Church must satisfy herself that the candidate actually possesses the requisite qualities. The Church could not at once promote an excommunicated person, such as Philip, to the supreme dignity; neither could she longer be deprived of a protector. The Pope was, therefore, obliged to decide in favour of Otho. With regard to the complaint concerning his legate, Innocent declared he was neither elector—for he in no manner effected the election of one or the other—nor judge—for he delivered no judgment; he was simply to report upon the two candidates, and in so doing had in no manner overstepped his powers. The Pope fully recognised the right of the electors to choose their king, and they must equally recognise his right to examine into the fitness of the candidate before consecrating him to the empire.[10]

In case of a disputed election to the German kingdom it would become the duty of the Pope (1) to admonish the princes to reëstablish concord; (2) if his admonition failed, to decide in favour of one of the claimants; and this that the Church might not longer remain without a protector.[11]

This is nothing but the consistent development of the distinction between the German kingdom and the empire, and in no manner prejudicial to the German kingdom, which could exist alone. Nothing but a complete misunderstanding of the historical and legal circumstances of the case could lead any one to see here an injustice.[12]

---

[1] Hefele, v. 675, 677 seq.

[2] Reg. de Negot. Imper. Ep. 1 seq. Migne, t. ccxvi. p. 995 seq.

[3] Cf. Innoc. III. l. i. Ep. 25 (Migne, t. ccxiv. p. 20).

[4] Reg. de Neg. Imp. Ep. 32 (Baluz. i. 702; Migne, l.c. p. 1036): ' Auctoritate Dei omnipotentis, nobis in B. Petro collata, te in *regem* recipimus, et *regalem* tibi praecipimus de caetero reverentiam et obedientiam exhiberi, praemissisque omnibus quae de jure sunt et consuetudine praemittenda, regiam magnificentiam ad suscipiendam *Romani imperii* coronam vocabimus et eam tibi dante Domino humilitatis nostrae manibus solemniter conferemus.' Cf. Ep. 33, p. 704 seq.; and the deliberation, Ep. 29, p. 1025 seq.

[5] Reg. Ep. 61, 62, p. 1063 seq. c. xxxiv. Venerabilem, i. 6, de Elect. Phillips's K.R. iii. § 127, p. 194 seq. Hefele, v. 695 seq.

[6] If the Pope speaks of a translation of the empire from the Greeks to

the Germans, this is only to be understood as meaning that Leo III. transferred to Charles that authority which extended from the East over the West, whence follows, of course, that Charles, after his coronation by the Pope, was preëminently protector of the Church. The expression 'translation' was long in use. Thus Otto of Freising says of the coronation of Charles the Great: 'Exhinc regnum Romanorum, quod a Constantino usque ad id tempus in urbe regia s. Cpli. fuit, ad Francos *derivatum* est' (Chron. v. 31). And of the coronation of Otho I.: 'Exhinc regnum Romanorum, quod post Francos et Longobardos ad Teutonicos vel ut aliis videtur, rursum ad Francos, unde quodammodo elapsum fuerat, *translatum* est.'

⁷ Gosselin, ii. pp. 320, 321.

⁸ This does not refer to the College of Electors, which did not exist at that time. The first traces of it appear after the election of William of Holland and Rudolph of Hapsburg. Phillips, p. 199 seq.

⁹ 'Rex Romanorum in imperatorem promovendus.' The expression here employed by the Pope is found also in the golden Bull of Charles IV. of 1356, c. i. § 1, 2, and is used also by other Popes. S. Olenschläger, Erläuterung der goldenen Bulle Urk. p. 46. C. ii. § 1 of the Bull gives: 'Rex Romanorum futurusque Caesar.' We read in the Reg. Innoc. Ep. 15, p. 1010: 'Cum imperialis corona sit a Romano Pontifice concedenda, eo rite prius electo in principem et prius in regem legitime coronato, talem secundum antiquam et approbatam consuetudinem libenter ad coronam suscipiendam vocabimus.'

¹⁰ Ep. 62, p. 1065: 'Jus principum nolumus nobis vindicare. . . . Sed et principes recognoscere debent et *utique recognoscunt, sicut iidem in nostra recognovere praesentia*, quod jus et auctoritas examinandi personam electam in regem et promovendam ad imperium ad nos spectat, qui eum inungimus, consecramus et coronamus.'

¹¹ Innocent recalls to mind Conrad III., who in 1127 made himself king in opposition to Lothair, but was obliged to submit when the latter was made emperor. Conrad had received the iron crown in June 1128 at Monza, from the Archbishop of Milan; but the See of Rome decided in favour of Lothair.

¹² Huber, p. 18.

§ 11.

We do not find that any serious attempt was made to confute the legal view taken by the Pope. Philip only sought to enter into fresh negotiations with Rome.¹ He employed many artful and cunning devices, and in 1207 was absolved from his excommunication.² After Philip's assassination in 1209,³ Otho retained undisputed possession of the kingdom, and was crowned emperor by the Pope in 1209. But he was ungrateful to the Pope, to whose protection he himself acknowledged he owed almost everything.⁴ He did not keep to his solemn oath,⁵ and endeavoured to subjugate the whole of Italy, even including the

States of the Church, which he had repeatedly engaged to protect,[6] and Naples, the inheritance of the boy Frederick, who was
under the guardianship and protection of the Pope. In consequence of all these misdeeds he drew upon himself the Papal
excommunication in 1211.[7] A diet of princes held at Nuremberg pronounced his deposition. Otho was unable to resist the
decree, and in 1212, Frederick, son of Henry VI. and the Pope's
ward, received the crown of the kingdom of Germany.[8]

[1] Vide his detailed statement, Reg. Innoc. III. Ep. 136, 140, p. 1132
seq., and his Promissio, in Pertz, t. ii. Leg. p. 108 ; Migne, ccxvii. p. 295,
Ep. 9.
[2] Hefele, v. p. 698 seq. 711 seq. Reg. Ep. 142, 143, p. 1142.
[3] Report of Cardinal Ugolino, Reg. Ep. 152, p. 1146.
[4] His letters in the Registr. Innoc. Ep. 19, 20, 53, 54, 81, 106, 160,
187, 189, 190, 193, pp. 1016 seq. 1054 seq. 1087 seq. 1108, 1150, 1157,
1169 seq. 1172.
[5] Reg. Inn. Ep. 77, 189, pp. 1084, 1169.
[6] Hefele, pp. 692, 720.
[7] Cf. Innoc. III. l. xiii. Ep. 210. Migne, t. ccxvi. p. 375 ; l. xiv. Ep.
78, 79, 101, pp. 439 seq. 465.
[8] His 'Promissio' of 1213 is in Pertz, Leg. ii. 224. Walter, Fontes Jur.
Eccl. pp. 76-78.

PART II. CONFLICT OF FREDERICK II. WITH THE CHURCH.

§ 1. His proceedings until the death of Honorius III.   § 2. His excommunication.   § 3. His pretended war against the Saracens.   § 4. His
'peace' with them rejected by the Pope. § 5. Frederick's hypocrisy and
contradictions.   § 6. Peace of San Germano. § 7. Violation of treaties
and conduct in Italy.   § 8. Release from the oath of allegiance.   § 9.
Frederick's war against the Pope. § 10. The Council prevented. § 11.
Louis IX. of France. § 12. Council of Lyons, 1245.   § 13. Frederick's
crimes.   § 14. Election of an opposition king.

§ 1.

Frederick II. was solemnly crowned by the Archbishop of
Mayence on the 25th July 1215, whilst the vanquished Otho
wore away his days ingloriously on his paternal estates in Brunswick.[1] Frederick promised solemnly in 1216 that after receiving the imperial crown he would give up Sicily to his son as a
kingdom separate from the kingdom of Germany. This was a
matter of the first importance for the material safety of the See
of Rome.[2] He also renewed all the promises made formerly by
Otho IV.

But after the death of the great Pope Innocent III.,[3] Frederick showed himself as false as Otho, and nearly as despotic as his grandfather.[4] At his coronation by Honorius III. on the 22d Nov. 1220, he had again taken up the cross, as he had promised to do at Aix-la-Chapelle in 1215, and had vowed shortly to begin the campaign.[5] But it was not his real intention to execute his promise, and he sought constantly fresh reasons for postponement. When in 1219 Damietta, which the Crusaders had gained at so much cost, had to be given up again to the Sultan of Egypt, Honorius deeply grieved, reminded Frederick (19th November 1221) of his promise. The blame of the misfortunes of the Crusaders had already been attributed to the Pope, because he had not by means of the ban forced the emperor to fulfil his promises.[6] Frederick excused himself on the ground of the pressing necessities of his dominions, and again promised shortly to undertake the campaign. He renewed the promise in 1222[7] and 1223, when he once more vowed his willingness to enter upon the carefully prepared Crusade in less than two years.[8]

In spite of the serious nature of his grievances the Pope showed Frederick the greatest indulgence. Frederick already treated the subjects of the Pope as his own, oppressed the clergy in Sicily, and appeared unwilling to recognise the Papal right of confirmation of the nomination of bishops by the emperor.[9] The Pope hoped that Frederick's marriage with Iolantha, heiress of the kingdom of Jerusalem, would serve as a fresh motive to induce him to save that kingdom from its threatened subjection ; but the emperor applied to his father-in-law to obtain for him a fresh postponement, because he feared an insurrection of the Lombards, who were, however, quieted by the intervention of the Pope. The Pope then despatched Cardinals Pelagius and Gualo of St. Martin with distinct proposals with regard to the repeatedly postponed expedition. At the treaty of San Germano (July 1225) Frederick undertook to furnish a certain supply of money, troops, and ships, and to engage in the Crusade within two years ; he swore that if he had not fulfilled these engagements within the appointed time he should be excommunicated, and that he himself and his dominions should, by a just judgment, be at the Pope's disposition.[10]

[1] Hefele, pp. 721, 724.

[2] Pertz, Leg. ii. 228 seq. Bréholles, Hist. Diplom. Frid. II. t. i. p. 469 seq. Rayn. a. 1215, n. 38 : 'Ne forte pro eo, quod nos dignatione divina sumus ad imperii fastigium evocati, aliquid unionis *regnum* ad *imperium* quovis tempore putaretur habere, si nos simul *imperium teneremus et regnum, per quod tam Apostolicae Sedi quam haeredibus nostris aliquod posset dispendium generari.*' Migne, ccxvii. p. 305, Ep. 19.

[3] His letters to Innocent, Pertz, Leg. ii. 223, 224. Migne, l.c. p. 310 seq. Ep. 16, 17.

[4] Cf. Hefele, Conc. v. p. 812 seq., who also exposes Schirrmacher's very partial explanation.

[5] Honor. Ep. ad Ep. Alban. Raynald. a. 1220, n. 53, 21 seq. Hefele, v. 811 seq.

[6] Raynald. a. 1221, n. 6, 18 seq. Cf. letters addressed to the Pope after the conquest of Damietta from the king and the Patriarch of Jerusalem, from the Grand Masters and other Crusaders (Petr. Bles. Ep. 195 ; Migne, ccvii. pp. 478, 479), as well as the Papal letters consequent thereon (ib. Ep. 196, pp. 479-481).

[7] Richard a. S. Germano, Chron. a. 1222. Honor. III. Ep. ad Pelag. ap. Rayn. a. 1222, n. 2, 4.

[8] Honor. Ep. ad Reg. Franc. Rayn. a. 1223, n. 4. Spondan. h.a. n. 1. Hefele, l.c. p. 819.

[9] Rayn. a. 1221, n. 32; 1222, n. 26 seq.; 1223, n. 15, 19. Huillard-Bréholles, Hist. Diplom. Frid. II. t. ii. pp. 139, 200, 239, 258, 272 seq. 431.

[10] Rayn. a. 1225, n. 1-7. Bianchi, t. ii. l. vi. § 4, n. 1, pp. 418-420. Döllinger, Lehrb. ii. p. 196 seq. Hefele, v. 819 seq.

§ 2.

When Honorius, towards whom Frederick had alternately shown himself hostile and friendly, died in March 1227, Cardinal Ugolino, who was very active in favour of the Crusades, and for whom Frederick had testified much esteem, was made Pope under the title of Gregory IX. He immediately entreated the emperor most pressingly to fulfil his promises,[1] admonished him fervently, and as Frederick still procrastinated,[2] threatened him with excommunication.[3] Through Frederick's fault a fine army of Crusaders, assembled in Lower Italy, melted away. The Landgrave Louis of Thuringia and some bishops died in the summer of a sickness that arose at that time ; rumour reported that the landgrave had been poisoned by the emperor. Frederick was pleased at the miscarriage of the enterprise, and, feigning illness, retired to the baths of Puzzuoli. Deeply grieved at the frustration of the hopes of Christendom, Gregory IX., on the 29th Sept. 1227, pronounced sentence of excommunication upon the faithless Frederick, who even on his own showing had deserved it long since.[4] He still wished, as Frederick at first endeavoured to excuse his conduct, to show him indulgence if he would only give proof of a serious conversion. The emperor's tyranny in Sicily, his leaning towards the Saracens, and his immoral life, for which Gregory had rebuked him on former occasions, had caused him to be the object of much mistrust, and had given ground for many complaints against him. Soon now too he published most malicious libels against the Church of Rome.[5] On the 23d March 1228, the Pope renewed his excommunication in a Synod held at Rome, as Frederick persisted in his obstinacy and committed fresh crimes (robbery of the Knights Templars and Hospitallers; for example, of Count Roger and others), and the places at which he sojourned were laid under an interdict.[6] Still no sentence of deposition was pronounced,[7] and the Christians in Palestine considered Frederick as an excommunicated person indeed, but not as having lost his authority.[8]

[1] Greg. IX. l. i. Ep. 2. Rayn. a. 1227, n. 18, 20 seq.
[2] Richard a. S. Germano, Chron. a. 1227. Vita Greg. IX. l. i. Ep. 165, ad Frid. Rayn. h.a. n. 14.
[3] Letters of 8th June 1227. Rayn. h.a. n. 21 seq. H. Bréholles, iii. p. 7 seq.
[4] The Encyclical of Oct. 10, which Böhmer declares to be a noble document, is given in part in Brischar Stolberg's K.G. vol. lii. p. 120 seq.
[5] Bréholles, iii. pp. 37 seq. 48 seq. Böhmer, Regesten, p. 138.
[6] Vita Greg. IX. Ep. ad Episc. Apul. Rayn. a. 1228, n. 2. Mansi, xxiii. 162. Hefele, p. 855 seq.
[7] Bossuet, Defens. P. i. l. i. sect. 2, c. xxix. p. 167 ; l. iv. c. vi. p. 347, with reference to Gregory's words : ' Imp. Fridericum excommunicatum, quamquam inviti, publico nunciamus et mandamus ab omnibus arctius evitari, contra ipsum, si contumacia ejus exegerit, gravius processuri.'
[8] Matth. Paris. a. 1228, pp. 349, 351. Bossuet, l.c.

§ 3.

The Frangipani, who were in league with the emperor, excited an insurrection in Rome against the Pope, which obliged him to

fly.   Frederick, in mockery of the excommunication, entered
upon a mimic war[1] against the Saracens with a paltry army,
whilst he left behind him a strong force, amongst which were
some Saracens, to make war upon the States of the Church.
His conduct towards John of Ibelin at the island of Cyprus,
his secret negotiations with the Saracens, the treaty he entered
into with the Sultan Camel on the 19th February 1229, as well
as all his measures in Palestine, were not calculated to place him
before the world in a better light.   Gregory, constrained to take
up arms by the attack made by Duke Rainald upon the Papal
States, assembled an army under John of Brienne, who drove
back the duke and seized several Neapolitan towns.[2]   In the
mean time, Gregory IX. had, on the 30th August 1228, released
all the inhabitants of the kingdom of both Sicilies from their
oath of allegiance to Frederick ;[3] he was justified in this as
feudal sovereign of the kingdom on account of the felony of the
vassal after the invasion of Rainald his lieutenant in July.[4]

[1] In this sense he expressed himself to the Saracens (Wilken, Gesch.
der Kreuzzüge, vi. 420, n. 12.
[2] Richard, Chron. a. 1228.   Greg. IX. Ep. ad Mediol. et ad Duc.
Austr.   Rayn. a. 1229, n. 2, 23.   Jordan. ib. n. 31.   Gerold. Hieros. ap.
Matth. Paris. et Rayn. a. 1229, n. 3 seq. 15.
[3] Bréholles, iii. p. 494.   Hefele, p. 857 seq.   Bianchi, l.c. n. 4, pp.
425, 426, supposes that towards the end of the year 1228 Gregory had released all Frederick's subjects from their oath of allegiance.
[4] Bréholles, l.c. p. 75.   Letter of the Pope of Aug. 5.

§ 4.

How can we regard it as otherwise than extremely disin-
genuous of Professor Huber[1] to place before his readers the
entry of the Pope's army into Apulia, keeping absolute silence
on the prior invasion of the Papal States by the army of Duke
Rainald,[2] which had devastated and pillaged the country ?   What
a history a Frenchman might make of the war of 1870 if he
made similar omissions !   Frederick himself acknowledged that
Rainald was the aggressor in this instance, at the same time
asserting that it had been done without his knowledge ;[3] which
is hard to believe, for no one dared to stir hand or foot in his

dominions without his permission.[4] That Frederick, whilst he
was under excommunication, should have entered upon a Crusade was an act of rebellion and defiance of the Church, and he
continually showed that these were his dispositions. The Pope
could not absolve him from the excommunication as long as he
manifested no repentance, but despised the Pope's censures, and
flung to the winds his warning against fulfilling his vow before
being reconciled to the Church.[5] It is not true that the Pope
wished to nullify the results of Frederick's Crusade, for Frederick
himself did not intend any results to ensue : he undertook the
campaign with only a hundred knights, and had no single passage of arms with the Saracens ; on the contrary, he entered into
negotiations with them upon a most friendly footing,[6] and concluded by no means a ' favourable peace,' but only an armistice,
which was injurious to the Christians,[7] and was condemned by
the majority of his contemporaries.[8] Huber says that the Pope
' rejected the arrangement because it conceded the right of entering Solomon's temple to the Moslem ;' whereas this reason,
which is here misstated, was far from being the only one. For
not merely admission to, but the custody (custodia) of, the temple
(templum Domini) was granted to the Saracens; in consequence
the Christians found themselves subject to many annoyances
when visiting it. This templum Domini had been the cathedral
of the Patriarch, and was now to serve for both the Moham-
medan and Christian worship.[9] Patriarch Gerold had considered
this a great injury to the Christians.[10] Then the Pope gives
further reasons for his rejection of the treaty. These were, that
Frederick had yielded to the Sultan of Babylon, as a mark of
lasting friendship, the sword which had been taken from St.
Peter's altar, thus, as it were, pledging the honour of the empire
to undertake no further measures against the unbeliever; that,
by the armistice, he exposed the town and district of Antioch,
the territory of Tripoli, and other Christian possessions without protection to the unbeliever; finally, that he had bound
himself by oath to resist by force of arms, at his own expense,
any one who should oppose this treaty ; thus placing himself in
the position of an enemy to any Christian army which should

take the field for the liberation of the Holy Land.[11]   All this
was the more injurious to the Christians, by exposing them de-
fenceless to the Sultan of Damascus, who was not a party to the
treaty.   Frederick eventually treated the Patriarch of Jerusalem
as a prisoner, and suffered several mendicant friars who defended
the Church to be torn from the pulpit and ill-treated.[12]   The
evil consequences soon manifested themselves.   In 1230 Jerusalem, whose walls had not been rebuilt, was overrun by a
horde of Saracen fanatics, who killed many Christians, and laid
the place in waste.   The defeat of Marshal Richard in the island
of Cyprus was a death-blow to Frederick's authority in the
East, A.D. 1232.[13]

[1] P. 28.
[2] For the authority conferred upon him in June 1228, vide Bréholles,
t. iii. p. 63 seq.
[3] Thus Gregory IX. in the letter of 23d Oct. 1236. Bréholles, iv.
914 seq.
[4] Bréholles, v. p. 295 seq.
[5] Bréh. iii. p. 482.
[6] Matth. Paris, who was not inclined towards the See of Rome, says
this also, p. 302 : 'Conglutinata est anima imperatoris cum anima Soldani
indissolubili cemento dilectionis,' &c.
[7] Natal. Alex. saec. 13 et 14, c. i. a. 3, p. 28 : 'Exitiosum Christianae
rei foedus.' Patriarch Gerold found in this 'principis hujus malitiam
evidentem.'
[8] Vide the testimonies in Wilken, vi. p. 508 seq.
[9] Greg. IX. Ep. ad Aep. Mediol. 13 June 1229. Raynald. h.a. n. 2.
[10] Hefele, v. p. 863. Very damaging to Frederick are the reports of
the Patriarch Gerold, in the letter of the 26th March 1229. Bréholles,
iii. pp. 102-104.
[11] Bréholles, iii. p. 147 seq.
[12] Ib. p. 135 seq. Brischar, in Stolberg's K.G. vol. lii. p. 160 seq.
Hefele, v. p. 865.
[13] Wilken, vi. pp. 512 seq. 526 seq.

§ 5.

Frederick, in a speech made at Jerusalem on the 17th March
1229, excuses the Pope for having excommunicated him, saying,
'that otherwise he (the Pope) could not have escaped the invec-
tives and insults of men.'[1]   These words contain almost as
striking a justification of the Pope as it were possible to con-
ceive, coming from one of his enemies ; and also, as the utterance of a ruler who well knew the mind of his contemporaries,

make it incredible that 'the whole world was horrified at the Pope's conduct.' This, in reality, appeared not only justified, but called for, by what had gone before. It has become a principle with some 'that Gregory waged a war of extermination against the Hohenstaufen' (Huber, p. 27), and they trouble themselves little about these words of Frederick's, though at other times they consider the words of the emperor, without indeed the replies of the Pope, and the testimony of his adherents, without indeed the opposing testimonies, well worthy of attention and notice. The Italians knew much more of Frederick II. than the Germans did ; for he passed far the larger portion of his time in Italy. The German bishops were on his side, because he conceded to them certain privileges, by which a great step was taken toward their future sovereignty,[2] the unity of the kingdom was impaired, and the splendour of the throne considerably diminished. Frederick's own letters were to many Germans the only sources of information on which they could form a judgment on his proceedings in Italy and Palestine. This was the case with the Provost of Auersperg,[3] who, like others, had been won by Frederick's bounty,[4] and who, with others, was at some distance from the theatre of the events related to them.[5] These letters of Frederick's were composed, for the most part, in his name by Petrus de Vineis, the same whom Frederick in after years suffered to perish miserably in a dungeon. They are said to place his 'sincerity' beyond doubt ; whereas, in fact, they not only contradict other witnesses, but are convicted of falsehood by Frederick's own deeds, and show in themselves a mass of falsehoods, hypocrisy, and contradictions. He had, for instance, contrary to an engagement entered into by oath,[6] effected the union of the kingdoms of Germany and Sicily ; when, in 1220, he suffered his son Henry, who had been made King of Sicily, to be elected also in Germany, he put everything off upon the princes, whom he had prepared beforehand,[7] and promised the further separation of both kingdoms, a promise which he was never willing to execute. He gave as his reason the maintenance of peace; but it is difficult to see how that could be attained by a boy still under age.[8] He had repeatedly expressed himself full of gratitude·

towards the Church of Rome,[9] which under Innocent and Honorius had done so much for him; but in 1226 he denied this,[10]
then again admitted it,[11] and then on the 6th December he complained that always, even under Innocent, the Church of Rome
had shown herself but a stepmother towards him.[12] Whilst he said
at one time that he should long since have gone to the assistance
of the Holy Land had not the Pope impeded the pacification of
Lombardy; at another (1241) he blamed the Pope for not having
averted the danger threatened by the Tartars, although he had
spurned all the Pope's offers.[13]　He excused the invasion of the
Papal States, saying that it was to seek a paternal reception and
apostolic counsel from the Pope before employing all his forces
against the enemies of the Faith.[14]

[1] Letter of the Grand Master of the Teutonic Order, who was active
on Frederick's side, and translated at the time his Italian speeches.　Bréholles, iii. p. 100.　Cf. Hefele, v. p. 862.

[2] Böhmer, Reg. Imp. p. 238, n. 237.　Hefele, v. 880.

[3] Huber, p. 27 seq., gives his words leaving out his admission : ' Sicut
idem imperator in epistolis suis rescripsit principibus Alemanniae.'　On
which Natal. Alex. l.c. p. 27, remarks : ' Partium studio horrendum in modum
abreptum esse oportuit hunc auctorem, qui S. Pontifici tam insolenter in-
sultat *nec aliunde* probat Friderici innocentiam quam *ex ipsiusmet literis.*'

[4] Bianchi, l.c. § 4, n. 8, pp. 434, 435. Pandolf. Cillenut. Hist. Neapol.
l. iv. pp. 149, 158, follows the authority of the Provost of Auersperg and
Matthew Paris.

[5] The reports of Salimbene of Parma (Chronicle of 1212-1287) and also
of Richard of San Germano, who was a strong Ghibelline (Potthast, Bibl.
Hist. Medii Aevi, Berol. 1862, p. 512), often have quite a different tenor.

[6] Huillard-Bréholles, i. 469 seq.

[7] Ibid. p. 803.

[8] Hefele, v. pp. 813-815.

[9] Bréholles, i. 636 seq.　Rayn. a. 1220, n. 18.　Walter, Fontes, p. 76.

[10] Bréh. ii. 588 seq. in the words of Frederick's there cited.

[11] Raynald. a. 1226, n. 23 seq.

[12] Bréh. iii. 36 seq. 48 seq.

[13] Hefele, v. p. 957, with note 3.

[14] Bréh. v. 1139 seq.　Hefele, p. 958, No. 1.

§ 6.

It is quite a false assertion that the Pope, seeing the universal horror caused by his proceedings, was obliged at last to
conclude a peace with Frederick.　The latter feared a coalition
between the followers of the Church and the enemies of his

house,[1] but the Pope had always declared himself willing to enter into negotiations for a reconciliation with Frederick if he would perform satisfaction and promise amendment. In June 1229, on his return to Italy, Frederick found it advisable to be reconciled to the Church. Finally, on the 23d June 1230, peace was concluded at San Germano. Frederick undertook to submit to the Church on all those points which had led to his excommunication ; to make restitution of whatever he had robbed from the Roman or any other Church ; to recall the exiled bishops ; to grant an amnesty to those who had assisted the Church against him; to leave free the Church elections in Lower Italy ; to indemnify all spoliations ; to take all necessary precautions for the Holy Land. On this Frederick visited the Pope at Anagni, and in his letters to the princes praised his beneficent and noble demeanour, which had extinguished all his animosity.[2] Gregory also gave free expression to his joy over the reëstablished concord.[3]

[1] Stolberg-Brischar, l.c. p. 176 seq.
[2] Raynald. a. 1230, n. 3-16. Pertz, Mon. iv. Leg. ii. pp. 269-276.
[3] Raynald. h.a. n. 41 seq. Bréholles, l.c. p. 224 seq. Extract in Brischar, l.c. p. 180 seq.

§ 7.

But the perfidious Frederick broke this treaty, like so many others. Soon afterwards he allowed himself to be seduced by his councillors into persecuting those who had taken the Pope's part against him ; he wished especially to be revenged upon the Knights of St. John and the Knights Templars, although these were expressly included in the treaty. He deprived them of their possessions, and continued his hostilities towards them until Gregory was obliged to remind him of the engagements he had entered into.[1] Whilst the Pope, in many ways, was assisting him in carrying out his schemes,[2] he issued, in 1231, his new code of laws[3] for the kingdom of Sicily, which encroached in many particulars upon the rights of the Church, and he took in very ill part the Pope's reclamations, upon which the Pope, for the sake of preserving peace, sought to appease him.[4] In the year 1232 the emperor condescended to approve of the inter-

vention of the Papal legate between him and the Lombards,
because he had really no sufficient force ; he did not, however,
await the result : persecuted some Catholics whom he was displeased with because, he said, they were heretics, and allowed
his Saracens at Lucera to pillage a church ; he also chose to
regard the Lombards, because there were amongst them some
Cathari, as heretics, whom he said he must exterminate ; and
because the Pope had favoured them he reproached him with it,
and called him ' favourer of heresy.'[5] He was displeased at the
Pope's decision of the 5th June 1233, in the matter of his dispute
with the Lombards ; Gregory defended it (12th August), saying
that it had been issued with the advice of the cardinals, and
was in accordance with law and equity, but offered to retract it,
and let everything revert to its former position.[6] Frederick
would not agree to this, and gave his consent to the Pope's
decision.[7]

Very different was the assistance which the Pope rendered
to Frederick, when his son Henry, for the second time, rebelled
against him,[8] from the lukewarm assistance Frederick had rendered to the Pope, on the occasion of a rebellion in Rome in 1234,
when Frederick was in secret league with the Pope's enemies,[9]
and the latter felt it his duty not to decline his help.[10] The
situation would have been highly perilous for the emperor if the
Pope had given his support to Henry, whose causes of quarrel
were not wholly unreasonable, nor the means at his disposal
insignificant ; but Gregory threatened to excommunicate him, and
gave such efficient help to Frederick that the latter succeeded at
last in placing Henry in confinement, and kept him until his death
in 1242 a close prisoner. Such was the end of Frederick's eldest
son, who had been raised to be King of Germany in violation
of the promise given to the Holy See.[11] Frederick in spite of
this aid remained an implacable enemy of the Papacy, and
never abandoned his scheme for subjugating the whole of Italy.[12]
In the year 1236 he made vigorous war upon the Lombards,
and rejected all intervention ; in 1237 he was at the summit of
his power, with strength sufficient to set at naught the supremacy of the Church and the feudal suzerainty. His replies to

the complaints of the Pope were sometimes evasive, sometimes insolent; so that Gregory, on the 23d October 1236, repeated all his grievances, at the same time representing to Frederick his position with regard to the Church, and reproving him for his want of respect.[13] Intoxicated by his victory over the Lombards at Cortenuova, 27th November 1237, the emperor drove them by his tyranny to the resistance of despair,[14] took every pretext for jeering at the Pope, and multiplied his outrages against the Church.[15] It was a source of much sorrow to the Pope that Frederick's officers in Sicily should, in 1236, have intercepted and imprisoned a nephew of the King of Tunis who had been converted by the Dominicans, and was travelling to Rome, there to receive baptism. Frederick, however, refused to set him at liberty, pretending that the prince had been unduly influenced, and that he could not become a Christian without the consent of his uncle.[16] Many other grievances were added to these, viz. that he had violated the treaty of San Germano, incited the Romans to rebellion against the Pope, illtreated and banished several prelates; that he had put priests cruelly to death; that he prevented the filling up of vacant sees, had employed Saracens to destroy Christian churches; that he had rendered vain all endeavours to secure the Christian supremacy in the East; that he had conferred upon his natural son Enzio[17] the island of Sardinia, which he had himself acknowledged to belong to the Church of Rome; that he led a dissolute life, and was strongly suspected of heresy and unbelief.[18] With regard to the latter point the Pope reserved to himself a more searching investigation. The charge of unbelief was denied by Frederick,[19] as well as by his biographers; but the suspicion has always attached to him, since his whole course of action seemed to justify it. Over and above these grievances, he took prisoner Peter the Saracen, who was sent to the Pope on the part of Henry III. of England, and refused to permit Cardinal Palestrina, who was commissioned to Provence, to pass through his dominions on the way thither.[20]

[1] Raynald. a. 1230, n. 17; a. 1231, n. 2.
[2] Hefele, v. p. 880.

[3] This is treated in detail, of course exactly according to his point of view, by Pietro Giannone : Istoria Civile del Regno di Napoli, t. iv. l. xvi. c. viii. p. 48 seq. ed. 1821, Italia (place of publication not given).

[4] Raynald. a. 1231, n. 10 seq.

[5] Cf. Hefele, l.c. p. 833.

[6] Bréh. iv. p. 447 seq.

[7] Ib. p. 451 seq.   Cf. Brischar, l.c. pp. 281-283.

[8] Hefele, p. 885.

[9] Raynald. a. 1234, n. 4 seq.

[10] Vita Greg. IX. p. 580 : ' Imperator. . . . Reate concitus nec invitatus advenit, Ecclesiae causam, quam *ut advocatus ex imperii debito et vassallus ex homagio regni Siciliae* gemino tenebatur defendere juramento, cum supplicatione suscipiens D. Papae et fratribus de ipsius fide dubitantibus prosequendam.   Fecerat enim eorum judicia futuri profectus incredula mentitae saepius offerentis fidei conjectura.   Quod prudenter tandem summi praesulis cautela permisit, *eligens potius felicem deesse negotio successum, quam recusare debitum imperatoris ipsius obsequium, per quod, cum ex conditione regni et imperii teneatur, grave poterat Ecclesiae praejudicium generari.'*

[11] Bréh. iv. pp. 473 seq. 530 seq.   Brischar in Stolberg's K.G. vol. lii. p. 340 seq.

[12] Sigon. de Regno Ital. Hist. i. 18, p. 180, ed. Venet. 1591. Döllinger, l.c. ii. p. 205.

[13] Bréh. iv. 906 seq. 914 seq.   Brischar, l.c. pp. 378-394.

[14] Even Matthew Paris, who was so favourable to Frederick, remarks, p. 400 : ' From this time forward the emperor lost the affection of many hearts, for he showed himself an implacable tyrant ; whilst the Milanese, on account of their submissiveness, deserved to have been raised and strengthened.'

[15] Brischar, pp. 398-407.   Hefele, v. p. 892 seq.

[16] Raynald. a. 1236, n. 22 seq.

[17] Raynald. a. 1238, n. 68.

[18] Various utterances of Frederick's are reported, whose contradictions are not surprising considering his sceptical tendencies.   Even if the Book of the Three Impostors be not his work, everything makes it credible that he spoke like that book.   Not merely Gregory IX. (Mansi, xxiii. 79 seq.) and his biography, but also the Chron. Augustan. a. 1245, ed. Freher, t. i., the Compilatio Chronol. ap. Pistor. Scr. g. i. p. 1102, a. 1249, have the same, as well as the Hist. Langrav. Thuring. c. 1. ib. p. 1327.   An utterance concerning the Eucharist is reported by Alberic. ap. Leibniz. Access. Hist. ii. 568 ; Pistor. Struve, in M. Chron. Belg. t. iii. p. 244.   Cf. Bianchi, l.c. § 4, n. 7, pp. 432, 433 ; and Ricordano Malespini, Istor. Fiorent. c. cxxxii. (Murat. R. J. Scr. viii. 966).   Arabian authors confirm the accusation (Reinaud, Extraits des Hist. Arabes relatif aux Guerres des Croisades, Paris, 1829, p. 431).   The Journal Asiatique, Paris, Mars 1853, pp. 240-274, gives the questions laid by Frederick before the Mussulman doctors and the answers of Abu Muhammed Ibn Sabin.   The words of Gregorovius, quoted by Huber, p. 35, really offer no counter testimony.

[19] Petrus de Vineis, lib. i. Ep. 31.   Frederick in any case was obliged to

disavow unbelief before his contemporaries (Döllinger, Kirche und Kirchen, p. 52).

[20] Rayn. a. 1239, n. 6. Bréholles, v. 271 seq.

§ 8.

If after all this Gregory IX. did, on the 20th March 1239, renew Frederick's excommunication, and release his subjects from their oath of allegiance so long as he should be under the ban,[1] who could ascribe it to 'the immoderate claims of the Papacy, to motives of worldly policy, to blind passion,'[2] when the many and grievous crimes Frederick had committed, backed up as they were by his outrageous manifestoes,[3] are given their due weight? The excommunication was used as a measure of defence, in the Church's direst necessity, and as the fulfilment of an imperative duty. Frederick asserted, and his followers sought to gain credence for the idea,[4] that the Pope excommunicated him with a view of favouring the rebellious towns of Lombardy, and that the other reasons he gave were mere pretexts; but the facts of the case, as shown by the Pope, and which no one has ever contradicted, amply refute the assertion. Although the Lombards had been very negligent in support of the Pope, Gregory had, after peace had been concluded in 1230, shown himself full of consideration towards them,[5] but he could not vanquish their mistrust of a despotic ruler, which Frederick certainly fully justified. The emperor respected the Papal decision of 1233 just so long as he had need of the Pope; and new discords presently arose, which Gregory desired to adjust on the 25th July 1235.[6] Frederick, in reply, declared that if before Christmas the Pope had not arrived at an arrangement honourable to the emperor and advantageous to Germany, he should, in April of the following year, invade Lombardy simultaneously from two quarters.[7] Gregory, upon this, desired the Lombards to send their plenipotentiaries to him by the 1st of December, to lay their cause before the Church, otherwise they would have only themselves to thank for the evils which delay would bring upon them. He charged the Master of the Teutonic Order to prevail if possible upon the emperor to remove from his decrees the condition unfavourable to peace.[8] The

Lombards, having before their eyes the fear of such tyranny as that practised in Sicily, began by a renewal of their League,[9] which caused a delay in the arrival of their plenipotentiaries in Rome ; in consequence of which the Master of the Teutonic Order, as envoy of the emperor, left the city and refused to return, even when messengers were sent after him announcing the arrival of the Lombard plenipotentiaries, and explaining the reason of their delay.[10]   Frederick paid no attention to the request the Pope sent on the 21st March 1236,[11] that these same ambassadors might return without delay for the negotiations, although Gregory represented to him in what a bad light he would appear before the world, if without further parley he were to attack the Lombards ; also that these might think they had been deceived by the Church.   Gregory also wrote to many of the nobles who surrounded Frederick, and admonished the Lombards by the Bishop of Ascoli to effect a peace with the emperor.[12]   Frederick, whose forces were well prepared, was dissatisfied with the peace concluded by his grandfather, and was bent on a war of subjugation, which he sought to cover with the pretence of making it a religious war for the extirpation of heresy.[13]   Gregory's further letters, and the mission of Cardinal Palestrina, were of no avail.[14]   As the Lombards had never refused to enter into negotiations, Gregory could not censure them, as Frederick wished him to do ; subsequently the shocking acts of violence perpetrated by Frederick made all hope of peace impossible.

---

[1] 'Donec fuerit vinculo excommunicationis adstrictus' (Raynald. a. 1239, n. 15).   Cf. Bréholles, t. v. p. 286 seq.

[2] Huber, p. 26.

[3] Bréholles, v. 295 seq. 307, 348 seq.

[4] In the letter to the cardinals of 10 March 1239, and in the Encyclical from Padua (Bréholles, v. pp. 282 seq. 307).

[5] Bréholles, iii. p. 244 seq.

[6] Bréh. iv. 490, 735 seq.

[7] Ib. p. 759 seq.

[8] Ib. pp. 479 seq. 776 seq.

[9] Bréholles, iv. 796 seq.

[10] Ib. p. 830, n. 5.   Annal. Wormat. h.a. p. 165.

[11] Ib. pp. 870 seq. 904 seq.   Vita Greg. p. 581.

[12] Ib. p. 827, n. 1.

§ 9.

Frederick took his stand on a despotic law of King Roger, a law revolting to all free men in the Middle Ages,[1] which declared it sacrilege to dispute the judgments, deeds, ordinances, counsels of a king, or the fitness of those chosen or appointed by him.[2] He even applied this law to the Pope, when Gregory declared a bishop appointed by Frederick to be unworthy of the office; and Gregory very justly complained of this.[3] Frederick asserted that the Pope had no power to excommunicate him. Gregory declared this to be heretical[4] according to the existing law, and on account of the denial of the spiritual power of the Holy See. Frederick wrote to the Romans inciting them against and insulting the Pope,[5] telling them that he had absolved the towns of the march of Ancona and of the duchy of Spoleto from their oath of allegiance to the Pope, as it was his intention permanently to separate these districts from the States of the Church.[6] His conduct was like that of Napoleon I. in 1806, and Victor Emmanuel in 1860 and 1870: especially the proclamations and letters of Napoleon show a striking likeness to the manifestoes and letters of Frederick II. Frederick mocked at the intercessory processions held in Rome by the Pope in his great need in 1240, as comedies played by boys and old women.[7] More than 100 Italian nobles were outlawed by him on the 13th June 1239, for having joined the cause of the Church,[8] and he persecuted religious orders and all followers of the Pope with the utmost cruelty.[9] Many German princes remained faithful to the Pope,[10] and in Italy Frederick found himself unable to take the towns either of Milan or Bologna; he was obliged to content himself with ravaging the surrounding country. Whilst besieging Ascoli, in the summer of 1240, he entered into an armistice which included the Lombards; he then besieged Faenza from the end of August of that year till April 1241; he was drawing nearer and nearer to Rome. Thus at the very time when the German Empire was being assailed by the Tartars, the

Christian emperor waged a furious war against the Head of
the Church, and rejected all overtures of peace.[11]   Whilst Frederick was assuring his followers in Germany, who were not at
this time very numerous, that he was anxious for peace, and that
he considered it imminent, in a confidential letter to his son
Conrad he says that, in spite of the Pope's fair offers, he should
bring the affair to an issue by the sword; that he should, with
his great army, humble the pride of the high priest, and treat
him in such a manner that in future *he would never venture
to open his mouth against the emperor.*[12]   Whilst Frederick himself acknowledges the Pope's desire for peace, Dr. Huber (p. 29)
represents him as living and dying inexorable and unappeased.
Shortly before his death Gregory sent Bartholomew of Trent to
Frederick; but Frederick would not hear of repentance.[13]   If
the Pope had given him absolution without requiring satisfaction, it would have been contrary to all the rules of the Church,[14]
and would have disgraced Gregory in the eyes of his contemporaries and of posterity.   There was more than worldly policy to
be considered; the situation was one that involved the whole
position of the Church.   There is no difficulty in comprehend-
ing the reason of the Pope's order to his legate in Hungary
that the Crusaders should fight against Frederick instead of in
Palestine,[15] since if the Holy See should be permanently deprived of power and liberty by Frederick, the cause of the Holy
Land would be hopeless.

   [1] Joh. Sarisb. Polycr. l. vii. c. xx. p. 688 seq., nearly a hundred years
previously depicts the servile fawning ecclesiastics, slaves of tyrannical
princes, and together with Barbarossa's favourite words places these in
their mouth: 'Sacrilegii instar est dubitare, an is dignus sit, quem princeps elegerit.' He shows how these tyrants made their servants into
bishops, who indulged them in every way and counselled them to evil;
whilst courageous champions of truth appeared to them as enemies of
princes. He says of such princes, p. 691: 'Hi, qui divinam evacuare ni-
tuntur, ut suam statuant auctoritatem, sine liberis moriuntur aut eos
relinquunt degeneres et ignavos. Procul dubio quisquis ecclesiasticam
deprimit libertatem, aut punitur in se aut punitur in sobole. Amittunt
ergo filii etiam propria, cum his quae favore eorum paterna impietas occu-
pavit.' This was fulfilled in Frederick II.
   [2] Bréholles, iv. 9.
   [3] Ib. 914 seq.

[4] Ib. v. 339, 340.
[5] Ib. iv. 901 seq.
[6] Hefele, v. 950.
[7] Brćh. v. 840 seq.
[8] Ib. p. 318 seq.
[9] Ib. pp. 343 seq. 435, 785, 866, 903.   Giov. Villani, Chron. Flor. l. vi.
Flav. Biondo, ii. Dec. 7.   S. Antonin. Sum. Hist. tit. 19, c. vi.
[10] Hefele, v. p. 948.
[11] Hefele, v. 957, 952, 953.
[12] Brćholles, v. 1003, 1005, 1007.
[13] Hefele, v. 958.
[14] Cf. the passages from the Fathers in Gratian, c. xxxiii. q. 3, and
Joh. Saresb. Ep. 219, ad Alex. III. p. 244.   Polycr. l. v. c. v. p. 548.
[15] Hefele, v. 956.

§ 10.

On the 9th August 1240, Gregory, in the hope of obtaining
peace, complied with Frederick's demand of the preceding year,[1]
and summoned a General Council for Easter 1241 ;[2] but Frederick,
who had nothing personally to hope from it, hindered its assem-
bling with all the authority and means of intimidation at his disposal.   On the 3d May he caused the prelates travelling to Rome
to be made prisoners with great violence,[3] that is, more than
a hundred bishops and delegates, the deputies from Lombardy, and three cardinals, Bishop Jacob Pecorara of Palestrina (who to avoid Frederick's snares had travelled in the dress
of a pilgrim to Genoa, and from there to France,[4] and was
returning by Genoa), Otho of St. Nicholas, and Gregory of
Romania.   The emperor boasted of this crime, and for a long
time did not release the prisoners.[5]   When, on the 21st August
1241, the heart of the magnanimous and aged Pope broke with
all the misery he had endured, Frederick informed the princes
of his death in coarse terms that befitted neither a knight nor
an emperor.[6]   After the death of the Pope, whilst the Holy See
was still vacant, he devastated the States of the Church,[7] as if to
show more and more that the Pope was justified in his conduct,
and to prove that the true object of his attack was not so much
the person of Gregory IX. as the Holy See.   Frederick's deeds
and his letters are Gregory's noblest apology.   The Gallicans[8]
—for instance, Natalis Alexander—avowed this, and it is only
questioned by some professors of our day, no true Catholics.

[1] Bréholles, v. p. 301 seq.

[2] Spondan. a. 1241, n. 1.

[3] Bréh. v. 1112 seq. 1118 seq.

[4] Richard a S. Germ. a. 1239. Rayn. h.a. n. 38.

[5] Richard a S. Germ. a. 1241. Matth. Paris, l.c. Spond. a. 1241, n. 11. Bianchi, l.c. n. 9, pp. 436, 437.

[6] Bréh. v. p. 1165 seq. Hefele, p. 963.

[7] Hefele, pp. 964, 965.

[8] Natal. Alex. H. E. saec. 13 et 14, c. i. a. 3 : 'Concilium, cujus sententia se exutum iri imperio praevidebat Fridericus, celebrandum prohibere studuit, minis deterrens episcopos a Romano itinere. Per Gregorium non stetit, quin sacerdotium inter et imperium pax iniretur, si Fr. arma feritatemque deponere et Ecclesiae satisfacere voluisset. Tartarorum enim in Ungariam irruptio illataque Belae Ungariae et Colomano Ruthenorum regibus clades pontificium pectus urgebat ad pacem optandam offerendamque perduelli adversus eam imperatori, ut deinde ad propulsandos Tartaros omnium arma verterentur. Id constat ex Ep. Greg. IX. ad Carinthiae ducem et ad Belam regem Ungariae 91 et 108, l. xv. At pacem Frid. recusavit, rebus secundis insolens et Romae totiusque Italiae dominationi inhians.'

§ 11.

These professors appeal to St. Louis, King of France, who they say supported Frederick's cause, and showed himself wholly in his favour. Let us look at the facts. On the 10th May 1232, at a time when Frederick was at peace with the Church, Louis IX. entered into a friendly league with the emperor at Pordenone, when each pledged himself to join no enterprise injurious to the other or his heirs in life or honour, to assist the other against his enemies, and permit no war to be made upon him.[1] The more jealous and passionate Frederick was, the more care did the chivalrous and generous Louis take to avoid giving him any offence, and to set his actions before him in a pleasing light ; his letters to the emperor always breathe a deep piety. In 1236, Frederick complained to Louis of the partiality shown by the Pope to his prejudice in favour of the Lombard rebels, and insisted that the interests of all sovereigns required the subjection of rebels such as these.[2] Thus he spread distrust of the Pope, and succeeded in gaining credit in France by his vehement protestations of innocence. Moreover, we only know what the English chronicler Matthew Paris tell us ; but he has been shown to be untrustworthy,[3] and good critics say that his chronicles 'are so full of gross errors, that except when supported by contemporaneous testimony or documentary evidence they have been long recognised as unworthy of any, or of any but the slightest, credence ;'[4] moreover, not a few of the documents he brings forward are suspicious. Therefore the only testimonies we have are such as criticism must take exception to.

It is very questionable whether Gregory IX. actually had the intention which Matthew Paris ascribes to him of conferring the empire upon Prince Robert of France, brother of King Louis ; no other trace of such an intention is to be found. If it be true that the French refused the Pope any support against Frederick, how comes it that the same author tells of the return from France of the Cardinal-legate Jacob with so considerable a sum of money that it sufficed to pay the expenses of the war ?[5] If the French nobles (or Louis himself) said that the emperor had no superior or equal,[6] how could the French ambassadors, in the face of the imperious Frederick, have declared that their king was higher than any emperor constituted merely by election ?[7] If, subsequently, Gregory entered into fresh negotiations with Frederick, how could he have declared that Frederick's well-known crimes had condemned him so utterly and irrecoverably that he could never be reinstated ?[8] How can it be asserted with even a shadow of foundation that the Pope, on receiving the money from France, commissioned Cardinal Colonna to put an end to the truce which had been concluded on account of the Council, when it is established that such a truce never existed at all ?[9] How could it be said in letters from the French nobles that Frederick had never comported himself in a hostile manner against France, when we are told elsewhere of his hostile schemes in the year 1238 ?[10] But even supposing that we could unreservedly accept these letters as genuine, they prove only that the French nobles (not the king) declare that *it appeared to them* that Frederick was innocent ; they had observed nothing wrong in him ; they would send ambassadors to him, who should investigate the state of his mind with regard to the Catholic faith (an inquiry likely to be frustrated by Frederick's talent for hypocrisy). Should they discover that he was in bad disposi-

tions, they as well as the Pope would persecute him even unto·
death.[11]   If he had merited deposition they thought that the
sentence should be delivered against him only by a General
Council.[12]   The reason of this was that it might be quite clear
that the decision was an impartial one, and properly conducted,
as the Pope was suspected of partiality.[13] If these letters are genuine, they are certainly a weapon for those who hold that princes
can be deposed by the Church on account of heresy.[14] It is certain
that later Louis modified very much his favourable opinion of
Frederick, when he learnt his violent conduct towards the bishops
on their way to the Council, amongst whom were many French.
He repeatedly wrote to Frederick on the subject,[15] at last with·
threats,[16] till he had obtained their release.[17] Frederick yielded
to save appearances, while he still kept Cardinals Jacob and
Otho in confinement,[18] and after the death of Celestine IV. impeded the election of his successor.   If the letters of Louis on
this subject are genuine,[19] he was convinced of the guilt of
Frederick, from whom the cardinals were entitled and bound to
demand the security of the conclave and the release of their imprisoned colleagues.[20]

[1] Bréholles, iv. 353 seq. Pertz, Leg. ii. 293.

[2] Bréh. iv. 873 seq.

[3] Raynald. a. 1213, n. 71; a. 1239, n. 39 ; a. 1254, 71, 72. Spondan. h.a.
n. 13. Natal. Alex. H. E. saec. 13 et 14, c. iv. a. 3, n. 4, t. xv. p. 250, ed.
Bing. 1789. Aub. Miraeus, Auctor. de Script. Eccl. c. cccciii. Oudin.
Com. de Script. Eccl. t. iii. saec. 13, a. 1240, p. 200 (al. p. 530): 'Omnes
secat, universos pungit, ac si nulli mortalium aut parcere aut condonare
rigidissime sibi proposuisset.' Cf. Baron. a. 996, n. 54 ; a. 1197, n. 17.

[4] Thus Döllinger, Lehrbuch d. K.G. (1843), ii. p. 219, No. 1. Cf. Potthast (l.c. p. 438 seq.) : 'It is proved that three writers are hidden under
the name of Matthew Paris : Roger of Wendover, who is the most trustworthy, the continuator William Rishanger, and standing in time between
them Paris himself, who in many details cannot be absolved from the reproach of *premeditated inventions* and of a love of *anecdote*, very dangerous
to historical truth.' Wattenbach (Deutschlands Gesch. Quellen, Berlin,
1858, p. 420) observes : 'Matthew Paris was very prone to sharp judgments
and unsparing reprobation ; he attacks no one more severely than the Holy
See whilst glorifying Frederick II.'

[5] Matth. Paris, ad a. 1240.

[6] Tantum principem, quo non est major, imo nec par inter Christianos.

[7] Credimus enim D. nostrum regem Galliae, quem linea regii sangui-

nis provexit ad sceptra Francorum regenda, excellentiorem esse aliquo imperatore, quem sola electio provehit voluntaria.

[8] ' Scelera enim praedicti Friderici multiplicia, sicut jam novit mundus, eandem *irrestaurabiliter* condemnarunt.' This mode of expression is altogether exceptional.

[9] Cf. also Raynald. a. 1240, n. 52 seq.; Spond. a. 1240, 1241.

[10] Guillelm. de Nangiaco Chron. a. 1238 : ' Quemadmodum malitiosus et seductor aliquid satagebat in regem et regnum Franciae machinari.'

[11] Matth. Paris, a. 1239 : ' Et si nil nisi sanum invenerint, cur infestandus est ? Sin autem, et ipsum, imo etiam ipsum Papam, si male de Deo senserit, usque ad internecionem persequemur.'

[12] Ib. ' Si (Frid.) ab apice imperiali meritis suis exigentibus deponendus esset, nonnisi per Concilium generale cassandus judicaretur.'

[13] Bossuet, l.c. p. 348, believes this answer to have been one reason for convoking the Council.

[14] Cf. Gosselin, ii. p. 109.

[15] Bréholles, vi. 18, 59 seq.   Rayn. 1242, n. 5.

[16] Regnum Franciae non est adeo debilitatum viribus, quod se vestris permittat calcaribus perurgeri.

[17] Guill. de Nang. a. 1240; Nicol. Giles, Annales de France, a. 1240. Frederick was not absolutely deprived of the empire, and could still be treated as emperor. The letters in De Vineis, i. 12, 13, some think have been altered (Bianchi, l.c. n. 14, pp. 445-448).

[18] According to Matth. Paris, he liberated them for the election of the new Pope, stipulating that they should afterwards return into captivity. But Richard of S. Germano and others say this was not the case, and in April 1242 they were still not at liberty.

[19] Bréholles, vi. pp. 68, 70.   Böhmer, Regesten, p. 352, doubts their authenticity.   Cf. Hefele, v. 965.

[20] Bréholles, vi. 204.

§ 12.

At length, on the 25th June 1243, Cardinal Sinibald Fiesco was elected at Anagni, under the title of Innocent IV. He immediately sent plenipotentiaries with the fairest proposals to Frederick, with whom he had once been on terms of friendship. His principal appeal was for the release of the captive prelates, promising to take this as a special token of his willingness to be reconciled to the Church. He left it to the emperor to arrange what he would do as satisfaction on his release from the excommunication, and declared himself ready to repair any wrong that he could prove had been done him by the Church. The decision on the matter was to be intrusted to a large assembly of civil and spiritual princes, and all adherents of the Church were to be included in the peace.[1]   Frederick did not

entertain those proposals, but alleged a host of grievances, which
Innocent in a letter (26th August) to his plenipotentiaries discussed in detail. During the negotiations Frederick continued his
hostilities, laid siege to Viterbo, and alleged as a fresh grievance
against the Pope that some of his followers had been robbed
and maltreated ; although he was obliged to confess that not
only were the Pope and his legate, the Cardinal-deacon Otho,[2]
quite innocent of the affair, but that the latter had interfered to
prevent the crime at some risk to his own life.   However, when
the falling off from his cause had become more universal, he
entered into fresh negotiations at the end of the year 1243.
Finally, on the 31st March 1244, peace was solemnly sworn to
at Rome by Frederick's representatives.[3]   But Frederick interpreted it differently from the Pope,[4] excited disturbances in
Rome by means of the Frangipani,[5] and refused to give up the
occupied territory or to release the prisoners until he had received absolution.[6]   He must have known that could not be
done, and that to ask it was an insult to the rules of the Church.
The whole proceeding was only another added to the long list
of his deceptions of the Holy See.[7]   Innocent sent Cardinal
Otho to the proposed conference at Narni, for he had been
warned of Frederick's knavery; he himself fled from Sutri
through Genoa to Lyons, where, on the 3d January 1245, he
convened a General Council to be held on the Feast of St. John,
which was to compose the dispute between Frederick and the
Church.   Frederick was invited to appear personally, or by
plenipotentiaries.[8]   Only after fruitless negotiations and fresh
postponements,[9] Innocent took the measure of pronouncing
sentence at Lyons.   Dr. Huber is silent on all these prelimi-
naries ; he only says (p. 29) : 'Innocent IV. immediately (!)
renewed at the Council of Lyons the sentence of excommunication and deposition.'

[1] Raynald. a. 1243, n. 14.   Bréholles, vi. 112.
[2] Hefele, v. p. 966 seq.
[3] Raynald. a. 1244, n. 16 seq.   Bréholles, l.c. p. 168 seq.
[4] Frederick says this in the memorial of the summer of 1244. Bréholles,
l.c. p. 203 seq.
[5] Bréholles, l.c. pp. 183-188.

⁶ Frederick's memorial, just mentioned, shows this. Cf. Döllinger, Lehrbnch, ii. p. 237 seq.
⁷ Phillips, K.R. iii. § 128, p. 129 seq.
⁸ Mansi, xxiii. 608 seq. Rayn. a 1245, n. 1.
⁹ Bréholles, vi. 222, 282. Hefele, v. 972, 988 seq.

§ 13.

The crimes Frederick was charged with, and which his advocate Thaddeus of Suessa was unable to argue away, were almost the same as those which occasioned the loss of the empire to his predecessor in the purple, Otho IV.;[1] namely (1) many perjuries ; (2) sacrileges, especially with regard to the imprisoned prelates ; (3) unbelief, and intercourse with Saracen women and Saracens ; (4) his tyrannical government in the kingdom of Sicily, with violation of all feudal duties, retaining the feudal tax, obliging vassals to fight against their lord paramount. His crimes even exceeded those of Otho, whose deposition Frederick had acknowledged to be a righteous act.[2] In the same way Rudolph of Hapsburg recognised later that Frederick's deposition was lawful, when he only confirmed the privileges conferred by him before the Pope's sentence of deposition and excommunication.[3]

[1] Richard a S. Germano, Chron. Murat. R. It. Scr. vii. 989.
[2] C. 2, Ad Apostolicae, ii. 14, de Sent. et re Jud. in 6. Mansi, l.c. p. 613.
[3] Böhmer, Reg. Imp. ii. p. 54.

§ 14.

The Pope regarded as hypocritical and deceitful snares all such proposals of the emperor's as the following : To effect the subjection of the Greek Empire to the obedience of Rome, which was a task beyond Frederick's strength, and one which he had never furthered in the slightest degree ; to undertake a new Crusade, when for sixteen years, to the great loss of Christendom, he had refused to engage in one ; to fight against the Mongols, who had invaded and were devastating Germany, when his duty as ruler already made it incumbent upon him to resist them. These high-sounding promises, made at Lyons by Thaddeus of Suessa, might have had some effect if Frederick had at least in

some measure performed those he had previously sworn to at
Rome ;[1] but as he had not executed what was light and easy, how
could great and arduous things be expected of him ?   After the
sentence Frederick declared, in a memorial of the 31st July
1245,[2] that he acknowledged the Pope's supremacy in spiritual
things ; but not his right to take kingdoms at will, and inflict
the loss of their kingdoms upon kings and princes, least of all
upon the German emperor, who was independent of all laws.[3]
He asserted that all the proceedings against him were informal
and illegal.   In maintaining that his condemnation could be upheld neither by divine nor human laws, Frederick overlooked the
fact that with regard to Sicily he had acknowledged in public
documents that he was the Pope's vassal ; he also overlooked
the whole development of the public law of Christian States. His
anger knew no bounds.   He demanded a third of its revenue
from every diocese for the expenses of the war against the Pope
and the Lombards, shamefully maltreated the followers and relations of the Pope, banished all priests who obeyed the sentence
of Lyons, persecuted especially the Franciscans and Dominicans,
even commanding that they should be bound together in couples
like foxes to be burnt.[4]   Nothing could be hoped for from such
a tyrant : the Pope, attacked to the uttermost, had to adopt extreme measures in his defence.   In the spring of 1246, public
opinion in Germany had so far undergone a reaction against
Frederick, that the followers of the Pope united to choose an
opposition king in the person of Henry Raspe of Thuringia, who
was victorious on the 5th August 1246, near Frankfort, over
Frederick's son Conrad.[5]   From 1247, when William of Holland
was elected in Germany, the fortune of war deserted Frederick
also in Italy.   As to the endeavours for a reconciliation set on
foot by Louis IX. of France,[6] it is certain that Innocent IV.
knew the deposed emperor far better than the French king did ;
at the very time of his memorials and his cunningly devised
letter to Louis of September 1245, Frederick had issued commands and undertaken affairs in direct contradiction to the sentiments therein expressed ; but by this time he was too well known
and his schemes were too plainly deceitful.[7]   The Pope, and

especially the Council of Lyons (can. 14-17),[3] did their utmost to remedy the loss of the Holy Land and the defencelessness of Germany against the Mongols, whilst Frederick applied himself only by words to both these important matters. Not till he saw death approach did Frederick testify any repentance, and he then endeavoured to repair many a grievous wrong. His influence might have been as profitable as it was rendered fatal through his sensuality, cruelty, faithlessness, and tyranny. The only fruit of the splendid education he had received from his guardian, Innocent III., was that he fostered learning and education. In the early part of his career he cannot be said to have contributed to the prosperity of cities, for he framed laws prejudicial to their autonomy; only in the last five years of his reign did he show himself more favourable towards them.[9] His life was a grand misuse of his gifts and powers.

[1] Hefele, v. 984.

[2] Bréholles, vi. 331.

[3] Per quam (sententiam) imperator Romanus in laesae majestatis crimine dicitur condemnatus per quam ridiculose legi subjicitur, qui legibus omnibus imperialiter est solutus.

[4] Bréholles, vi. 357 seq. 366, 374, 375, 581, 701, 702. Cf. Höfler, Friedrich II. p. 227.

[5] Hefele, l.c. p. 1007 seq. 1009.

[6] A meeting between the King and the Pope took place at Clugny in Nov. 1245; further endeavours followed in the April and in the autumn of 1246 (Hefele, pp. 1005, 1008). Huber (p. 31 seq.) refers to Daunou, Essai Historique sur la Puissance Temporelle des Papes, i. 212. The report of the conversation, which Döllinger (Lehrb. ii. p. 219) thinks very questionable, comes from Matth. Paris.

[7] 'In omnibus se reddidit incredibilem' are words reported of the Pope by M. Paris. Later, Louis promised if it were necessary to defend the Pope and the Church by force of arms. Hefele, p. 1012.

[8] Hefele, pp. 993-996.

[9] Bréholles, iii. 445 seq.; iv. 286 seq.; vi. 366. Hefele, pp. 880, 882.

PART III. THE EMPIRE FROM FREDERICK II. TILL ITS FALL.

§ 1. Rudolph of Hapsburg. § 2. Adolphus of Nassau and Albert. § 3. Henry VII. § 4. The emperor's oath and the rights of the Pope. § 5. Henry VII.'s quarrel with the Pope. § 6. Declaration of Clement V. § 7. The imperial vicariate in Italy. § 8. Louis of Bavaria and Frederick of Austria. § 9. Louis excommunicated. § 10. Louis de-

clared to have forfeited the empire. § 11. His campaign in Italy.
§ 12. Louis and Benedict XII. § 13. The controversy as to Louis.
§ 14. Election of Charles IV. § 15. From Charles IV. to Charles V.
§ 16. Disputes with Charles V. § 17. Abdication of Charles V. § 18.
Fall of the ancient German Empire.

§ 1.

From the deposition of Frederick II., A.D. 1245, till the
coronation of Henry VII., A.D. 1312, there was no lawful emperor.[1] Innocent IV. endeavoured to obtain recognition for
William of Orange, who had been elected by the Church party
in Germany, and who, after the death of Frederick (December
13th, 1250), and after having conquered Conrad IV.,[2] had a
meeting with the Pope at Lyons, and made some progress in
Germany. After William's death in 1256, the German princes
again split into two parties, who respectively elected Prince
Richard of Cornwall and Alphonso X. of Castile. Of these the
former came to Germany but for a short time, the latter never.
Almost all the princes of the empire showed themselves to be
corrupt, selfish, and fickle.[3] The Pope positively forbad the
proposed election of the boy Conradin, because the Hohenstaufen were enemies of the Church, and the Holy See could
not choose as her protector one who had insulted her.[4] Alexander
IV., who was applied to by both candidates, gave no decision
concerning the disputed election.[5] Urban IV., elected in 1261,
invited both parties to Rome, there to state their case.[6] But both
accepted the invitation as implying their right to be undoubted,
that their summons to Rome signified that their election would be
confirmed by the Pope, and that they should be crowned by him.
Urban upon this rejected both candidates, and justly, for how could
his decision carry weight if he were denied the right to decide ?
Alphonso was the first to take this step, and Richard's ambassador
followed. The Pope endeavoured to negotiate an understanding
between the parties. His successor, Clement IV., at once took
up the affair ; both sides prevaricated, and the German princes,
contrary to the Pope's advice, meditated a fresh election. When
Alphonso, after the death of Richard in 1272, demanded the
imperial crown of Pope Gregory X., the latter declared that he

must first hear the German princes who had elected Richard, for that their rights should not be encroached upon. Alphonso was offended at this, and conceived the project of sending an army into Italy. But as his supporters in Germany were dead, and he now enjoyed little consideration there, the time seemed come to end the strife, and Gregory advised the princes to make a new and unanimous election, otherwise with the help of the cardinals it would be his care to provide an emperor.[7]

Rudolph of Hapsburg was elected in 1273, and on the 26th September 1274, was recognised at Lyons by the Pope as King of the Romans. Later, when Alphonso had shown himself inclined to give way, Rudolph was invited to receive the imperial crown. He met the Pope, Gregory X., at Lausanne, in October 1275, and took the customary oaths;[8] but he never came to Rome to be crowned. Rudolph died in 1291. In 1279, under King Rudolph and Pope Nicholas III., many princes of the empire expressly acknowledged it to be a special favour from the Holy See that the king they elected was also chosen to be future emperor. The codes of law known as the Sachsenspiegel and the Schwabenspiegel are identical with the Pope's view of public law.[9] The latter maintained that the emperor should exercise his authority to procure due obedience for the Pope in case of necessity by the imperial ban. The Germans elect the King of the Romans[10] and enthrone him at Aix-la-Chapelle, but the Pope by his consecration confers the full power of the empire and the imperial title.

<hr>

[1] Phillips, K.R. iii. § 123, p. 123.

[2] 'Such bitterness had the Pope created in men's minds,' exclaims Huber (p. 32), 'that even German prelates had sworn to murder their king.' But the prelates in question (the Bishop of Ratisbon and the Abbot of St. Emmeran) had suffered very much from the Hohenstaufen, and were thus exercising a private revenge upon Conrad, whom besides they did not recognise as their lawful king. It is nowhere shown that Innocent IV. had any share in the sudden attack made on Conrad at Christmas 1250; he had only expressed himself against Conrad, who appeared to be following his father's example only too closely.

[3] Hefele, vi. p. 10 seq.

[4] Alex. IV. Const. 7, Firma, to the Archbishop of Mainz, July 1256, § 1: 'Quanta vigilantia debet adhiberi, ubi de advocato Ecclesiae agitur, de ipsius defensore tractatur, ne pro advocato impugnator et pro defensore

assumatur offensor.' Cf. Card. Vinc. Petra, Com. in Const. ap. t. iii. p. 116 seq.; Urban IV. ap. Rayn. a. 1262, n. 5 (not Urban VI., as we find it in Huber, p. 23). By the election of Conradin, who was at that time only four years old, the existing condition of rebellion against law and order would not have been ended but increased. The same reasons held good now as at the death of Henry VI.

[5] Raynald. a. 1257, n. 8 ; 1263, n. 40, 41, 43.

[6] Cf. Bianchi, t. ii. l. vi. § 8, n. 3, p. 555 seq.

[7] Böhmer, Fontes, ii. p. 112. Cf. Ricord. Malasp. Hist. Flor. c. cxcviii.; Villani, Chron. l. vii. c. xliii. ; Naucler. Gen. c. xliii.

[8] Raynald. a. 1274, n. 7, 12, 51, 54 ; a. 1275, n. 37 seq.

[9] Pertz, M. G. Hist. iv. 421 : ' Complectens ab olim sibi Romana mater Ecclesia quadam quasi germana charitate Germaniam illam eo terrenae dignitatis nomine decoravit, quod est super omne nomen temporaliter tantum praesidentium super terram, plantans in ea principes tamquam arbores praeelectas et rigans illas gratia singulari, illud eis dedit incrementum mirandi potentia, ut ipsius Ecclesiae auctoritate suffulti, velut germen electum per ipsorum electionem illum, qui frena Romani teneret imperii, germinaret.'

[10] Cf. Senkenberg, in the preface to the Schwabenspiegel, § 20; Eichhorn, Deutsche R. und Rechts-Geschichte, vol. ii. ; Gosselin, ii. p. 323 seq. Vide the passages in Friedberg, p. 29, No. 5 ; p. 87, No. 1.

[11] The land law of the Sachsenspiegel, b. iii. a. 57, § 2, and the feudal law of the same code, art. 4, § 2, mention expressly the seven electors. The English ambassadors in Rome under Urban IV. mentioned them in their judicial statement in favour of Richard of Cornwall, according to Urban's letter to Richard (Raynald. a. 1263, n. 53). Cf. Hefele, vi. p. 18, No. 1. Nicholas of Cusa thought they had been appointed by the Emperor Henry II. with the consent of the nobles and people. Cf. Düx, Nicholas of Cusa, vol. ii. p. 303. Thomassin (P. iii. l. i. c. xxx. n. 18) places their origin in the second half of the thirteenth century.

§ 2.

Adolphus of Nassau could not aspire to the empire ; he was a man of small account. Albert of Austria, who conquered and slew him in 1298, was acknowledged King of the Romans for the first time in 1303.[1] He despatched a letter to Rome, promising fidelity and obedience, and fully recognised that the Roman See had conferred upon the German princes the power of electing the King of the Romans and future emperor.[2] He promised also not to send any imperial vicar to Tuscany or Lombardy for five years without the consent of the Pope, and to fight against the enemies of the Church. On the 1st May 1308, Albert was murdered by his nephew John.

[1] Rayn. a. 1302, u. 2 seq. Böhmer, p. 231 seq. 243.

[2] Rayn. a. 1303, n. 8-13. Pertz, ii. 483, 484. Böhmer, p. 235. Albert acknowledged: 'Quod jus elegendi Romanorum regem in imperatorem postmodum promovendum certis principibus ecclesiasticis et saecularibus est ab eadem Sede (sc. Ap.) concessum, a qua reges et imperatores, qui fuerunt et erunt pro tempore, recipiunt temporalis gladii potestatem ad vindictam malefactorum laudem vero bonorum.' He avows: 'Quod Romanorum reges in imperatores postmodum promovendi per Sedem eamdem ad hoc potissime ac specialiter assumuntur, ut sint S. Romanae Ecclesiae advocati, Catholicae fidei ac ejusdem Ecclesiae praecipui defensores.' Albert also fully acknowledges what appears to Huber (p. 37) as Papal usurpation.

§ 3.

Philip the Fair of France endeavoured to obtain the vacant imperial throne for his brother Charles of Valois; but the Pope, through Cardinal Prato, brought his influence to bear upon the spiritual electors,[1] and in 1308, Henry of Lutzelburg was unanimously elected. Henry's ambassadors took the customary oaths relative to the protection of the Pope and of the Church,[2] and he renewed them in person at Lausanne in October 1310. On the 6th January 1311 he was crowned King of the Lombards at Milan, and received the imperial crown from the hands of the cardinal delegates at the Lateran on the 29th June 1312.[3] Henry thought that as emperor he was monarch of all the world, and that all kings were subject to him; but as he was not powerful enough to maintain his position over the various parties in the empire, he shortly found himself merely leader of the Ghibellines. He quarrelled with King Robert of Naples, whom he treated as a simple vassal, whereas he was so only as far as his earldom of Provence was concerned. When (before Henry's coronation as emperor) Clement V. bade both him and Robert conclude a peace and recall their troops from Rome, appealing to the oaths each had taken to the Holy See, Henry, surrounded as Frederick Barbarossa used to be with a crowd of lawyers,[4] protested that in their opinion it was quite unlawful to put him and his vassals on a par, and to ascribe to him an oath of fidelity which he had never sworn, and thus to slight the imperial dignity. At the same time he declared himself willing, from affection for the Pope, not to make war upon

Robert for the space of one year, and to send a stately embassy to Avignou.[5]

[1] Christophe, Hist. of the Papacy during the Fourteenth Century (Germ. Trans.), vol. i. book iii. pp. 173, 174.
[2] Pertz, Leg. ii. p. 492 seq.   Rayn. a. 1309, n. 10 seq.
[3] Hefele, vi. 383 seq.   Phillips, K.R. iii. § 132, p. 276 seq.
[4] Barthold. Römerzug Heinrichs VII. vol. ii. p. 279.
[5] Raynald. a. 1312, n. 44 seq.   Hefele, vi. p. 489.

§ 4.

That the German emperor was never considered a *vassal* of the Pope, that his oath was not the same as a *feudal* oath of allegiance, appears from the following considerations : (1) No Pope at his accession ever thought of requiring that the emperor should apply to him for a renewal of his investiture, as a feudal lord might have required from a vassal.   (2) The oath taken by the emperor was an oath of homage, but not a feudal oath. If it had been a feudal oath it would have stated that the emperors held their dominions from the Holy See, whereas it only lays down the obligation of protection and fidelity towards the Holy See, and contains the promise of defending her.[1]   The difference may be seen by comparing the oath which Robert Guiscard took for Naples[2] with the oath taken by the German emperors.[3]   The form of oath which Gregory VII., after the death of Rudolph (15th October 1080), sent to Bishop Altmann of Passau and Abbot William of Hirscham to be sworn by the new king was intended only to insure to the Pope security against schism and against the antipope set up by Henry IV. ; it promised obedience ' as befitted a Christian.'   Rudolph also had promised this.[4]   The words ' champion (miles) of St. Peter and of the Pope' show no special feudal relation.[5]   (3) As the Pope in conferring the title of emperor upon Charles the Great and Otho the Great gave them no new territory, but only a dignified office and a preëminence over other princes, and laid upon them the obligation of protecting the Church, this obligation is naturally the chief matter of the oath.[6]   Henry VII. took precisely the same oath.[7]   We find feudal investiture only in the case of Lothair II. receiving from Innocent II. Mathilda's in-

'heritance for himself, his daughter, and his son-in-law,[8] as well as in the investiture with the kingdom of Sicily. The marks of reverence prescribed by custom[9] were not accounted humiliating in the Middle Ages. Some were in use only during a short period; for instance, the 'adoration,' which later became obsolete. All these acts are quite independent of feudal investiture.

[1] Phillips, K.R. iii. § 119, p. 58 seq.

[2] Hefele, Conc. iv. 768; v. 139. Formulas of 1059 and 1080, the latter post Greg. VII. l. viii. Ep. 1, p. 574 seq. Pag. a. 1080, n. 5.

[3] Vide the oath of Otho I. in c. xxxiii. d. 63, Pertz, M. G. iv. 29. Also Phillips, l.c. § 123, p. 115 seq. 125 seq. Of Henry II. we read in Dietmar, Chron. l. vii. Baron. a. 1014, n. 1: 'Ad Ecclesiam S. Petri, Papa exspectante, venit et antequam introduceretur, ab eodem interrogatus, si fidelis vellet Romanae patronus esse et defensor Ecclesiae, sibi antem suisque successoribus per omnia fidelis, devota professione respondit et tunc ab eodem inunctionem et coronam . . . . suscepit.' The coronation oaths of 1111 and 1133 (Pertz, l.c. pp. 68, 82) are equally different from feudal oaths.

[4] Greg. VII. l. ix. Ep. 3, p. 608: 'Providendum est ergo, ut non minus ab eo, qui est eligendus in regem, inter tot pericula et labores sperare debeamus.' Ib.: 'Sanctae Ecclesiae humiliter devotus et utilis, quemadmodum Christianum regem oportet.'

[5] Although the word 'miles' is often used of vassals (l. iii. Feud. tit. 1, § 1), in itself it is much more comprehensive. So too 'ligium' and 'homaginm' are both used in different senses. The use of the words 'fidelis' and 'dominus' neither prove an oath of vassalage (Friedberg, l.c. pp. 82, 83). Bossuet, l. i. sect. 1, c. xii. p. 110, makes his case very easy by giving no proofs. It all depends upon the obligations entered into. In this case these are: (1) Obedience to the Church as befits a Christian; (2) agreement with the Pope concerning the ordinatio ecclesiarum and concerning the territory and prerogatives of the Holy See; (3) defence of the Church. There is no word of a feudal tribute. Cf. Bianchi, t. i. l. ii. § 12, p. 328 seq. In Bernold, 'miles' and 'fidelis' are used as general terms (Phillips, p. 132, No. 45). Baldwin I., who notified to Pope Innocent III. in a letter in 1204 his election as Emperor of Constantinople, called himself 'Dei gratia imperator et semper Augustus,' and at the same time 'miles Papae' (Innoc. III. l. vii. Ep. 152; Migne, ccxv. p. 447).

[6] Murat. Liturgia Romana vetus, Venet. 1748, f. t. i. p. 455. Cf. Dissert. de Reb. Liturg. c. vi. pp. 72-77.

[7] According to Clement V. c. Romani principes, ii. 9, in Clem., the oath was quite the same as the formula in Muratori: 'Ego Henricus Romanorum rex, annuente Domino futurus imperator, promitto, spondeo et polliceor atque juro coram Deo et B. Petro, me de caetero protectorem et defensorem fore summi pontificis et hujus S. Rom. Ecclesiae, in omnibus necessitatibus et utilitatibus suis, custodiendo et conservando possessiones, honores et jura ejus, quantum divino suffultus adjutorio fuero, secundum

scire et posse meum, recta et pura fide.   Sic me Deus adjuvet et haec
sancta Dei evangelia.'
   * Cf. Hefele, v. p. 375.
   * Pipin exercised the 'officium stratoris' for the Pope's horse towards
Stephen II., and the Emperor Louis II. towards Nicholas I.   Vita Steph.
II. et Nicol. I. (Baron. a. 753, n. ult. a. 858); also in 1095, Conrad,
son of Henry IV. (Pertz, x. 474).   The Sachsenspiegel says it symbolised
the union of both powers and the help rendered by the civil power.   Cf.
Friedberg, l.c. p. 84, No. 2.

§ 5.

Henry was right in maintaining he had taken no oath of vassalage to the Pope, and was not, like Robert, the Pope's vassal.
Both were defenders of the Church, but with different rights
and for different reasons.   He was, however, wrong in repudiat-
ing the oath of fidelity, which he confused with the feudal oath
(homagium).   He had promised fidelity, if not the fidelity of a
liegeman.   It appertained to the oath of fidelity which he had
sworn to the Pope that he should not engage in war with any
of the Pope's vassals.[1]   Henry, however, maintained the alliance with King Frederick of Sicily, and prepared for war against
Robert.   After an abortive undertaking against Florence, he
laid the ban of the empire upon Robert, and sentenced him to
capital punishment.[2]   The Pope, with the utmost consideration,
intreated Henry VII. to retract the hasty order; at the same
time the Kings of France and England requested him immediately to declare the emperor's sentence to be null and void.
Any further measures of Henry's were frustrated by his early
death on the 24th August 1313.[3]

   [1] That is also to be found in Rudolph's oath.   Vide Raynald. a. 1274,.
n. 9.
   [2] Pertz, iv. 544 seq.
   [3] Raynald. a. 1313, n. 24.

§ 6.

Pope Clement V. saw that the emergency required that he
should enter more fully into the matter in two decretals.   He
declared that the oath which Henry had taken was an oath of
fidelity,[1] like those of former emperors and kings;[2] Robert lived
in Naples, and there was the Pope's vassal; the Pope was his

ordinary judge, therefore Henry could not summon Robert before his judicial tribunal outside the kingdom. The judgment had been delivered against an absent and undefended person, who was under no obligation to appear, least of all in a place that would not have been safe for him; it was a usurpation of jurisdiction, especially as it condemned the king to the loss of his kingdom, which was not held under the emperor, but under the Holy See.

[1] C. an. Romani principes, ii. 9, de jurejur. in Clem.
[2] The Pope quotes l.c. § Praefatis itaque, the formula in decretis (c. 33, Tibi Domino, d. 63), also the others used at the coronation, § Postque idem, and the promises collectively, § Porro praeter. He also calls to mind the promises of Rudolph and Albert. The Pope only speaks of the juramentum fidelitatis, nowhere of the vassal's oath (Huber, p. 39). The former was common to both princes, not so the latter. Clement V. describes the difference between them in the words: 'Cum ipsi reges ejusdem Ecclesiae specialissimi filii sibi juramento fidelitatis et alias multipliciter essent adstricti.'

§ 7.

After the death of Henry VII., the Pope appointed King Robert, during the vacancy of the empire, imperial vicar in Italy,[1] the crown of Italy being quite distinct from the crown of Germany. In this he acted in accordance with customary law, and followed the example of earlier Popes; by whom, to take one example, King Charles in 1268 was appointed imperial vicar.[2] The customary law attributed the care of the empire during an inter-imperium to the successor of St. Peter,[3] whose authority would, better than any other, restrain contending parties.[4] The imperial vicar should guard the imperial prerogatives, but relinquish his office as soon as the Pope should have confirmed as emperor the elected King of the Germans.[5] In Italy several petty dynasties usurped the authority of imperial vicar, had allegiance sworn to themselves, and occasioned much disorder. John XXII. rejected these would-be imperial vicars as interfering with the Papal prerogative, and threatened those who resisted with the ban and interdict.[6]

[1] Raynald. a. 1314, n. 2: 'Nos, ad quos Romani vacantis imperii regimen pertinere dignoscitur.'

² Raynald. a. 1267, n. 5-9. Bzov. h.a. n. 1. Bianchi, l.c. n. 4, pp. 559, 560. Spondan. h.a. n. 3, 4 ; a. 1268, n. 6. Ricord. Malesp. c. clxxxv. clxxxviii. Villani, l. vii. c. xv. xvi. xxi. Leon. Aret. l. ii. S. Antonin. Sum. Hist. tit. 20, c. i. § 5.
³ Bianchi, t. ii. l. vi. § 8, n. 1, pp. 552, 553. Phillips, pp. 288, 289.
⁴ Raynald. a. 1267, n. 9.
⁵ Rayn. a. 1314, n. 2 (Clement V. to King Robert, 14th March 1314).
⁶ C. Si fratrum, tit. 5. Ne Sede vacante, in Xvag. Joh. Rayn. a. 1317, n. 27 seq.; a. 1319, n. 6. Cf. Phillips, p. 290 seq.; Bianchi, l.c. n. 5, p. 561 seq. The words ' Cui in persona B. Petri terreni simul et coelestis imperii Deus jura ipse commisit,' are like similar earlier utterances of Popes, not to be taken to mean that the spiritual and temporal sovereignty are intrusted to him *alike*, and that all kingdoms are subject to him in temporal affairs. The rights of both are intrusted to the Pope's care, and he is bound to watch over them. With regard to the Holy Roman Empire, he had, however, special rights as having reconstituted it.

§ 8.

It was during the period that intervened between the death of Clement V. and the accession of his successor, John XXII., that the unfortunate double election occurred in Germany, when Louis of Bavaria was crowned at Aix-la-Chapelle and Frederick of Austria at Bonn, A.D. 1314.

Louis had the majority of votes. His election was made at the customary place, and he had been crowned at Aix-la-Cha-pelle. So much was in his favour. But his coronation had been performed by the Archbishop of Mainz, whilst Frederick had been crowned, though not in the right place, yet by the right person, the Archbishop of Cologne.[1] As the Papal chair was then vacant, Louis' electors wrote to the future Pope concerning the election (in which there was a question as to the rights of the Bohemian, Saxon, and Brandenburg electors),[2] demanding recognition for Louis and his coronation as emperor.[3] There was at that time no law in favour of the majority; neither of the parties would give way, and both were anxious to try the fortune of war. The Papal decision did not now carry all the force which it possessed in the time of Innocent III., for the influence of France was suspected in the decrees of the Papal court of Avignon. Neither was it now quite easy to arrive at a decision, for the balance of justice did not turn decidedly against either claimant.[4]   John XXII. rightly found it impossible to decide in favour of Louis without hearing the other side.   On the very day of his coronation (September 5, 1316) he wrote to Louis and Frederick, as well as to the princes of the kingdom, admonishing them to an amicable arrangement of the dispute.[5] A king unanimously elected by the German princes at that time would have been invited by the Pope to receive the imperial crown.   But they could not agree ; they hesitated, and some desired to remain neutral until the Pope should have confirmed one or other of the claimants.[6]   Until 1322 the fortunes of war were also indecisive.

As early as 1315, Louis appointed an imperial vicar for Italy, in the person of John of Belmont ;[7] and he also supported Galeazzo Visconti of Milan, who was in open insurrection against the Church, and had been visited with censure,[8] against Robert of Naples.   When Louis informed the Pope of his victory at Mühldorf in June 1322, John, by his friendly congratulations, invited him to further advances.[9]   But Louis would submit to no examination of his claim by the Pope, and demanded instant recognition ; he had, in fact, acted as King of the Romans, and even as emperor, contrary to all ancient principles and the ideas of most of his contemporaries.[10]   He suffered his army in Italy to act against the Papal vicar ; wherefore the Pope solemnly warned him, under pain of excommunication, to desist within three months from administering the empire, and to revoke all his acts in Italy.[11]

[1] Hefele, vi. pp. 510-512.
[2] Raynald. a. 1314, n. 24, 25.
[3] Ep. apud Rayn. h.a. n. 23 : 'Eapropter Sanctitati vestrae tam humiliter quam devote voto unanimi supplicamus, ut ipsum electum nostrum in regem Romanorum paternis ulnis amplectentes munus inunctionis et consecrationis eidem conferendo de sacrosanctis manibus vestris sacri imperii diadema dignemini loco et tempore favorabiliter impertiri.'
[4] Phillips, § 133, p. 292 seq.
[5] Raynald. a. 1316, n. 10.
[6] Mutii Chron. Germ. l. xxiv. p. 866 : 'Plurimi exspectabant confirmationem, interea neutri adhaerere volebant.'
[7] Ficker, Urkunden z. Gesch. des Römerzugs K. Ludwig d. B. 1865, p. 1 seq.

[8] Raynald. a. 1322, n. 8 ; 1324, n. 9 seq.

[9] Ib. a. 1323, n. 15.

[10] Mutii Chron. Germ. l.c.: 'Tanta Romanae Sedis auctoritas et religio erat apud plerosque, ut non judicarent nec appellandum censerent imperatorem nisi prius unctus, coronatus et confirmatus esset.' Gerard de Roo, l. ii. p. 88 : ' Et Pontificis auctoritas ea apud plerosque reverentia erat, ut ab ejus confirmatione imperatoria dignitas penderet.'

[11] Raynald. a. 1323, n. 30.

§ 9.

The Pope on Louis' entreaty granted him a longer term.[1] But whilst the negotiations were still pending Louis declared war upon Frederick's adherents, and protested against the proceedings of the Pope. He refused to admit the Pope's right, which had always been acknowledged, of examining into the election of the King of the Romans before conferring the imperial crown. He loaded the Pope with all manner of reproaches, especially for having favoured heretics, and he demanded a General Council.[2] Louis had fallen into the trap laid for him by the heretical Franciscan spiritualists, who found in him a powerful ally against the Pope.

At length, on the 23d March 1324, the Pope excommunicated him. Louis, on this, issued through the spiritualists a new and still more violent manifesto against the Pope, in which he was even spoken of as a heretic.[3] Everything was done to nullify the Papal sentence, and the electors were especially told that he was encroaching upon their rights. John XXII. declared that to be a falsehood.[4] He had demanded nothing new, and maintained merely the privileges always exercised by his predecessors. A king like Henry VII., unanimously elected, had never been rejected by the Pope; but when the votes were divided custom had always given to the Pope the right of deciding, since this right did not by law rest with the majority. The electors often paid more heed to the money given for their votes than to the welfare of the empire and the Church ; hence the importance of the Pope's examination of the candidate before his coronation as emperor.

[1] Raynald. a. 1324, n. 3.

² Herwart ab Hohenburg, Ludovicus IV. Imp. defensus, p. 245. Rayn. n. 1323, n. 34-36. Böhmer, Regesten K. Ludwig's, p. 218.
³ Rayn. a. 1324, n. 14. Böhmer, p. 42. Cf. Hefele, vi. p. 515.
⁴ Raynald. a. 1324, n. 17. Christophe, l.c. book v. p. 282.

§ 10.

As Louis, besides making arbitrary appointments to bishop-rics and persecuting the Archbishop of Salzburg[1] and the Bishop of Strasburg, persisted in his hostility, John, on the 11th July 1324, issued a fresh decree, in which, after detailing his griev-ances and admonitions, he declared Louis to have forfeited all right to the empire, and summoned him to appear in the following October before his tribunal.[2] At this juncture Duke Leopold of Austria concluded a treaty with Charles IV. of France, with the object of procuring the imperial crown for the latter. John concurred in the arrangement, but it was pro-secuted with negligence on all sides, and was finally abandoned by the King of France.[3] Louis, in January 1325, was van-quished by Duke Leopold; and, forsaken by many princes, he found himself in much distress. He set his imprisoned ad-versary, Frederick, at liberty under hard conditions, which were not recognised either by the Pope or by Duke Leopold. Louis desired, in September 1325, to share the government and the title of king with his former adversary, with whom he was now reconciled, and who had returned into captivity; but the princes declared that both had lost their right to the kingdom, and Leopold continued the war. On the 7th January 1326, Louis, being in great difficulties, declared at Ulm that he was willing to resign the kingdom to Frederick, whilst retaining the im-perial crown and Italy.[4] Frederick did everything to gain over his brothers. Leopold died on the 28th February. As the treaty of Ulm decreed, the Pope's ratification was sought for Frederick, but the Pope declared that he could not grant it until the authentic proofs confirming his better right were laid before him. Louis after this believed himself to be no longer bound by the Ulm treaty, and this led to a dispute betwixt him and Frederick.[5]

[1] Raynald. a 1324, n. 21.   Christophe, l.c.
[2] Rayn. a. 1324, n. 17, 21 seq.   Böhmer, p. 216.
[3] Christophe, p. 285 seq.
[4] Raynald. a 1325, n. 6.
[5] Hefele, vi. pp. 515-517, where the books on this subject are specified.

§ 11.

Louis' Italian campaign, his acts of violence towards the Pope's adherents in Italy, his close alliance with Marsilius of Padua, John Giandone, and the Fraticelli, his acceptance of their heretical doctrines,[1] his coronation at Milan by two excommunicated and deposed prelates, his anointing in Rome by an apostate bishop, when Sciarra Colonna, the notorious companion of Nogaret, placed the crown upon his head in the name of the Roman people, his continuing to call himself emperor, his attempted occupation of the States of the Church and the kingdom of Naples, the deposition he pronounced on the 18th April 1328 of John XXII., his appointment of an antipope,[2] together with a number of heavy crimes against the Church, could only widen the breach.   In 1328 the German princes were inclined to agree to the demand of the Pope and proceed to a new election, but did not do so owing to a want of unanimity.[3]   On the 4th August 1328, Louis, much mortified, was forced to leave Rome, and by the end of 1329 he found himself obliged to abandon Italy also.[4]   In Germany, after the death of Frederick (13th January 1330), Louis again showed himself extremely untrustworthy and uncertain.[5]   Whilst still openly defying the Pope, he began to treat with him through some princes in Avignon (May 1330).   He declared himself willing to sacrifice the antipope, to relinquish his appeal to a General Council, to recall all he had done against the Church, to acknowledge the justice of his own excommunication, if only his authority were guaranteed.[6]   But the antipope had already submitted, and the schism had terminated ignominiously.   Louis had made no promises with regard to the Fraticelli, and it appeared impossible to allow him to retain an authority he did not rightfully possess. So limited a submission could not satisfy the strict principles of law to which John XXII. so tenaciously adhered.   The Pope:

declared that as Louis still protected heresy and performed no satisfaction, any agreement with him was out of the question, and the election of a new king was required.[7] The only way for him to prove the reality of his repentance, which must precede his release from excommunication, appeared to be the renunciation of the imperial dignity which he had usurped, and of which his continuance was a continual misprision of the existing law. As in 1333, Louis seemed ready to agree. The Pope sent envoys to him with an amicable letter.[8] In 1334, John XXII. died.[9]

[1] Cf. Christophe, p. 288 seq.; W. Schreiber, in Die polit. und relig. Doctrinen unter Ludw. d. B. 1858, p. 24 seq.
[2] Christophe, pp. 292-307. Hefele, p. 518 seq.
[3] Hefele, p. 520, and the authors cited in note 2.
[4] Christophe, p. 310 seq.
[5] Von Weech also admits this weakness (K. Ludwig d. B. und K. Joh. von Böhmer, mit. urkundlichen Beilagen, 1861).
[6] Raynald. a. 1330, n. 28, 34, 35. Böhmer, Reg. p. 194.
[7] Martene, Thes. ii. p. 800. Rayn. a. 1330, n. 29, 33 seq. Christophe, vol. ii. b. vi. p. 17.
[8] Raynald. a. 1334, n. 19-22; admonition to repentance of June 28.
[9] Hefele, vi. 521 seq. Christophe, ii. pp. 17, 18. Phillips, p. 300.

§ 12.

The gentle Benedict XII. lost no time in informing Louis of his willingness for a reconciliation, but to this the Kings of France and Naples, and later those of Bohemia and Poland, offered opposition. The Pope's efforts were impeded by the policy of France, whose object was facilitated by Louis' changeable demeanour. Louis finally declared, in a constitution of the 8th August 1338,[1] that the imperial authority (as then existing) was derived immediately from God, a proposition which neither Popes[2] nor theologians[3] of that time could accept; also that the emperor could not be judged by the Pope, but that the Pope could be judged by a General Council. The document ascribed to the Kurverein (electoral assembly) of the 6th July 1338, which also alleges that the imperial dignity comes immediately from God, and that he whom the electors chose is lawfully to be and to be called king, the contrary to be accounted high treason, must be regarded as unauthentic, neither can the letter of the electors to the Pope be looked upon as genuine.[4] Most critics, on the other hand, recognise the genuineness of the document of the 16th July, which declares that he whom the majority have elected is to be acknowledged as lawful king. This obviated the necessity for a unanimous election, enforced the submission of the minority to the majority, and rendered ratification by the Pope superfluous. Whether the princes, if they did not observe the other duties incumbent upon them as electors, were entitled to force upon the Pope as future emperor *every* candidate whom they might have elected, is another question, answered not as they would wish by the traditional custom of the empire to which they appeal. Least of all could it be employed retrospectively in favour of Louis, whose election was not unanimous, and who was under the excommunication which had so many times been inflicted upon him. Indeed, these same electors afterwards ceased to acknowledge Louis as lawful king, and agreed to the Pope's proposal of electing another.[5] The King of Bohemia took no share in the declaration extorted at that time from Louis.[6] This declaration was in contradiction with those of former emperors and electors, as well as with Louis himself,[7] especially with the promises and confessions he had made in 1336, when he undertook to refrain from any enactments in Italy,[8] and to acknowledge his coronation as emperor to have been illegal.[9]

---

[1] Böhmer, Reg. Ludw. p. 120.   Hartzheim, Conc. Germ. iv. 328 seq.

[2] Raynald. a. 1343, n. 43 seq.; a. 1346, n. 3 seq.   Clem. V. c. Romani principes cit.; Joh. XXII. Const. Si fratrum cit.

[3] Alvarus Pelag. de Planctu Eccles. l. i. c. lxvi.   Alex. a S. Elpidio, O.S.A. de Jurisd. Imper. et Auct. Pontif.   Petrus de Palude, de Causa immed. Eccles. Potest.   Cf. Almain. de Supr. Eccl. Pot. c. i.; Pighius, l. v. de Eccl. Hier.; Bellarm. de Laic. iii. 6; Suarez, de Leg. iii. 2, 3; Gravina, de Jure natur. et gent. § 18; Charlas, de Libert. Eccl. Gall. t. ii. l. vii. c. iv.

[4] Böhmer, Reg. p. 241 seq.   Ficker, Der Churverein zu Rhense (Report of Session of the Academy of Vienna, 1853, vol. xi.).   Weech, l.c. p. 69 seq.   Hefele, vi. p. 559.   In one notarial instrument the proposition is expressly accepted: 'Papa major est imperatore, quia dominus spiritualium et animarum est, iste vero dominus corporum et rerum.'

[5] Phillips, pp. 297, 298.

* Raynald. a. 1338, n. 10.   Spondan. h.a. n. 23.   Bianchi, t. ii. l. vi.
§ 8, n. 6, p. 562.
⁷ Bianchi, l.c. 563 seq.   Rayn. a. 1338, n. 12.
⁸ Raynald. a. 1336, n. 23: ‘Quod non ingrediemur partes Italiao nec
in eis nec de eis per nos vel alium sivo alios aliquid administrabimus aut
quomodolibet disponemus, donec probationem apostolicam personae nostrae fuerimus assecuti.’
⁹ Ib. n. 35: ‘Nos assumpsisse titulum imperialem et unctionem in
Roma perverse, male et injuste et a potestatem non habento, item . . . .
quod credimus, quod ad summum pontificem spectat hoc facere, et non ad
alium.’

§ 13.

If in the controversy with Louis writers who sided with the
Church express themselves very strongly,[1] those of his contemporaries who defended him exhibit equal one-sidedness
and exaggeration. They confused the empire and the kingdom ;
Occam and Marsilius denied that the Pope had power to depose
the emperor, whom they even called his lord ; and they said
that the emperor could with far better right depose the Pope.[c]
Neither side could view the circumstances in the light of history ; but the attitude of Louis' party, which included many
heretics, could not alter the rights of the case, and the principles of the Church for some time still retained their ascendency.[3]
But by degrees the King of Germany was called emperor, without regard to his coronation by the Pope ;[4] and as time went
on, this custom became more frequent. Later writers have more
and more misconceived the legal principles of the case. Warnkönig is right in the main point when he says : ‘Of lasting importance was the principle established by the constitution of the
Carolingian empire—that any one cut off from the Church by
excommunication had no right to the empire ; whence follows,
as a matter of course, that an excommunicated emperor was
legally incapable of reigning. Excommunication was the Pope's
chief weapon against the emperor, and one which for the deposition of the emperor he believed himself all the more qualified
to wield, *because the imperial dignity was created by the Pope,
and it was necessary that the German king should be crowned by
the Pope in order to become emperor.* They had also a *de facto*
power, because through the development of the feudal system,

especially after fiefs had become hereditary, the Pope excommunicating an emperor could count upon adherents amongst
the opponents of the emperor.'[5]

[1] Thus Augustinus Triumphus (†1328), Summa de Potestate Ecclesiac·
ad Joh. P. XXII. (Abridgment in Friedberg, l.c. pp. 237-244, 30, 31, and
elsewhere), who speaks of the emperor as ' minister Dei, ergo et Papae,'
and circumstantially develops the rights of the Pope over the empire; also
Alvarus Pelagius, de Planctu Ecclesiae, 1. i. c. xli. xliv. xlvi. lvii. lxviii.
(cf. Schwab, Joh. Gerson, especially p. 26). For the rest, it is admitted
even by the former (q. 39, a. 3) that ' quod imperator statim electus
absque Papae auctoritate possit administrare saltem in *regno Alaman-
niae.*'

[2] Occam, Quaest. octo decis. q. 3, c. ii.; q. 1, c. xvii. Dial.l. vi. c. xcii.
Gold. ii. 347, 332, 610 seq. Friedberg, p. 74 seq. No. 7. Marsilius requires
a General Council for the deposition of an emperor : Def. Pac. P. ii. c. xxv. ;
Gold. ii. 282 ; Jacob Almainus, de Potest. Eccl. et Laica, q. 2, ad c. viii.
doctoris Occam, distinguishes two cases in which the emperor could be
deposed: (1) ' propter crimen spirituale,' such as heresy; (2) ' propter crimen civile, quando negligit administrare justitiam.' Only in the first of
these cases the Pope could depose him, ' cum habeat plenam potestatem
in puniendis peccatis spiritualibus.' That is, according to c. xii., ' relaxare·
et jus declarare.'

[3] Friedberg, p. 69 : ' Etsi vero medii aevi temporibus maximi aestima-
bant plurimi, jam juris Romani praecepta sccuti, imperatoriam majestatem, tamen juris publici regulam fuisse vidimus, imperatores a Papis deponi posse, atque *singulos tantum viros* hasce doctrinas impugnasse.' Anton
Rosellus (†1466), Monarch. P. iv. c. xl. p. 255, ed. Gold., teaches that the
Pope could depose the emperor, ' causa haeresis subsistente rel simili.'

[4] So the later glosses to the Sachsenspiegel (vol. iii. art. 52), to the·
Saxon Weichbild (art. 3), in Friedberg, p. 85, No. 4, 5.

[5] L. A. Warnkönig, Die Staatsrechtliche Stellung der kathol. Kirche
in den kath. Ländern des deutschen Reichs, Erlangen, 1855, pp. 8, 9.

§ 14.

Germany was in a miserable condition; but Louis' opposition to the Roman See was not shared universally. Great displeasure was occasioned when Louis, who from having been on
the English side went over in January 1341 to the French side,.
dissolved the marriage of Margaretha, heiress of Carinthia and
Tyrol, with Prince John Henry of Bohemia in virtue of ' imperial sovereignty,' and espoused her to his son Louis of Brandenburg, who was related to her in the third degree, thus
offending at once the Church[1] and the house of Luxemburg.[2]

Clement VI., on the 12th April 1343, issued a severe Bull against him.[3] Louis delayed beyond the time appointed in the Bull, but in September found it necessary to enter into fresh negotiations. His envoys made a humble recantation, but Louis did not ratify it, and in 1344 the princes of the empire declared against it. Still, they wished to have no further dealings with a ruler who had brought ruin upon the empire.[4] Five electors on the 11th July 1346 chose Prince Charles of Bohemia, the former pupil of the Pope, to be their king; but after the death of Louis (11th October 1347) the Bavarian party opposed to him Count Gunther of Schwarzburg. On the death of the latter, 14th June 1349, all agreed in recognising Charles IV. As Aix-la-Chapelle barred its gates to him, he received the crown of Germany at Bonn on the 26th November 1346. He had already renewed to the Pope all the promises of former kings, and had made further promises of his own.[5]

[1] Occam (de jurisdictione Imperatoris in causis matrimonialibus) wrote in defence of this unusual proceeding. Goldast. i. 21. Cf. Marsil. Defens. pac. concl. 19, tract. Consultationis super divortio matrimonii. Launoi follows them in his work, Regia in Matrim. Potestas, Paris, 1674, c. ii. a. 1, P. iii., which was condemned at Rome on the 10th Sept. 1688. No law of the fourteenth or fifteenth century ventured to follow the example of Louis. Cf. Friedberg, p. 121.

[2] Raynald. a. 1341, n. 15. Phillips, pp. 301, 302. Döllinger, Lehrb. ii. p. 267.

[3] Rayn. a. 1342, n. 6 seq.; a. 1343, n. 42 seq. Böhmer, Reg. pp. 144, 231.

[4] Christophe, vol. ii. b. vii. p. 75 seq. Hefele, vi. p. 581 seq.

[5] Rayn. a. 1346, n. 19-24; 1347, n. 1.

§ 15.

At Easter 1355, in Rome, Charles IV. received the imperial crown from two delegated cardinals,[1] and fulfilled his promises.[2] In 1355 and 1356, by the Golden Bulls the rights of the electors were permanently regulated, and it was established that the majority of votes sufficed for the election of a king.[3] The emperor's quarrel with Innocent VI. was only temporary: it arose from his desire arbitrarily to undertake the reform of the German clergy.[4] Urban VI. had acknowledged Charles' son Wen-

zel as King of the Romans[5] on his election, 26th July 1378, by
the German princes. Wenzel, as well as his father, who died
shortly after (Nov. 29), declared himself against the Antipope
Clement VII.,[6] and in these terms expressed the purpose of the
empire : that as the bark covers and protects the tree, forming
with it but one substance, so the emperor, placed with the civil
sword on the outer surface of the Church, must protect her if
need be with his own blood.[7] Wenzel was deposed by the
princes in 1400, and Ruprecht of the Palatinate was elected : his
election was confirmed by Boniface IX. in 1403.[8] He died in
1410, without having been crowned emperor. Wenzel lived till
1419 : his dominions were limited to Bohemia. Sigismund, in
1433, received the imperial crown in Rome from Eugenius IV.
Albert II., elected in 1435, after the death of Sigismund, reigned
only two years, and had no time to receive the imperial crown
from the hands of the Pope. Frederick III., on the contrary,
was solemnly crowned emperor by Pope Nicholas V., 1452.[9]
He was succeeded in 1493 by his son Maximilian, whom he
had caused to be elected and crowned Romano-German Emperor in 1486. Julius II. in 1508 gave Maximilian the title
of 'Roman emperor-elect,' which was thenceforth borne by the
rulers of Germany.[10] Charles V. alone was crowned emperor
by Clement VII.[11] At his election Charles had sworn to a
capitulation, whereby he bound himself and others to protect
the Church and the Pope ; thenceforward written capitulations
remained in use.[12]

[1] For detailed account of the ceremony, vide Raynald. a. 1355, n. 2-17.
[2] Raynald. a. 1355, n. 19.   Christophe, l.c. b. x. p. 202.
[3] Rayn. a. 1356, n. 13-25.   Hefele, p. 608 seq.
[4] Christophe, ii. pp. 241-243.
[5] Rayn. a. 1378, n. 41.
[6] Hefele, vi. pp. 672, 673.
[7] Rayn. a. 1379, n. 40 seq.   Hefele, p. 676.
[8] Rayn. a. 1403, n. 1 scq. 8.   Hefele, p. 741 seq.
[9] Concerning this coronation, see Card. V. Petra Com. in Const. 5,
Imperator.   Nicol. V. t. v. p. 38 seq.
[10] Raynald. a. 1530, 1538.   The Popes use the expression : 'In Romanorum imperatorem electus ;' then, 'Electus [in contradistinction to
coronatus] Romanorum imperator.'   Thus Pius VI. in the Briefs to Leopold II. and Francis II. (Collect. Brev. Pii VI. Paris, 1798, pp. 557, 561).

Maximilian himself, in his letter in 1508 to the cities of the German kingdom (Daht, de Pace Publica, l. iii. c. vii. n. 30), tells them that he has taken the title of Roman emperor-elect in consideration of the right of the Pope over the coronation, and that his Holiness 'was well pleased' ('dess ein gut gefallen gehabt').

[11] Charles, as well as Frederick III., performed the 'officium stratoris,' although the Pope would have prevented it. Rayn. a. 1529, n. 84; 1530, n. 39. Thomassin, P. ii. l. iii. c. lxv. n. 9.

[12] Rayn. a. 1519, n. 27. Dumont, Corps Diplom. Univ. t. iv. P. i. p. 298. Gosselin, ii. p. 344 seq.

§ 16.

Besides his quarrel with Clement VII. before his coronation,[1] Charles V. had quarrelled with Paul III. This Pope has been much blamed[2] for having, especially at the commencement of his pontificate, been too solicitous for the elevation of his family (Farnese), and it was far from being the intention of the author of Anti-Janus to justify either his efforts for this end or all the measures by which he sought to compass it. Paul III. has also been reproached for faithlessness towards Charles V., with having broken the League of 1545 and 1546, with having conspired against him, with having in the spring of 1547 expressed his pleasure that Protestants were holding their ground against him, and with having found it well that they should be supported against him.[3] But on the other hand we must not forget (a) that the French reports[4] are anything but trustworthy, and (b) that the Pope had numerous and just grievances against the emperor. For (a) there is no doubt that French diplomacy not only sought in the Pope's conduct a justification of its own negotiations with German Protestants, but left no measure untried to dissolve the league between Pope and emperor, and explained and applied every action and every word to its own advantage. The Saxons and Hessians were repeatedly told by the French that a breach between Pope and emperor was inevitable, and that the former would soon be deprived of the means of carrying on war.[5] (b) Further, the Pope's grievances against the emperor were such as to render alliance with him very distasteful, and even to undermine all reliance upon Charles' sincerity.[6] As supreme Head of the Church it was impossible the Pope should permit Charles to assume the right to decide and command in affairs relating purely to the Church,[7] as he had done in first thwarting, then ignoring and partially resisting, the decree on justification published at Trent (13th Jan. 1547), also in violently resisting the postponement of the Council, a measure agreed upon (11th March) by a majority of the prelates.[8] The emperor also made exorbitant claims as to the subsidy from Church property in Spain for the prosecution of the war. Even the Madrid government under Prince Philip protested, and Charles found it necessary to abate these claims in some measure.[9] Further, he refused to acknowledge the feudal dependence of Parma and Piacenza upon the Papacy, though it was attested by so many records. Also he suffered his new viceroy in Milan, Fernando Gonzaga, always an enemy of the Pope's family, to make constant war upon Pier Luigi Farnese, who was killed at last on the 10th September, not without the participation of Fernando.[10] Spanish ascendency in Italy was an oppression at that time as well as under Clement VII.[11] Paul III., both as Pope and as an Italian prince, accounted the exclusive power of Spain in the peninsula to be dangerous. 'Naples and Milan in the grasp of Spain was the destruction of Italian independence'.[12] The emperor was already laying his hand upon other domains in Italy.[13] He concluded treaties with the Protestants, and made concessions to them which increased the Pope's distrust and induced him to refuse new support.[14] Besides all this, notwithstanding his alliance with the Pope, he acted in the most arbitrary manner, and without so much as consulting his allies or their ambassadors.[15] The Venetians had declared that they would refuse passage through their dominions to the Papal troops.[16] Charles' violent and impatient demeanour and his threats of retaining the Council in Rome with an army must have largely contributed to the breach between him and the Pope.[17] If the Pope, when the fate of the war was already decided in the middle of November,[18] withdrew his troops,[19] it was under the circumstances a very comprehensible act. The Papal policy should not bear all the blame; certainly no lesser share should fall upon the emperor.

There can be no question of a breach of faith on the part of the Pope, for his auxiliary troops had been granted only for six months, and this period had elapsed in December 1546, when he considered whether he should continue the league or not.[20] The Papal treasury was exhausted by the expenses of the Council, by the advancement of a hundred thousand ducats for the Turkish war,[21] and by the last equipment; whilst Charles had at his disposal not merely the considerable sums furnished by the Church in Spain,[22] but the heavy contributions levied from the conquered rebels.[23]

But as the war appeared likely to break out again between France and Germany, it became necessary for the Pope to take into consideration the protection of the States of the Church, for which material means were needed, and also the neutrality which the See of Rome, especially between 1525 and 1542, had often declared to befit her in a war between two Catholic princes.[24] The Pope for these reasons sent Gerone Bertano to the emperor, counselling him to keep peace with France; the envoy, detained by illness on the journey, reached Ulm, where Charles was, on the 27th January 1547. The emperor set forth his grievances with much violence, and showed himself by no means inclined to peace. The Papal envoy, however, was able to show good cause in justification of his master.[25] Even after disputes had arisen the Church made many concessions of subsidies to the emperor, and did things, especially with regard to the Council of Bologna, to prevent the conflict at least from increasing.[26] Even before the death of Paul III. better relations existed between Charles and the See of Rome. Charles at the end of his life had time to repent of his former wild impetuosity.

¹ Cf. Pallavicini, Hist. Conc. Trid. l. ii. c. xiii-xvi. Ranke, Päpste, iii. p. 241 seq.; i. 103 seq.

² Pallav. l.c. l. xi. c. 6, n. 4.

³ Huber, p. 40 seq.

⁴ Ribier, Lettres et Mémoires d'état, i. 637-639. The ambassador Dumortier often formed very wrong estimates of the Pope.

⁵ W. Maurenbrecher, Karl V. und die Deutschen Protestanten, 1545-1555, Düsseldorf, 1865, pp. 133, 134 (note 18), 135.

⁶ Maurenbrecher, l.c. p. 113.

⁷ Ibid. p. 149. Cf. Döllinger, Beiträge, i. p. 60.

⁸ Farnese's letters to Cervinus dated the 3d, and to the legates dated

23d July 1546 (Pallavic. l. viii. c. v. n. 3-5), show that it is false that the Pope had long wished to dissolve or transfer the Council. On the 3d or 4th of August he first consented to the proposal, but with the condition that it should be if the majority of the Fathers willed and desired it. He also proposed the town of Lucca, which was quite submissive to the emperor, required that preliminary information should be imparted to the emperor, and that the discussion on the doctrine of justification and on residence should be terminated (ib. c. viii. n. 3). Only after he had learnt the manner in which his legates had been mortified by Madrucci, together with the wish of many bishops, did he show himself inclined to the translation; still he did not yet give way to the legates (c. x. n. 5 ; c. xv. n. 1 seq.). At the beginning of the year 1547, Paul, from consideration for the emperor, had not yet granted his consent (ib. l. ix. c. iii. n. 4 fin.).

[9] Maurenbrecher, pp. 123, 140, 152.

[10] Ib. p. 115 seq. 160 seq. Ranke, Päpste, i. 256 seq. Deutsche Gesch. im Zeitalter der Ref. vol. v. p. 11.

[11] Ranke, Päpste, i. 100 seq.

[12] Maurenbrecher, p. 114.

[13] Ib. p. 159.

[14] Ib. p. 128.

[15] Maffei to Cervinus, 4 Dec. 1546, 23 Feb. 1547. Pallavic. l. ix. c. iii. n. 1. Charles to Don Diego Hurtado de Mendoza, d.d. Ulm, 11 Feb. 1547, in Maurenbrecher, appendix v. 11, p. 86* seq.; ib. p. 128 seq. The memorial sent to Berallo. Pallavic. l.c. n. 5.

[16] Maurenbrecher, p. 124.

[17] Ib. pp. 54, 170, 171, especially note 6.

[18] Ib. p. 111.

[19] Charles to Mendoza, 11 Feb. 1547, where he says the Papal troops were of little service (ib. p. 89*).

[20] Pallavic. l. viii. c. i. n. 3 ; l. ix. c. iii. n. 1 seq. 5.

[21] Maurenbrecher, p. 64.

[22] Concerning such subsidies, vide Charles' letter to Philip, of 24th April 1546, in Döllinger, Beitr. i. p. 44. Charles demanded in Rome the secularisation of half the Spanish Church property, which could not have been granted (Maurenbrecher, p. 131 seq.).

[23] Pallav. l.c. n. 2. Maurenbrecher, pp. 127, 128.

[24] The Nuncio Rorarius to Sadolet, 14 Feb. 1525 (apud Lömmer, Mon. Vat. p. 22) : ' Havendo SS. deliberato gerere se tamquam patrem omnibus communem e servar la neutralità (Maurenbrecher, p. 54 ; Pallavic. l.c.).

[25] Pallavic. l.c. n. 9, 10. Charles to Mendoza, 11 Feb. 1547 (Maurenbrecher, app. v. 11, pp. 86*-89*).

[26] Ranke, Deutsche Gesch. v. p. 115 seq.

§ 17.

But a fresh quarrel was occasioned by Charles' abdication. ' Paul IV.,' says Huber, ' regarded the abdication of Charles and the election of Ferdinand as invalid on the ground that the Popes

had removed the empire from the Greeks to the Germans, and possessed full supremacy over the imperium.'¹ Certainly it must have
appeared strange to the Pope that Charles should have entered
into long negotiations concerning his abdication with the electors,
amongst whom were some who employed menacing expressions
towards the Church of Rome,² whilst he was not consulted; and
that the abdication was delivered into the hands of the electors,
not into those of the Pope.³ It is true that Ferdinand was with
the consent of the Pope recognised by the majority of the electors
as ' King of the Romans,' with the right of succession to the
empire ;⁴ but upon this he called himself ' Roman emperor-elect
(erwählter),' whilst for the Pope, Charles V. was alone emperor.
Paul IV. did not immediately receive Ferdinand's ambassador,
Martin Guzman, and then only as a private individual, and proposed four questions for discussion to the cardinals : I. Whether
the ambassador had to give the reasons for Charles' abdication ;
II. whether the abdication was valid without the consent of the
Pope ; III. whether the bad education of his son Maximilian
ought to weigh against Ferdinand's recognition ; IV. what course
was to be adopted with regard to the heretical electors. The
Sacred Congregation decided according to the existing law
that the abdication was invalid, that it was the duty of the
Pope to prevent any one who was incapable of defending the
Church receiving a right over the empire, and that heretical
electors were deprived of their office.⁵ This decision was not
arbitrary; it was founded upon the clear law of the decretals,
which had been always acknowledged by earlier emperors, and
whose validity no German had ever before disputed.⁶ Although
John Gropper, at that time living in Rome, advised making concessions, the Pope held firmly to the old law. On the death
of Charles V., the 21st September 1558, he assumed that the
empire had fallen vacant by death. Paul IV. is only open to
the charge, often preferred against him,⁷ of too great severity, and
of an uncompromising adherence to the letter of the law ; his
successor, Pius IV., immediately received Ferdinand's ambassador,⁸ not wishing to decide the matter according to strict law,
for which Ferdinand I. expressed his gratitude.'⁹

[1] Huber, p. 46.
[2] Ranke, Deutsche Gesch. v. p. 413 seq.
[3] Ranke, l.c. pp. 420, 421.
[4] Pallavic. l. iii. c. ix. n. 2, 3.
[5] Raynald. a. 1558, n. 8, 10.   Pallavic. l. xiv. c. vi. n. 5-14.   Bromato,
Vita di Paolo IV. t. ii. p. 431.   The individual motives, arguments, and
votes are not the important thing, but the legal decision.
[6] Ranke, l.c. p. 422.
[7] Pallavic. l.c. c. xi. n. 1.
[8] Raynald. a. 1559, n. 42.
[9] Pallavic. l.c. c. xii. n. 1.

§ 18.

The Roman emperor, henceforward no longer 'crowned,' but 'elect,' had from that time scarcely any relations with the Holy See beyond those of other sovereigns.   The empire had become a mere phantom.   The election was always signified to Rome by the elected prince, and Rome always in return acknowledged it. Enfeebled and unmeaning, the empire after a life of a thousand years expired in the person of Francis II. in 1806, in consequence of the ascendency of the French and of the confederation of the Rhine.   Sixty-four years later it revived not merely in a new guise, but with a new spirit and new foundations, in some sort a new creation.   Time will show whether the new foundations are more lasting than the old.   Would that in looking onward we might hope that the Ghibellines and the Guelfs had laid their arms down for ever, that those who so recklessly impugn the past would not more recklessly embroil the present and the future, and that the statesmen of these times would judge the Catholic Church by her deeds and her fruits, not by party-spirited perversions and misrepresentations of her doctrine !

ESSAY X.

THE POPES AND THEIR VASSAL KINGDOMS.

AFTER the eleventh century many princes entered into feudal relations with the Church of Rome, and the rights of the Pope over such princes were much greater than over other rulers. He had not only an ecclesiastical, but also a temporal jurisdiction over them. The lord superior had the right to judge those princes who were his vassals, in any case of violation of fealty (felony) to depose them, and to give away to others the fiefs that escheated to him in these cases. The Popes in using their right of lord paramount to support their spiritual power acted in conformity with the general feeling of the Middle Ages, according to which the material sword served as an aid to the spiritual. The exercise of their power may appear frequently to have been imprudent, immoderate, even hard and oppressive; but there was no violation of law or usurpation of jurisdiction. We must not blame a judge who rests his judgment on the principles of jurisprudence prevailing in his time only because they do not find the same acknowledgment in our day. This principle is always recognised, except when in the case of the Popes. This is the less reasonable, as it was precisely the justice of their authority which caused their contemporaries most highly to esteem and most strongly to support it. To meet the complaints made on this subject against the Popes, we will consider the Papal fiefs—I. in Italy; II. out of Italy.

PART I. PAPAL FIEFS IN ITALY.

§ 1. Feudal connection of the South Italian kingdom with the Pope. § 2. From 1251-1282. § 3. From that time till 1302. § 4. Till 1372. § 5. Till the eighteenth century. § 6. Sardinia and Corsica. § 7. Parma and Piacenza.

§ 1.

The Normans in Lower Italy and Sicily were the first who entered into a feudal connection with the Church of Rome, and in spite of many vicissitudes this connection continued.[1] Calixtus II. received homage in 1121 from the nobles of Lower Italy.[2] Innocent II. recognised Roger as King of Sicily, July 27, 1139, on condition of his taking the oath of allegiance and paying a tribute.[3] As William II. (1154) caused himself to be crowned without application to the Roman See, Hadrian IV. protested, and at the peace of 1156 the king admitted his feudal dependence.[4] Under Clement III. (1187-1191) the question was discussed whether his heirs were to render allegiance to the Popes in every new pontificate, which, according to strict feudal law, could of course be demanded ; the Pope, however, decided that the one act of allegiance was sufficient for each king.[5] Under the Emperor Henry VI. the kingdom passed to the house of Hohenstaufen. Innocent III., though guardian of the young Frederick, both protected the claims of his ward to the South Italian kingdom and the undisputed rights of suzerainty of the Church of Rome, and provided for a regular administration there.[6] The successors of Innocent interceded more than once with this tyrannical ruler for the oppressed people. When in the history of Frederick II. we are told that 'the Papal pretension to power was without any legitimate title and utterly exorbitant,'[7] the fact is entirely overlooked that the feudal subjection under which Frederick, as King of Sicily, stood to the See of Rome was in itself a very important and very legitimate title. A single breach of faith, such as Frederick himself committed by the hundred, would have sufficed in his eyes for the immediate degradation of any of his vassals.

[1] Baron. a. 1059, n. 70. Cf. Leo Ost. Chron. Cassin. iii. 12; Cenni Monum. Domin. Pontif. ii. 48 seq.; Urban. II. ap. Mansi, xx. 659.
[2] Jaffé, Reg. n. 5034, pp. 536, 537.
[3] Baron. a. 1139, n. 12. Mansi, xxi. 396. Jaffé, n. 5734, p. 588.
[4] Baron. a. 1156, n. 4, seq. Mansi, l.c. p. 801. J. n. 6941, p. 667.
[5] Mansi, xxii. 556. J. n. 10,279, p. 885 : ' Haeredes tui, qui nobis vel alii successorum nostrorum juraverint, alii postea minime jurare compel-

lantur, Catholicis tamen successoribus nostris et hominii et fidelitatis puri-
tatem, ac si juraverint, teneantur observare.'
    * Raynald. a. 1198, n. 67.   Innoc. III. l. i. Ep. 410-413 (Migne, ccxiv.
p. 387 seq.) ; Ep. 507-515 (ib. pp. 510-521) ; l. ii. Ep. 167, 179 (ib. pp. 717,
729) ; Ep. 187, 200, pp. 736, 749 ; l. vi. Ep. 52-54.
    ⁷ Huber, p. 35.

§ 2.

After the deposition of Frederick II. the kingdom of the Two
Sicilies reverted as a vacant fief, even according to imperial law,
to the Church of Rome ; his successors had forfeited their right,
and could only be readmitted as vassals by an act of favour.
Innocent IV. also expressed this view in 1251.[1]   In the mean
time Conrad IV. came to Apulia in 1252, conquered many towns,
behaved most ungratefully to his bastard brother Manfred, and
most injudiciously to the towns which had allied themselves to
the Church of Rome.   In order to put a check to Conrad's further
progress Innocent, as lord paramount, offered the Sicilian crown
in the summer of 1253 to Prince Charles of Anjou ; and as this
came to nothing, to the English Prince Edmund, whose father,
Henry III., accepted the offer, but then failed to send an army
as stipulated.[2]   When the Counts of Savoy and Montfort tried
to effect an understanding between Conrad and the Pope, Innocent did not reject it ; but Conrad died, May 20, 1254, before
further negotiations could be brought about.[3]   Being still quite
free as to the disposal of this fief, the Pope, while reserving his
rights, could still declare that he was inclined to show favour to
Conrad's child when he should be of proper age, and already
acknowledged him as Duke of Swabia and King of Jerusalem ;[4]
but he did not pledge himself to maintain the former Hohenstaufen provinces in Italy in their full integrity.   Manfred in
the mean time sought a reconciliation with the Pope, acknowledged his overlordship, and was confirmed as viceregent of
Lower Italy.   However, shortly after he faithlessly renewed
hostilities, and Innocent IV. soon died.[5]   His successor, Alexander IV., revived the negotiations with England, but without
better result ; he also wrote to the mother and grandmother of
Conradin, telling them of the favourable dispositions he enter-

tained towards him: his object was to find a faithful vassal and neighbour, well disposed towards the Church, and competent for the position. He was obliged to interfere against Manfred, who had already proved faithless, and was even now (1258) being crowned king at Palermo, and so sorely pressing the Pope that another nomination to the fief was becoming an urgent necessity.[6] Urban IV., in many difficulties, and pressed by the creditors of the Papal States, did not by any means refuse to be reconciled with Manfred, but the proposals of peace made by the latter were of such a nature that the Pope, straitened on all sides though he was, could not accept them.[7] At that time England was torn by civil wars, and Edmund was not in a position to undertake the kingdom of Sicily ; he soon resigned his claims to it, and on July 28, 1263, Urban declared them extinct.[8] He then turned his attention to France, and Charles of Anjou, brother of St. Louis, accepted the proposal, urged thereto by his own ambition and by his wife, Beatrix of Provence. St. Louis at first hesitated. The King of England had besought him to use his interest for his son Edmund, and he imagined that after Conradin, Edmund had the best claim. But the Pope represented to him that the former had no right on account of the felony of his grandfather, and the second on account of his having failed to fulfil the accepted conditions. Louis then gave his consent, and even allowed a tithe to be levied on the clergy, in order to help his brother to take possession of his throne.[9]

Almost the whole of Italy was at that time in the hands of Manfred, so much so that Cardinal Guido Fulcodi, elected Pope under the name of Clement IV., February 5, 1265, could only travel through Italy in the dress of a simple monk. Charles came to Italy in this year (1265), and after the confirmation of the Papal overlordship was crowned king (January 6, 1266). Manfred's army was overcome, he himself killed in battle. But the Roman See was cruelly deceived in the wicked brother of St. Louis. In Rome he acted in an arbitrary manner, levying heavy contributions on the Papal States, allowing many outrages to be committed by the troops. Clement IV. had bitter cause to complain of his tyranny.[10] It must be acknowledged, says Raumer,[11] that this Pope supported him most laudably and persistently in all good, and candidly blamed his faults. Huber indeed tells us, ' No advocate of Papal politics can clear Clement IV. of a moral participation in the execution of Conradin at Naples (Oct. 29, 1268)' [12] But the Pope acted only according to strict justice when, after first earnestly warning, he excommunicated Conradin, who since 1262 had been unopposed Duke of Swabia,[13] but since 1266 had acted as King of Sicily, and in 1267 had, in spite of the dissuasions of his nearest relations, undertaken his adventurous expedition to Italy, which was very dangerous for the Papal States. The Pope urged Charles of Anjou to be merciful, and it was not his fault that his admonitions were disregarded ;[14] it grieved him bitterly. In many other cases he experienced similar mortifications.

[1] Raynald. a. 1251, n. 11. Cf. a. 1253, n. 2.
[2] Lingard, Hist. Eng. vol. ii. pp. 420, 421, 5th edit. 1849.
[3] Hefele, Conc. vi. p. 8 seq.
[4] Raynald. a. 1254, n. 46, 47. Raumer, Gesch. der Hohenstaufen, iv. 352.
[5] Hefele, vi. p. 7.
[6] Hefele, vi. p. 13 seq.
[7] Hefele, vi. p. 14.
[8] Rymer, Foed. i. 769. Lingard, p. 425. Pauli, iii. p. 758 seq.'
[9] Daniel, Hist. de France, t. iv. a. 1264, 1265. Velly, Hist. de France, t. v. p. 328. Michaud, Hist. des Croisades, t. v. p. 42.
[10] Martene, Thes. ii. 136, 172, 267, 298, 306. Raynald. a. 1266, n. 7, 9.
[11] Gesch. der Hohenstaufen, iv. 565.
[12] Huber, p. 34.
[13] Böhmer, Reg. v. 1196 seq. p. 283 seq.
[14] Rayn. a. 1268, n. 32 seq. n. 86.

§ 3.

The 'Sicilian Vespers' (March 31, 1282) were a result of the hard yoke laid by Charles I. of Anjou upon his new subjects. After the expulsion of the French, King Peter III. of Aragon, who had married Manfred's daughter Constantia, was chosen and crowned King of Sicily. Charles could only maintain the territory north of the Faro. Pope Martin IV. excommunicated

King Peter, and forbade the single combat that had been agreed upon. As Peter despised the censure, he issued a fresh severe edict against him, at the same time dispossessing him of the kingdom of Aragon, which he offered to the French Prince Charles of Valois.[1] He made use of his spiritual power as Pope to release Peter's subjects from their oath of fidelity, and of his temporal power as lord superior in endeavouring by every means to protect his vassal Charles in Naples. Peter, however, was left conqueror in the struggle with Naples and its allies ; the eldest son of Charles of Anjou, afterwards Charles II., was captured by the Aragonese.[2] During this time Pope Honorius IV. (1285 till 1287), as lord superior, published wise laws for the continental territory of the kingdom, which, after the way the people had been oppressed, afforded them great relief.[3] Nicholas IV. also sought in vain to induce the Sicilians to return to the authority of the dynasty of Anjou, and in vain urged James II., Peter's second son, crowned at Palermo in 1286, to renounce the crown of Sicily. When, by the death (1291) of his elder brother, Alphonso III., James II. succeeded to the throne of Aragon, the third brother, Frederick, took possession of the island, and was crowned, in spite of the treaty concluded between his brother in Aragon and Charles II. After this (1302) peace was made, and it was agreed that Frederick, by a marriage with Eleanora, daughter of Charles II., should remain for his life king in Sicily. Boniface VIII. ratified the peace, and arranged that Frederick should be called King of Trinacria (to avoid confusion of titles), and should remain a vassal of the Church of Rome.[4]

[1] Raynald. a. 1283, n. 15 ; a. 1284, n. 2 seq.
[2] Hefele, vi. p. 190.
[3] Rayn. a. 1285. Lunig. t. ii. Cod. Diplom. Ital. p. 1023. Giannone, Istoria Civile del Regno di Napoli, t. v. l. xxi. c. i.
[4] Raynald. a. 1303, n. 3 seq. n. 25. Hefele, p. 256.

§ 4.

Soon afterwards dissensions again arose between King Robert of Naples and Frederick of Trinacria, of whom the former

was on the side of the Guelfs,[1] the latter of the Ghibellines.[2]
John XXII. excommunicated Frederick and laid the island
under an interdict, 1321, because the king refused all peaceful
mediation. After the death of Frederick, his son, Peter II.,
took upon himself the government of the island, contrary to
former agreement, and disregarded the censures of Pope Benedict XII., who therefore, in 1339, declared his authority to be
forfeited and Trinacria an escheated fief. Nevertheless the
house of Aragon succeeded in asserting its authority. After the
death of the wise King Robert of Naples (1343), his grand-
daughter Joanna succeeded. She had married her cousin, the
Hungarian Prince Andrew, who soon became odious to her and
to her court, and was at last murdered at Aversa in 1345. As
Joanna was suspected of participation in the murder, her brother-
in-law, King Louis of Hungary, demanded her deposition by
Pope Clement VI. But Clement, having anathematised the
murderers and ordered a strict inquiry, could not agree to this
without further evidence ; therefore the King of Hungary came
down with an army on to the kingdom of Naples, and made
such progress that Joanna fled by sea to Nice, January 13,
1348. At Avignon she justified herself completely in consistory, and was recognised as lawful queen.[3] As the tyranny
of Louis excited the Neapolitans to revolt he soon returned to
Hungary, and she maintained the possession of her kingdom
and sold Avignon to the Pope,[4] for which Charles IV., as lord
superior of the kingdom of Arles, gave his permission. After a
fresh expedition by King Louis (1350) and a fresh inquiry into
Joanna's guilt, a peace, ratified by the Pope, was concluded between Hungary and Naples.[5] At last under Pope Gregory XI.,
1372, an understanding was brought about between the courts
of Naples and Palermo. The Aragonese conquest was recognised
as well as the separation of Sicily from Naples. The conditions
of the separation of the kingdom of Trinacria from that of
Naples were that the rulers of the former were to be arrière
vassals of the Pope and the immediate vassals of the King of
Naples, rendering to them feudal support and paying a yearly
tribute of 3000 ounces of gold.[6]

¹ Robert always acknowledged his feudal dependence upon the Holy
See (Raynald. a. 1335, n. 47 seq.).
    ² Hefele, vi. p. 489.
    ³ Hefele, vi. p. 585 seq.
    ⁴ Christophe (Hist. of the Papacy in the Fourteenth Cent. ii. doc. 4, 5)
gives the documents.
    ⁵ Christophe, ii. b. vii. pp. 83-110 (Germ. ed.).
    ⁶ Raynald. a. 1372, n. 3.   Christophe, l.c. 306 seq.

§ 5.

The feudal dependence of the South Italian kingdom on the
Papal See was acknowledged until the eighteenth century, and
regular payment generally made of the feudal tribute agreed
upon after the treaty of 1268 with Charles of Anjou.   Pius II.,
1458, acknowledged Prince Ferdinand as king; Julius II.
granted the investiture to King Ferdinand of Aragon; Leo X.
to Charles V.; Julius III. to Philip II., son of Charles V., the
conditions being always the same.   The latter took the oath of
allegiance at Brussels, October 1, 1555.   Philip III. of Spain
took it for Naples through his ambassador, 1599, under Clement
VIII. ; Philip IV., 1621, under Gregory XV.   Marianne of
Austria, mother and guardian of Charles II., caused homage
to be rendered for him by Cardinal Frederick Sforza, 1666, to
Pope Alexander VII.   In the War of the Spanish Succession
both Philip V. and the Archduke Charles wished to pay
tribute and take the oath of allegiance; Clement XI. accepted
nothing from either side till the end of the struggle.   Innocent XIII. afterwards conferred the investiture on Charles
VI. for the usual tribute of 7000 ducats and a white palfrey
(1722).   When afterwards Charles of Bourbon came into
possession of the country and paid homage through Cardinal
Aquaviva, Clement XII. bestowed the investiture upon him on
May 10, 1738, with the remission of the long-unpaid tribute,
and with the reservation of his right of lord-superior.[1]   The
payment of the tribute was discontinued under Ferdinand IV.
and his violent minister Tanucci, who even seized the Papal
enclaves Benevento and Pontecorvo, and only restored them in
1774.[2]   The Concordat of 1791 was never carried out; it stipulated for an alteration in the payment of the tribute :[3] in the

stormy years that followed this payment was almost entirely discontinued. Joachim Murat again, in 1815, submitted to this contribution, but soon after declared war. King Ferdinand, when reinstated as ' King of the Two Sicilies,' would not hear of feudal subjection. Since the year 1816 the See of Rome protested against this breach of ancient obligation, which had been acknowledged by Ferdinand himself in 1806.[4]

[1] Clem. XII. Const. 233, *Ad excelsum*, Bull. t. xv. pp. 189-194, with complete enumeration of historical data (Artaud, Vie de Pio VII. vol. ii. 2, cap. xxii.).

[2] Theiner, Hist. du Pontificat de Clément XIV. t. i. pp. 345, 346, n. 36 seq.; t. ii. p. 467.

[3] Moroni, Dizionario, v. Concordato, t. xvi. p. 39.

[4] Artaud, l.c. chap. xxix. xxxii. xxxiv.

§ 6.

The Popes moreover asserted their old feudal right over the islands of Corsica and Sardinia.[1] In the year 1297, Boniface VIII. bestowed both these islands on King James of Aragon as Papal fiefs, thereby inducing him to relinquish Sicily, upon which his brother Frederick took possession of it ; the Pope in this case expressly stipulated for the freedom of ecclesiastical elections.[2] Under Benedict XII., King Alphonso distinctly acknowledged that he received these islands as a fief from the Pope.[3] When, according to the conditions of the Quadrupal Alliance of 1718, Victor Amadeus II. of Savoy received the kingdom of the island of Sardinia, the Roman See asserted its right, and did not acknowledge the new ruler to be entitled to the exercise of any patronage such as formerly the Spanish kings had possessed.[4] In the negotiations with Rome in 1725 the court of Turin asserted that Victor Amadeus as a descendant of Charles V.[5] ought to be ranked in the same line as the Spanish King Philip V., and being therefore included in the succession of Aragon and Sardinia required no investiture ; that as to the clause of the union of Sardinia with the Aragonese crown, the Pope in his new Indult could either modify it or, in surrendering the clause, make a protest defending the rights of the Holy See ; that the court would be prepared with a counter-protest, but would be ready to accept any equitable arrangement. The cardinals resisted the acknowledgment of the new king—first, because the interference of two heretical powers (England and Holland) was very offensive to them ; and secondly, because it appeared to be a favourable opportunity for the renewal of the Papal right and for the attainment of greater compliance in ecclesiastical matters. The Republics of Venice and Genoa sided with the cardinals, as it was extremely disagreeable to them to have an Italian prince raised to the dignity of a king. Mgr. Lambertini (afterwards Benedict XIV.), who was very popular at foreign courts on account of his liberality and love of peace, had to overcome many objections at Rome before the Indult for the right of presentation was granted to the king and his successors, October 25, 1726, the other rights of the Holy See being reserved. The crafty diplomatist D'Ormea obtained great concessions from Benedict XIII. for the Sardinian court.[6] There were also Papal fiefs in the continental possessions of the king : for instance, Alessandria, which had been built in honour of Alexander III. and had always been subject to the Holy See ;[7] also the principality of Masseran and the marquisate of Crevacour, which had been restored to the Papal See in 1658 by the family of the Fieschi, who had had possession of it since 1394.[8]   Alexander VII. accepted the restitution, 1659, and in 1661 forbade the alienation of this property, enlarging the Bull of Pius V. against alienation of property from the Church of Rome.[9] When, after this, Prince Charles Bassi-Ferrari-Fieschi sold this estate, without the consent of the Roman See, to Victor Amadeus II., who was then duke, Innocent XI. as lord superior declared the sale null and void, February 26, 1686.[10]   Considerable contentions arose, and for a long time all efforts at arrangement were fruitless.   At last the dispute was adjusted by Benedict XIV., 1741 ; he adopted a plan formerly entertained of conferring an apostolic vicariat *in temporalibus* on the King of Sardinia under certain conditions, viz. of rendering homage and presenting a gold chalice worth 2000 scudi every year on the feast of St. Peter, which continued to be the custom till the French Revolution.[11]

[1] Innocent III. says of Sardinia : ' Tota Sardinia dominii juris et proprietatis Apostolicae Sedis existit.' Ap. Raynald. a. 1200, n. 49, l. iii. Ep. 35, pp. 917, 918 (to the judex of Cagliari, whom he reproaches with his crimes and calls to account, at the same time commissioning the bishops to this effect). Ib. Ep. 36, p. 918, l. v. ; Ep. 124, 125, pp. 1126-1128 ; l. vi. Ep. 29, p. 31 : ' Cui (Rom. Eccl.) tam in spiritualibus quam in temporalibus est subjecta.' Cf. Ep. 30, p. 32 ; l. vii. Ep. 109, p. 391 ; l. ix. Ep. 63, p. 876. Rudolph I., 1274, also acknowledged Corsica and Sardinia to be possessions of the Holy See (Pertz, Mon. Germ. iv. 403, 404).

[2] Raynald. ad a. 1297, n. 2. Mariana, de Rebus Hisp. l. xiv. c. xiv. n. 17. Thomassin, P. ii. l. ii. c. xxxvii. n. 5.

[3] Raynald. ad a. 1335, n. 39.

[4] Carutti, Storia del Regno di Vittoria Amadeo II., Turino, 1856, p. 105. Rigant. in Reg. ii. Canc. § 1, n. 20, t. i. p. 209.

[5] Katherina, sister of Philip III. of Spain, married Duke Charles Emmanuel of Savoy (1580-1630), who was great-grandfather of Victor Amadeus II.

[6] Carutti, l.c. pp. 412-415 seq. 427 seq. 483 seq.

[7] For the documents see Ughelli, Italia Sacra, t. iv. p. 442 ; Migne, PP. Lat. ccxv. 621. Cf. letter of Innocent III. of 1206, l. ix. Ep. 93 (ib. p. 910).

[8] Moroni, Dizionario, v. Masserano, t. xliii. pp. 237, 238.

[9] Alex. VII. Const. Cum sicut, May 8, 1659 ; Const. Inter, Feb. 1, 1661 (Bullar. Rom. vi. v. p. 1 seq. 127).

[10] Innoc. XI. Const. Cum sicut, Bull. viii. 381 (al. xi. pp. 481-483, Const. 149).

[11] Carutti, Storia del Regno di Carlo Emanuele III., Torino, 1859, vol. i. pp. 153, 154. Docum. n. 3, pp. 347-352. Moroni, l.c. p. 238.

§ 7.

Parma and Piacenza were also among the Papal fiefs ; in 590 they had become united to the exarchate of Ravenna, and with it became part of the Papal States, and afterwards devolved once more upon the Roman See with the rest of Matilda's inheritance.[1] On the 6th August 1545, Paul III. gave these duchies as a Papal fief, in exchange for a yearly tribute of 9000 ducats, to his son Pier Luigi Farnese, born before he entered holy orders, and after him to Pier's son Ottavio. The Farnese took their oath of allegiance, and, after the acknowledgment of Philip II. in 1552, remained in undisturbed possession.[2] At the beginning of the Spanish War of Succession, Duke Francis Maria mounted the Papal arms for greater security from the belligerents. When in 1707 the emperor's party declared Parma an imperial fief, laid it under contribution, and oppressed the clergy, Clement XI. (August 1, 1707) issued severe decrees against the usurpation.[3]　The house of Farnese expired with Duke Antonio, January 20, 1731, when Clement XII. declared that if the widowed Duchess Henriquetta should die without male heirs the country would revert to the Holy See, according to the law of investiture made by Paul III.[4]　Germany and Spain, however, strove for possession.　The Infant Don Carlos, son of Philip V. of Spain, and Elizabeth Farnese, niece of the last duke, received the duchy, and later (in 1735) the kingdom of Naples.　The peace of Aix-la-Chapelle (October 18, 1748) assured the duchy to him and his male heirs, on condition that if ever he ascended the Spanish throne he should cede it to his brother Philip.　The rights of the Roman See were totally despised, and the power of protesting was all it now possessed. On the death of Duke Philip (July 18, 1765), and during the minority of his son, W. du Tillot conducted the government and made many laws inimical to the interests of the Church.　The bishops expostulated, and Clement XIII. as lord superior declared the laws void and issued a severe admonition (1768), which excited the greatest anger in the Bourbon courts.[5]　History shows after what fashion these were really good 'Catholic' courts at that time; they treated the Roman See worse than any non-Catholic States, and oppressed Clement XIII. till he died.[6]　His successor, Clement XIV., ended the dispute by granting a dispensation to the young duke for his marriage with Maria Amalia of Austria, and without entering upon what had gone before, appearing tacitly to retract the past.[7]　Later events, such as the dethronement of Duke Ferdinand and the French occupation, forced the questions of right more and more into the background; but every year on the feast of St. Peter the solemn protest was renewed in Rome.

---

[1] With regard to this inheritance, Innocent II., 1133, without renouncing his right, had been very compliant to Lothair II.; Hadrian IV. demanded it back in 1159 from Frederick I., who at last, in 1176, promised Alexander III. to return it, but in later negotiations endeavoured to evade his promise (cf. Hefele, v. 375, 495, 620, 622, 629, 643).　Innocent III. successfully made good his right to the Tuscan territory.　L. i. Ep. 15, p. 14, he writes: 'Cum ducatus Tusciae ad jus et dominium Ecclesiae Ro-

manae pertineat, sicut in privilegiis Rom. Eccl. oculata fide perspeximus contineri, nullam inter se sub nomine societatis colligationem facere debuissent episcopi et consules civitatum Tusciae, nisi salvo per omnia jure pariter et auctoritate SS. Rom. Sedis.' L. vii. Ep. 64, p. 344, he commissions the Bishop of Mantua to take possession, for the Roman See, of those portions of Matilda's inheritance which were within or on the borders of his diocese.

² Nicholi, Dissert. istorico-politica e legale sopra la natura e qualità delle città di Parma e Piacenza. Ragioni della S. Sede sopra il ducato di Parma e Piacenza. Della istoria del dominio temporale della Sede Ap. nel ducato di Parma, Roma, 1720. Theiner, Hist. du Pontificat de Clément XIV. t. i. p. 114 seq. Moroni, v. Parma, t. li. pp. 212 seq. 222 seq.

³ Carutti, Vittorio Amad. II. c. xiii. p. 209; c. xvii. pp. 280, 281.

⁴ Const. 39, Cum bonae, Bull. ed. Lux. xiv. pp. 154, 155.

⁵ Theiner, l.c. p. 115 seq. Moroni, l.c. p. 232 seq. The hatred of these courts had reached to such a height at that time that the life of the writer of the admonition, Mgr. Antonelli, who was made later a cardinal-deacon, was sought after. The hired assassin, however, murdered another prelate, by name Mgr. Antonelli Velletri, whom he mistook for the other. Pacca, Memorie Storiche, P. ii. c. ii. pp. 160, 161, ed. 1830. Several of Du Tillot's decrees may be found in Münch. Conc. i. 498 seq.

⁶ Cf. R. A. Menzel, Neuere Gesch. der Deutschen, xi. pp. 453, 455.

⁷ Theiner, l.c. pp. 286, 287.

PART II. PAPAL FIEFS OUT OF ITALY.

§ 1. Question as to feudal dependence of the Spanish kingdoms. § 2-4. England. § 5. Magna Charta. § 6. Scotland. § 7. Other tributary kingdoms. § 8. Kingdoms under the protection of St. Peter. § 9. Conduct of the Pope with regard to feudal subjection. Clement V. and Venice. § 10. The losses of Rome in land and power.

§ 1.

It is much to be doubted whether Portugal was ever really in feudal connection with the Apostolic See. Even supposing that Innocent III. had called it a tributary kingdom, and had placed it under his own and St. Peter's protection, still that shows no kind of feudal relation between them ; tribute can be paid freely and out of devotion, not necessarily only from a vassal.¹ Neither is it any proof that Innocent IV. appointed a regent to the kingdom, as the appointment can be explained on other legal principles, and in the decree itself there is no mention of feudal relations.² As far as Aragon is concerned, we know that Peter II. of Aragon was crowned in 1204 by Innocent III., that he made his kingdom subject to the Apostolic See, and paid a yearly tribute.[3] At the same time it is very much disputed whether the tribute and the dependence were of a feudal nature.[4] The oath which the king took at his coronation was only a simple oath of fidelity. The annual tribute might be intended as an expression of the king's religious dependence. The feudal dependence of the King of Aragon was only mentioned by Innocent III. with regard to certain castles.[5] After the revolt of the Sicilians against Charles of Anjou, in 1282, Martin IV. excommunicated King Peter III. of Aragon, who had seized the throne, deprived him of both kingdoms, and made over Aragon to Philip the Bold, for one of his sons. Philip accepted it, and sought to make good his right at the head of an army. With regard to Sicily, the Pope acted as lord superior ; some historians[6] have asserted that he also acted thus in regard to Aragon ; others[7] deny this. He by no means acted ‘ as using a divine right,’[8] but appealed mainly to the fact that the King of Aragon was specially bound to fidelity to the Apostolic See.[9] He pronounced those who despised his condemnation to have forfeited all the lands, fiefs, and rights which they derived either from the See of Rome or from any other sees, but not all their possessions in general.[10] He thus resisted a revolution, and the deposition of a legitimate prince, with all the weapons left at his command ; if in any way he overstepped the limits of moderation, it is open to any one to blame him ; even an ‘ Ultramontane theologian’ can do so without danger of offending against a dogma ; but in itself this struggle was perfectly just. The feudal relations of the Spanish peninsula with the Roman See only concerned particular places ; if they were more extended, it was only for a time and by single rulers.

[1] Aug. Barbosa (J. U. D. Lusitanus), de Officio et Potestate Episcopi, P. i. tit. 3, c. ii. n. 64 seq. ed. Romae, 1623 : ‘ Devotionis causa, solum ut tamquam Christi milites devoti et grati sub illius utpote ejusdem vicarii protectione militarent et Maurorum expulsioni et Christianae fidei propagationi incumberent.’

[2] Innoc. IV. c. ii. de Suppl. Neglig. Prael. i. 8, in 6.

[3] Innoc. Reg. xvi. Ep. 87. Raynald. a. 1204, n. 71, 72. Fleury, t. xvi. 1. lxxvi. n. 10. Thomassin, P. iii. l. i. c. xxxii. n. 8. Hurter, Innocenz III. i. p. 598.

⁴ J. D. Mansi, note in Natal. Alex. H. E. sacc. 13 et 14, c. i. a. 4, pp. 43, 44, t. xv. ed. Bing. Phillips (Kirchenrecht, v. § 236, p. 556), however, supposes distinct feudal relations.

⁵ L. viii. Ep. 97, p. 667, a. 1205. The Papal legates are commissioned to bestow upon this king personaliter *in feudum* the castrum Scurae, which he had reconquered from the heretics : ' Ita tamen quod ex eo fidelitatem Ecclesiae Romanae faciat et in recognitionem, quod ejusdem castri proprietas ad jus B. Petri pertineat, certum censum statuat solvendum nobis nostrisque successoribus annuatim.' Cf. l. ix. Ep. 103, p. 916.

⁶ Zurita, Ind. rer. ab Arag. Reg. gest. h.a.: ' XI. Kal. April. Martiuns P. M. Urbe Veteri de Collegii sententia Petrum Ar. uti Ecclesiae subditium et perduellionis convictum regno ac ditionibus omnibus mulctat.' Natal. Alex. sacc. 13 et 19, c. i. a. 4, p. 64. Fleury, Hist. Ecclés. t. xxiii. l. lxxxviii. n. 10, 19. Daniel, l.c. t. iv. a. 1283. Velly, t. vi. p. 386.

⁷ Mansi, note in Natal. Alex. H. E. sacc. 13 et 14, c. i. a. 11, p. 43.

⁸ Janus, p. 15.

⁹ Specialiter Sedi Apostolicae fideles et obnoxios teneri.

¹⁰ Natal. Alex. l.c. p. 64.

§ 2.

The manner in which England became a Papal fief under Innocent III., and the means by which it was effected, have led to many complaints against this Pope. In 1206 he decided the dispute which had arisen shortly before, about the right of election for the primacy of Canterbury, in favour of the monks (canons) who lived there, and against the bishops ; and Stephen Langton, having been elected on his recommendation, was consecrated by him at Viterbo in 1207. King John was indignant at this, because he had wished to raise the Bishop of Norwich to the archiepiscopal see : he drove the monks from Canterbury, seized their goods, and forbade the reception of the new primate.[1] The Roman See had always treated him with great consideration, but he was more defiant and regardless of her than any other prince of his time.[2] The Pope charged the English bishops to lay the country under an interdict if John remained obstinate. The Bishops of London, Ely, and Worcester pronounced the interdict over the whole of England in March 1208, and subsequently fled to France, where Archbishop Langton also was staying.[3] Most of the clergy strictly observed the interdict,[4] which caused John to take more violent measures against the clerical power ; and in 1209, Innocent excommuni-

cated him by name.[5]   The endeavours which the Pope made to
reconcile the king with the Church were fruitless.   In 1211 an
insurrection broke out, which John suppressed with shocking
cruelty.   At last, in 1212, Innocent released John's subjects
from their oath of allegiance, and opened to the King of France
a prospect of the throne of England in case John did not
submit.[6]   After all we have not the text of the Papal condemnation, and Matthew Paris, often quite untrustworthy, is our
only source of information.[7]   Philip Augustus resolved on a war
with John, who soon found himself in great difficulties.   On the
13th May 1213, at Dover, he swore to submit to the Pope's
judgment, and despatched ambassadors to him with letters.[8]
Stephen Langton, the persecuted bishops, clergy, and laity, received security and compensation for their losses ; the crowns
of England and Ireland were surrendered to the Pope as lord
superior, with the promise of a yearly tribute.[9]   After this any
attack on England by the French king was forbidden by the
Pope.   A moment's thought would make this appear quite
natural,[10] and in no way ' a breach of faith' with France.[11]   If
the Pope had refused to be reconciled with a king ready to
submit to the Church and make satisfaction, then he would
have deserved just blame, and would have been guilty of arbitrary tyranny.   The object of ecclesiastical censures was the
correction of offenders : if ineffectual, then, as a last measure,
release from the oath of fealty and deposition, or rather (as it
was not irrevocable) suspension from government, was added :
the censures and their consequences ceased when they had
attained their object, the amendment of offenders.   This was
how Innocent III. understood it, and plainly showed his object[12]
by giving John the title of king even after he had censured
him.[13]   Ranke says very truly, that ' as soon as the Pope was
acknowleged as lord superior, not only must all hostility cease,
but it became his duty to take the kingdom under his protection.'[14]   It was known also in France that the Pope only intended Philip Augustus to take permanent possession of the
country if John remained obdurate ;[15] if Innocent had ceded it
unconditionally, we must have admitted that he did not act for

the good of the Church in England, or in a way to insure its stability. The proposed feudal sovereignty, which, moreover, had been temporarily acknowledged by Henry II.,[16] gave the Pope the means of protecting the dioceses and the subjects from any heavy oppression, and beyond the payment of the tribute was hardly at all felt.[17] Edward II. afterwards acknowledged himself to be a vassal of the Roman See,[18] while Richard II. denied the feudal subjection.[19]

[1] Hefele, Conc. v. pp. 645, 725-727. Lingard, Hist. Eng. ii. p. 316, 5th edit. 1849.

[2] Innoc. III. l. x. Ep. 219, p. 1328 : ' Cum nos in tali casu tantum honorem nulli principium detulerimus, quantum tibi, tu nostro tantum derogare attendis honori, quantum in simili casu nullus princeps derogare praesumpsit.' Cf. l. xi. Ep. 87, 89, 90, 91, p. 1403 seq.; Ep. 141, 211 seq. pp. 1455, 1526 seq.; Ep. 221, 223, p. 1535 seq.

[3] Innoc. III. l. ix. Ep. 34 seq. 205, 206; l. x. Ep. 113, 159 seq. Acta Innoc. n. 132 (Murat. Rer. it. Scr. xiii. 561). Rigord. in Gest. Phil. Aug. n. 1212. Lingard, l.c. pp. 317, 318.

[4] The terms of the interdict in the Supplem. ad Innoc. III. Epist. n. 136 (Migne, t. ccxviii. p. 190).

[5] Innoc. l. xii. Ep. 57.

[6] Hefele, p. 728. That it was proposed actually to depose the king is disputed by Natal. Alex. H. E. saec. 13, c. i. a. 1, n. 13.

[7] Bossuet (P. i. l. iii. c. xxi. p. 317) also can only refer to Matthew Paris (a. 1212, p. 232), who no more gives the actual words of the judgment than of the letter to the French king.

[8] Raynald. a. 1213, n. 74.

[9] Rymer, Foed. i. 1, p. 129.

[10] Hefele, l.c.

[11] In July 1215, Innocent expressly called upon the French king to attend to the warnings of the Cardinal-bishop of Tusculum, who had been sent to England, and to reëstablish peace with King John (l. xvi. Ep. 83, pp. 884, 885).

[12] In the letter of Aug. 15, 1215. The Pope's letter refutes the account given by Paris that John had taken the oath of allegiance ' juxta quod Romae fuerat sententiam.'

[13] L. xv. Ep. 234, p. 772 seq.

[14] Engl. Geschichte, i. p. 66. He also remarks : ' It appears, moreover, that in the beginning the barous approved the act of the king, though they did not give a formal approval. They asserted that they had risen for the rights of the Church, and looked upon the Pope as of their party.' This is corroborated by the passage in Rymer, i. 185 ; Innoc. l. xvi. Ep. 77 : ' Communi consilio baronum nostrorum.'

[15] Rigord (properly his continuator, William Brito), Gest. Phil. Aug. a. 1213 : ' Causa, quae Philippum regem magnanimum moverat ad hoc, ut vellet in Angliam transfretare, fuit, ut episcopos, qui diu a sedibus suis

ejecti in regno suo exulabant, suis Ecclesiis restitueret, ut *divinum servi-lium*, quod jam per septennium in tota Anglia cessaverat, *faceret renovari* et ut ipsum regem Joannem . . . . *vel poenae condignae subjiceret vel a regno prorsus expellens* secundum agnominis sui interpretationem omnino *efficeret sine terra.*'

[16] This king wrote to Alexander III.: ' Vestrae jurisdictionis est reg-num Angliae et quantum ad feudatarii juris obligationem vobis dumtaxat obnoxius teneor et adstringor' (Baron. a. 1173, u. 10). Cf. Hefele, l.c. pp. 612, 613; Thomassin, P. iii. l. i. c. xxxii. n. 4.   Cf. Vita Alex. III. ap. Murat. R. J. Scr. iii. 1, pp. 462, 24.   Cf. Innoc. III. l. xvi. Ep. 79-82, p. 881 seq.   Matthew Paris (a. 1215) himself recounts the vain hopes which were at that time generally raised by this step: ' Speraverant omnes et singuli, Angliam quasi Acgyptiaco jugo . . . . liberntam pace et securitato gaudere,' &c.   He says (a. 1216) of the barons complaining of the rex tributarius : ' Peccantes inexpiabiliter, cum scriptum sit: Principi non maledices . . . . cum Deo servire regnare sit.'

[17] Thomassin, l.c. c. xxxii. n. 5.

[18] Eduardi II. Diplom. ap. Raynald. a. 1316, n. 24.

[19] Richard II. in 16 ; Richard III. c. v.   Brun's Eccles. Can. s.v. Su-premacy.

§ 3.

After King John was absolved from the ban of excommuni-cation, and the interdict had been withdrawn, he endeavoured to regain the English possessions on the Continent, but unsuc-cessfully, and a truce of five years was concluded.[1]   Soon, how-ever, John was threatened at home, for on his refusal to grant the privileges bestowed by Henry I. upon the barons, they joined together, and took up arms to recover them.   In 1215 they forced from him the confirmation of their liberties, the so-called *Magna Charta libertatis ;* and when John appeared to be going to abolish this, they again threatened him.[2]   The king appealed to the Pope.   ' The rebellious nobles discovered that the Pope was not only ready to protect the king, his feudatory, against foreign attacks, but also against civil agitations.'[3]   The unruly barons sent Eustachius de Vescy, the most distinguished of their number, to Rome, to gain the Pope to their side, ac-knowledging him positively as the lord of England.[4]   When the Pope decided against them they did not yield, but, on the contrary, chose Prince Louis of France as king.   The Pope endeavoured to persuade Philip Augustus to prevent the depar-ture of his son for England ;[5] however, Prince Louis entered

London, and was excommunicated by the Papal legate.[6] Innocent III. died at this time (1216), and King John also in
the same year.[7] His son and successor, Henry III., found the
Papal protection very useful in the early days of his reign :
peace was concluded with the French Prince Louis, who subsequently applied for and obtained from the mild Honorius III.
the repeal of the Papal Brief issued against his expedition.[8]

[1] Hefele, pp. 728-732.
[2] What Paris says about John's delay from May 1215 contradicts the
documents apud Brady and Rymer (Lingard, ii. p. 361, n. 3).
[3] Ranke, l.c. i. p. 68.
[4] Maucler, Literne de Negotio Baron. ap. Rymer, Foed. i. 185. Ranke,
i. 69 : ' Magnates Angliae—instanter D. Papae supplicant, quod cum ipse
sit dominis Angliae, vos—compellat, antiquas libertates suas—eis illaesas
servare.'
[5] Hefele, p. 810.
[6] The interdict in England did not by any means fall ' powerless to
the ground' (Huber, p. 16) ; Matthew Paris even does not say that: it was
only London (sola civitas Londinensis) that despised the censures, whilst
they were published per totam Angliam in brevi.
[7] What Matthew Paris says of John's inclination to accept his kingdom
in fief from the sultan of Morocco, we consider—although he refers to
Robert of London, a clerk of the royal chapel—to be a malicious invention ;
and also the answer of Miramolinus, so shocking to Christians, appears
hardly credible. Lingard (ii. pp. 324, 325) endeavours to defend the account ; Pauli (iii. p. 882) rightly condemns it.
[8] Honor. III. Ep. ap. Raynald. a. 1217, n. 79.

§ 4.

Innocent III. had protected the rights of John and his son,
particularly as the former was his vassal, and had taken the
cross. He could neither be expected to repel John in 1213 with
severity after his submission and to refuse any reconciliation, nor
to allow John in 1215 to be oppressed by rebels or turned out
of his country by foreigners. The Papal condemnation of 1212
was intended to bring the misguided king back to his senses
and to save his throne for him. The feudal superiority given
over to the Pope was likewise intended to protect the king
against the power and the revenge of the rebels, to free the kingdom from foreign invasion, and to maintain the lawful succession. If Innocent had repelled the king in 1213, would it not

have been said that he wished the destruction of a sinner, not that he should be converted and live ?[1]   Had he declared himself on the side of the barons against John in 1215, would he not have been accused of openly favouring rebellion, of siding with rebels, of violating duties newly undertaken ?   And would not these accusations be much better founded than those which now it is alone possible to raise ?

[1] When Innocent III. (1199) absolved Markwald he declared : ' Ad reconciliationem et receptionem Marcowaldi *debitum officii pastoralis, quo tenemur omnes ad viam rectitudinis revocare ac redeuntes recipere,* nos induxit et optata regni tranquillitas invitavit, ut simul et humiliaremus hostem et humiliatum et poenitentem *ejus* reciperemus exemplo, qui non vult mortem peccatoris, *sed ut magis convertatur et vivat,* qui Chananaeam et publicanum non solum vocavit ad poenitentiam, sed et traxit' (l. ii. Ep. 167, p. 716, ed. Migne).   In another place, he had accepted him ' ne se poenitentem, sicut videbatur . . . . recipere negaremus, non Christi vicarii videremur vel successores Apostolorum principis, sed inexorabiles potius nostrarum injuriarum ultores' (ib. Ep. 179, p. 729).   In the same way at the absolution of the King of Leon (l. vii. Ep. 94, p. 376, ed. cit.).   As early as in 1207, Innocent III. described the object of his measure against John : ' Ut *medicinali manu* sanatus in gratiarum nobis actiones assurgat.'   Innocent III. (l. xvi. Ep. 80, p. 882 ; Ep. 81, p. 883) expressly mentions the words of Scripture (Ezech. xviii. 23 ; xxxiii. 11 ; 2 Peter iii. 9).

§ 5.

Let us hear an impartial historian concerning Magna Charta. L. Ranke says : ' By the Charta the barons usurped a power of compulsion over the king, which was set aside, with other weighty claims, in the reign of Henry III.[1]   It is not the original Magna Charta of John which is the foundation of English liberties, but the one revised in the reign of Henry III.[2]   Magna Charta was the project of an agreement, the execution of which was to be the subject of dispute for centuries.'[3]   Pauli[4] and the ' decidedly Catholic' Lingard[5] will be cited against us, but they do not say anything essentially different.   They mention the numerous alterations which the Charta has undergone.[6]   Lingard only says it was considered as the basis of English freedom ; and Pauli, that ' as the kings repeatedly perjured themselves, and vainly strove to demolish the principles of Magna Charta,

the whole fabric of English freedom was considered as linked
with Magna Charta.'[7]

[1] Ranke, Engl. Gesch. i. p. 72.
[2] Ib. p. 75.
[3] Ib. p. 76.
[4] Pauli, Geschichte von England, iii. 424.
[5] Lingard, Hist. of Eng. ii. 349.
[6] Ib. p. 359.
[7] Pauli, l.c.

§ 6.

With regard to Scotland, Boniface VIII. is alleged to be the
first who declared that it belonged to the Roman See.[1] This is
certainly untrue. The Scotch Church was subject in early times
to the metropolis of York, and this led to many disputes,[2] especially as the Kings of England made use of the ecclesiastical
dependence of Scotland to bring about its political dependence.[3]
Innocent II. had in 1131 confirmed its dependence upon the
see of York;[4] but Celestine III. in 1192 cancelled this arrangement at the prayer of King William, and placed the Scotch
Church directly under the Apostolic See,[5] to which also the
country now sought to unite itself more closely. There were
continual wars between the English and the Scotch. Henry II.
tried to gain influence among the latter, and to overthrow the
Scotch king. John Lackland accepted the feudal oath from
King William and his son Alexander in 1209 and 1212; Henry
III. also received it from the latter. The Scotch on their side
were only willing to acknowledge the feudal supremacy of England for a few counties, and not for the crown of Scotland itself.
King Alexander III., although married to an English princess
(1251), avoided taking the oath at York; and in 1256 the
English king expressly acknowledged the complete independence of the Scotch crown. When, in 1290, Alexander III. died,
leaving no male heirs, and sanguinary disputes broke out in the
country between the families of Bruce and Baliol,[6] England,
under Edward I., sought to bring about the absolute feudal dependence of Scotland. Edward I. begged Nicholas IV. to confirm the claims of the crown of England; but the Pope declared
that it was not in his power, as he could not deprive the Roman

See of an overlordship which belonged to it.[7] Most probably the Scotch, in order to avoid the English claims, had already many times declared that their kingdom should only be dependent on the Roman See. Boniface VIII. by no means refused the King of England every right, but he wished to have it proved by plenipotentiary in Rome. He demanded, above all, the liberty of the clergy and the rights of the Church,[8] and only repeated the statements of the Scotch agents, who in Rome had eagerly maintained that Scotland belonged to the Roman See. He did not decide about it in any definitive manner. The feudal union of Scotland and Rome was scarcely ever touched upon again ; it never came into active existence.

[1] Huber, p. 37.
[2] Hefele, v. pp. 348, 616 seq.
[3] This is a difficulty which had already occurred to several countries. With reference to Moravia, cf. Dudik, Mähr. Gesch. i. p. 156 seq.
[4] Jaffé, Reg. n. 5357, 5387 seq. pp. 565, 567.
[5] Mansi, xxii. 613. Jaffé, n. 10,361, p. 891.
[6] Pauli, Gesch. Englands, iii. pp. 171 seq. 349 seq. 505 seq. 638, 665, 703 ; iv. 53 seq. Lingard, ii. 320 seq. 401 seq. 525 seq.
[7] Spondan. a. 1290, ex Reg. Vat. Ep. 102 : 'Se non posse in regno Scotiae Sedi Apostolicae obnoxio Ecclesiae Romanae derogare ejusque fiduciarios regi Anglo submittere' (Lingard, ii. p. 560, n. 2).
[8] Rymer, ii. 844 seq. Lingard, ii. p. 559 seq. Pauli, iv. p. 248 seq.

§ 7.

Of other kingdoms we only know that they paid a yearly tax to the Roman See ; for instance, Sweden, under Popes Anastasius IV.[1] and Innocent III.,[2] and under the latter Poland[3] also, whose Duke Boleslav drew down many rebukes upon himself on account of his tyranny (1206).[4] In 1295, Boniface VIII. made Duke Przemysl II. of Kalisch king of all Poland ; and in 1319, John XXII. declared, after continued contests between that country and Bohemia, that Poland stood directly under the protection of the Roman Church.[5] Some towns also paid a similar tax for the special protection of the Roman Church ; for example, Marseilles under Gregory IX.[6] Under Honorius III. the Isle of Man was made subject to the Church of Rome by King Reginald.[7] Under Gregory IX. the neophytes of Gothland were

pronounced independent of Sweden and Denmark, and only subject to their bishop.[8]   Later, Lithuania was marked out as the
property of the Roman See.[9]   Vulcan, King of Dalmatia and
Dioclea, took an oath of allegiance to Pope Innocent III., and submitted himself and his country.[10]   Kalojohn, King of Bulgaria
and Wallachia, in order to be independent of other princes, placed
himself under the Roman See.[11]   He begged from Rome a crown
and imperial honours, such as (in the tenth century) his predecessors Peter and Samuel had received.[12]   In 1204, Innocent
sent Cardinal Leo of the Holy Cross to anoint and crown the
king acknowledged by him, and to receive the acknowledgment
of the Papal jurisdiction.[13]   He determined the rights of the
primate, and gave further instructions.[14]   On the whole, this
submission had only a transitory importance.   The Popes were
generally careful not to insist on feudal subjection where it had
been quite voluntary, and especially when the princes of later
times opposed it.[15]

[1] Jaffé, Reg. n. 6819, 6820, p. 658, d. 28 Nov. 1154.
[2] Innoc. III. Supplem. Ep. 230. Migne, ccxvii. p. 265.
[3] Innoc. III. l. ix. Ep. 219, p. 1063. Thomassin, P. iii. l. i. c. xxxii.
n. 11.
[4] Ib. Ep. 217, p. 1060 seq.
[5] Thomas. l.c. Joh. XXII. ad Acp. Gnesn.: ' Tam vos per episcopum
et literas quam idem episcopus per se ipsum cum multa nobis instantia
supplicastis, ut cum regnum praedictum esset nobis et Ecclesiae Romanae
nullo mediante subjectum, et in signum subjectionis ejusmodi census, qui
denarius B. Petri vocatur, nobis et eidem Ecclesiae annis singulis debere-
tur,' &c.
[6] Raynald. a. 1230, n. 29.
[7] Raynald. a. 1219, n. 44.
[8] Thomassin, l.c. n. 11.
[9] Raynald. a. 1254, n. 27; a. 1255.
[10] Innoc. III. l. i. Ep. 176, 526, 527, pp. 725 seq. 481 seq.
[11] Gesta Innoc. n. 70, p. 126.
[12] Innoc. l. v. Ep. 115, p. 1112 seq. Cf. l. vi. Ep. 143, 144, pp.
156-158.
[13] L. vii. Ep. 1, p. 277 seq., where it says: ' Populos Bulgarorum et
Blachorum, qui multo jam tempore ab uberibus matris suae alienati fuerunt, in spiritualibus et temporalibus providere volentes ejus auctoritate
confisi, per quem Samuel David in regem innuuxit, *regem te statuimus*
super eos et per dil. fil. Leonem tit. S. Crucis presb. cardinalem Ap. Sed.
legatum sceptrum regni ac regium tibi mittimus diadema ejus quasi nostris tibi manibus imponendem, recipiendo a te juratoriam cautionem, quod

nobis et successoribus nostris et Ecclesiae Rom. devotus et obcdiens per-
manebis et cunctas terras et gentes tuo subjectas imperio in obedientiae
devotione Sedis Ap. conservabis.' Cf. Ep. 12, p. 295.
[14] Ib. et Ep. 2, 3, Aep. Trinovit. p. 280 seq.; Ep. 7-11, p. 292 seq.
[15] Thomassin, l.c. c. xxxii. n. 1.

§ 8.

To say that Innocent III. or his successors considered and
treated *all princes* as his vassals[1] is one of those assertions which,
often brought forward, are never proved, and which never can
be proved in face of the Papal Briefs.   Let any one look, for
example, at the Papal Briefs addressed to John Lackland before
taking the feudal oath,[2] to Philip Augustus of France,[3] to the
Kings of Denmark,[4] Castile,[5] Hungary,[6] &c.   The form 'to take
under the protection of St. Peter,'[7] that is continually recurring,
does not refer to vassalage, which indeed is shown by its being
applied to the princes who undertook a Crusade.   The only effect
of this protection was that injuries done to any one thus protected would be considered sacrilegious, and censured in the
same way as if they had been done to the Church of Rome.[8]

[1] Huber, p. 18.   Friedberg, p. 27 seq.
[2] Innoc. l. v. Ep. 160, pp. 1175-1177.   Cf. l. vi. Ep. 63, a. 1203,
мссxv. p. 61; l. vii. Ep. 171, a. 1204; ib. t. 484, seq. n. 8, Ep. 166, p. 747.
[3] L. i. Ep. 171, 348, 355; l. ii. Ep. 24; l. vi. Ep. 150, 182.
[4] Cf. l. vi. Ep. 181, pp. 194-198; Ep. 193, p. 771; l. x. Ep. 41; l. xi.
Ep. 10.   The Archbishop of Lund was commissioned in 1204 to collect
the census B. Petri in Denmark and Sweden (l. vii. Ep. 155, p. 461).
[5] L. vi. Ep. 80, 94, pp. 82, 99; l. viii. Ep. 50, 203, pp. 616, 617, 782
seq.; l. xiv. Ep. 4, p. 380; Ep. 154, 155, p. 513 seq.; l. xv. Ep. 183,.
p. 703.
[6] L. viii. Ep. 126-128, p. 410 seq.; l. viii. Ep. 36-42, p. 595 seq.;
Ep. 88, 107, 127, pp. 668, 675, 702; l. ix. Ep. 74, p. 893; l. x. Ep. 39, p.
1132.
[7] The common form was : 'Tuis justis precibus grato concurrentes
assensu personam tuam cum omnibus bonis, quae impraesentiarum ratio-
nabiliter possides, specialiter autem . . . . aut in futurum justis modis Deo
propitio poteris adipisci, sub B. Petri et nostra protectione suscipimus et
praesentis scripti pagina communimus.'   Thus, for example, l. ii. Ep. 182.
R. Comiti Licii, p. 733.   It is declared (l. vii. Ep. 177, p. 489), that being
taken under the protection of St. Peter does not withdraw the clergy and
laity from the jurisdiction of their bishops.
[8] L. x. Ep. 149, Regi Francorum, p. 1247: 'Nos, ut securius his possis
intendere, terram tuam et homines tuos ac eorum bona interim sub B.

Petri et nostra protectione suscipimus, et si quis (quod non credimus) to
vel tuos nequiter molestare praesumpserit, tantam injuriam, quam reputa-
remus Sedi Apostolicae principaliter irrogatam, curaremus per censuram
canonicam vindicare.'

§ 9.

Though several princes offered their countries to be held as
fiefs from the Popes it was done voluntarily and without compulsion, and, as a rule, the Popes only accepted when they were
convinced that the rights of no third party were injured by their
so doing.[1]   Accordingly Innocent IV. (1244-45) declined the
offer made by Prince David of Wales to place himself under the
feudal sovereignty of the Pope because he was a vassal of England ;[2] and then again he accepted, in the interests of the propagation of Christianity, the subjection of his country to the
chair of Peter, proposed by the Grand Duke of Lithuania, and
he allowed him to be invested by the Bishop of Culm with the
insignia of authority.[3]

Whoever carefully examines the actions of the Popes will
find that their object was not to aggrandise their earthly possessions,[4] but conscientiously to preserve the rights that had been
transmitted to them, and to increase their influence in the
interests of the Church.   Some may have gone too far in this,
or their measures may have been too violent.   Clement V., for
whose mode of government we are not responsible, acted with
great severity towards the Venetian Republic, which, however,
was not disputing with him 'the possession of Ferrara,'[5] but
had violently usurped the territory which Francesco, Duke of
Reggio, held as lawful feudatory under Papal authority.   The
admonitions of Clement V. had no effect ; his ambassadors in
Venice were grossly insulted, and the right of the Church of Rome
utterly disregarded.   If the Pope took such measures against the
obstinate islanders as before had only partially been taken,[6] it was
but a severe carrying into effect of the public law of those days;[7]
the object was to protect the international principles of the
Middle Ages against insolent encroachments, and to brand the
disturbers of such principles as common and public enemies.
In the Middle Ages whoever was a declared obstinate enemy of

the Church was a public enemy as long as he was not prepared to make requisite satisfaction.[8]

[1] According to the old canonical rule, ' Ne laedatur jus tertii.'
[2] Rymer, i. 425. Lingard, ii. pp. 403, 404.
[3] Raynald. a. 1251, n. 45 ; 1254, n. 27. Thomassin, P. i. l. i. 59, n. 5.
[4] Not only De Maistre (Du Pape, l. ii. c. vi. pp. 241, 55) has shown this, but also Michaud (Hist. des Croisades, t. vi. p. 231).
[5] Huber, p. 39. Schulte, i. p. 37 seq.
[6] When the citizens of Piacenza had shamefully ill-treated their bishops and plundered the churches, Innocent III., 1204 (l. vii. Ep. 173, pp. 487, 488), ordered the Lombard bishops: ' Quatenus cives jam dictos, ad quem-cumque locum provinciae Mediolanensis devenerint, in colloquiis, hospitiis atque contractibus tamquam excommunicatos faciatis arctius evitari et tenere etiam bona eorum, ubicumque illa contigerit inveniri, donec per satisfactionem condignam reconciliari Ecclesiae mereantur.' Cf. l. ix. Ep. 131, pp. 948, 949 ; Ep. 166, 167, p. 995 seq. And before that, when the citizens of Treviso murdered the Bishop of Belluno, burnt churches, prac-tised many cruelties, and despised censures, Innocent threatened to remove the bishopric, to forbid trading and intercourse with them, to seize their merchants and confiscate their goods (l. ii. Ep. 27, pp. 355-358). After satisfaction was promised, then (1200) absolution was assured to them upon certain conditions (l. iii. Ep. 39, p. 922).
[7] Bishop Fessler (pp. 50, 51) justly considers it ridiculous to wish to make a dogmatic proposition out of an ' edictum judiciarium,' as does Schulte (i. p. 37, n. 5) when he says : 'The Pope can make *slaves* of Christian subjects and *dispose of them*, when their ruler or rulers have been excommunicated ;' and as do the 'German theologians' in the Allge-meine Zeitung of June 19, 1870, A. B. n. 8 : ' The Pope can, *according to divine right* [where is that to be found ?], give up, without distinction, whole Christian nations to slavery because of some measure enacted by one of their princes.'
[8] Some jurists of that time carried the matter to its logical results and said: ' Ad servitutem *accidentalem* juste potest Papa rebelles damnare.' Thus Augustine Triumphus, Sum. de Potest. Papae, q. 22.

§ 10.

Few other rulers would have been contented to lose so many temporal possessions as easily as the Popes did in the course of centuries. Long after the foundation of the States of the Church Papal authority was ill-established, Papal possessions were often occupied by powerful noble families ; in the twelfth century they were threatened by the efforts of the republicans, and later by the Ghibelline party. Innocent III. first brought about a stronger and firmer government in the State, while recognising the ancient liberties of the towns.[1] When the consuls and the people of Montebello submitted to him as to their sovereign, they declared that[2] 'no one can deny that our town belonged to the dominion of the Duchess Matilda. But formerly the Church of God could not exercise its authority in this place, having been weighed down by the civil power. Now, however, in our time, as ordained by Almighty God, the prodigal sons return to the bosom of their mother, and desire in everything to maintain the authority of their father. We all unanimously beg and entreat for your government and desire to swear fidelity to your Holiness ; and we do so the more faithfully, as we confidently believe that you have the Spirit of God, and through it receive the power to lead everything by your wisdom back to its right condition.' Then came the request that the ancient and modern rights of the township should still be granted, which was accorded. Individual municipalities retained their privileges, and were only laid under trifling obligations.[3] In the struggles with Frederick II. the greater part of the Papal States was lost again, and the French Popes at Avignon could not remedy these losses. Cardinal Ægidius Albornoz (1353-1368) alone stands out as a statesman and legislator of any importance.[4] The power of the Holy See in the Papal States, and especially in Rome, was not more firmly established until the fifteenth century, when it was restored by Julius II.[5] Parts of the States were frequently alienated to vassals, vicars, or relations. Gregory IX. had caused such alienations to be dependent on the consent of the cardinals,[6] and the Council of Constance renewed that condition.[7] Paul III. and Paul IV. still practised such alienations.[8] The Bull of March 29, 1567, issued by Pius V. put a bar to such proceedings for ever.[9] After the incorporation of Ferrara (1596) and Urbino (1631)[10] the States of the Church continued the same till the French Revolution ; but then Venaissin, which had belonged to the Popes since 1274,[11] and Avignon, which they had bought in 1348, were incorporated with France, without the smallest indemnification, by a decree of September 14,

1791, both territories having been temporarily taken away, 1768-74. The forced peace of Tolentino (February 19, 1797) moreover took away the three legations, which were only re-stored in 1815, with certain diminutions. The revolution, after several short-lived triumphs, destroyed the States of the Church in three successive attacks in 1859, 1860, and 1870. The nineteenth century has swept away all old feudal relations, and has reduced the Popes to political impotence. The enemies of the Church rejoice at all feudal links being broken, and at the destruction of the States of the Church, and mock at the Papacy reduced to such temporal weakness ; nevertheless they affect to show an unconquerable dread of the spiritual and moral power of this same Papacy, and to believe that with the dogmas which the world derides it will once more conquer the world and bring all kingdoms into subjection !

[1] Cf. Döllinger, The Church and the Churches, pp. 342-347, Eng. trans. 1862.

[2] Innoc. III. 1. i. Ep. 47 (Migne, ccxiv. p. 44).

[3] Döllinger, l.c. p. 347.

[4] Döllinger, p. 353.

[5] Döllinger, p. 356.   Ces. Cantù, Storia Univ. l. xv. P. i. c. iv. v.

[6] Greg. IX. Const. 6, Rex excelsus, Bull. i. 76.

[7] Conc. Const. Mansi, xxviii. 270, 368. Hausmann, Gesch. der Päpstl. Reservatfälle, p. 219 seq. A remedy was sought in capitulations of the German emperor (Döllinger, Lehrbuch, d. K.. Gesch. ii. n. 349, 353, 357 seq.).

[8] Döllinger, The Church and the Churches, p. 361 seq.

[9] Pius V. Const. 35, Admonet nos, Bull. ii. 236.

[10] Döllinger, l.c. p. 358.

[11] Hefele, Conc. vi. p. 118.

ESSAY XI.

BONIFACE VIII. AND PHILIP THE FAIR.

SELDOM has a Pope been so much calumniated, both during his life and after his death, as Boniface VIII., who before his pontificate had distinguished himself as a jurist. The Colonnas, the Italian Ghibellines, Nogaret and Peter Flotte, the French jurists, the fanatic monks, all used every effort to dishonour his memory,[1] and heavily did the Pope pay for his delusive hope of finding a Catholic king of the old sort, and a worthy successor of St. Louis, in Philip the Fair of France. His principal object was to restore peace throughout Europe, and to lead the allied strength of the Christian princes against the infidel;[2] but the mutual hatred of these princes was too great and too selfish for them to give ear to his peaceful admonitions, and in the States of the Church the powerful Colonnas were preparing the most serious difficulties for the Pope.[3]

Pope Boniface VIII. had specially to defend the rights and liberties of the Church against Philip IV. the Fair of France.

[1] Spondan. Ann. a. 1301, n. 2; 1303, n. 8, 14. Bianchi, t. i. l. i. § 10, p. 91 seq.
[2] Raynald. a. 1295, n. 43. Hefele, Conc. vi. p. 254.
[3] Christophe, Hist. du Papauté au 14me siècle, Germ. transl. i. p. 65 seq.

PART I. BONIFACE VIII. AND PHILIP THE FAIR UNTIL THE PUBLICATION OF THE BULL 'UNAM SANCTAM.'

§ 1. Attempt of the Pope to mediate between the Kings of England and France. § 2. Bull 'Clericis laicos.' § 3. Measures of the king against it. § 4. Bull 'Ineffabilis.' § 5. Apparent adjustment of the quarrel. § 6. Principles of the two parties. Judgment of the Pope as arbitrator. § 7. Further violent acts of Philip. § 8. Mission of the Bishop of Pamiers. § 9. Papal decrees of 1301. Difficulties of the Pope. § 10. Bull 'Ausculta fili.' § 11. Forging a false Bull. § 12. Convention of

the States-General.   § 13. Letters of the clergy and nobility.   § 14.
Answers from Rome.   § 15. Justification of the Pope.   § 16, 17. His
speech.   § 18. Synod at Rome, and its results.

§ 1.

If Boniface wished Philip the Fair and the King of England
to allow their differences to be adjusted by him,[1] surely that
was by no means unjust—it was far better than quietly to sit
by and watch the war of the two princes ; and for many centuries
the Pope had been acknowledged as umpire between the different countries.[2]   In numberless letters (1295) he admonished
both the kings, particularly Edward I. of England, whom he
reminded of his youthful ardour for the Holy Land.[3]   Edward
explained to the legate that he could not conclude a peace himself without the consent of his ally, the German King Adolphus.
The Kings of England and Germany seemed inclined to accept
mediation,[4] but the French king raised difficulties and frustrated
the whole.   At that time Philip most faithlessly took prisoner
the Count of Flanders and his wife ; and only set them free
on their consenting to leave behind their daughter, who was
betrothed to the son of Edward of England.   He allied himself to the Scotch king against England, and once more a violent
war broke out.[5]   Boniface, who considered it a sacred duty to
prevent the shedding of blood amongst Christians, again, in
1296, exhorted them to make peace, and obliged the princes to
sign a truce, and obtained from Edward and Philip a declaration
that they were ready to allow him to mediate between them.[6]

[1] Huber, p. 37.
[2] Alex. III. (Baron. a. 1167, 1168 ; Petra, Comment. t. ii. p. 43).
Innoc. III. l. vi. Ep. 68, 163, 166. Coelest. V. Rymer, Foed. i. ii. p. 811.
[3] Raynald. l.c. Rymer, l.c. p. 817.
[4] Later the Popes often undertook such an office, as for instance John
XXII. 1317, 1320, 1324 (Rymer, ii. i. pp. 317, 431, 558).
[5] Hefele, Conc. vi. p. 258 seq.
[6] Raynald. a. 1296, n. 18-21. Bianchi, t. ii. l. vi. § 5, n. 1-3, pp. 449-
454.

§ 2.

Both kings carried on their wars principally by money obtained from the arbitrary taxation of the Church. Many French

prelates sent a petition to Rome for protection against the
numerous extortions practised by the royal officers,[1] and at the
same time the Count of Flanders complained to the See of
Rome of the forcible retention of his daughter. With regard to
the latter complaint Boniface commissioned the Bishop of
Meaux to remonstrate with Philip, and in case of a refusal to
summon him to justify himself;[2] with regard to the former he
published, with the consent of the College of Cardinals, the
Bull ' Clericis laicos' of February 25, 1296,[3] which forbade under
pain of excommunication that any tax should be levied or demanded on the income and goods of ecclesiastics and their
churches without the consent of the Apostolic See. The clergy
were forbidden under pain of deposition to submit to such im-
positions, and to pay anything without the express permission
of the Holy See.

[1] To be found in Christophe, vol. i. doc. 3, pp. 324-326.
[2] Simon Vigior, Hist. du Différeud, p. 3. Baillet, Hist. du Démêlé,
p. 21. Christophe, l.c. p. 76 seq.
[3] C. 3, de Immunit. iii. 23, in 6. Cf. Bianchi, l.c. n. 4 seq. p. 454 seq.;
Phillips, K.R. iii. § 130, p. 243 seq. The introduction on the enmity of
the laity towards the clergy recalls can. 9 of the Synod held at Nantes in
1264 (Hefele, vi. p. 74), and the introductory words of the Synod of Châ-
teau-Gontier, 1268 (ib. p. 100). According to the Synod of Tours, 1282,
c. 11, there were lords who even forbade their dependents to hold intercourse with priests (ib. p. 202).

§ 3.

The Bull was based both on the aforesaid petition of the
prelates referring to heavy oppression,[1] and also on the ancient
ecclesiastical laws, which were recognised even in France. The
third Lateran Council, 1179, had already, in canon 19, decreed
that Church property should be burdened with extra taxes only
when the bishops and clergy recognised their necessity or advantage ;[2] the fourth Lateran Council, 1215,[3] required that the
Pope should be consulted even as to voluntary contributions of
the bishops and clergy.[4] Moreover the second Council of Lyons,
1274, directed that whoever, through being the founder or
through custom, had any right of advocacy or any similar
rights over churches, monasteries, and charitable foundations,

was not permitted to abuse them or to claim any of the revenues, except during the time of vacancy.[5] Philip the Fair, suspicious and irritable, imagined a special attack on his crown in the Bull of Boniface, which was really published in general for the whole Church ; he ordered that no foreigners should be allowed to engage in trade in France, that gold, precious stones, arms, and provisions should not be exported without the written permission of the king.[6] This measure was directed against the sums of money despatched to Rome, also against donations for the Holy Land, legacies to the Holy See, &c., and was meant to loosen the ties which united French ecclesiastics to the Head of the Church.

[1] As in the Bull the 'trepidantes ubi trepidandum non est, transitoriam pacem quaerentes, plus timentes majestatem temporalem offendere quam aeternam' were mentioned, so were also in the petition the ' propriae prudentiae innitentes et humanam amittere gratiam formidantes ;' the Bull forbade taxes to be imposed ' absque auctoritate Sedis Apostolicae,' and in the petition it was asked that they should only be demanded ' prius interveniente Romani Pontificis consilio, cujus interest communibus utilitatibus providere ;' as in the Bull it is brought forward that the laity ' in clericos ecclesiasticasve personas vel bona sit interdicta potestas,' in the petition it was ' cum eis (laicis) super his nulla sit attributa facultas nec auctoritas imperandi.' These words of the petition, that the clergy were worse off than the Egyptian priests under Pharaoh, are taken from the third Lateran Council (vide the following note), to which Boniface VIII. plainly refers.
[2] C. Non minus, 4, de Immunit. Eccl. iii. 49.
[3] C. Adversus, 7, h.t. (Mansi, xxii. p. 1030).
[4] The words ' cujus interest communibus utilitatibus providere,' just quoted from the petition to Boniface VIII., are taken from this Council. If the Pope was once asked, his answer was decisive. Innocent also declared constitutions contrary to this to be void. Cf. Hausmann, Gesch. der Päpstlichen Reservatfälle, p. 194 seq. The Council of Constance afterwards repeated the same provision.
[5] C. Generali, 13, de elect. i. 6, in 6.
[6] Dupuy, Hist. du Diff. Actes et Preuves, p. 43. Baillet, l.c. p. 26.

§ 4.

Boniface VIII. remonstrated with the king, especially in the Bull ' Ineffabilis' of September 25, 1296,[1] over this encroachment on the rights of the Church. He conjured him to respect them.[2] Philip, he said, could find no excuse for his decree in the Bull

of February 25, because for the most part it only contained
what had been long since established by other canonical sanctions. It did not forbid the payment of contributions in money
for the defence of the king and the country on the part of the
clergy, but only required the Papal authorisation for such payment, in order to abolish the abuses practised by the royal
officers, against which many complaints had already been raised.
When it was really necessary for the country, the Apostolic See
would not only approve of such contributions by the prelates
and other ecclesiastics, but even order them; and in case of
urgent necessity would rather allow the sacred vessels and the
crosses of the churches to be sold, than expose to danger a kingdom so glorious and so much beloved by the See of Peter.
Further on Philip was reminded how dangerous it would be for
him if Rome were to side with his two enemies,[3] the King of
the Romans and the King of England, who were both disposed
against him—the former on account of his having retained some
territories belonging to the empire, the latter on account of some
contested provinces—both ready to accept the judgment of the
Holy See,[4] and both asserting that Philip was in fault. Moreover, the Pope expressly declared that his Bull in no way concerned the service and tribute which proceeded from the feudal
relation, and that he had already explained this by word of
mouth to the king's ambassadors and confidants; but he also
protested that he and his brethren were ready to suffer persecution, exile, and even death itself, for the liberty of the Church.[5]

[1] Raynald. a. 1296, n. 25 seq. Dupuy, l.c. p. 15.
[2] ' Et si (quod absit) fuerit condentis (legem) intentio, ut ad nos et
fratres nostros Ecclesiarum praelatos ecclesiasticasvo personas et ipsas
Ecclesias ac nostra et ipsorum bona non solum in regno tuo, sed constitu-
torum ubilibet extendatur, hoc non solum fuisset improvidum, sed insanum,
velle ad illa temerarias manus extendere, in quibus tibi saecularibusquo
principibus nulla est attributa potestas' (Words of Innocent III. c. x. de
Const. i. 2); ' quin potius ex hoc contra libertatem eamdem temere veni-
endo in excommunicationis sententiam promulgati canonis incidisses.'
Bossuet, P. i. l. iii. c. xxiii. p. 322, considers these words are exaggerated.
But as far as Church property is concerned the Church alone has the right
to dispose of it, as she has oftentimes declared. Honorius III. excommunicated those laymen who published statutes against ecclesiastical liberty,
c. xlix. Novit. v. 39, de Sent. Excom.

[3] Bossuet, l.c. p. 323, does not consider these intimations as either Papal or fatherly, though really they are perfectly intelligible when made to such a prince as Philip the Fair: for on the one hand, Philip treated his subjects neither in a fatherly nor royal manner, and did not behave to the Pope as a son of the Church; and on the other hand, it might well be possible, even necessary, on just grounds for the Pope to declare in favour of Philip's adversaries, which would give them an increased moral weight. It is not a question of assistance rendered by material weapons.

[4] Raynald. l.c. n. 9: 'Numquid super iis dicti reges denegant stare juri? Numquid Apostolicae Sedis, quae Christicolis omnibus praeeminet, judicium vel ordinationem recusant?'

[5] Cf. the analysis of the Bull, apud Hefele, vi. pp. 267-269.

§ 5.

But King Philip was able to insure the execution of his orders, for he had just gained a victory over the English, and by oppression and craft had learnt to keep his subjects in hand. A deputation also which was sent to Rome was successful. In 1297 the king and the French clergy received from the Pope new explanations modifying his Bull, which was not to forbid the levying of subsidies in cases of necessity. The Kings of France—or during a minority the States-General—were to determine the existence of a case of necessity.[1] Boniface did all he could to appease the king;[2] he approved the ready support given to the king by the prelates, shown in their agreement to pay him the tithes for two years. He granted him further privileges, and on August 11 completed the canonisation of his grandfather, Louis IX.[3] This gave general satisfaction in France, and Philip then stayed the execution of his orders, and allowed the Papal agents to send the revenues of the Apostolic Chamber to Rome. Towards the beginning and during the course of the year 1298, harmony between Rome and France seemed once more restored.[4]

[1] Dupuy, p. 39. Thomassin, l.c. n. 9, remarks: 'Huic Bonifacii constitutioni Joannes Ferrant in tract. de juribus et privilegiis regni Francorum, Privil. iv., superstruxit illud regum privilegium, ut a clero exigant nomine mutui, doni, subsidii charitativi ad defensionem regni sine nova permissione Papae.'

[2] Rayn. a. 1297, n. 45 fin. 46 init. n. 50 fin.

[3] Rayn. l.c. n. 46, 58.

[4] Baillet, l.c. p. 56. Daniel, Hist. de France, t. v. p. 56.

§ 6.

But though to all appearance the Pope and the king were nearly reconciled, they were in reality farther apart than they themselves knew : a fundamental principle separated them. The former desired to maintain the rights which, as Head of the Church militant, he had received from his predecessors ; the latter, on the contrary, desired to be free from all ecclesiastical control, and to exercise his civil power quite independently of all spiritual power. The differences of principle were not removed by the peace in such a way as to prevent their revival when an opportunity should present itself.[1]

A truce was concluded, January 6, 1298, between France and England, and both kings chose the Pope as arbitrator between them ; not, however, as Pope, but only as a private individual. He gave his judgment as Benedict Gaetani, and published it in open consistory, June 27, as Boniface VIII.[2] The Pope's judgment was carried out, though not at once, in all its parts ;[3] and though it was perfectly just, Philip was dissatisfied. He unjustly[4] accused the Pope of partiality towards the King of England. However, when the Pope added his Papal sanction to the judgment he had given as private arbitrator, Philip did not complain.[5]

[1] Christophe, l.c. p. 81.
[2] Raynald. a. 1297, n. 42 ; a. 1298, n. 1 seq. Dupuy, p. 41. Rymer, Foed. pp. 893, 894. Cf. Spondan. a. 1298, n. 1 ; Bianchi, l.c. § 5, pp. 471, 472 ; Leibnitz, Cod. Jur. Gent. Prodr. n. 16.
[3] Rymer, pp. 899 seq. 904 seq.
[4] Boutaric, l.c. p. 99 seq.
[5] Hefele, vi. p. 280.

§ 7.

Complaints of the oppression practised on the Church were continually on the increase in France. The Vicomte Amaury of Narbonne, refusing to take the oath of allegiance to his lord superior, the archbishop of that place, received from Philip a rescript in his favour. Philip seized the county of Melgeuil, which belonged to the Bishop of Maguelone, without any right or reason, and many of his vassals followed his example.[1] Philip

not only took for himself the revenues of vacated sees and of
the so-called royal abbeys, but he also laid hands on their landed
property, ordered forests to be cut down, &c.   To this prerogative he superadded the 'sauvegarde royale' over all remaining
vacated bishoprics and abbeys.   Thus he, in fact, received the
revenues of all vacated benefices ;[2] but he also did the same by
benefices that were not vacant.   When, in 1298, Boniface VIII.
suspended the Bishop of Laon, the king took possession of the
property of that see, as though it were vacated.   Some property,
left by Cardinal John of St. Cecilia in his will for charitable
purposes, was seized by Philip's order for the exchequer.[3]   Count
Robert, Philip's special favourite, occupied the town which belonged to the Bishop of Cambray.   For a long time, and in
spite of the Pope's remonstrances, Philip would not deliver up
the sequestrated lands to the newly-elected Archbishop of Rheims.
The Indult granted to him by Boniface, by which, in order to
enable him to meet the expenses of the war, the firstfruits of
the year of all provostships, archdeaconries, and other benefices, were adjudged to him for as long as the war should last,
was enormously abused by the royal officers : the bitterest complaints ensued,[4] which obliged the Pope to remonstrate, January
1299.[5]   Added to this, the war with Flanders was renewed,
Count Guido deceived, and his country governed by French
officials.   Guido appealed to the Pope for assistance in 1300,
but he died in captivity; even a victory gained by the Flemish
over the French in July 1302 did not procure them their freedom.[6]

Whilst the Pope was using every effort to forward the interests of Philip's brother, Prince Charles of Valois, designating
him to be emperor at least of the Greek Empire,[7] Philip himself
was entering into a close compact (December 8, 1299) with
the German King Albert, who, on account of the violation of
an oath to Adolphus of Nassau, was not yet acknowledged by
the Pope.[8]   He was also receiving into France several rebellious
members of the Colonna family, who spread the most injurious
reports about Boniface.[9]   Whilst in Rome Boniface was solemnly
celebrating the great jubilee, and, as the result of many favourable circumstances, cherishing in his mind new hopes for the

deliverance of Palestine,[10] at the French court the one idea was to gain increase of power, and plans were formed which had the complete subjugation of the Papacy for their object.[11]

[1] Raynald. a. 1300, n. 30. Bianchi, l.c. n. 11, p. 475.
[2] Hefele, l.c.
[3] Rayn. a. 1299, n. 22, 23. Bianchi, n. 11, p. 474.
[4] Rayn. l.c. n. 25. Cf. the complaint of Bishop William of Anjou to the king, D'Archery, Spicil. nov. ii. p. 190 seq.; Bianchi, l.c.; Hefele, l.c.
[5] Const. Dudum celsitudini. Rayn. a. 1299.
[6] Christophe, l.c. p. 83.
[7] After the earlier negotiations of 1298 he summoned Prince Charles at the end of 1300 to Italy, in order to win back Sicily and settle all the disturbances. After the death of his wife, Margaretha of Naples, he effected his marriage with Katharina, only daughter of the titular Emperor Philip of Constantinople, who possessed some Greek territory (Raynald. a. 1300, n. 20, 21; Spondan. 1301, n. 2). In July 1300, Charles of Valois was in Milan (Coirus, Hist. Mediol. P. ii.), and in September in Anagni, where the Pope received him with honour, appointed him prefect and captain-general of the States of the Church, and afterwards imperial vicar in Tuscany. According to Villani, l. viii. c. xlii., he is said to have thought of giving him the crown of the Holy Roman Empire, as he had refused it to the German King Albert. But this must not be considered to be proved. Cf. Raynald. a. 1301, n. 3, 11, 13; Hefele, pp. 256, 281, 288; Bianchi, l.c. § 5, n. 12, pp. 476, 477.
[8] Hefele, p. 283 seq. Christophe, p. 84 seq.
[9] Hefele, pp. 327, 404, 406. Cf. also Hist. du Differ. p. 34; Bianchi, § 5, p. 470 seq.
[10] Hefele, pp. 284-287. Bianchi, l.c. § 6, n. 1, p. 479.
[11] Cf. also the record of the year 1300 discussed by Schwab (Tüb. Quartalschr. 1866, II. 1), which was probably drawn up by Peter Dubois of Coutances. Hefele, p. 285 seq.

§ 8.

It was impossible that the Pope, who was both bound and resolved to maintain his dignity, could remain indifferent to all this. The *ecclesiastical*, and not the *political*, grievances principally occupied his mind. In 1301 he sent the Bishop of Pamiers, Bernhard de Saisset, to France as his nuncio, in order to promote the projected Crusade, and to exhort the king to apply the Church tithes thereto, as he was bound, and also to remonstrate against the many violations of ecclesiastical privileges.[1] This prelate, when he was Abbot of Pamiers, had previously, in 1294, had a dispute with the king, and as Bishop

of Pamiers he was also unpopular at the court.   In the mean
time he had proved himself full of zeal for the Church.   There
is no proof that he behaved with arrogance.   Philip wanted
some scandal in order to throw the odium on the Pope, and he
looked out for a favourable opportunity.[2]

Whilst the bishop was finishing his mission the king had
him rigorously watched and twenty-four witnesses examined,
of whom the most important was his personal enemy, the Comte
de Foix.   In the middle of the night (12th July 1301) he was
summoned to Paris, robbed of his papers and possessions, separated from his chaplains and servants.   The latter were put to
the torture, to extort from them confessions which would tell
against him.   At the end of two months he was conducted to
the court, and brought before the Council of State at Senlis
on October 24th.   Peter Flotte, Philip's confidential adviser,
appeared as the public complainant.   The defendant was found
guilty of high treason, and delivered over to the Archbishop of
Narbonne, who was desirous to keep him till the Papal decision
should arrive.   The bishop had protested against the competency
of the assembly, and also against the assertions which he had
been accused of making.[3]

[1] Spondan. a. 1301, n. 5.   Bianchi, l.c.   Boutaric, p. 103.
[2] Christophe, p. 86.   Hefele, p. 290 seq.
[3] Preuves du Différend, pp. 628, 631.   Martene, Thesaur. Anecdot. t. i.
p. 1320, s. 1320.   Christophe, pp. 87, 88.   Hefele, pp. 291, 292.

§ 9.

On December 5, 1301, Boniface VIII. demanded from the
king the freedom and the possessions of his nuncio, who was to
be judged by the Church.   He charged the Archbishop of Narbonne to release the bishop, and to allow him to travel to Rome
with the legal documents of the trial.[1]   He then convoked the
bishops, doctors, and magistrates of France, as well as the chapter,
which was to be represented by procurators, to attend a Council
at Rome, and he invited the king to appear, either in person or
by proxy, also the superiors of orders.[2]   In the Bull 'Salvator'
of December 4,[3] the Pope recalled all privileges with regard

to tithes[4] and Church properties, which had been specially
granted to the king in times of war, now that such wars had
ceased, and so many abuses were practised. The Bull 'Ausculta
fili carissime' is dated December 5.[5] In it the Pope exhorts
the king to listen as a son to his precepts, tells him of his paternal love, and reminds him of his duties as a Christian.[6]
Among other things the Pope said: 'God has placed us, although
unworthy, over kings and kingdoms.'[7] He specially called attention to the fact that the king did not allow canonical appointments to ecclesiastical offices to take effect, and set up his own
nominees instead ;[8] that, acting as judge in his own cause, he
was both plaintiff and judge at the same time, and laid hands
on the property and rights of the Church at pleasure; that he
summoned prelates and other ecclesiastics to appear before his
courts, taxed them, hindered spiritual jurisdiction over convents
and other religious places, oppressed the Church of Lyons,
which did not belong to his kingdom, took the revenues of vacated cathedral churches without moderation, and even exhausted
them.[9] There was only too much reason for these complaints.
The French kings of former times never thought of such an extensive royal prerogative, and only had the patronage of a few
benefices.[10] Also, it was not customary in all the French sees
for the royal officers to take charge of the Church property after
the death of a bishop ;[11] the further extension of such a custom
was forbidden by the second Council of Lyons, 1274: it had
originated in the fiefs held by the Church ; even after Philip
the Fair many of the sees, and indeed entire provinces, were
exempt from it.[12] Louis IX. had many rights of patronage,
which when he went to Egypt he gave over to the Bishop of
Paris ;[13] but Philip, by virtue of 'royal right and custom,' desired to have not only the presentation, but also the collation
of all benefices belonging to the bishops when a see should
become vacant, even where he had no patronage and no privilege.[14] It was an ecclesiastical principle of the old canons
that the revenues of vacant sees belonged to the Church, and
not to temporal princes,[15] and also that the laity could not of
themselves bestow offices of the Church without a special con-

cession by the Church.[16]   The Popes had to keep a firm hold
on existing rights, and Boniface now acted as a guardian of the
laws of the Church, and with full knowledge of the condition of
things and the state of the law in France; he was ready to
make many concessions, only as a matter of principle he desired
and was bound to preserve the rights of the Church.[17]

The Pope further complained that a prohibition had been
laid not only on the resident prelates and ecclesiastics, but also
on those who were merely travelling through France, by which
they were forbidden to export their movable possessions out of
France, thereby experiencing much loss and an oppressive bond-
age; he also complained of the debasement of the coinage,[18]
and other injuries and oppressions put upon the king's subjects;
also of infraction of the liberty and immunity of the Church,
against which many complaints had been brought to the Apostolic See, and general disapprobation evinced.

[1] Raynald. h.a. n. 27, 28.   Hist. du Différend, pp. 637, 661.   Tosti,
Storia di Bonifacio VIII. 1846, ii. p. 128.   Bulacus, Hist. Univ. Paris, t. iv.
p. 13.

[2] Rayn. h.a. n. 29.   Dupuy, Actes et Preuves, pp. 53, 54.

[3] Rayn. l.c. n. 30.   Dupuy, p. 42.   Cf. Hefele, p. 293.

[4] These abuses often happened in France, especially under Philip
Augustus. Peter de Blois wrote in 1188 (Ep. 20, Migne, ccvii. 74): 'Sanc
sicut audivimus, exiit edictum a Philippo rege, ut describeretur Gallicus
orbis, et oneraretur Ecclesia decimationibus recidivis. Sic paulatim tran-
sibit decimatio in consuetudinem et praesumpta semel abusio iguominiosam
Ecclesiae servitutem infliget.' He wished Bishop Rainald of Chartres,
who was related to the king, to be stirred up to an energetic resistance.
As Peter foresaw, decimation became a general practice. Choppin de
Doman. 1. iii. tit. 23: 'Neglecto sacrarum expeditionum consilio nihilo
secius decimantur sacerdotiorum reditus et decimae in annuas fisci ra-
tiones patrimonii instar reservantur.' Peter expresses himself very
strongly in a letter to the Bishop of Orleans, Ep. 112, p. 335 seq., whom
he calls upon to make a stand against the plundering of the Church practised on the pretext of the Crusade.

[5] Raynald. l.c. n. 31-34.   Bull. M. ed. Lux. ix. 121.   Dupuy, l.c. p. 48.
Bulacus, l.c. p. 7.   Ap. Christophe, i. pp. 327-332, doc. 4.   For this and
other documents, vide Bianchi, t. ii. l. vi. § 6, n. 3, pp. 483-485.   Phillips,
K. R. iii. p. 252 seq.

[6] The whole passage, 'Campum siquidem militiae humanae mortali-
tatis ingressus, renatus sacri fonte baptismatis, renuncians diabolo et
pompis ejus, non quasi hospes et advena, sed jam domesticus fidei et civis
sanctorum (Eph. ii 19) effectus, ovile dominicum intrasti, colluctaturus

non solum contra carnem et sanguinem, sed etiam contra aëreas potestates .... (Eph. vi. 12) sic veri Noe es arcam ingressus, extra quam nemo
salvatur,' &c., shows how the Pope wished to assert his *spiritual* power.
⁷ The early Popes used the passage, Jer. i. 1, almost as a regular
formula, as did also Innoc. III. c. Solitae, 6, de M. et O. i. 33; l. vi. Ep.
143, p. 156; l. vii. Ep. 1, p. 277; Ep. 14, p. 297 (cf. Vulcan. Dalm. Ep. ad
Innoc. 1199, l. ii. Ep. 176, p. 725); previously Alex. III. Ep. 1356, ad Aep.
Pisan. (Migne, cc. p. 1184); even John VIII. Ep. ad Basil. (Baron. a. 878,
n. 111; a. 879, n. 26), and most of the writers of the Middle Ages, S. Bern.
Ep. 238, ad Eug. III.,'and others. How Huber, p. 37, can bring this up as
anything peculiar to Boniface VIII., is incomprehensible. According to
the context there is no reason for assuming that the Pope as ' actual
superior' was also to provide for the good government of the French kingdom in *temporal matters*.
⁸ Vecerius, in Vita Henr. VII. Imp.: ' Ad hoc Philippus, ne quid impo-
tentiae praetermitteret, sacerdotales Galliarum titulos a Pontificibus antea
pro decretis proque more S. Matris Ecclesiae componi solitos ipse ordinare
citra consensum praesidis Romani statuit, quae ubi summus antistes intellexit, gravissime tulit injuriam, pessimi exempli id quod erat existimans,
si vel antecessorum recte instituta rescinderentur vel auctoritatem pontificiam laicus princeps profanasset.' Mutius, in Chron. Germ. l. xxii.: ' Rex
ubi intellexit, Pontificis animum a se alienatum .... jus ecclesiasticum,
quod Papae erat, sibi vindicabat, sacerdotia et episcopatus conferebat
quibus placuit, quos praelatos cognoverat Pontifici patrocinari, deposuit,
eorum praelaturas aliis conferens; diripuit etiam opulentiores episcopatus.'
⁹ Innocent III., 1207, had already denounced such abuses of the royal
prerogative in the Church of Auxerre to Philip II. l. x. Ep. 71, p. 1169
seq.: ' Idem rex audito quod b. m. Hugo Aep. naturae debitum exsolvisset,
statim fecit per servientes suos episcopales res, quas vocat *regalia*, occu-
pari, qui more praedonum debacchantes in eis crudeliter Ecclesiae nemora
passim fecere succidi, eadem venalia omnibus exponentes; stagna quoque
fecerunt dirui et penitus expiscari,' &c. See also Innocent III. l. x.
Ep. 195, p. 1300; l. xiii. Ep. 190, 191, p. 357 seq.; l. xiv. Ep. 52; l. xv.
Ep. 39, 40.
¹⁰ Bianchi, l.c. n. 5, p. 490 seq.
¹¹ Register of the royal chamber, ap. Pasquier, lib. iii. Disquisit.
Francic. c. iii. De Marca, de Conc. viii. 4, 4.
¹² Bianchi, l.c. p. 494.
¹³ Duchesne, t. v. p. 423.
¹⁴ Hist. du Différend, pp. 90, 93.
¹⁵ Photii Nomocan. tit. x. c. iii. De Marca, l.c. c. xviii. n. 11. Thomassin, P. iii. l. ii. c. liv. lv. Hincmar, Ep. 9, ad Episc. Prov. Rhem.
c. xli. Baluz. cap. ii. 1286: ' Sicut episcopus et suas et Ecclesiae facultates in vita sua dispensandi habet potestatem, ita facultates Ecclesiae
viduatae post mortem episcopi penes oeconomum integrae conservari
jubentur futuro successori ejus episcopo, quoniam res et facultates Ecclesiae non in imperatorum atque regum potestate sunt ad dispensandum
vel invadendum vel diripiendum, sed ad defensandum atque tuendum.
Sunt enim sanctuaria et haereditas Domini.'

[16] Conc. Oecum. viii. c. 22. Greg. VII. l. iv. Ep. 22. Hugo Flavin. (Migne, PP. Lat. cxviii. 786). Thomassin, P. ii. l. i. c. lv. Ruzaeus, Praef. Tract. de Jure Regal. p. 5, n. 4. Joh. Ferraldus, de Privileg. Reg. Franc. c. viii. Others, ap. Thomassin, l.c. n. 7. The 'deliberatio magistri Petri de Blois contra assertas literas Bonif.' (Hist. du Différend, p. 45) appeals to the apocryphal Canon Hadrianus, d. 63, Sigel. Gembl. Chron. a. 773 (cf. Baron. a. 774, n. 13 seq.; Petrus de Marca, de Conc. viii. 12, n. 8, 9 ; Natal. Alex. saec. 8, c. i. a. 9 ; Pag. Crit. a. 774, n. 13 ; Bianchi, t. ii. l. v. § 10, n. 1, p. 288), which was never in force in France. Bianchi, l.c. l. vi. § 6, n. 9, pp. 498, 499.

[17] Boniface himself declared to the French delegates in consistory (Hist. du Diff. p. 77): 'Volumus rex faciat licite, quod facit illicite. Volumus super hoc sibi facere omnem gratiam, quam poterimus, quia certum est et omnia jura clamant, quod *collatio* beneficiorum non potest cadere in laicum, ita quod habeat jus seu potestatem conferendi.' Cf. Alex. III. Ep. 28, ad Episc. Angl. Conc. Later. iii. 1179, can. 9, 14 ; Innoc. III. l. xv. Ep. 192.

[16] Daniel, Hist. de France, t. v. p. 124, ed. 1755. Drumann, ii. p. 165. Hefele, p. 295, n. 1. The coin possessed accordingly in reality only one-third of its nominal value. The first Lateran Council, 1123, protested, c. 15, against this, as did also many local Synods, such as those held at Salzburg, 1281, and at Würzburg, 1287. On the great evils which at that time arose through debasing the currency, vide Hüllmann, Städte-wesen. ii. p. 19.

§ 10.

The whole rage of Gallicanism was unloosed[1] against this Constitution, which abounds in biblical quotations and allusions. It has been alleged against it that it is injurious to the majesty of kings and offensive to Philip the Fair, and that it contains the maxim, unheard of before the time of Boniface VIII., that the Pope, as vicar of God on earth, is the lord of all the king-doms of the world.[2] We have read and reread this Bull, but could find in it neither presumption nor insults nor menaces. It is true that its tone is forcible, but moderate,[5] even when re-proaching. Boniface does not say that the Pope is the lord of the world, but that he is raised over those who govern the world, in order to oblige them to walk in the way of justice. And, indeed, how could the doctrine of the Bull 'Ausculta fili' astonish Philip the Fair, when modern historians, enemies to the Catholic Church, have not hesitated to declare openly, ' that it would be much better for the people if sovereigns would recognise over them a power descended from·heaven, which would hold them back from crime,⁴ and that it were to be wished that the Church should recover her authority, and kings and kingdoms be made to tremble by interdict and excommunication, as in the days of Gregory VII.'�)⁵ But this monarch was surrounded by corrupt men, who strove to disfigure the truth, in order to make it hateful ; and the worst of these was Peter Flotte. He triumphed on this occasion. The Pope did not overstep his lawful powers in what he *commanded*. He spoke only as Head of the Church, and desired only to exercise a spiritual power ; his grievances referred *altogether* to the rights of the *Church*, which had hitherto been acknowledged by the whole of Europe. Even when any matter had both an ecclesiastical and civil character, the Pope could consult and negotiate about it from an ecclesiastical point of view. For that purpose Boniface did not wish only to publish decrees, but also to advise with the French bishops as well as with the procurators of the king.⁶

¹ Christophe, l.c. p. 91 seq.
² Hist. du Différend, p. 10.   Baillet, l.c. p. 96 seq.
³ Tosti, Storia di Bonif. VIII. vol. ii. p. 131.
⁴ Sismondi, Hist. des Républiques Ital. t. iv. p. 139.
⁵ Leibnitz, Lettre ii. à M. Grimaret.
⁶ Bianchi, l.c. n. 4, pp. 487-490.

§ 11.

Although the document 'Ausculta fili carissime' was dated the 5th December 1301, it was nevertheless discussed once more in consistory, and delivered over in the beginning of the following year by the Archdeacon of Narbonne, Jacques de Norman. But at the audience on the 10th February 1302 the Comte d'Artois, Philip's cousin, snatched the Bull away from him and threw it into the fire.¹ Instead of that one, a so-called short document² was published, drawn up by the French statesmen (probably from previous information received from the ambassadors at Rome), in which it was plainly said that the king was to be subject to the Pope in spiritual *and in temporal matters*.

The forgery of this document is now, as Hefele³ says, universally acknowledged, except by Huber,⁴ who briefly attributes the sentence above quoted to the Papal Bull. Style and tone do not correspond with those used at Rome, but accord exactly with the answer drawn up in Philip's name. Jacques de Norman—who had had charge of the real Bull—and the cardinals denied that Boniface had ever written to the king that he was subject to him in *temporal matters*,[5] and the Pope denied it himself. Peter Flotte it was who thus forged and deceived, not, however, without the king's knowledge and consent,[6] as was afterwards recognised at Rome. The author of the forgery borrowed a few phrases from the Bull for his composition, made the Pope refuse unconditionally all royal prerogative with regard to interim cases and all the king's rights of conferring ecclesiastical preferments, and endeavoured to excite the pride of the French nation against ' Papal aggression.' He succeeded but too well. ' The well-grounded discontent of thousands over the misrule of the king seemed forgotten, when once it appeared necessary to protect the independence and honour of the French crown.'[7] It is easy to imagine how, by the intrigues of Peter Flotte, all ranks of the people were brought to believe that ' Boniface claimed supreme authority in political affairs;' and with characteristic vivacity at once took the part of their crafty sovereign.

[1] Christophe, i. p. 92. Hefele, p. 297.
[2] Dupuy, Preuves du Diff. p. 44. Bulaeus, iv. 7.
[3] Hefele, p. 298. Christophe, l.c. Cf. Spondan. a. 1301, n. 11 ; De Marca, de Conc. Sac. et Imp. iv. 16 ; Bianchi, l.c. § 6, n. 4, p. 485 ; Döllinger, Lehrb. der. K.G. ii. p. 239 seq. ; Phillips, K.R. iii. § 130, p. 253.
[4] Huber, p. 37.
[5] Preuves du Différend, pp. 63, 73, 75.
[6] Drumann, ii. pp. 24-26. Boutaric, l.c. p. 106. Hefele, l.c.
[7] Hefele, p. 300.

§ 12.

In order to win the clergy to his side, and to make it appear that he greatly esteemed the laws of the Church, Philip allowed the imprisoned Bishop of Pamiers and Archdeacon Jacques to withdraw ; both of them were to leave the country as soon as possible.[1] A letter, pretending to be an answer from the king[2] to the forged Papal document, and written in the same terse style, was published in France; but, naturally, not officially forwarded to Rome.[3] As the publication from Rome had been met by an answer from the king, so against the Council to assemble on All Saints a French National Assembly was summoned. On the 10th April 1302, Philip assembled a parliament of the three estates of his kingdom in Notre Dame. Peter Flotte brought forward bitter complaints against the Pope, whom, he said, not only heavily oppressed the Church in France by taxes, gave away benefices to foreigners, and arrogated all authority to himself, but also endeavoured to subject the king to himself *in temporal matters*, and wished to become temporal ruler of France. As a friend the king begged, and as a sovereign he commanded, that they should stand by him. The nobility, guilty of the same oppressions and having the same interests as Philip, determined in secret conclave with the third class, till now very much oppressed, to sacrifice property, life, everything, for the preservation of the rights and liberties of the nation, and to stand nobly by the king. The clergy, who had originally desired to deliberate longer, were intimidated,[4] accused of treachery to their country, and were at last induced to write to the Pope as the king desired, whilst the nobles and citizens addressed special letters to the cardinals.[5]

[1] Christophe, p. 94.
[2] Dupuy, Preuves, p. 44.
[3] Hefele, p. 301 seq. Natalis Alex. II. E. sacc. 13 et 14, diss. 9, a. 2, n. 5 (t. xvi. p. 321, ed. Bing.) says of this letter, though at other times he so warmly defends the king: 'Inscriptio et priora verba, quae immodesta et contumeliosa sunt, aeterna oblivione delenda potius quam in historiam referenda.'
[4] The French prelates of that time, with but few exceptions, were far from maintaining the resolute bearing of their predecessors. About 1172, Archbishop Rotro of Rouen wrote: 'Regiae majestati non congruit depopulari quod suum est aut illas expugnare Ecclesias, quarum tutor est et patronus. Si alius nos infestaret, non aliunde remedium quaereremus' (Petr. Bles. Ep. 23, p. 68).
[5] Christophe, pp. 96, 97.

§ 13.

The letter written by the clergy[1] announced these events to the Pope, 'not without grief and bitter tears,' as well as the prohibition laid by the king and his barons on their going to Rome. In the insolent letter sent by the nobles to the cardinals, they avoided calling Boniface VIII. Pope, and enumerated the king's grievances, which were : (*a*) the presumptuousness of the words used in the Papal Brief and by the ambassadors, that the king was subject to Boniface *in secular matters*, and held his kingdom from him ; (*b*) the summons of the bishops, abbots, and doctors to Rome, when it was felt to be so necessary that the king should be at the head of any reform ; (*c*) the bestowal of the most important ecclesiastical posts, for good sums of money too, upon unknown, treacherous, and incapable persons ; (*d*) the endeavour to deprive the king of the power of disposing of the benefices belonging to him, with the object of further burdening the country. The writers of the letter did not wish to believe that the Pope had been able to take such intolerable measures with the consent of the cardinals, and begged them urgently, as *partakers in the government of the Church*, each to help to bring these proceedings, begun in so disorderly and wanton a manner, to a good termination, so that, preserving and increasing the love between the Church and France, a Crusade might become possible.

¹ Dupuy, Actes et Preuves, p. 67. Bulaeus, t. iv. p. 19 seq. Christophe, pp. 332-335. Cf. Hefele, pp. 302, 304.

§ 14.

On the 26th June the cardinals wrote a detailed and dignified answer to the French nobles.[1] They spoke of their grief at the contents of the document addressed to them, of their agreement with the Pope, and the wish they shared with him for the preservation of the close alliance between the Roman Church and France ; also of their conviction that *an enemy* had been sowing tares, and had thereby occasioned the dispute. They emphatically contradicted the statement that the Holy Father had ever written, or allowed his nuncios to say, that King Philip was subject to him *in temporal matters as regarded his kingdom*, and that he had received it as a fief from him.[2] The convocation of the prelates and other Frenchmen was nothing new—a proof, like the Papal Bull, of good-will and paternal solicitude. If the Pope had injured the French Church in the matter of temporal possessions, it had been done *only upon application from the king,* and to oblige him. Bishoprics had only been disposed of to two foreigners, Italians, and distinguished men.[3] Lastly, the cardinals censured the improper way in which the Pope was mentioned in the document sent by the nobles, and which almost seemed to imply that they did not wish to recognise him as Pope.

The Pope, personally most deeply insulted by the events in Paris, and by the offensive reply which was published in France with the forged Brief, could not contain his indignation at the thought of the disgraceful treatment he had met with, and of the inconstancy shown by the French prelates, *many of whom had previously appealed to him* against the oppressions of their king; he showed his feelings in his answer to the French clergy.[4] In bitter irony he turns Peter Flotte, the originator of the intrigue, into ridicule,[5] lashes the cowardice of the prelates, and threatens canonical punishment in case of further disobedience to the instructions of the Apostolic See.[6]

[1] Bulaeus, iv. p. 26. Dupuy, p. 63. Hefele, pp. 306-308.
[2] Volumus vos pro certo tenere, quod D.N. summus Pontifex numquam scripsit regi praedicto, quod *de regno suo sibi subesse temporaliter illudque ab eo tenere deberet,* et Mag. Jacobus archidiaconus Narb., notarius et nuntius, sicut constanter affirmat, ipsi D. Regi hoc ipsum vel simile numquam verbaliter nunciavit aut scripto. Unde propositio, quam fecit Petrus Flotte, arenosum et falsum habuit fundamentum et ideo necesse est quod cadat aedificium.
[3] These were Aegidius of Rome, an Augustinian, pupil of St. Thomas, sometime professor in Paris and tutor to King Philip, at whose wish Boniface raised him to the archbishopric of Bourges; and Gerard Pigalotti, likewise professor in Paris, who received the see of Artois.
[4] Raynald. a. 1302, n. 12. Bulaeus, l.c. p. 24. Dupuy, p. 65. Hefele, p. 308.
[5] Semividens corpore, menteque totaliter excoecatus—Belial.
[6] Christophe, p. 99.

§ 15.

In August 1302 the envoys of the king and of the clergy of France were present at a great consistory, which was opened by the Cardinal-bishop of Porto, with a speech concerning the existing subjects of dispute.[1] He represented that no difference of opinion existed between the Pope and the College of Cardinals, and the Bull 'Ausculta fili' had been issued with the consent of the cardinals, after mature deliberation ; that numerous complaints had come from France to the Holy See of the way in which the liberty of the Church was abused and despised, and therefore it had become necessary to admonish the king. He praised the Papal Bull, which contained the words of a loving father, but did not contain the sentence attributed to it—that the king must consider his authority *as bestowed by the Church*, which Archdeacon Jacob had also never said ; he denied that another writing (the so-called short Brief 'Deum time') had been issued by the Pope or the cardinals. 'If prelates are called to Rome to deliberate, it is not the opponents of the king, but his special confidants who are summoned; and not to the end of the world, but to Rome ; nor to remain there for a long time, but to return home as soon as the business is finished. With regard to the giving away of benefices, the right of patronage with presentation must be distinguished from collation with putting into possession. The latter can never be allowed to a layman. If it is anywhere said that the king has further right of patronage, at least it is impossible that anything beyond what the Church bestows (ministerialiter) can belong to him.[2] But if it is said that he has the right by prescription, then I ask, Why (supposing he can dispose of the benefices by his own authority) does he apply to the Church for a concession ?' Further, it was especially shown that in cases of sin the Pope has to decide about temporal matters ; and it was shown that the possession of the temporal jurisdiction belonged by right to the Pope, but by custom and in practice to the temporal princes; this was illustrated by the simile of the two lights in the firmament of heaven.[3] In conclusion, the cardinal said that King Philip had no ground of complaint, and that he and the other cardinals would pray to God for his enlightenment, and for his return to the position of a true son of the Church.

[1] Dupuy, l.c. p. 73. Bul. p. 28 seq. Hefele, pp. 309-311. Natal. Alex. l.c. n. 6, pp. 321, 322.

² Hefele explains: 'So far as in the quality of Papal minister or vicar it had been granted him by the Pope.' To me it seems that the 'by concession of the Church' is put in opposition to the 'jus proprium,' the rights inherent in the crown.

³ 'Scriptum est: Fecit Deus duo luminaria magna. . . . Jurisdictionem spiritualem principaliter habet summus Pontifex et jurisdictionem temporalem habent imperator et alii reges, tamen de omni temporali habet cognoscere S.P. et judicare *ratione peccati.* Unde dico quod jurisdictio temporalis potest considerari prout competit alicui *de jure* [in contradistinction to ratione actus et usus]. . . . Unde jurisdictio temporalis competit summo Pontifici, qui est vicarius Christi et Petri, de jure. Et qui contrarium sentit, impingit in illum articulum: *Judicaturus est vivos et mortuos* et in illum: *Sanctorum communionem.* Sed jurisdictio temporalis *quantum ad usum et executionem actus* non competit ei, unde dictum est Petro: *Converte gladium in vaginam.'* These are the ideas of St. Bernard as they are represented by Aegidius of Rome (de Eccl. Pot. l. i. c. ix.): 'Ecclesiam habere decet materialem gladium *non ad usum,* sed ad nutum.' Thus in France they were by no means so new and unheard of as necessarily to cause offence.

§ 16.

The Pope, referring in his speech to the passage of Scripture, 'What God hath joined together let no man put asunder' (Matt. xix. 6), showed how France had been benefited by the alliance between her kings and the Church since the time of the baptism of Clovis. Peter Flotte was the man (the enemy) (Matt. xiii. 28) who desired to separate what God had joined together, and his companions were the Count of Artois and the Count of St. Pol. Flotte had falsified the Papal Bull, or had given out its contents falsely,[1] as, for instance, that the king must consider his kingdom as a Papal fief. Concerning this, Boniface remarks, 'It is forty years since we mastered jurisprudence, *and we know that God ordains that there shall be two powers;* who then can or dare believe that *such a foolish sentiment* came from us? We declare that *we do not desire to trespass on the king's jurisdiction in anything.* But neither the king nor any other Christian can deny that *in matters of sin* he is subject to us.'[2] With regard to the giving away of benefices, the Pope observes that from zeal for truth, and for the salvation of the king, he had often said to the royal ambassadors: 'We desire that the king do lawfully what now he does unlawfully. We desire to show him the greatest possible amount of favour: for

it is certain and all laws proclaim that the collation of benefices
in itself cannot belong to a layman, for he would then have a
right to transfer the spiritual power. He can only receive the
right of collation with the consent, tacit or express, of the Holy
See.' We have, he continued, allowed the king to appoint a
canon in each of the sees of his kingdom; we entirely made
over to him the appointing of the prebends to the Church of
Paris, on the condition that he disposed of them only to masters
of theology, or doctors of law, or other learned persons, and not
to nephews and relations of this or that person. But neither
the king nor any prelate had bestowed a benefice on a master of
theology, but only on worthless favourites. Although Boniface
felt he was perfectly right, still he declared himself ready, in
case he had gone too far, to make amends for the fault. He
proposed the cardinals as arbitrators between himself and the
king, and also that the latter should despatch some of the upright members of the nobility (not the satellites of wickedness),
perhaps the Duke of Burgundy, the Count of Brittany, and suchlike, who could tell him in what he had erred and whom he had
troubled. He would redress the grievances according to their
judgment, and make even still greater concessions with regard
to the patronage of benefices.

¹ Qui literam nostram falsavit vel falsa de ea confinxit. Cf. De
Marca, de Conc. iv. 16, 5. Bianchi also says (l.c. § 7, n. 11, p. 530) : ' I
sentimenti di questo Pontefice stranissimamente allora ed oggi travolti ed
interpretati.'

² Hefele (p. 298) justly remarks that Boniface, in the Brief Ausculta, according to the tenor of the whole, only claims a subjectio ratione peccati;
according to which it is not the government transactions in themselves, but
only those which contain a peccatum, which are laid under the cognisance
of the Pope. '*This proves a great difference in principle ;* for even now, in
the completely altered state of the world, it can be said : however independent a Catholic king may be from the Church in his administrative
transactions (in temporalibus), still as to the sins which he commits in regard to those transactions he is in a certain degree of subjection to his
confessor. The latter has the right and the duty to admonish, to blame,
and to lay a penance upon him for such sins, and this not only when he
voluntarily accuses himself, but also when the matter in question is publicly known. During the Middle Ages, however, the Pope considered
himself the spiritual director of the Christian princes.' He is in fact the
superior, who gives directions for the guidance of consciences even to

confessors; he is the interpreter of the divine law. 'Innocent III. had already in 1204 .... laid down the same principle and the same distinction.'

§ 17.

This very fair offer would have made a most suitable conclusion to the Papal address. *If the whole speech is genuine,* Boniface said much that was offensive to French ears. He showed that the king would scarcely have a firm hold on the throne without the Pope; that when necessary he was ready to depose the king, as his predecessors had before deposed three kings of France;[1] that the prelates were obliged to appear in Rome, under pain of deposition,[2] &c. But several words do not thoroughly accord with former expressions in the speech; we cannot be certain whether the record of the Pope's speech, found in the codex of the convent of St. Victor in Paris, corresponds to the *real contents.*[3]

[1] 'Our predecessors have deposed *three* Kings of France; you have it in your chronicles, we have it in ours, and one of them is to be found in the Decretals' (Gratian, cau. Alins, c. xv. q. 6. Cf. Ivo, Decr. P. v. c. 378, concerning the case of Childeric III.). It is not evident what other cases were alluded to in the speech. *Three* cases of this sort were never brought forward. This passage, like others in the speech, has the look of being spurious.

[2] 'If some do not come, the words of the Song of Solomon (ii. 12) will apply: Tempus putationis advenit.' This text is also used in the same way by St. Bernard (Ep. 240, c. ii. ad Eugen. III. p. 433).

[3] We have in other preserved allocutions of this Pope considerable variations in the manuscripts. Cf. J. D. Mansi, note in Natal. Alex. l.c. a. 2 fin. p. 332. Much still remains here to be accomplished.

§ 18.

The Duke of Burgundy's attempted mediation bore no fruit. Philip IV. had forbidden the clergy and laity to leave France without the royal permission, and also the export of gold and money, ordered the property of thirty-nine bishops and six abbots, who in spite of all had attended the Synod at Rome, to be confiscated. The decrees of the Synod opened in Rome on the 30th October 1302 are lost. We only know of two Bulls as the result of the consultations in Rome. By the first all those who detain or otherwise injure any persons travelling to or returning from the Holy See are excommunicated;[1] the other, the Bull 'Unam sanctam,' declares, without special reference to France, the duty of obedience towards the Pope to be general.

[1] Dupuy, p. 83. Raynald. a. 1302, n. 16. Mansi, xxv. p. 98 seq. Cf. c. un. Rem non novam, ii. 3, de dolo et contum. in Xvagg. com. Several Synods had formerly protested against this; for instance, the Synods of Ofen, 1279, can. 58; Würzburg, 1287, c. 25 (Mansi, xxiv. 299, 861; Hefele, vi. pp. 176, 221).

PART II. THE BULL 'UNAM SANCTAM.' CONTINUATION OF THE DISPUTE.

§ 1. Substance and object of the Bull 'Unam sanctam.' § 2. Personal conflict with the Pope. His attempts at mediation. § 3. The king's reply. § 4. New treaties. § 5. Open complaints against the Pope. Appeal for a Council. § 6. Measures taken by the Pope. § 7. The outrage at Anagni. § 8. Release and death of the Pope. § 9. The position of Benedict XI. § 10. The king's document. § 11. Indictment of the deceased Pope. § 12. Mitigation of earlier decrees. § 13. Bull 'Flagitiosum scelus.' § 14. Transactions concerning Boniface VIII. § 15. Council of Vienne. § 16. Judgment upon Boniface VIII. § 17. Efforts of Philip IV. to raise the civil over the spiritual power.

§ 1.

The Bull 'Unam sanctam,'[1] which has been so much discussed, explains that Christ is the Head of the one Holy Catholic and Apostolic Church,[2] and that St. Peter and his successors, to whom the Lord has intrusted *all* His sheep, are His representatives. Referring to St. Luke xxii. 38, the Bull says further that there are two swords within the power of the Church, the spiritual and the material sword. The latter is drawn *for* the Church, the former *by* the Church; this one by the hands of the priests, the other by the hand of kings and warriors, but according to the will of the priests and only as long as they allow it.[3] One sword, however, must be subject to the other, and temporal authority must be subject to spiritual power; the Apostle says (Rom. xiii. 1): 'For there is no power but from God; and those that are, are ordained of God.' But they would not be ordained if one sword was not

subject to the other, and if the inferior was not drawn upwards
by means of the other (superior).[4] As truth testifies, the spiritual power has to teach (instituere) the civil power.[5] If
'instituere' is to be translated to appoint instead of to direct,[6] at
all events it can only apply to the anointing and crowning, and
not to the elevation to the dignity; Boniface VIII. expressly
acknowledges *two powers ordained by God.* At the conclusion follows the precise definition that every human creature
has to submit to the Roman Pontiff.[7] As Christophe remarks,[8]
this constitution was clearly dictated with the view of declaring
'that in the Christian Church there is only one power instituted directly by God; further, that as the society of the faithful also comprises the society of citizens, this power is twofold,
if I may so express myself, since it divides itself into spiritual
and civil, the former being represented by the Pope, the latter
by the princes. Given this principle, it naturally follows as a
result that the spiritual power is raised above the civil on account of its superiority; the civil is dependent on the spiritual,
is obliged to follow its lead, and perhaps even to be corrected
by it. There is no question here of special ordinances for
France, but of general principles applicable to all Christian
States.[9] Boniface does not assert that the authority which he
has over kingdoms is the same as that of a feudal lord over a
fief; he only claims the superior power of judging princes with
regard to the administration of their States (in as far as this
affects the Church), and to correct their faults by means of
apostolic decrees; and such a claim certainly had its origin
in the public law then in force. Philip the Fair, who with such
determination, rejected this claim as unheard-of, ought to have
remembered that the great Innocent III. in his struggles with
Philip Augustus considered it an indisputable privilege of the
successors of St. Peter.[10] With regard to the conclusion of the
Bull, in which it is said that every human being is subject to
the Popes, it is certain that it is not stronger than what goes
before. The Gallican Bossuet[11] and P. de Marca are astonished
at its moderation.[12] Is it not an unexceptionable article of
Catholic faith that every Christian should be subject to the

Vicar of Christ? If individuals are subject to the highest jurisdiction, why should princes be exempt from it?'[13]

[1] C. i. de M. et O. i. 8, in Xvagg. Com. Rayn. a. 1302, n. 13. Ap.
Christophe, p. 335 seq.

[2] The Bull says : 'She is the seamless garment of the Lord, which
was not torn, but for which lots were cast (John xix. 23, 24).' Similarly,
Petri Bles. Ep. 28, pp. 96, 97 ; Innoc. II. Ep. ad Episc. Gall. 1140, de
Erroribus Petri Abael. (Epist. Bernard. n. 194, p. 360, c. i.).

[3] '*Ad nutum* et ad patientiam sacerdotis.' St. Bernard (infrà, Essay
xiii. P. i. § 3) also has the first expression (ad nutum sacerdotis), and from
him the passage is taken ; he, however, adds : ' et jussum imperatoris.'
John of Paris explains the ad nutum: ' Quia in hoc non habet auctoritatem jubendi vel compellendi, sed solum innuendi, si voluerit et imperator'
(ap. Natal. Alex. l.c. a. 2, n. 11, p. 327). Anselm of Canterbury also says:
' Nota, *duos gladios* esse *in Ecclesia :* alter materialis, alter spiritualis,
sed spiritualis nonnisi volentes, materialis vero etiam cogit nolentes' (Com.
in Matt. c. xxvi.), but he does not carry the similitude so far as St. Bernard. Sigismund's words in the Council of Constance are analogous to
the above. Cf. Gregory IX. 18 May 1233, ad German. Patr. Cpl. Mansi,
xxiii. 59, and Aegidius of Rome, de Eccles. Potestate, l. i. c. vii.-ix.

[4] Aegidius Romanus, de Eccles. Potest. l. i. c. iii. : ' Non est potestas
nisi a Deo, sed et omnis habet ordinata esse, quoniam .... quae sunt a
Deo, oportet ordinata esse. Non essent autem ordinata, nisi unus gladius
reduceretur per alterum et nisi unus esset sub altero.'

Cf. Aegid. l.c. :

Quoniam, ut dictum est per Dionysium,
hoc requirit lex divinitatis, quam Deus dedit universis rebus creatis, et hoc requirit
ordo universi, i.e. universarum rerum cre-
ataram, ut non omnia aeque immediate
reducantur in suprema, sed infima per
media et inferiora per superiora. Gladius
ergo temporalis tamquam inferior redu-
cendus est per spiritualem tamquam per
superiorem, et unus ordinandus est sub
altero, tamquam inferior sub superiori.

Boniface VIII. :

Nam secundum B. Diony-
sium lex divinitatis est, infima per media in suprema
reduci. Non ergo secundum
ordinem universi omnia aeque ac immediate, sed infima per media, et inferiora
per superiora ad ordinem
reducuntur.

John of Salisbury (Polycr. vi. 25, p. 626) expresses the idea of the Areo-
pagite writings thus : ' Sic ergo cohaereant inferiora superioribus, sic
universa membra se subjiciant capiti, ut religio servetur incolumis.'

[5] Aegid. l. i. c. iv. : ' Quod spiritualis potestas instituere habet terrenam
potestatem, et si terrena potestas bona non fuerit, spiritualis potestas eam
poterit judicare.'

The Bull continues : ' Thus the prophecy of Jeremias : See, I have this
day set thee over the nations and over the kingdoms, &c., is true of the
Church and of the ecclesiastical power.'

Even in 431, at Ephesus, Bishop Theodotus of Ancyra used this passage from Jeremias in the same sense, when in the introduction to his
third Homily (Migne, PP. Gr. t. lxxvii. p. 1385) on ecclesiastical power he

says : ' *Priests also have a sword*, not in order to wound, but to cure. Grace has already announced this in the words of Jeremias : See, I have this day set thee over the nations and over the kingdoms, &c. For holiness cannot be sown *till wickedness has been rooted out.*' The passage was used in the same way in the Byzantine Synod, under Mennas, 536, act. 4 (Hard. ii. 1260), and in a letter from Oriental bishops to Pope Symmachus in 512. Jer. i. 10 is combined with Matt. xvi. 18 (Baron. a. 512, n. 50) in the same way in a letter of the Patriarch of Jerusalem to John II. of Constantinople (Hard. ii. 1243).

Again the Bull continues : ' Therefore should the earthly power transgress, it is judged by the spiritual power ; should the spiritual power transgress, the lesser is judged by the higher ; but if the highest spiritual power should transgress, it can be judged by God alone and not by man.' Cf. Aegidius, l.c. : ' Si deviat ergo terrena judicabitur a potestate spirituali tamquam a suo superiori ; sed si deviat potestas spiritualis et potissime potestas summi pontificis, a solo Deo poterit judicari.'

The Bull goes on : ' As the Apostle attests : He that is spiritual judgeth all things, yet he himself is judged of no man (1 Cor. ii. 15).'

Later writers have followed the extensive use made of this text by Irenaeus (Adv. Haer. l. iv. c. xxxiii. n. 1 seq., specially n. 7). Thus Hugo a S. Victore, de Sacram. l. ii. P. ii. c. iv. Aegid. Rom. (l.c. c. ii.) : ' Quod summus pontifex est tantae potentiae, quantae est ille spiritualis homo, qui judicat omnia et ipse a nemine judicatur.' Against this remarks Joh. de Parisis (ap. Natal. Alex. l.c. n. 14, p. 327) : ' Licet illa auctoritas *frequenter* assumatur et in diversis casibus pro auctoritate D. Papae, tamen non est ad propositum, quia non accipitur ibi homo spiritualis de spirituali potestate, quam habet ecclesiasticus judex, quum habens interdum hanc potestatem spiritualem sit *animalis*, ut ibi accipitur, sed dicitur animalis homo vita vel sensu. . . . *Vita* quidem dicitur spiritualis, qui secundum Deum habens rationem animam suam regit ; spiritualis autem *scientia* est, qui non secundum humanum sensum, sed Spiritui S. subjectus per fidem de Deo judicat certissime et fideliter. Unde talis judicat omnia,' &c. Anonym. de Pot. Papae (ib. p. 328) : ' Apostolus non loquitur ibi *de judicio jurisdictionis*, quod competit alicui per supremam impositionem, sed *de judicio discretionis*, quod habetur per internam inspirationem.'

* Hefele, p. 317. Berchtold, p. 28. Schulte, i. p. 31. Allg. Zeit. 26 Dec. 1870.

7 From Thom. Aqu. Opusc. c. Graec. c. xxv. p. 257.

8 Christophe, l.c. i. pp. 102, 103.

9 Petrus de Marca, Concord. Sac. et Imp. l. iv. c. xvi. n. 3.

10 The view taken in the introduction is based on c. Novit de judiciis (infrà, c. xiii. P. i. § 14 seq.), Spondan. a. 1302, n. 11, Bianchi, t. i. l. i. § 10, n. 2, p. 93, against Bossuet, l. iii. c. xxii. pp. 319, 320, who wrongly says that the Decretal Novit is not to the point here. The principle is quite the same ; the potestas indirecta is understood under the figure of the material sword.

11 Defens. Decl. Cleri. Gall. l. iii. c. xxiii. p. 326 : ' Eo viam sibi parasse videbatur, ut Rom. Pontifici omnem potestatem esse subditam, etiam in temporalibus, pro certo fidei dogmate definiret. *At profecto non eo usque*

processit ; hoc enim tantum habet *definitio : Porro subesse Rom. Pontifici omnem humanam creaturam declaramus, dicimus, diffinimus et pronunciamus omnino esse de necessitate salutis,* quod quidem est verissimum et apud Catholicos certum, si de spirituali potestate intelligatur.'

[12] Also Natal. Alex. (l.c. a. 2, n. 10, p. 324) does not find in the Bull the view which the Frenchmen of the time pretended that it contained ; but he only finds in it the ' indirecta in temporalia regum potestas,' which indeed he equally disputes.

[13] Christophe, l.c.

§ 2.

The Dominican John of Paris[1] and others[2] subsequently attacked this Bull, which they interpreted in the sense of a direct power over temporal matters, and sought to invalidate its argument. But far from carrying on the dispute as a question of *principles*, Philip's party turned it into a *personal* quarrel. They desired to make a more direct attack upon the Pope, to stigmatise him as an unlawful Pope, a heretic, and a simonist, and to heap up accusations against him. After the deaths of the Comte d'Artois and Peter Flotte, William of Nogaret, keeper of the seals and closely bound up with the Colonnas, remained the Pope's chief enemy. In the mean time Philip had it announced in Rome that he no longer acknowledged the Pope as arbitrator in his war with Flanders and England.[3] The Pope was said to have excited both these countries against Philip ;[4] but there are proofs of his conciliatory dispositions. In an attempted mediation[5] the following conditions for a peace were demanded :[6] 1. That the king should recall the prohibition which he or his officers had laid on the journey to Rome, together with the penalties attached to it. 2. That he should acknowledge the Pope's original right to bestow ecclesiastical offices, and the necessity of his tacit or expressed consent to the appointments being made by a layman,[7] and also 3. the right of the See of Rome to send legates into particular States without needing the permission of any one. 4. That he should likewise acknowledge the right of the clergy in the administration of ecclesiastical property, and the Pope's right of supreme direction over it and over any taxation laid on it. 5. No layman, not even a prince, should have the right to lay hands on the possessions of the clergy, to burden them with a rent, to summon ecclesiastics before his courts of justice, or to arrest them on account of personal conduct or on account of immovable goods, unless these were feudal possessions. 6. That as the king allowed Papal documents with portraits of the Princes of the Apostles to be burnt in his presence, he must either account for such an unheard-of act or receive punishment for it, particularly by forfeiting the privileges bestowed upon him by the Holy See. 7. That the king shall no longer abuse the so-called regalian rights, seize vacant churches, or keep the interim revenue of future bishops. 8. Spiritual jurisdiction must be given back to the prelates again, but without detriment to acquired privileges, so that in some cases the laity might exercise such jurisdiction. 9. That as the debasement of the coinage and the extortions of the royal officers had done great damage to the clergy and the people, the king must make them some indemnification. 10. Further explanations would be necessary of the bad reception given to the nuncio Jacques Norman and to the Bull of December 5 which he brought with him. 11. The town of Lyons must be acknowledged to belong to the archbishop, and not to the king. If no amendment was made within the time agreed upon by Prince Charles and the ambassadors, the Pope would take more severe measures.

[1] Tract. de Potestate Regia et Papali (Goldast. Mon. ii. 108 seq.) denies the direct power, but allows an indirect one, *e.g.* p. 132 : ' Papa non instituit regem, sed uterque est a Deo institutus suo modo ; nec cum dirigit *per se*, ut rex est, sed *per accidens*, in quantum convenit regem *fidelem* esse, in quo instruitur a Papa de fide, non de regimine.' Cf. about this, Neander, K.G. ii. pp. 685-687, 3d edit.

[2] Thus the author of the ' quaestio in utramque partem disputata de potestate regia et pontificali' (Gold. ii. 95 seq.). Cf. Neander, l.c. p. 684 seq.

[3] Dupuy, p. 84. Notices et Extraits de ms. de la Bibl. Imp. xx. 145.

[4] Nicol. Trivet, Annal. p. 396. Rayn. a. 1302, n. 17 fin. Hefele, p. 319.

[5] Baillet, p. 172. Spondan. a. 1303, n. 2. Raynald. h.a. n. 15. Christophe, p. 104.

[6] Dupuy, Preuves, p. 90. Raynald. l.c. n. 34. Hefele, pp. 319, 320. Christophe, pp. 104, 105.

[7] In quibuscumque beneficiis ecclesiasticis conferendis, vacantibus in curia vel extra curiam, Rom. Pontificem summam et potiorem obtinere potestatem, et quod per collationem cujusvis laici in ipsis vel eorum aliquo non potest alicui jus acquiri sine auctoritate vel consensu Sedis Apostolicae tacitis vel expressis.

§ 3.

Philip caused a reply to be made to these articles.[1] 1. The prohibition made against travelling out of the country was occasioned by the pressure of the times, the war in Flanders, and the necessity of preventing possible revolutions. Against 2, 4, 5, 7, he appealed to the usages and examples of his predecessors. He disapproved of the abuses practised by his officers, and would redress them. With regard to the question of the burnt Bull, Philip pretended to have misunderstood article 6, and treated it as if it referred to quite another document. It was evident that the Court was ashamed of that act.[2] Concerning the complaints of the debased coinage and extortion (art. 9), it was replied that State necessities had compelled them to it; part of the distress suffered by his subjects was already alleviated ; measures should be taken to remove all complaints. As to art. 11, the king deplored the troubles of the Church of Lyons, but laid them all to the refusal of the archbishop to take the feudal oath, and he declared himself ready to negotiate. He professed himself to be ready to abide by the judgment of the Dukes of Burgundy and Brittany, who were highly esteemed by the Pope.

[1] Dupuy, p. 92. Baillet, p. 175 seq. Natal. Alex. l.c. diss. 9, a. 3, n. 2, pp. 334, 335. Christophe, p. 106 seq. Hefele, p. 320 seq.
[2] Döllinger, Lehrbuch, ii. p. 244.

§ 4.

The moderate tone of this document, so much praised by the Gallicans,[1] clearly shows cunning calculation and crafty deceitfulness, but no upright and conciliatory dispositions. Hefele says : 'Notorious actions were simply denied or all the guilt laid on the officers, the complaints made by the Pope were arbitrarily explained, even intentionally misunderstood, the real point in question was evaded, apparent concessions were made in the vaguest manner.'[2] French diplomacy showed itself in that conflict, as it has in innumerable cases since, dishonest and faithless, as well in the undecided and evasive manner in which it answered as in that which it left unanswered. In the Brief of April 13, 1303,[3] addressed to Prince Charles of Valois and the Cardinal-legates, Boniface described Philip's answer as very unsatisfactory; for the rest he was perfectly ready to accept the mediation of both the dukes. Beyond this he sent two Bulls to the legates, one of which summoned those French prelates who had not appeared in Rome to come there within three months,[4] but the other announced that King Philip, in spite of his exalted rank and privileges, would incur the penalty of ex-communication, which would fall on every one who should pre-vent the journey to the Apostolic See.[5] Probably the publica-tion of this latter constitution was intended only to take place if the king had rejected all reconciliation, and had thus driven the Pope to severity.[6] If he made no kind of satisfaction, the Pope believed he would be obliged to interfere with all the weight of his spiritual and temporal power (spiritualiter et temporaliter). But it is historically false that just after the Bull 'Unam sanctam' the Pope *deposed* King Philip, and released his subjects from their oath of allegiance.[7]

[1] Natal. Alex. (l.c. art. 3, n. 2, p. 334) says : 'Rex incredibili modestia temperatum responsum dedit.'
[2] Hefele, p. 321.
[3] Dupuy, pp. 95, 97. Raynald. a. 1303, n. 34.
[4] Dupuy, p. 88.
[5] Dupuy, p. 98. Raynald. a. 1311, n. 39 : 'Per processus nostros.'
[6] Bianchi, l.c. p. 533. Christophe, p. 108.
[7] Berchtold, p. 29.

§ 5.

But already before the publication of this Bull the passion and blind hatred of the French statesmen had hurried them on to extreme measures. In an extraordinary sitting of the State Council held in March 1303, William Nogaret challenged the king to protect the Holy Church against Boniface, the inter-loper, false Pope, thief and robber, heretic and simonist, and to convoke a General Council in order to effect his deposition.[1] Philip ordered the bearer of the Papal document to be arrested. The protest of the cardinal-legate remained unnoticed, and he himself was treated with indignity and obliged to escape from

France.[2]   The peace concluded with England on May 20[3] left Philip free to oppress the liberty of Flanders and to humiliate the Pope, which he desired still more. The Pope being made acquainted with these events endeavoured to improve his cause thus endangered, and to lessen the number of his powerful opponents.[4]

On June 13, 1303, some thirty prelates who had submitted to the king, several barons and lawyers, were collected together at the Louvre, whereupon the Chevalier William Plasian (du Plessis), Lord of Vezenobre, delivered a lengthy accusation against the Pope, declared himself ready to prove all the statements and to take his oath on the Gospels, and at the same time begged the king as protector of the faith to assemble a General Council. The twenty-nine counts[5] which he alleged on the following day contained the vilest calumnies;[6] for instance, that Boniface did not believe in the immortality of the soul, eternal life, or transubstantiation, that he did not hold fornication to be a sin, compelled priests to violate the seal of confession, practised simony and sodomy, encouraged idolatry, did not keep the fast-days, was possessed with a wicked spirit, consulted soothsayers, was guilty of the loss of the Holy Land as well as of the death of his predecessor Celestine V.,—almost all things which had been noised about for years by the Colonnas, some French priests, and other enemies of the Pope. Plasian declared that he appeared as a complainant against the Pope, not from hatred or passion, but from zeal for the welfare of the Church. He was supported by Count Louis of Evreux, the king's son, Count Guido of St. Pol, and Count John of Dreux. The king assured them that he would direct his efforts to assemble a General Council merely as a matter of conscience and without prejudice to the honour of the Holy See, called upon the prelates to coöperate, and then and there appealed to the future General Council, to the future true Pope, and to anything that could be appealed to. A like proceeding had never before occurred in the French Church. Laymen came forward with the most absurd charges against the head of the bishops.[7] The king, who promised to attend in person at the Council, desired to sit in judgment over him.[8]   An appeal of this kind had never before been brought, except in the case of the Emperor Frederick II., and never at all by France; it was in complete contradiction to the principles of the Church.[9]   Five arch-bishops, twenty-one bishops, and a few abbots declared that they appealed beforehand to the General Council and to future rightful Popes against any censures of Boniface ; all possible steps were taken to obtain the agreement of the Paris University,[10] of the clerical corporations, and of the towns and provinces.[11] Nearly seven hundred addresses of agreement were obtained by the royal commissioners sent about for that purpose.[12]   Any one who did not voluntarily subscribe to these addresses was forced to do so.   John, Abbot of Citeaux, was imprisoned for refusing, as were also the Abbots of Clugny and Premontré, and many Italian monks.[13]   The Dominicans of Montpellier were deprived of royal protection in consequence of their opposition, and were ordered to leave the kingdom within three days.[14] Whoever did not consent to this audacious and unecclesiastic appeal was considered a traitor to his country, and what slander had begun was accomplished by violence.[15]   Philip then wrote to the other princes and prelates of Europe concerning his pro-jected Ecumenical Synod, and also to the cardinals, to whom he hypocritically protested his fervent and devoted love to the Church.[16]

[1] Dupny, p. 56. Baillet, p. 169. Drumann, ii. p. 68 seq. Christophe, p. 109. Hefele, p. 322.

[2] Spoudan. a. 1303, n. 7. Natal. Alex. l.c. a. 3, n. 3, 4. Hefele, p. 322 seq.

[3] Pauli, Gesch. Engl. iv. p. 156 seq.

[4] Christophe, pp. 109-113.

[5] Dupuy, p. 101 seq. Bulaeus, l.c. p. 42 seq. Hefele, pp. 323-325.

[6] Natal. Alex. l.c. a. 4, n. 1, p. 336: 'Immania accusationum, immo calumniarum capita.'

[7] Against the complaints of laymen, specially those which are person-ally hostile against bishops, are directed c. 1-3, 14 seq. c. ii. q. 7 ; c. 8, c. vi. q. 1 ; Chalc. c. 21 (c. 49, c. ii. q. 7) ; Conc. Aquisgr. 789, c. 30 (Labbé, ix. 17 ; Hefele, iii. 624).

[8] Bianchi, l.c. n. 12, p. 535.

[9] Gelas. I. c. 16, 17, c. ix. q. 3 ; Conc. Rom. 800, sub Leone III. (Hard. iv. 936, 937). Petrus de Marca, l.c. iv. 23 : 'Numquam admissa est in Ec-

clesia provocatio a Papa ad Concilium.' Mansi, Animadvers. in Nat. Alex.
l.c. pp. 355-362.
    [10] It acquiesced in these words : 'Appellationi praefati D.
Regis adhaeremus, *quantum de jure possumus et debemus secundum Deum et justitiam et sanctae permittunt canonicae sanctiones ;* supponentes nos ac nobis
adhaerentes et adhaerere volentes et universitatem nostram protectioni
divinae et praedicti Concilii generalis ac futuri veri ac legitimi pontificis.'
Dupuy, Preuves, p. 17 ; Natal. Alex. l.c. a. 4, n. 3, p. 337.
    [11] Boutaric, p. 29 seq.
    [12] Bulacus, iv. 46 seq.   Dupuy, p. 112 seq.
    [13] Const. Super Petri solio, Preuves, p. 184.   Christophe, p. 115.
    [14] Hist. du Diff. p. 154.   Natal. Alex. l.c. n. 7, p. 338.
    [15] Christophe, l.c.
    [16] Boutaric, p. 111.   Hefele, p. 327 seq.

§ 6.

At the news of these proceedings in France, Boniface VIII.
cleared himself of the charges brought against him by a solemn
oath in a consistory held at Anagni (August 1303), and then
issued several Bulls referring to them, well knowing that all the
authority of the Church would be annihilated if Philip's proceedings were to gain strength.[1]   In one of the constitutions
he declared any one who should put difficulties in the way of
the publication of the Papal summonses to be excommunicated.[2]
Those doctors of the university who, partly mislead and partly
ill-treated by the king, agreed to what he proposed or gave him
advice, were deprived by the Pope of the power of conferring
the right to teach and the academical degrees in theology and
in civil and canon law, till such time as the king should offer
satisfaction to the Apostolic See.[3]   He then suspended the
right of election to all ecclesiastical corporations, and reserved
the disposal of all ecclesiastical benefices in France to the
Apostolic See.[4]   In another constitution[5] he censured the accusations and slanders current in France, as well as the appeal to
a General Council, the right of convoking which belonged to
the Pope alone, and he threatened the king with the punishments of the Church.   Therefore Boniface had *not yet excommunicated the king by name ;* he still wished to allow him
time.

    [1] Spondan. a. 1303, n. 9-11.   Bianchi, l.c. § 7, n. 15, pp. 542, 543.

² Whatever spiritual or temporal dignity they might hold. Const. Rem non novam aggredimur. Dupuy, p. 161. Raynald. a. 1303, n. 40. Tosti, ii. p. 309.
³ Const. Sedes Apostolica. Dupuy, p. 163. Raynald. a. 1303, n. 38.
⁴ Dupuy, l.c. Raynald. l.c. n. 39.
⁵ Const. Super ad audientiam, ap. Dupuy, p. 166. Bulaeus, iv. p. 55 seq. Raynald. l.c. n. 36. Cf. a. 1311, n. 40.

§ 7.

The publication of the Bull[1] of excommunication which, in the mean time, was being prepared never took place. Brutal and treacherous violence was to overcome Boniface VIII. Ever since April, Nogaret had been staying in Italy, gaining followers and soldiers by the means of rich bribes, organising together with Sciarra Colonna a powerful anti-papal party, preparing a cunning attack upon the Pope, who was staying at Anagni. At break of day, Sept. 7, 1303, Nogaret, accompanied by armed men, whom, to his still greater shame, he ordered to carry the standard of the Church of Rome, appeared before Anagni, where he already had an understanding with some of the members of the nobility. Adenolfo, son of Maffeo, who had been an enemy of the Pope for a long time, treacherously opened the gate to him, and with the cry, 'Long live the King of France! Down with Boniface!' they rushed into the town. A rabble collected together, for the most part bought over, and thinking only of the plunder, joined themselves to the enemy, who soon lined the streets and public squares and repulsed the Papal adherents. The town authorities, either from bribery or surprise, took no part in the proceedings; panic reigned everywhere; the cardinals all fled but two. The Papal palace and the church of the Mother of God close to it were surrounded, the latter taken possession of, and the doors and windows of the former broken open; the palace was plundered, everything of any worth stolen, even the archives destroyed. Many valuable documents were perhaps lost amongst them, for which those preserved in France can offer no adequate compensation. The Pope, who was nearly eighty-six years old, maintained his dignity and resolution; in face of the rough soldiery pouring in his only thought was to die worthily. He cried out to the persons round him : ' Open the doors to my apartments, for I will suffer martyrdom for the Church of God. . . As I am taken like Christ by treachery, I will die as Pope.' He waited for his murderers, seated on the Papal throne in all the splendour of his dignity, surrounded by the Cardinals Nicholas Boccasini, Bishop of Ostia, and Peter d'Espagne, Bishop of Sabina. At sight of the reverend old man the intruders were deeply moved, stood still, and did not venture to lay a hand upon him.[2]   But Sciarra and Nogaret stepped boldly up to the Pope and overwhelmed him with abuse, to all of which he maintained a dignified silence. Nogaret, who, it is said, prevented his companion from actively ill-treating the Pope, presented him with the resolutions of the Paris Assembly, and threatened to have him carried in chains to Lyons, there to be judged and deposed by a General Council. Boniface then said : ' Here is my head, here my neck. For the liberty of the Church I will submit, as a Catholic, as lawful Pope, and as Vicar of Jesus Christ, to be condemned by Patarini ; for I desire martyrdom for faith in Christ and His Church.' These words keenly affected Nogaret, for his grandfather had been burnt for the Albigensian heresy. He is said by some to have moved away abashed; but according to others he is said to have pulled the Pope down from the steps of his throne, amidst scornful cries from his comrades of ' Maledictus Malefacius' (Cursed malefactor), and allowed Sciarra to ill-treat him. No certainty can be attached to Nogaret's later denials, for he has contradicted other things which cannot be doubted. The Pope and his suite were made prisoners ; he was kept without food for a long time, in the hopes of forcing him to abdicate or to recall his Bull; and his followers were insulted, robbed, and ill-treated.[3]

---

[1] Dupuy, p. 182 seq.   Bulaeus, p. 57.   Raynald. a 1311, n. 44.   Spondan. a. 1303, n. 11.   Natal. Alex. l.c. a. 5, n. 1, p. 342.   Many do not hold the Bull to be genuine (Bianchi, l.c. n. 15, p. 544).

[2] Giov. Villani, Istoria Fior. l. viii. c. lxiii.   S. Antonin. Summa Hist. t. iii. tit. 20, c. viii. p. 21.   Franc. Pipini, Chron. l. iv. c. xli.   Thomas Walsingham, Hist. Angl. in Eduard. I. l. i.   Ferrettus Vicentin. in Bonif.

l. iii. p. 1002.   Istoria Pistolesi (Murat. t. xi. p. 529), Chron. Parm. a. 1303, p. 848.

[3] Christophe, pp. 119, 120.   Drumann, ii. p. 114 seq.   Hefele, p. 330.

§ 8.

The blow had succeeded; but the conspirators were undecided what was next to be done. It appears that they did not consider it advisable to carry the Pope away from Anagni, for fear of being attacked on the way by his adherents. Two days were thus let to pass away. But on the third day the citizens of Anagni made an effort, roused by the outrage done to their countryman and benefactor, and led by Cardinal Lucas del Fiesco. Amidst cries of 'Long live the Pope! Death to the traitors!' they drove away the French and the Colonnas party, and set the Pope at liberty with every mark of respect.[1] In the evening of the same day, it is said that Boniface, who in a time of utmost need had shown extreme courage,[2] held a consistory, and pardoned the rioters of Anagni, with the exception of the robbers and traitors. The Pope also pardoned Reginald da Supino, who had held him prisoner, and who now in his turn was seized, together with his children, and also the faithless Cardinal Richard of Sienna, and Napoleon Orsini.[3] 'I do not know,' says Christophe,[4] 'any more touching, high-minded, or heroic trait in history than of this venerable old man, who had no other answer to the unheard-of outrage, which he might have sought to avenge, than the words: "I forgive." And it must not be forgotten that this old man is the "passionate," "implacable," maligned Boniface.' At this turn of events the conspirators united with all the enemies of the people of Anagni, with Ferrentino and Alatri, and inflicted what harm they could on the town; whereupon all participators in the imprisonment of the Pope were banished from the town, and those who interceded for them were punished.[5] For centuries the remembrance of this outrage remained alive in Anagni,[6] and Dante[7] has vividly described it. Soon afterwards Boniface returned to Rome, accompanied by armed men who had been sent from there to protect him; he was received with lively joy, but soon found himself watched and tyrannised over by the powerful Orsini. Enfeebled in body but strong in mind, he died of a violent fever on October 11, 1338,[8] having again made a solemn confession of faith. The idea that he killed himself in madness and despair[9] is a fiction invented by his enemies; when his coffin was opened, October 9, 1605, no trace of a wound was discovered.[10]

[1] Pappencordt, p. 338.
[2] Pipini, Chron. 1. iv. c. xxi. : ' Magnanimitatem et constantiam semper ostendit.' Natal. Alex. l.c. a. 5, n. 2 : ' Conjuratos incredibili magnanimitate exspectavit.'
[3] Thom. Walsingham, l.c. Joh. Rubeus, Bonifacius VIII. et familia Gaetanorum principum, Romae, 1651, p. 216.
[4] L.c. pp. 120, 121.
[5] The edict ap. Rubeus, l.c. pp. 338-341.
[6] Fr. L. Alberti, Descrizione di tutta l' Italia, 1550, f. 146. Pappencordt, l.c.
[7] Dante, Purgat. xx. 86.
[8] Christophe, p. 121. Pappencordt, pp. 338, 339. Hefele, pp. 330, 331.
[9] Ferret. Vicentin. p. 1005 seq.
[10] Spondan. a. 1303, n. 16. Raynald. h.a. n. 44. Rubeus, l.c. p. 346 seq. Wiseman, Essays on various Subjects, iii. 219 seq.

§ 9.

Boniface VIII., who after his famous 'Liber Sextus' is chiefly celebrated for the institution of jubilees and for the establishment of the Roman University,[1] was followed even beyond the grave by the hatred of the French. Unfortunately his immediate successor, the pious Nicholas Bocassini, of the order of the Dominicans, under the name of Benedict XI., only carried on the pontificate from October 22, 1303, to July 7, 1304. He endeavoured in the mildest and most conciliatory manner possible, without detriment to justice, to reëstablish peace. He was in a very critical position in Rome ; they were divided into many parties there, and even in the College of Cardinals French influence threatened to become powerful. The Colonnas had reappeared ; the Ghibellines raised their heads defiantly.[2] Benedict abolished the condemnation published by his predecessor against the Colonnas, gave them back those of their possessions which had not passed into other hands ; but he forbade the rebuilding Palestrina, and did not allow the two cardinals of the family to take part in the functions of the Sacred College.[3] He also wished to reëstablish peace with France, without violating the dignity of the Apostolic See. Prior Peter de Paredo, who had been sent to Italy by King Philip on different commissions, delivered a memorial of complaints against the late Pope, in which the resolutions drawn up at Paris in June were given, and the convocation of a General Council at Lyons, or any other town agreeable to the king, was proposed. Benedict gave no official answer to these unauthorised agents, but he let Nogaret understand by means of a French prelate that the state of things was no longer the same since the change in the pontificate, no steps were to be taken till new instructions should be agreed upon, and he declared his desire to adjust the unhappy discord. In Paris it was decided to send a new ambassador to the new Pope.[4]

[1] Christophe, p. 122.
[2] Christophe, p. 125 seq.
[3] Hefele, pp. 345-347. Cf. c. Dudum, v. 4, de Schismat. in Xvagg. Com.
[4] Dupuy, Hist. du Diff. p. 25 ; Actes et Preuves, p. 200 seq. Baillet, p. 235 seq. Christophe, p. 138 seq. Hefele, p. 348 seq.

§ 10.

The outrage at Anagni had caused great indignation even in France against Nogaret and the king.[1] Nogaret therefore advised an explanation to be made with the Holy See; but also at the same time a vindication of the outrage to be attempted. In the eyes of contemporaries this could be done best by condemning Boniface VIII. as a heretic, as well as by treating him as the originator of the strife ; if that could be made out, Philip and Nogaret would no longer be offenders, but true knights and deliverers of the Church. The king agreed to this plan, and did everything to further it.[2] He congratulated the Pope on his accession ; in his letter to the Pope[3] he contrasted him very favourably with his predecessor, and whilst abusing Boniface showered praises on Benedict: the former was to be branded in every kind of way, while the latter was to be won over. The king recommended himself, his kingdom, and the French Church very warmly to his favour. Some of the followers of Boniface VIII. who had been imprisoned were set free, not without ransoms, however ; and preparations were made for the mitigation of the prohibition laid on exportation.[4]

[1] The memorial (Notices et Extraits des mss. xx. 2, p. 150 seq.), probably drawn up by Nogaret at this time, shows this. Cf. Schwab, in the Tüb. Quartalschrift, 1866, i. p. 23 seq.
[2] Hefele, p. 349.
[3] Dupuy, p. 205.
[4] Hefele, pp. 349, 350.

§ 11.

In the presence of the French ambassadors Benedict absolved the king from all excommunication, for whatever reason it had been incurred, and sent him the intelligence in a friendly letter on April 2, 1304. But he expressly describes his act as one of apostolic clemency towards an erring sheep,[1] and admonished the king to receive it in all humility, and to be obedient to the Church. With regard to the convocation of a General Council for the judgment of Boniface, the Pope declared in consistory that he reserved the decision to himself. In the mean time Philip's ambassadors endeavoured for this purpose to win over each cardinal separately, and with seven they appear to have succeeded.[2] Besides this, a memorial to the king, drawn up by Dubois, a lawyer, was published in France, to demand protection (or rather vengeance—which surely had been more than sufficiently executed) against the attacks made by the *deceased* Pope on the liberty and sovereignty of the kingdom, and to cause him to be condemned as a heretic.[3] Thus they always acted on the supposition that Boniface had raised *new* and *quite unheard-of* claims, had been the *first* to endeavour to extend the power of binding and loosing to temporal matters, and had desired to make himself the absolute master of France. The *direct* power of the Church in civil affairs was now combated in detail. It was said that according to the Divine Will, kingdoms and priesthoods must be, and always have been, separate ; that Christ Himself did not

exercise any civil power, did not demand obedience from Pilate
and Herod, but, on the contrary, commanded that unto Cæsar
should be given the things which were Cæsar's; that in like
manner neither Peter, nor Paul, nor Clement, nor any of their
successors, had claimed a power over civil matters, with the
exception of that bestowed by Constantine the Great;[4] that
Boniface VIII. was the first to go so far.

[1] Dupuy, p. 207 : 'Quanta nos, fili carissime, ad tui directionem sollicitudo impulerit pastoralis officii, quantave paternae pietatis dilectio ad
salutem tuam super te viscera mansuetudinis nostrae commoverit, absolu-
tio, quam tibi nuper absenti et non petenti ab omnibus excommunicationum
sententiis, quibus ex quacumque causa forsitan tenebaris adstrictus, in
tuorum nunciorum praesentia te in benedictionibus dulcedinis praeveni-
entes impendimus, manifestat. Id ne sanguis tuus de nostris requiratur
manibus, fecisse laetamur; id egisse non poenitet, et quod plus est, illud
etiam facere debebamus. Sumus namque illius vicarius, qui dixit hominem
illum, qui fecit coenam magnam, servo suo dixisse: Exi in vias et sepes et
compelle intrare, ut impleatur domus mea (Luc. xiv. 23). In hoc para-
bolam illam implevimus, secundum quam habens centum oves, relictis 99
in deserto, vadit ad illam, *quam deviasse putabat,* donec inveniat eam, et
inventam imponit in humeros suos gaudens (Luc. xv. 4, 5). Numquid
igitur te, etiamsi nolles, non cogemus intrare? Numquid tantam ovem,
quanta tu es, sic nobilem, praecipuam et praeclaram relinquemus, quin
impositam nostris humeris reducamus?'
[2] Dupuy, pp. 219 seq. 231 seq.
[3] Dupuy, p. 214 seq. Hefele, p. 351.
[4] 'From the point of view of the Donatio Constantini, which is here
accepted as genuine, it would have been difficult to refute the alleged
claims of the Pope' (Hefele, l.c. note 2).

§ 12.

Pope Benedict XI. published two decrees at Viterbo, on the
18th and 19th April 1304, in which he cancelled the suspension from the right of teaching and of conferring academical
decrees, as well as the reservation of all French benefices, which
had been enacted by his predecessor in the previous August.[1]
Then on May 12th he moderated the constitution 'Clericis laicos'
at Perugia, so that only the demand, and not the payment, of
taxes by the clergy to the laity was condemned, and the payment of contributions for State objects, in times of necessity,
should be allowed in moderation after previous consultation
with the Pope, in accordance with the fourth Lateran Council.[2]

Some days later he absolved all the French priests and laymen who had been excommunicated by Boniface, or by any previous Pope, on account of having put difficulties in the way of communication with the Holy See, and likewise all those who had taken part, either by word or deed, in the imprisonment of his predecessor or of his legates, Nogaret alone being excepted, his absolution being specially reserved.[3] Further, he pardoned the disobedience of all the prelates, abbots, and doctors who had not obeyed the summons to the Roman Synod of 1302;[4] then he cancelled the enactments of his predecessor by which the privileges bestowed on France were recalled or granted to others to the prejudice of the former, or by which any one had been exempted from his obligations towards the king; everything was to return to the same order as before the dispute, with the exception of anything which Boniface VIII. had ordained against Nogaret.[5] Benedict not only secured the old favours to the king, but even added new ones, such as the grant of a half-yearly tithe from ecclesiastical possessions, and the exemption of the court chaplains from the jurisdiction of the Bishop of Paris and the Metropolitan of Sens; he also promised to help the plans of Charles of Valois on Constantinople, which he claimed as the husband of Katharine Courtenay, heiress of the Latin emperor of that place.[6] It appears as if the Pope by these measures hoped to dispose King Philip to accept patiently the energetic blow which he was preparing to deal against the leaders of the attempt at Anagni. At Perugia, where Benedict thought himself sufficiently safe, he ordered the Bull 'Flagitiosum scelus' to be published. After narrating the acts of violence committed by Nogaret, Sciarra, Reginald da Supino, and their accomplices, of which he himself had been a witness, Benedict continued : ' Who is so hard-hearted as not to be able to shed tears over this ? Where the opponent who would feel no pity ? Where the judge, however weak he might be, who would not rise up to condemn that by which security has been violated, the inviolable assailed, the Papal dignity dishonoured, the Church and her Bridegroom degraded ? O crime never to be atoned for! O unheard-of violence ! O unhappy town of Anagni, which suffered it patiently without averting it!' After this complaint the Pope declared all participators, abettors, and assistants in this attempt to be excommunicated, and summoned them to appear before the Apostolic See before June 29th, to receive judgment.[7] If they did not appear they would incur severe anathemas.[8] In the mean time, Benedict XI. died at Viterbo, and so suddenly as to cause a belief that he was poisoned.[9] Some accused the Colonnas of being the perpetrators of this crime, others accused the Gaetanis, others the Florentines, again others a party amongst the cardinals, and others Nogaret's accomplices Ferreta of Vicenza,[10] Philip the Fair himself, the Franciscan monk Bernard Delitiosi and some of the clergy, as to whom John XXII. afterwards (1319) caused investigations to be made. The prelates deputed by the Pope did not find quite sufficient proof of the murder, but condemned the Franciscan monk to perpetual and severe imprisonment; and John, in spite of the objection raised by the royal procurator that the sentence was too light, confirmed the judgment.[11]

[1] Dupuy, l.c. p. 209. Const. Ut eo magis, p. 229.
[2] C. un. Quod olim, de Immunit. Eccl. iii. 13, in Xvagg. Com. Cf. Raynald. a. 1304, n. 12 ; Bzov. h.a. n. 4 ; Phillips. K.R. iii. § 131, p. 261 seq.
[3] Dupuy, p. 208. Const. Sanctae matris Ecclesiae.
[4] Dupuy, p. 229. Const. Dudum Bonifacius.
[5] Ib. p. 230, Ad statum tuum. In the constitution Sanctae matris, Benedict gives as reasons for his leniency : '(1) utilitates et commoda, quae ex eodem regno (Franciae), dum in ipsius Ecclesiae devotione persistit, Ecclesiae praedictae proveniunt ; (2) quod propter evitandum scandalum, praesertim ubi multitudo delinquit, severitati est aliquid detrahendum.'
[6] Hefele, p. 353.
[7] Dupuy, p. 232. Raynald. a. 1304, n. 13-15. Tosti, vol. ii. doc. S. p. 313. Christophe, p. 141.
[8] Spondan. a. 1303, n. 21. Bzov. a. 1304.
[9] Drumann, ii. p. 164.
[10] Ferret. Vicent. (Murat. R. It. Ser. ix. 1018).
[11] Natalis Alexander (l.c. art. 6, n. 2, 3, pp. 345-347) gives, from the Inquisition archives of Carcassone, the Papal decree concerning the preliminary arrangements of the inquiry and then the result in short. Cf. Baluz. Vita Pap. Aven. t. ii. p. 341.

§ 13.

The Frenchman Bertrand de Got, Archbishop of Bordeaux, was chosen Pope, under the name of Clement V., by the conclave at Perugia, after a long contest between the French and Italian parties; he was crowned at Lyons on November 14, 1305, and took his seat in France, so that the Papal See then fell into an irksome dependence on the Parisian court.[1]   As soon as the coronation festivities were concluded, King Philip wished that the new Pope might listen to the proofs of the heresy of Boniface, and then condemn his memory.   Clement V. endeavoured to gain time,[2] and in the mean while to content the king in some other way.   He not only renewed the absolution pronounced by Benedict XI., not only chose nine of the new cardinals from among Frenchmen, and restored all their rights to the two Colonna cardinals, not only granted an ecclesiastical tithe to the king for five years,[3] but he even went much further than Benedict in recalling and modifying the decrees of Boniface VIII., and appeared to make all the interests of the French sovereign his own.   He entirely cancelled the Bull 'Clericis laicos' by a new decree,[4] retaining, however, the old decrees, specially those of the Lateran Council; on February 1, 1306,[5] he declared with regard to the dogmatic Bull ' Unam sanctam,' that it should in no way prejudice Philip or his kingdom, nor alter his relations with the Holy See concerning the obedience which he owed to it.   By this, Philip's grievance only was removed, or rather the decretal was cleared of the false meaning which had been imputed to it by the French.[6]   Besides this, Clement granted a Church tithe for·two years to Charles of Valois, to help to carry out his plan on Constantinople, by which it was hoped that the Holy Land might the more easily be conquered, and asked for contributions from the Italian States for this expedition so ardently desired by him.[7]

[1] Hefele, pp. 357-369.
[2] Dupuy, pp. 298, 368.
[3] Raynald. a. 1305, n. 14.   Christophe, p. 155.   Hefele, p. 370.
[4] C. un. Quoniam ex constitutione, iii. 17, de Immunit. Eccl. in Clem. Dupuy, Preuves, p. 287.
[5] C. 2, Meruit, v. 7, de Privil. in Extravagg. Com.   Dupuy, p. 288.
[6] Bianchi, t. i. l. i. § 10, pp. 97, 98, against Bossuet, l.c. c. xxiv. p. 327. Phillips, iii. p. 266.
[7] Raynald. a. 1306, n. 2-5.   Hefele, p. 370.

§ 14.

Clement V. remained a whole year from February 1306 at Bordeaux, where he was ill for a long time.[1]   In May 1307 he met King Philip at Poitiers, when the latter repeated his proposal for the trial of the memory of Boniface VIII. At last the Pope obtained a promise that he would leave it to him to see what should be done against Boniface;[2] notwithstanding this, Philip still urgently and frequently renewed his request. The strongest measures of intimidation were employed by means of the suppression of the order of the Templars.[3]   Clement was ready to make the greatest sacrifices, because of his helpless condition[4] and the violence of the king. The Pope was obliged to begin with the least possible delay legal investigations, and to listen to the accusers of the deceased Boniface. In the edict of citation of September 13, 1309, the Pope declared his personal conviction of the innocence of Boniface, but nevertheless promised to listen to his accusers.[5]   The trial began with a public consistory held at Avignon, 16th March 1310. The accusers made very extreme charges. They asserted the invalidity of the resignation of Celestine V., from which followed the illegitimacy of Boniface; and they accused him of heresy, simony, and immorality, and maintained the complete innocence of Nogaret and his comrades. There was no want of witnesses against Boniface; everything had been prepared for seven years. If the extant drafts of the proceedings were not arbitrarily falsicated, not a few of the witnesses, both lay and clerical, appear to have been very abandoned men.

The defenders of Boniface desired above all things that Nogaret and his companions should be excluded from the proceedings, as they were personal enemies of the accused, and at the present time under the ban of excommunication. So far Clement agreed with them when he declared on May 13, 1310, that he was of opinion that it was erroneous that an excommunicated person was absolved by the mere fact that the Pope held conversation with him.[6] They protested against the arrangements made with regard to the examination of witnesses; likewise against the right to judge a Pope, which belonged only to a General Council, and when it was question of heresy. As their main effort was to contest the right of their opponents to bring an accusation at all, they cared less to refute the actual charges, and only discussed some of them; for example, the false statement that Boniface had refused the sacraments on his deathbed.[7]

[1] Christophe, p. 160.
[2] Hefele, pp. 372, 373.
[3] Boutaric, Notices et Extraits, xx. 2, pp. 165 seq. 175 seq. La France sous Philippe le Bel, p. 133 seq. Hefele, p. 381.
[4] Cf. Christophe, p. 170. In the May of 1308, Philip repeated the proposals he had made in the previous May for the commencing a process against Boniface; he consented first in 1311, that at the General Council, which on August 12, 1308, was called for October 1, 1310, at Vienne (Mansi, xxv. p. 369 seq.; Raynald. a. 1308, n. 4), both the great matters should be negotiated: 'De quibus Templariorum et Bonifacii negotiis poterit vestra sanctitas, interim examinata plenius veritate, in Concilio feliciter ordinare.' Ep. Philippi ap. Dupuy, Preuves, p. 299. That which is related of the advice of the Cardinal of Prato (Christophe, i. p. 171 seq. according to Villani, viii. 91) is only put in the wrong place, but really quite conceivable.
[5] Raynald. a. 1309, n. 4. Dupuy, p. 368 seq.; Redemtor noster.
[6] Hefele, p. 397.
[7] Dupuy, p. 512 seq. Only a part of the protest.

§ 15.

In December 1310, the Pope adjourned the proceedings till Mid-Lent Sunday of the following year.[1] In February 1311, Philip at last committed the whole affair to the Pope, with the condition that reparation must be made to himself. The king was pronounced free of all guilt in the unhappy occurrences at Anagni, and all decrees disadvantageous to the king and his kingdom were cancelled. At the Council of Vienne, which was opened on the 16th October 1311, the affairs of the Templars appeared to be the most important matter; still the case of Boniface was brought to a conclusion.[2] The much-abused Pope was defended by three cardinals and several learned men in France and he was also acknowledged to be a rightful Pope.

[1] Hefele, p. 402.
[2] Giov. Villani, l. ix. c. xxii. Pipini, Chron. l. iv. c. xli. xlix. MS. Vat. ap. Raynald. a. 1311, n. 54. Mansi, Conc. xxv. 403. Hefele, p. 472 seq.

§ 16.

The German chroniclers speak on the whole very favourably of Boniface. The monk of Furstenfeld considered him to be a Pope hated by many on account of his sense of strict justice, who, had he lived longer, would have remedied many imperfections in the Church.[1] Nicholas of Siegen is astonished at his courage, which was without equal.[2] And indeed, says Schwab,[3] after quoting this testimony, there is no mistaking a certain loftiness of mind in the bold words which he said to the cardinals in his distress: 'And if all the princes of the world were united against us, and against this (Roman) Church, we would regard them as straws, if we had truth on our side and were responsible for it. But if we had not truth and justice on our side, then indeed we should have reason to be afraid.'[4] It can reasonably be said of him, ' What he desired to effect was explained by the principles on which the Popes had acted for a long time. The failure of his plans did not lie with him, but in the important changes of the time. When the Papacy was obliged to descend again from the heights to which it had attained in the twelfth and thirteenth centuries, it could not have been done with more dignity than by Boniface VIII., and in the manner in which he conducted himself during his pontificate.'[5] The sacrilegious outrage against him did not remain unpunished.[6]

[1] Böhmer, Fontes rer. Germ. i. p. 24.
[2] Chronicon Eccles. ed. Wegele, Jena, 1855, p. 372.
[3] Schwab, Gerson, pp. 4, 5.
[4] Alleg. D. Papae pro confirmando rege Rom. Alberto ap. Marca, de Conc. l. ii. c. iii. p. 111, ed. Baluz.
[5] Möhler's Church History, edited by Gams, ii. pp. 472, 473.
[6] Bianchi, t. iii. l.c. § 7, n. 15, p. 546 seq. When Philip IV. died in 1314, many priests had to be forced to say Masses for his soul. Raynald. a. 1314, n. 26. In 1316 his son, Louis X., was poisoned, and in 1328 the throne passed to the line of Valois.

§ 17.

The question concerning the indirect power of the Church over temporal matters in a Christian State was not yet decided; it was further discussed in its various aspects. But in the person of Philip IV. the State was already in opposition to the

Church, having separated itself from her and raised itself above her,[1] and France, which once was the glory and faithful support of the See of Rome,[2] now reduced it to a state of servitude, and the fundamental principles of the mediæval Christian State were put an end to. Regal pride and national egotism joined hands in the work, and the world was taught by experience that regal pride was not appointed as the protector of the Church, and that national egotism was in principle irreconcilable with the idea of a universal religion. The origin of many of the claims of the civil power must therefore be looked for in that unhappy time, and by degrees from that time they have received an historical form, and have been received as a part of positive law. The Church indeed at that time was still deeply rooted in the faith of nations; till then she had been the leader of general politics, and her institutions had a part in all the circumstances of life; but everything was preparing for the great breach which was to separate the life of the State from the life of the Church,[3] in order that the civil should be raised over the spiritual power.

In his struggle with the Church, Philip IV. was greatly assisted by the widely-spread discontent against spiritual jurisdiction, which was very extensive. Incessant bickerings took place between the royal and episcopal courts, and the strain became so great that King Philip VI., the first Valois, ordered several conferences to be held in his presence at Paris and Vincennes (the end of 1329 and the beginning of 1330).[4] The royal councillor, Peter de Cugnières, made a speech, alleging a passage[5] from St. Matthew xxii. 21, in which he endeavoured to prove with the help of sixty-six arguments that no civil jurisdiction belonged to ecclesiastics, but that they had taken almost entire possession of it.[6] Then the Archbishop of Sens, who, it should be said, did not recognise the assembly as a competent authority, in the name of the prelates made a speech founded on 1 Peter ii. 17. Later on, Peter Bertrandi, Bishop of Autun, endeavoured to refute the arguments of Peter de Cugnières in detail, and defended the indirect power of the Church in civil affairs. The prelates defended the principle of the jurisdiction which appertained to them, but allowed that in practice some abuses had crept in amongst the Church officers, which they promised to put down. The king demanded a written deposition of the statement of the case by the bishops ; they presented him with a short explanation in French, in which they begged him to leave the Church in possession of her rights. He expressed his strong desire to protect the rights of the Church, and then, when Peter de Cugnières had drawn up a fresh memorial, for the limitation of ecclesiastical jurisdiction,[7] and had been forcibly answered by the Bishop of Autun, who begged for a clear declaration on the part of the king, Philip repeated that he did not intend to diminish any ecclesiastical right, he would rather increase the liberties of the prelates. The edicts of the royal officers, which the bishops pointed out as offensive, were declared by the king to be invalid and published without his orders ; on the other hand, he made the fulfilment of the promise to remove the acknowledged abuses a condition for granting his future protection to spiritual jurisdiction and his forbearance from further interference. Philip VI., who was praised by Pope John XXII. on account of his bearing towards the Church,[8] showed that he was not moved by the same spirit which animated Philip IV., and which did not revive till later at the French court.

[1] Phillips, K.R. iii. § 131, p. 267.
[2] Cf. Greg. IX. et al. ap. Raynald. a. 1229, n. 53, 56; 1227, n. 60; Innoc. III. l. xii. Ep. 27 (Migne, t. ccxvi. p. 36).
[3] Phillips, l.c. p. 268.
[4] Phillips, l.c. p. 269 seq. Hefele, vi. p. 549 seq. The Libellus D. Bertrandi adv. Mag. Petrum de Cugnières, in Max. Bibl. PP. Lugd. t. xxvi. p. 109 seq.; also in the Traités des Droits et des Libertés de l'Eglise Gallicane, 1731, t. i. Raynald. a. 1329, n. 75 seq. Mansi, xxv. 883 seq.
[5] Each of the speakers, whether bishop or layman, took a verse from the Bible as a text.
[6] Hence the expression 'reintegrare temporalia.'
[7] Not for the introduction of the 'appel comme d'abus,' which was first instituted in the fifteenth century. Phillips, p. 271.
[8] Joh. XXII. Ep. iii. Non Jun. : 'Literas regias fervorem magnae devotionis et fidei, quibus erga Deum et Ecclesiam praefulgere regalis serenitas noscitur, recensentes delectabiliter et responsum perversis detractoribus laedere sinceritatem regiam circa praemissa molientibus factum, sicut Catholicum et orthodoxum decebat principem, describentes, recepimus laeta manu.' Cf. Natal. Alex. H. E. saec. 13 et 14, cap. x. a. 7, t. xv. p. 556 seq.

ESSAY XII.

WE have already seen, in the case of Gregory VII., how unjustly has been attributed to him the opinion that the Pope can
at pleasure bestow on others lands which are not his own. Let
us now examine the remaining cases brought forward in proof
of this supposed Papal doctrine.

The forged donation of the Emperor Constantine is especially pointed out as the basis of the extensive spiritual and
temporal jurisdiction of the Pope, and was, according to *Janus*
(p. 142 seq.), a Roman fabrication, in order to move the King of
the Franks to act in favour of Rome, and bestow upon her fresh
gifts.

PART I. GIFTS OF LAND MADE BY THE POPES.

§ 1, 2. Writers on Papal rights over individual and especially heathen
lands. § 3. Bull of Alexander VI. 'Inter cetera.' § 4. Slavery. § 5. In
what sense the Bull implies a gift. § 6. In any case it is no definition of faith. § 7. Pope Nicholas V. on the possessions of Mahometans.
§ 8. Clement VI. on the Canary Islands. § 9. Alexander III. on the
Saracens. § 10. Ireland given to the English king by Hadrian IV.
§ 11. Whether in fief. § 12. Possibility of obreptions and subrep-
tions, which are not inconsistent with the doctrine of Infallibility.
§ 13. Falsifications of Papal deeds severely punished. § 14. The
Papal power not based on falsifications.

§ 1.

It cannot be denied that certain writers (defenders of the
direct power of the Church in matters temporal) have claimed
for the Pope full sovereignty over all kingdoms of the world, in a
sense never put forward by the Apostolic See itself. Others again
were of opinion that the Pope might dispose at will of heathen

lands. Some have held the same opinion as to the power of the emperor; and under this idea Albrecht of Apeldern, 1198-1229, obtained for Livonia certain rights from Philip and Otto IV.[1] Even though there may have been no foundation for this opinion,[2] it is never made a subject of reproach to those who, acting upon it, asked and obtained for themselves heathen lands from the emperor. But in the Middle Ages the authorisation of the Pope was sought far more eagerly than that of the emperor; and meeting with readier acknowledgment from the whole of Christendom, it offered far better means of defence against internal and external foes. It remains to be seen whether and to what degree this opinion may have been in truth founded not merely upon isolated general expressions, but upon certain determinate acts of the Popes.

[1] Döllinger, Lehrbuch der Kirchengeschichte, ii. p. 110.

[2] Many authors agree in this view that the universal empire exercised by ancient Rome, based upon the subjugation of many nations, was justified by the good end which it served. Dante, de Monarch. 1. ii. c. vi.: 'Declaranda . . . . duo sunt, quorum unum est, quod quicunque bonum reipublicae intendit, finem juris intendit, aliud est, quod Romanus populus subjiciendo sibi orbem bonum publicum intendit.'

§ 2.

Although certain ancient writers, such as the Cardinal Bishop Henry of Ostia (died 1271), Ægidius of Rome, Alvarus Pelagius, and Augustinus Triumphus, deny to unbelievers the right of possession, yet the greater number of theologians dispute this,[1] and teach, with St. Thomas, that unbelievers retain their dominions; that the Church cannot depose and deprive of their territory unbelieving princes who have never been her subjects; those only who, having at one time accepted the Faith, have fallen away from it, may, if needful, be declared by judgment of the Church to have forfeited their dominions.[2] On the other hand, the Church claims an absolute right of preaching the Gospel in every place, thus fulfilling the duty laid on her by Christ in virtue of the power given to Him in heaven and on earth, of going out into all the world, teaching and baptising all nations (St. Matt. xxviii. 18, 19). Moreover, according to Hugo

Grotius,[3] unbelievers have no right to hinder the preaching of the Gospel and persecute preachers. In such case Christian princes may protect missionaries with the sword, forcing unbelievers to suffer them to preach freely, and at least to tolerate converts to Christianity in their land.[4]

On this point the doctrine of the Middle Ages was in agreement with the Fathers of the Church,[5] especially with Gregory the Great, who, though usually so gentle, commended the Exarch Gennadius of Africa for waging a successful war for the spread of Christianity.[6] Since the conversion of heathen nations cost the lives of many missionaries and neophytes, the protection of Christianity was one of the chief duties of Christians in authority; and a war undertaken in defence of the faithful was fully justified, especially if it put an end to severe persecution, and chastised injustice done to fellow-countrymen and co-religionists, even though the war should end in the subjugation of heathen princes.[7] This view found expression not only in the Crusades and in the wars against the heathen Prussians, but in our own days also, when the Christians were massacred in Syria, China, and Cochin-China, and when, in Abyssinia, Englishmen and Germans were imprisoned and ill-used. For causes far more trifling have Indian princes been deprived of their dominions by England; and often not only diplomatic notes, but fleets and armies, have been set in motion by the ill-treatment of a single Jew.

[1] Molina, de Justitia et Jure, t. i. tract. 2, disput. 29, n. 15, p. 60 : 'Per adventum Christi in mundum non amiserunt homines sua jura et dominia neque ab illo, quatenus homine illa acceperunt,' &c. Cf. Cajetan, 2, 2, q. 66, a. 8, resp. ad 2 ; Franc. Victoria, Relect. de Indis. P. i. ; Didacus Covarruvias, Relect. super Reg. Peccatum, P. ii. § 10 ; Barthol. Cassanus, Apologia pro Indis. Domin. ; Bannez, in S. Thom. 2, 2, q. 12, art. 10.

[2] S. Thom. 2, 2, q. 12, a. 2 : '*Infidelitas secundum se ipsam non repugnat dominio*, eo quod dominium introductum est de jure gentium, quod est *jus humanum;* distinctio autem fidelium et infidelium est *secundum jus divinum per quod non tollitur jus humanum*. Sed aliquis per infidelitatem peccans potest sententialiter jus dominii amittere, sicut etiam quandoque propter alias culpas. Ad Ecclesiam autem non pertinet punire infidelitatem in illis, *qui numquam fidem susceperunt*, secundum illud Apostoli : Quid mihi de his qui foris sunt? (1 Cor. v. 12.) Sed infideli-

tatem illorum, *qui fidem susceperunt*, potest sententialiter punire, et con-
venientur in hoc puniuntur, quod subditis fidelibus dominari non possint.
Hoc enim vergere posset in magnam fidei corruptionem, quia, ut dictum
est, *homo apostata pravo corde machinatur malum et jurgia seminat in-
tendens hominem separare a fide.* Et ideo quam cito aliquis per sententiam denunciatur excommunicatus propter apostasiam a fide, *ipso facto*
ejus subditi sunt absoluti a dominio ejus et juramento fidelitatis, quo ei
tenebantur.'

³ Hugo Grotius, de Jure Belli et Pacis, l. ii. c. xx. § 49, n. 1.
⁴ St. Thomas, l.c. q. 10, a. 8, in corp. Joh. Major, in l. ii. sent. dist. 44,
q. 2, 3. Cajetan, in 2, 2, q. 10, a. 8. Alphons. a Castro, de justa Haeret.
punitione, l. ii. c. xiv. Dominicus a Soto, in l. iv. dist. 3, q. un. art. 1.
Antonius a Corduba, Quaestion. l. i. q. 57, dub. 4. Gregorius de Valentia,
t. iii. disput. 1, q. 10, punct. 6, p. 525 seq. Cf. punct. 8, p. 542 seq.;
Solorzan. de Jure Ind. l. ii. c. xx.; Toletus, in Sum. l. iv. c. ii. n. 3;
Ledesma, t. ii. Sum. tract. 1, c. v.; Sanchez, in Sum. t. ii. l. ii. c. i. n. 4;
Suarez, de Fide, disput. 18, sect. 2, n. 8; Beccan. in Sum. t. ii. q. 4, c. xiii.
n. 12.
⁵ Bianchi, t. ii. l. vi. § 9, p. 569 seq. against the Defensio Declar.
Cleri. Gall. P. i. l. i. sect. 1, c. xv. p. 117 seq.
⁶ Greg. M. l. i. Ep. 75, al. 73, ad Gennad. Patr.: 'Quatenus Christi
nomen per subditas gentes fidei praedicatione circumquaque discurrat.'
Cf. ibid. Ep. 74, al. 72.
⁷ Covarruvias, P. xii. in Regul. Peccatum, § 10, n. 13, v. Quanto
licitum, § 11, v. Fateor plane; Bannez, O.S.D. in Sum. 2, 2, q. 10, a. 10,
v. concl. 3; L. Molina, l.c. disp. 105, 106, t. i. p. 181 seq. de Fide, q. 10,
a. 8; Azor, and others (Bianchi, l.c. n. 4, p. 574). The Protestant Grotius, l.c. n. 1, 2, teaches the same, and cites on this point the wars of the
ancient Roman emperors against the Persians. At the time of the Council
of Constance it was disputed whether conversions might be made by force
of arms (Hefele, Conc. vii. p. 241).

§ 3.

No Pope has ever taught, nor has any grave theologian ever
maintained,¹ that the Pope has authority to bestow the dominions of unbelieving princes upon believers merely at his own
discretion, and to give away at will lands not belonging to him.
The Bull ' Inter cetera' of Alexander VI. (1493),² which is specially cited in proof of this claim, was by no means intended to
partition the world, but to direct the course of Spanish ships,
to hinder disputes between Christian princes, especially between
Spain and Portugal; and, on the other hand, to secure the
spread of Christianity. In all matters concerning the acquisition of territory and voyages of discovery made by Christian
kingdoms the Pope, as their recognised arbiter, had the right

of decision ;[3] and in matters concerning the spread of Christianity in newly-discovered lands he had the same right, as Head of the Church. Just as patents are now given for inventions, and copyrights granted for compositions in literature and art, so in former days a Papal Bull and the protection of the Roman Church were found convenient means for securing fruits acquired with toil and difficulty, all other claimants unjustly desirous of taking them for themselves being held back by the censures of the Church. All this was completely in accordance with the spirit of the Middle Ages, by which Spain and Portugal were at that time still guided.[4]

[1] Bianchi, l.c. p. 582: 'Noi non ammettiamo tal potestà nel Romano Pontefice, sicchè gli sia lecito conceder quello che non è suo, nè dare ai rè Christiani i regni degli infedeli.'

[2] C. i. libri sept. i. 9, de Insulis Novi Orbis. Bullar. M. ed. Luxemb. t. i. p. 454. Raynald. a. 1493, n. 19.

[3] Hugo Grotius acknowledges this in the treatise, de Mari Libero, c. iii., published 1609. He wrote to defend the right of the Dutch to sail to certain islands in the neighbourhood of the East Indies, a right disputed by Spain and Portugal, and in so doing he answered one of the objections raised against the Bull Inter cetera. Cf. Bellarm. de Rom. Pont. l. v. c. 2 v. fin. Franc. Victoria, Relect. de Indis. p. 131, ed. 1565. Bianchi, l.c. § 9, n. 6, p. 581. Mamachi, l.c. pp. 176, 177.

[4] Civiltà Cattolica, 1865, ser. vi. vol. i. p. 662 seq.

§ 4.

The Bull of Alexander VI. is by no means answerable for the tyranny to which the natives of America were subjected by the Spaniards—a tyranny well-nigh outdone indeed by that exercised ' in the interests of civilisation' by the English settlers, even in our own day, upon the North American Indians and Australian natives, now fast dying out.[1] The Church had power to mitigate and lessen slavery, but she could not put an end to it by a single blow.[2] The religious orders, with perfect self-devotion, did all in their power to put down abuses.[3] Councils[4] and Popes[5] had the freedom of the natives greatly at heart. The violence of the conquerors was neither caused nor favoured by the Bull of Alexander VI., which was directed to the conversion,[6] and therefore to the true welfare, of the natives.

[1] Cf. extract from observations of Rev. W. Schmidt, June 1842, Byrne, Emigrant's Guide, p. 70; R. Salvaldo, O.S.B. Memorie Storiche dell' Australia, Roma, 1851.·

[2] Margraf, Kirche und Sklaverei seit der Entdeckung Amerika's, Tübingen, 1865, p. 5 seq. Civiltà Cattolica, 1865.

[3] Margraf, l.c. p. 57.

[4] Councils of Mexico, 1545 and 1585; of Lima, 1583 and 1585. Margraf, pp. 107 seq. 116 seq. 120.

[5] Pius V. 7 and 8 Oct. 1567, to the Archbishop and the Viceroy of Mexico (Raynald. h.a.). Clement VIII. for Peru (Solorzano, Polit. Ind. ii. 1, n. 12). Urban VIII. Constit. Commissum, April 22, 1639. Benedict XIV. Constit. Immensae, Dec. 28, 1741. Gregory XVI. Constit. In supremo, Dec. 3, 1839. Cf. Lämmer, im Archiv. f. Kath. Kirchenrecht, 1864, vol. xii. p. 177 seq.

[6] The first sentence of the Bull shows this, in which it is set down as specially pleasing to God, and most desired by the Pope: 'Ut fides Catholica et Christiana religio nostris praesertim temporibus exaltetur, ubilibet amplietur et dilatetur,' &c.

§ 5.

The express mention in the Bull of the word 'gift' (donamus) has given special offence. The Pope then, it is said, gave what did not belong to him, and thus set at naught the independence and freedom of the American Indians.[1] Even presuming it to have been a mere donation, it would be easy to reply that the transaction was far better than the treaties of modern States. ' It is asked,' writes Ferdinand Walter,[2] ' what right the Pope had to dispose of foreign countries; but, judged by private law, it is equally unsatisfactory whether this is done by the Pope, or, according to the new international law, by a European treaty. The Pope gave that right, as is proved by the Bull in question, that the natives might by mildness and gentleness be converted to Christ. But in modern treaties of this sort little is said in the interests of the conquered people; there can be no doubt therefore on which side lies the gain for humanity.' To this it might be added, that a Papal constitution in that day had as much force as a European treaty in our own, and even more. It may be observed further: (1) That in treaties and public documents doubtful expressions are to be understood according to reason, justice, and honour. It would have been unreasonable and foolish for the Pope to give away that which was not his own; it would have been unjust and dishonourable

to deprive whole nations of their freedom, even though they
were unbelievers ; moreover, it would have been contrary to the
teaching of mediæval theology. Since, then, the Pope was entitled neither by his temporal nor by his spiritual power to
make any such unlimited donation, the word *donamus* must be
understood in the limited sense of the law then recognised ; it
is to be applied only to coast-stations and settlements acquired
by just title, and to other territory in the islands then in question ; and in this sense it was understood by those living at the
time—Cajetan, Dominicus Soto, and also by later and even by
Spanish theologians.[3] (2) In the year 1497, King Emanuel of
Portugal sought from the same Pope Alexander VI. a like grant
of West Africa. The Pope made use of the same formula, *donamus*, but with the condition of the voluntary subjection of the inhabitants ;[4] which condition, since it was implied in the law itself,
was to be understood equally with other legal principles, even
though not expressed ; and thus a donation was indeed expressed
as against all other European princes,[5] but not as against the
natives of the New World. Monarchs receiving this grant had
a right of priority in the territory of which they were the dis-
coverers. (3) The Pope does indeed say that the land in question
is bestowed as a free gift, and from the fulness of his apostolic
power ; but the choice of Alexander as arbiter was founded in
the first place on the authority possessed by him as Pope, and
on the reverence felt by Catholic sovereigns for his dignity as
Head of the Church ; and hence he was authorised to give his
decision not only with perfect freedom and full knowledge of
the case, but, moreover, in virtue of the apostolic power, which
had moved even kings to commit to him the decision in a matter
so weighty. So little did he arrogate to himself absolute sovereignty over these lands, that he expressly declared in his
Bull his desire to be in no way prejudicial to Christian princes
who, before the Christmas of the preceding year, 1492, had
taken possession of those islands and territories.[6] He thus
made it understood that the one single aim of his decree was
the prevention of strife between the Kings of Spain and Portugal, who had of their free will chosen him as arbiter ; and that

he in no way made himself judge between them and other sovereigns, by whom his intervention had neither been asked nor
accepted. Moreover, the circumstance that Alexander VI. addressed his decree not to the whole Church, nor even to all
princes, but to Ferdinand and Isabella alone, proves he had no
desire to dispose of the lands in question as absolute lord, but
as an arbiter, who confirmed his sentence with his authority as
Vicar of Christ, and with the usual forms ; and in this he acted
precisely according to the intentions of the Spanish sovereigns.[7]
(4) When Paul III.,[8] in two Briefs, took under his protection
the freedom of the American natives, he had not the least
thought of derogating from the Bull of Alexander VI., which
he understood precisely in the sense given above. Moreover,
the Spanish laws go upon the supposition of the freedom of the
Indians.[9] It is to be remembered, that the proclamations made
by the Conquistadores to the natives of the discovered and conquered lands, telling them of the universal supremacy of the
Pope, and the duty of submission to the kings sent out by him,
did not proceed from the Pope, but were fabricated by officials
and adventurers.

[1] Robertson's History of America, vol. ii. Büschung, Erdbeschreibung,
vol. xxxi. Marmontel, Les Incas, Préf. p. xxviii. seq.; and others.
[2] Lehrbuch des Kirchenrechts, § 342, p. 607, note 8, 11th ed.
[3] Suarez, disput. 18, de Fide, sect. 1, n. 7. Lugo, disp. 13, de Fide,
n. 102. Salmanticenses, tract. 21, de Decalogo, P. ii. n. 9. Conink,
disput. 18, de Fide, n. 160. Morelli, in Ord. Apost.: 'Quia concessio,
quantumvis ampla et absoluta sit verbo, restricta debet intelligi *ad terminos juris et aequi.*' The general rules for privileges apply here, on
which vide Schmalzgrueber, in l. v. Decret. tit. 23, § 4, specially n. 128, 129.
[4] Raynald. a. 1497, n. 33 : 'De civitatibus, castris, locis . . . . infidelium, quae tibi ditionique tuae subjici et quae te in dominum cognoscere
seu tributum solvere *velle* contigerit . . . . districtius inhibentes *quibuscunque regibus*, quibus jus quaesitum non foret, ne se contra (illos) se tibi
subjicere *volentes* quovis modo opponere audeant.'
[5] But rights already gained by them were respected ; the Bull applied
only to 'terras quae sub actuali dominio temporali aliquorum domino-
rum Christianorum non essent.'
[6] Decernentes nihilominus, per hujusmodi donationem, concessionem
et assignationem nostram nulli Christiano principi, qui actualiter praefatas
insulas et terras firmas possederit, usque ad dictum diem Nativitatis
D.N.J.C., jus quaesitum sublatum intelligi posse aut auferri debere.
[7] Gosselin, ii. p. 272 seq.

[8] Pastorale officium, May 23; Veritas ipsa, June 2, 1537.
[9] Recopilacion de leyes de los regnos de las Indias, 1. iii. tit. de la Guerra, 1. iv. tit. 7; 1. i. tit. 4, 1. viii. (the two last laws of Charles V.).

§ 6.

But even presuming it to have been the opinion of Alexander VI. that the Pope may dispose of heathen lands for the sake of their conversion, or even that unbelievers are wholly incapable of lawfully possessing dominions, still this his own personal opinion, expressed in granting a privilege to one dynasty, would be in no way binding, and should any one consider this an error on the part of the Pope,[1] he would be guilty of no offence against the dogma of Papal Infallibility.[2] A merely temporal donation cannot be considered as a definition of doctrine, and a practical enactment by the Pope differs widely from a binding expression of his supreme teaching office in matters of revelation.[3]

[1] Gregory of Valentia is not far from this when he says, l.c. punct. 7, p. 540, ad 2: 'Alexander VI. (si in eo facto particulari, ad reges illos tantum et ad illas insulas pertinente non erravit) solum concessit illis regibus jus quoddam superintendentiae et patrocinii in infideles illos, postquam debito modo essent ad fidem conversi. Nec enim potuit infideles illos dominio suo privare propterea solum, quod essent infideles.'
[2] Card. du Perron. Repl. 1. i. c. xci. p. 545.
[3] Fessler, p. 50.

§ 7.

Pope Nicholas V. is reproached[1] with having in 1454 empowered King Alphonsus V. of Portugal to enslave foreign nations merely because they were not Catholic, and to take for himself the possessions of all the Mahometans and heathens of West Africa,[2] which grant was confirmed by Calixtus III. in 1456 and Sixtus IV. in 1481.[3] In this case also it was presupposed that the limits of the principles of justice then universally acknowledged were to be observed. The intention was to ward off the attacks of the enemies of Christendom (Portugal had been many times forced to go to war), to protect converted negroes, to retain lands lawfully won, and to afford means for the free preaching of the Gospel. The Pope thus confirmed the prohibition of Alphonsus V., by which no one might sail to those islands and coasts except with Portuguese ships and sailors, after payment of a fixed tribute and permission received from the king; and this was done that an undertaking begun with just reason and so favourable to civilisation might not be injured, and that disputes and wars might be prevented. The legally-established titles by which slavery was justified could neither be changed nor abolished by the Popes; they were forced to be content with condemning the deeds of violence by which, contrary to justice, negroes and other barbarians were deprived of their freedom; they could not forbid conquests made in wars against Mahometan and other infidel princes, and could only strive to make them serve the interests of civilisation and of Christianity.

[1] Defensio Decl. Cleri. Gall. l. i. sect. 1, c. xiv. p. 116. Schulte, i. p. 36 seq.
[2] Const. Romanus Pontifex, Jan. 9, 1454 (Bull. Rom. iii. iii. p. 70); Const. Nuper. (Raynald. a. 1454, n. 8 seq.).
[3] Calixt. III. Const. Inter cetera, 1456; Sixt. IV. Const. Aeterni Regis, 1481. Cf. Cyr. Morelli, Fasti Novi Orbis, p. 58.

§ 8.

In the year 1344, Luis de la Cerda had caused the sovereignty of the newly-discovered Canary and other islands to be delivered over to him by Pope Clement VI.,[1] who gave them on condition that no other Christian princes had won for themselves a special right over these islands.[2] The King of Portugal and Alphonsus of Castile did make good such a claim, but relinquished it out of love of the Apostolic See.[3] This case may possibly have been influenced by the fact that there had before been question of various islands bestowed upon the Roman Church by Constantine the Great, and also of the necessity of a Papal authorisation for the spread of Christianity, and for any addition to the number of Christian princes; moreover, the kings of the Pyrennean peninsula had long before obtained from the Papal See an authorisation for the conquest of lands occupied by unbelievers.

[1] Raynald. a. 1344, n. 39 seq.   Döllinger, Lehrbuch, ii. p. 271.

[2] Raynald. l.c. n. 39: 'Omnes praedictas insulas et earum quamlibet, *dummodo in eis non sit alicui Christiano specialiter jus quaesitum*, in omnibus juribus ac pertinentiis suis .... in feudum perpetuum .... concedimus et donamus teque praedicto feudo per sceptrum aureum praesentialiter investimus.'

[3] Ib. n. 47 seq. 50.

§ 9.

Alexander III. in 1179 confirmed to Alphonsus of Portugal, together with kingly rights, all those places he might take from the hands of the Saracens, provided no claim could be laid to them by the neighbouring Christian princes.[1]   Applications of the same kind had been already made to the Roman See under Gregory VII., and had been granted by him.[2]   Great security was thus gained for the newly-won territory, and at the same time all question as to the lawfulness of the occupation was set at rest, as it might have been thought that the Moors, who had ruled the southern half of the Peninsula since 712, could not merely by the natural law be expelled.   Public law had long recognised the widest distinction between Jews and Saracens.   Jews showed themselves willing to serve and to obey; Saracens persecuted Christians in all ways and drove them out of their own territories;[3] to live at peace with them was then impossible, and it was especially necessary and allowable to pursue the Moorish pirates to the utmost.[4]   The Mahometans occupied territory belonging to Christians which had never been legally surrendered to them; they misused and injured in every way those professsing Christianity, and not only blasphemed their faith, but went all lengths in fighting against it.

[1] 'Omnia loca, quae de Saracenorum manibus eripuerit, in quibus jura sibi non possint Christiani principes circumpositi vindicare.' Sousa, Provas da Historia Genealogica da Casa real Portugueza, Lisboa, 1739, i. 7. Brandão, Monarchia Lusitana, Lisboa, 1690, iii. 295. Jaffé, Reg. n. 8725, p. 786.

[2] See Essay viii. (on Gregory VII.) part ii. § 5.

[3] Can. 2, Dispar. c. xxiii. q. 8 (Alex. II.); also Ivo, P. x. c. lxx.; Pann. viii. 20.

[4] Cf. can. 12, Praeterea, c. et q. cit. (Joh. VIII.).

§ 10.

Special stress is laid on the claim of Pope Hadrian IV. to all islands converted to Christianity as possessions of the Roman Church; and in particular on his gift of Ireland to the King of England on condition of a yearly tribute.[1] King Henry II. had expressed to the Pope his desire to extend the kingdom of Christ and to civilise barbarous nations,[2] and had made known to him especially his resolution to bring the inhabitants of Ireland within the pale of the law. In many parts of this country Christianity was well-nigh exterminated, and murder, debauchery, and complete lawlessness reigned.[3] According to the English chronicles, the bishops of Ireland assented to this plan of Henry's.[4] Hadrian IV. merely gave his consent that Henry should land in the island, that the people should receive him with respect and acknowledge him as their lord.[5] The island, once subjected to the kingdom of Christ, was to be guarded by the Church; it was the property of St. Peter, as the king himself acknowledged to the Pope;[6] but no mention was made of a temporal right or of a real donation. The yearly tribute offered by Henry and accepted by the Pope is no proof of temporal possession; England herself paid such a tribute without having up to that time acknowledged the Pope as her temporal sovereign.

[1] Bossuet, Defensio Decl. Cleri. Gall. t. i. l. i. sect. 1, c. xiv. p. 116; l. iii. c. xviii. fin. p. 313. Schulte, i. p. 38, n. 5.

[2] This appears from the letters of the Pope to the king. Hadrian, Ep. ad Heuric. II. (Mansi, xxi. 788; Jaffé, n. 6908): ' Ad dilataudum Ecclesiae terminos ac declarandum indoctis et rudibus populis Christianae fidei veritatem et vitiorum plantaria de agro Dominico exstirpanda sicut Catholicus princeps intendis et ad id convenientius exsequendum consilium Apostolicae Sedis exigis et favorem.'

[3] The island was still in a most lawless condition under Alexander III., successor to Hadrian IV.; vide Alex. III. Ep. 1002 (Migne, t. cc. p. 883): ' Quae (sens Hibernica) divino timore post posito tamquam effrenis passim per abrupta deviat vitiorum et Christianae fidei religionem abjicit et virtutis, et se interimit mutua caede. . . . Novercas suas publice introducunt et ex eis non erubescunt filios procreare; frater uxore fratris, eo vivente, abutitur: unus duabus se sororibus concubinis immiscet et plerique illorum, matre relicta, filias introducunt,' &c.

[4] Thomassin, P. iii. l. i. c. xxxii. n. 4, 5, fin.: ' Archiepiscoporum et episcoporum Hiberniae consensum auctor est Rogerius Pontifici ostensum

fuisse.'   Alexander III. subsequently took for granted the voluntary subjection and allegiance of the Irish princes to Henry, which secured peace
and order in the island.   Alex. III. Ep. 1003, p. 884 seq.: ' Ubi communi
fama et certa relatione primum nobis innotuit, quod vos . . . . regem Angliae
illustrem in vestrum regem et dominum suscepistis et ei fidelitatem jurastis,
tanto ampliorem in corde laetitiam concepimus, quanto per ejusdem regis
potentiam in terra vestra cooperante Domino major pax erit atque tranquillitas et gens Hibernica, quae per enormitatem et spurcitiam vitiorum
adeo videbatur longius recessisse, divino cultu propensius informabitur et
melior Christianae fidei suscipiet disciplinam. . . . Unde super eo, quod
tam potenti et magnifico regi . . . . vos *voluntate libera* subdidistis, provi-
dentiam vestram digna laudis commendatione prosequimur, cum exinde
vobis, Ecclesiae et toti populo illius terrae utilitas speretur non modica
proventura.'

    [5] Hadr. IV. l.c.: ' Nos itaque pium et laudabile desiderium tuum cum
favore congruo prosequentes et petitioni tuae benignum impendentes assensum, gratum et acceptum habemus, ut pro dilatandis Ecclesiae terminis,
pro vitiorum restringendo decursu, pro corrigendis moribus et virtutibus
inferendis, pro Christianae religionis augmento insulam illam ingrediaris et
quod ad honorem Dei et salutem illius terrae populus honorifice te recipiat
et sicut Dominum veneretur, jure nimirum ecclesiastico salvo, illibato et
integro permanente et salva B. Petro et SS. Rom. Ecclesiae de singulis
domibus unius denarii pensione.'

    [6] Ibid.: ' Sane Hiberniam et omnes insulas, quibus sol justitiae Christus
illuxit, et quae documenta fidei Christianae ceperunt, ad jus B. Petri et
SS. Rom. Ecclesiae (quod nobilitas tua recognoscit) non est dubium pertinere.'   Many learned writers say that, according to the words of the Pope,
Ireland did not belong to St. Peter as a property to a master, but as a
flock to a shepherd.   Thomassin, l.c. n. 4, speaking of Hadrian's words
quoted above, says: ' Quod de filiali subjectione et religiosa obedientia intelligi nil prohibet. . . . Cum non facile justitiae color et species affingatur
iis bellis, quae gentibus quietis . . . . vixque cognitis inferuntur, suadet
ipsa ratio et sapientia, ut ea religionis vertici et parenti omnium fidelium
ante approbentur, a quo re perpensa illud pronuncietur, illud reapse curetur,
ut ne ambitione serviant ejusmodi expeditiones, sed pietati dilatandae et
summi verique Dei cultui ac lumini barbaris nationibus inferendo.'   Also
Bianchi, t. ii. l. v. § 13, n. 10, pp. 350-353; Gosselin, t. ii. c. iii. a. 1, § 2,
p. 246 seq.

§ 11.

It may still be objected that this explanation is scarcely
satisfactory, since John of Salisbury, at whose request Hadrian
IV. issued his decree, bases the Papal constitution upon the
donation of Constantine, and relates how the Pope sent the king
through him a gold ring with a splendid emerald, as a sign
of investiture.[1]   It may well be said in reply that Innocent III.
sent a precious ring to King Richard I. of England,[2] when there

was no question of feudal relations between them ; that John of
Salisbury gave a reason for the investiture which accorded with
the views of the day and the intention of the king, but of which
the Pope never said a word ; and that the English writer may
easily have gone beyond the intention of the Pope. Moreover,
it is extremely probable that Henry II. may have desired from
the Pope an outward sign which would right him in the eyes of
the bishops and chiefs of Ireland, and may even have wished to
receive the land in fief from the Roman Church. When afterwards, in 1172, Alexander III. admonished the king to restore
order and Christianity, to root out crime, and to improve the
condition of the island, he declared that the Roman Church
had rights in the island distinct from those which were hers in
the great countries on the Continent ; and he demanded that
where the Church possessed no privileges, the king should
bestow such upon her.[3]

[1] Joh. Saresb. Metalogr. l. iv. c. xlii. p. 945 : 'Ad preces meas illustri
regi Anglorum Henrico II. concessit et dedit Hiberniam jure haereditario
possidendam, sicut literae ipsius testantur in hodiernum diem. Nam omnes
insulae de jure antiquo ex donatione Constantini, qui eam fundavit et
dotavit, dicuntur ad Romanam Ecclesiam pertinere. Annulum quoque
per me transmisit aureum smaragdo optimo decoratum, quo fieret investi-
tura juris in gerenda Hibernia.'
[2] Innoc. III. l. x. Ep. 218 ; Reg. Imp. Ep. 5, p. 1001.
[3] Alex. III. Ep. 1002, p. 884 : ' Et quia, sicut *novit* tuae magnitudinis
excellentia, *Rom. Ecclesia aliud habet jus in insula, quam in terra
magna et continua*, nos eam de tuae devotionis fervore spem fiduciamque
tenentes, quod jura ipsius Ecclesiae non solum servare velis, sed etiam
ampliare, et *ubi nullum jus habet, id debes sibi conferre*, magnificentiam
tuam rogamus et sollicite commonemus, ut in praescripta terra jura B.
Petri studeas sollicite conservare, et si etiam ibi non habet, tua magnitudo
eidem Ecclesiae jura *constituat et assignet*, ita quod exinde regiae celsitu-
dine gratias debeamus exsolvere copiosas et tu primitias tuae gloriae et
triumphi Deo videaris offerre.—Dat. Tuscul. xii. Kal. Oct. (1172).'

§ 12.

Hadrian IV., himself an Englishman, did not foresee the
abuses to ensue from the English rule, and he cannot be held
responsible for them. His rescript, which was the cause of
much perplexity to the Irish in later times,[1] may have been obtained on the English side by *obreption* (giving a false reason)

and by *subreption* (suppressing the truth).   In spite of the resistance of the Irish, no steps seem to have been taken formally
to rescind the rescript.[2]

The supposition of obreption and subreption is in fact still
admissible, and the dogma of the infallibility of the doctrinal
definitions of the Pope by no means binds us to consider every
Papal publication without distinction as a rule of faith and
morals.   The right of the Pope to dispose at will of foreign
lands, whether Christian or infidel, has never been in this sense
defined.   It is still possible that Papal Briefs may be obtained by
corrupt and unjust officials; that information may be falsified,
and abuses tolerated; all this in no way affects the article of
faith, which teaches that the holder of the supreme teaching
office, by the supernatural assistance of God, will never be suffered
to propose to the acceptance of the faithful in a binding form
error in the place of religious truth.   Above all things it is
necessary in the Church to distinguish between the divine element and the human element.   In spite of the sins of men,
Catholic Christendom persevering in strict obedience to its
Head will never be led away from the true faith or into error;
for this we have the Word of God.   A Council, in spite of the
human failings of its members, has the assistance of God, though
only as regards the actual definition; and in like manner all the
faults of the Popes and their surroundings do not set aside the
assistance promised and granted to the successor of St. Peter,
not for his own benefit, but for the benefit of the Church, and
to preserve the purity of the Faith.

---

[1] Döllinger, Papstfabeln, p. 80, note, quotes White, Lynch, Lanigan,
and MacGeoghegan.

[2] Innoc. III. l. vi. Ep. 75 (Migne, ccxv. pp. 70-71): ‘Quia per statuta
canonica sententia Sedis Apostolicae non negatur in melius posse commu-
tari, cum aut surreptum aliquid fuerit, aut ipsa pro consideratione temporum et aetatum seu necessitatum gravium aliquid dispensatorie ordinare
decrevit, et secundum jura civilia principes contra res judicatas in audi-
torio suo examinari restitutionem in integrum permiserunt.’   Cf. c. xx. de
Rescript. i. 3; c. v. de J.J. Rest. i. 41.   Peter the Venerable, l. i. Ep.
34 (Migne, clxxxix. p. 170), writes to Cardinal Aimericus as to a Papal order
burdensome to the monastery of Clugny: ‘Laborate, obsecro, ut in melius
sententia commutetur quia mirum sapientibus videri non debet, si homini
tantis totius mundi curis in diversa distracto quilibet sua quaerens *subri-*

pere potuit, sed valde mirum videbitur, si postquam perniciosum cognoverit, tantus pastor ovibus non providerit.' Cf. S. Bern. Ep. 46, ad Honor. II. p. 153 ; Ep. 231, c. iii. ad Card. Episc. p. 419 ; Ep. 268, ad Eugen. III. p. 472.

§ 13.

Many complaints have been made as to the falsification of Papal Bulls and Briefs. Long ago Martin I. had punished the Archbishop Paul of Thessalonica for this offence,[1] and the eighth Council renewed the statute published in 649, against the falsifications of Photius ;[2] from the time of the Carolingians they became more frequent,[3] and were indeed carried on as a business.[4] The Popes, especially Innocent III., upon whom a deception had been attempted, enforced severe penalties for falsification.[5] The Synod of Trêves in 1227 treated the falsification of Apostolic Briefs as a reserved case to the Pope,[6] and the *Bulla Coenae* afterwards did the same.[7] Many documents were falsified to the prejudice of the Apostolic See, especially at the time of the dispute on investiture and the combats between the Church and civil rulers ;[8] nor where they always recognised at once in their true colours. Are we to believe that the Popes, who for seven centuries took such strong measures against falsifications, themselves made use of them to extend and exalt their power? Everything considered, is this probable, or even credible?

[1] Mansi, x. 834 seq. 847 seq.

[2] Can. 6, Mansi, xvi. pp. 163, 164, 402.

[3] Caroli, Antichità Italiche, v. 61. Hurter, Innoc. III. vol. i. p. 108. For examples, vide Joh. Saresb. Ep. 129 ; cf. Ep. 89 ; Phillips, Kirchenrecht, iii. § 154, pp. 648-650 ; Petrus Bles. Ep. 53, p. 92, ed. Mog. 1600 ; cap. Super eo, 2, de Crimini Falsi, v. 20 ; cap. Ad audientiam, 3, h.t.

[4] Raumer, Gesch. der Hohenstaufen, vi. p. 190. Neander, Kirchengeschichte, ii. p. 442 seq. 3d ed.

[5] Gesta Innoc. III. n. 42, p. lxxxv. Hurter, l.c. p. 116 seq. Martene, Coll. Amplissima, i. 1031. C. Dura saepe, 4, h.t. C. Licet ad regimen, 5, h.t. C. Quam gravi, 6, h.t. C. Ad falsariorum, 7, h.t. Cf. Schmalzgrueber, in l. v. tit. 20. Many of the Pope's letters are on this subject : vide l. i. Ep. 235, ad Aep. Rhem. p. 202 ; l. i. Ep. 262, 349, pp. 221, 322, 324 ; l. ii. Ep. 29, p. 359 ; Supplem. Ep. 234 (Migne, ccxvii. p. 273 seq), l. xv. Ep. 223, p. 755 seq.

[6] Conc. Trevir. 1227, c. 4. Mansi, xxiii. p. 28. Hefele, v. p. 842.

[7] Cap. iv. h.t.; v. 9, in Libr. Sept. Many of the Popes took strong

measures against this crime : vide Bzovius, Ann. Eccl. a. 1490; Nota in Natal. Alex. H. E. saec. 15 et 16, c. i. a. 10, t. xvii. p. 49, ed. Bing. For the question, cf. Hausmann, Geschichte der Päpstlichen Reservatfälle, p. 136 seq.

⁸ Vide Anti-Janus, p. 121, especially n. 118, 119. To these belongs the first French Pragmatic Sanction ascribed to Louis IX., of which Rigant. in Reg. Cancell. i. § 1, n. 15, says : 'Apud cordatiores Gallos suspecta et spuria est;' it has been denounced as spurious by Thomassy, Lenormant, Affré, and others (Ami de la Religion, 5 Sept. 1854, p. 562). Its spuriousness has been proved by Rösen (Die Pragmatische Sanction, Münster, 1854), and by Ch. Gérin (Les Deux Pragmatiques Sanctions, 2d edit. Paris, 1869).

§ 14.

We have seen that the great political power wielded by the Popes in the Middle Ages came into being naturally from the mutual working of the spiritual and temporal law, and was based upon principles which had been long in existence. It had long been exercised before any one troubled himself to examine into its origin and make reflections upon it, for it was only from the middle of the twelfth century that this was done to any great extent. No one believed, and no one could have believed, that the extensive powers of the Pope had been obtained by a formal system of deceit, of falsification, and of usurpation, as has since been imagined by the centuriators of Magdeburg and other Protestants, in the last century by Febronius, and in our own day by *Janus.* It was reserved for the modern spirit to devise this aburdity,[1] and even to attempt to prove that falsifications existed before and after Pseudo-Isidore, from Gratian up to the Dominicans, and from them on to the Jesuits. In the chapter of *Anti-Janus* which treats of these falsifications[2] I have examined these hypotheses, which are all more or less untenable ; on very few points has any refutation of my statements[3] been attempted, and these with but poor success. The Pseudo-Isidore question has been discussed by numerous writers,[4] who have come to conclusions very different from those of *Janus.* Of still less weight is the allegation that St. Thomas Aquinas suffered himself to be taken in by spurious editions of the Fathers, in his doctrine of the Papal authority and teaching power.[5] In general the proofs brought forward have been

very weak. When an alteration in a text might most easily
have arisen from bad handwriting or from an error, it has
been at once set down to intentional deceit, while no pains
have been taken to prove that any falsification was intended.[6]
When the possibility of such an intention was the utmost
that could be conceded, its existence in fact has been without further inquiry admitted and presumed. This has indeed been carried so far, that, contrary to all rules of justice,
ancient authors, who have quoted from still earlier writers texts
not perfectly correct, have been for this reason accused of general
falsification, without its being thought necessary to bring forward any convincing proof; and while the proof of mere possibility is sufficient for the accusers, they will not admit that
of an exactly contrary possibility in favour of the accused.[7]

[1] J. Shepherd (The History of the Church of Rome to the End of the
Episc. of Damasus, London, 1851) maintained that even before 500 a large
number of documental proofs, *e.g.* Cyprian's letters, were forged as a foundation of the Roman supremacy; this is declared even by Guericke, Kirchengeschichte, i. p. 259, n. 1, 9th ed., to be a monstrous assumption.

[2] Eng. trans. ch. viii.

[3] Cf. also the Laacher Stimmen on the Ecumenical Council, i. Part vii.;
Das Concil and der Neu-Jansenismus, p. 27 seq.

[4] All the writings on canon law, from Ballerini down to Möhler, Walter,
Schulte, Richter, Phillips, and Hinschius, supply proof of this.

[5] On this assertion, cf. Anti-Janus, p. 116; my criticism of Dr. Döllinger's declaration, pp. 31, 32; and Dr. Raich, Die Auflehnung Döllinger's
Gegen die Kirche, Mainz, 1871, p. 61 seq. The Dominicans, R. Bianchi
and Alex. Reali, as also Dr. Uccelli, have written in Italian against it. Dr.
Uccelli found in the Vatican library the codex used by St. Thomas. Its
publication will be thorough proof of the absurdity of the supposition of
intentional falsification.

[6] Gratian's c. vi. d. 19 is termed a gross falsification by Janus, p. 120,
the Correctores Romani having before Janus' time added the true text of
St. Augustine, concerning whom he says nothing. Melchior Canus, de
loc. Theol. l. v. c. v. § Dicamus igitur, seq. 168, says on this point: ' Ubi
Gratianus [or still more his predecessors Anselm and Gregory] Augustini
sententiam non est assecutus. Cui errori causam fortasse praebuit codex
quispiam depravatus. . . . Id quod ante nos . . . . alii viri diligentissimi
deprehenderunt.' An intentional falsification is still less admissible in the
case of Gratian, because early and later authorities stand equally high
with him; the text of Pope Nicholas I., cited can. 1, is quite sufficient for
him, and other passages prove the same; *e.g.* Jaffé, n. 3479, pp. 398,
898, ex Ivonis Decret. v. c. xxxi. Mansi, xix. 979: ' Alex. II. Philippo
regi Francorum scribit, Sedis Apostolicae decreta eodem loco cum canoni-

bus habenda esse.' Cardinal Deusdedit is accused by Janus, p. 119, of falsifying the words of Pope Agatho, which falsification according to others was adopted also by Gratian, c. ii. d. 19 ; but no proof is offered that these are not a distinct utterance independent from the text of the Roman Synod, and they were in truth so understood by Jaffé, p. 167, n. 1629.

⁷ A single quotation of a spurious passage is made ground for vehement accusations ; but such accusations pass unnoticed in persons who agree with the accusers ; *e.g.* Professor Schulte, who cites the false letter of the Council of Nicea to Pope Sylvester (iii. p. 28), and even gives it a first place among his proofs. On the letter, vide Hefele, Conc. i. p. 421 seq.

PART II. THE DONATION OF CONSTANTINE.

§ 1. In what it consisted.   § 2, 3. The question as to the time and place of its origin.   § 4. Its extension in the eleventh and twelfth centuries. § 5. Seldom used by the Popes.   § 6. Its genuineness disputed since the fifteenth century.   § 7. Its insufficiency as an explanation of the Papal power.

§ 1.

Many searching inquiries have been made into this document in latter times, and it has been much used against the Church ;[1] but the Roman See has never thought its rights were menaced by the result of these inquiries, nor looked on this apocryphal document as its 'strongest bulwark,' and the 'foundation of the system of universal sovereignty exercised by the Popes for a thousand years.'[2]

The document, which exists in various Latin and Greek ver-sions,[3] grants to the Pope and the Roman clergy : (1) certain marks and insignia of honour ; to the Pope, the tiara, the lorum, and imperial robes ; to the clergy, the dress of the highest imperial officials, the right of riding on horses with white trappings, together with the privileges of the imperial senate, —on these points the author enters more into detail, having apparently such things most at heart ;[4] (2) the ecclesiastical supremacy of the Pope above other patriarchs, and above all other Churches, and his office of judge in questions of faith and worship ; (3) temporal sovereignty over Rome and the provinces, towns, and castles of all Italy, or the western regions. In this last part the different versions vary much.

¹ Döllinger, Die Papstfabeln des Mittelalters, München, 1863, p. 61 seq.

² Schulte, p. 68.
³ Biener. de Collect. Canonum. Eccl. gr. 1827, pp. 72, 79. Döllinger, l.c. p. 65.
⁴ Döllinger, p. 72.

§ 2.

Respecting the time and place in which this document had its origin, and respecting its author, as many hypotheses have been made, as in the case of the Pseudo-Isidore Decretals, with which it also has found a place.

The fact, so important in its bearing on later times, that the first Christian emperor, instead of choosing Rome as his seat, made a new dwelling for himself on the Bosphorous, so that in the old capital of the world the splendour of the Pontificate might be developed more fully, unhindered by the majesty of the emperor, gave rise to the renowned tales and legends of Constantine, which took fantastic shapes, and later gave rise to the documents in their present shape.

The first trace of the gift has been thought to have been found in a letter of Pope Hadrian I. in 777. But the likeness between an expression in this letter and the spurious document is far from justifying the conclusion that Hadrian made use of the document; its composer may quite as well have adopted phrases out of the letter of Hadrian. Hadrian merely says that Constantine exalted the Roman Church, and invested her with rights in Italy ;[1] it cannot in fact well be doubted that from times as early as these she was in possession of considerable revenues drawn from landed possessions, and even of temporal power.[2] Hadrian's words prove that he knew nothing of the document. He would not most surely have made appeal, both before the Frankish and Greek courts, to isolated and comparatively insignificant donations, had he had by him so extensive a deed of gift from the most renowned of emperors, devised expressly in order to claim from these courts for the Roman Church larger possessions in land. He would have contradicted himself had he, in one and the same Brief, attributed to himself on the one hand unlimited power over all Italy by reason of the supposed donation of Constantine, and had then spoken only of patrimonies in certain regions as gifts from various emperors and other Christians.[3]

Neither did Hadrian's immediate successors know of this document. The hypotheses by which it is said to have been devised in 767 under Paul I.,[4] or perhaps even in 752,[5] have no real foundation. The prudent Popes of that time, so weak in political and military matters as to be forced almost continually to claim the aid of the Frankish kings, could never have entertained the adventurous project of obtaining for their See a dominion over all Italy; mention is everywhere made of certain specified territories, never of North Italy or Lombardy. After 774 there was no longer any cause for the deception,[6] and before 752 it could have had no success,[7] and the same may be said also of the intermediate space of time.[8]

[1] Cod. Carolin. Ep. 59 (al. 49), Cenni, Mon. Dom. Pont. i. 305 : ' Sicut temporibus B. Sylvestri Rom. Pontificis a.s. rec. piissimo Constantino magno imp. per ejus largitatem S. Dei Cath. et Apost. Romana Ecclesia elevata atque exaltata est, et *potestatem in his Hesperiae partibus* largiri dignatus est, ita et in his vestris felicissimis temporibus atque nostris S. Dei Ecclesia, i.e. B. Petri Apostoli germinet atque exultet et amplius atque amplius exaltata permaneat.' The expression *hae partes Hesperiae* is not identical with the *occidentalium* regionum *provinciae,* and *potestatem* is not necessarily to be translated by ' *the* power;' moreover, Hadrian does not say, ' urbem Romam et omnes totius Italiae et occidentalium regionum provincias, loca, et civitates,' which are the words of the document according to Mansi, ii. 603 seq. Floss (Die Papstwahl unter den Ottonen, Urk. pp. 9-23) gives the facsimile of the text of the Donatio.

[2] Zaccaria, Dissert. de Rebus ad Hist. et Antiqu. Eccl. pertinentibus, Fulgin. 1781, t. ii. p. 75 seq. dissert. 10.   Gosselin, vol. i. pp. 230 seq. 242 seq.; ii. p. 421.

[3] Cf. Gosselin, ii. pp. 420, 421 ; Civiltà Cattolica, May 7, 1864, ser. v. vol. x. p. 305 seq. ; Chilianeum, vol. v. p. 63 seq. Hadrian's words l.c. are : ' Sed et cuncta alia, quae *per diversos imperatores, patricios etiam et alios Deum timentes* pro eorum animae mercede et venia delictorum *in partibus Tusciae, Spoleto, seu Benevento atque Corsica,* simul *et Sabinensi patrimonio* B. Petro Apostolo sanctaeque Dei et Apostolicae Rom. Ecclesiae concessa sunt et per nefariam gentem Longobardorum per annorum spatia abstracta atque ablata sunt, vestris temporibus restituantur ; *unde et plures donationes in sacro nostro scrinio Lateranensi recordatas habemus.*'

[4] Petrus de Marca, de Conc. Sac. et Imp. l. iii. c. xii. n. 3. Cf. Pag. ad Baron. a. 324, n. 16.

[5] Döllinger, l.c. p. 67.

[6] Ib. p. 69.

[1] Ib. p. 67.
[8] Civiltà Cattolica, l.c. p. 315 seq.

§ 3.

The questionable document first confronts us in the so-called Colbertine collection, which is somewhat older than Pseudo-Isidore,[1] and certainly of Frankish origin. The three authors by whom this document was first cited in the ninth century belong also to the Frankish kingdom—Æneas, Bishop of Paris (about 868),[2] Ado of Vienne (died 875),[3] and Hincmar of Rheims (died 882).[4]

There are many grounds for believing that Charles' coronation as emperor, which was ill received in the East, and also the loss of the Greek dominion in Italy, had to do with the origin of the false document. That its author intended it for the Greeks is plain from the passages against the Greeks, quoted also by Æneas, on the transference of the imperial throne to Byzantium, and the relinquishing of Rome to the Pope, the expressions as to the reverence due to the Papal chair, and the mention of the four Eastern Patriarchs, as to whom the West was almost indifferent.[5] The author for the most part placed the ancient legend of Sylvester in the mouth of the Emperor Constantine, and at the same time gave expression in a rude form, and with glaring exaggerations, to the ideas of his own time.[6] There is nothing to prove the author to have been a Roman ecclesiastic;[7] he is quite as likely to have lived in France, to which conclusion all early traces of the work would lead us. Up to 1053 the document is never found to have been made use of in Rome ; and up to that date it is most certain that Rome made no endeavour to circulate it.[8]

[1] Ballerini, de Antiquis Collectionibus et Collectoribus Canonum, P. ii. cap. viii. u. 4 ; P. iii. c. vi. § 5, u. 19 (Migne, PP. Lat. t. lvi. pp. 143, 255).
[2] Tractatus adv. Graecos, c. ccix. (D'Archery, Spicil. vii. p. 111 ; Migne, t. cxxi. p. 758). He adds : ‘Cujus (donationis) exemplaribus Ecclesiarum in Gallia consistentium armaria ex integro potiuntur.'
[3] Adonis Chronicon. Actas vi.
[4] Hincmar, Ep. 3, c. xiii. : ‘Constantius M. imp., Christianus effectus, propter amorem et honorem SS. Apostolorum Petri et Pauli sedem suam,

urbem scil. Romam, Papae Sylvestro *edicto privilegii* tradidit et sedem
suam in civitate sua, quae antea Byzantium vocabatur, nominis sui civitatem ampliando aedificavit.'
    ⁵ Zaccaria, diss. cit. de Patrimoniis, S.R.E. cap. ii.: 'Nec fortasse
a vero aberraret, qui renovatum a Leone III., Carolo M. imperatore coronato, occidentale imperium ejus fingendi Constituti Gallo cuipiam scriptori
occasionem, sub saeculi ix. initia, dedisse conjiceret, ut Constantini M.
auctoritate Graecorum Italiae a suo imperio defectionem ea Caroli inau-
guratione confirmatam aegre ferentium impetum ferociamque comprime-
ret.' Cf. Thomassin, P. i. l. i. c. v. n. 14. 'Commentitio quidem hoc
diplomate excidebant imperatores Graeci spe recuperandi occidentis imperii; at cum ante ejus evulgationem Pipinus Carolusque M. Romanae
Ecclesiae tam multa donassent, tam multa sibimet vindicassent, quae imperii ante fuerant, non magnopere de titulis et jure decertandum sibi
Graeci existimarunt, qui re vera tam amplas imperio suo abscindi provincias sive ignavia sive virium inopia passi erant' (Hincmar, tom. ii.
p. 206).
    ⁶ The idea arose early that it was the destiny of Rome to become, in-
stead of the capital of the ever-decreasing Roman Empire, the capital of
Christendom, which was daily on the increase. Leo M. (Sermo 82, al. 80,
cap. i.) says on the city of Rome : ' Isti (Petrus et Paulus) sunt, qui te ad
hanc gloriam provexerunt, ut gens sancta, populus electus, civitas sacerdotalis et regia, per sacram Petri sedem caput orbis effecta latius praesi-
deres religione divina quam dominatione terrena.' Prosper. Carm. de In-
gratis : ' Sedes Roma Petri, quae pastoralis honore Facta caput mundo,
quidquid non possidet armis, Religione tenet.' Cf. Auct. de Vocat. omnium
Gentium, l. ii. c. xvi.
    ⁷ Döllinger, p. 67.
    ⁸ Ibid. p. 76.

§ 4.

It was in the eleventh century that the false document first
became more widely known. Bruno, Bishop of Toul, a native
of Lorraine, when he became Pope Leo IX., cited for the first
time, in his letter to Michael Caerularius,[1] long passages from
this deed, the validity of which he never doubted ; after him it
was appealed to by Peter Damiani ;[2] Gregory VII. never made
use of it.[3] The apocryphal document was held in far higher
esteem in the twelfth century, especially after Gratian's disciples
incorporated it into his Decretal.[4] In the contest between the
convent of Farfa and the Roman nobles (1105), it was by no
means maintained that Constantine ' could only have meant to
give spiritual rights in Italy'[5] to the Pope ; the assertion disputed
was that the emperor delivered over to the Holy See the whole
of Italy, with all the rights of the empire, and the rights o

private persons.[6] The words of the unsuspected document were taken now in a wider, now in a more restricted sense, as this or that clause was cited according to the special aim or occasion.[7] The Greeks who came to know of the document treated it as authentic ; the Western heretics also took its validity for granted, even those among them who insisted on complete poverty for the clergy, such as the Waldenses, the Beguards, the followers of Dolcino and of Wicliffe ; as a rule they merely maintained that Constantine had erred in endowing the Church with earthly possessions.[8] Also the defenders of the civil power in the Middle Ages for a long time felt no doubt as to the authenticity of the deed, and only raised various objections against its legality and its binding power.

Many attempted to make out that the gift was extravagant and unjust, and that Constantine in making it had failed in his duty as emperor, and that only into the hands of the Roman people could he have resigned his power.[9] The legality of the document, far more than its authenticity, was called in question.[10]

[1] Ep. ad Caerul. c. xiii. xiv. Will, Acta et Scripta, pp. 72-74. Constantine here gives Sylvester 'tam palatium nostrum quam Romanam urbem et omne Italiae seu occidentalium regionum provincias, loca et civitates.'

[2] Opusc. iv. Opp. iii. p. 33. Hard. Conc. vi. 1122.

[3] Döllinger, l.c. pp. 77, 78, 84. Janus indeed declares this to be an error (p. 114), but gives no proof of his assertion ; there is no mention of the donation in the Pope's letters. In relation to Corsica there were many other documents to which Gregory might appeal.

[4] Palea, in can. 13, 14, dist. 96.

[5] Döllinger, p. 81.

[6] The monks amongst other things say : ' Postquam aeternam postestatem per B. Petrum Apostolum Rom. Sedes adepta est a Christo, *temporale* etiam suscepit *privilegium* ab Imperatore Constantino, quod jure possidere creditur aeterno .... quia Constantinus *non jura privatorum nec ex toto terreni imperii dominium* B. Sylvestro concessit .... *non omnis* ergo *Italia* in terrenis facultatibus patrimonium B. Petri Ap. Ecclesiae exstitit nec unquam Pontificum Romanorum *ex toto* dominium fuit' (Murat. Rer. Ital. Scr. ii. ii. pp. 648, 637 seq.).

[7] Robert Abolant speaks only of a privilegium left to the Popes ; Sicard of Cremona only of regalia ; Ptolomy of Lucca only of the rights and privileges of the senate, granted by Constantine to the Roman clergy ; Amalrich Angerii of the grant of the imperial insignia, and the sovereignty of the city of Rome, which last is also quoted by the Belgian monk Bald-

win of Ninnove; Lucas of Tuy speaks of the Regnum Italiae; Gervasius
of Tilbury says the emperor endowed the Pope with kingly but not imperial power over the western provinces; the author of De Regimine
Principum, l. iii. c. x. that he resigned the imperial power to the Pope;
the compiler of the Ottimo Commento on Dante (c. 1333) that he gave
over to him all the dignities of the empire; another commentator on
Dante, about 1375, that he gave him the States of the Church as they
existed in the fourteenth century; a third says the patrimony in Tuscany;
while Canon Pandulf Colonna of Siena speaks once again of Rome, Italy,
and all the western kingdoms (Döllinger, pp. 86-88, 90, 93 seq.).

    ⁸ Friedberg, l.c. p. 24 n. quotes Reinerii Summa, ap. Martene et Du-
rand. v. 1775. Cf. Moneta, iv. 412, tract. de Haer. Pauper. de Lugd. ap.
Mart. l.c. p. 1779; Pseudo-Reiner. c. Wald. Bibl. Max. PP. xxv. 264;
Pillichdorf, c. Eosd. ib. p. 278; La Nobla Leizon, ap. Raynouard, Choix
des Poésies, Paris, 1816, ii. p. 79. Cf. Döllinger, p. 101 seq.; Friedberg,
p. 56 seq. Wicliffe's prop., thirty-third of the forty-five condemned at
Constance, says: 'Sylvester Papa et Constantinus imperator errarunt
Ecclesiam dotando.' Dante (Inferno, c. 19), Marsilius, Occam, and Gre-
gory of Heimburg, also set themselves against these donations (Admon.
Gold. i. 560).

    ⁹ Glossa ad tit. 6, Auth. Coll. i. Quomodo oportet ad voc. generi.
Gloss in book iii. art. 63, of the Sachsenspiegel. Auct. anon. de Henr.
VII. apud Dönniges; Acta Henr. VII. ii. 158. Nikol. Dubois ap. Dupuy,
Hist. du Differ. Preuves, p. 46. Dante, de Monarch. 1. iii. c. x. p. 277, ed.
Schard. Anton. Rosell. c. lxiv. Gold. i. 290. Anon. de Jurisd. Imp. Döl-
linger, pp. 96, 97. Cf. Friedberg, p. 53 seq.

    ¹⁰ Molina, tract. de Justit. et Jure, ii. disp. 25, n. 4, p. 52.

§ 5.

The document being so generally acknowledged, no surprise
could be felt had the Popes of the Middle Ages, following the
example of Leo IX., appealed frequently to it; but as a fact
they seldom did so. Innocent III., who might so often have
had occasion to use it, makes no mention of it in his Decrees
and Briefs, and cites it only in a speech on St. Sylvester.¹
Gregory IX. made use of it in 1236, when reminding his adversary Frederick II. of the devotion of the great Emperors Constantine and Charles towards the Church.² Innocent IV. (1245)
declared to same emperor that it was not Constantine who *first*
gave temporal power to the Apostolic See, for he pointed out
that its germs were in fact contained in the fulness of power
bestowed by Christ upon St. Peter, and he therefore represented
the gift of Constantine rather as a surrender than as a gift.³

Nicholas III. (1278) mentions only the ceding of the city of Rome to the Pope ;[4] and John XXII., ' in his refutation of Marsilius of Padua, makes merely a passing reference to the fact that Constantine gave over the imperial throne to Sylvester.'[5] Clement V. likewise had mentioned only the rights granted to the Roman Church by the emperors, and in the first place by Constantine.[6]

[1] Sermo de S. Sylvestro, Opp. i. 97, ed. Venet. 1578.
[2] Bréholles, t. iv. p. 914 seq. Rayn. a. 1236, n. 24. Hefele, v. 891.
[3] In Raumer, Hohenstaufen, iv. 178. ' Cf. Alvar. Pelag. de Planetu Eccl. l. i. c. xliii. He says: ' Fertur dixisse.' The passage is not wholly free from doubt. Aug. Triumph. Summa de Eccl. considers the donation as a restitution.
[4] C. 17, Fundamenta, i. 6, de Elect. in 6.
[5] Raynald. a. 1327, n. 31. Döllinger, p. 93.
[6] C. un. ii. 9, Jurejur. in Clem.

§ 6.

These few quotations from the false document are all that occur in Papal publications; the Popes place upon entirely different grounds the powers exercised by the Apostolic See; moreover, from the fifteenth century the authenticity of the document was on many grounds called in question with the full knowledge of the Popes. It still found defenders in the sixteenth and seventeenth centuries ;[1] but from the time of Baronius their number continually decreased.[2] A decided majority of theologians sided with him ;[3] and at length the document was acknowledged by all to be a forgery.

[1] Amongst others Albert Pighe, Augustin Steuchus, John Faber, &c., quoted by Pichler, ii. pp. 689, 690.
[2] Baron. a. 324, n. 108-110 ; a. 1191, n. 52 ; a. 1192, n. 73.
[3] Pag. a. 324, n. 13. Ceillier, Hist. des Ant. t. iv. p. 177 ; t. viii. p. 145. Cenni, Monum. Dominat. Pontif. t. i. p. 304 seq. Zaccaria, diss. de reb. ad H. E. pertin. t. ii. ; diss. 10, c. ii. n. 4, 5. Daude, Hist. Univ. et Pragm. Wirceb. 1754, t. ii. p. 177 seq.

§ 7.

The Papal power was in the main based not upon individual documents, but upon principles and ideas which held universal sway. However closely the mediæval documents may be examined, it must be conceded, in the words of a non-Catholic theologian,[1] that 'the moral power upon which the temporal sovereignty of the Popes rested was no other than the power of the ideal, to which nations educated in Christianity were highly susceptible.'

[1] C. B. Hundeshagen, 'Ueber einige Hauptmomente in der geschichtl. Entwicklung des Verhältnisses zwischen Staat und Kirche,' in Dove's Zeitschrift fur Kirchenrecht, vol. i. p. 259.

ESSAY XIII.

THE DOCTRINE OF THE SUPERIORITY OF THE CHURCH AND OF HER AUTHORITY IN MATTERS TEMPORAL.

THROUGHOUT the Middle Ages it was maintained as a doctrine that two powers have come down from God, the spiritual and the temporal, both indispensable to mankind, and appointed to work together in peace.[1] Concord between the two was recognised as the foundation of the well-being of peoples and kingdoms, and discord as their ruin.[2]

The Church and State, distinct in aims and means, in extent and compass,[3] are nevertheless to work together for the well-being of mankind, mutually supporting and aiding one another.[4] But although both powers are coördinate and independent in their own domain,[5] still a certain order of precedence must exist between them, since they do not precisely coincide ; and in case of conflict preference must be given to one over the other; and in this case the preference was given to the Church. Let us now examine more closely—I. the doctrine of the superiority of the Church, and II. of her authority in matters temporal.

[1] Bossuet, Defens. Decl. Cleri. Gallic. l. i. sect. 2, c. xxxiii. ; and he often quotes witnesses on this point, especially Popes Gelasius I. and Nicholas I., Isidore of Seville, and others, who may also be found in Gratian, dist. 10 and 96, and elsewhere. See also Just. Nov. 6; Praef. Nov. 42; Capit Franc. v. 119; Conc. Paris, vi. 829, l. i. c. iii. Dante (de Monarch. l. iii. ap. Schard, de Jurisd. p. 283) says : ' Opus fuit homini duplici directivo secundum duplicem finem : sc. summo pontifice, qui secundum revelata hominum genus perduceret ad vitam aeternam, et imperatore, qui . . . ad temporalem felicitatem dirigeret.' The Greeks also continually represented the two powers as given by God (Theod. Stud. l. i. Ep. 16, p. 961, Nicephoro Imp.).

[2] Ivo Carnot. Ep. ad Paschal II. (Duchesne, Scr. Fr. iv. 241) : ' Novit paternitas vestra, quia cum regnum et sacerdotium inter se conveniunt,

bene regitur mundus et floret et fructificat Ecclesia. Cum vero inter se
discordant, non tantum parvae res non crescunt, sed etiam magnae res
miserabiliter dilabuntur.' Cf. S. Bernard. serm. 46, in Cant. Cantic.
³ Cf. Pignatelli, Consult. can. t. ix. cons. 61, p. 113 seq.; consult.
62-66, p. 117 seq.
⁴ Bianchi, t. iii. l. i. c. i. § 1, n. 4, p. 8 seq.
⁵ Innocent III., in a letter to the King of France, 1207, speaks of the
two powers as coördinate (1. vii. Ep. 79; Migne, ccxv. pp. 361, 362); also
to the princes of Germany, several years earlier (Reg. super Negot. Imp.
Ep. 2; Migne, ccxvi. p. 997 seq.).

PART I. THE DOCTRINE OF THE PRE-EMINENCE OF THE CHURCH.

§ 1. As maintained by the Fathers.   § 2. The figure of the two swords.
§ 3. St. Bernard.   § 4. The material sword in defence of the Church.
§ 5. Utterances of the Popes.   § 6. The preëminence of the Church
defended throughout and beyond the Middle Ages.   § 7. Each power
independent in its own sphere.   § 8. Distinction between them.   § 9.
Separation of Church and State to be rejected on principle.   § 10. The
State has not to fulfil the highest end.   § 11. Even Protestants defend
the superiority of the Church.   § 12. Decisions of Popes on the scope
of her power.   § 13. Ideal of the truly God-fearing State.   § 14. The
Decretal 'Novit.'   § 15, 16. Opinion of Innocent III.   § 17. The Church
necessarily able to judge of sin.

§ 1.

The doctrine of the superiority of Church over State is by no
means a speciality of the Middle Ages, as has often been asserted ; it belongs rather to the patristic age, and was defended
by the Fathers of the Church. Thus St. John Chrysostom says :
' The Church is above the State, in the same way as the soul is
above the body[1] and heaven above the earth,[2] and indeed far
more.' Gregory of Nazianzen unites the two comparisons when he
says to those holding civil dignities (dynasts and archons) :
' Take not amiss my freedom of speech : the law of Christ subjects you to my power and to my throne ; for we bishops also
exercise a sovereignty, and, moreover, I add, a greater and more
perfect sovereignty ; or is perchance the spirit to be inferior to
the flesh, the heavenly to the earthly ?'[3]   St. Isidore of Pelu-
sium writes : ' The government of the world rests on kinghood
and on priesthood : although the two differ widely—for one is
as the body, the other as the soul—they are nevertheless des-

tined to one end, the well-being of their subjects.'[4] The sovereignty exercised by bishops is, according to him, more sublime and more arduous than that of kings.[5] The dignity of the priesthood is expressed by St. John Chrysostom in yet another way : ' Those who are rulers on earth have indeed the power of binding, but it affects bodies merely ; but the priestly power of binding touches souls, and penetrates heaven ; what priests do here below is confirmed by God above, and the judgment of the servants is approved by the Lord (St. John xx. 23 ; St. Matt. xviii. 18). What power can be mightier ? All judgment has been given by the Father to the Son (St. John v. 22) ; and I know that the disciples received all judgment from the Son ; a power as much exalted above earthly power as heaven above earth and the soul above the body.'[6]

This figure of the body and soul was employed also in the Middle Ages.[7] Precisely similar to the image of heaven and earth is that of the sun and moon, made use of by Popes Gregory VII. and Innocent III.,[8] and by many other writers.[9] Moreover, the words of Pius IX., so ill received by the public press, in which he said that the Church was stronger than heaven, are used by St. John Chrysostom.[10]

---

[1] Chrys. hom. 15, in 2 Cor. n. 5 (Migne, l. xi. 509) : ὅσον οὖν ψυχῆς καὶ σώματος τὸ μέσον, τοσοῦτον πάλιν αὕτη διέστηκεν ἐκείνης ἡ ἀρχή. Thus also Constit. Apost. ii. 34 : ὅσῳ ψυχὴ σώματος κρείττον, τοσούτῳ ἱερωσύνη βασιλείας. Cf. Chrys. de Sacerd. iii. 1 (Migne, xlviii. 6, 41) : τοσοῦτον ἀνωτέρω βασιλείας, ὅσον πνεύματος καὶ σαρκὸς τὸ μέσον. The spiritual power is called by him ἀρχὴ πνευματική, hom. 3, in Coloss. n. 5 (Migne, t. lxii. p. 323).

[2] Chrys. hom. cit. n. 5 (p. 507) : Αὕτη γὰρ ἡ ἀρχὴ τοσοῦτον τῆς πολιτικῆς ἀμείνων, ὅσον τῆς γῆς ὁ οὐρανὸς, μᾶλλον δὲ καὶ πολλῷ πλέον. Thus also as early as the second century the Jewish-Christian writings (Testamenta xii. Patriarcharum Test. Judae, c. xxi.), in which Neander (Kirchengeschichte, i. p. 201, n. 1, 3d ed.) discovers already the Hildebrandian principle : ὡς ὑπερέχει οὐρανὸς τῆς γῆς, οὕτως ὑπερέχει θεοῦ ἱερατεία τῆς ἐπὶ γῆς βασιλείας. Also Pope Stephen V. (al. VI. 885-891), Ep. ad Basil. Imp. (Mansi, xvi. 421) : ὅσον διάφορον οὐρανοῦ πρὸς τὰ ἐπὶ γῆς.

[3] Naz. Orat. xvii. n. 8, pp. 322, 323, ed. Maur.

[4] Isid. Pelus. l. iii. Ep. 249.

[5] Id. l. iv. Ep. 219. Cf. Chrys. hom. 34, in Hebr. n. i. : ὅσον καὶ τὸ τῆς ἀρχῆς μεῖζον καὶ ὑψηλότερον : hom. 4, in verba Isaiae, Vidi Dominum, n. 5 (Migne, lvi. 126) : μείζων ἡ ἀρχὴ αὕτη, with reference to 2 Paral. xxvi. 18. Naz. Or. ii. n. 10, p. 17.

[6] Τοσούτῳ μείζονα ἐξουσίαν, ὅσῳ γῆς τιμιώτερος ὁ οὐρανὸς καὶ σωμάτων ψυχαι, l. iii. de Sacerdot. n. 5 (Migne, xlviii. 643).

[7] Vide Ivo Carnot. Ep. 106 (al. 51), ad Henric. Reg. Angl. p. 50 : ' Sicut sensus animalis subditus debet esse rationi : ita potestas terrena subdita esse debet Ecclesiae regimini, et quantum valet corpus, nisi regatur ab anima tantum valet terrena potestas, nisi informetur et regatur ab ecclesiastica disciplina.' Hugo, de Sacram. Fid. l. ii. P. ii. c. iv. : ' Quanto autem vita spiritualis dignior est quam terrena et spiritus quam corpus, tanto spiritualis potestas terrenam sive saecularem potestatem honore ac dignitate praecedit.' Honor. Augustod. de Praecell. Sacerd. ap. Pez. Thes. Anecd. ii. i. p. 180. Innoc. III. Resp. in Consist. ad Nuntios Philippi, Baluz. Epist. Innoc. t. i. pp. 647, 692. Reg. Ep. 18. Alex. Halens. p. 3, q. 40, m. 2 : ' Quamvis in ordine potestatum saecularium nullus est major rege vel imperatore quemadmodum in ordine potestatum spiritualium nullus major est Papa, sed tamen collatione facta potestatis spiritualis ad saecularem potestas spiritualis est supra corporalem, spiritus supra corpus.' Thom. 2, 2, q. 60, a. 6, ad 3 : ' Potestas saecularis subditur spirituali sicut corpus animae, et ideo non est usurpatum judicium, si spiritualis praelatus se intromittat in temporalibus, quantum ad ea, in quibus ei subditur temporalis potestas.' Cf. Auct. de Regim. Princip. l. iii. c. x., and Auct. Quaest. in utramque Partem Disput. a. 3 (falsely ascribed to Ægidius Romanus in Goldast. Mon. ii. 100) : ' Nam quantum distat oriens ab occidente, corpus ab anima, corporalia a spiritualibus, tantum distat auctoritas Summi Pontificis a culmine imperialis aut regiae dignitatis.' Vide also Gerson, Opp. iii. 1083 ; Bellarm. de Rom. Pont. v. 3, de translat. Imp. i. 13 ; Occam, Quaest. Octo Decis ; Goldast. ii. 331 ; Somm. Virid. ap. Gold. i. 77.

[8] Greg. VII. l. vii. Ep. 25. Cf. l. viii. Ep. 21. Innoc. III. c. Solitae, 6, § Praeterea, de M. et O. i. 33 ; l. i. Ep. 401 ; Reg. Ep. 32, p. 1035.

[9] Gerhoch, de Corrupto Eccl. Statu. praef. c. iii. (Galland. Bibl. PP. xiv. 549) : ' Spiritualia, quibus praeest Dominus Papa, diei, et temporalia, quibus praeest Dominus Imperator, nocti comparantur. Ecce duo luminaria,' &c. Berengos. serm. de Myst. Lig. Dom. (Bibl. Max. PP. xii. 374) : ' Isti (rex et pontifex) sunt enim qui ex antiquo divinitatis dispensatione bifaria, in firmamento Ecclesiae quasi duo magna convenere luminaria, quatenus in his, quae sunt saeculi, et in his, quae sunt Dei, luminare minus nocti et luminare majus debeat praeesse dici,' &c. Alvarus. Pelag. de Planctu Eccl. l. i. c. xxxvii. ; Friedberg, de Finium inter Eccl. et Civitatem Regundorum Judicio, l. i. § 3, p. 17: ' Ita erat medii aevi tempore usitatem, ut Frid. II. imp. non dubitaret, in exordio legum regno Neapolitano constitutarum se cum luna, cum sole Papam comparare atque se minorem illo proclamare' (Canciani, Leg. Barb. i. 305). Innoc. III. l. i. Ep. 401 (Migne, PP. Lat. ccxiv. p. 377) : ' Sicut universitatis conditor Deus duo magna luminaria in firmamento coeli constituit, luminare majus, ut praeesset diei, et luminare minus, ut nocti praeesset : sic ad firmamentum universalis Ecclesiae, quae coeli nomine nuncupatur, duas magnas instituit dignitates : majorem, quae quasi diebus animabus praeesset, et minorem, quae quasi noctibus praeesset corporibus : quae sunt pontificalis auctoritas et regalis potestas. Porro sicut luna lumen

suum a sole sortitur, quae revera minor est illo quantitate simul et quali-
tate, situ pariter et effectu : sic regalis potestas ab auctoritate pontificali
suae sortitur dignitatis splendorem, cujus conspectui quanto magis inhae-
ret, tanto majori lumine decoratur, et quo plus ab ejus elongatur aspectu,
eo plus proficit (deficit) in splendore.'

¹⁰ 'Η *ἐκκλησία οὐρανοῦ ἰσχυροτέρα.* Serm. antequam iret in exilium,
Opp. iii. 429, ed. Migne.

§ 2.

The figure of the two swords is also much used in the Middle
Ages. Abbot Godfrey of Vendôme¹ employs it even before St.
Bernard, to whom Bossuet ascribes its first use,² but not with
quite so wide an application. The spiritual and the material
sword were both to serve for the defence of the Church ; and the
material sword was to support the spiritual. Bishop Hildebert
of Mans, when unjustly kept prisoner by the Count of Perche,
wrote to Bishop Herlo : ' Most surely it was not without reason
that two swords were found on the Apostles (St. Luke xxii. 38),
since both are still to be found on the members of Christ's body ;
as the priest is a member of Christ, so likewise is the king.³
I am speaking to one who has knowledge ; thou knowest the
meaning of the sword of the king and the sword of the priest :
the first is the penalty imposed by the courts of justice ; the
second, the severity of Church discipline. If any one would
set me free with the sword of the king, I would not ask that on
my account the sword of the priest should be drawn.'⁴ Frederick Barbarossa appealed to Hadrian IV. on the precise ground
that it was to these two swords that God had delivered the government of the world.⁵ According to St. Richard, Archbishop
of Canterbury, these two swords seek mutually for aid, and the
one lends to the other its own power.⁶ Other writers also make
use of this figure ;⁷ and in Gratian may be found a passage imputed (though questionably) to Pope Nicholas I., in which the
bishops of Gaul received an order to force plunderers of Church
property to make restitution, both by the spiritual and material
sword.⁸ Innocent III. also employs the figure to point out the
necessity of mutual support between the two powers, which in
a certain sense complete each other.⁹ Thus in 1208 he called
upon the King of France to unite his sword with that of the

Church, for the chastisement of evildoers, since the spiritual and material sword have to aid each other.[10]

[1] Goffr. Vindocin. Opusc. iv. (Migne, PP. Lat. clvii. p. 220): ' Voluit .... spiritualem et materialem gladium esse in defensionem Ecclesiae.'

[2] Bossuet, l.c. l. i. sect. 2, c. xxxvii. p. 181. This is corrected by Leroy, l. iii. c. xvi. p. 308 ; and Fleury, Hist. Ecclés. t. xiv. p. 301 ; t. xvii. p. 41.

[3] Sacerdos in the Middle Ages usually meant bishop.

[4] Hildeb. Opp. l. ii. Ep. 18 (Bibl. PP. xxi. 136).

[5] ' Qui (Deus) in passione Christi Filii sui duobus gladiis necessariis regendum orbem subjecit.' Radev. de Gest. Frid. i. 10. Baron. a. 1159, n. 52. Cf. Ep. ad Manuel. Comm. ap. Goldast. Constit. Imper. iv. 72.

[6] Richard. Cant. Ep. ad Omn. Episc. Angl. inter Petri Bles. Ep. 73, Opp. i. 110, ed. Paris (Migne, ccvii. p. 226 seq.).

[7] Alan. ab Insulis Distinct. Diction. Theol. v. Gladius (Migne, ccx. p. 803) : ' Hi duo gladii significant duos judices, sc. judicem fori et judicem poli, i.e. regem et sacerdotem.' PetrusVener. l. i. Ep. 17, Gerhoch, l.c. ; also in Bennettis, Privileg. S. Petri, t. vi. pp. 555, 556.

[8] C. 2, Auctoritatem, c. xv. q. 6. Cf. Jaffé, Reg. n, 2027, p. 238. Another passage attributed to him, c. 6, c. xxxiii. q. 2, says : ' S. Dei Ecclesia .... gladium non habet nisi spiritualem.'

[9] L. vii. Ep. 54, Regi Bohemorum, p. 339 : ' Sic sibi spiritualis et materialis gladius mutuae mutuant subventionis auxilium, et vicissim, communicant vires suas, ut defectus ope vicaria suppleant et uterque alterius perficiat imperfectum.' L. x. Ep. 141, Comitibus et Baronibus Siciliae, p. 1235 : ' Unde cum spiritualis et materialis gladius mutuo se debeant adjuvare juxta quod legitur : Ecce duo gladii hic, idem rex (Frid.) nobis humiliter supplicavit, ut eos, qui terrenam non metuant potestatem, per censuram ecclesiasticam cogeremus ad exhibendum sibi subsidium opportunum.' In an inverted order he says, l. vii. Ep. 212, p. 527 : ' Gladium quem Petrus per semetipsum exercet, non metuunt, qui sunt extra ovile Domini constituti ;' it is therefore necessary, ' ut saecularis gladius potestatis, qui ad malefactorum vindictam a regibus et principibus bajulatur (Rom. xiii. 4) ad vindicandam evaginetur injuriam Salvatoris.' He says that the spiritual sword is often despised unless supported by the material. Reg. Ep. 79, l. ii. Ep. 1, p. 539. Innocent asks the Polish Duke Ladislaus in 1206, l. ix. Ep. 217, p. 1060: ' Did the Lord give to thee the sword, that thou mightest turn it against the bowels of thy mother ?'

[10] L. xi. Ep. 28, pp. 1358, 1359. Cf. l. xii. Ep. 69, p. 77 : ' Quia, sicut ab orthodoxis doctoribus et Catholicis expositoribus perhibetur, non solum spiritualis gladius, quo utitur sacerdotalis auctoritas, sed etiam materialis, quem exerit saecularis potestas, est necessarius ad vindictam malefactorum, laudem vero bonorum.'

§ 3.

Even stronger are the words of St. Bernard, in which he calls upon Pope Eugenius III. to draw the two swords, which

both belong to Peter : one to be drawn at his command, the
other by his hand, as often as is needful.[1] In his great work
dedicated to the same Pope, he says: ' He who denies to thee
the (material) sword does not seem to have weighed sufficiently
the words of our Lord, "Put thy sword into the scabbard." It is
thy sword, and is to be drawn on a sign from thee, although not
with thine own hand. For if it in no way belonged to thee,
the Lord of the Apostles, when they said to Him, " See, here are
two swords," would not have made answer, "It is enough," but
" It is too much." Both swords therefore, the material and the
spiritual, belong to the Church; the first to be drawn *for* the
Church, and the second *by* the Church.'[2]

According to St. Bernard the material sword belongs, in the
first place, to civil rulers : but it must in any event be used according to the advice and counsel of the Church. It does not
belong to the Church absolutely, but only in a certain sense,
and in so far as it is bound to give her aid, to support and defend her. The figure is meant to show forth, in the first place,
the necessary harmony of the two powers, and also the principle
that earthly power has for its end the well-being and furtherance of the kingdom of Christ. John of Salisbury,[3] and many
other writers,[4] teach the same thing; the Emperor Frederick II.
also employed this figure in the same sense,[5] and many Popes
have done the same.[6]

This teaching was opposed for the first time in the fourteenth century, by the champions of the civil power, who maintained that the allegory had no weight as proof ; that it might
easily bear quite another meaning;[7] and that even supposing the
two powers to be intended by the two swords, it by no means
necessarily followed that both belonged to St. Peter, or to any
other Apostle.[8]

---

[1] Bern. Ep. 256 (Opp. i. 257, 258): 'Exercendus nunc uterque gladius
in passione Domini, Christo denuo patiente, ubi et altera vice passus est.
Per quem autem nisi per vos? Petri uterque est: alter suo nutu, alter
sua manu, quoties necesse est, evaginandus. . . . Tempus et opus esse
existimo ambos educi in defensionem orientalis Ecclesiae.'

[2] De Consider. l. iv. c. iii. (Opp. i. 438): ' *Tuus* ergo et ipse, tuo forsitan nutu, etsi non tua manu evaginandus. Alioquin si *nullo modo* ad te

pertineret et is, dicentibus Apostolis: *Ecce duo gladii hic*, non respondisset Dominus: *Satis est*, sed: Nimis est. Uterque ergo Ecclesiae, et spiritualis sc. gladius et materialis; sed is quidem *pro* Ecclesia, ille vero *ab* Ecclesia exercendus, ille sacerdotis, is militis manu, sed sane ad nutum sacerdotis et jussum imperatoris.' Cf. ad Milit. Templi. Exhort. c. iii. Marsilius, P. i. c. xxviii. (Goldast. ii. 229), calls these words a contradiction because St. Bernard had said: 'Quid tu denuo *usurpare* gladium tentas, quem semel jussus es reponere in vaginam?' and *usurpare* is used of what does not belong to one. But apart from the various meanings of the word, the material sword, according to St. Bernard, is only to be denied to the Pope *secundum quid*, inasmuch as it is not to be used by him *propria manu*, and St. Bernard is therefore guilty of no contradiction.

³ Polycrat. l. iv. c. iii.

⁴ Henricus Gaudav. Quodlibet, vi. q. 33. Cf. Huet. Henri de Gand. p. 186; Alvar. Pélag. de Planctu Eccl. l. i. c. vi.; Memoriale Pot. Reg. ap. Murator. R. It. Scr. viii. 1078; Durand. Specul. Jur. de Leg. 50, i. 50, ed. Venet. 1576; Berthold. in Grimm, Freidanks Bescheidenheit, l. ix.; Schwabenspiegel, c. i,; Ruprecht von Freising, Rechtsbuch, c. ii. p. 11, ed. Maurer.

⁵ Const. a. 1220, § 7 (Walter, Fontes, p. 80): ' Et quia gladius materialis constitutus est in subsidium gladii spiritualis,' &c.

⁶ Greg. IX. ap. Matt. Paris, a. 1237. Innoc. IV. ap. Höfler, Friedrich II. p. 223.

⁷ This is not denied even by Bellarmine, de R. Pont. v. 5, de Verbo Dei, iii. 3. Joh. de Paris, de Pot. Reg. et Pap. c. xx.: ' Quod dicitur de duobus gladiis, non est nisi quaedam allegatio allegorica, ex qua non potest sumi argumentum, quia secundum Dionysium mystica theologia non est argumentativa. Et Aug. dicit in Ep. ad Vincent., quod allegoria non sufficit ad probationem alicujus, nisi quum ejus habeatur aliunde auctoritas manifesta. Possum etiam dicere, quod per illos duos gladios intelligunt omnes mystice verbum Dei juxta illud Apostoli Eph. vi. 17: *Accipe loricam fidei et gladium spiritus, quod est verbum Dei*. Quod autem dicitur duo gladii, propter vetus et novum testamentum, et per duos gladios intelligunt gladium verbi et gladium instantis persecutionis . . . (Luc. ii. 35; 2 Reg. xii. 10). . . . Et horum unus erat Apostolorum passive, qui ab eis sustinendus, sc. gladius persecutionis, alius autem erat eorum proprie, quia ab eis pro tempore competente evaginandus, sc. gladius verbi Dei.'

⁸ Ib.: ' Dato autem, quod per illos duos gladios, quos habebant Apostoli, intelligantur duae potestates, sc. spiritualis et temporalis, quae licet dicantur ibi esse, tamen non dicuntur ambae esse Petri vel alterius Apostoli. Nam unum eorum non tetigit Petrus, sc. saecularem, qui suus non erat. Alium vero tetigit, sc. spiritualem, quem solum Dominus dixit esse suum, et tamen non statim evaginandum a Petro (Joh. xviii. 11), quia certe non debet statim, sed cum magna deliberatione et in necessitate magna judex ecclesiasticus uti suo mucrone spirituali, ne contemnatur. Posito igitur, quod per illos duos gladios mystice illae duae potestates intelligantur, pro nobis est, quia cum essent duo, Petrus non habuit suum nisi unum (vide Matt. x. 34, gladium; Ps. xliv. 4; Apoc. i. 16, xix. 15). Ecce ergo quod a Christo non habet nisi unum.' Some writers merely contend that the

Church can make use of the earthly sword only on just grounds, with much deliberation and in grave necessity, which was never called in question by the writers most strictly for the Church; while others ascribe this sword to the Pope so far as to allow him authority to set it in motion for the Faith. Ant. Rossellus (Gold. ii. 280) : ' Gladius temporalis est Petri et Papae quantum ad potestatem, quem habet faciendi ipsum moveri pro fide, non pro aliis, et hoc modo dicitur esse Ecclesiae et esse Papae, ut verba secundum certam materiam capiantur.' The two swords were also ascribed to the Church in the sense that ecclesiastics are not incapable of possessing temporal power, and do in fact receive such by permission and concession of princes. Joh. de Paris, l.c. : ' Potest nihilominus dici, quod duo gladii ibi dicuntur fuisse et ad Apostolos pertinere, quia unus Apostolis et eorum successoribus convenit per se, quem a Christo habent, alius vero suus est aptitudine quia eis non repugnat et ex commissione et permissione principum suus erat futurus.'

§ 4.

The principle is the same set forth by the Fathers, that God has given power to emperors and kings that they may serve His kingdom, coöperate in the aims of the Church, and promote the worship of the Almighty, and that earthly kingdoms may serve the cause of the heavenly.[1] Gregory the Great expresses this in a letter to the Emperor Maurice : ' For this end has power over all mankind been bestowed by Heaven upon the piety of my sovereign, that those who strive after good may be supported, that the path to heaven may be widened, that the earthly kingdom may serve the heavenly.'[2] In the same way Leo the Great warned the Emperor Leo that the imperial power was not given him merely for the ruling of the world, but also for the protection of the Church.[3] No thought is more prominently put forward by the Fathers than that of the civil power (the material sword) being intended for the protection and furtherance of the Church.[4] Thus Bishop Ivo of Chartres writes to King Henry I. of England :[5] ' We admonish your highness, with urgent entreaties, to suffer the Word of God to be preached without hindrance in the kingdom intrusted to you, and to be ever mindful that the earthly kingdom must be always subordinate to the heavenly kingdom, intrusted to the Church.' Paschal II. (April 2, 1117) writes to the King of Denmark :[6] ' Power is rightly used when the eye is fixed on God, by whom it has been bestowed; therefore have God ever before thine eyes; and as thou hast received power from God, strive ever to please Him through His grace. Honour the churches and priests of God, in joy and humility; protect orphans and widows; be active in administering justice, and repress with thy might all who strive against it. Suffer not any one to plunder the goods of the Church, for this is a crime of sacrilege, and for such guilt thou art responsible; since it must not be that what is bestowed for the good of many should be plundered by the violence of one. In the repression of this crime and others let the bishops of thy kingdom be thy fellow-workers, supporters, and helpers. The world is well governed when the priestly power acts in concert with the kingly.'

[1] Aug. Ep. 185, al. 50, ad Bonif. n. 19 (Opp. ii. 651, Maur.): 'Quomodo ergo reges serviunt in timore (Ps. ii. 2) nisi ea, quae contra jussa Domini fiunt, religiosa severitate prohibendo atque plectendo? Aliter enim servit, quia *homo* est, aliter quia *rex* est. In hoc ergo serviunt Domino reges, *in quantum sunt reges*, cum ea faciunt *ad serviendum illi, quae non possunt facere nisi reges.*' C. Crescon. Gram. iii. 51 (t. ix. p. 463): 'In hoc reges sicut eis divinitus praecipitur, Deo serviunt, in quantum reges sunt, si in regno suo bona jubeant, mala prohibeant, non solum quae pertinent ad humanam societatem, verum quae pertinent ad divinam religionem.' L. v. c. xxiv. de Civ. Dei: 'Felices eos dicimus, si juste imperant . . . . si suam potestatem ad Dei cultum maxime dilatandum majestati ejus *famulam* faciunt.' Isid. Sent. iii. c. liii. (c. Principes, c. xxiii. q. 5): 'Principes saeculi nonumquam intra Ecclesiam potestatis adeptae culmina tenent, ut per eamdem potestatem ecclesiasticam disciplinam muniant.'

[2] Greg. M. l. iii. Ep. 65 (J. n. 903): 'Ut terrestre regnum coelesti regno *famuletur.*'

[3] Leo M. Ep. 156, c. iii. p. 1323, Baller. He also praises the emperor for his services in religious matters; Ep. 157, c. i. p. 1339: 'Qui supra curam rerum temporalium religiosae providentiae *famulatum* divinis et aeternis dispositionibus perseveranter impenditis, ut sc. Catholica fides, quae humanum genus sola vivificat, sola sanctificat, in una confessione permaneat et dissensiones, quae de terrenarum opinionum varietate nascuntur, a soliditate illius petrae, supra quam civitas Dei aedificatur, abigantur.' Cf. Ep. 164, c. i. p. 1345: 'Agnosce igitur, auguste et venerabilis imperator, in quam totius mundi praesidium divina sis providentia praeparatus et *quid auxilii matri tuae Ecclesiae debeas,* quae te filio maxime gloriatur.' Ep. 48, ad Pulcher.: 'Res humanae aliter tutae esse non possunt, nisi quae ad divinam confessionem pertinent, et regia et sacerdotalis defendat auctoritas.'

[4] Fulgentius (Relatus Conc. Aquisgran. 836, cap. iii. can. 2): 'Prae omnibus ita se (princeps) S. Matris Ecclesiae Catholicae meminerit filium, ut ejus paci ac tranquillitati per universum mundum suum prodesse faciat

principatum. Magis enim Christianum regitur ac propagatur imperium, dum ecclesiastico statui per omnem terram consulitur, quam cum in parte quacumque terrarum pro temporali securitate pugnatur.'
    ¹ Ivo Carnot. Ep. 106, ed. Duret.
    ⁴ Jaffé, Reg. Rom. Pontif. n. 4842, p. 515.   Temporal sovereigns speak in precisely similar terms of their duties.   Thus Charlemagne styled himself ' devotus sanctae Ecclesiae defensor humilisque adjutor' (vide Capitul. 789, Walter, Fontes, p. 46), in a letter to Leo III., 796 (Mansi, xiii. 196) ; thus also Louis the Pious, 833 (Baluz. Capit. i. 675, ed. 1677).   Louis the German, 870, wrote as follows to Hadrian II. (Floss, Leonis P. viii. Privileg. Frib. 1858, p. 75) : ' Omnipotens Deus vos, ut veridice credimus, ideo praefecit in apostolatus culmine, ne spiritalis ordo sine jure et lege laberetur in voragine confusionis, nosque vestrae pietati clementer constituit consortes, ut quod religio reprimere non valet, terror ac disciplina saecularis per nos opitulante Christo emendet.'

§ 5.

The preëminence of the spiritual power has also been set forth by the Popes.   Thus Pope Gelasius wrote to the Emperor Anastasius : ' There are two powers by which the world is principally governed, the consecrated authority of the bishops and the authority of the king.   Of these two, the burden of the bishops is the heavier, since they have to render account for kings themselves before the judgment-seat of God. If thou by thy dignity hast precedence amongst men, still must thou bow thy neck in obedience to ecclesiastical superiors ; thou hast to direct thy course according to their judgment, not to lead them according to thine own pleasure.   Still more hast thou to submit to the Bishop of the Roman See, set over all by the voice of Christ, and ever acknowledged with reverence as her head by the Church.'¹   Pope Symmachus declares to him : ' If thou be a Christian prince, thou must hearken patiently to the voice of every bishop.   When the dignity of emperor is compared to the dignity of bishop, the difference between them is as great as between the charge of things human and of things divine.'²   Gregory IV. impressed upon the Frankish bishops that the charge of souls, a bishop's office, is higher than the imperium, which is merely temporal.³   According to Ambrosiaster, nothing like the episcopal dignity is to be found ; compared to it the splendour of kings and the diadem of princes are as lead to gold.[4] Treating of this, Erasmus of Rotterdam himself says : 'Weighed in a just balance, no king is so exalted, in virtue of his kingship, as not to be beneath the dignity, I will not say of a bishop, but even of a simple pastor of souls, in virtue of his pastoral charge.'[5] 'In the hour of death,' observes Gregory VII.,[6] 'no one calls for the assistance of an earthly king, but for that of a priest; priests are the fathers and teachers even of kings and princes, and Constantine himself considered them as his judges;[7] indeed a simple exorcist has greater power than civil rulers; for the exorcist has sway over devils, while rulers often obey them.'

[1] Ep. ad Anast. Imp. Mansi, viii. 31 (c. x. d. 96).
[2] Symmach. Libell. Apol. Mansi, viii. 213-215.
[3] Ep. ad Episc. Franc. Roccab. Bibl. Max. Pont. ii. 2.
[4] Ps. Ambros. de Dignit. Sacerd. c. ii. Opp. Ambros. iv. 569, ed. Paris, 1845, ap. Placid. Pez. Thes. Anecd. ii. 2, p. 134.
[5] Erasmus, de Ratione Concionandi, t. i. p. 67, ed. Basil. It is not therefore to be wondered at if, as Schulte brings forward (Die Macht der Röm. Päpste, p. 31, n. 2), Urban II. said in a sermon in 1096, that the lowest priest had a preëminence over every king (Migne, PP. Lat. clxxiii. Landulf, Jun. c. xxvii.).
[6] Greg. VII. l. viii. Ep. 21, pp. 597, 598.
[7] Greg. I. l. iv. Ep. 31, ad Mauric. Imp.

§ 6.

Throughout the Middle Ages, and long afterwards, the preeminence of the Church over every earthly kingdom was uncontested.[1] It was recognised that the order or rank of societies differed according to their end or aim;[2] that the end of the Church was the higher, indeed the highest conceivable,[3] and that the temporal must be subservient to the spiritual. The principle put forward by St. Augustine was maintained, that without true justice, which is the foundation of kingdoms, no government can endure;[4] but that true justice exists only where the true faith reigns, where Christ is king.[5] It was remembered in the Middle Ages that the Fathers had set forth the insufficiency of political and social institutions,[6] and had referred the Bible prophecies concerning the kingdom of David, and the eternal kingdom never to be overthrown, to the Church.[7] The

words of Holy Scripture as to the chastisement of the mighty
who despise the law of God were ever before men's eyes (*e.g.*
Wisd. vi. 2, 10),[8] and the passages as to the passing nature of
all earthly power and greatness (*e.g.* Eccl. i. 1 seq.) ;[9] and they
were used to see the first place conceded to the kingdom of
God above all others.

[1] Auctor de Modis Uniendi ac Reformandi Ecclesiam (1410), c. ii.
(Gerson, Opp. ii. 163) : ' Ecclesia Christi est inter omnes respublicas aut
societates recte ordinatas a Christo superior, nobilior ac diligibilior.'
Bossuet himself (Defens. P. i. l. i. sect. 2, c. xxxiii. p. 174), after quoting
the words of Pope Symmachus, allows : ' Potuisset dicere honorem sacer-
dotalem superiorem esse honore regio, h.e. praestantiorem, sublimiorem,
digniorem, *neque quisquam negasset Christianus ;* ac in aequalitate utriusque potestatis S. Pontifex merito acquiescit.' But he only says : ' Ut
non dicam superior, certe aequalis est honor.' In the preceding century, Pietro Giannone himself (dell' Istoria Civile del Regno di Napoli,
t. i. l. i. c. xi. p. 52, ed. 1821) writes : ' Presso di noi il sacerdozio è riputato
tanto più alto e nobile dell' imperio, quanto le cose divine sono superiori
alle cose umane e quanto l'anima è più nobile del corpo e de' beni temporali.'

[2] Arist. Ethic. Nicom. i. 1. Polit. i. 1. Thom. de Reg. Princ. i. 14 :
' Ei, ad quem finis ultimi cura pertinet, subdi debent illi, ad quos pertinet
cura antecedentium finium, et ejus imperio dirigi.' Cf. ib. c. xv. Thus
even Dante, de Mon. p. 172, ed. Schard. Auctor Somnii Viridar. (Gold. i.
71). Auctor quaest. in utramque partem disput. (ib. ii. 196). Joh. de
Paris, ap. Schard, pp. 193, 200.

[3] As indeed followed from its being the ' finis ultimus,' and was admitted by all authors.

[4] No work exercised greater influence upon educated men in the
Middle Ages than St. Augustine's de Civitate Dei. In l. iv. c. iv. we
read : ' Remota justitia quid sunt regna, nisi magna latrocinia? Quia et
ipsa latrocinia quid sunt nisi parva regna ?'

[5] Aug. C. D. ii. 21 : ' Vera autem justitia non est nisi in ea republica,
cujus conditor rectorque Christus est.' L. xix. c. xxv. he shows : ' Quod
non possunt ibi esse verae virtutes, ubi non est vera religio.' C. xxiii. fin. :
' Ubi non est ista justitia, ut secundum suam gratiam civitati obedienti
Deus imperet unus et summus, ne cuiquam sacrificet nisi tantum sibi, et
per hoc in omnibus hominibus ad eamdem civitatem pertinentibus atque
obedientibus Deo, animus etiam corpori atque ratio vitiis ordine legitimo
fideliter imperet, ut quem ad modum justus unus, ita coetus populusque
justorum vivat ex fide, quae operatur per dilectionem . . . . ubi ergo non
est ista justitia, profecto non est coetus hominum juris consensu et utili-
tatis communione sociatus.' Cf. c. xiii. xiv. ; also Auct. de Regim. Princ. iii.
10 : ' Sicut ergo corpus per animam habet esse, virtutem et operationem,
ita et temporalis jurisdictio principum per spiritualem Petri et successorum
ejus.' Dante, l.c.

⁶ Aug. de Civ. Dei, l. xix. c. v-vii.

⁷ Aug. de Civ. Dei, l. xvii. i. 8-10, 16, 20; xviii. 29 seq. 48. Hieron. in Isai. xxii. 9-10. Euseb. in Ps. xlvii. 2.

⁸ Petr. Bles. Ep. 124, p. 371, ed. Migne.

⁹ Alan. al. Insulis Lib. Sentent. c. xxxvi. (Migne, ccx. p. 249) : 'Quid mundanae potestates, nisi potestatum histriones? Quid saeculares digni-tates, nisi dignitatum larvae et simiae? Quid terrena bona, nisi bonorum phantasiae? Certe bona terrena bona non sunt; si bona essent, num-quam deessent, non abessent justis, non adessent injustis.'

§ 7.

It is the teaching of theologians and canonists, that although the political power of sovereigns is the highest of its kind in all that concerns the material aims of life and the well-being· of society, and is in its own sphere second to none, still it by no means follows that in all which relates to a more sublime end it has not been subjected to another power.[1] From a Christian point of view, the end of the State is not the final and most lofty ; it is inferior to the end of eternal salvation ; the natural order is surpassed by the supernatural.[2] The Church ever sets before men the highest end ; and it is precisely by their ends that the relation of various societies to each other is determined. Earthly well-being, which it is the duty of the State to promote, is for the Church merely a means to her own end, the attain-ment of eternal salvation for her members. So long as it is not denied that this life is to be referred to a future life ; so long as the immortality of the soul, and the final destiny of man be-yond the grave, are maintained ; and so long as it is conceded that the aim of the Church is to prepare and direct mankind for this destiny, it must likewise be conceded that in questions relating to the higher end, eternal salvation, the civil power must be subordinate to the spiritual, even as the end of the one is subordinate to the end of the other.

But in things temporal the dependence of the Church upon the State is often felt most pressingly ; according to Pope Nicholas I., Christian emperors, in order to attain eternal life, stand in need of the Pontiffs, while they, on their side, make use of the imperial laws in earthly matters.[3] This mutual need brings with it a mutual dependence in all things which extend beyond the distinct province of each power.

[1] Pignatelli, Consultat. canon. t. ii. consult. 56, n. 6 seq. p. 111 seq. Bianchi, t. i. l. iii. § 17, n. 1, p. 512.
[2] Molina, de Justit. et Jure, tract. 2, disp. 21, n. 4, p. 45: 'Cum nobilitas et eminentia cujusque facultatis ex objecto et fine potissimum pensanda sit, sane pro quantitate excessus supernaturalis finis ad naturalem, salutisque spiritualis animae ad temporalia commoda pacificumque ac tranquillum hujus vitae statum judicanda erit nobilitas et eminentia potestatis ecclesiasticae supra potestatem laicam.'
[3] Nicol. I. Ep. 8, ad Mich. III. Imp. (c. vi. d. 96). St. Basil says the same, Ep. 225, a. 375 (Migne, xxxii. 840): οἱ νόμοι, καθ' οὓς πολιτευόμεθα τὰ ἀνθρώπινα.

§ 8.

Nevertheless, the Church being a direct institution of God, while the State has been only indirectly instituted by God,[1] the Church once more takes precedence ;[2] she has, moreover, greater firmness and endurance, wider extension, more influence both on the heart and actions of men.[3] Even French Councils pronounced the higher dignity and preëminence of ecclesiastical over civil power ;[4] and as late as the beginning of the seventeenth century this was a received principle with all Catholic authors.[5] Whether the civil power owed its origin to the ecclesiastical was indeed disputed, but never that it was beneath the ecclesiastical in dignity.[6]

[1] Permaneder, Kirchenrecht, § 29, p. 37, 2d ed.
[2] Bellarm. de Eccl. Milit. iii. 6. Charlas, de Libert. Eccl. Gall. l. iv. c. iv. n. 11. Bianchi, l.c. c. i. § 1, p. 6 seq. Bennettis, Vindic. Privil. S. Petri, P. iii. t. vi. p. 9 seq. Cf. Grotius, de Jure Belli et Pacis, l. i. c. iv. § 7, n. 3.
[3] Card. Turrecremata, Summa de Eccl. l. i. c. xc. proves the superiority of the Church: (1) ex antiquitate temporis (the Church began in Abel); (2) ex nobilitate originis (the Church comes direct from God); (3) ex singulari dignitate (soul and body, &c.); (4) ex majoritate auctoritatis; (5) ex nobilitate finis; (6) ex caussalitate; (7) ex jurisdictione; (8) ex superioritate praelationis; (9) ex amplitudine principatus; (10) ex firmitate et fortitudine.
[4] Conc. Senon. a. 1527 (Labbé, xix. 1154, ed. Venet.): 'Verum ex sacris literis coercitus est delirantis hujus haeretici (Marsilii Patavini) immanis furor, quibus palam ostenditur, non ex principum arbitrio dependere ecclesiasticam potestatem, sed ex jure divino, quo Ecclesiae conceditur leges ad salutem condere fidelium et in rebelles legitima censura animad-

vertere; iisdem quoque literis aperte monstratur, *Ecclesiae potestatem longe alia quavis laica potestate non modo superiorem esse, sed et digniorem.*'
    [5] Suarez, de Leg. l. iv. c. ix. : ' Dicendum est potestatem ecclesiasticam non solum esse in se nobiliorem, sed etiam superiorem et habere sibi sub-ordinatam et subjectam potestatem civilem. Est conclusio haec certa et communis apud Catholicos.'
    [6] Thus Joh. de Parisiis (died 1304) ap. Natal. Alex. saec. 13 et 14, diss. 9, a. 2, n. 12, t. xvi. p. 328 : ' Has potestates ordinem habere *digni-tatis*, non *causalitatis*, quum una non sit ab alia, sicut angeli a Deo sunt producti ordine quodam dignitatis, in quantum unus in naturalibus est nobilior altero, sed non est ibi ordo causalitatis, quo unus sit ab alio, quum omnes sint a Deo immediate creati. Intentio tamen Apostoli videtur esse de ordine cujuslibet ad finem suum proprium, non de ordine cujuslibet ad alterum. Quod patet ex hoc, quod subjungit de principe, quod minister Dei est in vindictam (Rom. xiii. 4).' Even Bluntschli (Sybel's Zeitschrift, 1861, pp. 35, 55) allows that although the deductions drawn from this doctrine were disputed, and its application restricted, still no one ventured to attack the real principle, ' the spiritual nature of the Church, and the earthly nature of the State ;' also that the Ghibellines, like the Guelfs, were 'in-clined' to imagine, inferior to God, from whom ecclesiastical and civil power were derived, a Christ, and that the Pope in virtue of his religious calling stood clearly in closer relation to 'this God' than the temporal emperor (the Arian Bluntschli does not of course look upon Christ as God).

§ 9.

From a Christian point of view the superiority of the Church is seen to be all the more needful from the fact that otherwise the true relation between the two orders, the natural and the supernatural, would be wanting.[1]   Seen in the light of the Catholic faith, the separation of Church and State, lately become a principle, is the tearing of the world from God, of the crea-ture from the Creator, the turning away of society from its highest end ; the dividing and dismembering of each individual, by separating the characters of churchman and citizen, in a way opposed to the nature of things, and which entails endless col-lisions of duties, being contrary to the text, ' That which God has united let not man put asunder' (St. Matt. xix. 6).[2]   In practice it presents immense difficulties, things temporal and things spiritual not being always easy to divide ; for the points of contact and connection between the religious and civil domains are endless,[3] and the boundary line has not in all cases been discerned, much less determined. ' If the Church,' says an able French writer,[4] ' were merely an institution for prayer, and the State for police; if religion confined itself entirely to speculative opinions, mystical feelings, and secret meditations, while the State had to do only with the good order and cleanliness of cities and streets; if the spiritual sphere comprehended only the innermost relations of each soul to God, the temporal only the prevention of misdeeds and plunder among men; it would then indeed be easy to separate completely two spheres which would neither have, nor be likely to have, any points of contact, and to preserve freedom to two powers knowing nothing of, and never coming across, one another. But facts overturn all these imaginary barriers and boundary lines. Religion is by no means a hermit enclosed in a cell; neither is the State contented with the part of a district policeman or beadle. Both powers aim far higher, and as yet, even without overstepping the sphere transmitted and belonging to each, neither of the two have been able to stir a step without being brought into mutual contact.' Everywhere in life they come across one another, and the one can neither avoid nor ignore the other. This being the case, it cannot be but that one should honour the other as superior. Even if it does not follow, as was maintained of old,[5] from the principle of unity in the government of the universe, that two powers, not merely distinct, but, moreover, entirely independent of each other, cannot by possibility exist side by side,[6] it may still be seen from their actual relations, that either the State must guide the Church or the Church the State; a mean between State supremacy and a so-called theocracy is no longer conceivable. Since earthly wellbeing is to lead to heaven, all else must be subordinate to man's final end; and the rulers of Christian States, as believers, being bound by the same duties as their subjects, a Catholic State cannot avoid acknowledging the superiority of the Church, and must necessarily look upon it as a healthful and strengthening influence, as a safeguard of its own welfare and prosperity.

[1] Martin Gerbert, de Legit. Eccl. Potestate, S. Blas. 1761, l. iv. c. i. n. i. p. 611: 'Dubitandum non est, cum finis spiritualis regiminis sit longe praestantissimus, ac hominis ad aeternam vitam destinati ultimus et supremus, ei omnes alios subordinari debere et cedere, si quae collisio officiorum contingeret. . . . Quodsi ergo in regimine saeculari sit aliquid, quod

spirituali obsit, cedat necesse est potiori juri nobiliorique fini, quidquid contra prodest, et facit ad consecutionem finis praestantioris, ex parte ignobiliore inferioreque consecrandum est, et deferendum parti superiori.'

² Cf. M. Liberatore, La Chiesa e lo Stato, c. i. pp. 4, 55, 175. '

✝ This is dwelt on by Mr. Gladstone, a witness beyond suspicion. He says : ' Even in the United States, where the severance between Church and State is supposed to be complete, a long catalogue might be drawn of subjects belonging to the domain and competency of the State, but also undeniably affecting the government of the Church ; such as, by way of example, marriage, burial, education, prison discipline, blasphemy, poor-relief, incorporation, mortmain, religious endowments, vows of celibacy and obedience. In Europe the circle is far wider, the points of contact and of interlacing almost innumerable.' Vatican Decrees, pp. 41, 42. [Tn.]

⁴ Albert de Broglie, La souveraineté pontificale et la liberté, Correspondant, 25 Oct. 1861.

⁵ Auctor. Quaest. in utramque part. disput. Gold. ii. 102-105. Dante, de Monarch. p. 279, ed. Schard. Alvar. Pelag. l. i. c. xxxvii.

⁶ A protest against any such conclusion was raised, as early as the fourteenth century, by the author of the Somnium Viridarii, c. cii. (Gold. i. 91), and of the Quaestio in utramque partem disput. de pot. reg. et Pont. a. 5 (ib. ii. 103-105), and afterwards by Bossuet (Def. l. i. sect. 2, c. xxxiii. p. 173 seq.). He merely regards the two powers as societate foedere, pace conjunctae, with reference to Zach. vi. 12, 13 ; 2 Paral. xx. 11. But, observe others, if they be so united, the State acknowledges the superiority of the Church in all things relating to eternal salvation ; and if it does not acknowledge this, then they are not thus united.

§ 10.

Christianity of necessity brought with it a change in the conception of the State. The State is no longer a final end to which, according to the ancient idea, individuals must devote themselves, and personal rights be sacrificed ; on the contrary, individuals have essential aims, independent of the State, which they may never sacrifice to it.[1] To them the State is not above all else, but is subservient to the institutions ordained for the salvation and highest destiny of mankind.[2]

Christianity may thus seem to have withdrawn from the State a portion of its dignity, but it has in reality increased it. According to the Christian conception, the State is an ordinance of God for the maintenance of peace and justice, a figure of the moral government of the universe in this lower world. The majesty and power of rulers is based upon their receiving a

charge from God, and being His representatives; and it is their
calling to do all in their power for the increase of God's kingdom, and the training of man for his supernatural destiny.[3]

[1] Cf. Aug. de Civ. Dei, xiv. 28; xv. 4.
[2] Walter, Naturrecht und Politik, § 515, p. 515.
[3] Walter, l.c. p. 516. Cf. Liberatore, l.c. c. i. a. 6, § 3, pp. 85-88.

§ 11.

Let us hear a professor of Protestant theology. The ecclesiastical privy councillor of Baden, C. B. Hundeshagen, writes:[1]
'Within the pale of Christianity there is no point of view from
which it is not accepted as a certain truth that heaven is superior, earth inferior and subordinate; that the salvation of souls
is incomparably above all earthly well-being; that the majesty
of holiness is immeasurably beyond all other majesty; that aid
in attaining heaven, in the very nature of things, takes precedence of any kind of aid towards the end of this earthly life.
This is and will ever be the Christian view of life. It is absolutely inconceivable that, so long as Christianity exists, this
view of life should ever cease to exercise its influence upon the
hearts and minds of men.[2] Striking practical proof in support
of this assertion is given us in the fact that the destiny of man
for something higher than this every-day world, and that which
it brings with it, has so completely taken possession of the mind
of all ages of Christendom, that even such times and societies as
have long ago got rid of all thought of "the undiscovered
country from whose bourn no traveller returns," still have not
been able to free themselves from a remnant of Christian idealism. In many regions of the great world of civilisation, as is
well known, there often remains, of that which constitutes the
real meaning of Christian hopes and aspirations, merely a dull
colourless deposit. It is nevertheless acknowledged that spirit
is above matter, the soul higher than the body, the world of
thought more exalted than the world fashioned by our hands;
that the ideal, though invisible, and merely an object of faith,
takes precedence of all that is visible to our eyes, that may be
felt, that stands before us and flatters our senses, that is the

object of sensible experience. It is not necessary, for this, to mix with men of a higher stamp ; in most cases even those of a coarser nature will confess that in theory at least, above money and land, above property and pleasures, above the loaves and fishes of this earthly life, stand ideal goods : conscience, honour, freedom, right, love, truth, art, and science. They will at least allow that such a view of the world, if perhaps not "practical," is still "beautiful." This remnant of idealism has still, there can be no doubt, a certain value. Reverence for the sublime, the noble, and the beautiful, in contrast with the mean and the base, forms most surely a notable point of union between the un-Christian civilised world and the Christian, with its high conception of things sacred. It is at the same time a testimony of the permanent influence of the Christian view of life, even in such regions as have in all else rejected the Christian view ; and in this respect it is a remarkable sign. Suffice it to say that the magic by which New Rome won the hearts of men to her system of the government of the State by the Church was no other than this sense of ideal good so strongly and universally awakened in mankind by Christianity.' And this, forsooth, is called theocracy !³

¹ Abhandlung über die Entwicklung des Verhältnisses zwischen Kirche und Staat, in Dove's Zeitschrift für Kirchenrecht, Berlin, 1861, vol. i. p. 259 seq.

² Also the view that the end of the world's history is a holy Christian kingdom, is not purely mediæval, as Bluntschli seems to suppose (Kirchenfreiheit und Kirchenherrschaft in der Geschichte, in Sybel's Histor. Zeitschrift, 1861, P. i. p. 54) ; in a thousand ways, even in the Chiliastic views of the earliest Christian ages, this conviction has expressed itself.

³ Strictly speaking, the Jewish kingdom was the only instance of theocracy ; never elsewhere has the government been directly divine.

§ 12.

Theocracy, in this sense, can never be uprooted ; it is inseparably bound up with Christianity ; it is the ideal of Christians truly filled with faith and trained at the same time in mind. It will make itself felt amid all forms of human development as long as men have faith in Him who has said : ' Heaven and earth shall pass away, but My words shall not pass away.' But even among Christians it is an ideal but seldom, and in part, realised. In a sense it is the same as with Christian perfection and the Evangelical Counsels. The heathen of old, especially Julian the Apostate, made sport of them, above all of St. Matthew xix. 21, as impolitic and conducive to the ruin of human society, which could not exist together with them. Amongst other answers it was urged in reply[1] that though, of course, perfection was to be desired for all, still as a fact it was not to be found in all, while virtue had ever fewer followers than vice, and wealth found more supporters than poverty. But supposing the luxury of life, the search and pursuit of earthly pleasure, the serving of mammon completely done away with, all society would be raised, ennobled, and transformed into a more sublime community. In the same way, were an end put to all wars, were all laws moulded upon the eternal justice of God, the supernatural everywhere preferred to the natural, and all spiritual claims satisfied, the pathway to the Church triumphant would be thrown open for the Church militant, and earth would be the antechamber of heaven ; a true kingdom of God would arise, not indeed rendering earthly kingdoms superfluous, but raising them to a higher unity. Christ did not set aside His counsels because few were found to follow them, and in like manner the ideal of the truly God-fearing State, because it can be but seldom and approximately realised, is not therefore to be passed over in silence, and this all the less because, from a religious point of view, it is here not a question of a counsel merely, but of a duty.[2] For as the individual has to subject himself to God and to His revelation, so also has society, domestic as well as political, the family as well as the State. Christ has given to the community the same way of salvation as to the individual ;[3] and as the body has its life from the soul, so the soul has its life from God, in whom we live and move and have our being.[4] The admonition ' Seek first the Kingdom of God and His justice, and all these things shall be added to you' (St. Matt. vi. 33), applies as much to the community as to individuals ;[5] earthly blessings will follow after.[6] Some there are who deny the divinity and sovereignty of Christ, and withdraw their necks from His yoke ;

but the King and Lord of all things does not therefore cease to possess this sovereignty ; His right and His majesty are in no way impaired by this disobedience.[7] Christ is and must ever be the King of kings, and the Church is His Kingdom, to which all are bound to belong.[8]

[1] Photius, Quaest. Amphil. 100, p. 168 seq. ed. Athen. 1858; q. 101, p. 616 seq. ed. Paris (Ep. 187, ed. Mout.; Ep. 66, ed. Bal.).

[2] Moreover the counsel and the duty may become one. In so far as concerns *positive enactments*—leaving out of the question special legal relations—the union of the civil with the spiritual power is a counsel ; but in so far as the *negative* side of the question is concerned—namely, that nothing shall be demanded or prescribed which hinders the attainment of the supernatural end—it is also a duty. Suarez (de Leg. 1. iii. c. vii.) : ' Dico potestatem civilem (etiam prout est in principibus Christianis fidei conjuncta) non extendi in materia vel actibus suis ad finem supernaturalem s. spiritualem vitae futurae vel praesentis, licet legislatores fideles in suis legibus ferendis *possint et ex parte debeant* naturalem finem et actum ipsum ferendi legem in supernaturalem finem *referre*.' He then observes : ' Hanc *relationem* posse dupliciter fieri : Primo *per positivam ordinationem*, et sic regulariter erit *in consilio*, nisi speciale praeceptum vel necessitas ad illum obligaverit. . . . Secundo intelligi potest *per negationem tantum* s. per circumspectionem nihil statuendi per hanc potestatem, quod sit contrarium fini supernaturali vel ejus consecutionem impedire possit ; quae observatio et prudens cautio ex fide procedit et virtualis quaedam relatio in ultimum finem dici potest. Estque non tantum in consilio, sed etiam *in praecepto*, maxime proprio Christiani et Catholici principis, ut constat '

[3] ' Non aliunde beata civitas, aliunde homo, quum aliud non sit civitas, quam concors hominum multitudo' (Aug. Ep. 155).

[4] Joh. Saresb. Polycr. iii. 1, p. 477 : ' Caro vivit ab anima, cum aliunde corpori vita esse non possit, quod semper inertiae suae torpore quiescit, nisi spiritualis naturae beneficio moveatur. Haec autem habet et ipsa vitam suam. Deus enim vita animae est. Quam sententiam modernorum quidam graviter quidem et vere, licet metrica levitate complexus est : Vita animae Deus est, haec corporis ; hac fugiente Solvitur hoc, perit haec destituente Deo,' according to St. Aug. C. D. 1. xiii. c. ii. ; xix. c. xxvi.

[5] Chrys. hom. 22, ad 13, in Matt. n. 3 (Migne, l. vii. 305) : Ζήτει . . . . τὰ μέλλοντα καὶ λήψῃ καὶ τὰ παρόντα· μὴ ζήτει τὰ ὁρώμενα καὶ πάντως αὐτῶν ἐπιτεύξῃ.

[6] Aug. (de Civ. Dei. 1. v. c. xxv. xxvi.) points this out in the cases of Constantine and Theodosius I.

[7] Cyrill. Alex. l. vi. c. Julian. Migne, PP. gr. lxxvi. p. 829, D.

[8] Christus et ejus Ecclesia = rex et civitas quam condidit. Thus continually in St. Augustine, de Civ. Dei. Cf. *e.g.* l. xvii. c. xv.

§ 13.

The practical consequences arising from the superiority of
the Church are by no means such as have been deduced from it,
that is to say, it does not follow that the whole domain of civil
rule devolves upon the Church; never has she claimed for herself so unlimited a competency. The Popes themselves, when
engaged in the decision of weighty questions, have fully set
forth the limits of their power. This is the case, for example, in
the Decretal of Innocent III., 'Per venerabilem' (1202).[1] The
Pope here clearly and emphatically expresses his high respect
for the authority of temporal princes.[2] Count William of
Montpellier had petitioned the Pope to legitimatise his illegitimate children, and amongst other examples appealed to that of
the French King Philip Augustus. Innocent thereupon made
answer : ' The King of France, since he acknowledges in matters
temporal no superior, could, without violating the rights of a
third party, submit himself to our judgment, as he actually did ;
some may even think that he himself in his own person might
have given the dispensation, not as a father to his own children,
but as a prince to his subjects. But thou (William) art, as thou
knowest, subject to other princes ; hence perhaps thou couldst
not submit thyself to us without prejudice to them if they
should withhold their consent ; and thy authority is not such
as to give thee personally in such cases the right of dispensation.'[3]

---

[1] C. 13, Qui filii sint legitimi (iv. 17). Innoc. III. l. v. Ep. 128. Migne,
ccxiv. pp. 1130-1134.

[2] In connection with this Decretal, the canonists explain the légitimatio
per rescriptum principis, and teach that, except in the States of the
Church, the Pope cannot, regulariter loquendo, legitimatise bastards ad
successionem hereditariam et ad munera mere temporalia, except only in
a case of real necessity, touching the validity of a marriage, dispensatio
in radice, or the weighty affairs of a country or province.

[3] Ib. p. 1132 : 'Insuper enm rex ipse superiorem in temporalibus minime
recognoscat, sine juris alterius laesione in eo se jurisdictioni nostrae subjicere potuit et subjecit in quo forsitan videretur aliquibus quod per se ipsum, non tanquam pater cum filiis, sed tanquam princeps cum subditis
potuerit dispensare. Tu autem aliis nosceris subjacere. Unde sine ip-

sorum forsitan injuria, nisi praestarent assensum, nobis in hoc subdere non posses, nec ejus auctoritatis existis, ut dispensandi super his habeas potestatem.'

§ 14.

Here also mention must be made of the celebrated Decretal 'Novit,' called forth by a complaint made by the King of England against Philip Augustus of France. The feudal relation between the continental possessions of the English kings and the crown of France had often led to disputes and wars, always most disastrous, but especially so in the time of King John of England. The murder of his nephew Arthur was universally laid to his charge ; and, at the suit of the Duchess Constance, Prince Arthur's mother, and of the nobles of Aquitaine, the French king summoned John before the feudal court to make his defence. John neither appeared himself nor sent representatives. The court of French peers declared him guilty of felony, and his feudal estates in France forfeited. Philip Augustus, with a strong force, invaded Normandy, and took one by one all John's continental possessions.[1] John, unable to withstand his enemy, applied to the Roman See, complaining that the King of France had violated a sworn treaty, had begun the war before the expiration of the time agreed upon, and had violently seized from him his dominions. These incessant feuds between great kings were, as Alexander III. had before declared, Sept. 6, 1173,[2] most displeasing to the Holy See, especially as they harassed and divided the powers of Christendom, and thus rendered impossible all joint undertakings, especially Crusades. Innocent III., who had not been remiss in admonitions and warnings, and had made unceasing efforts to keep peace between the two kings,[3] sent the Abbots of Casamario and Tre Fontane as legates to induce them to lay down their arms and make peace, and the rights of each party being reserved, to lay that country under an interdict whose ruler should refuse compliance. The legates were sent to both princes, who were admonished to put an end to the war.[4] The letters of the Pope, in which similar words are used to both kings, show an equal sense of his own duty, and of the respect due to their high dignity. 'Since it is well known to thy kingly highness,' he says, 'that with us there can be no respect of persons, we are convinced that thou wilt not take it ill if even towards thee we fulfil the duty of our pastoral office, lest, together with the offence against the Divine Majesty of which negligence would make us guilty, our office may incur the censure of men by our omitting in the case of kings and princes something of that which ought to be done, making more account of their wishes than of their well-being. The word of God in our mouths must never be bound, but must be wholly free, that we may freely correct the turbulent, and as often as is profitable fulfil the word of the Apostle, which applies to us all the more the higher the office held by us in the Church.'[5] John, in the midst of so many difficulties, was ready to submit, even though the bitterest truths were told him ; but Philip Augustus, who had no wish to be deprived of his victory, first delayed his answer, then deliberated with his council, and at last replied, that in matters of fiefs and vassals he was not bound to render account to the Pope, who had moreover no concern with the disputes of kings. Thereupon the Pope wrote back to Philip that nothing more nearly concerned his pastoral charge than the admonishing of Christian princes to keep the peace, that he might thereby hinder pillage, sacrilege, and other evils arising from war ; that the King of England had complained to the Holy See of grievous injustice suffered at the hands of Philip, by reason of which, having in vain sought redress, he had turned to the Church ; to her the king must perforce hearken, since it was a question involving grievous sin.[6] The Pope wrote in detail on the same subject to all the bishops of France in 1204, setting forth the right and justice of his interference.   Hence arose the celebrated Decretal ' Novit.'[7]

[1] Pauli, Geschichte von England, iii. p. 314 seq.

[2] Ep. ad Henric. Rhem. Bouquet, xv. 938. Jaffé, n. 8283, p. 758.

[3] Innoc. III. l. i. Ep. 130, p. 117 ; Ep. 346 seq. p. 319 seq.; l. ii. Ep. 23, 24, p. 552 seq.

[4] Innoc. l. vi. Ep. 68. Brequigny, Diplom. P. ii. t. i. p. 278.

[5] Raynald. a. 1203, n. 54. Cf. a. 1202, n. 25. Spondan. a. 1202, n. 7, 8, l. vi. Ep. 68, 69. Migne, ccxv. pp. 64-66.

[6] L. vi. Ep. 163, pp. 176-180. Cf. ib. Ep. 164-167.

[7] L. vii. Ep. 42. Brequigny, t. ii. p. 478 ; c. xiii. de Judic. ii. 1.

§ 15.

Innocent declares that he has the honour and well-being of the King of France so much at heart, that he considers the exaltation of his kingdom as the exaltation of the Holy See, and that he was far from intending in any way to injure him ; that, burdened already with duties beyond his strength, he had no thought of encroaching upon the jurisdiction of the king,[1] and neither would the king desire to do anything to the prejudice of the Pope's jurisdiction ; that he had merely made use of the spiritual jurisdiction possessed by the Church (St. Matt. xviii. 15-17) ; that when brotherly admonition and correction before witnesses were fruitless, the sinner was to be brought before the judgment-seat of the Church, and if found guilty and wanting in submission, was to be cast forth and treated as the heathen and the publican ; that the right of correction, even in the case of Christian princes, had ever been inherent in the Church ;[2] that he had no intention of judging in a question of *fiefs*, but in a question of *sin*, to censure which was beyond doubt the duty of the Pope ;[3] that moreover this was a case of treaties of peace confirmed by oath and broken before the appointed time ; and that it was the duty of the Church to take cognisance of oaths.

The principle of the Decretal is that *directly* the Church has to pass judgment as to the violation of the moral law, *indirectly* as to the temporal matters involved. The Pope was not directly concerned in the execution of the sentence of the French feudal court, nor in the sentence itself, but grievous offences against the moral law fall under the judgment of the Head of the Church, who has power to proceed against the culprit with spiritual punishments. This is a power given not by men but by God, the power of binding and loosing given to St. Peter and affecting all Christians without respect of persons ; kings even are subject to it, and all the more because, with this exception, they acknowledge no superior. The Pope has not to speak of temporal matters *as such*, and can only touch them *indirectly* when they are connected with a violation of the moral law.[4] The Pope in this case is merely a subsidiary judge.[5]

¹ The Pope here clearly sets forth the independence of the king *in temporalibus.* Cf. suprà, § 13, n. 1, 3.

² The Fathers often rebuked emperors and kings, especially St. Ambrose (Orat. c. Auxent. de basilicis; Ep. 21, 29 ; Theod. H. E. v. 17), St. Martin of Tours (Sulpic. Sever. Vita S. Mart. l. i. c. xxiii.), St. John Chrysostom (Theod. H. E. v. 28). Earlier Popes had in former times rebuked the Byzantine emperors (Anastasius, Leo III. &c.) and other Christian princes. When Charles the Bald complained of the undeserved censure of Pope Nicholas I. the Pope replied, in 863 : ' Scimus tamen nos, ex qua radice contra dilectionem vestram haec virga processerit ; percuteris, imo pulsaris, fili, ut cautior et sollicitior valeas inveniri' (Mansi, xv. 296; Jaffé, n. 2056, p. 242). The king willingly submitted himself, as is seen by the Pope's next letter (Jaffé, n. 2066).

³ Non enim intendimus *judicare de feudo,* cujus ad ipsum spectat judicium . . . . sed *decernere de peccato,* cujus ad nos pertinet sine dubitatione censura, quam in quemlibet exercere possumus et debemus.

⁴ Phillips, Kirchenrecht, iii. § 129, specially p. 226. Bossuet (Defens. l. iii. c. xxii. p. 519) considers the Decretal as not applicable in the case, because it does not treat of the deposition of kings ; but he overlooks the fact that the theologians with whom he is disputing have in this case only the general principle in view. He observes, in conclusion : ' Ceterum *in foro conscientiae,* ubi habemus confitentem ac poenitentem reum, quo pacto quaecunque peccata sunt etiam in temporalibus (sive illa sunt ambigua sive certa, sive publica sive occulta) clavibus Ecclesiae subdantur, quatenus quidem peccata sunt, nemo sanus objiciet neque ad rem ullo modo pertinet. Quod propter tardiores aut cavillatores monitum esse volumus.' Modern writers indeed, who are horrified at the wide domain of morals (Schulte, i. p. 26), do not seem willing to allow this. The text in St. Matt. xviii. 15 seq. cannot rightly be applied to the secret tribunal of conscience. Gosselin (ii. p. 253 seq.) interprets the Decretal according to his theory of the directing power.

⁵ Glossa, Jurisdictionem nostram, in Phillips, p. 233, n. 20.

§ 16.

This was the principle applied by Alexander III. in a question as to legitimacy¹ when appeal was made from a temporal judge to the Roman See,² and by Honorius III. in the dispute as to the right of succession of the Queen of Cyprus.³ Innocent accurately distinguishes the question of civil law from that falling within his own jurisdiction. In the particular case before us King John had brought Philip's offence under the notice of the Church, and had offered to come forward himself as a witness. Philip, as the Pope admonished him, should now have called to mind the example of pious princes, such as the Emperor Valentinian, who desired ever such a supreme pastor as would

recall him to the right path by his rebuke, when he through
human frailty erred ;[4] Theodosius II.[5] and Charles the Great[6]
directed that if one of two contending parties desired to lay his
case before the Church he should be suffered to do so. The
promotion of peace was the Pope's unquestioned duty ; a short
time before it had been beneficial to the French king ; and since
he had himself desired the Pope to mediate for peace with Richard
Cœur-de-Lion, he had no just ground for now withstanding a
like endeavour.[7] But beyond the question of the truce came
that of its confirmation by oath, upon which the Church had an
acknowledged right of judgment. The Pope could not appear
to favour such a state of disturbance between the two kings, or
to lean to one side rather than the other. His legates were to
move the King of France to make a new treaty, or failing this,
in conjunction with the Archbishop of Bourges[8] to make inquiry into John's grievances. John sent no representative to the
Synod held by the legates at Meaux in 1204, while the French
prelates appealed to the Pope.[9] The Pope received the appeal,
though he would not hold them bound by the obligation they
had undertaken of obeying the summons within an appointed
time under pain of suspension ; he was satisfied with the attend-
ance of a few.[10] Those who made their appearance were the
Archbishops of Sens and Bourges, the Bishops of Paris, Meaux,
Châlons, Nevers, and other ecclesiastics ; they defended the
right of their king, and were prepared, in case they had fallen
under suspicion, to undergo canonical purgation. The Pope released them from this, and took no further steps on the side of
John, who again had sent no representative to Rome.[11] By
1206, John had lost his dominions on the Continent. When,
in 1205, the Bishops of Normandy inquired of the Pope whether
they were to take the *fidelitas* demanded by the French king,
i.e. the oath of allegiance, Innocent III. replied that they must
judge for themselves according to their knowledge of the circumstances, and that he could give them no answer on the subject.[12]

---

[1] C. 7, Causam, iv. 17, Qui filii sint legitimi : ' Nos attendentes, quod
ad regem pertinet, non ad Ecclesiam, *de talibus possessionibus judicare,*

ne videamur juri regis Anglorum detrahere, qui ipsarum judicium ad se asserit pertinere, fraternitati vestrae mandamus, quatenus regi possessionum judicium relinquentes de causa principali, videl. utrum mater praedicti R. de legitimo sit matrimonio nata, plenius cognoscatis' (Migne, cc. p. 1185, seq. Ep, 1360).

² C. 7, Si duobus, § 1, de Appell. ii. 28 : ' Tenet quidem in his, qui sunt nostrae temporali jurisdictioni subjecti ; in aliis vero, etsi de consuetudine Ecclesiae tencat, secundum juris rigorem credimus non tenere.' Cf. Phillips, l.c. p. 234 seq.

³ C. 3, Tuam, ii. 10, de Ord. Cognit. Louis VIII. of France was petitioned not to decide as to the right of succession until the judgment of the Church had been given as to the disputed legitimacy of the queen (Migne, t. ccxvi. p. 985, n. 15).

⁴ C. 3, d. 63.

⁵ C. 35, c. xi. q. 1 ; i. 1, Cod. Theodos. de Episc. Judic.

⁶ Capit. vi. 366 ; c. Volumus, 37, c. et q. cit.

⁷ Phillips observes (§ 139, p. 419) that Innocent III. did not go so far as Luther, who in 1542 ordered the Prince Elector John Frederick and Duke Maurice of Saxony to desist from their contest for the city of Wurzen, and admonished their vassals to refuse their feudal service. K. A. Menzel, Neuere Geschichte der Deutschen, ii. p. 296 seq.

⁸ Phillips, p. 237 seq. Hefele, Conc. v. p. 708 seq.

⁹ Innoc. l. vii. Ep. 134, p. 425, ed. Migne.

¹⁰ He expressly declared : 'Nolumus vos hoc titulo tenere legatos, sed apellationem interpositam prosequamini, prout regno et sacerdotio noveritis expedire : quia non ita volumus sacerdotii jure integra conservare, ut etiam regni jura custodiamus illaesa.'

¹¹ Acta Innoc. III. n. 130. Muratori, R. It. Scr. iii. 561. Mansi, xxii. 545 seq.

¹² L. viii. Ep. 7, p. 564.

§ 17.

The Decretal ' Novit' was everywhere, even in France itself, accepted as part of the canon law.¹ In 1329, Petrus Bertrandi, at that time Bishop of Autun, set forth these principles in the name of the clergy before the officers of the crown, making appeal to this very Decretal ;² the same had been done before by the renowned Augustinian Ægidius of Rome, Archbishop of Bourges (died 1316), who defended the jurisdiction of the Church in mixed matters in the sense of the Decretal ;³ even the author of the *Somnium Viridarii* (c. 1382), though so little in favour of ecclesiastical claims, maintains the same ; the differences of opinion mentioned by him scarcely affect the material question.⁴ St. Bernard also taught that in certain contingencies (incidenter) and for cogent reasons the Church may intervene in temporal matters,[5] and the same has been taught by the majority of theologians since his time.[6] But this did not imply that all temporal power was delivered over to the Church, or that the two powers were blended into one. The Church punished crimes which fell under her cognisance with spiritual penalties, while the State came in with temporal penalties. The State dealt with temporal cases inquisitorially and by means of its officials; the spiritual power only after a denunciation, or by reason of the publicity of the guilt, in so far as lay within its domain. The Church, whose aim was the amendment of the offender, only punished the obstinate (contumax), who, in spite of all warnings, did not amend; the State punished those who had done wrong, even when they had repented of their crime. The chastisements of the Church were intended to heal the soul (medicinal), and not primarily to expiate the crime (vindicative).[7] But the Church could not justly punish unless the sin was proved; she must take cognisance of it. Therefore kings, though subject to no vindicative punishment, and having in matters temporal no superior over them, were still not free from the spiritual power and from the healing punishments of the Church in case they sinned publicly and with grievous scandal, or misused their power to the injury of religion and of souls.[8] It did not follow that every question of law could be brought at pleasure before the spiritual court under pretext of grievous sin; if fraud (dolus) were proved, the spiritual judge was bound to refuse to hear the question in dispute.[9] Moreover, the competence of the civil judge, when real, did not cease because the Church also took cognisance of the case of a Christian guilty of public and grievous sin.[10]

¹ The Gloss on art. 1 of the Sachsenspiegels (Friedberg, p. 28, n. 6) says : 'The Pope may intervene in matters temporal to pass judgment on public sins.'

² Respons. ad Petrum de Cugnières in disputat. cum officialibus regni (Bibl. Vet. PP. Lugd. 1677, t. xxvi. p. 109 seq.) : 'Nullus dubitat, quin cognitio de peccato ad personas ecclesiasticas pertineat. . . . Ecclesia, quae habet judicare de spiritualibus, potest et merito de temporalibus judicare, et hoc satis deducitur Xvag. de Judic. c. 13, Novit.' The royal official supposed the Decree to hold good only de facto regis Franciae, qui superiorem non habet, 'sed in aliis dicebat secus.'

³ Cf. F. X. Kraus, in the treatise ' Ægidius von Rom' (Oesterreichische Vierteljahrschrift für Kath. Theologie, Vienna, 1862, i. Jahrgang, p. 1 seq.), in which further proof is given of the spurious character of the document printed after Ch. Jourdain's example (Un Ouvrage inédit de Gilles de Rome, Paris, 1858) by Goldast (Monarch. S.R.J. ii. p. 95 seq.), de utraque potestate s. quaestio in utramque partem disputata de potestate regia et pontificali ;' a document to which Bossuet (Defens. l. iii. c. xxv. p. 329 seq.) and many others appeal.   In the Quaestiones disputatae, art. 4, it is said : ' Rex Franciae secundum jura non subest summo Pontifici nec ei tenetur respondere de feudo suo, potest tamen ei subjacere *incidenter et casualiter, ratione connexionis alicujus causae spiritualis,* sicut habetur extravag. de judiciis cap. Novit. . . . Causae *mixtae* (it says) sunt causae temporales, quae connexionem quamdam habent cum spiritualibus.'   Cf. Friedberg, p. 63, n. 1.   In his writing, de Ecclesiastica Potestate (Kraus, l.c. p. 14), Ægid. teaches (P. iii. c. v.) : ' Quod si temporalia fiant spiritualia vel annectantur spiritualibus, vel e contrario temporalibus spiritualia sint annexa, sunt spirituales casus, per quos Ecclesia jurisdictionem temporalem dicitur exercere.'   Cf. ib. c. vi-viii.

⁴ Somnium Virid. (Gold. i. 59 seq.) : ' Concedendum est, quod principatus papalis concernit temporalia, prout de necessario concernit spiritualia, *cum ab eorum usu vel abusu surgit peccatum,* prout dicunt textus : *ratione peccati* omnes causae spectant ad forum ecclesiasticum cap. *Novit* de judiciis.   Tamen *principaliter* disponendo et auctorizando nihil spectat ad Papam quantum ad temporalia. . . . Non debet se (potestas eccl.) de depositione imperatorum seu regum intromittere, quantumcumque rex vel imperator sit dignus depositione propter defectum quemcumque vel crimen, quod *non est inter spiritualia crimina* computandum, et ideo si imperator vel rex committit crimen delapidationis vel destructionis imperii sive regni vel tyrannidis vel quodcunque aliud, propter quod non immerito deponi meruit, Papa non debet eum deponere, sed populus, a quo suam recepit potestatem tacite vel expresse, *nisi illi, ad quos pertinet nollent aut non possent facere justitiae complementum.* . . . Fatendum tamen, quod Papa potest transferre imperium vel regnum *casualiter,* ut quia non est alius superior vel alter, aut imperium vel regnum est transferendum de gente in gentem *propter aliquod crimen spirituale gentis,* puta si gens illa inficiatur haeretica pravitate vel ad legem Judaeorum vel ad ritum gentilium vel sectam aliam converteretur.   Si transferendum esset imperium vel regnum propter crimen spirituale, dicunt quidam, quod Papa potest *jure divino* transferre imperium seu regnum, quia *in spiritualibus et annexis eis* habet plenitudinem potestatis *quantum ad ea, quae sunt de necessitate facienda.*   Alii dicunt, quod Papa in hoc casu non potest transferre imperium seu regnum, nisi laici fuerint damnabiliter negligentes vel faventes genti, a qua transferri necesse est imperium vel regnum, sed in hoc casu spectat ad Papam, *de crimine spirituali* cognoscere et denunciare illis, ad quos spectat, ut ipsum deponant ; quodsi noluerint vel non potuerint, *jure divino devoluta est potestas ad summum pontificem,* et hoc quia ipse habet plenitudinem potestatis quantum ad omnia, quae sunt de necessitate facienda.'

⁵ S. Bern. de Consid. l. i. c. vi. n. 7 : ' Quaenam tibi major videtur et

dignitas et potestas, dimittendi peccati ad praedia dividendi? Sed non est comparatio. Habent haec infima et terrena judices suos, reges et principes terrae. . . . Quid falcem vestram in alienam messem extenditis? *Non quia indigni vos, sed quia indignum vobis* talibus insistere, quippe potioribus occupatis. Denique *ubi necessitas exigit,* audi quid censeat Apostolus : *Si enim in vobis judicabitur hic mundus, indigni estis qui de minimis judicetis !* (1 Cor. vi. 2.) Sed aliud est, *incidenter* excurrere in ista, *causa* quidem *urgente,* aliud ultro incumbere istis, tamquam magnis dignisque tali et talium intentione rebus.'

[6] W. Occam himself teaches, Quaest. Octo Decis. q. 8, c. v. (Gold. ii. 385), that the Pope *casualiter,* in urgent need or for the public service, may intervene in temporal matters. Much earlier again, Petrus Bles. (Specul. Jur. c. xvi.) wrote : ' Canonum enim vigor se extendit ad causas saeculares, ex quibus et in quibus animae periculum versatur. Quantum enim *ad hoc, ut animae provideatur,* omnes personae spectant ad forum ecclesiasticum, et in talibus judiciis, secundum meum judicium, videtur per canones legibus et consuetudinibus derogatum.' That even the opponents of the Popes often shared their principle is acknowledged by Friedberg himself (pp. 39 seq. 48, 52, n. 4).

[7] Petrus Vener. l. vi. Ep. 28, ad Eugen. III. (Migne, clxxxix. p. 442) : ' Sed quamvis Ecclesia non habeat imperatoris gladium, habet tamen super quoslibet minores, sed et super ipsos imperatores, *imperium.* Unde ei sub figura prophetici nominis dicitur : Constitui te super gentes et regna, ut evellas et destruas, et disperdas et dissipes, et aedifices et plantes (Jer. i. 10). Qua de re *si non potest occidere, potest evellere, si non potest occidere, potest destruere.'*

[8] Bianchi, t. ii. l. vi. § 3, p. 403 seq.

[9] Navarr. Relect. cap. Novit, Notab. 6, n. 19 seq. Opp. ii. p. 158 seq. ed. Lugd. 1589. Phillips, l.c. p. 236.

[10] Navarr. l.c. n. 18. Phillips, pp. 234, 235.

PART II. THE POWER OF THE CHURCH IN MATTERS TEMPORAL.

§ 1. Three theories on this point. § 2. (a) Direct power of the Church in matters temporal. § 3. This theory untenable. § 4. (b) Indirect power. § 5. Bellarmine's teaching. § 6. Ground for this opinion. § 7. This power has ever been used by the Church. § 8. Teaching of the Fathers. § 9. Cardinal Turrecremata. § 10. This teaching the most general. § 11. Attacks upon Bellarmine's teaching. § 12. Objections. § 13. Replies. § 14, 15. Teaching of the Jesuits. § 16. (c) Directing power. § 17, 18. Relations of this theory to the preceding. § 19. Superiority of ecclesiastical over civil legislation.

§ 1.

In relation to the power of the Church in matters temporal were formed three systems based upon the notions expressed in the Decretal ' Novit,' upon the idea prominent even in the first ages of Christianity that the spiritual power was above the temporal, and upon the theory and practice of the Middle Ages : (*a*) the system of the direct power of the Church in matters temporal ; (*b*) that of the merely indirect power ; (*c*) that of the merely directing power.

(*a*) *The system of the direct power of the Church in matters temporal (Potestas directa Ecclesiae in temporalia).*

§ 2.

The main doctrines of this system were as follows : God has given to the Pope, as His Vicar, endowed with the unlimited power of binding and loosing, authority to rule the world in temporal as in spiritual matters, but in such manner that the spiritual power is to be wielded by him in person, while the civil power is to be delivered over to princes, who in reality are merely servants of the Church, receive their power from her, are responsible to her, and in case of misconduct may be deposed by her. Thus the Pope comes to be the supreme head in spiritual and temporal matters, to whom, as Vicar of Christ, the King of kings, all nations and kingdoms are directly subject, and earthly kings must in turn be his representatives.[1]

This opinion, strongly combated by Bellarmine,[2] was held by Henry of Segusia, Cardinal Bishop of Ostia,[3] Augustinus Triumphus (1320),[4] Alvarus Pelagius (1340),[5] and others.[6] The learned John of Salisbury (1159), who is in some respects considered as the first defender of this system,[7] has by no means made use of the strong expressions employed by late upholders of this view. His opinion seems to have been shared by St. Thomas à Becket.

[1] Bossuet, who in the Defens. (l. i. sect. 1, c. i.) gives the first of the four articles of 1682, states like Bellarmine this view as follows (c. ii.) : ' Rom. Pontificem Christi regis vicarium directo et jure divino regem regum esse ac totius orbis dominum ; quare exorta pontificia dignitate statim regna atque imperia omnia in ejus imperium concessisse, reges omnes nonnisi Papae vicarios esse, gladium temporalis aeque ac spiritualis potestatis proprie ejus esse, vicaria licet manu exercendum, atque ita in Pontificem omne translatum esse dominium, ut principes etiam infideles deturbare solio eorumque regna jure suo donare possit quibuscumque voluerit fidelium.'

[2] Bellarm. de Rom. Pont. 1. v. c. i. seq.; to which Bossuet also l.c. makes appeal.
[3] Henric. Ost. in cap. Quod super his, t. iii. p. 129 (p. 334, § 2, n. 1).
[4] Aug. Triumphus, Sum. de Pot. Eccl. q. 23, a. 1 seq. p. 136, ed. 1584.
[5] Alvar. Pelag. de Planctu Eccl. 1. i. c. xiii. p. 3, ed. 1560.
[6] Panormit. in c. Novit, cit. Sylvester in Summa de Peccatis v. Papa, § 2, f. 223, ed. 1619.　Nicolaus Cevolus ex Marchionibus de Sarreto. Consult. Theol. Jurid. p. 11 (cf. Bossuet, l.c. Anton Arnauld, lettre 221, t. iii. p. 408, ed. 1727).　Alex. Carerius of Padua, lib. de Potest. Rom. Pontificis adv. impios Politicos, c. v. seq. ix. seq. pp. 51 seq. 58 seq. ed. Patav. 1599.
[7] Gosselin, ii. 440 seq.

§ 3.

The large majority of theologians have perceived this doctrine to be untenable, and have proved it in detail to be so.[1] They point out that though Christ is possessed of all power in heaven and upon earth, and though the Pope must be regarded as His Vicar, still this vicariate extends over the religious domain only, and includes no unlimited temporal sovereignty, although the temporal sovereignty of a determinate district has been advantageously united with it.　Unbelieving princes do not belong to the fold of Christ (St. John xxi. 15 seq.), and the Church has in general no jurisdiction over unbelievers (1 Cor. v. 12); the Pope would not most surely appoint heathens as his vicars.

Neither are the keys of earthly kingdoms committed to the Pope, but those of the Kingdom of Heaven; so that Christian rulers by the acceptance and introduction of Christianity have not forfeited their sovereign power, and Christ, who bestows the heavenly, does not deprive them of their earthly kingdom.[2] Were the Pope a universal ruler, the bishops would necessarily be everywhere rulers in their own cities and dioceses; the practical consequences of this doctrine prove its absurdity.[3]　The Popes have never laid claim to any such power, but have on the contrary fully acknowledged the jurisdiction of temporal princes.[4] Even Innocent III., to whom men love to attribute the most exorbitant pretensions, distinguished perfectly between his complete and unlimited spiritual jurisdiction and his limited temporal power.[5] The Popes, when claiming the care of the heavenly

and earthly kingdom, have never said that the two were subject
to them in precisely the same manner; and in maintaining the
superiority of the spiritual power they have still never said that
temporal power must everywhere and in all cases be subject to
it, or that the temporal had its origin in the spiritual. Some
are astonished at the saying of Innocent III., that Christ gave
to St. Peter the government not of the whole Church, but of
the whole world;[6] but in this he surely said nothing more than
had been already said by Eugenius III., that Christ had delivered to St. Peter the rights of the earthly and of the heavenly
kingdom.[7] The point which Innocent desired to prove was, as
the whole context shows, that the primacy of the Pope has no
territorial limits.[8] The power of the Pope extends to all Christian lands, not merely on earth, but also in heaven; by this is
meant spiritual power only, of which it had been before said:
'Power is given to princes on earth, but to priests in heaven
also.'[9]

[1] Bellarmine (de Rom. Pont. l. v. c. ii-iv.) contradicts in detail the assertion: 'Papam esse dominum totius mundi, dominum totius orbis terrarum, habere jurisdictionem temporalem directe.'

[2] Kirchenhymnus von Sedulius, Dec. 28: 'Non eripit mortalia, qui
regna dat coelestia.'

[3] Mamachi (Ord. Praed.), Orig. et Antiqu. Chr. Romae, 1752, t. iv.
pp. 175-179.

[4] P. c. Novit cit.; Per venerabilem (Baluz. Ep. Innoc. I. p. 676).

[5] Innoc. III. l. ii. Ep. 4 (to the consuls and people of Jesi in the States of
the Church), p. 541, ed. Migne: 'Cum Apostolicae Sedis, *jurisdictio spiritualis nullis terminis coarctetur*, imo super gentes et regna sortita sit potestatem: *in multis* etiam per Dei gratiam ejus *extenditur jurisdictio temporalis*, quae, licet aliquando visa fuerit propter quorumdam violentiam co-
arctari, nunc tamen eo faciente nobiscum signum in bonum, qui imperat
ventis et mari . . . redit in potentatum antiquum et de die in diem amplius
dilatatur.' He is referring to the regained territory of the States of the
Church, Perugia, Camerino, &c. Again (l. viii. Ep. 190, p. 767). he writes:
'Licet pontificalis anctoritas et imperialis potestas diversae sint dignitatis
et officia regni et sacerdotii sint distincta, quia tamen Rom. Pontifex illius
agit vices in terris, qui est rex regum in terris et dominus dominantium,
sacerdos in aeternum secundum ordinem Melchisedech, non solum *in spiritualibus* habet *summam*, verum etiam in *temporalibus magnam* ab ipso
Domino potestatem.' The temporal sovereignty of the Pope, like that of
other princes, has its origin in God. The sentence immediately following
shows that he alludes to this temporal sovereignty: 'Cum igitur episcopatus Firmanus [the letter demanded from the clergy and people of Fermo

in the States of the Church obedience to the new bishop; tam in spiritualibus quam etiam temporalibus ad eum nullo pertineat mediante, nos . . . . electionem illius . . . . auctoritate curavimus apostolica confirmare ipsumque postmodum per vexillum de regalibus investire.' Cf. also ib. Ep. 191.

⁶ L. ii. Ep. 209, Patr. Cpl. p. 759, ed. cit. : (Chr.) 'Petro non solum universalem Ecclesiam, sed totum reliquit sacculum gubernandum.'

⁷ Jaffé, n. 6362, p. 629 : ' B. Petro, coelorum regni clavigero, terreni simul et coelestis imperii jura commisit.' Gregory VII. and Nicholas II. (p. 140, n. 1, 2) had before declared the same.

⁸ Immediately afterwards (p. 760) he says : ' Nam cum aquae multae sint, populi multi, congregationesque aquarum sint maria, per hoc quod Petrus super aquas maris incessit, *super universos populos* se potestatem accepisse monstravit.' Nothing else is meant than that Peter 'universum orbem susceperat *gubernandum.*' *Gubernare* is used in relation to the helm of a ship, and the Scripture narratives of Peter walking on the water are brought forward ; while the others remained in the ship, he hastened *sine beneficio navis* to the Lord ; thus making known that to him is committed not individual churches or provinces but the whole world. The words of the Pope (Baluz. i. 547, 548) : ' Singuli (principes) singulas habent provincias et singuli reges singula regna ; sed Petrus, sicut *plenitudine*, sic et *latitudine* praeeminet universis, quia vicarius est ejus, cujus est terra et plenitudo ejus,' &c. (Ps. xxiii. 1), imply merely that the power of the Pope in extent as well as in plenitude excels all earthly power.

⁹ Cf. on this point Gosselin, ii. p. 248 seq.; also Petr. Dam. Opusc. v. ad cler. pop. Mediolan. ; also Mamachi, l.c. p. 183. Innocent again expresses the same thoughts in l. vii. Ep. i. p. 279. The interpretation of the word *gubernandum* urged by Hundeshagen (l.c. p. 264) is quite inadmissible. Innocent has in this case the words of St. Bernard (de Consid. l. ii. c. viii. n. 16) before his eyes, which are : ' Signum singularis pontificii Petri, per quod non navem unam, ut ceteri quique suam, sed *saeculum ipsum susceperit gubernandum.* Mare enim saeculum est, naves Ecclesiae. Inde est altera vice instar Domini gradiens super aquas *unicum se Christi vicarium designavit,* qui non uni populo, sed cunctis praeesse deberet; siquidem *aquae multae, populi multi* (Apoc. xvii. 15). Ita cum quisque ceterorum habeat suam, tibi una commissa est grandissima navis, facta ex omnibus ipsa universalis Ecclesia, toto orbe diffusa.'

(*b*) *The theory of the indirect power of the Church in matters temporal* (*Potestas indirecta in temporalia*).

§ 4.

The second system, which has the largest number of followers, teaches that the Church has direct spiritual power, but no direct temporal power ; she is appointed to govern the faithful in the supernatural way of salvation ; spiritual matters alone are in themselves subject to her, and in worldly matters she takes no part. In so far only as temporal matters are opposed to the supernatural end, or are necessary for its attainment, has the Church to concern herself with them, and to exert her power.[1] She has in that case to correct and to guide the worldly power, and if necessary to chastise it when it turns aside from the right path of divine law, hinders the attainment of the supernatural end, and endangers the stability of religion and of the Church.[2] Neither the Pope nor the Church can directly depose a prince, but they can where the highest interests of religion are concerned declare the duty of obedience towards him to have ceased. A prince, bound by oath to maintain religion, who has broken this oath by apostasy or by persecution of the Church, who hearkens to no warnings and despises ecclesiastical penalties, may not be dethroned by his people, for this would strengthen and justify all rebellion; but the people must be declared free from their oath of allegiance by sentence of a General Council or of the Head of the Church.

This indirect power of the Church in matters temporal in general, and in relation to the dethroning of princes in particular, is not a temporal but a spiritual power. It is exerted in matters temporal only in so far as they intrench upon religion, and in this way cease to be purely temporal. Thus Innocent IV. said that the Church passed judgment in a spiritual manner on temporal matters (spiritualiter de temporalibus);[3] and in his contest with Frederick II. he declared that he was making use not of the temporal but of the spiritual sword.[4] Some theologians have attributed to the Pope in certain cases power to depose a prince; but the distinction is rather in the words than the matter;[5] they required the same conditions, and merely took the consequences of the act for the act itself; instead of the power of declaring the right of sovereignty forfeited, they supposed him to have the power of deposing (potestas deponendi, instead of potestas declarandi).[6] In general it was held that all things temporal were to be directed towards eternal goods, and that earthly goods were to be used with a view to heavenly, otherwise they would be merely abused.[7]

At first the title 'indirect power' appeared to many strange and contrary to the common teaching; and for this reason Bellarmine's book putting it forward was placed on the Index under Sixtus V.; but before long the conviction spread that the matter of the book was sound, and that the expression 'indirect power' was well chosen ; Urban VII. therefore, in 1590, had the book erased from the Index.[8]

[1] Bellarm. de Rom. Pontif. v. 6 : 'Spiritualis potestas non se miscet temporalibus negotiis, sed sinit omnia procedere, sicut antequam essent conjunctae, dummodo non obsint fini spirituali aut non sint necessaria ad eum consequendum. Si autem tale quid accidat, spiritualis potestas potest et debet coercere temporalem omni ratione ac via, quae ad id necessaria esse videbitur.'

[2] Bellarm. l.c. c. vii.: 'Finis temporalis subordinatur fini spirituali, quia felicitas temporalis non est absolute ultimus finis, et ideo referri debet in felicitatem aeternam. . . . Non recte asseritur spiritualia pendere a temporalibus, ergo temporalia a spiritualibus pendent illisque subjiciuntur.' Bossuet (Def. l. i. sect. 1, c. ii. p. 87) thus gives the doctrine : ' Primum : temporalia omnia ad spiritualia referri ut ad finem, i'sque per sese subordinata esse ; tum : ita subordinari facultates ut subordinantur fines ; atque ideo qui fini praesit, eum etiam praesidere mediis, adeoque posse et imperare omnia, quae fini adipiscendo necessaria videantur, et ea amovere quae impedimento sunt, quare omnem saecularem potestatem *eatenus* in temporalibus esse Papae subjectam, *quatenus* abusio aut negligentia Christianorum regum circa temporalia nata sunt impedire finem spiritualem, in quem habet Papa universalem Ecclesiam dirigere. Quam Papae potestatem ideo *indirectam* vocant, quod non se extendat *directe* ad temporalia, sed indirecte, *quatenus ex temporalibus spiritualia vel promoventur vel impediuntur.*'

[3] Bréholles, Diplom. t. vi. p. 496 seq. Hefele, v. 1006.

[4] Ep. ad Capitul. Gen. Cistere. ap. Bréholles, l.c. p. 346. Hefele, l.c. p. 1007.

[5] Mamachi, l.c. pp. 182, 183.

[6] Jac. Almain. de Potest. Eccl. et Laica, q. 1, c. ix. ad c. cxci. Occami : ' Christus numquam dedit auctoritatem Petro aliquem regem a jurisdictione sua deponendi, et non dedit potestatem laicos suis dominiis et proprietatibus privandi, *nisi in casu* si contingeret principem saecularem *abuti* re sua in perniciem Christianitatis vel fidei, ita quod ille abusus in maximo esset nocumento pro consecutione felicitatis aeternae, et non negat Doctor, quia *in tali casu* Papa *possit eum deponere* etsi alii Doctores hoc negent, quamvis doceant, *habere solum potestatem declarandi* ipsum principem esse deponendum.'

[7] Auct. Quaest. in utramque Part. Disp. a. 5 (Gold. ii. 103): ' Dicendum, sicut temporalia sunt propter corpus, et corpus propter animam, ita quod haec omnia inferiora debent ad bonum animae ordinari. *Aliter non recte uteretur homo temporalibus, sed potius abuteretur.* Sic potestas temporalis *quodam modo* ordinatur ad spiritualem, in his, quae ad ipsam spiritualitatem pertinent, i.e. in spiritualibus.'

* Sachini, Hist. Soc. Jesu, P. v. t. i. p. 499. Vita Rob. Bellarmini, Auctore Fuligato, l. ii. c. vii. D'Avrigny, Mémoires pour servir à l'Hist. Ecclés. du 17 siècle, Nov. 1610.

§ 5.

Bellarmine treats of the indirect power of the Church in a triple application : (1) *Quantum ad personas* ; (2) *quantum ad leges* ; (3) *quantum ad judicia.* In relation (1) to persons, he teaches that in an ordinary way, as *judex ordinarius*, the Pope cannot depose temporal princes as he can bishops, but can only, in virtue of his right as head of Christendom, dispose of all things necessary to the salvation of souls.[1] All the schoolmen were agreed upon the main point, that in case of threatened destruction to faith and the exercise of religion, or where the preservation of the Church is concerned, this power may be exercised, especially in a case of apostasy from the faith.[2] (2) In relation to laws, the Pope, as Pope, cannot release from civil laws or abolish the laws of temporal princes except only when it is necessary for the good of souls, or when an existing temporal law is dangerous to salvation, and when at the same time princes refuse its repeal.[3] (3) As judge he can pass sentence in temporal matters only when absolutely necessary for the salvation of souls.[4]

[1] Bell. l.c. c. vi. : ' Quantum ad personas non potest Papa ut Papa *ordinarie* temporales principes deponere, *etiam justa de causa*, eo modo, quo deponit episcopos, i.e. tanquam ordinarius judex : tamen potest mutare regna et uni auferre atque alteri conferre tanquam summus princeps spiritualis, *si id necessarium sit ad animarum salutem*.'

[2] Bianchi, t. i. l. i. § 14, pp. 116-121, where it is shown how vain is Bossuet's appeal to Melchior Cannus, who expressly says : ' Scholae communem consensum nonnisi impudenter et temere rejici ; haeresi proximum esse, concordi theologorum scholae de fide vel moribus sententiae contradicere' (de loc. Theol. viii. 4, concl. 2. Cf. Sfondrat, Regal. Sacerd. l. i. § 17).

[3] Bellarmin. l.c.: ' Quantum ad leges, non potest Papa ut Papa ordinarie condere legem civilem vel confirmare aut infirmare leges principum, quia ipse non est princeps Ecclesiae politicus, tamen potest omnia illa facere, si aliqua lex civilis sit necessaria ad salutem animarum et tamen reges non velint eam condere, aut si alia sit noxia animarum saluti et tamen reges non velint eam abrogare. . . . At quando materia leges est res temporalis nec concernens animarum periculum, non potest lex pontificia abrogare legem imperatoriam, sed utraque servanda est, illa in foro eccle-

siastico, ista in foro civili.'   Also Gloss to c. ii. Possessor de Reg. J. in 6.

⁴ Ibid.: ' Quantum ad judicia, non potest Papa ut Papa ordinarie judicare in rebus temporalibus. .... At nihilominus in casu quo id animarum saluti necessarium est, potest Pontifex assumere etiam temporalia judicia, quando nimirum non est ullus qui possit judicare, ut cum duo reges supremi contendunt, vel quando qui possunt et debent judicare, non volunt sententiam ferre.'

§ 6.

In further support of this opinion the following proofs were brought forward : Christian princes form, as is universally allowed, part of the flock of Christ confided to St. Peter (St. John xxi. 15) ;[1] the charge of them consists in so leading them that they may attain eternal salvation. But how can they attain it if the supreme pastor has not the means either of leading back erring sheep to the fold or of hindering the rest from going astray? This he cannot do if he is forced to look on while a prince is raging unpunished against the Church, and leading or forcing the subjects bound to him by oath away from the true religion into error. The Pope must take the necessary steps against him by censures, and if his obstinacy require it, also against those who obey his evil orders, and who have dealings with him in his official position. In case of extreme obstinacy, which is made a condition by all theologians,[2] the Pope may declare the oath taken to a prince to be no longer binding, for the purpose of moving him to amendment. No oath binds in such a way that it cannot be loosed if it endangers the salvation of souls, and no end may be preferred before the highest and last end of man.[3]

---

[1] Petav. de Hierarch. Eccl. l. iii. c. ix. Dogm. t. iii. p. 853 seq. ed. Paris; Bossuet, Defens. P. i. l. i. sect. 1, c. iii.; and elsewhere. Also Dante (de Monarch. l. iii. p. 284, ed. Schard), highly as he esteems the power of the emperor, insists that he should show reverence to the successor of St. Peter, 'qua primogenitus filius debet uti ad patrem, ut luce paternae gratiae illustratus virtuosius orbem terrae irradiet.' Upon which Friedberg (p. 61, § 4) remarks: ' Minime discrepans hac in re a Bellarmino, qui nihil nisi hanc reverentiam Papae vindicans tamen omnibus illum imperare praedicat.' Cf. Bernold. Rat. Apolog. c. viii. seq. p. 1222, ed. Migne.

[2] Even Joh. Saresb. Polycrat. l. v. c. vi. p. 549: ' Nec tamen licitum est favore novorum recedere a sanguine principum, quibus privilegio di-

vinae promissionis et jure generis debetur successio liberorum, si tamen, ut praescriptum est, ambulaverint in justitiis Domini. Si vero a via paulisper deflexerint, *non statim usquequaque dejiciuntur,* sed patienter corripiuntur in justitia, *donec fiat conspicuum eos pertinaces esse in malo.*
 Thom. de Regim. Princip. l. i. c. xiv. p. 295, ed. 1587.

§ 7.

The Church, even in the earliest times, exercised an indirect power in matters temporal. How was it else that she forbade the faithful to undertake and administer certain employments and offices prejudicial to the welfare of their souls,[1] and that later, when persecution had ceased and the danger was lessened, she still required ecclesiastical approval for the administration and exercise of such offices and professions, though they were no longer prohibited?[2] Christians who held the post of city duumvirate, and were thus brought into close contact with heathen rites, had to remain away from church during their year of office.[3] Under Constantine, however, the Synod of Arles, 314, directed that Christian *praesides* were to bring with them into their provinces letters of communion from their bishop, and only in the event of their acting contrary to the laws of the Church were they to be cut off from communion by the bishop of the place in which they were holding office.[4] By an exercise of the same power, persons performing public penance were excluded from civil as well as military offices (militia togata et paludata), and even when it was over, these offices might not be resumed under pain of perpetual exclusion from them.[5] It is manifest that the Church has ever had the right of imposing public penance upon Christians, however high their dignity; from the penance it resulted that such persons forfeited their office and dignity; and thus in an indirect manner she deprived them of temporal power. The well-being of private persons was not more important in the eyes of the Church than that of Christian princes; she imposed penances upon the one as upon the other, even when they were not voluntarily undergone. This is one of the earliest forms in which the indirect power was exercised. Again, in time of persecution the Church enjoined upon the faithful flight,[6] and complete withdrawal from contact with the heathen world; and this flight was permitted even when forbidden by the heathen rulers, and although public burdens were thus avoided; and in this way she interfered indirectly in the domain of the State. This was indeed only a conditional and provisionary measure; but the same is true of all other cases of indirect interference, which only continue so long as the danger exists, so long as the sinner refuses amendment, so long as is required by the all-important end of the salvation of souls.[7]

[1] Tertull. de Idolol. c. xvii. xviii. ; Apol. c. xlvi. ; Minuc. Felix, in Octav., and others, in Mamachi, t. iv. p. 46.
[2] Bianchi, t. i. l. lii. § 2, n. 3, p. 452 seq. Bennettis, Vindiciae Privil. S. Petri, t. vi. p. 627 scq. Mamachi, l.c. p. 186.
[3] Conc. Eliber. c. 56. Hard. i. 256. Cf. Hefcle, i. p. 151.
[4] Conc. Arelat. i. c. 7. Hard. i. 263. Hefele, i. p. 177.
[5] Morin. de Discipl. in Admin. Sacram. Poenit. l. v. c. xxiv. n. 2, p. 318, ed. Paris. Bianchi, l.c. n. 4, p. 453. Mamachi, l.c. p. 187 seq.
[6] Bossuet (P. i. l. i. sect. 2, c. xv. p. 147) cites such passages as S. Matt. xx. 28, S. Luc. xxi. 16, 17, S. Matt. x. 23, which are, however, no proof that at all times only flight is to be employed against the oppressors of the Church. The faithful were warned not to expose themselves rashly and without necessity to the anger of their foes, to be always on their guard (Conc. Eliber. c. 60; Athan. Apol. de Fuga sua ; Cypr. Ep. 15, ed. Pamel. ; Aug. Ep. 185, c. iii.), and not to sacrifice life for religion where both might be retained.
[7] Bianchi, l.c. § 4, n. 5, pp. 482-484.

§ 8.

: The Fathers laid it down as a rule that all public temporal regulations are to be observed which are not a hindrance to religion or contrary to the commandments of God.[1] In case of danger to salvation all is to give way, according to St. Matthew xvi. 26, v. 29. He who is charged with the guidance of the faithful in the way of eternal salvation must be able to know and to set aside the hindrances to salvation. The preservation and furtherance of spiritual good, which is the charge of the Church, requires from time to time the sacrifice of some earthly good or interest, and therefore the power intrusted with earthly and temporal interests must give way before the power intrusted with spiritual and eternal interests. Civil society rests upon the observance of natural law, distributive justice, and freedom of intercourse. By an abuse of power legitimate authorities may become illegitimate; when this happened, nations threw off such authorities in virtue of the judgment of the Church; and what she did was not by her own power to set aside a rightful sovereign, but, when a sovereign had become illegitimate, to declare him to be such.[2]

[1] Ang. de Civ. Dei, xix. 17: 'Si religionem non impedit;' c. xix: 'Si non est contra divina praecepta.' Thus St. Chrys. hom. 70, al. 71, in Matt. c. xxii. n. 2 (Migne, lviii. 656), says: 'That which is due to the emperor must be given to him τὰ μηδὲν τὴν εὐσέβειαν παραβλάπτοντα, otherwise the tribute would not be the emperor's but the devil's.'

[2] Bianchi, t. iii. l. i. § 4, n. 2, p. 478 seq.

§ 9.

Cardinal Bellarmine is usually spoken of as the originator of this doctrine; but before his time the majority of theologians taught the same. Cardinal Turrecremata of the Dominican order (died 1468) states[1] two opinions: (1) the Pope has power in spiritual matters alone, and not in temporal, with the exception of that which the Church has acquired by the gift of the faithful or of princes; (2) the Pope, as Vicar of Christ, has full jurisdiction over the whole earth in matters spiritual and temporal. The cardinal himself holds neither of these opinions, but teaches, in accordance with the system spoken of above, that the Pope has jurisdiction in temporal matters *only so far as may be necessary* for the preservation of spiritual good in himself and others, or so far as is required by the needs of the Church or the duty of the pastoral charge in the correction of sinners.[2] If it be objected from Scripture[3] that Christ had no worldly power, and desired none, and that therefore His Vicar has none, the answer is: (1) that no such power is in itself ascribed to the Pope; (2) that to our Saviour is given *all* power in heaven and on earth.[4] He is the King of kings, Lord over all, and this even as man; but He did not avail Himself of His power because He came to be an example of humility and poverty.[5] Before Pilate, Christ expressly declared Himself to be a king ; He did not say that His kingdom is not *in* this world, but only that it is not *of* this world ; He was but declaring the high origin and sublimity of His kinghood.[6] When Christ paid the tribute for Himself and Peter, it was not most surely done because it was due, but to avoid scandal (St. Matthew xvii. 26).[7] In driving the buyers and sellers from the Temple,[8] Christ exercised the spiritual power, which extended to earthly things, since He paid no regard to the worldly loss of those whom He expelled.[9]

---

[1] Summa de Ecclesia, l. ii. c. cxiii.

[2] Ib. p. 263, ed. Venet. 1561 : ' Quantum necesse est pro bono spirituali conservando ipsius et aliorum, sive quantum Ecclesiae necessitas exigit aut debitum pastoralis officii in correctione peccatorum exposcit.'

[3] St. John xviii. 36 ; St. Luke xii. 14 ; St. John vi. 15. These texts are appealed to by Marsilius Patav. Defens. Pacis. P. ii. c. iv. (Goldast. ii. 195, 196) ; Auctor Somnii Virid. c. xii. (ib. i. 63) ; Joh. Gaudun. (ib. p. 20) ; Occam, Quaest. Octo Dec. q. 1, c. vi. (ib. ii. 320) ; Gregor. Heimburg. de Injusta Usurpat. (Gold. i. 559). Cf. Determinat. Univ. Paris. apud Bulaeum Hist. Univ. Par. iv. 944.

[4] Alvar. Pelag. l. i. c. xiii.: ' Dicit *omnis ;* ergo nihil excipit.' Cf. de Regim. Princip. iii. 10. For other authors, vide Molina, de Justitia et Jure, tract. 2, disp. 28, n. 2, p. 54.

[5] Joh. XXII. Extrav. Cum inter nonnullos, 4, de V. S. tit. 14. Distinction must be made between *dominium* and *usus.* Friedberg, l.c. p. 41 : ' Nemo scriptorum non confitetur, omnia regna Christo tradita esse, Dei filium Dei praeditum fuisse potestate ; tamen saeculare imperium numquam eum *exercuisse* probare student. Praeter omnes homines excelluit Christus, sed *auctoritate* tantum, *non executire,* Somnii Viridarii auctor ait (c. xii. 65, Gold. i. 63, 80), *dominus* quidem fuit *dominantium, dominans* numquam.' According to Joh. de Paris (c. ii. p. 162, ed. Schard), he reigns per fidem in cordibus, non in possessionibus. But because a right is not used, it by no means follows that it does not exist.

[6] Aug. tract. 114 et 115, n. 2, 3, in Joh. Chrys. hom. 83, ab. 82, in Joh. n. 4 (Migne, lix. 453) : οὐκ ἔστιν ἐκ τοῦ κόσμου τούτου ἡ βασιλεία αὐτοῦ . . . . οὐχ ὅτι οὐ κρατεῖ καὶ ἐνταῦθα, ἀλλ' ὅτι καὶ ἄνωθεν ἔχει τὴν ἀρχὴν, καὶ οὐκ ἔστιν ἀνθρωπίνη, ἀλλὰ πολλῷ μείζων ταύτης καὶ λαμπροτέρα. Cyrill. Alex. l. xii. in Joh. c. xviii. (Migne, lxxiv. 620). S. Thom. ap. Turrecrem. l.c. f. 271, 6, · Sum. p. 3, q. 59, a. 2-4, in Ep. ad Hebr. c. ii. lect. 2. Pilate, according to St. Joh. xviii. 37, interpreted the words of Jesus in the affirmative sense, and our Lord did not contradict him. Aug. tr. 25, in Joh.: ' Quid ? non erat rex, qui timebat fieri rex ? Erat omnino, nec talis rex, qui ab hominibus fieret, sed talis qui regnum daret. . . . Praedixerunt autem prophetae regnum ejus, etiam secundum quod homo factus est Christus.'

[7] Cf. Alvar. Pelag. l. i. c. xxxvii. Bellarm. de Cler. i. 19.

* Some see in this the exercise of the priestly office, or that of the Os-
tiarius (Auct. Quaest. in utramque Partem Disput. a. 5; Occam, l. vi. c. iii.;
Rosell. l.c. c. xliv.; Gold. ii. 104, 509; i. 282). Others, *e.g.* Joh. de Paris,
l.c., consider that Christ here intended to teach that both powers have
their origin in Him; Peter of Blois (tract. Quales sunt, P. iv. c. xii. p. 1048):
'Rex ejicit ejiciendos, ejiciendos ejicit pontifex. . . . Ille unus gladium
utrumque, quando placuit, exercuit.'
* On the text Rom. xiii. 1 seq. vide Greg. VII. l. i. Ep. 22, ad Carthag.
p. 306, ed. Migne: 'Cum ergo *mundanis* potestatibus obedire praedicavit
Apostolus, *quanto magis spiritualibus* et vicem Christi inter Christianos
habentibus.' Also Pope Symmachus, Ep. cit.: 'Si *omnis potestas* a Deo
est, magis ergo, quae rebus est praestituta divinis. Defer Deo in nobis, et
nos deferemus Deo in te. Ceterum si tu Deo non deferas, non potes ejus
nti privilegio, cujus jura contemnis.' Cf. Bianchi, t. i. l. iii. § 4, n. 6-8,
pp. 485-489. S. Bernard. Ep. 42, ad Henric. Aep. Senon.: 'Omnis anima,
inquit, potestatibus sublimioribus subdita sit. Si omnis, et vestra. Quis
vos excipit ab universitate? Si quis tentat excipere, conatur decipere.'
He is speaking of subjection to ecclesiastical authorities. Bianchi, t. iii.
l. i. c. i. § 7, n. 8, pp. 61, 62. The text is thus quoted also by Innocent
III. in l. xi. Ep. 20, p. 1351, and by St. Anselm of Canterbury, Com. in
Ep. ad Rom. h. 1.

§ 10.

The more closely the ancient theologians are examined the
more clear does it become that Bellarmine and the Jesuits—
who were moreover especially admonished to keep, if possible,
to the common teaching of the theological schools[1]—were not
introducing any new doctrine, but were on this point completely
in accordance with the other religious orders. The teaching of
the great theologians of the Middle Ages—St. Bonaventure, St.
Thomas, and others—differs in no essential point from theirs.[2]
The Dominicans in the time of Bellarmine taught the same;
e.g. amongst others, Francis Victoria (died 1546) says: 'The
Pope in matters temporal may not interfere with the civil power,
unless where there is danger of grievous loss to souls.'[3] Precisely
the same was taught by theologians of various nations, religious
orders, and positions, throughout the sixteenth and seventeenth
centuries;[4] the same again in the eighteenth,[5] although these
controversies were then shortly supplanted by others of quite
another type.

[1] Institut. S.J. ed. Prag. 1757, vol. ii. p. 181 seq. Buss, Die Gesellsch.
Jesu, Mainz, 1853, p. 440.

[2] S. Bonavent. de Eccles. Hierarch. P. ii. c. i. p. 274, ed. Romae, 1596 : ' Jam vero possunt Pontifices ex causa amovere reges et deponere imperatores, sicut saepius accidit et visum est, quando scil. eorum *malitia* hoc *exigit* et reipublicae necessitas sic requirit.' Cf. in l. ii. d. 37. S. Thom. in l. ii. dist. 44, q. 9, a. 2 ; Sum. 2, 2, q. 12, a. 2 ; q. 60, a. 6, ad 3. Hugo a S. Victor, de Sacram. Fid. l. ii. P. i. t. iii. p. 607, ed. 1648. Alex. Hal. Sum. P. iii. q. 40, m. 1, a. 3, p. 159 seq. ed. 1575. Alex. a S. Elpidio, tract. de Eccles. Potest. c. iv. seq. ed. Taur. 1496. Roccab. Bibl. ii. p. 17, ed. 1698. Henricus Gandaveus, Quodlib. vi. q. 23. A long list of writers is cited by Card. Sfondrato, Gallia Vindicata, dissert. 2, § 2, n. 25, p. 458, ed. St. Gallen, 1702 ; and Bianchi, t. i. l. i. § 11, p. 104 seq.; § 20, n. 3, p. 174 seq.

[3] Franc. Victoria, Relect. de Potest. Eccl. sect. 5, n. 12, pp. 36, 37, ed. 1565. Cf. sect. 7, n. 8, p. 48.

[4] Joh. Driedo, de Libertate Christ. l. ii. c. ii. Albert. Pighe, Hierarch. Eccl. l. v. Cajetan, in Apol. c. xiii. ad 6. Gretser, Defensio Controvers. Bellarmin. l. v. c. vi-viii. t. ii. p. 151 seq. ed. 1609. Mart. Becanus, de Republ. Eccles. l. iii. c. iv. Privil. 5, n. 48, p. 265 seq. ed. 1619. Refutatio Torturae Torti, Parad. 6 seq. t. ii. p. 531. Refut. Apol. Jacobi, Reg. Angl. P. ii. p. 493, ed. Lugd. 1621. Nic. Sander. de Monarchia Eccles. l. ii. c. iv. p. 77 seq. ed. 1571. Ad. Schulken, Pro Illustr. D. Roberto Bellarmino, S.R.E. Card. adv. librum falso inscriptum Apologia, 1613. Bzovius, O.S.D. de Praest. Offic. Auctorit. Rom. Pontif. c. xlii. seq. ed. Colon. 1619. Mauclor, de Monarchia Divina, Eccl. et Saecul. P. iv. l. iv. c. xiii. p. 2048 seq. ed. Paris, 1622. Card. du Perron, Harangue au tiers état (Œuvres Div. p. 595 seq. ed. 1622). Baron. Annal. a. 800, n. 6 seq. Roccaberti, de Rom. Pontificis suprema in Temporal. Potest. l. i. c. i. seq. t. iii. ed. 1683. Aguirre et Dubois, in Schulken, Apol. de Potest. Pont. Max. adv. Widringt. p. 52 seq. Charlas, de Libert. Eccl. Gallic. l. iv. c. i. seq. p. 155 seq. ed. Leod. 1684. Sfondrat. Gallia vindicata, diss. 2, § 1 seq. p. 491 seq. ed. 1687. Thom. Stapleton, t. i. Controv. 3, de primo subjecto potest. Eccl. q. 1. a. 2, Paris, 1620 (dedicated to Paul V.) : ' Ad puniendos atque etiam privandos regno principes saeculares a fide devios potestatem spiritualem Rom. Pontifex habet.'

[5] Bianchi, op. cit. l. i. c. i. seq. ed. Romae, 1745. Mamachi, Orig. et Antiqu. Christ. t. iv. P. i. c. ii. p. 181 seq. ed. Romae, 1752. Card. Vincent. Petra, Comment. in Const. Apost. Venet. 1741, t. i. n. 27, 28 seq. pp. 177, 178 : ' The Pope has power in temporalia indirecte et secundario, quatenus conducunt ad finem supernaturalem.' T. ii. p. 120, in Innoc. III. Const. iv. n. 1 seq. : ' The Pope cannot without cause (nulla existente causa) appoint other kings.' Cf. also Roncaglia, Animadvers. in Natal. Alex. H. E. saec. 11 et 12, dissert. 2, t. xiii. pp. 605-626, ed. Bing.

§ 11.

On comparing the expressions of Bellarmine, and the Jesuits who succeeded him, with those of more ancient theologians, it will be found that, far from seeking to render the prevailing view more strict, these later theologians strove rather to modify it; not only

did they, in opposition to the theory of a direct power in matters
temporal, defend the merely indirect power, but even to this
they put many limitations. Bellarmine was attacked on either
side: by some he was blamed for granting to the Church too
little power; by others, especially by Anglicans and Gallicans,[1]
for granting her too much.[2] The earlier French writers had
disputed the direct power only,[3] as may be seen in the controversy under Boniface VIII., who, as they supposed, desired to
reduce France to the condition of a feudatory kingdom;[4] the
later writers since the seventeenth century disputed the indirect power also. Until 1615 this was still considered the
prevailing doctrine;[5] but the sentence (afterwards revoked)
passed by the Paris parliament in 1610, condemning Bellarmine's work, *On the Power of the Pope in Matters Temporal,
against William Barclay,*[6] was followed by the censures of the
Sorbonne in 1626 on the Jesuit Anthony Santarelli and the
Dominican Malagula for the same doctrine;[7] and the first of
the four Gallican articles of 1682 rejected altogether any power,
whether direct or indirect, on the part of the Church in the
civil government of kings and princes.[8]

[1] L. El. Dupin, de Antiqua Eccles. Disciplina, dissert. 7, p. 433, ed.
1688. Natal. Alex. Hist. Eccl. saec. 16, dissert. 5, J.B. Bossuet, Defensio
Declar. Cleri. Gall. P. i. l. i. p. 89 seq. Maimbourg, Traité Hist. de l'établ.
et prér. de l'Eglise de Rome, c. xxvi. p. 303 seq. ed. 1685.

[2] Adolph. Schulken especially wrote in defence of Bellarmine: 'Pro
illustrissimo D. Rob. Bellarmino S.R.E. Cardinali adversus librum falso
inscriptum apologia' (c. iii. p. 59 seq. ed. 1613).

[3] Joh. Major. in l. iv. d. 24, ad arg. 4: 'Si dicatur Maximus Pontifex
esse dominus omnium et omnes alii principes ejus vasalli, et posse instituere et destituere, hoc judico falsum. Sed si intelligatur habere dominium
in temporalibus *casualiter* et multum posse agere ad depositionem regum
suadendo, consultando, imo alios ad gladium provocando in eos, quando
sunt labefactores fidei et reipublicae Christianae prorsus inutiles, hoc
mitius ferendum est nec alienum a dictis nostris.' Cf. d. 44, q. 3. Joh. de
Paris, tr. de Pot. Pap. et Reg. c. vii.: ' Papa vero, qui est supremum caput
non solum clericorum, sed et generaliter omnium fidelium, ut fideles sunt,
tamquam generalis informator fidei et morum, *in casu summae necessitatis
fidei* et morum, in quo casu omnia bona fidelium sunt communia et com-
municanda, etiam calices ecclesiarum, habet bona exteriora fidelium dispensare et exponenda decernere, prout expedit necessitati communis
fidei.'

[4] Bianchi, t. i. l. i. § 11, n. 3, 4, pp. 108, 109.

⁵ Cf. Bossuet, l. i. sect. 1, c. iii. p. 91 seq. (speech of Prince Henry of Condé-Bourbon before Louis XIII.).

⁶ Fuligatti, Vita del Card. Rob. Bellarmino, Romae, 1624, p. 76. Gaillard, Notices et Extraits, vii. p. 340 seq.

⁷ Bossuet, Defens. l. i. sect. 1, c. iv. v. pp. 93-95.

⁸ Ib. c. i. pp. 85, 86.

§ 12.

Various objections have been brought forward against the indirect power. (1) The highest civil authority was from the beginning a lawful power;[1] it had its origin in God, and could lose nothing of its power by the institution of the ecclesiastical hierarchy:[2] Christ Himself tells us to render to Cæsar the things that are Cæsar's (St. Matt. xxii. 21). (2) Moreover, the early Popes and bishops had no thought of exercising any such power: the Fathers were all in favour of obedience, even to apostates such as Julian, who was obeyed by Valentinian,[3] except in matters relating to the heathen superstition : they excommunicated princes and authorities, but never so much as thought of deposing them.[4] (3) The system of indirect power brings with it the direct, for which it serves as a mask. All cases would become subject to the Pope, primarily, indeed, heresy and idolatry ; but from the eleventh century simony was called heresy, and covetousness also is idolatry (Eph. v. 5) ; incapacity was likewise made a reason for deposition. The rule which held good for princes must also hold good for individuals; and all temporal matters without distinction must be subject to the Pope, since it is easy to make out that any temporal matter has connection with the spiritual end of man.[5] (4) The consequences of this doctrine are such as to disturb the peace of princes and people, to put an end to security in the administration of justice, and even to endanger the life of the ruler ; since if a deposed ruler desired to regain his kingdom by force, his murder would be considered allowable.[6]

¹ Bossuet, op. cit. l. i. sect. 2, c. i. seq. p. 122 seq.

² Ib. c. vi. p. 130 seq.

³ Theodoret, H. E. iii. 16, p. 136, ed. Cantabr.

⁴ Bossuet, l.c. c. xxvi. seq. p. 161 ; l. ii. c. i. seq. p. 183 seq.

⁵ Ib. l. i. sect. 1, c. ii. pp. 87-90. Cf. Huber, p. 55 ; Bluntschli, p. 79.

⁶ Bossuet, l.c. p. 90 ; c. iii. pp. 91, 92 ; c. vi. p. 95.

§ 13.

To these arguments the following replies have been made : (1) The sovereignty even of heathen princes may be lawful,[1] and as such even Christians are bound to render it obedience in all things not contrary to conscience.[2] Civil authority is, within its own domain, independent, and may exist without the Christian religion, but never on so true and firm a basis as is given to it by Christianity.[3] The power bestowed by Christ upon the Apostles includes that of feeding the flock, and the power of the keys, under which head must be reckoned the right of excommunication, and the loosing of oaths injurious to salvation.[4] (2) It by no means follows that because at a certain time no use was made of a power, therefore the power was not in existence. The Church may have had many reasons for not proceeding against apostates such as Julian : in the first place, the impossibility of effecting any good, and the danger of increasing the evil,[5] for Julian was in full possession of power ; then again the short period of his reign, and the at least apparent justice shown by him in the beginning ; the fact also that Julian did not himself pass and publicly enforce laws directly contrary to Christianity ; that he did not compel its abjuration, and that he did not make the profession of Christianity, but pretended crimes, the pretext of his frequent barbarity.[6] Moreover, Christianity had not as yet penetrated so deeply into the life of society as to have affected the whole of civil legislation. Where censures would fail of their effect—the amendment of the offender—and would even be the cause of evils still greater, it would seem mere prudence to abstain from the most severe punishments, and rather to suffer the existing evil.[7] (3) Between the two systems, that of direct and that of indirect power, there is the widest distinction : the first gives to the Pope *a real sovereignty* in temporal matters ; the second imparts to his spiritual power in certain cases only a decisive influence, which has certain results within the civil domain. If excommunication brought with it, as a natural consequence, the forfeiture of earthly sovereignty, the Church would have direct power in temporal matters, and not merely indirect;[8] but for this last it suffices that the Church should act upon the subjects in such manner that loss of power to the ruler ensues;[9] as by release from the oath of allegiance, which does not of itself necessitate the withdrawal of obedience.[10] Moreover, the power of the Pope is primarily restricted to the case of crimes endangering religion, to which class belong all the known historical cases. (4) As to the consequences of the doctrine, the Pope can by no means, at his own pleasure and on every occasion, depose princes; he is able only to declare in what cases citizens are released from the oaths taken to them; for such princes as are the cause of extreme danger to religion and the salvation of souls deprive themselves of their rights by their own acts. Since judgment on these points cannot be passed by individuals or by nations, this doctrine rather serves as a safeguard to rulers and a restraint to subjects. The Pope leaves to the dethroned prince, as long as he gives prospect of amendment, the hope of regaining his kingdom; therefore, that this hope may be realised, the Church is bound to protect and defend him against his subjects.

No theologian has ever ascribed to the Pope power over the lives of princes; and permission granted for their murder is inconceivable. Bellarmine expressly says: 'It is unheard of that the murder of a prince should ever be permitted, even were he a heretic, a heathen, and a persecutor, and even were monsters to be found capable of committing such a crime.'[11]   ·

---

[1] Bianchi, t. i. l. i. § 3, p. 21 seq. Mamachi, t. iv. pp. 195, 196.
[2] Bianchi, t. i. l. iii. § 4, pp. 475, 478.
[3] Mamachi, l.c. p. 196.
[4] Bianchi, t. i. l. iii. § 1, n. 2, pp. 436, 437. The meaning of the keys in Scripture is proved by texts such as Isaias xxii. 21, 22, Apoc. i. 18, iii. 7, and by the numerous passages of the Fathers cited by Bennettis, Vindic. t. i. p. 49, to which may be added many classical passages (Passaglia, de Praerogat. B. Petri, Ratisb. 1851, l. ii. c. viii. p. 486). Even Protestant synods often rest their rules and prohibitions on the binding and loosing power; this was expressed by the Synod of Alain in 1620 in its formula of excommunication: 'Nous ministres de la parole de l'Evangile de Jésus-Chr., que Dieu a armés d'armes spirituelles, puissantes de par Dieu a la destruction des fortesses qui s'opposent contre lui, auxquelles le Fils éternel de Dieu a donné la puissance de lier et de délier sur la terre, déclarant que ce que nous aurons lié sur la terre sera lié dans le

ciel, voulant nettoir la maison de Dien,' &c. (Actes ecclés. et civ. de tous
les Synodes nationaux de l'Eglise réformée de France, ii. 181, 182. Cf. i.
160, 176).
    ⁵ This held good also in the case of the Arian emperors. Cf. Bingham,
Orig. et Ant. Chr. l. xvi. c. iii. § 6.
    ⁶ Bianchi, t. i. l. iii. § 9, p. 549 seq.; t. iii. l. i. c. i. § 4, n. 6, p. 41
seq.   Mamachi, l.c. pp. 202-204.   Cf. S. Thom. 2, 2, q. 12, a. 2, ad 1.
    ⁷ Ang. c. Parmen. iii. 2, Lib. ad Donat. post collat. c. xx.; quoted also
by Kober, Kirchenbann, pp. 114-116.
    ⁸ Bianchi, t. i. l. iii. § 1, n. 7, p. 446.
    ⁹ Joh. de Parisiis, tract. de Potest. Papali et Regali, c. xii.: ' Si esset
(princeps) haereticus et incorrigibilis et contemptor ecclesiasticae censurae,
posset Papa aliquid facere in populo, unde privaretur ille saeculari honore
et deponeretur a populo, et haec faceret Papa in crimine ecclesiastico, cujus
cognitio ad ipsum pertinet, excommunicando scil. omnes qui ei nt domino
obedirent, et sic populus ipsum deponeret et Papa per accidens.'
    ¹⁰ Bianchi, t. i. l. i. § 10, n. 4, p. 97, on the passage of Joh. de Paris
quoted above.
    ¹¹ Ep. ad Blackwellum, presb.

§ 14.

Even those Jesuits who are said to have boldly developed
this doctrine to its uttermost consequences¹ have defended
the indirect power alone.   Louis Molina discusses the question whether Christ, as man, was temporal king and lord of
the whole earth,² and lays down the following propositions: (1) The Pope has no temporal power of jurisdiction of
such kind as to make him lord of the whole earth ; the kingly
power is altogether distinct from that of the Pope, and in their
own sphere kings are independent.³   Hence, in the ordinary
course of things, it does not belong to the Pope to appoint or to
depose kings ; the Pope has not power directly to decide purely
temporal disputes between princes.⁴   (2) Although the Pope
has general jurisdiction over the temporal goods of the Church,
still he is not lord over them, but administrator and director,
and may not therefore dispose of them at will, but only on prudent grounds for the benefit of the Church.⁵   (3) To the spiritual
power of the Pope, bestowed for the supernatural end, is united
the highest and most extensive power of temporal jurisdiction⁶
over all princes and other subjects of the Church, *in so far as
is required by the supernatural end*, for which the spiritual
power was ordained.

Hence the Pope can, if it be required by the supernatural end, depose princes and deprive them of their kingdoms.[7] He can also decide between them in temporal concerns, invalidate their laws, and amongst Christians order all things, not anyhow, but in the way recognised according to wise judgment as absolutely necessary[8] to the general spiritual welfare, and may enforce his commands not merely by censures, but also by public punishments and by force of arms, like any other temporal prince; although it is for the most part more suitable for the Pope to do this not of himself, but through temporal princes. In this sense is the Pope said to have both swords and both powers, the spiritual and the temporal. This doctrine was based on the ordinary grounds.[9] Again and again was it pointed out that the Pope, as a rule, was to make use of the spiritual power alone, and only where this proved insufficient, or where there was danger in delay—thus only in extraordinary cases—was he to draw the temporal sword.[10]

[1] Huber, p. 42.

[2] Molina, de Justitia et Jure, tract. 2, disput. 28, t. i. p. 34 seq. ed. Antwerp, 1615.

[3] L.c. n. 17: 'Non eo modo reges pendent a potestate S. Pontificis, quo episcopi constituti per diversa loca, quos et creare et amovere potest tamquam supremus in spiritualibus Ecclesiae pastor ac moderator, tametsi sine rationabili causa eos amovere non debeat. Neque item pendent ab eo perinde ac optimates regni pendent a rege ac perinde atque reges vel alii principes ab imperatore non exempti ab eo pendent, esto ab imperatore amoveri nequeant. Quin potius tam reges ab imperatore exempti quam imperator ipse supremae sunt potestates in temporalibus a nullo alio dependentes.'

[4] N. 19-21. Proofs from Alexander III., Innocent III., St. Bernard (pp. 405 seq. 409).

[5] N. 22, pp. 60, 61.

[6] N. 23: 'Supremam et amplissimam potestatem jurisdictionis temporalis.' It is afterwards observed that this power, 'cum non ad temporalia ipsa, sed ad supernaturalem finem ordinetur,' is not mere 'temporalis,' but 'spiritualis ex parte finis,' and should therefore be called not temporal but ecclesiastical power, '*jurisdictionis tamen temporalis*,' in order to distinguish it from the purely spiritual, to which it is annexed.

[7] N. 28. Molina here appeals to Sotus and Victoria.

[8] Huber translates 'necessaria' by suitable, pp. 42, 43, and omits altogether 'non utcumque, sed simpliciter.' The 'simpliciter necessarium' is repeatedly and expressly taught by Molina, n. 24. The kingly power is 'quoad finem suam naturalem in se spectatum independens a summo

Pontifice.' The Pope may not intervene in their government 'quatenus praecise respicit finem reipublicae politicum et naturalem,' but only 'eatenus quatenus deviat ab eo, quod finis supernaturalis *omnino* postulat.'

* N. 24. Cf. n. 37, p. 63, ad 2 : 'Potestates laicas omnino subjici in temporalibus S. Pontifici, quantum *necesse est* ad finem supernaturalem. *Eatenus* nempe respublica temporalis subordinatur reipublicae spirituali Ecclesiae et *in ea quasi includitur; secundum se* autem respublica temporalis integra quaedam respublica in se est, cujus potestas summa est princeps temporalis.' N. 24-27, pp. 61, 62.

¹º Ib. n. 33, according to Victoria and Sotus, whom Molina follows throughout.

§ 15.

The same is taught by Salmeron, who opposes the direct power, defends the indirect, and, like Molina, appeals to Dominicans, such as Turrecremata, Victoria, and Soto.¹ Anthony Santarelli defended the indirect power alone, although in a more emphatic form ;² the other religious orders,³ the secular clergy, and the jurists, maintained the same doctrine ;⁴ it was, moreover, defended by the Sorbonne. It was only on the 8th of May 1663, after many intrigues on the part of the parliament and the court,⁵ that a declaration⁶ was passed to the effect that the Pope has no authority in the temporal concerns of kings, and that subjects could in no case be dispensed from the allegiance due to the king. This was based upon former royal edicts, sentences of the parliament,⁷ and declarations of the Sorbonne,⁸ which, however, merely declared the independence of the French crown ; and this had been before acknowledged even by the Popes. Shortly after the Declaration of March 19, 1682, on June 10, 1683, the Inquisition of Toledo,⁹ in opposition to it, condemned as erroneous and schismatical the proposition : ' The Pope or the Church have neither direct nor indirect power in the temporal concerns of kings, and these cannot be deprived of their dominions ; nor can their subjects, upon whatsoever ground, be pronounced free from their oath of allegiance.' The Dominican Carena pronounced even impious and heretical the opinion of the Calvinists and the Magdeburg Centuriators, who denied to the Pope any power, direct or indirect, in matters temporal.¹⁰ As this was a question of a doctrine universally defended in the schools,¹¹ the Jesuits, especially in their delicate relations towards the Dominicans, could not, without the gravest reasons, have taken a different view; moreover, they followed always the common teaching of the schools.[12]

[1] Opp. t. iv. P. iii. tract. 4, in Matt. c. xvi. p. 410, ed. Colon. 1610 seq. After saying that the Pope in certain cases has to instruct and admonish princes, he continues : ' Cui Pontificis praecepto tamquam Christi verbo habent principes obedire et si resistant, potest eos tamquam contumaces punire et si in Ecclesiam et Christi gloriam aliquid moliantur, potest eos tanquam contumaces punire et regno privare vel eorum ditiones alteri principi tradere et eorum subditos ab obedientia illis debita et juramento facto absolvere.' He then cites Jer. i. 10, and brings forward the proofs against the ' potestas directa,' and for the ' indirecta.' Herr Huber quotes him as saying that ' the Pope may order the execution of a prince ;' but where is the sentence to be found? Until the passage is accurately given, and proof of its genuineness produced, it must be rejected as a misrepresentation.

[2] Tract. de Haeresi. Roccab. iv. 462. The Paris theologians censured the passage : ' Summum Pontificem posse poenis temporalibus punire reges et principes, eosque deponere et suis regnis privare ob crimen haeresis, eorumque subditos ab illorum obedientia liberare, eamque semper in Ecclesia fuisse consuetudinem, et propter alias causas, ut pro delictis, si expedit, si principes sint negligentes, propter insufficientiam et inutilitatem suarum personarum. . . . Pontificem jus et potestatem in spiritualia simul et omnia temporalia habere, et in eo esse de jure divino, utramque potestatem,' &c.

[3] Amongst the Dominicans, François d'Enghien in Louvain opposed Natalis Alexander, and the theologians of the other religious orders in the place were on his side—Auctoritas Sedis Apostolicae in reges . . . . adversus P. Natalem Alexandrum. Against this Natalis wrote, H. E. saec. 15 et 16, a dissertatio apologetica, t. xviii. pp. 304-401, ed. Bing.

[4] Alphons. Alvarez Guerrerus, J.C., de Jure ac Potest. Rom. Pontif. Imper. Regum ac Episcoporum, Colon. Agripp. 1586, c. xvi. p. 108 : ' Habet (Rom. Pontifex) potestatem in temporalibus ex consequenti, et hoc proprio jure, sc. quantum necessarium est ad conservationem rerum spiritualium, ad directionem hominum in salutem aeternam, ad correctionem peccatorum, et ad conservandam pacem in populo Christiano.'

[5] Cf. Recherches historiques sur l'Assemblée du Clergé de France de 1682, par Charles Gérin, Paris, 1869.

[6] In Latin in D'Argentré, Collect. Judiciorum, t. iii. P. i. p. 90; in French in Dupin, Manuel du Droit public ecclésiastique Français, Paris, 1847, p. 103.

[7] Thus upon that of Dec. 2, 1561 ; Jan. 4, 1549 ; Jan. 7 and 20, 1595 ; of 1610 (May 27 and Nov. 26) ; July 27, 1614.

[8] Of 1413, 1561, 1595, 1610, 1611, 1620.

[9] Bianchi, l.c. § 15, n. 2, p. 126.

[10] Carena, de Offic. S. Inquisit. P. i. tit. 1, de Potestate Summi Pontif.

in Tempor. § 5 : ' Prima sententia est impia et haeretica.' Thus Alphonsus
Ciaconius, in Vita Leonis III. says : ' Si quis neget Romani Praesulis
auctoritatem in imperium, plane impius et infidelis et rerum ecclesiasti-
carum plane rudis esse convincetur.' The defenders of the direct power
likewise considered it heretical to dispute the primacy of the Pope ' super
spiritualia et temporalia.' Augustin. Triumph. Prooem. Lib de Pot. Eccles. ;
Durandus, Ep. Meldensis, de Orig. Jurisdiction. in fine ; Petrus Bertrandi,
de Orig. et Usu Jurisdict. q. 3 ; passages in Bianchi, l.c. n. 1, pp. 122-124.

   11 To contradict the ' concors scholae sententia' is ' temerarium, haeresi
proximum.' Thus Melchior Canus, de Loc. Theol. l. viii. c. iv. concl. 2 ;
Sfondrat, Regale Sacerdot. l. i. § 17.

   12 Suarez, de Fide, disput. 20, sect. 3, n. 1, 26.   Gregor. de Valentia,
t. iii. disp. 1, q. 12, punct. 2, pp. 568 seq. 575 seq.

(c) *The system of the directing power (potestas directiva).*

§ 16.

Other theologians, as a modification of the theories described,
taught that the Church has only a directing power (a guiding
but not a constraining power) over civil authorities ; that is to
say, it is her right and her duty, by doctrinal decisions, by
warnings, declarations, counsels, and commands, to enlighten
the consciences of princes and people ; to remind them of their
duty towards God and religion, to instruct them as to the scope
and limit of their duties, and in case of a collision of duties to
pass judgment as to what is to be done to satisfy God and
conscience.   Therefore she must be the judge of human laws
which contradict the divine law, she must strive for their im-
provement when dangerous to salvation, satisfy inquiries in
cases of conscience, and when her voice is unheeded she must
defend herself to the utmost against the evils arising from this
neglect.[1]

   Numerous early examples were brought forward in support
of this view : e.g. the conduct of the great Pope Gregory I.,
who endeavoured to obtain from the Emperor Mauricius the
withdrawal of a law injurious to the interests of religion.[2]
Gregory approved the first clause of the said law (of 592), by
which active State officials were not to undertake ecclesiastical
offices ; the second clause, by which these same officials were
not to become monks, he desired so far modified as that they

should be obliged first to render account of their service, and in general to fulfil all former obligations; the third clause, by which all military persons were entirely prohibited from taking holy orders, he rejected, as closing to many the way of salvation.[3]

Looking at it from this same point of view, Bossuet also considered the much-discussed reply of Pope Zacharias as to the accession of Pipin in the light of a counsel given by the Pope, and not a command.[4]

---

[1] Fénélon, Dissert. de Auctoritate Summi Pontificis (Œuvr. t. ii. ed. Vers. 1820), espec. c. xxvii. xxxix. In detail Gosselin, Le Pouvoir du Pape au Moyen Age, Louvain, 1845, vol. ii. (German ed. Münster, 1859). Gosselin tries even to show, p. 335 scq., that Bossuet adopted this doctrine in the main; and he quotes also in its favour De Maistre, the Lyons theogian Van Gils (died 1834), Möhler (Symbolik, 6th cd. p. 392), Receveur (Hist. de l'Eglise, t. v. p. 127), and others.

[2] S. Greg. Vita Recens Adornata, l. ii. c. x. Fleury, l.c. t. viii. l. xxxv. n. 31.

[3] Greg. M. l. iii. Ep. 65, 66 (vol. ii. 2, 62, 65). Jaffé, n. 903, 904.

[4] Bossuet, l.c. c. xxxiii. p. 246, ed. Mogunt, 1788.

§ 17.

In accordance with the expression of Gerson and Fénélon, this power has been called a directing or guiding power (potestas directiva et ordinativa);[1] but it is a matter of dispute whether Gerson's directing power is not the same as that called by others indirect power. Gerson teaches that the Church is so to restrain her power within limits as to acknowledge also the independence of the civil power, so long as the civil power is not by an abuse made the means of attacking the faith, blaspheming God, and openly oppressing the power of the Church; should such be the case, it becomes the duty of the Church to guide and direct the civil power.[2] But has anything essentially different been maintained by the supporters of the indirect power? Have they placed other limits to the independence of civil authority? and is not this a question rather of words than of things? the word may be better chosen, but the thing is essentially the same. There is, however, a distinction between Gerson and Fénélon: Gerson speaks of a superiority, a dominion, of the spiritual power, in case of abuse of the civil power; Fénélon allows only a directing power, consisting mainly in instruction and counsel. The question remains, how far this last power may go, and what are its limits. These limits are determined by Fénélon and Gosselin chiefly according to prevailing public law and according to special legal titles, which were frequently united with ecclesiastical titles in the person of the Pope; consequently the exercise of this directing power must necessarily differ at different times, and regard must be had to contemporary circumstances and legal relations; its expression and its consequences will differ, while its fundamental principle—supremacy in all questions affecting religion—necessarily remains ever the same. The Head of the Church will ever have the right of judging whether, and how far, religion is injured by this or that civil law; thus the principle remains, though the form in which it is carried out may vary with the times.[3]

[1] Fénélon, Diss. Cit. c. xxvii. p. 334: 'Haec autem potestas, quam Gersonius *directivam et ordinativam* nuncupat, in eo tantum consistit, quod Papa utpote princeps pastorum, utpote praecipuus in majoribus moralis disciplinae causis Ecclesiae director et doctor, de servando fidelitates sacramento populum consulentem edocere teneatur. De cetero nihil est quod pontifices regibus imperare velint, nisi ex speciali titulo aut possessione aliqua particulari id sibi juris in aliquem regem feudatarium Sedis Apostolicae adepti fuerint.'

[2] Gerson, de Potest. Eccles. consider. 12, Op. ii. pp. 246-248, ed. 1706: 'Potestas ecclesiastica non ita habet dominia et jura terreni simul et coelestis imperii, quod possit *ad libitum suum* de bonis clericorum, et multo minus laicorum, disponere, *quamvis concedi debeat*, quod habet in eis *dominium regitivum, directivum, regulativum,* et *ordinativum.* . . . Postremo suis se terminis ita potestas ecclesiastica coerceat, ut meminerit, potestatem saecularem etiam apud infideles sua habere propria jura, suas leges, sua judicia, de quibus occupare se ecclesiastica potestas non praesumat, *nisi dum redundat abusus saecularis potestatis in impugnationem fidei et blasphemiam creatoris et in manifestam potestatis ecclesiasticae injuriam; tunc enim ecclesiastica potestas habet dominium quodam regitivum, directivum, regulativum et ordinativum.*' Cf. Schwab, Gerson, pp. 734, 735, P. iv. Serm. de Pace et Unit. Graec. Consid. v. t. ii. p. 147: 'Omnes homines, principes et alii, subjectionem habent ad Papam, *in quantum eorum* jurisdictionibus, temporalitate et dominio *abuti vellent contra legem divinam, naturalem,* et potest superioritas illa nominari *potestas directiva et ordinativa potius quam civilis et juridica.*' Cf. Schwab, p. 261.

[3] Bianchi, l. iii. § 1, n. 1, pp. 435, 436.

§ 18.

In principle the doctrines of the indirect and of the directing power do not in all points differ widely.[1] Let us consider them under Bellarmine's three heads. (1) In respect to persons (quoad personas): it is universally admitted that the Head of the Church may admonish and correct princes guilty of crime, and, with a view to their amendment, may lay them under censures. As to the deposing of princes *in extreme cases*, the defenders of indirect power, far from making the doctrine that princes might be deposed stand and fall with their general theory, do not even make this doctrine a necessary and abiding expression of the indirect power; while the defenders of the directive power limit deposition to the one case where the public law of the country in question authorises it ; in such a case both theories agree that the Pope can declare the right of governing to have been forfeited. According to the teaching of both parties it belongs to the Pope, under certain conditions, to declare non-binding the oath of allegiance, and this in virtue of the rights of the Church, since he is the supreme guide of consciences within her. On this point, however, a controversy exists as to whether the condition of belonging to the Catholic Church, which in the Middle Ages was attached to the election and accession of the sovereign, rested, as the defenders of the indirect power believe, upon the natural law, or only upon the positive human law, as is held by Fénélon and the upholders of the directing power.[2] It would follow from the first of these opinions, that at the present time the deposition of such princes would be justified, even though not absolutely commanded ; according to the second, the right of deposing would cease when not sanctioned by the public law of the land in question. Theologians have not yet come to an agreement upon this disputed question.[3]

(2) In respect to laws (quoad leges) : surely in common fairness the Church has at all times the right of declaring any given State law injurious to the interests under her charge ; precisely as the civil power may declare the same of a law of

the Church. As a matter of fact, and as we now experience, the State not only makes this declaration without real cause, but proceeds to measures grievously injurious to the Church. When civil laws are such as to endanger salvation, the Pope, as Head of the Catholic Church, has without doubt the right to declare them to be such, to denounce them emphatically; and if denunciation be fruitless, to proscribe them as powerless to bind the conscience; he is indeed as much bound in duty to this as were the Apostles and first bishops to prohibit the faithful from taking part in the serving of idols, and from obeying those commands of the State which they could not fulfil without betraying God. However hard it may from circumstances become for the Pope, he is still bound by the sanctity of his office to condemn whatsoever is contrary to the faith and morals of the Church, and to declare with apostolic freedom that the Church, far from justifying such laws, is ever bound to reject them.

(3) In respect to sentences (quoad judicia): the Church's right of judgment is inseparably united with her right of legislation. The same power which enables her to pass laws within her own domain enables her also to apply them, and to watch over their application. When a question comes before her judgment-seat which has relation to the supernatural end under her charge, she has full power to pass judgment; and temporal matters also fall under her control, *when and in so far as* they relate to the fulfilment of her great charge. Here again the words of Cardinal Antonelli apply : ' The Church has received from God the sublime charge of guiding men, whether as individuals or united in societies, to a supernatural end; thence comes her power and her obligation of passing judgment upon all matters, whether inward or outward, in their relation to the natural and divine laws. But since every action, whether commanded by a higher power, or proceeding from the freedom of the individual, is necessarily invested with this character of morality and justice, it follows that the judgment of the Church, as it is *directly* concerned with the morality of the action, extends also *indirectly* to all things with which this morality is bound up. But the Church does not therefore directly interfere in political

matters, which by the ordinance established by God, and by the teaching of the Church herself, come within the domain of the civil power, and are completely independent of any other authority.'[4]

[1] Many even of Bellarmine's most ardent opposers agree to the directing power. Even Caron, Remonstr. Hibernorum, P. ii. c. viii. pp. 81, 82, allows the weight of the words used by Hugh of St. Victor and Alexander of Hales : ' Sicut spiritus constitutus est ad dirigendum corpus, ita spiritualis potestas constituta est ad dirigendam terrenam ;' and only asks whether ' dirigere' goes so far as ' deponere.' He then observes : 'Thomas Waldensis (Doctrin. Fid. 1. ii. a. 3, c. lxxviii.) expresse docet, idem esse vinculum reges ad coronam, quod mariti ad uxorem, h.e. juris utrinque divini inseparabilem unionem, adeoque sicut sacerdos vinculum matrimonii solvere nequit, sed tantum dijudicare, si tenent nec ne, sic de potestate terrena summus sacerdos habet de illa judicare, si recta sit, judicare, inquam, non praejudicare.' ·

[2] Cf. Gosselin, ii. pp. 447, 448.

[3] But the second, as will later be seen, is to be maintained as the right opinion.

[4] Card. Antonelli to the Nuncio Chigi, March 19, 1870.

§ 19.

If, indeed, Stahl were in the right when he wrote that one or the other must be the case : either the Pope must have indirect power in temporal matters, or princes must have indirect power in spiritual matters : there is no third alternative[1] (which, however, many would by no means allow[2])—the question may fairly be asked : Which is most supported by Christian and historical principles, which is most profitable to the free development and the highest interests of mankind : the indirect or directing power in matters temporal maintained by the earlier theologians, or else the direct or indirect power of the State in ecclesiastical matters defended by the later legists and regalists ? In the present day only one case of practical importance can occur, that of a contradiction between a positive civil law and a law of the Church. In our day laws are often passed by party intrigue, hastily, intended to last only a short time, with corrupt aims, and often with the sacrifice of general to individual, interests ; thus in many cases the mediæval saying might be applied, by which laws were likened to the behaviour of Anacharsis with the cobweb.[3] Is it not plain that the legislation of the Church, based as it is upon high principles, is far superior, and that it might easily become her duty to encounter these modern laws with the words, ' This is unlawful for thee to do,' or ' Non possumus'? Or is the Church indeed at one time to approve the French laws of 1789, at another time those of 1793, then the Code Napoléon, then the Prussian Landrecht, and then again the Swiss Federal Constitution as at present revised ?[4] In so doing she would cease to be herself, she would destroy her very being, she would no longer be the Bride of the Lord. But the State, which is only negatively bound to demand from the faithful nothing contrary to conscience, and which has moreover in almost all lands guaranteed liberty of conscience, would contradict itself should it disallow this right of the Church. If in watching lest the State suffer injury (ne quid detrimenta respublica capiat) civil rulers consider themselves entitled to pass judgment on the laws of the Church, and to subject them to their Placet, they cannot deny that the rulers of the Church are in the same way bound to watch lest any injury be done to souls ; and that although they may on their side oppose no Placet[5] to that of the civil power, it is nevertheless the right and the duty of the Church rulers to declare that such and such a State law is contrary to the conscience of Catholics. Can it be that at the very moment in which a dogma of the Church is declared to be dangerous to States, the right of the Church is to be called in question of at any time declaring on her side a law of the State to be dangerous to the conscience of the faithful ?

[1] Stahl, Rechtsgutachten, p. 69, quoted by Phillips, Kirchenrecht, ii. § 115, p. 618, n. 21.

[2] Rintel, Der Protestantismus als polit. Princip. p. 113 seq.

[3] Joh. Saresbur. Enthetic. p. 997, Quod leges civiles comparantur aranearum telis :

> Retia solvuntur leviter, quae texit arachne,
> Arte tamen mira fila coire facit ;
> Impediunt eadem muscarum corpora parva,
> Magnaque si veniunt, quolibet ire sinunt ;
> Sic Anacharsis ait, cohibent civilia jura
> Invalidos, magnis quolibet ire licet.
> Non ita lex aeterna potens torquere potentes
> Atque fovens humiles, quos videt esse pios.

⁴ Even the ancients rejected the definition of law which said: 'Jus esse, quod ei, qui plus potest utile est.' Aug. de Civ. Dei, xix. c. xxi. n. 1, ex Cic. de Republ.

⁵ Such was thought of by the Portuguese Oliva, M. Schenkl, George Wanner, and others; while many writers acknowledge that in this matter the Church should have reciprocal rights. Cf. Henner, Die Kirchliche Frage in Bayern, 1854, p. 40.

ESSAY XIV.

ORIGIN OF THE CIVIL POWER AND THE RIGHT OF RESISTING IT.

WHAT is the origin of State authority? From what source do kings derive their right? Have the people the right to overthrow them? These are questions of great antiquity, which have been discussed a thousand times, and are still discussed from various points of view. Opinions are now, as in old times, greatly divided on the subject. A glance at the various works elicited by the discussion shows that the same views have often been both held and opposed by Catholics and Protestants.

A number of charges have been raised on this question against Jesuits and against mediæval writers, and have been made use of to cast suspicion upon the Church. Let us examine these charges.

PART I. ORIGIN OF THE CIVIL POWER.

§ 1. Gregory VII. and Innocent III. § 2. Civil power derived from God. § 3. Whether mediately or immediately? § 4. Authority to be distinguished from the holder of the authority. § 5. Doctrine of the sovereignty of the people as held by theologians. § 6. Not originated by Jesuits. § 7. Inadequacy of the doctrine. § 8. It holds the mean between absolute despotism and the modern sovereignty of the people.

§ 1.

Many mediæval writers, and especially Popes Gregory VII. and Innocent III., are charged with having taught that civil power had its origin in evil, and that royal authority rose from human violence. But Gregory VII. and Innocent III., like other writers, are not treating of the authority itself, but of its tyrannical exercise. They follow the early Fathers, who lay down that by nature all men are equal, having no dominion over other men but only over animals (Gen. i. 26); that dominion over man was established by the justice of God as a consequence of sin;[1] that Nimrod, the man of violence, was the first king[2] (Gen.x. 8) ; that the old monarchies were nearly all founded on force,[3] and that the origin of the Jewish kingdom was connected with a revolt against God[4] (1 Kings viii. 7). Gerson considers sin to have been the efficient cause of the establishment of an authority to govern and punish.[5] Theologians say that without sin there had been no need of coercive or penal authority.

[1] Aug. de Civ. Dei, xix. 15: ' Rationalem factum ad imaginem suam voluit (Deus hominem) nisi irrationabilibus *dominari* non hominem homini, sed hominem pecori. . . . Prima ergo *servitutis* causa *peccatum* est, ut homo homini conditionis vinculo subjiceretur, quod non fit nisi Deo judicante.' Cf. l. iii. 14, 15 ; iv. 4-7; v. 12 ; xvi. 17 seq. ; xviii. 2; de Doctr. Christ. l. i. (expressly cited apud Greg. VII.l. viii. Ep. 21, p. 598). Greg. M. Regul. Pastor. P. ii. c. vi. l. xxi. Moral. in Job, c. xv. seq. n. 21, 22.

[2] Aug. de Civ. Dei, xvi. 3, 4. Cf. Iren.l. v. c. xxiv. n. 2 init.

[3] Aug. l.c. xviii. 2. Sulpic. Sever. Chron.l. ii. c. iii. seq. Cf. Turrecremata, Sum. de Eccl. l. i. c. xc. n. 2.

[4] Greg. M. in l. i. Reg. l. iv. c. iv. v. n. 4, 38. (The Jews desired a king with the tyrannical authority of the heathen kings : Bianchi, t. iii. l. i. c. i. § 11, pp. 103-107.) Aug. de Civ. Dei, xvii. 6. Theodoret, q. 14, in l. i. Reg. Phillips, K.R. ii. § 94, p. 367.

[5] Gerson, Serm. ad Reg. Franc. pro Justitia (Opp. iv. 648) : ' Causa efficiens (dominationis et coercitivi dominii) fuit peccatum, causa finalis fuit pax, tranquillitas et sufficientia in vita civili.'

§ 2.

But nevertheless theologians and the Fathers always maintain that civil power is of God,[1] and they all appeal in behalf of this opinion to the clear testimony of Scripture (Rom. xiii. 1 seq.; Wisdom viii. 15 ; Prov. vi. 3 ; Dan. iv. 14, v. 21 ; Jer. xxvii. 3). Innocent III., in spite of his remarks upon the origin of the Jewish kingdom,[2] nevertheless always regarded royal authority as bestowed by God.[3] Gregory VII. acknowledged it in letters to Henry IV.[4] Authority in general is not denied to have a divine origin because individual rulers are not held to have received their authority immediately from God;[5] but apart from this there is a very clear distinction between these two propositions : (1) ' Kings and dukes are descended from those who with pride, robbery, and perfidy usurped a despotic authority ;' and (2) 'the origin of civil authority and its foundation is not of God but of Satan,' as some heretics taught.[6]   Gregory VII., following the Fathers, uttered the former proposition in private letters, without any intention of imposing it as a doctrine or prescribing its acceptance ; he not only did not utter the latter proposition, but distinctly stated the contrary.   The former is an historical assertion founded on Bible history;[7] the latter, a theological error which the Church has at all times rejected.

[1] Aug. de Civ. Dei, v. 1: 'Prorsus divina providentia regna constituuntur humana ;' c. xi. : '(Deus) nullo modo credendus est regna hominum corumque dominationes et servitutes a suae providentiae legibus alienas esse voluisse.' Cf. c. xxi. iv. 5; Confess. iii. 8; Leo M. Ep. 43, ad Marcian. Aug.: 'Christum, qui regni vestri, est *auctor* et rector.' Cf. Job. Saresb. l.c.; Gerson, l.c.

[2] Migne, ccxvi. 1073 seq. With reference to 1 Kings, chap. viii. he said of the Jewish people that their kingdom arose *per extorsionem humanam ;* and later, p. 1074, *ad petitionem humanam extortum.*

[3] L. vii. Ep. 212, p. 527 : 'Ut gladium, quem *Dominus* tibi tradidit, a quo est omnis potestas, non videaris sine causa portaro (Rom. xiii. 4), oportet, ut apprehensis armis et scuto causam Dei alleges,' &c.

[4] Greg. VII. l. ii. Ep. 31, ad Henric.: 'Quem *Deus* in summo rerum posuit culmine.' Cf. l. iii. Ep. 7 ; l. vii. Ep. 21, 23, 25.

[5] Bianchi, t. i. l. i. § 1, 2, p. 5 seq. Phillips, l.c. § 103, p. 457 seq.

[6] Iren. v. 24, n. 2, 3. Aug. de Natura Boni adv. Manich. c. xxxii. Opp. viii. 509, ed. Maur. Bianchi, l.c. n. 11-13, pp. 13-16, § 3, n. 1, 2, pp. 21, 23. Mamachi, t. iv. p. 61.

[7] Upon 1 Kings viii. 7, theologians observe : God did not renounce His right of supreme ruler of the Jewish people—this is inconceivable—but He deprived them of the special care He had formerly bestowed upon them. An abandonment on the part of God refers not to His power but to His favour. In contempt of His saints God sees Himself contemned, as in honour paid to them He is honoured : Cypr. Ep. 59, ad Cornel. ed. Vet.; Cyrill. Alex. l. x. in Job. c. xxxvi. Moreover, it was a sin to desire a king like the heathen kings, whose tyrannical government was denounced by the prophet : Bianchi, t. iii. l. i. § 11, p. 108 seq.

§ 3.

It would be hard to find a Catholic theologian who has opposed the doctrine that sovereignty is of God. The only vexed question is whether it is of God immediately, or mediately through human agency—the choice or consent of the people.[1] Both views have met with numerous supporters amongst Catho-

lics and also amongst Protestants.[2] Those who support the
opinion that royal authority only comes from God mediately
appeal to the testimony of the ancients,[3] and the history of
the peoples and empires of antiquity,[4] from which they learn
the lesson reason also teaches, that our natural wants as well as
the necessity of order and self-preservation have led and must
lead men to form societies, and invest one or more persons with
the social authority. To prove that authority comes immediately
from God, it should be shown that God alone can confer it.
Now Saul and David are the only kings of whom it can be said
that God directly appointed them.   Further, the doctrine of
the immediate divine appointment of kings leaves unexplained
the origin of the authority possessed by an aristocracy or a
democracy; it makes any change in the form of the constitution an offence against God, and directly favours despotism.[5]
Holy Scripture proves the divine origin of authority, but not
that it comes immediately from God ; St. Paul (Rom. xiii. 1
seq.) speaks not merely of the supreme civil authority, but of
any authority, including many subordinate offices of human appointment, for instance Pilate (John xix. 11).

[1] Bianchi, t. i. l. i. § 1, n. 1 seq. p. 5 seq.   Mamachi, t. iv. l. iv. c. ii.
§ 2, p. 57 seq.
[2] Supporters of the immediate divine appointment of kings are found
principally in France and Germany, amongst whom may be named the
author of the work de Modis Uniendi Ecclesiam, c. 1410 (Gerson, Opp. ii.
179 seq.) ; Petrus de Marca, Concord. Sacerd. et Imp. l. ii. c. ii. n. 1
seq. ed. Francof. 1708; Victor, Relect. de Pot. Civ. n. 8, ap. P. de
Marca, l.c.; Caron, Remonstrantia Hibernorum, P. ii. c. iii. § 1; Dupin, de Ant. Eccl. Discipl. diss. 7, c. ii. § 1 ; Pierre Nicole, de l'Unité
de l'Eglise, l. iii. ch. x. p. 399 ; Renat Choppin, de Sacra Politia, l. i. tit.
7, § 9, p. 135 seq. ed. 1609; St. Baluz. not. ad. Ep. 8 ; Lupi Ferrar.; Joh.
Frid. Hornius, de Civ. l. ii. c. i. Francof. 1672; J. Ad. Osiander, Observat.
in Grot. l. i. c. ccclxvii. p. 478.   Also the tract of the unknown Benedic-
tine, de Finibus utriusque Potestatis, Ratisb. 1781, c. iv. p 80 seq.
    In opposition to these are numerous advocates of the merely mediate
divine appointment.   Thus Bellarm. de Laicis, l. iii. c. vi., who in this follows earlier authors like Durandus, tract. de Jurisdict. Eccles., and Jacob
Almainus, who, de Auctor. Eccl. et Conc. Gener. (Gerson, Opp. ii. 977,
978, ed. Antwerp), says : 'Nam, ut dicunt Doctores, . . non est intelligen-
dum, quod auctoritatis regis saecularis sit a Deo sic, quod eam *immediate*
commiserit alicui regulariter, sed quia secundum rectam rationem, quam
Deus hominibus indidit, est alicui commissa. Et non videtur, a quo sit

principi collata, nisi ab ipsa communitate.' The same doctrine is taught by Dominicus Soto, l. i. q. 1, art. 3; Ledesma, P. ii. q. 18, art. 3; Covarruvias, in Pract. c. i.; Suarez, de Leg. l. iii. c. iii.; Defens. Fid. Cath. l. iii. c. ii.; the Theologi Salmanticenses of the Carmelite order, particularly Antony of St. Joseph, Compend. Salmantic. Romae, 1779, tract. 3, de Legibus, cap. ii. punct. 1, inq. 2; Billuart, Theol. Moral. tract. de Legibus, art. 4; Charlas, tract. de Libert. Eccl. Gallic. l. iv. c. iv. p. 165, ed. 1684; Roncaglia, in Natal. Alex. H. E. saec. 13 et 14, c. ix. a. 5, t. xv. p. 519 seq.; Bianchi, l.c. p. 6 seq.; Mamachi, t. iv. pp. 59, 60, 66; Zallinger, Inst. Jur. Natur. § 204. Amongst Protestants who take this view are Grotius, de Jure Belli et Pacis, i. 4, § 7, n. 3, Paris, 1625 (cf. Leo, Universalgesch. iv. pp. 155-157); Sam. Pufendorf, de Jure Naturae et Gentium, l. vii. c. iii.; J. Barbeyrac, note in h.l.; Noodt, Buddeus, and others.

[3] Cic. de Off. ii. 12: 'Mihi quidem non apud Medos solum, ut ait Herodotus, sed etiam apud majores nostros justitiae fruendae causa videntur olim bene morati reges constituti. . . . Nam cum premeretur inops multitudo ab iis, qui majores opes habebant, ad unum aliquem confugiebant virtute praestantem, qui cum prohiberet injuria tenuiores, aequitate constituenda summos cum infimis pari jure retinebat.' De Leg. iii. 2: 'Omnes antiquae gentes quondam regibus paruerunt, quod genus imperii ad homines justissimos et sapientissimos deferebatur.'

[4] See many examples apud Bianchi, l.c. n. 4, p. 7.

[5] Bianchi, l.c. n. 10, p. 12.

§ 4.

The origin of the power must properly be distinguished from the bearer of the power, the power itself from the person holding it. All are agreed that authority comes from God; but not its concrete form, nor him who holds it. St. John Chrysostom[1] compares it with marriage : marriage is of God. Man and wife are united by God (Proverbs xix. 14) because God has instituted marriage, not because He unites individually all who marry. Authority in general is in its essence of God ;[2] particular forms of government are left to man's pleasure.[3] Man is destined by nature to live in society,[4] and society requires a ruler who shall insure to it order, unity, and peace.[5] This is part of the natural law which is divine law ; authority, therefore, comes from God.[6] Many theologians teach that this authority is communicated by God to the people, that it rests immediately with the people, and that they can transfer it to one or more persons.[7]

[1] Chrys. hom 23, in Rom. n. 1 (Migne, lx. 615). Likewise Joh. Dam. in h.l. (ib. xcv. p. 545). St. Thomas, in Ep. ad Rom. c. xiii. : 'Omnis potestas a Deo est, sed potestas ipsa, at non potentes.'

² Ægid. Rom. in l. ii. d. 44, q. 1, a. 2 ; q. 2. a. 2 : 'a Deo . . . generaliter et in quantum ordo est.'

³ Bossuet, l.c. p. 126 : 'Civile imperium generatim tantum traditum est et hominum arbitrio forma relicta, sive illa monarchica, sive aristocratica sive popularis foret.'

⁴ Aristot. Polit. i. 1, § 9, p. 483, ed. Paris, 1848: ἄνθρωπος φύσει πολιτικὸν ζῷον. Cf. also Balmez, Catholicity and Protestantism, Eng. trans. chap. xlix. p. 238 seq. ; Cic. de Republ. i. 25 (Lact. Inst. vi. 10 ; Aug. Ep. 138, n. 10).

⁵ De Reg. Princip. l. i. c. ii. Alvar. Pelag. de Planctu Eccl. l. i. c. xxxvi. f. 152 seq. Cf. Card. Gerdil, Diss. de Principatu Civili (Nouv. Opuscules du Card. Gerdil, Rome, 1852, p. 16 seq.).

⁶ Bellarmine, l.c. : 'Praeterea haec potestas est de jure naturae ; non enim pendet ex consensione hominum, nam velint, nolint, debent regi ab aliquo, nisi velint perire humanum genus, quod est contra naturae inclinationem. At jus naturae est jus divinum ; jure igitur divino introducta est gubernatio, et hoc videtur proprie velle Apostolus, cum dicit Rom. xiii. : Qui potestati resistit, Dei ordinationi resistit.'

⁷ Bell. l.c. Suarez, de Leg. iii. 4. Concina, l.c. In England during the reign of Charles I., Henry Bane (The People's Case Stated ; cf. Ranke, Hist. Eng. iii. 162) taught that it depended upon the people whether and under what conditions they should transfer the authority to individuals.

§ 5.

Earlier theologians base the proposition, that political authority rests originally and directly with the people — the community—firstly upon reason. For, they say, this authority is of divine law ; but divine law having conferred it upon no individual, it must have been conferred upon the community ; also, that supposing positive law to be abolished, there is no reason, since all men are equal, why one more than another should invest himself with authority, which, therefore, must belong to the entire people. Again, because human society must be a perfect society, it must have the right of self-preservation and of punishing disturbers of the public peace.[1] The proposition was based, in the second place, upon many passages of Roman law concerning the transference of the power of the people to rulers.[2] Thirdly, upon passages from classical writers, especially Aristotle and Cicero.[3] Fourthly, upon the historical testimony of ancient states and nations.[4] Lastly, upon the concurrence of previous writers. This doctrine approved itself to the monarchs of the sixteenth century, whose thrones gained much security from the downfall of the feudal lords and the development of the democratic element, at that time entirely harmless. The people were a support to them against the attacks of a turbulent and powerful aristocracy, long unwilling to submit to the position assigned to them of mere courtiers; for until the monarchy had become an all-devouring despotism, the people could more confide in the moderation and sense of justice of the king than of the nobles.

[1] Bellarmine, l.c.: 'Secundo nota, hanc potestatem immediate esse tanquam in subjecto in tota multitudine. Nam hacc potestas est de jure divino; at jus divinum nulli homini particulari dedit hanc potestatem, ergo dedit multitudini. Praeterea sublato jure positivo non est major ratio, cur ex multis aequalibus unus potius quam alius dominetur; igitur potestas est totius multitudinis. Denique humana societas debet esse perfecta respublica; ergo debet habere potestatem se ipsam conservandi et proinde puniendi perturbatores pacis,' &c. Cf. Almain. l.c.: 'Communitas confert principi auctoritatem occidendi eos, quorum vita in perniciem reipublicae cedit. Ergo illa auctoritas est per prius in communitate, cum nemo alteri det, quod non habet. Et antecedens notum est, cum princeps a se auctoritatem illam non habeat, nec eam habet a Deo, saltem ut in pluribus.'

[2] L. ii. Dig. i. 2, de Orig. Juris; l. ii. ib. tit. 4, de Constit. Princ.: 'Quod principi placuit, legis habet vigorem, utpote cum lege regia, quae de imperio ejus lata est, *populus ei et in eum omne suum imperium et potestatem conferat.*' Inst. i. 2, § 6. Cf. Bianchi, t. iii. l. i. c. i. § 8, n. 5, pp. 9, 10; t. i. l. i. p. 8 seq. Mamachi, l.c. p. 61.

[3] Cic. de Rep. i. c. xxvi. seq. c. xxxiv. seq. Aristot. Polit. iii. 6.

[4] Bellarm. l.c. § Quarto nota, refers to Roman history: 'Et si causa legitime adsit, potest multitudo mutare regimen in aristocratiam aut democratiam et e contrario, ut Romae factum legimus.'

§ 6.

This doctrine has often been ascribed exclusively to Jesuits, and Cardinal Bellarmine has been described as the inventor of the theory of the sovereignty of the people in the sense of Rousseau and similar writers.[1] But all acquainted with literature know that the doctrine held by Bellarmine and the Jesuits did not differ from that of other schools and orders, nor from the doctrine of the earlier schoolmen, and that it was essentially different from modern revolutionary theories. F. Walter[2] points out that Bellarmine, and theologians who agree with him, derive political power from God,[3] whereas modern theories ascribe it *entirely* to man. The former hold it to be imparted by God to man, the latter consider it to come from man's agreement and creation; according to the former it is transferred to those in authority of necessity by virtue of the divine and natural law,[4] whilst the latter make the transfer a purely voluntary arrangement made by virtue of a contract. These theologians are far from holding the opinions of the Contrat Social,[5] neither do they accept the theory that man in his primitive condition roamed about like the animals, until some sage prevailed upon him to live a social life.[6] The doctrine of these theologians, that the people having once conferred authority have not the right to retract it when they like, makes a further distinction between them and the advocates of the modern theories of the sovereignty of the people.[7]

[1] Stahl, Der Protest. als polit. Princip. Berlin, 1853, p. 24 seq. Ranke, Päpste, ii. 184 seq. Trendelenburg, Naturrecht, § 154, note. Cf. Huber, p. 42.

[2] Walter, Naturrecht und Politik, § 252, p. 228, with note.

[3] Suarez, Def. iii. 1, 6: 'Principem politicum potestatem a Deo recipere, quod etiam absolute *de fide* est.'

[4] Bellarm. l.c.: 'Tertio nota, hanc potestatem transferri a multitudine in unum vel plures *eodem jure naturae*. Nam respublica non potest per se ipsam exercere hanc potestatem, ergo tenetur eam transferre in aliquem unum vel aliquos paucos, et hoc modo potestas principum in genere considerata est etiam de jure naturae et divino: nec posset genus humanum, etiamsi totum simul conveniret, contrarium statuere, nimirum ut nulli essent principes vel rectores.'

[5] Various expressions on this subject may indeed be quoted from Fathers and theologians, for example Aug. (Confess. iii. 8): '*generale* quippe *pactum* est societatis humanae obedire regibus suis.' But a *generale pactum* is here something quite different from Rousseau's contract ('pactum vinculum naturale est, stipulatio vero civilis est obligatio,' says Petr. Bles. Ep. 70, p. 218, in accordance with Roman law). St. Augustine elsewhere (de Civ. Dei, l. xix. c. xii. n. 2) says: 'Homo fertur quodammodo naturae suae legibus ad ineundam societatem;' and Pius VI. in a Brief of the 10th March 1791, to Cardinal de la Rochefoucault, says truly: 'Qua propter haec potestas non tam a "sociali contractu," quam ab ipso Deo recti justitique auctore repetenda est.' Ranke is an example of how our modern historians, even those who summarily condemn former Catholic men of learning, are far from having reached a firm conclusion on this subject. In his History of England, vol. i. p. 75, he says: 'Whether political relations amongst mankind have in general their origin in a contract is a question for speculative politicians, to whom we may leave its solution.' Against Rousseau's theory, vide Taparelli, Naturrecht, 1840, § 557-585; Walter, l.c. p. 62; Balmez, chap. 1. (vol. iii. p. 57 seq.); Gerdil, l.c. pp. 19-23.

* Bellarm. l.c. c. v. Gerdil, l.c. pp. 17, 18.
[†] Petavius, de Eccl. Hierarch. l. iii. c. xiv. p. 88, ed. Paris : ' Quod in omnibus imperiis ac regnis usuvenisse putant, qui de rebus publicis scripserunt, ut jus et potestas omnis a natura ipsi communitati conveniat, quae eam postea vel in plures magistratus ac rectores partiatur vel integram in unum aliquem transferat, pro eo ac plurium vel unius regimen elegerit, ex quo civilium per gentes et populos administrationum sunt orta discrimina. . . . Porro ubi jus auctoritatemque, quam habebat, in eum quem elegit principem transtulit, *non eam penes se retinet nec revocare amplius potest.*' Also Valentinian's address to the soldiers (Theod. H. E. iv. 5) : ' Vestrum fuit milites, cum imperator nullus esset, imperii habenas mihi tradere ; nunc postquam imperium ego suscepi, meum est de cetero, non vestrum, de publicis negotiis deliberare.'

§ 7.

The germ, at least, of the State undoubtedly existed in the family in primeval times ;[1] the family of the first-born may have been treated with most consideration, but could scarcely have maintained its preëminence everywhere and always.[2] Imagine a considerable number of families, equal in every way and quite unconnected, cast by a storm upon a desert island, their vessels wrecked, and themselves without any hope of reaching the land they had left or the shores for which they were bound, entirely cut off from the society of other men ; these families could certainly not live upon this island without some government, and yet no one there would have more claim than another to any authority ; but they certainly have the right to institute a government that appears to them necessary and suitable. Thus this multitude, represented by the heads of families or otherwise, possesses the right of civil power, and the privilege of conferring it upon one or more according to circumstances. It will not be easy for any one successfully to oppose Bellarmine's doctrine on this point.[3] It applies also when a ruling family becomes extinct ; when both *de facto* and *de jure* claimants of a throne are wanting, where nothing has previously been done to meet such a case, and where no one has any special. rights. The difficulty in the concrete is the obscurity which veils the early formation of States.[4] Many governments may· have arisen in usurpation, but have become legitimate when they·

attained stability and received the consent of the people.[5] There are undoubted cases in which the ruling prince derives his commission to exercise authority through a transfer from the people and through their consent. The theory fails, however, when it is carried too far. It must not be used as a universal rule to be applied always and in all cases.[6] Legitimacy may be original or acquired; it may spring from various legal titles, such as election, succession, and others.[7]

[1] Walter, Naturrecht, § 49, p. 59.

[2] It is impossible in a large empire where there are many nationalities. Balmez, chap. xlviii.

[3] Balmez, chap. xlix. We must observe that this doctrine, although *in abstracto* recognising the universal equality of men, does not do so *in concreto.* Cf. Civiltà Cattolica, Dec. 1, 1855.

[4] 'The origin of forms of government, like the origin of States, belongs to a period when, as far as we are concerned, all is darkness; we only know of their changes and their development. When in a nation the supreme power has been transmitted without change of form, and in unbroken succession, or where the changes of form have been effected by the coöperation or with the consent of the possessor of the power, then the government resulting from the change is in the fullest sense legitimate.' Walter, l.c. § 248, p. 220.

[5] Ib. § 250, p. 222 seq. Bellarmine, l.c.: 'Adde, saepissime regna esse justa et injusta, a Deo et non a Deo; nam ex parte ipsorum occupantium et invadentium regna sunt latrocinia et injusta, et proinde non a Deo, tamen ex parte divinae providentiae, quae utitur mala intentione hominum et illam ordinat vel ad peccata punienda vel remuneranda bona opera vel ad alios bonos fines, regna illa sunt justa et legitima.'

[6] Walter, § 252, p. 227.

[7] Petrus de Alliaco ap. Almain. de Potest. Eccl. et Laica, q. 2, c. i. § Quantum ad haec. Bianchi, t. i. l.c. n. 8, 9, pp. 11, 12.

§ 8.

This old theological doctrine may be imperfect and defective, but it is far superior to many later theories. It holds, to a certain extent, the mean between the doctrine of an absolute monarchy by divine right—which may impose any yoke upon the people, and treat the country as a private possession[1]—and the doctrine of the sovereignty of the people, which allows them at any moment to transform the constitution and overthrow the monarchy.[2] This old doctrine teaches, not merely that authority in the abstract and in general is instituted by God, but that in the concrete and *in particulari* it comes from Him, though mediately.[3] This doctrine lays no claim to be regarded as a dogma, and openly confesses that revelation is silent on the subject.[4] As Balmez justly observes, there are two questions : (1) The divine origin of political authority; (2) the mode in which God imparts it. 'The first is a point of doctrine. No Catholic can entertain any doubt upon it. The second is open to discussion, and various opinions may be formed upon it without interfering with faith.'[5] The question is analogous to many other legal questions. To respect the right of property, for example, is commanded by the natural and divine law ; it is inculcated by the Church, and required by the State ; but as to the component parts of property, as to the rights of individual owners, as to acquisition and transfer of property, as to the necessary limitations of the right of property, these are questions appertaining to civil law, with which the Church has no concern.

---

[1] Theologians teach that public authority can never be *dominium proprietatis*. They refer to Seneca (de Benef. vii. 5 : 'Omnia rex imperio possidet, singuli dominio ;' c. iv. : 'Ad reges potestas omnium pertinet, ad singulos proprietas') and other classical writers, to the distinction between 'proprietas' (dominium) and 'possessio' (l. xii. Dig. xli. 2 ; l. i. Dig. xliii. 17 ; Aristot. Rhetor. i. 5) to the nature of things and to reason. Cf. Gerson, Opp. iv. 598 ; Schwab, p. 42 ; Grotius, de Jure Belli, l. ii. c. vi. n. 7-9. To the same effect are the passages in the Old Testament concerning the Jewish kings who arbitrarily disposed of the life and property of their subjects.

[2] Fichte even declared that the people could never be rebels, but were rather the source and foundation of all other power (Grundlage des Naturrechts, Th. i. § 16, Werke, iii. 182).

[3] Bellarm. l.c. Quinto nota : 'Ex dictis sequi, hanc potestatem *in particulari* esse quidem a Deo, sed mediante consilio et electione humana, ut alia omnia, quae ad jus gentium pertinent. Jus enim gentium est qua si conclusio deducta ex jure naturae per humanum discursum. Ex quo colliguntur duae differentiae inter potestatem ecclesiasticam et politicam,' &c. Cf. Rintel, pp. 57-59. Vide likewise Suarez, de Leg. iii. 3 : 'In hac re communis sententia videtur esse, hanc *potestatem* dari *immediate a Deo ut auctore naturae*, ita ut homines quasi disponant *materiam* et efficiant subjectum capax hujus potestatis ; Deus autem quasi tribuat *formam dando* hanc potestatem.' He quotes Cajetan, Covarruvias, Victoria, and Soto.

[4] Suarez, Defens. l. iii. c. ii. : 'Sed quamquam controversia haec ad fidei dogmata directe non pertineat (nihil enim ex divina Scriptura aut

Patrum traditione in illa definitum ostendi potest), nihilominus diligentur tractanda et explicanda est.'

⁵ Balmez, chap. 1.

PART II. THE RIGHT OF RESISTANCE AGAINST THE CIVIL POWER.

§ 1. Duty of obedience. Right of resisting tyranny in general. § 2. John of Salisbury. § 3. St. Thomas Aquinas. § 4. Proceedings in the fifteenth century. § 5, 6, 7. Protestant theories and practice. § 8. Absolute obedience. § 9. Two currents in Protestantism. § 10, 11. Catholic League in France. § 12. Must Catholics not rather suffer death than offer opposition? § 13. The Jesuits. § 14. Mariana. § 15. Suarez. § 16. Gregory of Valentia. § 17. Molina and other Jesuits. § 18, 19. Complaints against the Jesuits.

§ 1.

As a general rule it was maintained that the teaching of Holy Scripture and of the Fathers[1] inculcated upon subjects the duty of obedience towards all authority, good or bad, Christian or heathen, and that neither the personal wickedness of the ruler[2] nor his profession of a false religion exempted them from this duty. It was no less unanimously maintained, that when a ruler abused his authority by commanding anything plainly incompatible with the divine or natural law, or with justice, or with the constitution, *passive* resistance is not merely a right, but, when divine or moral law is in question, a duty. No one should make himself in such cases the accomplice of a wrong, and disobedience violates no right appertaining to the prince; for he has encroached upon a domain in which he has no authority and beyond the limits of his proper sphere. Where there is no right to command there can be no duty to obey.[3] But it was a disputed point whether *active* resistance, carried to the length of deposition, expulsion, or death, might, in extreme cases, be lawfully employed against a legitimate prince who governed unjustly. At an early period it was pretty generally held that there were cases in which subjects might withdraw their obedience from a ruler so far as actively to resist him; namely, when he entirely misused his authority, was tyrannical and oppressive, and when the self-preservation of the people required it. The ancients said that when self-preservation was

in question all the bonds of society were loosed, paternal authority
ceased, as well as the authority of the husband over his wife, of
the master over his servant : the authority of the prince followed
the same course.[4] They looked upon the tyrant as an enemy of
the law and of the people, who forfeited, therefore, his authority.[5]
A tyrant with them was not merely one who usurped the
government unlawfully.[6] A lawful ruler also was a tyrant if he
governed unjustly, oppressed his subjects, and led to the ruin of
the commonwealth,[7] but especially if he used his power to
oppress citizens for his private advantage.[8] The question was
discussed in the schools of who possessed the right, and under
what conditions, of rebelling against a tyrant, whether usurping
or legitimate, and depriving him of his power to do ill. The
majority of theologians did not concede the right to private
persons, but reserved it to the whole people, who were often
regarded as the real holders of the sovereign power,[9] and to them
only when all endeavours had been exhausted. They considered
that in such cases the verdict of reason and natural law made it
allowable to offer forcible resistance, as an extreme measure, for
defence and protection against public oppression.[10] This doctrine has been often and violently attacked, but has seldom been
made the subject of study in its true meaning, and in relation
to the circumstances of the time.[11] Let us hear on the subject
some learned men of the Middle Ages, who all start from the
principle that the rights of the king are not more holy and inviolable than those of the humblest subject, except so far as
they are intended for the protection of the rights of all others.[12]

[1] Vide Tertull. adv. Scapul.; Origen, l. ix. in Rom. n. 25 seq.; Chrys.
hom. 23, in Rom. c. xiii.; Aug. de Civ. Dei, v. 21, de Natura Boni, c.
Manich.; Catech. Rom. l. iii. de Quarto Praecepto, c. iii.

[2] Vide also Tacit. Hist. iv. 74 : ‘Quomodo sterilitatem aut nimios imbres
et cetera naturae mala, ita luxum et avaritiam dominantium tolerate;’ l.
vii.: ‘Bonos imperatores voto expetendos, qualescunque tolerandos.’ Seneca, in Trag.: ‘Aequum et iniquum regis imperium feras.’ Sophocles :
ἀλλ’ ὃν πόλις στήσει, τοῦδε χρὴ κλύειν καὶ σμικρὰ καὶ δίκαια καὶ τἀναντία.
Bianchi, t. i. l. i. § 3, n. 3, p. 23.

[3] Walter, Naturrecht und Politik, § 358, p. 327 seq. Cf. Martini, Lehrbuch des Staatsrechts, 1799, § 380; Dahlmann, Politik, § 202. Quite
similar is the teaching of St. Anselm. Cant. Com. in Ep. ad Rom. c. xiii.;
S. Thomas, Sum. 1, 2, q. 96, a. 4; Suarez, de Leg. l. iii. c. x.; Petrus

Bles. Ep. 131, p. 388. Aug. de Verb. Dom. sermo 6 (al. 62, n. 12, Opp.
v. 362): 'Si quid proconsul jubeat et aliud imperator, numquid dubitatur
illo contemto isti esse serviendum? Ergo si aliud imperator, aliud Deus
jubeat, contemto illo obtemperandum est Deo.' Thus Acts v. 29.
Mamachi, p. 68 seq., gives many older examples.

⁴ Vide passages apud Bianchi, l.c. § 4, pp. 24-29.

⁵ Hugo Grotius, l.c. n. 11 : 'Consistere enim non possunt voluntas imperandi et voluntas perdendi; quare qui se hostem totius populi profitetur,
in eo ipso abdicat regnum.' Cf. Barclay, l. iv. c. xvi. According to the
ancients a tyrant was the enemy of the law and of the people. Cic. de
Offic. iii. 19, 32, de Republ. i. 42: 'Quum rex injustus esse coeperunt
perit illud illico genus, et est idem ille *tyrannus*, deterrimum genus et
finitimum optimo.' L. ii. c. xxvi.: 'Simulac enim se inflexit hic rex (Tar-
quinius Superbus) in dominatum injustiorem, fit continuo *tyrannus*, quo
neque tetrius neque foedius nec Diis hominibusque invisius animal ullum
cogitari potest, qui, quamquam figura est hominis, morum tamen immani-
tate vastissimas vincit belluas. Quis enim hominem rite dixerit, qui sibi
cum suis civibus, qui denique cum omni hominum genere nullam juris
communionem, nullam humanitatis societatem velit?' Philipp. ii. : 'Omnes
boni, quantum in ipsis fuit, Caesarem occiderunt. Aliis consilium, aliis
animus, aliis occasio defuit, voluntas nemini.' Cf. Sueton. in Nerone, c.
xlix.; Arist. Polit. l. v. c. x. xi. The king, on the contrary, was regarded as
the father and benefactor of the people. Cic. de Rep. ii. 26 : 'Hic est
enim dominus populi, quem Graeci *tyrannum* vocant; nam *regem* illum
volunt esse, qui consulit ut parens populo, conservatque eos, quibus est
praepositus, quam optima in conditione vivendi.'

⁶ This is the usual meaning. Cf. Schwab, Gerson, pp. 615, 616.

⁷ A theologian of the fifteenth century says (Gerson, Opp. v. 867) :
'*Proprie* tyrannus est, quicunque reipublicae oppressor potentatu regali
et monarchica potentia abutitur despotice absque superiore repressore, sive
talis habeat vel usurpet titulum monarchici principatus sive non.'

⁸ Aristot. Polit. vii. 14, makes a distinction between power exercised
for the benefit of the rulers and that exercised for the benefit of the
governed. The former he calls despotic, the latter of the free. He does
not regard every government as a despotism (c. iii.). Tacit. Ann. l. xii.
represents the Emperor Claudius as admonishing the King of the Parthians
to have in his mind 'non dominationem et servos, sed rectorem et cives.'
The same idea made Augustus not wish to be called 'dominus' (Sueton.
in Oct. Aug. c. liii.). Gregory I. l. xiii. Ep. 31, thus states the difference
between pagan kings and the Roman emperor: 'Quod reges gentium
domini servorum sunt, imperatores vero reipublicae domini liberorum'
(Bianchi, t. iii. l. i. c. i. § 8, n. 3, 4, pp. 80-82). Ægidius Colonna, de Reg.
Princ. l. iii. P. ii. c. ii. defines the tyrant, 'per civilem potentiam oppri-
mens alios propter bonum privatum.' Thus Gerson, Opp. iv. 598-600.
Bossuet, Politique tirée des propres Paroles de l'Ecriture sainte, Paris,
1709, l. iii. a. 3, prop. 5: 'Le vrai caractère du prince est de pourvoir aux
besoins du peuple, comme celui du tyran est de ne songer qu'à lui-même.'
The two significations of the word 'tyrant' were not always clearly
distinguished, and thus the idea of tyrant was sometimes wider and some-

times more restricted. The word often appears in Scripture: Job xxxiv. 19 ; Dan. iii. 3; Wis. xvi. 4 ; also in the Fathers. Observe the words of Cicero, de Rep. i. 33 : 'Cur enim *regem* appellem Jovis Optimi nomine *hominem dominandi cupidum aut imperii singularis, populo oppresso dominantem*, non *tyrannum* potius ?' ii. 27: 'Hoc nomen (tyranni) Graeci *regis injusti* esse voluerunt.' Many distinguish the 'tyrannus secundum regimen et titulum' and the 'tyrannus secundum regimen tantum,' or the 'tyrannus quoad dominium et potestatem' and the 'tyrannus solum quoad regimen.' Cajetan, in Sum. 2, 2, q. 42, a. 2 : 'Quis sit autem modus ordinatus perturbandi tyrannum et qualem tyrannum, puta *secundum regimen tantum* vel *secundum regimen et titulum*, non est praesentis intentionis ; sat est nunc, quod ut utrumque tyrannum licet ordinate perturbare absque seditione quandoque, illum ut bono reipublicae vacet, istum ut expellatur.' Suarez, disp. 13, de Bello, sect. 8.

⁹ Many modern writers, such as J. H. Fichte (System der Ethik, ii. § 145), accept a twofold sovereignty, that of the people and of kings.

¹⁰ Cf. Haller (Restauration der St. Wissensch. Pt. ii. ch. 41). Upon this and Bluntschli and Dahlmann, cf. Walter, l.c. § 326, p. 335.

¹¹ Balmez, l.c. chaps. liv-lvi.

¹² In this sense writes Rintel against Stahl, p. 21 : 'According to the conservative principle, not merely the right of the ruling one or many, but the whole mass of rights within the State are Dei gratiâ—the expression of God's will. The smallest right of the lowest subject is in and through God as holy as the right of the king to his throne, and if the king violates the lowly right of his subject, the moral guilt, the breach of the divine law, the outrage against God, is no less than if the subject rise up against the king. (Compare the case of Achab, 3 Kings xxi. 1-25.) The right of the king is superior to that of the subject only in being the right to protect and defend all other rights ; but it is in no way the one sacred right in the State, and the only one coming from God.' The notion of 'divine right' as exclusively confined to kings is an invention of the time of the Reformation, especially of Henry VIII., who made his divine right a justification for the most crying tyranny.

§ 2.

John of Salisbury¹ says tyranny is above all things an abuse of the power conferred by God.² According to him, tyranny is not merely a public crime ; it is, if possible, more than this. 'The man who does not pursue a public enemy fails in duty towards himself and towards the whole human commonwealth.' 'The prince defends the laws and liberty of the people. The tyrant in every way sets the laws at naught, and seeks to bring the people into servitude.' 'The prince should be honoured and loved ; often the tyrant should even be put to death.'³ But he does not dispute that tyrants are servants of God, inasmuch as they chastise the sins of the people.[4] He says further : 'The will of the ruler depends upon the will of God, and causes no injury to liberty ; but the will of the tyrant serves greed, and in opposition to law—which fosters liberty—seeks to lay the yoke of servitude upon his fellow-servants.'[5] Gedeon, he says further, is the model of a good ruler ; for, although the deliverer of his people, he desired not his own government, but the government of God.[6] The tyrant is typified by Antiochus, who tore and burnt the books of the divine law, and raged against his subjects.[7] The history of Julius Cæsar and other pagan emperors illustrates the right of putting tyrants to death, in case no other remedy remains for preventing the continuance of tyranny.[8] The same thing, he says, is shown by the history of the Jews, especially the books of Judges and of Judith ;[9] but with the limitation that no one should aim at or strive for the downfall of one to whom he is bound by honour and oath, neither should poison be employed, and everything should be done without injury to religion or honesty.[10] Laws appear to be presupposed which permit tyrants to be put to death ; poisoning is inadmissible, on the ground that no law permits it.[11] Still, he thinks, pointing out the lamentable end of all tyrants, like Pharao, Achab, Sennacherib, Nabuchodonosor, Julian the Apostate, and others,[12] that the best and safest way of overcoming tyrants is for the oppressed to turn to God, and having purged themselves from sin to pray to Him for succour ; for the sins of the people are the tyrant's mainstay.[13]

[1] Polycrat. l. iii. c. xv. (Migne, cxcix. p. 512 seq.) : 'Undo et in saecularibus literis cautum est, quia aliter cum amico, aliter vivendum est cum tyranno. Amico utique adulari non licet, sed aures tyranni mulcere licitum est. Ei namque licet adulari, quam *licet occidere*. Porro tyrannum occidere non modo licitum est, sed aequum et justum.'

[2] C. xviii. p. 786 : 'Est enim tyrannis a Deo concessae homini potestatis abusus.'

[3] C. xvii. p. 778 : ' Imago Deitatis princeps amandus (vide Aug. Quaest. 5, et N. Testamenti, q. 35), venerandus est et colendus ; tyrannus pravitatis imago plerumque etiam occidendus.'

[4] C. xviii. p. 785.

[5] C. xxii. p. 807.

[6] Ib. : 'Defertur honor dominii et recusat ; legi tamen subjicit, quos a

jugo servitutis absolvit. Patri filiorum successurus defertur honor ; at ille Deum maluit honorari.'
      [7] Ibid. p. 808.
      [8] C. xviii. p. 788 : 'Ex quibus facile patebit, quia semper tyranno licuit adulari, licuit eum decipere, et honestum fuit occidere, si tamen aliter coerceri non poterat ;' c. xix. p. 792 : 'Et haec quidem est descriptio tyranni, qua explicatur res quae latet in nomine. Sicut ergo damnatum hostem licet occidere, sic tyrannum.' Ib. c. xx. p. 793, he refers to his earlier work, de Exitu Tyrannorum.
      [9] C. xx. pp. 794-797.
      [10] P. 796 : 'Hoc tamen cavendum doceat historiae, ne quis illius moliatur interitum, cui fidei aut sacramenti religione tenetur astrictus. Sed *nec* veneni, licet videam ab infidelibus aliquando usurpatam, *ullo unquam jure* indultam lego licentiam. Non quod tyrannos de medio tollendos non credam, sed *sine religionis honestatisque dispendio.*' The chapter, p. 793, bears the title, 'Quod auctoritate divinae paginae licitum et gloriosum est publicos tyrannos occidere, si tamen fidelitate non sit tyranno obnoxius interfector aut alias justitiam aut honestatem non amittat.'
      [11] Gosselin, ii. p. 441, note.
      [12] C. xxi. p. 797 seq.
      [13] P. 796 (after referring to David's conduct in regard to Saul, his persecutor): 'Et hic quidem modus delendi tyrannos utilissimus est et tutissimus, si qui premuntur ad patrocinium clementiae Dei humiliati confugiant et puras manus levantes ad Dominum devotis precibus flagellum, quo affliguntur, avertant. Peccata etenim delinquentium vires sunt tyrannorum.'

§ 3.

St. Thomas Aquinas says that a tyrannical government is not a legitimate government, therefore a rising against it has not the character of a rebellion, except when its overthrow would work more harm to the nation than its continuance ;[1] the tyrant is, properly speaking, to be regarded as a rebel. If the tyranny be not immoderate, the saint recommends endurance as the best expedient,[2] for it cannot last for ever,[3] and its removal may often occasion greater evils than its existence.[4] Thus the question is limited to a despotism so extreme as to be insupportable. But even in this case the right to rebel does not, he says, belong to private individuals.[5] Before any measures are taken against tyrants, the verdict of the country to that effect should have been publicly expressed, and the various cases carefully discriminated. Tyranny can be proceeded against only when the public judgment of the entire society has been given.[6] Wherever the people have the right to elect their king, it cannot be unlawful for them to depose him if he is false to the obligations he entered into; or they may restrict his power for the time to come, as we see in Roman history.[7] When the right of appointing a governor appertains to some higher authority (for example, in vassal States), it is to this higher authority that an oppressed people should turn for relief, as the Jews applied to the emperor against Archelaus the son of Herod.[8] If all human succour is wanting against the tyrant, then recourse, he says, should be had to God, the King of kings, who might convert or displace him; prayer would be efficacious if sin, the source of all evils in the people, were removed.[9]

---

[1] Summa, 2, 2, q. 42, a. 2 ad 3 : ' Regimen tyrannicum non est justum, quia non ordinatur ad bonum commune, sed ad bonum privatum regentis, ut patet per philosophum ; et ideo perturbatio hujus regiminis non habet rationem seditionis nisi forte, quando sic inordinate perturbator tyranni regimen, quod multitudo subjecta majus detrimentum patitur ex perturbatione consequenti quam ex tyranni regimine ; magis autem tyrannus seditiosus est, qui in populo sibi subjecto discordias nutrit et seditiones, ut tutius dominari possit ; hoc enim tyrannicum est, cum sit ordinatum ad bonum proprium praesidentis cum multitudinis nocumento ;' ib. q. 69, a. 4 : ' Sicut licet resistere latronibus, ita licet resistere malis principibus, nisi forte propter scandalum vitandum.'

[2] De Regimine Principum, c. vi. : ' Et quidem si non fuerit excessus tyrannidis, utilius est remissam tyrannidem tolerare ad tempus, quam contra tyrannum agendo multis implicari periculis, quae sunt graviora ipsa tyrannide.'

[3] Ib. c. x.

[4] C. vi. Example of greater tyranny in Dionysius of Syracuse.

[5] Esset autem hoc multitudini periculosum et ejus rectoribus, si privata praesumptione aliqui tentarent praesidentium necem, etiam tyrannorum. Plerumque enim hujusmodi periculis magis exponunt se mali quam boni. Malis autem solet esse grave dominium non minus regum quam tyrannorum, quia secundum sententiam Salomonis, ' Dissipat impios rex sapiens.' Magis igitur ex hujus praesumptione immineret periculum multitudini de amissione regis, quam remedium de subtractione tyranni.

[6] Videtur autem magis contra tyrannorum saevitiam non privata praesumptione aliquorum, sed auctoritate publica procedendum.

[7] The means previously pointed out for the prevention of tyranny were : (1) election of a man who appeared unlikely to become a tyrant; (2) limitations of his power so as to hinder it from easily degenerating. A restrained monarchy or mixed government was always reckoned the best. Thom. Sum. 1, 2, q. 105, a. 1. Cf. Cic. de Rep. i. 29, 45; ii. 23; Bellarm. de Rom. Pont. i. 1-4; Suarez, de Leg. iii. 4.

¹ Cf. Sum. 2, 2, q. 64, a. 3.

² Quod si omnino contra tyrannum auxilium humanum haberi non potest, recurrendum est ad regem omnium Deum, qui est *adjutor in opportunitatibus in tribulatione.* Ejus enim potentiae subest, ut cor tyranni crudele convertat in mansuetudinem secundum Salomonis sententiam Prov. xii.: *Cor regis in manu Dei,* &c. (examples of Assuerus and Nabuchodonosor). Tyrannos vero, quos reputat conversione indignos, potest auferre de medio vel ad infimum statum reducere, secundum illud sapientis Eccli. x. 17 : *Sedes ducum superborum destruxit Deus et sedere fecit mites pro eis* (Pharao, Nabuchodonosor). Nec enim abbreviata manus ejus est, ut populum suum a tyrannis liberare non possit. . . . Sed ut hoc beneficium populus a Deo consequi mereatur, debet a peccatis cessare, quia in ultionem peccati divina permissione impii accipiunt principatum (Osee xiii. 11; Job xxxiv. 30). Tollenda est igitur culpa, ut cesset tyrannorum plaga.

§ 4.

On occasion of the murder of Duke Louis of Orleans by command of Duke John of Burgundy, the Franciscan Jean Petit, on the 8th March 1408, defended the proposition that it was lawful for a subject to kill, or to cause to be killed, a false vassal or perfidious tyrant.¹ This elicited an emphatic denial² of the proposition from the learned John Gerson, who cited John of Salisbury and St. Thomas Aquinas in favour of his view.³ Petit's assertions were condemned in Paris, 1414, by the bishop and inquisitor.⁴ At the 15th session of the Council of Constance⁵ the following proposition was condemned : ' Any tyrant may be lawfully and meritoriously slain by any one of his vassals or subjects, even by cunning or secret ambush, without hindrance from any oath he may have taken to the said tyrant his lord, or any engagement by which he may be bound to him, and without awaiting the sentence or receiving the commission of any judge.'⁶ The condemnation of a proposition like this, containing many errors, left room still for disputes on several points. Further inquiries were excited by the assertions of Wicliffe and Huss, that no one could exercise an authority or superior power who was in mortal sin, and the people might punish a sinful ruler according to their judgment.⁷

¹ Gerson, Opp. v. pp. 15-42, ed. Dupin. Schwab, Gerson, p. 430 seq. Hefele, Conc. vii. p. 176 seq.

² Opp. iv. pp. 657-680. Schwab, pp. 499 seq. 609 seq.

[3] Gerson had declared previously in favour of the right of resisting tyrants, and even of tyrannicide. Vide Decem Considerationes principibus et dominis utilissimae, Opp. iv. 622 seq.; Schwab, l.c. p. 426 seq.; ib. pp. 615-617.

[4] The document apud Natal. Alex. H. E. saec. 15 et 16, c. ii. a. 4, n. 3, t. xvii. p. 184 seq.

[5] Mansi, xxvii. 765. Schwab, p. 622. Hefele, p. 181.

[6] The judgment ran thus: ' Doctrinam hujusmodi erroneam esse in fide et moribus ipsamque tamquam haereticam, scandalosam, et ad fraudes, deceptiones, mendacia, proditiones, perjuria vias dantem reprobari et condemnari.'

[7] Articuli damn. 1418, n. 15, 17. Wiclef. art. 30. J. Hus. (Denzinger, Enchirid. definit. p. 187, n. 491, 493; p. 193, n. 550). In Wicliffe's time (in 1386) the English peers declared to Richard II. that if he did not, according to custom, govern by their advice, and if he estranged himself from the people, it would be their part to depose him with the consent of the people, and raise another member of the royal family to the throne. Richard was actually deposed by the Parliament, whilst earlier (in 1327) Edward II. had been forced to abdicate to insure the throne to his son. Schwab, l.c. p. 588. Ranke, Gesch. Eng. i. p. 103. Pauli, Gesch. Eng. iv. p. 636 seq.

§ 5.

Discussions on this question became still more animated after the rise of Protestantism.

In the conflicts of the Huguenots in France under Charles IX. and Henry III., in the Scotch risings after John Knox, in the revolutions in England long before the execution of Charles I., in the wars of the rebellious Netherlanders against the Spaniards, many followers of Calvin defended the proposition that the people might take up arms and expel, dethrone, or otherwise get rid of their rulers if they were bad or hostile, or threatened their religion. They preached the strictest obedience to princes who embraced the new doctrines, but armed resistance to those in authority who opposed the introduction of these doctrines.[1] The Scotch appealed to Calvin's doctrine,[2] in justification of their rebellion against Mary Stuart;[3] George Buchanan, tutor of James I., sought to justify rebellion by revolutionary theories;[4] many others have done the same.[5]

[1] Bossuet, Hist. des Variations des Eglises prot. l. iv. n. 1-3. Baudrillart, Bodin et son temps, Paris, 1853, p. 40 seq. Poynet, Bishop of Winchester under Edward VI., in his Petit Traité du Pouvoir politique,

1558, appears as one of the first ' Monarchomachi' (Barclay has the expression). Cf. Walter, l.c. § 534.

¹ Calvin, in Daniel c. vi.: 'Abdicant se potestate terreni principes, cum insurgunt contra Deum; indigni sunt, qui in numero hominum censeantur, ideoque in capita potius eorum exspuere oportet, quam illis parere.'

² Camden Annal. P. ii. a. 1571: 'Immo a Calvini auctoritate populares, ubique magistratus ad libidinem regum moderandam constitutos esse iisque licere malos reges carceribus coercere et regno exuere probaro conati sunt.'

⁴ Buchanan, de Jure Regni, p. 13 : 'Populo jus est, de sceptro regis pro debito suo disponendi;' p. 62 : ' Populus principem in jus capitis vocare potest.' Cf. Hist. Scot. l. vii.

⁵ Goodman, Lib. de Obed. p. 25 : 'Reges jus regnandi a populo habent, qui occasione data illud revocare potest.' Further on, p. 99, he says Mary of England must be put to death. Apol. pp. 14, 85 : 'Mali principes juxta legem Dei deponi debent, cumque magistratus officio suo fungi detrectant, tum liberum est plebi, ac si nullum haberet magistratum, et tunc tempus illi usum gladii concedit.' John Kanus, whom Calvin praises, Ep. 306, and Beza in the Icones compares with the Apostles, says in the Admonitio ad Not. et Popul. Scotiae : 'Si principes adversus Deum et veritatem ejus tyrannice se gerant, subditi eorum a juramento fidelitatis absolvantur. Illud audacter affirmaverim debuisse nobiles, rectores, judices populumque Anglicanum non solum resistere et repugnare Mariae illi Jezabel, quam vocant reginam suam, verum etiam de ea et sacerdotibus ejus et aliis omnibus, quotquot ei auxilium tulerunt, mortis supplicium sumere, ut primum coeperunt Evangelium supprimere.'

§ 6.

The work[1] (printed in Edinburgh in 1579) of Hubert Languet, a man of varied learning, was, together with other works,[2] greatly used in the Netherlands in defence of revolution. It laid down distinctly that the people were authorised to resist and punish the king, if he oppressed the true religion (Calvinism) and introduced idolatry (Catholicism). The Huguenots in France received express approval from their preachers for their wars of religion.[3] The famous preacher Jurieu, who ascribed all power to the people,[4] delivered the following doctrine in a pastoral letter as late as 1689 : 'Kings are responsible to the people for the maladministration of the sovereignty intrusted to them, which can be withdrawn from them and made over to others if the public welfare and the interests of religion require it.'[5] The manifestations made here and there, and more frequently as time went on, in opposition to this doctrine and in favour of

royal authority, and later even of blind obedience,[6] took place
under a different order of circumstances, when the party had
suffered considerable diminution.   They may in many instances
be attributed to the endeavour to excite hatred against Catholic
doctrines ; the Calvinists, for instance, in 1614, out of respect
for James I. and animosity against Rome, condemned at Ton-
neins the book by Suarez containing an attack upon this king.[7]

[1] Vindiciae contra tyrannos seu de principis in populum populique in·
principem legitima potestate, auctore Stephano Junio Brutto, 8; vide p.
318.   Cf. Leo, Univ. Gesch. iv. p. 151.

[2] Cf. Hotomanni Francogallia (also Cologne, 1575), Du Droit des
Magistrats sur leurs Sujets (1577 ; first in German, Magdeburg, 1550) ; De·
justa reipublicae christ. in reges impios auctoritate (Rose), 1590.

[3] Th. Beza, Ep. 37, 40, ap. Keller, de Regicidio, p. 80.   Beza, Hist.
Eccl. l. vi.   Castlenau, Mémoires, l. iii.   Jac. Aug. Thuanus (de Thou),
Hist. sui Temporis, t. iii. l. xxx. pp. 278, 280, ed. Paris, 1606.   Davila, Istor.
civili di Francia, l. iv.   Synodes nation. des Eglises réformées de France,
t. i. p. 43 seq.   Also to these belong the letters of the Nuncio Santa
Croce to Cardinal Borromeo, particularly of the 13 and 17 April 1562, 23
February and 22 March 1563, concerning the schemes of the Huguenots
relative to the seizing and imprisonment of the king and his counsellors,
published by the Protestant Joh. Aymon Craveta (Les véritables causes·
des progrès et des catastrophes de la religion réformée découvertes par la·
production de cinquante lettres anécdotes, qui furent écrites . . . depuis l'an
1561 jusqu'à 1565).   Cf. Bolsec, in Vita Calvini, c. xxi.; also the work,
Avis important aux réfugiés, sur leur prochain rétour en France, Amster-
dam, 1609.   At Rotterdam appeared an answer called Réponse à l'avis aux
réfugiés, par M. D. L. P.

[4] Jurieu (ap. Barante, Questions constitutionelles, 1849, ch. i.): 'Il
faut qu'il y ait dans la société une certaine autorité, qui n'ait pas besoin
d'avoir raison pour valider ces actes.   Or cette autorité n'est que dans le
peuple.'

[5] 'Que les rois ne sont que dépositaires de la souveraineté, qu'ils sont
justiciables du peuple pour la mauvaise administration de ce dépôt, que le
peuple est en droit de retirer ce dépôt, lorsque le bien public et l'interêt de·
la religion veulent ainsi, et de le confier à qui bon lui semble.'   Cf.
Traité de l'Eglise, chap. xxi.

[6] Synodes nat. des Eglises réformées de France, t. ii. p. 106, ch. iv.
xxiv.   Daillé said at the Synod at Loudon in 1600 : ' The first and foremost
article of the reformed faith is : Que les rois ont une autorité souveraine sur
toutes sortes de personnes, sans excepter aucun de ses sujets . . . et qu'il
n'y a pas d'autorité médiate entre la leur et celle de la toute puissance de
Dieu ;' the royal power was to be free of the spiritual, and no resistance to
it justifiable.   Pastor Ferrand declared at Alençon in 1637 : ' Que l'autorité
royale n'est pas d'institution humaine, que la puissance du roi vient im-
médiatement de la puissance de Dieu.'   Cf. Bianchi, t. i. l. i. § 6, n. 1 seq.

p. 49 seq. Later appeared the work, Traité du pouvoir absolu des Souverains, pour servir d'instruction, de consolation et d'apologie aux Eglises
réformées de France, qui sont affligées, Cologne, 1685.
[1] Synodes nat. des Eglises réf. de France, t. ii. p. 65.

§ 7.

David Pareus, professor in Heidelberg (died 1615), likewise
conceded to the people power over a bad prince in matters of
religion. James I. caused his commentary on the Epistle to the
Romans to be burnt in England; but Philip, son of David Pareus,
defended the doctrine as having been taught by all the Protestant
theologians.[1] Hugo Grotius also taught that royal power ceased
in extreme cases when it was employed to the destruction of the
people.[2] Gronovius declared emphatically that a war of religion
against princes was lawful.

[1] Schröckh, K.G. seit der Reform. v. pp. 271, 272. Bianchi, l.c. § 7,
pp. 66, 67.
[2] Hugo Grotius, de Jure Belli et Pac. l. i. c. iv. § 1, 5, 11.

§ 8.

Absolute obedience towards the sovereign was, as time went
on, more and more enforced in monarchical States: numerous
refutations of the contrary doctrine were published;[1] James I.
himself turned author in the cause.[2] But in 1649, Charles I.
was forced to mount the scaffold, and his execution was defended
by the poet Milton;[3] like that of Louis XVI. in 1793, it was
justified by appealing to the supreme power of the nation.[4] 'In
a certain sense,' says Henry Leo,[5] 'it is true that the development of revolutionary political theories was the necessary and inexorable consequence of the Reformation; revolutionary views
gained ground in proportion as the limitations imposed by the
Church upon civil authority were disregarded.' Bossuet particularly observes: 'The claims of the Pope over kings in civil
affairs serve as the pretext to Protestants for preferring their
own allegiance as subjects to the allegiance of Catholics. But
it can be made clear as noonday that if the two opinions must
be compared, the one subjecting sovereigns in civil affairs to the
Popes, the other subordinating them to the people, the latter

alternative, which would submit government to the domination of fury, caprice, ignorance, and passion, is inconceivably the most to be feared. Experience has shown the truth of this view, and our age, as one of those that has abandoned sovereigns to the cruel humours of the multitude, exhibits more numerous and more tragic examples of acts of violence against the person and the authority of kings than could be found in six or seven centuries amongst people who have acknowledged on this matter the authority of Rome.'[6]

[1] W. Barclay, de Regno et Regali Potestate adv. Buchananum, Brutum, Boucherum et reliquos Monarchomachos, Paris, 1600. Against Joh. von Althusen, prof. at Herborn (Politica Methodice Digesta, Herb. 1603), Henning Arnisäus wrote the Tract. de auctoritate principum in populum semper inviolabili, Francof. 1606. Jean Bodin (de Republ. l. ii. c. v.) taught : ' Nec singulis civibus nec universis fas est, summi principis famam, vitam aut fortitudinem in discrimen vocare, seu vi seu judicio constituto id fiat.' Cf. Walter, § 534, p. 548.

[2] Triplici nodo triplex cuneus, Lond. 1608. Apologia pro juramento fidelitatis, Lond. 1609. (Lancelot Andrews, Bishop of Chichester) Tortura Torti, Lond. 1609. Cf. Werner, Suarez, i. p. 41 seq.

[3] Apologia pro populo Anglicano, Opp. Compl. ed. 1759, pp. 279, 309.

[4] Salmas. Defens. Reg. p. 375 : ' Sic securim porrexerunt (Presbyteriani), quae regis cervicibus impacta est. Dici vere potest, victimam Presbyterianos ligasse, Independentes jugulasse.' For the transactions, vide Macaulay, Hist. Eng. from the Accession of James II. c. ix.

[5] Leo, Univ. Gesch. iv. p. 153.

[6] Bossuet, Défense de l'Hist. des Variations, n. 55. Artaud, Hist. des Souverains Pontifes, t. v. Paris, 1847, p. 337, after quoting from Sevelinge's Biogr. Univ. xxi. 352, where the wide spread of the doctrine of the indirect authority is attested : ' Ajoutons que des circonstances nouvelles, la profonde sagesse du Saint-Siège, les actes successifs et spontanés des Papes, depuis deux siècles, ont amené partout à cet égard pour les princes Catholiques absolument les mêmes résultats, les consuétudes et les reconnaissances les plus publiquement soutenues, et l'on en est arrivé là dans le Catholicisme sans tant de crime.'

§ 9.

There are in Protestantism two chief currents, which have done their work at different times and with varied force. Luther, at one time the bitter foe of tyranny,[1] was after the peasant war of 1525 no longer the man of the people, but preeminently the man of princes. In his 'Admonition to my beloved Germans' (1530), and in his work 'Against the Assassin in

Dresden' (Duke George of Saxony), he had endeavoured to silence scruples of conscience with regard to a war against the emperor and the empire.[2]

It was the opinion of Melanchthon, not merely that it was lawful[3] to resist a tyrant if he were grievously oppressive, and in case of necessity to put him to death, but that it were desirable a brave man could be found who should kill Henry VIII. of England.[4] Protestants, in general living under princes who had embraced the new doctrines, were extremely desirous of binding Catholics to an absolute obedience towards their rulers, but when they themselves lived under Catholic sovereigns they claimed the most complete liberty of conscience.[5] Rousseau's theories are supported on the one hand upon Grotius, Pufendorf, Thomasius, and Kant,[6] on the other hand upon Buchanan, Languet, Milton, Algernon Sydney, and Locke.[7] This is the groundwork of the French Revolution.[8] Revolution in theory and practice is not a product of the doctrine taught by Catholic theologians. Rousseau comes of a Protestant line, and his progenitors are some of the bitterest enemies of Catholicism.

---

[1] Sleidan, Vita Luth. l. v. p. 75. Bossnet, Hist. des Variations, l. ii.

[2] Luther's Werke, xvi. pp. 1950, 2062. Luther's Tischreden, Jena, 1603, fol. 482.

[3] Melancth. Arg. Psalm. liii. (Corp. Reform. xiii. 1125, ed. Bretschneider): 'Judicio humanae rationis verum est, concessam esse defensionem adversus tyrannum inferentem manifestam et atrocem injuriam. Et si in tali defensione tyrannus interficitur, defensor judicatur juste fecisse.'

[4] Id. Ep. ad Vit. Theod. (ib. iii. 1075): 'Anglicus tyrannus Cromwellum interfecit et conatur divortium cum Juliacensi puella. Quam vere dixit ille in Tragoedia, non gratiorem victimam Deo mactari posse quam tyrannum. Utinam alieni forti vero Deus hanc mentem inserat!'

[5] Bianchi, t. i. l. i. § 7, n. 7, p. 75. Balmez, l.c. chap. 1. says: 'Protestantism, departing from the teaching of Catholicity, has been thrown alternately upon two opposite rocks: wishing to establish order, it has done so to the prejudice of true liberty; and in its desire to maintain liberty, it has become an enemy to order. From the bosom of false reform have arisen the insane doctrines, which, preaching up Christian liberty, discharged the subject from his obedience to the lawful authorities; from the bosom of the same reform has likewise arisen the theory of Hobbes, which sets up despotism in the midst of society as a monstrous idol, to which all should be sacrificed, without regard for the eternal principles of morality, with no other rule than the caprice of him who rules, with no other bounds to his power than those marked out by the extent of his

strength. Such is the necessary result of banishing from the world the authority of God. Man left to himself can only succeed in producing slavery or anarchy; the same thing under two forms—*the reign of force.*'

[6] Stahl, Gesch. der Rechtsphilosophie, iii. iii. 7, p. 241 seq. 2d ed. On Grotius, cf. ib. pp. 145, 170 ; Walter, l.c. § 537, p. 557.

[7] Algernon Sydney, Discourses concerning Government, London, 1698. Locke, two treatises on Government, London, 1690. On the development, vide Stahl, l.c. pp. 284-292.

[8] Stahl, l.c. p. 285. Rintel, pp. 75-80.

§ 10.

Of course no one will dispute that some Catholics also have held dangerous theories and committed grave crimes. But these are in no manner the result of Catholic principles. Macchiavelli, with his immoral political theories, was an offshoot of paganism, and was always opposed by Catholic theology.[1] Paul Sarpi, who advised the Council of Ten in Venice to exterminate at any cost some party chiefs amongst the inhabitants of the mainland, and in case this proved a difficulty to employ poisoned weapons,[2] was a long way from the spirit of Catholicism, and more congenial with that of Protestantism.[3]

The wars of the League in France might be cited with more show of reason. When Henry III. at Blois in 1588 caused the assassination of the Duke of Guise and his brother the cardinal, the Catholic League, headed by the third brother, the Duke of Mayenne, declared that obedience was no longer due to the king; and the Sorbonne, in a document of the 7th January 1589, declared that the people were free from any duty towards him, and might take up arms in the cause of the endangered religion.[4] When the king, at length openly allied with the Huguenots, had been assassinated on the 1st August 1589 by Jacques Clément, the League of the Seize in Paris compared the deed with that of Judith, and wished to have the exclusion from the throne of the heretical Prince Henry of Bourbon proclaimed.[5] The parliament of Toulouse, in a decree drawn up by the jurists of the assembly, approved the bloody deed.[6] Fanaticism had become so strong in the violent struggles of the time, that it threatened to bear down all before it, and it was with difficulty that the more circumspect could preserve their peace. Still, not all who approved revolt against a king endangering religion approved assassination, and not all who held no heretic could mount the French throne were in favour of an armed revolt.[7]

[1] Ces. Cantù, Storia Univers. l. xv. P. i. c. x. Cf. Dr. Fehr, Ueber die Entwicklung und den Einfluss der politischen Theorien, Innsbrück, 1855 (where the theories are given in some detail from Pythagorus to Augustine, but he omits all from St. Augustine to Macchiavelli) ; G. Frapporti, Sugli intendimenti di Nic. Macchiavelli nello scrivere il Principe, Vicenza, 1855.

[2] Opinione del P. Paoli Servita, consultor di Stato. In Venezia appresso, Rob. Matthei, 1681.

[3] Cantù, l. xv. P. ii. c. vi. Cf. Armonia, 10 Apr. 1861.

[4] Respons. Facult. Theol. Paris, in Additions au Journal de Henry III. t. i. p. 317. Ranke, Päpste, ii. 188.

[5] Crétineau-Joly, Hist. de la Comp. de Jésus, t. ii. p. 404 seq.

[6] Arrêt du Parlement de Toulouse, 22 Août 1589. Mémoires de la Ligue, t. iv. p. 51. Dumoulin, Annotat ad Clementinas, l. iii. tit. 15.

[7] Ranke (Päpste, ii. p. 193) acknowledges that many Catholics assented to the doctrine of the divine right of the royal authority defended by Protestants (particularly in the work Explicatio controversiarum, quae a nonnullis moventur ex Henrici Borb. regis in regnum Franciae constitutione. Opus a F. Bercheto Lingonensi c gall. in lat. sermonem conversum, Sedani, 1590), and he cites particularly the work published in Paris in 1588, apud Capet, Collectiou Universelle des Mémoires, t. lvi. p. 44. Cf. Etienne Pasquier, Recherches de France, 341, 344.

§ 11.

The right of refusing obedience to lawful rulers was conceded by the judicial theory to the people in certain cases, in the interests of their temporal welfare; with greater reason therefore was it conceded when their eternal salvation was concerned.[1] Protestant theologians, setting aside the power of the keys, taught that Holy Scripture allowed the people, for religious motives, to depose their sovereign, or withdraw from him their allegiance. They could not therefore declare it to be unscriptural to dispense an oath by means of the power of the keys, which, up to a certain point, they recognised.[2] Moreover, in the case of Henry III. no such decision emanated from the Church; they appealed to reason and argument:—The Christian must rank his religion above his life, as is seen from Holy Scripture and the examples of the martyrs; therefore what is permissible for the preservation of life is permissible for the preservation of the faith. The people cannot be bound to obey the civil government when this is abused to endanger and destroy religion. An oath of obedience, in this case, is not binding; to keep it would be a grave sin against God and against His law, a partaking in an offence against the Creator; it would be placing a sword into the hands of a madman. Besides, the example of the king has an almost irresistible weight; from Jeroboam to Queen Elizabeth, a ruler imbued with animosity against religion has only too often succeeded in completely extinguishing it in the people. The strongest ties of human society are loosed when they are misused to offend God : the son is then no longer bound by paternal authority, the wife no longer owes obedience to her husband.[3] The tie that binds the subject to his sovereign is not stronger than these. The divine command to guard the faith and be steadfast to God till death is a higher command than that of obedience to civil authority.[4]

[1] W. Allen, Ad Persecutores Anglos pro Christianis Responsio, 1582 : ' Si reges Deo et Dei populo fidem datam fregerint, vicissim populo non solum permittitur, sed etiam ab eo requiritur, ut jubente Christi vicario, supremo nimirum populorum omnium pastore, ipse quoque fidem datam tali principi non servet.' Person (Andr. Philopat.) ad Elizab. Reg. Edictum Responsio, n. 162 : ' Non tantum licet, sed summa etiam juris divini necessitate ac praecepto (?), imo conscientiae vinculo arctissimo et extremo animarum suarum periculo ac discrimine Christianis omnibus hoc ipsum incumbit, si praestare rem possunt.' N. 160 : ' Incumbit vero tam maxime . . . . cum res jam ab Ecclesia ac supremo ejus moderatore Pontifice nimirum Rom., judicata est; ad illum enim ex officio pertinet, religionis ac divini cultus incolumitati prospicere et leprosos a mundis, ne inficiantur, secernere.' Cf. Bianchi, t. ii. l. v. § 1, n. 2, p. 43.
[2] Bossuet, Hist. des Variations, l. i. n. 1 ; l. vii. n. 1, 2 ; l. x. n. 24-56. Défense de l'Hist. des Var. n. 5, 15. Bianchi, t. i. l. iii. § 1, n. 5, pp. 440, 441.
[3] Innoc. III. c. Gaudemus, iv. 8, de Divort. Bellarm. de Rom. Pont. v. 7, § Tertia ratio.
[4] Bianchi, l.c. n. 5, pp. 43, 44.

§ 12.

But should not Christian subjects suffer death rather than offer resistance, even when they have the power of doing so ? Christian perfection would counsel this, but not as a duty to be performed under all circumstances. For the natural law allows resistance to be offered justly in self-defence, and recognises no duty of unconditionally renouncing such resistance. When religion as well as life has to be preserved, there is all the more reason for exerting every effort.[1] The example of the first Christians proves nothing in this instance. Their position was quite changed when once public order had become subservient to the interests of Christianity. The excuses that were valid for a heathen government do not hold good for one which in these days persecutes the Church. Moreover, a revolt would then have been quite unavailing, and would even have been injurious to the Christian cause.[2] The mode of defending religion is twofold.[3] It may be done after the manner of Eleazar (2 Macchab. vi. 18-31) by martyrdom, or after that of Mathathias (1 Macch. ii. 1 seq.), who aroused his friends and relations to resist the oppression of the heathen.[4] What the natural law permitted to the Macchabees under the old covenant cannot be, in similar conditions, prohibited under the new covenant. Wars against the Saracens, especially the Crusades, were universally held to be just. Luther's proposition that to fight against the Saracens was to withstand God, who used them to punish the sins of Christians, was condemned by Leo X.[5]

[1] Bianchi, l.c. § 5, n. 6, pp. 44, 45.
[2] Bellarmin. l.c.
[3] Bianchi, l.c. n. 7, pp. 45, 46.
[4] Gregor. Naz. Orat. 15, in Land. Maccab. t. i. p. 286 seq. ed. Maurin. Cf. Grot. l.c. l. i. c. v. § 7, n. 7.
[5] Leo X. Const. Exsurge Domine, May 16, 1520, prop. 34 (Denzinger, Enchir. p. 224, n. 658). No doubt other than religious motives, especially political motives, operated in the Crusades; for the Mahometans were the constant and dangerous enemies of Christian kingdoms (Bossuet, P. i. l. iv. c. xv. p. 366); but for the most part religious motives were prominent. The Mahometan princes of Egypt, Syria, and Palestine had done no injury to St. Louis, for instance, and yet he made war upon them. Spondan. a. 1248, n. 10. Bianchi, l.c. n. 8-10, pp. 46-48.

§ 13.

On the 7th May 1590, the University of Paris formally denounced Henry IV. as a heretic; and in 1591, E. Richer, subsequently so celebrated, sustained in the Sorbonne the thesis that

the estates of the kingdom were superior to the king, and that
Henry III., as a tyrant, had been lawfully assassinated.[1] Jean
Boucher, rector of St. Benoit, made similar assertions from the
pulpit ; his discourses were shortly after printed.[2] But when,
after the entry and triumph of Henry IV., the League (composed notoriously of all ranks of society, and allied to the
parliament, university, and city of Paris) was dissolved, all
these utterances were ascribed exclusively to the Jesuits, who
were charged with having originated the doctrine of tyrannicide.
Yet they had spoken only in the same manner as other theologians ; they had treated the subject merely theoretically and
as an abstract question, whilst their opponents, especially in the
university, had pointed out the particular tyrants. Every
one knew, as the famous Breton Procureur-général, La Chalo-
tais, declared,[3] that the Jesuits had not invented the doctrine of
tyrannicide ; that many of them, for instance the calumniated
Father Claude Mathieu,[4] had emphatically protested against it;
and that in general it was not in France, but in Spain, that
these questions had been mostly discussed by Jesuits. The
founder, St. Ignatius, desired that politics should be altogether excluded from his Society ; but in the sixteenth century all court
affairs, all diplomatic negotiations, and even wars, had more or
less of a religious stamp. They all tended either to uphold or
stamp out Catholicity. Jesuits were thus obliged to share in
the movement of ideas, social and political ; and when the
General Aquaviva demanded from Pope Sixtus V. that he
should issue a prohibition of any political activity on the part
of the Jesuits, the Pope did not accede to his request.[5]

---

[1] Card. Du Perron, Lettre à M. Casaubon, 15 Avril 1612 (Ambassade
du Card. Du Perron, p. 696 ; Pey, de l'Autorité des deux Puissances, ii.
p. 496) : ' L'an 1591, au mois d'Octobre, il (Richer) soutint publiquement
en Sorbonne, que les états du royaume étaient indubitablement par-dessus
le roi, et que Henry III., qui avait violé la foi donnée à la face des états,
avait été, comme tyran, justement tué. Ce sont les propres mots de ses
anciennes thèses, dont j'ai l'original imprimé entre les mains.'
[2] Sermons de Jean Boucher, Paris, 1594, esp. pp. 162, 194. Cf. Ranke,
Päpste, ii. pp. 186, 187.
[3] Compte-rendu au Parlement de Rennes, p. 209.
[4] He wrote on 11 Feb. 1583 : ' On ne peut pas, en conscience, attenter

à la vie du roi, et le Papo Grégoire XIII. a condamné ceux qui osent penser ou enseigner le contraire.' Mémoires de Nevers, t. i. p. 657. Crétineau Joly, l.c. p. 626.
> Crétineau-Joly, t. ii. c. iv. pp. 175, 395. Vide also ib. p. 397 seq. Aquaviva's letter, of Feb. 22, 1586, to P. Mathieu, to which tho latter (†1587) submitted.

§ 14.

The book of Mariana[1] (died 1624), written expressly for the Infant of Spain, occasioned much stir. His two last books, which treat of the education of princes, are still worthy of being read and laid to heart; but the first book, although written unmistakably with a good intention, is defective in many parts.

His chief errors, for which his devotion to the classical authors of antiquity may in great measure be made accountable, lie in his theory of the democratic origin of all monarchies, in his advocacy of the principle of the sovereignty of the people, and in his doctrine of the permissibility of tyrannicide. With regard to the last point, he always, as his whole treatment of the subject shows, presupposes a tyrant whose crimes are excessive and exceptional; he also presupposes entire unanimity of public opinion concerning the magnitude of the tyranny, the failure of all other measures for putting a stop to it, and security from the advent of greater evils ensuing upon the tyrant's death. His companions in the order were dissatisfied with his doctrine, especially in France. Père Richeome, Provincial of Guienne, lodged a complaint against it in Rome. Claudius Aquaviva, General of the Jesuits, published a decree[2] on the 6th July 1610, strictly forbidding members of the Society to teach or maintain that any one, under any pretext whatever of tyranny, was allowed to assassinate, or make a murderous attempt upon, any prince or king.[3] When Paul V. found fault with the parliament for burning the work, it was because this act was an encroachment upon the ecclesiastical authority.[4] It is untrue that Mariana justifies and extols the assassination of Henry III.:[5] he speaks of it, in the introduction to the sixth chapter, as a deed condemned by some, extolled by others. He simply states the view of either party.[6]

¹ De Rege et Regis Institutione, libri tres. Cf. Rissel, Die Aufhebung des Jesuitenordens, Mainz, 1855, 3d edit. p. 289 seq.

² Crétineau-Joly, t. ii. p. 420 seq. Buss, Gesellsch. Jesu, p. 901. Rissel, l.c. p. 298 seq. Rintel, pp. 63, 64.

³ He adds in the decree the reason : ' Ne videl. isto praetextu ad perniciem principum aperiatur via atque ad turbandam pacem eorumque securitatem in dubio vocandam, quos potius ex divino mandato revereri ac observare oportet tamquam *personas sacras a Domino Deo pro felici populorum gubernatione in eo statu constitutas.*' Its observation is to be strictly enforced by all provincials under pain of deposition from their office, that all may recognise what is the view of the Society on this point, and that the errors of an individual may not make the whole Society suspected of error.

⁴ De Brèves, 8 July 1610 (apud Gaillard, Notices et Extraits des MSS. Paris, 1804, p. 331) : ' Sa Sainteté m'a répondu, qu'elle ne pouvoit que blamer grandement semblables écrits, et confessoit qu'ils méritoient d'être brûlés et ceux que les font châtiés ; mais qu'il auroit été plus à propos que le dit livre eût été brûlé par ordre de l'évêque de Paris ou des cardinaux qui sont en France, que non par l'autorité et ordonnance de la dite cour.'

⁵ Huber, p. 44.

⁶ In conclusion he says : ' *Haec sunt utriusque partis praesidia*, quibus attente consideratis, quid de proposita quaestione statuendum sit, explicare non erit difficile.' Then begins the author's own discussion of the matter. To the question, ' an liceat tyrannum veneno occidere,' in c. vii., the answer is a decided negative ; and also the things said (c. vi.) are called a private opinion, possibly erroneous, for a rectification of which the author would be grateful. Cf. concerning him, Civiltà Cattolica, No. 133, Oct. 1855, p. 39 seq.

§ 15.

Suarez (died 1617) distinguishes strictly between an unlawful usurper and a legitimate but tyrannical ruler. The former may be removed, he says, by force, either by the whole nation or by individual members, whenever the conditions of a just warfare are present, when no other means exist for being rid of him, and when the consequences of his death will not be worse than the tyranny itself ;[1] at the same time he acknowledged that other learned men, for instance, the Jesuit Jodok Azov (died 1609), held a different opinion. But Suarez also teaches that a legitimate prince, how great soever his tyranny, must never be assassinated by a private individual ;[2] only the body and commonwealth of the nation, under the condition of a just warfare, and in self-preservation, might revolt against the tyrant.[3] But a struggle of the people against a prince who is

neither a tyrant nor a usurper he condemns as a wicked rebellion.[4] It has been particularly objected to Suarez[5] that he
assumes that a legitimate ruler who has been lawfully deposed
is to be treated as an illegitimate usurper, because, having been
rightly deposed, he has ceased to be a legitimate ruler. The
objection rests on a confusion of two distinct matters : the
question here is not so much who has the right of deposing a
prince, and whether such a right exists at all, as whether a ruler,
the legality of whose deposition is presupposed, should be
regarded as no more than a tyrannical interloper if he seeks to
regain the power he had lost. It is a question whether the
aforesaid supposition can be made, but if it is made, Suarez is
quite consistent. For the rest, he teaches that all action in
this matter should be gradual ; that a deposed king may not be
at once killed by any private person, and is not to be forcibly
expelled, unless this was declared specifically in the sentence, or
another sentence or command were issued to that effect.[6]

---

[1] Suarez, disput. 13, de Bello, sect. 8, prop. 2 : 'Quando priori modo
accidit tyrannis, tota respublica et quodlibet ejus membrum jus habet
contra illum, unde quilibet potest se ac rempublicam a tyrannide liberare.
Ratio est: quia tyrannus ille aggressor est et inique bellum movet contra
rempublicam et singula membra, unde omnibus competit jus defensionis.'

[2] 'Certe veritas est, contra hujusmodi tyrannum (quoad solum regimen)
nullam privatam personam aut potestatem imperfectam posse juste movere
bellum aggressivum, atque illud esset proprie seditio. Probatur : quoniam
ille, ut supponitur, verus est dominus ; inferiores autem jus non habent
indicendi bellum, semper singulis facit injuriam ; atque si invaderet, id
solum possent efficere, quod ad suam defensionem sufficeret.' We should
remark that Suarez, in the Defensio Fidei, notices some learned jurists,
like Paris de Puteo, counsellor of King Ferdinand I., and Anton Massa of
Naples, who go further, and would have conceded to every individual the
right of violent attack upon an insupportable tyrant. Werner (Fr. Suarez, i. p. 144 seq.) gives an exposition of the doctrine taught in the
Defensio.

[3] Disput. de Bello, l.c. : 'At vero tota respublica posset bello insurgere
contra ejusmodi tyrannum, neque tunc excitaretur proprie seditio (hoc
siquidem nomen in malam partem sumi consuevit). Ratio est : quia tunc
tota respublica est superior rege ; nam cum ipsa dederit illi potestatem, ea
conditione dedisse censetur, ut politice, non tyrannice regeret.' Defens. iii.
3 : 'Si rex justam suam potestatem in tyrannidem verteret, illa in manifestam civitatis perniciem abutendo, posset populus naturali potestate ad
defendendum se uti, hac enim numquam se privavit.'

⁴ Disput. de Bello, l.c. prop. 3 : 'Bellum reipublicae contra regem neutro modo tyrannum est propriisime seditio et intrinseco malum.'

⁵ Huber, p. 44.

⁶ 'Non tamen statim posse regem depositum a qualibet privata persona interfici, imo neque per vim expelli, donec eis praecipiatur vel generalis commissio haec in ipsa sententia vel jure declaretur.'

§ 16.

Like Suarez, Gregory of Valentia is accused of having taught the doctrine of tyrannicide, and 'that a lawful monarch who misuses his authority to the destruction of the State is a tyrant, who may be sentenced to death by a State tribunal, and exe-·cuted.¹ These words are nowhere to be found amongst his works. He follows the Dominicans, Cajetan and Soto,² in the usual distinction between the usurper and the legitimate mon-·arch who abuses his power : of the latter he only says no private person may attempt his life, and it is alone lawful that the commonwealth should resist him, and call in the aid of individuals against him.³ He does not say that an unlawful ·tyrant may be assassinated by any one who chooses to do so ; but without any reference to tyrants, makes an abstract exami-nation of the question whether a law could be passed granting to any one the right of killing an evildoer *before* he has been judicially sentenced. He denies it, as being contrary to the natural law, but says the case is quite different if, *after* the con-demnation, the sovereign or judge declare the criminal to be an outlaw.⁴ Gregory neither says, nor intimates in any way, 'that the Pope can declare a sovereign to be a tyrant.'

¹ Huber, p. 43, where t. iii. disput. 5, q. 8, punct. 3, is quoted.

² Cajetan, in S. Th. 2, 2, q. 64, a. 3.   Soto, de Justit. l. v. q. 1, a. 3.

³ Punct. 3, p. 1323 : 'Vel est tyrannus non per arrogatam sibi injuste potestatem sed solum *per pravum legitimae alioquin auctoritatis* usum in gubernando, aut est tyrannus *per arrogatam potestatem,* quam vi obtineat. Si est tyrannus *primo* modo, nulli particulari licet eum occidere.   Nam id pertinet ad rempublicam, *quae posset jure oppugnare illum et vocare in subsidium cives.*   Si autem esset tyrannus *secundo* modo, quilibet posset eum occidere, nam tota respublica censetur gerere bellum justum contra ipsum, et ita civis quilibet, ut miles quidam reipublicae, posset eum oc-cidere.'

⁴ Ib. p. 1325 : 'Si tamen esset jam aliquis *legitime condemnatus,* pos-set princeps vel judex facere facultatem cuilibet eum occidendi, ut v.g.

si reus aufugisset. Neque in tali casu posset reus se defendere; esset enim ei ablatum jus per judicem; alioquin jam bellum esset justum ex utraque parte, quod est impossible.'

§ 17.

The doctrine of other Jesuits does not differ from this essentially ;[1] they generally maintain the doctrine current in their day. This is the case with Molina.[2] After the decree of the General of the Society, Aquaviva, in 1610, we never again find tyrannicide defended. Werner truly observes :[3] 'Mariana alone has defended tyrannicide in the strict sense, that is, when a man takes upon himself to kill a legitimate ruler lawfully sentenced. The utterances and declarations of Jesuits upon the question of tyrannicide, debated so frequently during the sixteenth and seventeenth centuries, are connected with each other; the principles of Becanus, Janner, Escoban, Dicastillo, are the same as those of Suarez, whose teaching has even been modified by restrictions or explanations added by other Jesuits, and thus withdrawn from the danger of misinterpretation.' We may commonly find in the writings of later Jesuits these two propositions, which any moralist might subscribe : (1) It is not allowable to kill a lawful sovereign, even if his government be tyrannical and oppressive; (2) Neither is it allowable to kill a usurper who has attained to the possession of power; it is only allowable before he has attained to power, by the authority of the lawful sovereign, in war, and for the defence of the State.[4]

[1] Em. Sâ, Aphorismi Confessariorum, v. Tyrannus, Colon. 1690, p. 360 : '*Occupantem* tyrannice potestatem quisque de populo potest occidere, *si aliud non est remedium* ; est enim *publicus hostis*.' But he who is merely 'tyrannus administratione' can only be deposed by a public sentence, which, when it has received the force of law, may be carried out by any one. An admonition must, however, precede the sentence.

[2] He teaches that political power is from God by the natural law ; that forms of government (monarchy, aristocracy, or democracy) may be instituted in various ways ; that power once conferred upon a king may not be withdrawn or lessened by the people ; and that the king must not pass the established limits of power ; that if he does so, not individuals but the commonwealth of the nation may resist him. Tract. 2, de Justitia et Jure, disput. 22, n. 8, 9, 10, t. i. pp. 48, 49 ; disput. 23, n. 4, 11, 12, pp. 49, 50, ed. Antwerp, 1615 seq. ; ib. n. 5, 9, 10, p. 50 : ' Si tamen rex potestatem sibi non concessam vellet assumere, posset quidem *respublica* ei

tamquam *tyranno* ea *in parte* resistere, perinde ac cuivis alteri extraneo, qui reipublicae injuriam vellet inferre.' Here the limitation of royal authority is presupposed as long since put, and resistance is alone held permissible to a usurped authority.

³ K. Werner, l.c. i. p. 147.

⁴ Anton Escobar (†1669) apud Riffel, l.c. p. 290, n. 1. Busenbaum, Medulla Theol. Moral. l. iii. tr. 4, c. i. dub. 3, n. 8, pp. 138-140. Gury,. Theol. Mor. t. i. p. 152, n. 394, ed. Ratisbon, 1862.

The wrong of active resistance was recognised in proportion as the proposition gained ground that royal authority did not come from the people, and could not be withdrawn by them, and had no superior on earth ; and the more as experience showed that a few factious men made profit out of the pretext of tyranny, and inflicted more injury on the people· than anything they might have suffered before. Card. Gerdil, l.c. p. 25 :· ' Hinc nulla sive in privatis sive in ipsa communitate facultas aut jus remanet resistendi principi, etiam per speciem vel pretextum mali regiminis. Secus in communitate duplex vigeret publica et suprema potestas, quod' plane repugnare vel ipse Burlamaquius agnoscit. Est porro subjectorum maxime Christianorum officium, patienter id mali quidquid est potius tolerare quam adversus supremam potestatem rebellare ; nam et dyscolis etiam praepositis obediendum, S. Petrus omnino praecipit. Quod si ex historiarum monumentis rerum gestarum memoriam repetere volumus, comperiemus : (1) Quoties per speciem mali regiminis populi rebellarunt, in id eos semper a paucis factiosis incitatos esse, qui populorum credulitate abuti tentarunt ad privatum commodum et lucrum ; (2) In his civilibus bellis ac motibus multo atrocioribus cladibus populos afflictos esse, quam ea incommoda fuerint, propter quae arma sumpserunt.' Cf. Walter, Naturrecht, § 360, p. 329 seq., who also makes reference to many Catholic and Protestant authors ; e.g. Petrus Gregorius of Toulouse (†1617), de Republica, Lugd. 1586, l. xxvi. 7 ; Zallinger, Inst. Jur. Nat. § 213 ; Taparelli, Naturrecht, ii. § 1005-1045 ; Kant, Rechtslehre, § 49 ; Anm. A. Trendelenburg, Naturrecht, § 214, 215. Cf. Stahl, Philos. d. R. ii. 2, § 154 seq. 3d edit.

§ 18.

What is to be said of those who have made it their object to · brand Jesuits as defenders of regicide ?[1] Do they not know how much stronger were the assertions made by the predecessors of the Jesuits concerning tyrannicide—the only form of regicide ever in question ? Do they not know what the secular and regular clergy[2] and the Protestant theologians of the sixteenth and seventeenth centuries taught contemporaneously with the Jesuits we have cited ?[3] Do they not know that in countries like Germany and Spain, where individual Jesuits taught that, under greater or less limitations, tyrannicide was allowable, no · kings were put to death ; but that in France and England, .

where kings have been expelled and killed, Jesuits never taught that doctrine?[1] Do they not know that the greater number of Jesuit writers have strenuously combated the doctrine that tyrannicide is allowable, that Jesuit supporters of this doctrine are comparatively few, that these are amongst the earlier members of the Society, and that they guarded their doctrine by many prudent limitations? Will these accusers of Jesuits still appeal to pamphlets[5] which a wider learning has long since refuted? Will they still, in their battle against the Society, employ the weapons of lies and falsification made use of by those who concocted the *Monita Secreta*,[6] and who complain of the immorality of the obedience practised by Jesuits?[7]

[1] Thus Paul Sarpi, Ep. 31, 32 (apud Le Bret, Magazin, ii. 318, 322); Huber, p. 41 seq.

[2] Prof. Merkle, as early as May 1870, in the Angsb. Pastoralblatt, answered Herr Huber shortly and to the point, in the form of five questions. The second question ran thus : ' Why does Herr Huber merely name the Jesuits Molina, Salmeron, Valentia, Suarez, Mariana, and Santarelli? He might equally with these six have named eleven other members of the Society of Jesus, namely, Em. Sâ, Toletus, Delrio, Sales, Heiss, Lessius, Becan, Gretser, Janner, Castro Palao, and Escobar, who have all treated the question of tyrannicide (not regicide). The reason was, that it would have been too difficult to find in their writings anything to serve his purpose.'

[3] Documents historiques, critiques, apolog. concernant la Compagnie de Jésus, Paris, 1828, t. ii. p. 82 seq. The number of these authors is four times as great. Merkle, l.c.

[4] Cf. the discussion in full, apud Riffel, pp. 280-301. Concerning the complaints with regard to the attempt upon Henry IV., cf. Mathieu, Hist. de la Mort déplorable de Henri IV. p. 120 ; Dupleix, Hist. de Henri le Grand, p. 163; Crétineau-Joly, t. ii. p. 445 seq.; Buss, Die Gesellsch. Jesu, Mainz, 1853, ii. pp. 895 seq. 915 seq. Merkle inquires : Why does Herr Huber conceal the fact that the party which publicly announces 'that the world cannot prosper until the last king shall have been strangled with the entrails of the last priest' is the deadly enemy of the Jesuits? As an instance of the opinion of a writer not a Jesuit, but holding nearly the same view, we may quote Leibnitz, Letter to Freiherr v. Boyneburg : ' Concerning the great question still agitated of the power of sovereigns and the obedience due to them from the people, I think it would be well if the rulers were convinced that the people were justified in resisting them, and the people on the contrary believed that they were bound to a passive obedience. Nevertheless I nearly agree with Grotius in thinking that as a rule obedience is necessary, for generally rebellion is attended with far greater evils than the tyranny that called it forth. Still I allow

that the prince may so far overstep his authority and the welfare of the
State be so far endangered as to remove the duty of bearing the ill-govern-
ment. But this case is very rare, and a theologian who would permit any
attempt to be made under this pretext should exercise great discrimina-
tion and watchfulness lest he should fall into excess, for excess here is
far more dangerous than remissness' (Commerc. Epistol. Leibnitz, Selecta
Specimina, ed. Feder, p. 402). In 1710 he wrote thus to Thomas Burnett:
'Tell me whether the moderate Tories do not acknowledge that there are
extraordinary cases when passive obedience ceases and it is allowable to
resist the sovereign, and whether the moderate Whigs do not agree that
such resistance should not be lightly offered, but only for grave reasons?
The case is similar to that of the right of succession by inheritance, which
must not be departed from *except when the welfare of the country forces
such a course upon the people.* For it is mere superstition to believe that
these things are of inalterable divine right; even the Sabbath is not so
strict an ordinance' (Guhrauer, G. W. Frhr. v. Leibnitz, ii. 305 seq.).

⁵ Amongst these are Morale Pratique des Jesuites, by Arnauld derived
for the most part from the Teatro Gesuitico, a lampoon condemned in
Spain in 1655, and in Rome on 26 Feb. 1656; also a work quoted by many
modern writers (as by Gieseler, K. G. iii. ii. p. 628, n. 36), Extraits des assertions dangereuses et pernicieuses que les soi-disants Jésuites ont dans
tous les temps et persévérament soutenues, enseignées et publiées dans
leurs livres avec l'approbation de leurs supérieurs et généraux, verifiés et
collationés par les commissaires du Parlement, à Paris, 1762. Theiner
(Hist. du Pontificat de Clément XIV. t. i. p. 47) calls this work a 'sink of
lies.' The work written against it, published in Paris, 1763 (Réponse au
Livre: Extraits des Assertions dangereuses, &c.), proved 457 misquota-
tions from the Latin and 361 from the French; and other works refuted it
more fully (Nouvelles Observations sur les jugemens rendus contre les Jésuites, Bourdeaux, 1763; Kurzer Inbegriff der Anklagen wider die Gesellschaft Jesu in Frankreich nebst deren Beantwortung: from the French,
Augsb. apud Wagner, 1762). Many French bishops published pastorals
against the pamphlet, and it was condemned by Clement XIII. in 1764
(Büll. Clem. XIII. t. iii. pp. 9, 16, 17 seq.).

⁶ This was first published at Cracow in 1612, and revived in Paris in
1761 (at a time when the Order was undergoing violent attacks). The
Bishop of Cracow had proceeded against the author, and the composition
was condemned in Rome on 10 Dec. 1616 as a forgery. Cf. Barbier, Dic-
tionnaire des Anonymes et des Pseudonymes, t. iii. n. 20,985; Crétineau-
Joly, t. iii. pp. 372, 373; Bonner, Theol. Literaturblatt, 1867, No. 9, p.
329 seq., where the Leipzig edition of Parson Bergmann is treated of; [Mo-
nita Secreta of the Society of Jesus, by the Rev. T. B. Parkinson; the
Month, July-August 1873. Tr.]

⁷ The work of Dr. Weber, Der Gehorsam in der Gesellschaft Jesu
(Breslau, 1872), was fully refuted in the Laacher Monatschrift, vol. i. pp.
453-466, 548, vol. ii. p. 72 seq. Doctors of the Church from St. Basil to
St. Bernard have said quite the same of the obedience of regulars. [See
also Remarks on a late Assailant of the Society of Jesus, reprinted from
the Month and Catholic Review, Burns & Oates, London, 1875. Tr.]

§ 19.

To throw odium upon the Society, Jesuits are accused of appearing on the one hand to acknowledge the sovereignty of the people, by placing the source of royal authority in the people ; on the other hand, practically rendering this vain by asserting an act such as the institution of a king performed by the people only obtains validity through its ratification by the Pope, who properly can alone depose and appoint kings.[1]

But this is a misrepresentation of their doctrine. As a fact, they placed the source of royal authority in God, and taught that the Pope's ratification was by no means requisite in all cases ; neither did they ever attribute to him an unconditional right of deposing sovereigns. A doctrine moreover is attributed to Jesuits which had been taught by other writers long before the existence of this Society. Cardinal Vincent Petra teaches : The institution of kings arises primarily from the natural law, secondarily from public law ;[2] nations without a king may choose a king for themselves ;[3] heathen nations have no need of the consent of the Pope for this, though Christian nations should seek his consent at the elevation of new kings ;[4] a Christian nation cannot depose its king without the consent of the Pope.[5] A decision from the supreme guardian of Christian morality, a declaration from the Supreme Head of the Church is to be sought on occasion of the institution of a new king or of a new dynasty. The reasons are, that power once delegated to the sovereign no longer rests in the people ; obedience is due even to a bad ruler, and the right of withdrawing obedience from one who is the open and public enemy of the people, or who would coerce them into rebellion against God, is founded, not upon their possession of a superior right, but upon the law of self-preservation.[6] Other reasons are, that in this matter the nation is very liable to be misled by deceit and false strivings after liberty into immoral action,[7] and that even the plea of liberty of conscience may be converted into a firebrand ; lastly, that the deposition of a king is the dissolution of a tie sanctioned by religion. This view of the Papal office would, it is evident, impede, not facilitate, revolution; the Pope appears as the safeguard of legitimacy. His whole position obliges him to protect this, and to uphold everywhere the divine law. His decision, based upon fixed principles of justice, is opposed to the frivolity and caprices of the populace. The false religion of the sovereign would not be held sufficient reason for resistance or deposition, though the duty of maintaining the true religion against violent efforts to destroy and ruin it would be so.[8] This was the principle adhered to firmly in Catholic mediæval States, and all mediæval history is interwoven with its results.

[1] Huber, p. 42. Cf. Döllinger, in A.Z. March 1872.

[2] Comment. in Const. Apost. t. ii. p. 121, in Innoc. III. Const. iv. n. 4, 5, with reference to l. v. Ex hoc Jure Dig. de Just. et Jure, i. 1; Arist. Polit. iii. 4; Cic. de Rep. l. iii. ; Aug. c. Julian. iv. 12.

[3] Com. in Innoc. III. Const. 8, n. 3, t. ii. p. 132. Grot. de Jure Belli et Pacis, l. i. c. iii. n. 8.

[4] 'In creandis *novis* regibus indigent ejus assensu,' l.c. n. 5.

[5] Ib. n. 13, 14, p. 134.

[6] Bianchi, t. i. l. i. § 7, n. 5, pp. 72, 73.

[7] Justin. Hist. l. xviii. c. i.: ' Saepe libertas et speciosa nomina praetexuntur, nec quisquam alienum servitium et dominationem concupivit, ut non eadem ista vocabula usurpavit.'

[8] Bianchi, l.c. § 5, n. 1, pp. 40, 41 ; § 7, n. 5-7, pp. 73-75.

ESSAY XV.

ECCLESIASTICAL JURISDICTION.

MANY people in these days take offence at the extent of spiritual jurisdiction exercised in former times, especially at the exemption of the clergy from civil courts of justice ; and as the Popes are supposed to have been the chief supporters of such usurpations on the part of the hierarchy, they have to bear the brunt of the attack. Ecclesiastical jurisdiction was long since attacked by Protestants following Marsilius Patavinus, who wished to deprive the clergy of all jurisdiction,[1] and William Occam, who denied the Pope any coercive power ;[2] but on the other hand it has been acknowledged even by Protestants, and amongst them men like Samuel Basnage,[3] learned in Christian antiquity, to be founded on divine right, and to be therefore just.

[1] Goldast. ii. 310. Friedberg, de Fin. &c. pp. 63, 64.
[2] Friedberg, p. 64, n. 3.
[3] S. Basnag. Annal. Eccles. t. ii. diss. 4, de Eccles. Tribunali, § 1 : ' Tribunal Ecclesiae jubente Deo erectum fuisse faciles largimur Baronio. Etenim nulla societas consistere potest absque auctoritate poenas illis irrogandi, qui compositas sancitasque leges evertunt atque perfringunt. Propterea Apostolus (1 Tim. v. 17, 19) meminit presbyterorum, qui bene praesunt, et Timotheum monuit : accusationem ne recipito, nisi sub duobus aut tribus testibus. Quibus constitutum in reos judicium indicatur. . . . Neque a principum voluntate Ecclesiae tribunal, sed ab ipso Christo originem ducit.'

PART I. ECCLESIASTICAL JURISDICTION BEFORE THE THIRTEENTH AND FOURTEENTH CENTURIES.

§ 1. Ecclesiastical jurisdiction till the time of Constantine. § 2. After Constantine. § 3. In the East. § 4. In the Germanic Empire. § 5. Crimes of the clergy under the Roman emperors. § 6. Immunity and barbarism of the clergy. § 7. Charge of over-leniency in the punishments of ecclesiastics. Decretal of Celestine III. § 8. Charge against Alexander III.

§ 1.

Even before Constantine the Great, jurisdiction in civil and criminal causes was exercised by the Church.[1] The Apostle (1 Cor. vi. 1 seq.) forbade the faithful[2] to carry their causes before heathen judges ; and the bishops being endowed as successors of the Apostles with a spiritual power to judge and chastise,[3] appear as the natural judges of the faithful in all judicial matters. When Christians were in danger of being obliged to swear to the gods or deny their faith before heathen judges, the Church forbade them to accept civil offices or carry their causes before heathen judges, and withdrew them partially from the State, making use of the indirect power over temporal matters, and *per accidens* deciding temporal affairs.[4] When the emperors had been converted to Christianity the rule was still maintained that no Catholic should, under pain of excommunication, bring his cause before a judge holding any other faith,[5] and that no cleric under pain of deprivation should bring an action against another before a temporal judge.[6] The Church also later asserted her jurisdiction.[7] It was not first granted to her by the emperors, but sometimes with more, sometimes with less restriction they acknowledged it as already existing.[8]

[1] Constit. Apost. l. ii. c. xi. xii. xxxvii. xlii. xlv-xlix. Can. Apost. 3 seq. 74 seq. Tertull. Apol. c. xxxix. Cyprian, Ep. ad Cornel. (Labbé, Conc. i. 716, ed Venet.). Conc. Eliberit. 305, c. 74, 75. Cf. Thomassin, de Vet. et Nova Eccl. Disc. P. ii. l. iii. c. ci.

[2] Aug. Enchir. ad Laur. c. lxxviii.: 'Extra Ecclesiam judicia finiri Apostolus *terribiliter vetat*.' Serm. 24, in Ps. 118: 'Constituit enim talibus causis ecclesiasticos Apostolus cognitores, in foro *prohibens* jurgare Christianos.'

[3] 1 Cor. iv. 18; v. 1 seq.; 2 Cor. x. 6 seq.; xiii. 2 seq.; 2 Thess. iii. 14; 1 Tim. i. 20; v. 19 (cf. Theodor. H. E. i. 21) ; 2 Tim. iv. 15. Bianchi, Della Potestà e della Polizia della Chiesa. Roma, 1746, t. iv. l. ii. c. iv. § 1 seq. pp. 581 seq. 587 seq.

[4] Bianchi, l.c. n. 13, pp. 495, 496.

[5] 'Catholicus, qui causam suam sive justam sive injustam ad judicem alterius fidei provocat, excommunicetur.' Thus the so-called fourth Council of Carthage, 398, c. 87, more properly—cf. Hefele, Conc. ii. p. 63 seq.— Statuta Eccl. Antiquae, c. 30 (Ballerin. Opp. Leon. M. t. iii. p. 659).

[6] Council of Hippo, 393, c. 9 ; of Carthage, 407, c. 10 (st. 104). Hefele, l.c. pp. 53, 89 ; c. 43, c. xi. q. 1. Cf. Statuta Eccl. Ant. c. 1 seq. d. 90.

In the Synod of Mileve, 402, c. 2 (Cod. Afr. n. 87, 88; Hefele, ii. p. 74; cf. c. 1, de Judic. ii. 1), Bishop Quodvultdeus was excommunicated because he would not present himself before the provincial Synod.

[7] In the Synod of Aquileja in 381, St. Ambrose, with universal assent, uttered the anathema upon Bishop Palladius, and said amongst other things: 'Quoniam *et in hoc* ipso damnandus est, quod laicorum exspectat sentoutiam, *cum magis de laicis sacerdotes debeant judicare*' (Labbé, ii. 1174, ed. Ven.). Chifflet's doubts concerning the acts have long since been refuted. Hefele, Conc. ii. p. 34, No. 2.

[8] It has often been asserted that the ecclesiastical jurisdiction mentioned, 1 Cor. vi. 1 seq., was merely an arbitration (Bossuet, Defens. P. i. l. i. sect. 2, c. xxxvii. p. 180). But we must distinguish two classes of judges (*arbitri*), l. ii. Si arbiter, Cod. 7, 45, de sent. et interloc.; l. Pacisci, 1, Dig. xxiii. 4, de pact. dotal; ib. l. iv. tit. 8, de receptis qui arbitr. recep.; l. xxiv. Dig. xvi. 3, deposito vel non; l. xvii. Dig. de neg. gest. 3, 5). They were appointed either merely to arbitrate or else to pronounce judgment. The former were connected with the judicature, and the *actiones* were to be brought before them; not so the latter. If we understand the first class, how could Christians be bound to an arbitration which in its nature was free? If we understand the second class, how could Christians be forbidden to bring the action before the ordinary judge? (Procul. in l. iv. Societatem, § 1, Dig. xvii. 2, pro soc.; Schmalzgrucber, in l. i. Decret. tit. 43, n. 1 seq.; Bianchi, t. i. l. iii. § 4, n. 12, pp. 493-495). As a matter of fact the bishops administered justice, and considered themselves bound to do so (cf. Synes. Ep. 57, 58; Nyssen. in Vita Greg. Thaum.; Ambros. de Offic. i. c. xxix.; Const. Ap. ii. 45, 49 seq.; Aug. de Op. Monac. c. xxix. n. 37). The *arbitri* could refuse to act, not so the bishops.

§ 2.

Constantine the Great, whose estimation of the bishops was so high,[1] not only acknowledged ecclesiastical jurisdiction in purely spiritual matters, but passed a law[2] by which, after the beginning of a civil law-suit, the parties concerned might leave the lay court of justice and appeal to the episcopal court (in this case a court of arbitration), against which, under such circumstances, no further appeal could be made.[3] By a later law[4] he even insisted that if one of the parties had appealed to the ecclesiastical court, the other should follow even against his will. Julian deprived the Christians of their privileges, but the succeeding emperors restored them, and in the course of time many changes took place as the ever-increasing weight of business became too heavy for the bishops.[5]

[1] Eus. Vita Const. iv. 27: πάντος γὰρ εἶναι δικαστοῦ τοὺς ἱερεῖς τοῦ θεοῦ

δοκιμωτέρους (ἐπεσφραγίζετο). Rnfin. H. E. i. 2. Thomassin, l.c. c. cii. n. 1 seq.

² Const. a. 321. Sirmond. Append. Cod. Theod. l. xvii. Opp. i. 736. Haenel, xviii. Constit. quas J. Sirmondus, a. 1631, divulgavit, Bonn, 1844, p. 475. Cf. Eus. l.c. Soz. H. E. i. 9.

³ L. viii. 9, Cod. Just. i. 7 (last law of Arcadius and Honorius, 408).

⁴ Const. a. 331, Ablavio Praef. Praet. Sirmond. l.c. p. 717. Haenel, p. 445 seq., partially apud Gratian, c. 35, c. xi. q. 1, after capit. vi. 281, and Conc. Valent. 855 (Labbé, ix. 1160, d.). Gothofredus, Loysean, Eichhorn, and others, have disputed its authenticity, which has been defended on more convincing grounds by the following: Baron. a. 314, n. 33 seq.; Sirmond. in h.l. Vales, note in Eus. l.c.; Selden, Ux. hebr. l. iii. c. xxviii. de Synedr. i. 10; Cujacius ad Leg. 14, de dote prael.; Alteserra de jurisd. Eccles. Paris, 1705, l. i. c. vii.; Const. Constantini, de Episcopali Judicio vindicata, Tolos. 1672; Jean le Gendre, Episcopali Judicium adv. calumn. Gothofr. vindicatum, Paris, 1690; Bianchi, t. iv. l. ii. c. iv. § 10, n. 704 seq.; Haenel, l.c. Praef. de Const. quas J. Sirmondus edidit, Lips. 1840.

⁵ Aug. de Op. Monac. c. xxix. n. 37: 'Multo mallem manibus aliquid operari, quam tumultuossissimas perplexitates causarum alienarum pati de negotiis secularibus *vel judicando dirimendis vel interveniendo praecidendis*. Quibus nos molestiis idem afflixit Apostolus, non utique suo, sed ejus, qui per eum loquebatur arbitrio.'

§ 3.

The Emperor Justinian fully recognised the independent spiritual jurisdiction in civil causes. In general it was left to the choice of the parties concerned whether they wished to have their civil causes decided by the bishops;[1] bishops and priests were obliged to bring their causes to the ecclesiastical authority immediately above them;[2] laymen could only sue ecclesiastics before the bishop.[3] As to criminal matters, in cases of slight offences committed by the clergy the inquiry rested with the bishop, who also had to take cognisance of any violations of their office or order;[4] in cases of more serious crime the accusation might be brought before spiritual or lay judges. In the first case the bishop deprived the offender of his office and dignity, and then delivered him over to the lay judge for further proceedings; but if the complainant went first to the lay judge —which could only be allowed to a layman—the offender would then be sent over to the bishop to undergo deposition and degradation, the acts of his trial having been handed over; if the bishop did not agree to the verdict of the lay judge, both judges had then to refer to the emperor for a final decision.[5] In such a case both powers coöperated, and in this the Church had nothing to fear, since at that time both agreed to the same first principles. The State lent its aid in executing the sentences of the bishops,[6] whose power was by no means limited to the infliction of purely spiritual punishments. They had their own prisons (decanica), in which they could imprison the accused and condemned persons.[7] The use of corporal punishments was allowed,[8] fines might be inflicted,[9] and banishment pronounced.[10] Death was the only punishment they might not inflict.[11]

In the course of time many other changes were effected; for instance, in the Byzantine Empire, where, according to the prevailing idea of imperial omnipotence,[12] an exception was made in the case when any one appealed to the imperial tribunal; but still the free spiritual jurisdiction in principle remained the same.[13]

[1] L. xxix. § 4, Cod. Just. i. 4, de Episc. aud.

[2] Nov. 123, c. 8, 22.

[3] Nov. 79, 83, Praef. 123, c. 21. Phillips, Lehrb. d. K.R. § 175, p. 483 seq.

[4] Nov. 83, c. 1. Cf. Thomassin, l.c. c. ciii. n. 1 seq.; Bianchi, t. iv. p. 608.

[5] Nov. 83, Praef. § 2; Nov. 123, c. 21, § 1. Cf. Phillips, l.c. § 186, p. 524 seq.

[6] L. viii. Episcopale, Cod. i. 4, de Episc. aud.: ' Per judicum quoque officia, ne sit cassa episcopalis cognitio, definitioni executio tribuatur.' Cf. Bianchi, t. iv. l. ii. c. iv. § 9, n. 4, p. 683 seq.

[7] The Archimandrite Basilius and other monks complain to Theodosius II. in their petition (Conc. Eph. Labbé, iii. 976): κἀκεῖθεν τυπτόμενοι ἀπηγόμεθα ἐν τῷ δεκανικῷ κἀκεῖ γυμνοὺς ἡμᾶς ὡς δημίους καὶ ὑπευθύνους τιμωρίᾳ ἐκόλυσεν. Cf. l. Arcad. et Honor. 396, in the Cod. Theod. de Haeret.; l. iii. Cuncti, C. Just. i. 5; Nov. 79, c. 3. Cf. Gothofred. Com. in l. xxx. C. Theod. de Haeret.; Ciron. l. ii. Observ. c. li. et in Rubr. de Offic. ord. Joh. a Costa, c. iv. Extravag. de Jud. Filesac, in c. i. de Off. ord. § 16. Bianchi, l.c. n. 7, p. 692.

[8] Aug. Ep. 133 (al. 159), ad Marcellin. n. 2. Cyprian, in Vita S. Caesar Arel. ap. Surium, 27 Aug. t. iv. p. 927. Conc. Agath. 506, c. 38, 41; Matiscon. i. 581, c. 8; Narbon. 589, c. 13 (Hefele, Conc. ii. 638; iii. 33, 50 seq.). Pallad. Hist. Laus. c. vi. Gregory the Great, who (Ep. ad Joh. Defens. ii. 54, ed. Vet. c. 38, c. xi. q. 1) appeals to Nov. 123, decreed for the *sortilegi* that free men should be imprisoned and slaves should be beaten (l. ix. Ep. 65, ol. vii. 67), and decided that the Subdeacon Hilarius should be castigated publicly *verberibus*, and then banished (l. xi. Ep. 71, cl. ix. 66). Other examples, apud Thomassin, l.c. c. cii. n. 19.

* Conc. Carth. Labbé, ii. 1454. Aug. de un. Eccl. c. 17 (c. 35, c. xxiii. q. 5). Greg. M. l. iv. Ep. 26, ad Jan. Cal. Ep. 27. Cf. Salgado, de Reg. Protect. P. ii. c. iv.; Bianchi, l.c. n. 8, p. 694.

[10] Conc. Rom. Symmachi, Labbé, v. 504 (c. 3, c. iii. q. 5). Conc. Aurel. iv. 541, c. 29; Tolet. xii. 681, c. 11. Gonzalez, in c. i. de Calumn. v. n. 14. Bianchi, l.c. p. 693.

[11] Cf. Gerbert, de Legit. Eccl. Potest. l. iv. c. ii. n. 1 seq. p. 666 seq.; Molitor, Ueber canonisches Gerichtsverfahren, Mainz, 1856, p. 26 seq.

[12] Ἡ βασιλικὴ ἐξουσία πάντα δύναται ποιεῖν. Balsam, in Carthag. c. xv. (Migne, cxxviii. p. 73). Cf. Demetr. Chomaten. ad Const. Cabas. (Leuncl. i. p. 317).

[13] Heraclius gave on March 21, 629, to the bishops the exclusive jurisdiction over ecclesiastics both in civil and criminal matters. Voell. et Just, Bibl. Jur. Can. Vet. ii. 1361-1365. Leunclav. Jus. Gr. Rom. i. pp. 73-75. Syntagma Athen. ed. Rhalli et Potli, t. v. 225-229. Balsam, in Phot. Nomoc. ix. 1 (Migne, PP. gr. civ. p. 1093). Pitra, Jur. Eccl. gr. Mon. ii. p. 532, gives thus the tenor of the law : μήτε ἐπίσκοπον μήτε κληρικὸν μήτε μοναχὸν χρηματικῆς ἢ ἐγκληματικῆς χάριν αἰτίας παρὰ πολιτικῷ ἢ στρατιωτικῷ ἐνάγεσθαι ἄρχοντι, ἀλλὰ παρὰ μόνοις τοῖς ἰδίοις ἐπισκόποις· ἢ μητροπολίταις ἢ πατριάρχαις.

§ 4.

In the German Empire also the Church gradually obtained complete exemption from the civil forum. With regard to the disputes of ecclesiastics amongst themselves the episcopal court was always competent; when otherwise, the class of the defendant determined the matter. But a priest was not allowed to carry any sort of complaint before a civil judge without the permission of the bishop, any more than a layman could carry a complaint against an ecclesiastic before a civil judge without this same permission.[1] Mixed tribunals (*tribunalia mixta*)[2] existed in the Frankish kingdom for a time; later on the bishop decided all causes of ecclesiastics. In Germany it was a principle in law that if possible every one should be judged by his own equals, and, moreover, on account of the peculiar position of the clerical order, the Church could better punish the offences of its members. In the time of Charles the Great ecclesiastical penal jurisdiction over the clergy was always final.[3] The extension of spiritual jurisdiction as it appears in the Middle Ages was a necessity, because the Church had to supplement the action of the State where the latter was either not in a position to fulfil its office, or allowed part of its functions to be made over to the Church.[4] The spiritual jurisdiction, expressly recognised as it was by the emperors, even by Frederick II.[5] and Charles IV.,[6] was firmly maintained by Popes[7] and Councils.[8] All clerical causes belonged to the spiritual court,[9] and no priest could forego this right. Only feudal causes were consigned to the civil tribunal.[10] It was against all the notions of the period, and offensive to religious feeling, that laymen should sit in judgment upon the clergy. Tosi[11] says: 'Ecclesiastical immunity owes its origin to a religious feeling based on just grounds. The State may possibly oppose this feeling, but not without transgressing against natural reverence for religion and the Church, and even against common equity and gratitude, considering the immeasurable advantages it owes to the religious feelings of its members and to the effects of the influence of the clergy. Thus arose the general legal recognition of ecclesiastical immunity ; and when thus recognised this immunity formed an acquired right for the Church, to be respected like any other right, and only to be altered with the consent of its possessor, the Church.'

[1] Conc. Agath. 506, c. 32 ; Epaon. 517, c. 11 ; Aurel. iii. 538, c. 32 ; iv. 541, c. 20 ; Autissid. 578, c. 35 ; Matiscon. i. 581, c. 8 ; ii. 585, c. 9, 10 ; Paris, v. 614, c. 4 ; Rhemens, 625, c. 6 (Hefele, ii. 637, 663, 756 ; iii. 42, 33, 37, 63, 69).

[2] Chlotar. Const. 614, c. 4. Pertz, iii. 14.

[3] Caroli M. Capitul. 789, c. 38 (Pertz, iii. 60) : 'Ut clerici et ecclesiastici ordines, si culpam incurreriut, apud ecclesiasticos judicentur non apud saeculares.' Capitul. Francof. 794, c. 39 ; Capit. Longob. 803, c. 12 (Pertz, l.c. pp. 74, 110) ; Capit. v. 137 ; vi. 155.

[4] Phillips, Lehrb. d. K.R. § 175, p. 478. Cf. Thomassin, l.c. c. cv. seq.

[5] Frid. II. Auth. Statuimus, ad 1, 33, Cod. Just. i. 3 (Pertz, iv. 244) : 'Statuimus, ut nullus ecclesiasticam personam in criminali quaestione vel civili trahere ad judicium saecularo praesumat contra constitutiones imperiales et canonicas sanctiones. Quod si actor fecerit, a juro suo cadat, judicatum non teneat et judex ex tunc potestate judicandi privetur.' Cf. Raumer, Gesch. d. Hohenstaufen, iii. p. 350 ; Phillips, Lehrb. p. 486, No. 6.

[6] Cf. Card Petra, Com. in Constit. Apost. ; in Const. iv. Boniface IX. Justis, et Urbani VI. Const. Quia sicut, t. iv. pp. 189 seq. 198 seq.

[7] Alex. III. Ep. 350, ad Henric. Angl. Reg. p. 375, ed. Migne : 'Sicut clerici a viris saecularibus vita et habitu distinguuntur, ita et judicia clericorum a laicorum judiciis diversa penitus comprobantur.' Innoc. III. l. ii. Ep. 162, Capitulo et Clero de Matera, p. 714 : 'Ordinis clericalis immu-

uitas eo est libertatis privilegio insignita, ut cum suos judices habeat, sub quibus possit et debeat conveniri, a saeculari judicio penitus sit exemta, quae nimirum nullis publicarum functionum oneribus obligata jugum saecularis effugit servitutis.' Ep. 163, ad Popul. de Matera: ' Cum (clerici) secundum Apostolum suo Domino stent aut cadant.' Cf. Urban II. ap. Thomassin, P. ii. 1. iii. c. cxii. n. 4 ; likewise c. xvii. d. 28 (Nicol. I.) ; c. vii. d. 97 ; c. i. 2 ; c. xxi. q. 5.

⁸ Council of Nîmes, 1096, c. 14 (Mansi, xx. 936 ; cf. Hefele, v. p. 220) : ' Nec clericos nec monachos in curiam suam ad saeculare ullus cogat venire judicium, quoniam hoc rapina esset et sacrilegium.' Lateran, iii. 1179, c. 14 (Mansi, xxii. 226 ; Hefele, p. 635). Synod of Lambeth, 1261, c. 1, 4, 5, 7-10 ; of Cologne, 1266, c. 11, 13, 18 ; of Seyne, 1267, c. 7 ; of Bourges, 1276, c. 6, 7 ; of Angers, 1279, c. 1 (Hefele, vi. pp. 59, 79, 95, 159, 180), &c.

⁹ This had competence not merely *ratione materiae*, but also *ratione personae*. The Popes knew the distinction of ' causae, quae ratione personarum aut rerum de jure aut antiqua consuetudine ad forum ecclesiasticum pertinent' (c. iv. Quoniam, iii. 23, de Immunit. Eccl. in 6).

¹⁰ Alex. III. c. vi. et vii. de foro Compet. ii. 2. Conc. Constant. 1463. Hartzheim, v. 45.

¹¹ Vorlesungen über den Syllabus, Vienna, 1865, pp. 91, 92.

§ 5.

We are told that in contrast with the Middle Ages the early Church under the Roman emperors never disputed the jurisdiction of the State over civil offences of the clergy.[1] This statement is disproved by the testimony of the Fathers and the Councils ; and regarding the civil laws in this connection, there is no foundation for representing the early emperors as *always* subjecting all the civil delinquencies of the clergy absolutely and even exclusively to the civil court.[2] We see the Church continually striving to bring the criminal causes of ecclesiastics before her own tribunal, but in serious cases the co-operation of the civil power has often been very welcome to her.[3]

[1] Huber, p. 12.

[2] Cf. also Devoti, Inst. Jur. Can. l. iv. tit. 1, § 10, n. 1-5.

[3] If we are further assured that the mediæval canonists, and after them even Baronius, endeavoured to hide inconvenient facts by means of forgeries, we must especially remember that they at least did not forge the *corpus juris*, but guarded it intact ; that the Pseudo-Isidore forgeries merely attribute to Popes of the first three centuries what was said by Councils of the fourth and fifth—c. 1, Nemo (Cajus P.) ; c. 3, Clericum (Marcellin.) ; c. 7, Quacunque (id.) ; c. xi. q. 1, c. 14, Relatum (Alex. I.) ib. ; that the Capitularies of Charles the Great existed and were in use long before Pseudo-Isidore, and that the genuineness of the extracts therein taken

from the Codex Theodosianus has to this day not been disproved—c. Continua lege, c. et q. cit. (1, 3, de Episc. Judic. post Cod. Theod.). Testimony to the authenticity is given by Legendre, l.c. c. ii. n. 5; Bianchi, l.c. c. iv. § 8, n. 4, p. 666 seq. Gratian follows Anselm (iii. 109) and Polycarp (i. tit. 19).

§ 6.

But this exemption from the civil courts has, we are told, helped to make the clergy intractable and uncivilised. Should then this exemption never have arisen, or, if existing, have been abolished in the midst of general barbarism and feudal anarchy? Considering what the civil courts then were, would not the clergy have become rather more than less intractable and uncivilised by being compelled to appear before them? Were the clergy to be tried by judicial combat and ordeal?[1] Cases actually occurred when civil magistrates wished to force the clergy to take part in the judicial combat.[2] Several Synods have forbidden ecclesiastics to be brought for trial before a civil court on the ground that the means of proving innocence or guilt, for instance the red-hot iron, were barbarous and superstitious.[3] At a time when civil administration of justice was so deficient, rude, and uncivilised[4] that the Church had to come to its assistance, barbarism would have grown apace if the priests, who were almost the only persons of any high degree of cultivation, had in all penal cases been subjected to the civil judges of the time.

[1] Walter, K.R. § 190, p. 343 seq.
[2] Pauli, Geschichte Englands, iii. p. 144.
[3] Mansi, xxii. 702, c. v. Other Synods forbade all combats to ecclesiastics (Council of Noyon, 1344, c. 1, 3; Mansi, xxvi. 4; Hefele, vi. 591), as well as the arrest and trial of ecclesiastics to civil judges (Council of Rouen, 1231, c. 28; of Paris, 1347, c. 1; London, 1321, c. 5; Mansi, xxiii. 217; xxv. 676; xxvi. 4; Hefele, v. 896 seq.; vi. pp. 503, 531), &c. Popes were unwilling for ecclesiastics to be present at ordeals or to bless them. Innoc. III. 1. vii. Ep. 113, p. 344, complains: 'Cumque candentis ferri et aquae frigidae ac similia judicia lex canonica non admittat, benedicere ac interesse talibus compelluntur miseri sacerdotes.'
[4] Cf. the Protestant canonist Dove, de Jurisdictionis Ecclesiasticae apud Germanos Gallosque progressu, Berol. 1855, esp. pp. 23 seq. 70 seq. Upon the state of things in England, cf. Chron. Roger. et Matth. Paris, Mansi, xxi. 603, 604; Council of London, 1138, c. 10, ib. p. 512; Thomassin,

P. i. 1. ii. c. xiii. Hausmann, Gesch. der Päpstl. Reservatfälle, p. 63 seq., gives much information.

§ 7.

The procedure of the spiritual court, the mildness of the punishments inflicted on ecclesiastical offenders, who were even sometimes left altogether unpunished,[1] is an especial source of offence. As an example of the 'extensive use which the Popes made of this immunity, which nominally was for the freedom of the Church,' we are referred to a well-known Decretal of Celestine III.,[2] the substance of which is that ecclesiastics convicted of murder or theft (or perjury) should be degraded (deposed), and in case they did not amend, excommunicated (Huber puts 'excluded from the Sacraments'); if in spite of that they continued to be obdurate, they should be anathematised; and then at last, if this wrought no change of mind, they should be delivered over by the Church to the civil tribunal to be punished [then had they not already suffered any punishment?]. On this it is remarked : ' So it appears that an ecclesiastic who was a murderer or a thief could only receive capital punishment [from a civil judge] after he had relapsed *three* times. Such an administration of justice induces the supposition, that crimes for which laymen have to suffer death [what, even for every theft?] are less grievous when committed by the clergy.' Let us look closer at the Decretal. Its primary object is to maintain, according to the existing spiritual and civil law, the ecclesiastical . jurisdiction over all the clergy in its integrity as long as the Church had sufficient means at her disposal.to keep them within bounds.[3] These means were only too many in the opinion of Professor Huber, as it appears from expressions he has used in another place.[4] The Decretal orders the deposition of any ecclesiastic who was guilty of manslaughter (simple manslaughter not qualified),[5] theft, or perjury, in accordance with the older decisions.[6] Huber either did not know or overlooked the fact that the most ancient canons of the Eastern Church for one and the same crime punished the laity with excommunication, the clergy with deposition.[7] The latter was a very severe punishment, far more severe than excommunication was to the laity.

It commonly involved the loss of temporal means of sub-
sistence and personal status. It was the ancient ecclesiastical
punishment for the clergy, and since the earliest times of the
Church the axiom was held to : 'No bis in idem' (Neh. i. 9) ;[8] *i.e.*
the same offence is not to receive two punishments. Deposition
and excommunication was a double punishment, to be inflicted
therefore only when great severity was necessary. As a second
punishment for those who were found to be incorrigible excommunication was added, according to the old rule not only of
the Popes, but also of the Synods ;[9] this entailed not only exclusion from the Sacraments, but also—until the later modifications we have already mentioned—from all social intercourse.
If this were fruitless the case, as a last and extreme measure,
was delivered over to the civil power.[10] Further, the Decretal
does not presuppose the repetition of the offence—a relapse—
but only the incorrigible and stubborn state of the offender ;
there is no mention of a relapse. Later laws have ordained that
a guilty ecclesiastic should be immediately made over to the
civil court[11] in case of certain offences ; they were opposed to
the earlier practice, which was founded on a strict sense of
justice.

[1] Innoc. III. l. vi. Ep. 183, to the Archbishop of Lund, 1203 : ' Quod
cum praelati excessus corrigere debeant subditorum et publicae auctoritatis intersit, ne crimina remaneant impunita et per impunitatis audaciam
fiant, qui nequam fuerant, nequiores : non solum possunt, sed etiam debent superiores clericos illos postquam fuerint de crimine canonico condem-
nati, sub arcta custodia detinere,' &c.

[2] C. 10, Cum non ab homine, ii. 1, de Judic.

[3] This is shown in the context by the words, ' cum Ecclesia ultra non
habeat quod faciat.'

[4] Huber, pp. 75, 85.

[5] Reiffenstuel, in l. ii. tit 1, § 2, n. 6 : ' Ob unum *simplex* (non qualifi-
catum) homicidium curiae saeculari tradi non possit.'

[6] Bernard. Papiensis Summa Decretal. l. v. tit. 10, § 7, p. 223 (ed. Las-
peyres, Ratisb. 1860) : ' Poena homicidii voluntarii est secundum leges, ut
sublimiores deportentur, omnibus bonis ademtis, minores capite puniantur,
ut Dig. ad Leg. Cornel. de Sicar. l. iii. § Legis (§ 5) et l. penult. ; secundum
canones autem clericus deponitur, laicus excommunicatur, ut dist. l. c. Si
quis viduam (8) et c. Si quis voluntarie (44), ex Martino Brac.'

[7] Can. Apost. 32, 63, 64-66, 69, 70, 84 (al. 30, 62, 63-65, 68, 69,
83) ; Eph. c. 6 ; Chalc. c. 2, 8, 27 (Hefele, i. pp. 783, 793 seq. 799 ; ii.
194, 487, 493, 508). The third Synod of Orleans, 538, c. 8 (Hefele, ii. p.

754), decreed : ' A cleric guilty of theft or forgery shall be degraded from
his order, but not excommunicated ; one guilty of perjury shall be excommunicated for two years.'   Also Aug. Enchirid. c. lxxx. presupposes the two
punishments as parallel for the two classes : ' Multa mala . . . in apertam
consuetudinem jam venerunt, ut pro his non solum excommunicare aliquem
laicum non audeamus, sed nec clericum degradare.'   Cf. Bingham, Orig.
et Ant. Eccl. 1. xvii. c. § 51 ; Kober, Die Suspension, Tübingen, 1862, p.
5 seq.

⁷ Already Can. Ap. 25 (al. 24, Hefele, i. p. 781) appeals to this ; likewise Basilius, Ep. 188, c. 3 (Migne, PP. gr. xxxii. 672) ; also Balsamon, in
c. 1, Neocaes. (ib. t. cxxxvii. p. 1197).   The same in Basil, can. 51 (ib.
cxxxviii. 737), designates the ἔκπτωσις τῆς ὑπηρεσίας as properly the punishment for clerics.

⁹ Already Can. Ap. 29 (al. 27, Hefele, i. p. 782) decrees : ' A bishop,
priest, or deacon deposed for some crime who shall venture again to exercise his office is to be entirely excluded from the Church.'   Likewise
Conc. Ant. 341, c. 4 (Hefele, i. 495), &c.

¹⁰ This is treated, c. 18, Si quis, c. xi. q. 1 ; c. 43, De Ligaribus, c.
xxiii. q. 5 ; Innoc. III. c. 27, de V. S. V. 40.

¹¹ Reiffenstuel, in l. ii. tit. 1, § 4, n. 112, 113.

§ 8.

The charge has been renewed[1] against Alexander III. of
declaring adultery to be a slight sin, and that no priest ought
to be deposed or even suspended by his bishop on account of it.
The passage on which this charge is founded has been mistrans-
lated by Huber,[2] and no regard has been paid to the arguments
already brought forward by Scheeben and Merkle[3] against this
calumny.   Alexander III. himself declares that a priest convicted of adultery must be removed from his office ;[4] and in the
letters here in question to the Archbishop of Salerno, Alexander
III., far from abolishing this rule, presupposes it.   The guilty
ecclesiastics lost their office at the beginning of their penance,
and during its continuance they could neither practise nor
receive any such office ; but the question was whether, after
the penance was accomplished, pardon might be granted, especially when complete amendment had taken place in the
delinquent.   In cases of adultery[5] and other crimes, less serious
than murder and sins against God,[6] a bishop *can* dispense
ecclesiastics[7] *after the completion of their penance,* and *need not*
therefore permanently exclude them from office ; but having de-

posed a criminal, he is not obliged to make him over immediately
to the civil power. The passage in question contains nothing
more. Alexander III. was in truth very severe upon such
crimes, though he could be lenient when occasion required.

¹ Huber, p. 13. The charge was first made in the Allgemeine Zeitung,
13th March 1869. Cf. Anti-Janus, p. 15.
² In the Decretal the words *cum clericis* belong not to *episcopus* but to
dispensare. In the language of the Church, *dispensare cum aliquo* means
to dispense any one, *e.g.* c. 1, de Cler. Pugn. in Duello, v. 14: 'si cum
ipso (sc. clerico) episcopus duxerit misericorditer dispensandum.' Huber's
mistranslation has arisen from total ignorance of ecclesiastical termin-
ology.
³ An article by the latter in the Augsb. Pastoralblatt of the 15th May
1869 was referred to in Anti-Janus, note 17.
⁴ C. Significasti, v. de Adult. v. 16, to the Bishop of Chartres, Mansi,
xxii. 434; Ant. Augustin. Opp. iv. 310; Jaffé, Reg. ap. Migne, cc. p. 1321.
⁵ This is the case in point, c. 4, At si clerici, § 1, de Adulteriis vero,
ii. 1, de Judic.
⁶ Cf. c. 16, xxxii. q. 7: 'Quid in omnibus peccatis adulterio est gravius? *Secundum* namque in poenis obtinet *locum*, quoniam *primum* illi
habent, qui aberrent a Deo, etsi sobrie vixerint.'
⁷ In books of canon law as a rule the word *clerici* by itself means
those in minor orders, while those in greater orders are generally given
their proper names. Permaneder, K.R. § 124, p. 206, 2d ed.

PART II. ECCLESIASTICAL JURISDICTION SINCE THE THIRTEENTH AND FOURTEENTH CENTURIES.

§ 1. Encroachments upon ecclesiastical jurisdiction. § 2. England. § 3.
Germany. § 4. France. § 5. Spain and Italy. § 6. Reason of the
dislike to special courts for the clergy. § 7. Complaints with regard
to ecclesiastical jurisdiction over the laity. § 8. Ecclesiastical right
of sanctuary and its modifications. § 9. Later Concordats. § 10.
Possible revival of former claims.

§ 1.

After the Ghibelline wars of the thirteenth century the
magistrates in the Italian towns set themselves in opposition to
the clergy and their immunities.¹ Several Synods of the thirteenth and fourteenth centuries complained of such interference,²
which was becoming more common and more oppressive,³ especially since the provincial Councils had been held less often.⁴

Contrary to imperial and Papal laws, the civil and even the criminal causes of the clergy were committed to civil judges.[5] Priests and even bishops were often arbitrarily ill-treated, their relations imprisoned, and fines inflicted on those who wished to take their causes before spiritual courts.

[1] The town of Parma in 1220 would allow no justice to be done to any priest if he would not present himself before the civil judge. Raumer, Gesch. der Hohenstaufen, vol. iii. p. 341.

[2] *E.g.* the Council of Avignon, 1279; of Valladolid, 1322, c. 3; Avignon, 1326, c. 8-10; Noyon, 1344 (Hefele, vi. 168, 533, 540, 591 scq.), and others.

[3] Petrus Bles. Ep. 27, p. 95: 'Irruunt laici in sancta sanctorum; sanctuarii vero lapides disperguntur in capite omnium platearum.'

[4] Thomassin, P. ii. l. iii. c. cx. n. 12.   Affre, Appel comme d'Abus, p. 60.

[5] Friedberg, de fin. &c. pp. 141, 143 seq. Cf. also Hausmann, Gesch. der Päpstlichen Reservatfälle, pp. 170 seq. 178 seq.; Ecclesiasticae jurisdictionis vindiciae advers. Caroli Feureti et aliorum tract. de abusu susceptae ab Ant. D. Alteserra, U.J. Prof. et Dec. Univ. Tolos. Paris, 1702, 4, P. i. l. i. c. iv. v. p. 10 scq.

§ 2.

In England, Henry II. endeavoured to abolish altogether the independent spiritual courts.[1] The clergy themselves were under certain disadvantages through the milder punishments inflicted by the ecclesiastical courts, to which laymen in ecclesiastical crimes were subject. Even the murderers of St. Thomas were not executed;[2] those who murdered any of the clergy were only excommunicated, while the murderer of a layman expiated his crime by death.[5] The civil judges used many pretexts to draw the clergy before their tribunals. Nevertheless Edward II. (1307-1327) restored great privileges to the spiritual courts, and Edward III. fully recognised the jurisdiction of the Church over the clergy in criminal matters.[4] But in the fifteenth century the inconveniences increased. A Synod held at York in 1466 complained of the ill-treatment of those who sought to bring their cause before the spiritual courts;[5] and Pope Sixtus IV. renewed, in 1476, the ecclesiastical prohibition to sue clergy before civil judges.[6]

[1] Hefele, Conc. v. p. 548 seq.   He especially used for this object the

rights he had obtained for the crown (cf. Joh. Saresb. Ep. 145, ad Barthol. Exou. p. 135, and elsewhere). After the murder of St. Thomas of
Canterbury he was, however, obliged to relinquish them (1172), Hefele, l.c.
p. 611 seq.

² Petrus Bles. tract. de Institut. Episcop. Migne, ccvii. p. 1110.

³ This difference of treatment led to the murder of ecclesiastics being
very frequent. Archbishop Richard of Canterbury wrote about it to his
suffragans, and even moved that murderers of the clergy should be committed before civil judges, that the civil sword might supply for the de-
ficiencies of the spiritual (Petr. Bles. Ep. 73; ib. p. 224 seq.: 'Ecclesia
jurisdictionem suam prius exerceat et si illa non sufficit, ejus imperfectum
suppleat gladius materialis'). He held this no violation of the old axiom :
Ne bis in idipsum (ib.: 'Non enim iteratum videtur, quod ab uno incipitur
et ab altero consummatur'). This was accomplished, and then soon in
other matters spiritual jurisdiction was much curtailed.

⁴ Lingard, History of England, vol. iii. chap. iii.

⁵ Hard. Conc. ix. p. 1481.

⁶ Hard. l.c. p. 1496. Roscovány, Monum. i. pp. 115-117.

§ 3.

In Germany the principle of making over clerical offenders,
who were imprisoned, to their bishops was constantly enjoined.[1]
The Synod of Würzburg (1287) increased the severity of the
punishments for imprisoning and ill-treating ecclesiastics, and
desired that if the priest was not set free within eight days
the place of his imprisonment should be laid under an interdict.[2] Still more severe punishments were determined upon
at Aschaffenburg (1291) for the imprisoning and mutilating
the clergy, which extended to the descendants of those
who had been guilty of such crimes.[3] In Germany ecclesiastical jurisdiction was in general more respected than in
other countries;[4] for the most part it was only the lesser territorial magnates and towns who interfered with it;[5] but in the
fifteenth century interference became more frequent and important, for which reason several Synods, such as those held at
Salzburg in 1420, Freising, 1440, and Mainz, 1549, protested
against it.[6] In the last period of the old German Empire the
circle of lay jurisdiction was enlarged at the expense of clerical
jurisdiction.[7] The strict Constitution drawn up by Martin V.[8]
against such extension of civil jurisdiction, from which even
causes of a purely ecclesiastical character were not exempted,
did not have the desired effect. Ecclesiastics, even those in the

highest positions in the Church, were constantly imprisoned by the civil power.[9]

[1] Friedrich II. 1220 (Pertz, iv. 244); his son Henry, 1234 (ib. p. 302); Rudolph I. 1281, 1287 (ib. pp. 429, 450); peace of 1495, &c. (apud Friedberg, p. 133, note 3).

[2] Hefele, Conc. vi. p. 221. In 1260 the Synod of Fritzler had for the archdiaconate in question prescribed a *cessatio a divinis* in such cases (ib. p. 53). Likewise did the Synods of Magdeburg, 1261, c. 6 seq.; of Cologne, 1266, c. 1, 18; of Vienna, 1267, c. 5; of Salzburg, 1291, c. 13 (ib. pp. 70, 77 seq. 89 seq. 195).

[3] C. 14, 15. Hefele, l.c. p. 248. Similarly in the Council of Mainz, 1261, c. 43 (ib. p. 66).

[4] Thomassin, P. ii. 1. iii. c. cxiii. n. 4.

[5] Friedberg, pp. 149, 150.

[6] Thomassin, l.c.

[7] Warnkönig, Die staatsrechtliche Stellung der Kath. Kirche, Erlangen, 1855, p. 109 seq.

[8] Martin V. Const. 10, Ad reprimandas, a. 1428.

[9] The canonist Pignatelli gives, together with several legal documents, details upon the imprisonment of Cardinal Clesel in 1618. Consultat. Canon. t. ii. Cons. 63, n. 16-30, p. 129 seq.

§ 4.

From the fourteenth century the spiritual jurisdiction in France was growing more contracted.[1] There also Synods had several struggles against the impediments raised by civil magistrates[2] to the exercise of spiritual justice, against the imprisonment of ecclesiastics,[3] against the difficulties or impediments made to the right of appeal to an ecclesiastical judge.[4] The *appel d'abus*[5]—appeal against the abuse of spiritual authority—was introduced, the clergy and even bishops were prosecuted by civil judges.[6] The jurists invented a distinction between the *common* and *privileged* criminal causes of the clergy; in cases of the former they were left to the jurisdiction of the Church, but in cases of the latter they were carried before a civil court. 'Their interpretation of the distinction, however, gradually led, to this, that all cases of discipline were declared to be "common transgressions," but all more grievous cases were to be treated as "privileged transgressions." At last the principle was reversed, and the so-called common law became the exception, and the privileged law became the rule.'[7] Several Synods, such as those of Rouen, 1581, Rheims, 1583, Bourges,

1584, and Narbonne, 1609, declared themselves emphatically in favour of ecclesiastical jurisdiction, and the edict published by desire of the clergy defended it against the innovations of civil magistrates.[8] That the civil courts should assist the spiritual courts in the execution of their sentences was still recognised in France in the seventeenth century, and was quite in accordance with earlier legislation.[9] The parliament, however, soon endeavoured to extend its cognisance to every judicial cause, even though purely spiritual, which resulted in great confusion and uncertainty.[10] As early as 1463, Charles VII. was obliged to see that the limits of parliamentary jurisdiction drawn up in the Pragmatic Sanction of 1438 were kept, and in the times that followed the French kings often had by new measures to oppose the arbitrary will of the parliament, which assumed everything to itself.[11]

[1] Thomassin, l.c. c. cxii. n. 7 seq.

[2] *E.g.* Council of Tours, 1282, c. 7; of Notre Dame du Pré near Rouen, 1313, c. 4-8 (Hefele, vi. 201 seq. 498).

[3] Council of Macon, 1286, c. 2; Council of Nogaret, 1290; Council of Marciac, 1326, c. 52 (Hefele, vi. pp. 211, 232 seq. 548).

[4] Council of Anse, 1300, c. 17 (Hefele, l.c. p. 399). Several Synods of the sixteenth century (apud Roscovány, Mon. t. i. pp. 173-180).

[5] 'From Peter de Cugnières French jurists date the proceedings on account of misuse of ecclesiastical authority, proceedings by which the judicial supremacy of the State over the Church was asserted' (Bluntschli, p. 73). Friedberg, p. 152, note 4, places the introduction at 1385. Cf. Altesema, op. cit. P. ii. l. viii. c. viii. seq. Affre, De l'Appel comme d'abus, Paris, 1845, defends, pp. 68-78, the view that this appeal first arose in 1438. Cf. p. 332, note 7.

[6] This was complained of at the fifth Council of the Lateran. Hard. Conc. ix. p. 1776. Cf. Thomassin, l.c. n. 12. As in England, bishops received the movable property of condemned ecclesiastics, and the king the immovable property (Ord. Phil. III. 1274, c. 5; Friedberg, p. 138).

[7] Bluntschli, pp. 67, 68.

[8] Thomassin, l.c. n. 14.

[9] Edict of Blois, 1610, art. 5: 'Les juges séculiers doivent prêter assistance et main forte à l'exécution des sentences des juges de l'Eglise, sans pour ce entrer en aucune connaissance des oppositions prétendues formées à leur dicte assistance requise.' Likewise the Ordonnance of 1629, art. 31, and others (apud Pey, vol. ii. p. 502 seq.).

[10] Cf. G. de Champagny, Recueil général du droit civ. ecclés. français, 2d ed. Paris, 1854, P. i.; Beidtel, Das Canonisches Recht, p. 200 seq., and elsewhere.

[11] Friedberg, in Dove's Ztschr. f. K.R. iii. pp. 85, 87 seq.

§ 5.

The personal immunity of the clergy was maintained longer in Spain and Italy than in other States; but there, as elsewhere, certain cases were recognised in which a civil judge might arrest an ecclesiastic, as, for instance, when taken *in flagranti.*[1] Here also Synods upheld independent jurisdiction of the clergy, and protested against its violation.[2] In the kingdom of Spain the civil power interfered in many spiritual judicial causes,[3] at the same time recognising ecclesiastical principles. Nevertheless, the tribunal of the Nunciature[4] was, with some restrictions, still recognised in the eighteenth century.[5] Conflicts were not wanting either here or in Italy.[6]

In many things the Church was very compliant; for instance, in 1741 great concessions were made to the Neapolitan Government.[7] The immunity enjoined by the Council of Trent was maintained by the Church against great misuse and violation of spiritual rights, and protected by spiritual punishments.[8] When it was violently and arbitrarily abolished by the Liberals without any previous consultation with the Holy See, then the Pope protested, and had a right to protest.[8]

[1] Thomassin, l.c. c. cxiii. n. 5 seq.

[2] *E.g.* Council of Milan, 1287, c. 7; of Bergamo, 1311, c. 13; of Padua, 1350, c. 11 (Hefele, vi. 226, 457, 603 seq.); Provincial Council of Naples, 1699, tit. 12 (Collectio Lacensis, vol. i. p. 236).

[3] Archiv f. Kath. K.R. vol. x. p. 23 seq.

[4] Ib. p. 80. It could not, however, take cognisance in the first instance to the prejudice of the ordinaries, nor proceed against the officials of the Inquisition. Pignatelli, Consult. Can. t. viii. Cons. 121, pp. 199, 200; Cons. 129, n. 9, p. 206.

[5] Concordat of 1737, art. 20 (Archiv, l.c. p. 211); Brief of March 26, 1771 (ib. vol. xi. pp. 875 seq. 895 seq.).

[6] Such arose especially with the Republics of Genoa and Venice, which brought ecclesiastics guilty of the so-called *delicta atrocia privilegiata* (according to the French theory) before the civil courts, and in many ways encroached upon ancient ecclesiastical privileges. An interesting opinion upon a similar decree is to be found apud Pignatelli, t. viii. Cons. 40, p. 61 seq. ed. 1688. The obligation of civil authority to lend the *brachium saeculare* to the Church was in general perfectly acknowledged. Carvajal, de Judiciis, disput. 2, 97, n. 76. Vultejus, de Judic. l. iii. c. xiii. Salcedo, Prax. Jud. c. cl. n. 9, 10. Gonzalez, in l. i. Decret. tit. 31, c. i. n. 18. Fagnan, in h.l.

⁷ Concordato di S. Santita col Regno di Napoli, 2 Guigno 1741, capo iii. 55.

⁸ Hansmann, Geschichte der päpstlichen Reservatfälle, pp. 170-189, gives much good material.

⁹ *E.g.* in New Granada. The Allocution of 27th September 1852 complained of it.

§ 6.

The majority of our contemporaries have no longer any liking for a special court to judge the clergy, because they no longer appreciate the importance of the clergy. The distinction between clergy and laity, so odious to many infidels, is like to that between rulers and subjects, teachers and learners.[1] The False Decretals were not needed to refer back this distinction to the authority of St. Peter;[2] it has existed from the earliest Christian times, as even learned Protestants, Bingham in particular, have authenticated.[3] Neither is it true that the clergy were only regarded as men of the spirit, and the laity only as men of the flesh; the Church had long rejected the Gnostic distinction between pneumatics and sarcics.

However bad a prince may be, still, in consideration of his office, he has a higher dignity than the best of his subjects. So it is also with priests; they are raised above the laity by reason of their sacerdotal dignity and the indelible character of their ordination; they alone administer the Sacraments; but by no means does it follow that good people who are not priests will have a lower position in the Kingdom of Heaven than bad priests. Those who think the high position of the clergy only 'spiritual pride' forget that Christ, the Head of the Church, according to Holy Scripture (Eph. i. 22; v. 23; Col. i. 18) appointed those and their successors to be His representatives to whom He said, 'As the Father hath sent Me, I also send you' (John xx. 21). There can be no pride in exercising a conferred power. The ecclesiastical system, founded as it is on Scripture and tradition, must be utterly rejected if reproaches such as these are to be made against the Catholic Church.[4] In consideration of the important duties of the priesthood, the exalted character of its mission and position, all nations looked upon it as natural and fitting that priests should be subject only to a tri-

bunal of their equals; in the priesthood they honoured the representatives of religion; they acknowledged such an arrangement
as in accordance with the will and laws of God.[5] If the civil
power appropriated anything belonging to the ecclesiastical, it
was looked upon as robbery and sacrilege.[6]

[1] Phillips, K.R. i. § 33, p. 276 seq. ·
[2] Bluntschli, l.c. in Sybel's Zeitschr. 1861, p. 54.
[3] Bingham, Antiquit. et Origin. Eccles. Lond. 1708, t. i. 1. ii. c. i. § 2.
Cf. also Rudelbach, Ztschr. für Ges. Luth. Theologie u. Kirche, 1845, ii.
p. 106 seq.; Guericke, Archäologie, § 7, p. 20 seq. The expressions are
well known (apud Clem. Rom. Ep. 1, ad Cor. c. xl.: ὁ λαικὸς ἄνθρωπος, apud
Orig. hom. 7 et 11, in Jerem.; Tert. de Praescr. c. xli.; Clem. Strom. vi.
p. 793, ed. Oxon.; Paed. iii. 12). Cf. Thomassin, P. i. 1. i. c. li-liii.
[4] The election of some to spiritual dignities by no means implies the
reprobation of all others. Aug. Civ. Dei, l. vii. c. i.: 'Et cum eliguntur
in Ecclesia, qui fiant praepositi, non utique ceteri reprobantur, cum omnes
boni fideles electi merito nuncupentur. Eliguntur in aedificio lapides an-
gulares, non reprobatis ceteris, qui structurae partibus aliis deputantur.
Eliguntur uvae ad vescendum, nec reprobantur aliae, quas relinquimus ab
bibendum. Non opus est multa percurrere, cum res in aperto sit.' The
general interior priesthood of all Christians, as the Scripture teaches it
(1 Pet. ii. 5, 9; Apoc. v. 10; xx. 6; Exod. xix. 6), is also acknowledged by
the Church (Aug. de Civ. Dei, xx. 10; cf Const. Ap. iii. 15), but is as
little as under the old law in opposition to the particular exterior priesthood.
[5] Cf. Hirschel, in the Archiv f. K.R. 1862, vol. vii. p. 202 seq. Cf.
also Schneemann, in the Laacher Stimmen über die Encyclica, vii. p. 73
seq. § 82 seq.
[6] Petr. Bles. in Dial. inter Henric. II. Reg. et Abbat. Bonevallis,
p. 984: 'Rapina, imo sacrilegium est, quidquid in rebus ecclesiasticis
potestas civilis usurpat.'

§ 7.

Those who attack the extension of ecclesiastical jurisdiction
over the laity overlook the facts : (1) that in general this jurisdiction over the laity existed only in ecclesiastical causes;[1] (2)
that the Church has very often exerted a salutary influence on
the interests of the State, and by so doing has earned for herself a right of jurisdiction, not only in civil[2] but also in criminal
matters.[3] The Church was the first to legislate against several
grave violations of morality, and the State laws were only due
to her influence and example.[4] The Church refined the rude

notions of law, raised the State on a Christian foundation, and imbued it with Christian principles.

' When otherwise it was only founded upon custom and particular circumstances, and the clergy were forbidden to encroach upon the domain of the civil judges. Conc. Later. iv. c. 42 : ' Sicut volumus, ut jura clericorum non usurpent laici, ita velle debemus, ne clerici jura sibi vindicent laicorum. Quocirca universis clericis interdicimus, ne quis praetextu ecclesiasticae libertatis suam de cetero jurisdictionem extendat in praejudicium justitiae saecularis, sed contentus existat constitutionibus scriptis et consuetudinibus hactenus approbatis, ut quae sunt Caesaris, reddantur Caesari, et quae sunt Dei, Deo recta distributione reddantur.'

² Mittermaier, Grunds. des deutschen Privatrechts, 7th ed. i. p. 43.

³ ' The jurisdiction of the Church in criminal matters,' says Abegg (Die verschiedenen Strafrechtstheorien, pp. 106-108), ' has had especially in the Middle Ages a substantial importance and a beneficial influence upon the State and legislation. In its results it must still be acknowledged and not set aside with the remark that its theocratic character makes it no longer useful to us.'

⁴ ' The Synod of Montpellier, 1195, c. 3, found it necessary to oblige the bishops to engage civil rulers under threat of excommunication to take steps against bands of robbers and pirates. Mansi, xii. 668 ; Hefele, v. p. 672. It follows from Innocent III. (Const. 12, Ad liberandam terram sanctam, Bull. M. i. 62), that civil potentates often through negligence, often even from a secret understanding, favoured robbery and piracy. Civil authority was especially slow in punishing acts of violence against ecclesiastics, for it often committed them itself ; the Church was therefore obliged to help herself as she could (Hausmann, l.c. p. 104).

§ 8.

Ecclesiastical right of sanctuary, originally acknowledged by all[1] and resolutely defended by the bishops,[2] was attacked in course of time, when it was found not to fit with the new ideas of the functions and power of the State. The Popes have acceded to the request of rulers in granting limitations for particular countries, to suit the exigences of the times.[3] Gregory XVI. is much blamed for having withdrawn concessions made on this point by several of his predecessors.[4]

The accusation is specially directed against the Bull ' Cum alias' of 1591.[5] The principal object of the Bull was to meet the evils which had arisen on account of differences in the concessions granted by Pius V. and Sixtus V., and it met them completely, partly by following the old canon law and partly by extending its limits.[6] In spite of the opposition of some Italian governments, which, however, was soon withdrawn,[7] it was accepted by the faithful with universal joy and satisfaction.[8] It is quite untrue that by Gregory's Bull murder was only to be refused right of sanctuary when it had been committed in a consecrated place.[9] In this, as in all her jurisdiction, the Church has always complied with well-grounded remonstrances of governments. The restrictions laid upon the right of sanctuary in the States of the Church since the time of Gregory XIV. were in 1737 extended to Spain by Clement XII., and in 1741 and 1742 to Naples and Sardinia.[10] Clement XIV. limited it still more in certain countries at the request of the governments.

[1] Cod. Theod. ix. 45, c. i. iv. vi. Thomassin, P. ii. l. iii. c. xcv. xcvi.

[2] *In the East*, vide Neander, Chrysostomus, ii. p. 71 seq.; Vita S. Tarassii (of Epl.), c. vi. n. 25-27 (Migne, PP. gr. xcviii. p. 1403 seq.); Phot. Ep. 4, p. 68, ed. Montac.; Theod. Stud. l. ii. Ep. 202; Nicol. Mystic. Ep. 3, ad Simeon. Bulg. pp. 170-175, ed. Mai. *In the West*, vide Council of Carthago, 399; of Orange, 441, c. 5; of Orleans, 511, c. 1; Epaon, 517, c. 39; of Lerida (between 524-546), c. 8; of Orleans (iv.), 541, c. 21 (Hefele, ii. pp. 65. 276, 643, 666, 686, 760); of Clermont, 549, c. 22; Macon, 585, c. 8; Rheims, 624, 625, c. 7; Toledo, 681, c. 10; ib. xvi. 693, c. 5; Paderborn, 785, c. 2; Mainz, 813, c. 39 (Hefele, iii. pp. 5, 37, 70, 289, 319, 593. 710); and others. Thomassin, P. ii. l. iii. c. c.

[3] Innoc. III. c. 6, Inter alia, iii. 49, de Immun. Eccl. (ad reg. Scot.). Gregor. IX. c. 10, Immunitatem, h.t. Julius II. ap. Raynald. a. 1504, n. 35.

[4] Huber, p. 55.

[5] Constit. 17, Bullar. t. v. P. i. p. 271. There was at one time a controversy whether the Bull was published only for Italy or for the whole Church; the majority of canonists decided with good reason in favour of the latter view. Schmalzgrueber, in l. iii. tit. 49, § 2, n. 96-98.

[6] Bened. XIV. Instit. Eccles. instit. 41, § 4, p. 286, ed. Ingolst. 1751 : 'Cum Romani Pontifices, ac praesertim S. Pius V. et Sixtus V. petentibus principibus indulserint, ab Ecclesia eos quoque divelli, qui criminibus per leges minime cantis tenebantur, et cum maxima rerum perturbatio ex hoc dimanaverit, Gregorius XIV. literas apostolicas promulgavit, quibus concessiones principum gratia . . . . obsignatas abrogavit . . . . partim veteres canones secutus, partim ipsorum terminos *extendens*.' Cf. de Syn. Dioec. l. xiii. c. xviii. n. 12, 13.

[7] Pignatelli, Consult. Canon. t. vi. Cons. 4, n. 59 seq. p. 19 seq., gives several documents. The Congregation of the Immunities, on 10 May 1667 and 4 Sept. 1668, maintained the authority of the Bull in opposition to the reclamations raised concerning it by the senate of Milan

(2 July 1666), and by the royal council of Spain (15 April 1667). Especial faculties were granted in 1652 and 1668 to the nuncios of Florence and Naples with reference to the easier *extractio reorum.*

* It belonged, as Clement XIV. in a Constitution published for Spain (Const. 200, Ea semper, Bull. Rom. Contin. t. iv. p. 488 seq.) says, like the following of Benedict. XIII. (Const. 73, Ex quo divina, 15 June 1725, Bull. t. xii. p. 1), Clement XII. (Const. 171, In supremo, 1735, Bull. t. xiv. p. 17 ; t. xv. ed. Lux. pp. 14-18), and Benedict XIV. (Const. 29, Officii, 1750, Bull. Bened. XIV. t. iii. p. 160, ed. Ven. 1754), to those ' quae omnibus Christi fidelibus collaudantibus et plaudentibus in lucem prodierunt.'

* The Bull excludes from the right of sanctuary ' publici latrones, grassatores viarum, agrorum depopulatores, committentes homicidium in ecclesia *vel homicidium proditorium*' (this means every kind of assassination), ' assassini, rei laesae majestatis, haerescos,' &c.

¹⁰ Archiv f. Kath. K.R. vol. xi. p. 377 seq.

§ 9.

Janus has (p. 13) referred in the vaguest manner to art. 8 of the Concordat of 1863, drawn up 'with the free States of South America' according to which civil courts have to execute *every* punishment decreed by spiritual judges, *without any power of refusal.* I drew attention (*Anti-Janus*, p. 23) to the fact that no such article was to be found in those Concordats addressed to the different South American States with the text of which I was acquainted. I still maintain the same, after the explanation given (Huber, p. 76 seq.), that the Concordat concluded in 1863 with the Republic of Ecuador was the one *specially* referred to ; and that the *Revue des Deux Mondes,* not always to be trusted in such matters, was the source whence the statements concerning arts. 1, 3, 4, 8, 10, 11 were derived. As a matter of fact, the Concordat was concluded with the Republic of Ecuador on September 26, 1862, and, on the exchange of documents, was ratified in Quito, April 19. 1863. The remaining articles nowise differ from other conventions. Article 8 is the only one of special interest, but it does not, as *Janus* says it does, treat of the execution of *every* punishment decreed by spiritual jurisdiction, but only of such as were pronounced on *ecclesiastics,* and it was rendered necessary by the excesses of some of the undisciplined clergy of the country.¹ The government of the republic, which entered into detailed negotiations on this subject, was perfectly satisfied ; it was by

no means in its interest entirely to abolish the legal competence
of spiritual courts over the criminal causes of the clergy. The
day on which Cardinal Antonelli and the ambassador Ordonnez
signed the convention, the former gave four explanatory notes
to the latter, which were regarded on both sides as an integral
addition to the Concordat; two of these relate to spiritual penal
jurisdiction over the clergy.[2]   They are, like the entire convention, a sure token of the way in which the Holy See is ready
to meet the reasonable wishes of governments, and to make,
when it appears necessary, still greater concessions, as in Italy
earlier; for example, the Concordat with Tuscany, of 25th April
1851, by which the civil and ecclesiastical causes of ecclesiastics
were made over to lay jurisdiction,[3] which was also conceded to
many other countries.[4]

[1] The article runs : ' Omnes *ecclesiasticae* causae et praesertim matri-
moniales atque illae, quae respiciunt fidem, sacramenta, mores, sacras func-
tiones, officia et sacra jura tum personae tum materiae ratione, exceptis majoribus causis summo Pontifici reservatis ex S. Concilii Tridentini prae-
scriptis Sess. xxiv. c. 5, de reform. ad tribunalia ecclesiastica erunt unice
deferenda.   Idem erit servandum *in civilibus causis ecclesiasticorum* atque
in aliis causis, *quae delicta respiciant* comprehensa in criminali reipublicae codice.   In omnibus judiciis quae ad judices pertinent ecclesiasticos,
civilis magistratus omnem opem auxiliumque feret, ut sententiae ac poenae
ab ipsis judicibus latae observentur et executioni mandentur.'   There is
nothing in the text about ' no power of refusing.'

[2] The first note says : ' Coll' articolo 8 si è dichiarata et confermata
l'existenza del foro ecclesiastico per le cause si civile che criminali dei
Chierici.   A rendere per altro più efficace l' azione della giustizia punitiva
ed a prevenire la rinuovazione di scandali, che, provenendo da ecclesiastici,
sarebbero di pessimo esempio ai fedeli, V. Ecc. ha domandato, che si pren-
dano dalla S. Sede le opportune provvidenze, onde i processi e i giudizii del
foro ecclesiastico siano condotti a termine nel più breve spazio di tempo
ed in piena conformità alle leggi canoniche, come pure che si dichiarino
decaduti dal privilegio del foro eccl., sia civile sia criminale, tutti quei
chierici, i quali se rendono recidivi negli stessi delitti punibili secondo le
leggi dello Stato, e che a tale effetto debbano essere giudicati dal foro
laico.   A dichiarare poi la recidiva, la Ecc. V. propone che basti provare
innanzi ai tribunali dello Stato, che il Chierico commise lo stesso delitto
dentro lo spazio degli ultimi dodici mesi.   Riconoscendo il santo Padre le
giuste ragioni, che muovono il governo dell' Equatore a fare la suespressa
domanda, ha ordinato al sottoscritto di dichiarare a V. Ecc., come andrà
quanto prima a dirigere una lettera enciclica a tutti i vescovi dell' Equatore, imponendo loro di dar corso con ogni precisione e di conchiudere nel
più breve spazio di tempo tutti i processi, sia civili, sia criminali, dei

Chierici in piena conformità delle disposizioni canoniche ; ed al tempo stesso S. Santità condiscende che gli Ecclesiastici recidivi, giusta il senso da ›. E. indicato, siano privati per punizione del privilegio del foro, accordando le opportune facoltà, onde i giudici possano applicare loro le pene imposte dai ss. canoni, qualora per alcuni delitti, come di ubbriachezza, concubinato, mercatura ed altri simili, non si faccia menzione nel codice criminale dello Stato.'

The second note says : 'Il sotto scritto Card..... ha l' onore di accusare la nota in data di oggi, nella quale V. E. ha dichiarato che se nelle cause civili come nelle criminali per delitti contemplati nel codice penale della nazione .... per gravi ragioni e per ispeciali circonstanze fosse necessaria una modificazione o deroga al privilegio del foro, il governo dell' Equatore non prenderà provvidenza alcuna in proposito, senza averne preventivamente riportato il consenso della Santa Sede, la quale condiscenderà ad un amichevole accomodamento giusta il bisogno. Se frattanto nel caso di qualsiasi delitto politico fosse mestieri prendere misura contro gli Ecclesiastici delinquenti, il governo invocherà la debita autorizzazione del prelato diocesano per procedere contro gli ecclesiastici a' termini delle leggi vigenti. Quando occorresse assicurarsi del reo, l' arresto dovrà farsi con le cautele e riguardi dovuti all' eccellenza dello stato clericale ; ed i luoghi di prigionia saranno sempre i conventi o altri luoghi ecclesiastici, o se non altro luoghi distinti dalle pubbliche prigioni. Infine quando si tratti di sentenza, che importa la pena capitale, si osserveranno le prescrizioni canoniche.'

³ Art. 6 says : 'La S. Sede *consente*, che le cause *civili* risguardanti le persone ed i beni degli ecclesiastici, del pari che quelle che riguardano attivamente e passivamente il patrimonio della Chiesa e della causa Pia vengano deferite ai tribunali laici.' Art. 10: 'La S. Sede *non fa difficoltà*, che le cause *criminali* degli ecclesiastici per tutti i delitti contemplati dalle leggi criminali dello Stato, estranei alla religione, vengano deferite al giudizio dei tribunali laici, liquali applicano loro le pene dalle leggi stesse prescritte, che subiranno in locali separati ed ad essi specialmente destinati negli stabilimenti penali.'

⁴ Bavarian Concordat, 1817, art. 12. lit. c.; Neapolitan Concordat, 1818, art. 20; Convention with Sardinia of March 27, 1841, on criminal jurisdiction over the clergy (Annali delle Scienze religiose, t. xii. p. 420); Convention with Costa Rica of October 7, 1852, art. 14, 15 (Acta Pii IX. vol. i. p. 457); with Guatemala, cod. d. art. 15, 16 (ib. pp. 515, 516) ; with Austria, August 18, 1855, art. 13, 14 (ib. ii. pp. 470, 471); with Würtemberg, April 8, 1857, art. 5 (ib. p. 597), &c.

§ 10.

It is indeed said, although concessions have been made in consideration of the circumstances of the time, the right to take another course in altered circumstances has also not been given up. But so long as the circumstances remain unaltered the agreement holds good; and if it was made originally in the form of a treaty, a new negotiation is required for any alteration. How much soever the conduct of the Austrian government might have justified the Pope in cancelling the concessions granted in the Concordat of August 15, 1855, he has certainly not cancelled them. Moreover, the Church is without the material power necessary to regain her former jurisdiction; her servants are everywhere forced to be content if laws are not made in their disfavour, and if the sanctity of religious life, faith, and worship is not violated by the rude intrusion of the civil magistrate.

ESSAY XVI.

THE PUNISHMENT OF HERESY AND THE INQUISITION.

CRUELTY towards other religions, manifested chiefly in the Inquisition, is one of the current objections raised against the Church and the Papacy. Trials for witchcraft also are imputed to some Popes as a heavy charge. *Janus* and Huber both connect the doctrine of Infallibility with the Inquisition, as though the one were supported by the other. Let us examine these objections.

PART I. THE PUNISHMENT OF HERESY.

§ 1.

Offences against religion, namely, apostasy and heresy, were in the early ages of Christianity reckoned amongst the gravest crimes.[1] The Roman Empire, converted to Christianity, could not do otherwise than share this view of the Church, and rigorously repress the spread of errors, by which the peace of the empire also was menaced. As the Donatists, after the Synods of Rome and Arles, as well as after their trial by Constantine, did not submit, but persisted in their defiant demeanour and deeds of violence, the emperor issued in 316 a severe edict, depriving them of their churches, confiscating their property, and banishing the most stubborn of their leaders.[2] After the Council of Nicæa, in 325, he pronounced banishment upon Arius and two bishops of his party.[3] Further, the immunities of the clergy were limited to Catholics, heretical assemblies were forbidden, heretical writings sought out and destroyed.[4] Theodosius I. published an edict, in which he threatened heretics, required from all his subjects an acknowledgment of the Nicene Creed,[5] deprived the Arians in Constantinople of their churches, which he gave to Catholics,[6] and in 381 forbade heretics from possessing churches or holding divine worship in the cities.[7]

Laws still more severe were subsequently enacted against the Manichæans, against whom an edict had been issued by the Emperor Diocletian, A.D. 296, on account of their excesses and their immoral doctrines,[8] condemning their leaders to be burnt and the followers to decapitation or loss of property.[9] Theodosius declared the Manichæans to be infamous, to be incapable of inheriting or of making wills; those amongst them who were called Encratets to be punished with death.[10] The prætorian prefects should appoint *inquisitors*—the name first appears here —to discover and prosecute them.[11] Heretics were forbidden to hold assemblies, and to impart or receive holy orders, under penalty of a fine. These laws were followed by many others: heretics, especially Donatists and Manichæans, were declared incapable of holding public offices or enjoying civil rights.[12]

---

[1] The Apostles and their disciples clearly expressed their horror of heresy : 2 Tim. ii. 25 seq.; Tit. iii. 10, 11; Gal. i. 8; 1 Tim. i. 19; 2 Thess. ii. 11; Can. Ap. 38, al. 36, Ant. c. xx. (Hefele, i. pp. 786, 499.) Vide passages in Möhler's Patrologie von Reithmayr, pp. 116, 135, 141, 301, 456, 483, 610; Basil. Ep. 28, ad Neocaes. c. ii. p. 108. Cf. Döllinger, Christenthum und Kirche, § 121, p. 236.

[2] Aug. Ep. 88, ad Januar. n. 3; Ep. 93, ad Vincent. c. lit. Petil. l. ii. n. 205, Optat. de Schism. Don. l. ii. p. 47, ed. Paris, 1679. Fleury, Hist. Eccl. t. iii. l. x. n. 19. Thomassin, Traité des Edits, t. i. c. xi.

[3] The Arians were to be called Porphyrians, and their works to be burnt. Philostorg. Suppl. p. 539, ed. Mogunt, 1679. Socr. H. E. i. 9. Soz. i. 21.

[4] Cod. Theod. xvi. tit. 5, l. 1, 2, 43, 65. Eus. Vita Const. l. iii. c. lxiii-lxvi. Fleury, t. iii. l. ii. n. 31, 46. Thomassin, l.c. c. xxx. Cf. Basilic. l. i. tit. 1, n. 22 seq.

[5] Cod. Theod. xvi. 1, de Fide Cath. l. i. ii.

[6] Socr. v. 7; Soz. vii. 5.

[7] Cod. Theodos. xvi. 5, de Haeret. l. vi. Cf. Fleury, t. iv. l. xviii. n. 9.

[8] Aug. de Mor. Manich. Cf. Bossuet, Hist. des Variations, l. xi. n. 7.

[9] Baron. a. 287, n. 1. Hugo, Jus civile antejustin. Berol. 1815, t. ii. p 1463. Ambrosiaster, in 2 Tim. iii. 7. Cf. Neander, K.G. i. pp. 79, 278, 3d ed.

[10] Cod. Theod. l.c. l. vii. ix. Cf. Cod. Just. i. v. l. 5.

[11] He said: 'Sublimitas itaque tua det *inquisitores*, aperiat forum, indices denunciatoresque *sine invidia delationis* accipiat, nemo praescriptione communi exordium accusationis hujus infringat.'

[12] Cod. Theod. l.c. l. xlii. seq. xii. xxi. Soz. vii. 12. Cod. Justin. i. 5, de Haeret. l. ii. iii. iv.

§ 2.

The Emperor Theodosius II. sent Nestorius into banishment;[1] the Emperor Marcian was not less severe upon Eutyches and his followers; they were declared incapable of making wills or of inheriting, or of entering the army (except for frontier service); their clergy were banished, their books burnt, and the authors and distributors punished with loss of goods and banishment.[2]

Justinian, who incorporated in his code many of these more ancient laws, followed the example of earlier emperors in regarding heretics as transgressors of the law of the State, since the State law recognised and enforced the judgments of the Church; he confirmed the penalties of loss of honour and rights, banishment and loss of goods, for heretics of both sexes.[3] All provincial rulers should swear never to act in any way contrary to the Catholic Church, and hinder with all their strength the enterprises of her adversaries.[4] Equally severe were the laws against apostasy and sacrilege.[5] As early as 435 death was the penalty decreed for those who led others to adopt the errors of any sect.[6] These laws were accepted also by the Visigoths,[7] in Spain,[8] England,[9] and other countries.

[1] Mansi, v. 413, 418. Evagr. H. E. l. i. c. xii.

[2] Mansi, vii. 475 seq. 502 seq. Cod. Just. l.c. l. viii. Hefele, Conc. ii. p. 536 seq.

[3] Cod. Justin. l.c. l. xix.

[4] Liberat. Brev. c. xxiii. Fleury, t. vii. l. xxxiii. n. 1, post Justin. Novell. 8.

⁵ Cod. Justin. i. tit. 7.   Cf. Dig. xlviii. 13, l. vi. ix.
⁶ Cod. Justin. i. 5, l. v.   Thomassin, l.c. c. xxx. n. 2, 3.   Jac. Gothofred.
Proleg. ad Cod. Theodos. c. iii.   Canciani, Barbár. Leg. Ant. t. i. Praef.
p. 13.   Savigny, Gesch. des Röm. Rechts, vol. i. c. iii. seq.
⁷ Lex Visigoth. l. xii. tit. 2, § 2.
⁸ Conc. Tolet. vi. 636, c. 3; viii. 653, c. 10.   Hefele, iii. pp. 83, 92.
⁹ Beda Vener. Hist. Eccl. Angl. l. i. c. xxi.

§ 3.

We must be aware of the immense importance attained by the Roman law properly to estimate the principles upon which heretics were persecuted for over a thousand years, and the proceedings taken against them. Even jurists regarded heresy as an offence against civil society: ' What is done against the divine religion is an injury done to all.'[1] It was a graver crime than high treason : ' Far more grievous is it to offend the heavenly than an earthly king.'[2] In these days crimes against earthly kings are punished with extremest penalties, but crimes against the Majesty of God are punished scarcely or not at all, and blasphemy, once a capital offence, is disregarded ;[3] and it is very difficult for a mind imbued with these ideas to estimate at their proper value, or in any degree, these ancient laws, once approved universally, and esteemed of undoubted necessity.

[1] ' Quod in religionem divinam committitur, in omnium fertur injuriam.' Theodos. ii. 407, l. iv.   Cod. Just. i. 5, de Haeret.
[2] ' Longe gravius aeternam, quam temporalem majestatem offendere.' Auth. de Statu et Cens. post l. xix. l.c. ; repeatedly in c. x. de Haer. v. 7 (Innoc. III. l. ii. Ep. 1).
[3] Levit. xxiv. 16.   Just. Nov. 77, c. i.

§ 4.

Besides the codes of Theodosius and Justinian, the doctrine of St. Augustine had great influence. The great Bishop of Hippo was at one time adverse to the adoption of severe measures against heretics and schismatics, especially against Donatists ; but he tells us that he was led, from weighty reasons, from personal experience, and from the representations of his fellow-bishops, entirely to change his opinion.[1] The reasons that led to the change were the following : (1) The con-

sideration of the necessity for all to be members of the true
Church, a happiness outweighing all others, and which made it
of the greatest advantage to be able even to bring up the children
of Donatists in the true faith ; (2) the reflection that men are
often brought to a better mind by external means, such as
suffering, and are by it prepared for, and made more receptive
of, truth ; that by paternal chastisements they are more easily
led to obedience ; that when teaching fails a wise schoolmaster
employs force, and that when love is ineffectual fear may operate
for good, as God draws His perishing creatures to Him by sorrow.[c] (3) A third reason was the violence and outrages perpetrated
by the Circumcellionists, who constantly threatened the Catholics
of Africa with murder, fire, and rapine, and compelled them to
seek the protection of the State, which was an absolute necessity
to them, and one that could not be refused.[3] (4) Fourthly, there
was also the consideration that the State punished murder,
adultery, and other crimes, and could not, therefore, if it desired
to be Christian, leave unpunished the far graver crimes against
God.[4]

The same views are stated by St. Jerome,[5] by Leo the Great,[6]
Gregory the Great,[7] Isidore of Seville,[8] St. Bernard,[9] and others.[10]

[1] Aug. Retract. ii. 5 : 'Et vere tunc mihi non placebat, quia nondum
expertus fueram, vel quantum mali anderet impunitas vel quantum eis in
melius mutandis conferre posset diligentia disciplinae.' Ep. 93, al. 48, ad
Vincent. n. 17 : ' Mea primitus sententia non erat nisi neminem ad unitatem Christi esse cogendum, verbo esse agendum, disputatione pugnandum,
ratione vincendum, ne fictos Catholicos haberemus, quos apertos haereticos
noveramus. Sed haec opinio mea non contradicentium verbis, sed demon-
strantium superabatur exemplis. Nam primo mihi opponebatur civitas
mea, quae, cum tota esset in parte Donati, ad unitatem Catholicam timore
legum imperialium conversa est. . . . . Ita aliae multae, quae mihi nomi-
natim commemorabantur' (c. 3, § 1, c. xxiii. q. 6).
[2] Aug. c. lit. Petil. l. ii. n. 185 ; Ep. 185, ad Bonif. n. 21 ; de Civ.
Dei, l. xix. c. 16, v. fin.; Ep. 51, ad Macedon. (c. 4, c. xxiii. q. 5).
[3] Ep. ad Vincent. cit. n. 12, 16, c. Gaudent. l. i. c. xxiii. ; Ep. cit. ad
Bonif. n. 6 (c. 1, c. xxiii. q. 6) : ' Cur non cogeret Ecclesia perditos filios,
ut redirent, si perditi filii coegerunt alios, ut perirent ?' Other passages,
vide c. 2, 3, c. xxiii. q. 3, and c. 1, 2, cad. c. q. 5.
[4] C. Gaud. i. 20 ; ii. 19, c. Ep. Parmen. i. 16 ; Ep. 105, al. 166 ; tract.
11 in Joh.; Ep. 185 cit. : ' An fidem non servare levius est animam Deo
quam feminam vero ?'

[5] Hier. Com. in Gal. v. 8, Opp. vii. 489, ed. Vall. Gratian, c. 16, c. xxiv. q. 3.

[6] Ep. ad Rip. c. Vigil. 109, n. 3 (c. 13, c. xxiii. q. 8) : 'Non est crudelitas, crimina pro Deo punire, sed pietas.'

[7] Greg. M. l. i. Ep. 74. Gennadio Patr. (c. 48, c. xxiii. q. 4), Ep. 75, Opp. ii. 558, ed. Paris, 1705. Mansi, ix. 1078 seq. Jaffé, n. 778 seq. Cf. l. ii. Ep. 48, Mansi, ix. 1102, J. n. 835 (against the Donatists in Africa) ; l. iv. Ep. 34, Mansi, p. 1178, J. n. 839 (against the same) ; l. v. Ep. 8, Mansi, p. 1189, J. n. 957 (against the Manichæans in Sicily).

[8] Isidor. Hispal. Sent. iii. 51, 53 (c. 20, c. xxiii. q. 5).

[9] Bernard. serm. 76, in Cantic. n. 12 : ' Melius procul dubio gladio coercentur, illius videl. qui *non sine causa gladium portat*, quam in suum errorem multos trajicere permittantur. *Dei* enim *minister* ille est, *vindex in iram ei qui male agit.*'

[10] The general proposition of Petrus Dam. (Opusc. lvii. p. 819 seq. ed. Migne) is accepted by most : ' Inordinata sane pietas nutrit impietatem et timida manus medici vulnus auget aegroti. Facit enim exuberare putredinem, dum non secando, sed palpando quotidie superducit vulnusculo cicatricem.' Petrus Bles. (Ep. 113, p. 341) admonishes Archbishop Gaufried of York to combat heretics, saying : ' Accite clerum, congregate populum, ut ex eorum communi deliberatione, qui spiritum Dei habent, terribilis constitutio in vestra provincia promulgetur, quatenus tam gravi animadversione plectantur, qui hac peste laborant, ut ex eorum poena ceteri terreantur.' Peter the Venerable (tract. c. Petrobrus, p. 721) says to the French bishops : ' Vestrum est, et a locis illis, in quibus (haeresis) se latibula invenisse gaudet, et praedicatione, et etiam, si necesse fuerit, vi armata per laicos exturbare.'

§ 5.

Many Fathers are cited as having differed on various grounds from the doctrine of St. Augustine, which was incorporated in Gratian's decretal with other similar passages. Reference is made chiefly to St. Ambrose of Milan and St. Martin of Tours, who seriously disapproved of the presence of Bishop Ithacus and other prelates at the execution of the heretic Priscillian in 385.[1] But the clemency befitting the episcopal dignity would forbid a bishop from desiring the blood of evildoers, or from conducting an execution.[2] St. Augustine and St. Leo the Great were both opposed to this,[3] and it was forbidden by several Councils[4] and by the mediæval law.[5] St. Ambrose was of one accord with St. Augustine concerning the justice of punishing heresy, and clearly expressed his opinion.[6] It was the same thing with other Fathers.

[1] Sulpic. Severi Chron. ii. 50, p. 103 seq. Dial. ii. (iii.) 11-13, p. 208

seq. ed. Vindob. 1866. Ambros. Ep. 24, ad Valent.; Ep. 26, ad Iren. Cf. Neander, K.G. i. p. 813 seq.; and also J. Bernays, Ueber die Chronik des Sulpicius Severus, Berlin, 1861, p. 5 seq.

² Sulpic. Sev. l.c. p. 104 : ' Ithacius videns, quam invidiosum sibi apud episcopos foret, si accusator etiam postremis rerum capitalium judiciis astitisset.' Before (p. 103) Sulpicius says : ' Quorum (Idacii et Ithacii) studium super expugnandis haereticis non reprehenderem, si non studio vincendi plus quam oportuit certassent.'

³ Aug. Ep. ad Marcellin. 158, 159 (can. 1, 2, c. xxiii. q. 5). Leo M. Ep. 15, ad Turrib.

⁴ E.g. Conc. Tolet. xi. c. 6 (c. 30, c. xxiii. q. 8).

⁵ Innoc. III. (in Conc. Lat. iv. c. 18 ; Hefele, v. 792), c. 9, Sententiam, iii. 50, Ne clerici vel monachi. Cf. c. 13, Per venerabilem, iv. 17, Qui filii sint legitimi, § Tria quippe.

⁶ Ambros. de Fide, ad Gratian. c. vi.

§ 6.

But it is further objected, that many Fathers and writers of the Church have condemned all external pressure in matters of religion.¹ This is in a certain sense true ; but a great distinction has always been made between those who have never had the faith² and those who having received baptism have sinned against it. The Church has no authority over the former (1 Cor. v. 12), who must not and never might be forced into belief.³ This is the doctrine of St. Augustine,⁴ of all theologians and canonists, and even of the later Popes.⁵ With regard to the latter class, those who have received baptism, if they break their vows, if they neglect the duties they undertook at baptism, if they mislead others, being still subject to the Church, though in rebellion against her, cannot be treated like the unbaptised. The Church and the Catholic State still have authority over them.⁶ A rebel does not cease to be a subject because he in bold insolence renounces obedience, and attacks the State with all the means and weapons at his disposal. It is the right and the duty of the government to reduce this refractory member to obedience.⁷ The words of Pope Nicholas I., ' God desires only voluntary obedience,' refer to the enforced conversion of the heathen, with regard to whom St. Bernard⁸ and later Popes⁹ have expressed the same principle. In the Middle Ages the principle was always held sacred that no one should be forced into belief ; but

at the same time the right was maintained of punishing the
apostasy of those who had believed.[10]

[1] Huber (p. 20) appeals (without exact references) to Tertullian (he
must mean lib. ad Scapulam, c. ii.), to Lactantius (he must mean Inst. Div.
l. v. c. xiv.), and Athanasius. The words of the latter, Θεοσεβείας ἴδιον
μὴ ὀναγκάζειν, ἀλλὰ πείθειν (Hist. Arian. ad Monach. n. 67 ; Migue, xxv.
p. 773), are universally accepted. Many other similar passages could be
quoted from the Fathers.

[2] Lactantius speaks of these when he says : 'Non enim nos illicimus,
ut ipsi objectant, sed docemus, probamus, ostendimus. Itaque nemo a
nobis retinetur invitus ; inutilis est enim Deo qui devotione et fide caret.'
Natal. Alex. (H. E. saec. 13 et 14, diss. 3, art. 1, n. 11, t. xvi. p. 36 seq.)
expresses himself in full concerning Tertullian. To these may be added
Cassiodor. Var. ii. 27 : 'Religionem imperare non possumus, quia nemo
cogitur, ut credat invitus.'

[3] Conc. Tolet. iv. c. 56 (c. 5, d. 45).

[4] Aug. c. lit. Petil. ii. 83 (c. 33, c. xxiii. q. 5) : '*Ad fidem* nullus est
cogendus invitus, sed per severitatem, imo et per misericordiam Dei tri-
bulationum flagellis solet *perfidia* castigari.' Cf. tract. 20, in Joh. n. 2.

[5] S. Thom. Sum. 2, 2, q. 10, a. 8 : 'Infideles, qui numquam fidem ha-
buerunt, non vi compellendi, sed ii, qui quandoque fidem susceperunt.
Accipere fidem est voluntatis, sed tenere eam susceptam necessitatis.'
Cf. q. 11, a. 3. Gonzalez, in c. Ad abolendam, v. 7, de Haeret. n. 14.
Gregor. de Valentia, Com. Theol. t. iii. disp. i. q. 10, punct. 6, p. 526.
Card. Petra, t. iii. p. 3 seq. Benedict. XIV. ad Episc. Polon. 8 Aug. 1748
(Bull. M. Rom. xvii. 272, ed. Coquel.). Clemens III. 1190, says (c. 9, de
Judaeis, v. 6) : 'Statuimus, ut nullus invitos vel nolentes Judaeos ad bap-
tismum venire compellat.'

[6] Cf. on this point the Brief of Pius VI. of 10 March 1791, where, after
St. Thomas, quotations are made from Tertull. Scorp. c. ii. n. 15, Aug.
Ep. 93, ad Vincent., Ep. 185, ad Bonif. (Opp. ii. 237, 652, ed. Maur.), and
Benedict XIV. de Beatif. et Canon. l. iii. c. xvii. n. 13. Also Bellarm. de
Membr. Eccl. iii. 21 ; Suarez, de. Leg. l. iv. c. xix. n. 2 ; Petra, l.c.
p. 249.

[7] We shall speak later of the application of this principle to modern
times.

[8] Bern. serm. 66, in Cant. : 'Quia fides suadenda est, non impo-
nenda.'

[9] Innoc. III.1. ii. Ep. 191, p. 739, ad Christifid. in Saxonia et West-
phal. concerning Livonia : 'Sicut ecclesiasticae laesionis censura *compelli
non patitur ad credendum invitos:* sic sponte credentibus Apostolica Sedes
.... munimen suae protectionis indulget et fideles ad defensionem eorum
salubribus monitis exhortatur.'

[10] Conc. Tolet. vi. l.c.

§ 7.

The mode in which men generally reasoned was as follows :
according to the Apostle (Romans xiii. 1 seq.), lawful authority has

the power of punishing evildoers. He also says (Tit. iii. 10, and elsewhere) that the heretic is subverted, and sinneth : therefore rulers have the right of punishing heretics.[1] But this right is not a duty to be exercised under all circumstances. It may, however, become a duty to exercise it when indispensable for the protection of the faithful and when the State in union with the Church is appealed to for help.[2] The Church has only pronounced that it is permitted, and is in no manner unlawful to punish heretics as well as other malefactors with death ; she had not pronounced it to be necessary and always expedient.[3] The converted Waldenses, who had denied the lawfulness of punishments affecting life or limb, were only required under Innocent III. to acknowledge the lawfulness of such punishments.[4] Theologians say that heretics may (not 'must') be justly punished with death ;[5] it only follows from Leo X.'s condemnation of Luther's 33d thesis that it is not contrary to the spirit of Christianity to punish heretics with death by fire.[6]

It was always well known that as every heresy was not equally detestable, so every heretic was not equally guilty.[7] An error in faith, be it ever so small, provided it be joined with rebellion, suffices to hinder salvation ;[8] but a human tribunal must consider persons and circumstances, and the greater or less danger of infection ; the power of a heresy for disturbing the peace of the county is also, of course, an important consideration for the State authority. In general to apostatise from the Faith was accounted one of the gravest crimes against the State. 'The severity of the punishments inflicted in the Middle Ages for heresy was in proportion to the general severity of punishments at that time. The age was rude compared with our day, and the punishments partook of the nature of the age. They depended also in some measure upon the particular nature of the heretical opinions, some of which were as much at variance with sound reason as with true faith. Some, too, asserted that the true Christ had not yet appeared ; the Christ of history was the son of a sinful woman ; and there were other such perversions. Imagine the indignation they would excite in the Middle Ages, when people had not become accustomed through historical research to all manner of preposterous assertions, and blasphemy was still, as under the old law, a capital offence. It is perfectly intelligible how the punishment of death came to be decreed for heresy.'⁹

---

¹ Natal. Alex. l.c. a. 1, prop. n. 1.

² The Faculty of Paris, in 1526, thus worded the censure passed upon Erasmus of Rotterdam, de Poena Haereticorum, prop. 1 (Du Plessis d'Argentré, Coll. Judic. t. ii. P. i. p. 69): 'Cum sit Catholicum et fide tenendum, non solum licere, sed et oportere haereticos pertinaces extremo supplicio puniri, *quando citra jacturam atque periculum reipublicae id fieri potest nec valet aliter salus eorum aut ceterorum procurari ac conservari*, oppositumque sit error Catharorum, Waldensium et Lutheri generalibus Conciliis et legibus imperialibus damnatus, pii expositoris munus Paraphrastes minime executus est,' &c.

³ Ib. p. 70, on prop. 5, the censure runs thus : ' Quamvis Evangelium non expresse et aperte haereticos monstret exurendos, leges tamen civiles conformiter ad jus naturale, quod Evangelium non abrogat, morte plectendos atque concremandos juste decernunt.' The reply to prop. 6, 'An leges Ecclesiae sunt, quempiam ultricibus tradere flammis ?' was : ' Justas leges magistratuum temporalium pro exstirpatione haereticorum latas Ecclesia non reprobat, licet illas nolit per ecclesiasticos (qui divinis omnino officiis sunt addicti) executioni mandari.' On prop. 7, 'Veteribus episcopis ultima poena erat anathema,' the censure was: ' Propter infestationem tyrannorum in primitiva Ecclesia non poterant haeretici severiori poena mulctari, quam excommunicationis; postea tamen, quum principes saeculi Ecclesiae colla submisere, perspecta contumacia et impietate haereticorum, necessarium fuit, nedum conveniens, in illos gladio temporali animadverti.'

⁴ Formula apud Innoc. III. l. xiii. Ep. 94 (Migne, t. ccxvi. p. 291): ' Potestatem saecularem secundum leges officium suum in malefactores peragentem non judicamus neque ob hoc damnandam esse dicimus vel credimus.' Previously the Pope wrote, l. xii. eq. 69, ib. p. 77 : ' Illud vero tamquam erroneum nullus vestrum praesumat asserere, quod saecularis potestas sine mortali peccato non *possit* judicium sanguinis exercere, cum lex potius quam judex occidat, dummodo ad inferendam vindictam non odio, sed judicio, non incaute, sed consulte procedat. *Non sine causa*, &c. Romans xiii.'

⁵ S. Thom. 2, 2, q. 11, a. 3 : ' *Possunt* non solum excommunicari sed et juste occidi.' Also earlier, Alanus ab Insulis contra Haeret. l. ii. c. xxii. (Migne, ccx. p. 396) : 'De Judaeis dicimus, quod non sunt occidendi. Si tamen laborent illis criminibus, pro quibus lex dictat hominem occidendum, judex *potest* eos occidere, ut in hoc deserviat legi. Similiter haeretici propter haeresiu non sunt occidendi, sed propter characterem Christianum, quem habent, ad caulam Ecclesiae reducendi sunt. Si tamen illis peccatis laborant, quibus mors temporalis debetur, a judice saeculari *puniri possunt*, si tamen eos puniat intuitu justitiae, non ex ira vel animi rancore.'

⁶ Denzinger, Enchir. 4th ed. p. 224, n. 657. Huber, on the contrary,

p. 40, makes the Bull say that to burn heretics is a work of the Holy Ghost. The Sorbonne, in reference to Luther's proposition, declared: 'Haec propositio est falsa, contra voluntatem Spiritus divini asserta et errori Catharorum et Waldensium consona' (Du Plessis, t. i. P. ii. p. 373, tit. 14).

  [7] Ps. Athanas. quaest. 116, ad Antioch Duc. (Migne, PP. gr. t. xxviii. p. 672). Simeon Thessal. Dial. c. Haer. c. x. (ib. t. clv. p. 65).

  [8] Pelisson, Lettre à Mme. de Brinon, 4 Sept. 1690 (Œuvres de Leibnitz, par Foucher de Careil, vol. i. 73): 'L'Eglise croit qu'il y a des erreurs plus détestable les unes que les autres; mais elle soutient que la moindre erreur en la foy, accompagnée de rébellion, est détestable et peut priver du salut.'

  [9] Möhler, K.G. ed. by Gams, ii. p. 650 seq.

§ 8.

The emperors especially considered it their duty to seek out Manichæans, and in the West also laws remained in force sentencing them to death. Manichæans were burnt in Orleans in 1022;[1] and in 1052 several were executed in Germany by order of Henry III.[2] Similar sects continued to exist under various names, particularly in France, North Italy, and Germany. In the twelfth century they were very numerous, especially on the Rhine.[3] The people often rose against them in wrath, and fearing the clergy would treat them too leniently, sought to forestall their investigations.[4] They delivered up Peter de Bruis to the flames in 1120.[5] Many, however, in spite of their detestation of heretics, could not bear to put them to death; for instance, St. Hildegarde[6] and Peter Cantor, who appealed to the example of Pope Eugenius III. and the Council of Rheims in 1148, where a Manichæan was only punished with imprisonment.[7] However, in the latter half of the twelfth century the increase of the sects and the discovery of their wickedness, by which they had become a pest to society, led to the increased severity or reënactment of the civil and ecclesiastical legislation against them. Civil princes often took the initiative in the matter. Heretics who persecuted the Church, committing sacrileges and pillaging the temples of God, seemed to have incurred the punishment of death, both by divine and human laws; their conduct admitted of no defence, and the prince who did not proceed against them appeared to draw destruction upon himself.[8]

[1] Mansi, xix. 373 seq. 378 seq. 423 seq.   Hefele, iv. 642 seq. 648.

[2] Herman. Contract. a. 1052: 'Imperator Natalem Domini Goslare egit ibique quosdam haereticos, inter alia pravi erroris dogmata, Manichaea secta, omnis esum animalis exsecrantes, consensu cunctorum, ne haeretica scabies latius serpens plures inficeret, in patibulis suspendi jussit.'

[3] Hist. Trevir. ap. d'Argentré, t. i. P. i. 24.   Everini, Praepos. Ep. ad Bern. ap. Mabillon, Annal. t iii.   Ecberti, sermon. in Bibl. PP. Lugd. t. xxiii. 600 seq.   Giesler and Neander give many details.

[4] Guibert de Novig. de Vita sua, iii. 14.

[5] Petrus Vener. Praef. ad Tract. c. Petrobrus (Migne, clxxxix. p. 723): 'Sed post rogum Petri de Bruis, quo apud S. Ægidium zelus fidelium flammas Dominicae crucis ab eo succensas eum concremando ultus est, postquam plane impius ille de igne ad ignem, de transeunte ad aeternum transitum fecit, haeres nequitiae ejus Heinricus,' &c.   Everin of Steinfelden relates another example of summary justice executed by the people upon heretics (Du Plessis, t. i. P. i. p. 33).

[6] Hildeg. Ep. ad Cler. Colon. p. 166, ed. Colon.; Ep. ad Mogunt, p. 138.

[7] Petrus Cantor. Verb. abbreviat. p. 200.

[8] Joh. Saresb. Polycr vi. 13, p. 608: 'Sed prae ceteris omnibus *divino et humano jure* gravius feriuntur *sacrilegi* et hi qui variis perturbationibus impugnant Ecclesiam Dei, quibus *lex* non praecisionem dexterarum, sed poenam irrogat capitalem.   Si patrocinium illorum assumant Cicero et Demosthenes, si in defensionem eorum linguam acuat et totius ingenii sui vires exhauriat Quintilianus, *si jura viguerint,* quod post Deum in manu principis est, fortunas eorum et capita, quin legitimis suppliciis feriantur, tueri non poterunt.   Quod si gladium suum adversus tales non exserit princeps, *in se ipsum* procul dubio provocat gladium bis acutum, quem in ore suo gerit filius hominis (Apoc. i. 16), gladium utique, qui vivus et efficax est, qui corpus findit et animam (Hebr. iv. 12).'

§ 9.

Many Councils have forbidden the support and defence of heretics.   Thus, amongst others, Pope Lucius III. issued, in conjunction with the Emperor Frederick I., at the Council of Verona in 1184, his celebrated decree against heretics, especially against Cathari, Patarines, Humiliati, Passagii, Josephines, Arnoldists.[1]   This decree is only a collection of older imperial and local ordinances.

It is quite untrue that all those condemned for heresy and delivered up to the civil tribunal were punished with death. Very many were liberated, with a small fine or short imprisonment, and the amount of punishment was proportioned to the offence. The decree of Lucius III. only says that laymen, unless they forswear their heresy and perform satisfaction, shall receive from the civil judge a punishment corresponding to the character of their crime.

¹ Cap. ix. Adv. abolendam, v. 7, de Haer. Mansi, l.c. pp. 476, 488 seq. Cf. Hefele, p. 644 seq.

§ 10.

But the sects were ever on the increase, and for the most part had practically ceased to be Christian. They seemed to be waging with the Church a war of life and death, and had attained, especially in the south of France, a power which threatened to bear down all before it.¹ Alexander III., in 1180, had considered a Crusade against them there to be necessary;² and it was even more incumbent upon Innocent III. to use extraordinary measures for stemming the tide of danger.³ The bishops had no sufficient force to meet the sectaries, especially in the south of France, where a spirit hostile to the Church had already attained great power; and the bishops, partly by their own fault,⁴ had lost consideration.⁵ But something might be hoped from the labours of simple priests, who, poor but faithful and well instructed, and, moreover, armed with the authority of Papal legates, obtained the assistance and support of such of the nobles as were still Catholics.⁶ The legates sent in 1198 were instructed to endeavour, first of all, to convert heretics by argument;⁷ if this failed, to excommunicate them; if their obstinacy continued, to call in the aid of the civil power, which should confiscate their property and drive them into exile,⁸ according to laws that already existed, and which had been reënacted also in Lombardy.⁹ But all sermons and discussions on religion were very ineffectual. Count Raymond VI. of Toulouse practised many deceptions, pillaged churches and convents, and was a persecutor of Catholics.¹⁰ The guilt was imputed to him, from many suspicious circumstances,¹¹ of the murder of the legate, Peter of Castelnau, in January 1208; and besides he had performed many acts of violence and cruelty towards bishops and priests, and had been visited with excommunication and interdict. The Papal legate released him from these on the 18th June 1209, on his solemn vow of performing satisfaction.[12]

[1] Hefele, Conc. v. p. 732 seq.
[2] Ib. p. 741.
[3] The first Crusade against heretics is generally ascribed to him. Paramo, de Orig. Inquis. l. ii. tit. 1, c. iii. n. 1; Petra, in Const. 17, Innoc. IV. t. iii. p. 97.
[4] *E.g.* Berenger II., 1191-1212, Archbishop of Narbonne, was not merely inactive but covetous and simoniacal. Innoc. III. l. iii. Ep. 24, p. 903 seq.; l. vi. Ep. 75, p. 355. When the legates were about to proceed against him he appealed to Rome, but did not follow up the appeal, wherefore the Pope summoned him, 1205, to appear, l. viii. Ep. 107, p. 675. He appeared at length, promised amendment, and submitted to the penance, l. ix. Ep. 66, p. 883 seq. But he did not amend; and in 1207 fresh inquiries into his conduct were ordered, l. x. Ep. 68, p. 1164 seq.
[5] Neander, K.G. ii. p. 675 seq.
[6] Cf. Petr. Bles. Ep. 220. Migne, ccvii. p. 510.
[7] That was always held to be first and most important means. Petrus Vener. l.c. p. 721: ' Quia majorem operam eos convertendi quam exterminandi adhibere Christianam charitatem decet, proferatur eis auctoritas, adhibeatur et ratio, ut si *Christiani* permanere volunt, auctoritati, si *homines*, rationi cedere compellantur.'
[8] Innoc. l. i. Ep. 93, 94, 165; l. ii. Ep. 122, 123.
[9] Ib. l. i. Ep. 298; l. ii. Ep. 1, 228.
[10] Innoc. III. l. x. Ep. 69, p. 1166 seq.
[11] Ib. l. xi. Ep. 26, p. 1354 seq.
[12] The documents, apud Migne, t. ccxvi. p. 89 seq. Post Ep. 85, l. xii. Innoc.

§ 11.

The Council of Avignon endeavoured to ameliorate and set in order the spiritual condition of Provence.[1] The bishops were solemnly enjoined to administer with more zeal their office of preachers, and to appoint good preachers;[2] they were further commissioned to compel by censures all counts, governors, and burgesses to take an oath that they would expel heretics, and would punish those who persisted in heresy ; also to administer in every parish an oath to the priest and to several well-disposed laymen that they would report to the bishop and the civil authority any heretics who might become known to them, as well as their aiders and abettors.[3] This, as well as the decree that officials who were negligent in this matter should be punished with interdict and ban, was conformable to the decrees of earlier Councils, and to the statutes of Lucius III. It was also not new that defenders, protectors, and favourers of heretics were with them equally punishable.

Excommunication was by command of the Pope renewed against Count Raymond, who had performed no iota of the satisfaction which he had promised a second time in Rome. The war was violent, for political and selfish interests were concerned in it. Innocent III. found it difficult to bridle the ambition and avarice of the Crusaders.[4] After more fighting and renewed negotiations,[5] the Council of Montpellier in 1215 transferred the conquered district of the county of Toulouse to Earl Simon de Montfort, an arrangement approved only provisionally by the Pope, who awaited a definitive decision from the General Council he had summoned.[6] The enactment was, however, carried through by the prelates of the south of France, who declared that if the conquered territory were surrendered it would be impossible to subdue the heresy. A certain part was retained for Raymond's wife, and reserve was made of the claims of his son over the still unconquered lands. The Count of Foix's castles were subsequently restored to him; and after many vicissitudes Raymond's son eventually came into possession of a large portion of his father's territory.[7]

[1] Mansi, xxii. 783 seq. Hefele, p. 749.
[2] Can. 1. Later Councils (*e.g.* those of Arles, 1234, c. 2, and Beziers, 1246, c. 7) repeated this. Hefele, pp. 919, 1017.
[3] This was done also by the Councils of Montpellier, 1215, c. 46; of Narbonne, 1227, c. 14 ; of Arles, 1234, c. 5 ; of Beziers, 1246, c. 1 (Hefele, pp. 765 seq. 839, 919, 1017). The last-mentioned Council has likewise the decree concerning the oath of the barons and burgesses, can. 9 ; Arles, c. 3.
[4] Innoc. III. l. xv. Ep. 212, 213, p. 739 seq.
[5] Hefele, p. 757 seq.
[6] Ib. p. 766.
[7] Hefele, p. 806 seq.

§ 12.

The great Innocent III. has been frequently accused of cruelty and severity towards heretics.[1] If he is open to the charge, it might also be preferred against the Councils held in his day, and particularly the twelfth General Council. His penal sentences are not nearly as severe as later ones ; they are founded on the law in force before his time. He was very gentle with converted heretics, for instance Durand de Osca.[2] He inculcated patience with the weakness of the newly converted. He knew that many are more touched by admonitions than by threats, and more likely to be converted by leniency than by severity. He would have wine and oil poured upon their wounds, and severe measures applied only when infection of parts still sound was threatened.[3] He deeply grieved over those who persisted in their infatuation, and only extremest danger induced him to allow the rigour of the law to take its course.[4] In his reign he certainly did not fail in giving every opportunity for instruction and information, and in earnestly admonishing bishops[5] to a better discharge of the functions of their pastoral office ; it was with him a subject of great solicitude that the innocent should not suffer, and that for this purpose the most careful investigations should be made.[6] Even in the States of the Church the Pope had to combat artful heretics, with whose insolence he became later only too well acquainted.[7]

[1] Huber, p. 18.
[2] L. xv. Ep. 90, 93-96, p. 603, 608 seq.   Cf. l. xi. Ep. 198; l. xii. Ep. 17 ; l. xiii. Ep. 78.
[3] L. xii. Ep. 67, p. 74.
[4] Ib. Ep. 126, pp. 154, 155 : ' Ad exterminationem suam rerumque publicationem suarum *secundum constitutiones civiles et canonicas* est processum ut quemadmodum scriptum est, *impiorum spolia justi tollant et divitias thesaurizent eorum.*'
[5] L. vi. Ep. 239, pp. 269, 270; Ep. 242, 243, p. 272 seq.
[6] L. ii. Ep. 228 ; Ep. Veronensi, p. 788 seq.
[7] L. x. Ep. 130, p. 1220 seq.

§ 13.

Laws concerning spiritual things took precedence of all other laws in ancient codes, and in civil legislation laws against heretics ranked as the foremost and most important.[1] The Emperor Frederick II., on the day of his coronation in Rome, A.D. 1220, proclaimed amongst others two laws against heretics, by which they were declared infamous and outlawed. They were to be punished with confiscation of property, and the civil government was to dislodge them from their territory, which on the lapse of one year might be taken possession of by Catholics.[2]

[1] Raumer, Gesch. der Hohenstaufen, vol. iii. p. 352.
[2] Pope Honorius confirmed these laws, and in 1221 renewed the anathema over all heretics. Mansi, xxii. 1137. Pertz, Leg. t. ii. p. 243. Walter, Fontes, p. 84, § 5, 6, c. xlix. de Sent. Excom. v. 39. Vinc. Petra, Com. in Const. Apost. Venet. 1729, t. i. p. 196 seq. Fleury, Hist. Ecclés. t. xvi. l. lxxviii. n. 40.

§ 14.

In France, after the death of Louis VIII. (1226), the Albigenses again became more powerful, and Gregory IX. summoned Louis VIII.'s son and successor to resist them by force of arms.[1] Peace was at length (1229) concluded between Louis IX. and Count Raymond VII. of Toulouse, whereby the latter ceded to France a great portion of his territory, and promised to purify the remainder from heresy. In the territory that remained with Raymond, as well as in the provinces ceded to France, convicted heretics were to be punished without delay; the others were sought out and reported to the bishops or their officers, and the property of those who remained a year under excommunication was to be confiscated by the royal bailiffs. In the spring of 1233, Count Raymond VII. issued even more rigorous decrees against the Albigenses.

[1] Raynald, a. 1227, n. 61; a. 1228, n. 20 seq.

Part II. The Inquisition and Witchcraft.

§ 1.

The episcopal Inquisition as it long existed received its complete formation at the Synod of Toulouse[1] in 1229, according to which every bishop was to appoint to every parish a priest and two or three laymen, whose duty it should be to seek out heretics and denounce them to the civil and ecclesiastical authorities; the bailiffs also were to seek out heretics.[2] In order that no innocent person might be punished and no false charges made, no one should be punished as a heretic before having been declared such by a bishop or by some properly authorised ecclesiastic (such as the Cistercian legates and future inquisitors).[3] The case of a person publicly charged with heresy should be subject to a judicial investigation (*inquisitio*).[4] The rules of proceedings against heretics were, as time went on, more and more precisely regulated.

[1] Mansi, xxiii. 191 seq. Hefele, v. p. 872 seq.
[2] C. 1-3.   This is quite in accordance with the Council of Avignon, 1209, and with many others (supra, Part I. § 11, note 3); amongst them the Council of Taracona, 1233, c. 8; Tours, 1239, c. 1 ; Albi, 1254, c. 13 (Hefele, v. pp. 918, 960 ; vi. p. 41). The latter has the addition : ' Neither from fear, nor hate, nor favour, shall they suffer themselves to be misled in their office.'
[3] The Council of Taracona, 1233, c. 5, repeats this.
[4] Innoc. III. c. xxxi. de Simon, v. 3.   Cf. c. xxiv. de Accus. v. 1.

§ 2.

On account of the negligence and corruption of some inquisitors, as well as because the bishops were not sufficient, from the year 1232, Gregory IX. appointed the Dominicans as inquisitors,[1] with whom Franciscans were often associated in the office.[2] The institution found no favour in Germany, though Frederick II. took the inquisitors under his special protection, cast suspicions on the Pope of protecting heretics, and desired to extirpate them himself ; it came to an end with the murder of the secular priest Conrad of Marburg in 1233. Many pious men took an active part in the office, but some of the Dominicans became obnoxious from over zeal and excessive severity. Several inquisitors were murdered, others grievously ill-treated or expelled ; wherefore in 1237 the Pope suspended the performance of their official duty in the territory of Toulouse.[3] The Inquisition was introduced into the kingdom of Aragon in 1232-1234.[4]

[1] Bull. Ord. Praed. i. 37, 38. Mansi, xxiii. 74.
[2] Cf. Alex. IV. Const. 18, Cupientes, to the inquisitors of this order, Petra, t. iii. p. 149 seq.
[3] Hefele, pp. 882, 978.
[4] Bzovius, Annal. ad a. 1232, n. 8, 9.

§ 3.

The Inquisition was reëstablished in the south of France in the year 1241, after the death of Gregory IX., and whilst the Papal chair was vacant. The newly-elected Innocent IV. felt it his duty not to accede to the request of Raymond VII. of Toulouse, that the Inquisition should be resigned to the bishops ; he desired that the bishops and the inquisitors should coöperate together, especially in delivering sentence ;[1] episcopal supervision of the purity of the Faith was, however, in no manner withdrawn.[2] Innocent IV. in 1243 confirmed anew Frederick II.'s laws concerning heretics.[3] It cannot be proved that Frederick's severe laws were first held binding in Germany and Italy after the Bull of Innocent IV. ; the Pope specially enforced them in the parts of Italy most threatened.

[1] Schmidt, l.c. pp. 297-325. Hist. de Languedoc, iii. p. 446.
[2] Boniface VIII. c. xvii. de Haer. v. 2, in 6 : ' Per hoc, quod negotium haereticae pravitatis (inquirendae) . . . aliquibus ab Apostolica Sede generaliter . . . delegatur, dioecesanis episcopis, quin et ipsi auctoritate ordinaria vel delegata (si habent) in eodem procedere valeant, nolumus derogare.' Cf. Clem. V. c. i. de Haer. v. 3, in Clem.
[3] Const. 1, Cum adversus. Petra, Comment. in Const. Ap. t. iii. p. 1 seq. c. i. l. v. tit. 3, in l. Sept. Bullar. et Taur. iii. p. 503. Cf. ib. p. 552, Const. a. 1252.

§ 4.

Heretics brought to trial and found guilty were divided into three classes : those who being truly penitent were reconciled to the Church ; those who submitted to the Church but with doubtful sincerity and for form's sake ; and those who remained impenitent and obstinate. The first class were only given some ordinary and easy ecclesiastical penance.[1] The second class were those who although outwardly renouncing heresy held to it inwardly, and after their release endeavoured with much craft to mislead others. Except the very worst of this class, they were condemned to perpetual imprisonment,[2] but only after their sentence had received Papal confirmation. Those impenitent, amongst whom were included those who had relapsed after having renounced heresy, were delivered up to the civil tribunals. Those who refused to be converted were not to be sentenced forthwith, but were to be several times admonished by inquisitors and others, as the Synod of Beziers, for instance, ordained in 1246. After the laws enacted by Frederick II. in 1231 and 1238, death by fire was the usual sentence upon impenitent heretics.[3] These laws, published during the reign of Gregory IX., at the time when the fresh struggle against this Pope was breaking out, were certainly not issued by his direction and with his concurrence; neither is it true that Frederick's terrible laws against heretics were but in accordance with contemporary and previous Papal ordinances. Until Innocent IV. there is no Papal law of the kind, and previously death by fire was by no means universally sanctioned.

[1] Mansi, xxiii. 353 seq. Hefele, v. p. 979 seq.
[2] Hefele, v. p. 919. Raumer, Gesch. der Hohenst. vi. p. 298.
[3] Cf. Pertz, t. iv. p. 327; Land law of the Sachsenspiegel, Bk. ii. art. 14, § 7; Schwabenspiegel, § 313, p. 136, ed. Lassberg, 1840; Card. Albitius, de Inconstantia in Fide, c. xxi. n. 8; Card. Petra, Com. in Const. Ap. t. iii. p. 6, n. 11.

§ 5.

Formal heresy being, according to imperial law, not merely on a par with but a greater crime than high treason,[1] this principle was carried out into its juridical consequences, and penalties made for the crime of high treason were applied to the crime of heresy. (*a*) In cases of high treason all citizens, without exception, were bound to inform against an offender, and those in other cases not allowed to be accusers were admitted;[2] the same rule was decreed for heresy. Every one was bound to give information respecting heretics known to be such[3] (they referred to Rom. xvi. 17 seq.); criminals, *infames*, and those guilty of the same crime were allowed to accuse them; the only testimony accounted invalid was that which sprang from malice or enmity.[4] (*b*) Torture was employed to extort confession from those accused of high treason,[5] and Innocent IV. is especially reproached with this. But in the criminal lawsuits of that day torture was commonly employed, and was often used by civil judges even against thieves. This means was to be used, having regard to the person accused[6] and to the crime, not too frequently, and only with a view to completing the evidence by a full confession; it was in general employed much more mildly than in the civil courts.[7] Clement V., moreover, decreed that it should never be employed unless the bishop (or vicar capitular) and the inquisitor were agreed about it;[8] and this led to its being more seldom used. (*c*) Persons guilty of high treason suffered besides death[9] confiscation of their property, of which their children and heirs were likewise deprived.[10] The Councils also inflicted the punishment of confiscation in accordance with the older imperial laws;[11] but it was declared that it should not take effect without a special legal sentence.[12] The sons, and then also the grandchildren, of declared heretics[13] were, as in the case of high treason, deprived of their property;[14] but the grandchildren by the mother's side were excepted.[15] Confiscation was not inflicted upon persons merely suspected of heresy, nor upon heretics who were reconciled to the Church.[16] The dower of an innocent woman ignorant of her husband's heresy at the time of her marriage was exempt from confiscation.[17] The emancipation of children by persons guilty of high treason was held void,[18] and the same applied to heretics.[19] (*d*) For both offences also the names of the witnesses and of the accusers when needful, to shield them from danger, were withheld from the accused;[20] but he was at liberty to name his enemies, who were not allowed to bear witness against him;[21] subsequently witnesses were always made known to some honest men of standing versed in the law,[22] and their testimony subjected to close scrutiny.[23]

¹ Upon Frederick II. vide Schirrmacher, vol. ii. p. 250. [Formal heresy is when a person is a heretic through his own fault. Tr.]
² L. vii. viii. Dig. xlviii. 4, ad Leg. Jul. Majest. Joh. Sar. Polycr. 1. vi. c. xxiv. p. 627.
³ Cf. Tertull. Apol. c. ii. ; Devoti, Inst. Jur. Can. iv. tit. 8, § 11, p. 114. But private persons who were under no special obligation were not punished as *fautores* for omitting to give information. Petra, Com. t. iii. pp. 142, 143, n. 22-28.
⁴ Council of Narbonne, 1243, c. 24, 25 ; Hefele, v. p. 981. Alexander IV. c. 5, In fidei, v. 2, de Haer. in 6, lib. sept. c. 7, h.t.
⁵ L. iii. iv. Cod. ix. 8 ; Joh. Saresb. l.c. Innoc. IV. Const. Ad exstirpanda, 9, a. 1252, § 25 ; Urban IV. 1261.
⁶ For delicate people, fasting was considered equivalent to the torture. Passerin. in Clem. i. de Haer. n. 31 ; Petra, t. iii. p. 123, n. 9.
⁷ Carena, de Offic. S. Inquisit. Lugd. 1669, tit. 10, § 21. Bangen, Die Röm. Curie, p. 117 seq.
⁸ Clem. c. 1, §'1, de Haer. v. 3 : 'Duro tamen tradere carceri sive arcto, qui magis ad poenam quam ad custodiam videatur, vel tormentis exponere illos aut ad sententiam procedere contra illos episcopus sine inquisitore et inquisitor sine episcopo dioccesano . . . non valebit,' &c. Cf. Eymeric, Direct. P. iii. q. 47.
⁹ L. v. Cod. ix. 8, Inst. iv. 18, 3.
¹⁰ L. v. vi. Cod. ix. 8. Frederick II. in the law Inconsutilem : ' Sicuti per duellionis crimen'personas adimit damnatorum et bona et damnat post obitum memoriam defunctorum, sic et in praedicto crimine, quo Patareni notantur, per omnia volumus observari.'
¹¹ Synod at Albi, 1254, c. 26. Hefele, vi. 42. Pignatelli (Consult. Can. t. vi. Cons. 75, pp. 154, 155 ; t. viii. Cons. 68, p. 118) shows that it was not inflicted so readily as is generally supposed.
¹² Synod of Beziers, 1246, c. 3. Hefele, v. p. 1017. Bonif. VIII. c. 19, Cum secundum, v. 2, de Haer. in 6.
¹³ The heretic retained ' possessio' until 'lata sententia,' and made ' fructos suos.' Gonzalez, in c. Vergentis, h.t. n. 12 ; Pignatelli, Consult. Can. t. viii. Cons. 68 ; Petra, t. iii. pp. 45, 46, n. 4 seq.
¹⁴ Frider. II. L. Gazaros: ' Censentes, ut omnia bona talium confiscentur nec ad eos ulterius revertantur, ita quod filii eorum ad successionem eorum pervenire non possint.' Alex. IV. in c. 2, § 2, de Haer. v. 2 in 6: ' Filii usque ad secundam generationem ad nullum ecclesiasticum beneficium seu officium publicum admittantur.' Nevertheless, sons of heretics who were not heretical succeeded to entailed estates, if the entail had not been created by their fathers. Cf. Honor. IV. c. 5, de Haer. v. 3, in lib. sept.
¹⁵ Bonif. VIII. c. 15, Statutum, h.t. in 6. Only in Spain the privation extended to the second generation, which was not fully recognised at Rome ; dispensations were also granted.
¹⁶ The irregularity applied to the sons of heretics, but not the *infamia juris.* Petra, t. iii. pp. 87-91.
¹⁷ Innoc. IV. ap. Bonif. VIII. c. 14, Decrevit, h.t. in 6.
¹⁸ L. v. § 4, Cod. ix. 8.
¹⁹ Alex. IV. c. 2, § 4, de Haer. v. 2 in 6.

²⁰ Innoc. IV. Const. 15, § 3; Urban IV. Const. 2, a. 1262, § 9. Petra, t. iii. p. 169 seq. n. 12: 'Id speciale expostulabat delictum haeresis, cujus causa omnium majorum est maxima, ut sc. ne ob defectum probationum cum magno religionis et fidelium periculo impunitum pertransiret, ex quo testes eorum praepotentiam exhorrescentes contra eos testimonium dicere expavescerent, eorum nomina reo non publicarentur, idemque etiam ob gravitatem delicti servandum esse voluerunt in crimine laesae majestatis humanae Guazzin. et Piazza.'

²¹ Thus, according to the precedent of the Synod of Toulouse, 1229, the Synods of Narbonne, 1243, c. 22, and of Beziers, 1246, Instruct. c. 10 (Hefele, v. p. 1020); Petra, l.c. u. 14.

²² Bonif. VIII. c. Statuta, 20, de Haer. v. 2 in 6.; Eymeric, Direct. P. iii. q. 80. Petra, l.c. n. 13, pp. 169, 170: 'Verum ne id quod solo veritatis amore inductum fuerat, vergeret quandoque in ejus detrimentum cum periculo condemnandi innocentem, idcirco statutum, ut nomine testium exprimerentur aliquibus personis providis, honestis et religiosis,' &c.

²³ Petra, l.c. p. 170, n. 15.

§ 6.

Cases of heresy were no exception to the principle that, failing clear proof or confession, no one should be condemned, as it were better a crime should be unpunished than an innocent person condemned.[1] Clement V. decreed that a sentence of condemnation should be only issued conjointly by the bishop and the inquisitor.[2] The keeping of accurate records of the trial was enforced, and instructions were issued on this subject.[3] The procedure was never to be held altogether in secret. Competent judges were to be present at the actual condemnation,[4] and two conscientious men at the examination of the witnesses.[5] The inquisitors were subject to the vigilant control of the bishops;[6] however much a bishop might be suspected, inquisitors could never proceed against him without a special commission from the Pope.[7] In their laborious office they were always liable to the interference of the Holy See, which regulated their powers[8] very strictly, and forbade any excess whatever.[9] Minute directions were published for the officials and servants of the Inquisition. Inquisitors were to be forty years of age, and men of honour; they were subject to severe penalties for transgressions of their duty. They were also not to be confessors.[10]

[1] These are the very words of the Synod of Narbonne, 1243, can. 23, and the Instruction of Beziers, 1246, can. 11. Alexander III. also wrote

thus,.on Dec. 23, 1162, to Archbishop Henry of Rheims (de Burgensibus haereticis et in fide depravatis, Ep. 118, p. 187) : ' Cautius et minus malum est, nocentes et condemnandos absolvere, quam vitam innocentium severitate ecclesiastica condemnare, et melius, viros ecclesiasticos plus etiam quam deceat esse remissos, quam in corrigendis vitiis supra modum existere et apparere severos.' Clement V. (c. 1, § 4, de Haer. v. 3, in Clem.): ' Grave est quoque et damnatione dignissimum, malitiose insontibus eamdem imponere pravitatem.'

² Clem. V. c. 1, § 1. Urban IV. had already directed (Const. 2, Licet, 1262, Petra, iii. p. 168 seq.) : ' Neminem absque dioecesanorum consilio damnent.'

³ The Synod of Narbonne, 1243, mentions (c. 6) the records of the confessions of the guilty; the Synod of Albi, 1254, ordains (cap. 21) that they should be made in duplo, and that the duplicates should be preserved in a safe place. Clem. IV. (c. 11, § 1, de Haer. v. 2, in 6) directs accurate records of the trial to be made as well as strict examination of witnesses.

⁴ Alex. IV. Const. Cupientes, 1260, Petra, t. iii. p. 149 seq.

⁵ Urban IV. Const. 2, Licet, 1262, § 6. In Spain this was firmly upheld. Paramo, de Orig. Inquis. l. iii. q. 4, n. 50 ; Petra, l.c. p. 169, n. 6, 7.

⁶ In general the inquisitors had to act de episcopi (vel vicarii ejus) consilio ; Alexander IV. (1257) only allowed interference without requisition of the bishop in cases of haeretici judicialiter confessi et obstinati. Const. 9, Ad capiendum, Petra, t. iii. p. 122 seq. They had, as a rule, jurisdictio cumulativa cum episcopis (Urban IV. Const. Licet, § 3; Clem. VII. Cum sicut, § 2); in Spain, on the contrary, privativa. Petra, t. iii. p. 93, in Innoc. IV. Const. 16, n. 10, 11.

⁷ Bonif. VIII. c. 16, Inquisitores, h.t. in 6. Cf. Pius V. Const. 82, § 6; Card. Petra, t. i. p. 135, in Const. 2, Leonis IX. sect. l. n. 76, 82. Innocent XI. caused the censures of an inquisitor against a bishop to be declared null, Jan. 24, 1687 (Petra, l.c. n. 79, 80). In the same way the inquisitors could not take measures against the nuncios and officials of the Holy See (John XXII. c. 3, de Haer. v. 3, in Xvagg. com.).

⁸ To these powers belonged the right of punishing those clerics and religious who instructed heretics in false and] evasive answers (Alex. IV. c. 8, § 8, h.t. in 6) ; the right, in certain cases, of proceeding against the praedicatores quaestuarii (Clem. IV. c. 11, § 2, h.t. in 6) ; the faculty of absolving and of dispensing in irregularities crusaders against heretics (Petra, in Innoc. IV. Const. 17, n. 4, t. iii. p. 97), as well as each other mutually, in cases where their regular superiors could absolve and dispense (Urban IV. Const. 8, Ut negotium, Petra, t. iii. p. 194) ; the right of proceeding against all privileged and exempted persons, even regulars, who might hinder the execution of their office or fail to give the support they were bound to give ; the right of taking as their notaries fitting clergy, religious, or laymen, to all of whom an oath was to be administered (Alex. IV. Const. 22, Ne commissae, 1260, Petra, l.c. pp. 158, 159) ; the right of committing to others the citation of witnesses, the examination of the same, and the promulgation of the judgment (Urban IV. Const. 2, Licet, 1262, § 10).

* Eymeric, Direct. P. ii. c. i. p. 112, ed. Rom. 1587 ; Pegna, ibid.
¹⁰ Innoc. IV. Const. 9, Ad exstirpanda, § 3 ; Alex. IV. Const. 2, Cum secundum, 1255 (Petra, t. iii. p. 107 seq.) ; Clem. V. c. 2, de Haer. v. 3, in Clem. ; John XXII. Const. 9, Exigit, 1321 (Petra, t. iv. p. 34) ; Clem. V. in c. 1, 2, de Haer. v. 3, in Clem.

§ 7.

In the year 1255, Louis IX. begged Pope Alexander IV. to charge the Dominicans with the office of inquisitors in his inherited States ;¹ but soon the parliament showed itself hostile to them. The Inquisition was established in Poland under John XXII. and King Ladislaus ;² a proposal for its introduction into England was made for the first time by the clergy in 1400,³ when the Lollards were numerous, and severe measures were taken there against the sect ; at a Synod held at Oxford in 1408 a decree was published, confirmed by the Convocation of London of the following year, ordering that all persons tainted with heresy should be summarily proceeded against.⁴ In Italy, where the Republic of Venice alone offered a lengthened opposition to it, the Inquisition had subsequently its chief field of action ;⁵ for many heretics had fled from the persecution in the south of France⁶ to Lombardy, where they had considerably augmented the agitation caused there by the late political conflicts.

¹ Raynald. a. 1255, n. 34.   Fleury, Hist. Ecclés. s. 17, l. lxxxiv. n. 15.
² Bzovius, Annal. a. 1327, n. 18.   Later (1424) King Ladislaus Jagello issued still more severe laws against heretics. Januszowski, Statuta prawa Krak. 1600, f. 260.
³ Wilkins, Conc. Brit. iii. p. 252.
⁴ Hefele, Conc. vi. p. 847.
⁵ P. Sarpi, Discorso sull' origine dell' Inquisizione in Venezia, 1638, 4.
⁶ The number of condemnations was later not very considerable here. The Liber Sententiarum of the Inquisition of Toulouse shows, between 1307-1323, only nineteen sentences in this extensive jurisdiction ; of these, fifteen were men and four women.   Phil. a Limborch, Hist. Inquis. Amstelod. 1692 ; Gibbon, Hist. of the Decline and Fall, c. liv. note 31.

§ 8.

In 1250, Innocent IV. commissioned Cardinal Octavian and the two Dominicans, Peter (Martyr) of Verona and Vivian of Bergamo, to combat heresy in the north of Italy. But in April 1252, Peter was cruelly murdered by heretics at Como, and heresy, protected by the tyrannical Ezzelin (who died 1259), maintained the upper hand.[1] The Dominicans, sorely grieved, were desirous of abandoning the post of inquisitors, and besought that it might be taken from them ; but the Pope refused to relieve them of it, and endeavoured to animate their courage.[2] It was in vain that Innocent IV. published Constitutions[3] enforcing earlier laws ; the magnitude of the evil called for special measures. The coöperation of the civil power was imperatively required on behalf of the inquisitors.[4] Statutes hindering or retarding their operations were declared invalid ;[5] sentences passed by the inquisitors were to be executed by the civil power,[6] and the inquisitors were empowered to enforce this by threats of censure.[7] The lay judges could indeed *in causis mixti fori* (cases which fell under the cognisance of the lay as well as of the spiritual courts) demand the acts of the ecclesiastical process,[8] but they could not take cognisance of matters of heresy, which was a purely ecclesiastical offence,[9] and thus could not in cases of heresy demand the acts to be laid before them. The *podestàs* of the towns and villages of Italy were in 1265 required, under pain of interdict and excommunication, to incorporate in their capitularies the constitutions of Innocent IV. and Alexander VI. against heretics, which contained also the imperial laws.[10] Such measures, indeed, appear intolerable to the spirit of the nineteenth century. It is too much for modern enlightenment to recognise the Church as an independent power, to allow her the entire cognisance of heresy, the greatest ecclesiastical crime, to claim no *placet* and *appel d'abus*, and no control over her judicial proceedings, to lower the State authority to the position of 'jailer and hangman to the Church.'[11] But Popes and Councils maintained their right to call in the aid of the civil power against heretics; and Charles IV. in 1359 issued a severe declaration against the usurpations and innovations which civil princes permitted themselves towards the ecclesiastical jurisdiction. The energetic conduct of Popes succeeded shortly ' after 1300 in greatly reducing the number of the sectaries in Italy, and the adherents of older or later heresies became very few.[12]

[1] Hist. de Languedoc, iii. pp. 431, 446. Raynald. a. 1251, n. 32; a. 1252, n. 11; 1254, n. 35 seq. 40.

[2] Raumer, Gesch. der Hohenst. vi. p. 300.

[3] Const. Cum fratres Perugia, 11 May 1252; Const. 9, Ad exstirpanda, cod. a.; Const. 10, Cum venerabilis, 1253. Card. Vinc. Petra, Com. in Const. Ap. t. iii. p. 45 seq.

[4] Alex. IV. Const. 15, Exortis, 1258, to the authorities and bishops in the territory of Spoleto (Petra, iii. p. 140 seq.), with the addition: ' In iis tantum quae ad eorum munus pertinent.'

[5] Alex. IV. 1257, Const. 10, Implacida, to the Bishop of Modena (Petra, t. iii. p. 124 seq.); to Innoc. IV. Const. 9, § 38. Likewise Urban IV. 1263, c. 9, Statutum, h.t. in 6. Eymeric, Direct. P. iii. q. 34.

[6] Council of Albi, 1254, c. 22. Alexander IV. declared (c. 6, de Haer. in 6) : ' Superiors who are under excommunication, or whose jurisdiction is merely *de facto*, not *de jure*, should and must render the assistance of the temporal arm against heresy when required by the bishops or inquisitors, if these cannot apply to the higher powers.'

[7] Alex. IV. Const. 17, Ad audientiam, 1260; Petra, t. iii. p. 146 seq. Cf. Leo X. Const. 43, Honestis, § 3, ib. p. 149.

[8] Petra, l.c. p. 148, n. 12 seq.

[9] Boniface VIII. c. 18, Ut inquisitionis, h.t. in 6, where also mention is made of the laws of Frederick II.

[10] Clem. IV. Const. 6, Ad exstirpanda, 1265; Const. 8, 1266. Petra, t. iii. pp. 229 seq. 234 seq.

[11] Huber, p. 24.

[12] Muratori, Antiquit. Ital. dissert. 60.

§ 9.

The conciliar and Papal legislation of the thirteenth century exhibits throughout the most numerous and most severe decrees against heretics. This circumstance plainly indicates what was in fact the case, that heresy was most dangerous at this time. 'The sects of the Gnostics, the Cathari and Albigenses, against whom it was necessary to wage a sanguinary war,' writes Döllinger,[1] 'and who especially elicited the severe and inexorable legislation of the Middle Ages against heresy, were the socialists and communists of that time. They attacked marriage, the family, and property ; had they triumphed, the consequences would have been general ruin, a return to barbarism and heathen licentiousness.' Huber, on the contrary, adopts the cause of these sects, which may be fittingly compared with ' the Internationalists' of our day. He considers that their antagonism to civil order is highly questionable. He particularly lays down these propositions: that the reports of the crimes of the Albigenses are untrue; that in any case the Church had no right to instigate bloody persecutions against them, for that the wheat and the cockle should both be suffered to grow until the harvest (Matt. xiii. 30); and that there is no excuse for the maintenance and increased severity of the Inquisition over less dangerous sects.   Let us examine more minutely these assertions.

[1] Döllinger, Kirche und Kirchen, p. 51; Eng. trans. p. 54.

§ 10.

The likeness which Huber[1] seeks to point out between the ascetic doctrines of the Albigenses and the orthodox monastic system is disproved by the absolute contrast they present both in principles and results.   In Gnostic and Manichæan sects both extremes are met with; on the one hand excessive severity,[2] on the other terrible licentiousness.[3] There was immorality and there was danger to civil authority in their doctrine of the free propagation of the species; in their approval of suicide;[4] in their hatred of the wealth of the clergy and the adornment of churches, which was not merely theoretical but led them into sanguinary excesses;[5] in the dissimulation and falsehood, destructive of social honesty, by which they feigned outward submission to the Catholic Church, and declared it lawful to conceal their heretical doctrines.[6]

It was quite natural that the acts of the Inquisition should record the errors but not the excesses of the Albigenses; in discovering whether a certain person was or was not tainted with heresy the criterion would be, not immoral conduct, of which a true believer might equally be guilty, but false doctrine. Heresy was a crime by itself, without needing any other. Fundamental dogmas of Christianity were involved. These heretics denied that Christ was true God and true man;[7] they denied the resurrection of the body, personal immortality,[8] and that the creation was the work of God;[9] they despised the Old Testament, and attributed it to the devil.[10] These doctrines excited among the Christian peoples a deep and most reasonable horror and aversion. Contemporary testimony to the moral conduct of the sectaries applies only to particular localities; and this apparent morality was often merely hypocritical. As Hefele[11] justly remarks : ' The saying of Innocent III., that the Cathari were worse than Saracens, is certainly true ; for their principles were totally un-Christian, and the results they deduced therefrom, in spite, nay on account of the veil of Christianity in which they were enveloped, were more dangerous to Christian society and Christian life than the Koran.'[12] If some of the charges brought against the Albigenses appear absurd, and if similar charges were brought against the early Christians, let us remember that we may learn from the history of the Church that however absurd a thing may be it has its parallel and precedent somewhere ; in the primitive ages of Christianity Gnostics were guilty of many crimes which heathens laid to the charge of the true Christians. These heretics were essentially of one accord with the ancient Gnostics and Manichæans, and their deceitfulness was in striking contrast to the truthfulness of the early Christians.

[1] Huber, p. 19.

[2] Neander, K.G. ii. p. 642 seq. 3d ed.

[3] Natal. Alex. H. E. sacc. 13 et 14, c. iii. a. 1, § 2, t. xv. p. 135 seq. Ekbert von Schönau, apud Du Plessis d'Argentré, t. i. P. i. p. 45. Council of Rheims, 1157 (Hefele, v. p. 500). Bishop Roger of Châlons to Wazo of Liége ; Gesta Episc. Leod. c. lix. Martene et Durand. iv. 898 seq. Vincent of Beauvais, Specul. Hist. l. xxix. c. xxvi. Raumer, Gesch. der Hohenst. vol. iii. pp. 74, 273.

[4] Raumer, l.c. pp. 274, 283. Neander, l.c. p. 644. Hurter, Innoc. III. vol. ii. p. 220.

[5] Raumer, iii. 292 ; vi. 290. Hurter, l.c. p. 217 seq. Cf. Guill. Armoricus, de Gest. Phil. Aug. (Duchesne, v. 72 ; Du Plessis, l.c. p. 58), ou the ' Ruptarii.'

[6] Neander, p. 647.

[7] Alanus ab Insulis, c. Hacret. l. i. c. xix. seq. c. xxxii. seq. (Migne, ccx. p. 321 seq.). Rainer, c. Wald. c. vi. (Bibl. PP. Lugd. xxv. 266). Moneta, adv. Cath. et Wald. l. i. Bonacurs, ap. Du Plessis, Coll. Jud. t. i. P. i. p. 43.

[8] Alanus, l.c. c. xxv. seq. p. 326 seq. Moneta, f. 357, 362.

[9] Alanus, l.c. l. i. c. ii-viii. p. 308 seq. Bonacurs, l.c. Rainer, ib. p. 48.

[10] Alanus, l.c. c. xxxv. seq. p. 337 seq. Moneta, f. 111, 199.

[11] Hefele, l.c. p. 741.

[12] Alanus ab Insulis, Prolog. ad Libr. contra Haereticos (Migne, ccx.
p. 307) : ' Nostris temporibus novi haeretici, imo veteres et inveterati, ve-
terantes dogmata, ex diversis haeresibus unam generalem haeresim com-
pingunt, et quasi ex diversis idolis unum idolum, ex diversis monstris
unum monstrum, et quasi ex diversis venenatis herbis unum toxicum commune conficiunt.'

§ 11.

Though proceedings against heretics were often set on foot by
the civil power, the Church always regarded it as one of her
most sacred duties to resist them, and to employ her penal authority for this purpose.[1]   The Cathari appealed to the parable
of the cockle and the wheat.[2]   They were told in reply,[3] that
Christ did not desire that the cockle should be spared but only
the wheat; that when the cockle plainly threatened the destruction of the wheat, and when the wheat could be saved by no other
means, the cockle should be rooted up.   Christ taught that evil
should be suffered with the good so long only as the removal of
the evil would entail greater harm, so long only as the good would
be in danger of being rooted up together with the evil.[4]   Moreover, the parable if thus used would prove too much ; it would
forbid government the use of the sword, would put a stop to excommunication, and would abolish all discipline : the cockle signi-
fies not merely false doctrine but all manner of wickedness.[5]

[1] Cyprian, ad Florent. de Exhort. Martyr. c. v. (Migne, iv. p. 638).   Cf.
Phillips, K.R. vi. § 322, p. 584.
[2] Moneta, l. v. c. xiii. f. 519.
[3] By William of Paris, de Leg. c. i.   Cf. Neander, l.c. p. 648.
[4] Moreover, individuals cannot always decide with certainty whether
this or that one is of the cockle.   Hieron. Com. in Matt. xiii. 25 : ' Inter
triticum et zizania, quod nos appellamus lolium, quamdiu herba est
et nondum culmus venit ad spicam, grandis similitudo est et in dis-
cernendo aut nulla aut perdifficilis distantia.   Praemonet ergo Dominus
ne ubi quid ambiguum est, cito sententiam proferamus, sed Deo judici
terminum reservemus, ut cum dies judicii venerit, ille non suspicionem
criminis, sed manifestum reatum de sanctorum coetu ejiciat.'
[5] So also Calvin, in the refutation of the errors of Servetus, apud Natal.
Alex. diss. cit. t. xvi. p. 32.

§ 12.

Less dangerous sects, especially the Waldenses, were also
persecuted ; but in course of time, and as a result of their obstinate defiance of the Church, the Waldenses adopted many

other errors, notably those of the Cathari ;[1] and even originally they were dangerous enough. Again, to quote Döllinger :[2] 'As to the Waldenses, every historian is aware that their principles concerning oaths and the penal authority of the State were such as to deny them any status in the European world at that time.' Every heresy in the Middle Ages was revolutionary, as tending to destroy order and dissolve the existing connection between Church and State.[3] We find no trace of an increased severity on the part of the Inquisition with regard to less dangerous sects ; the climax of severity against heretics was attained in the Albigensian persecutions. It is true, however, that a number of Popes employed the Inquisition, for they saw in it a necessary institution suited to the needs of society, approved by experience, and needed in many Christian countries to prevent the dissolution of social order.[4]

[1] Stephan. de Borbone, O.S.D. lib de Septem Donis Spir. S.: 'Postea in Provinciae terra et Lombardiae cum aliis haereticis se admiscentes et errorem eorum bibentes et serentes haeretici sunt judicati infestissimi et periculosissimi, ubique discurrentes, speciem sanctitatis et fidei praese-ferentes, veritatem autem ejus non habentes.' The Confession of Faith prescribed by Innocent III. for converted Waldenses shows this also (Den-zinger, Enchirid. Defin. 4th ed. p. 159 seq. n. 366 seq.).

[2] L.c.

[3] Hausmann, Gesch. der Papstl. Reservatfälle, p. 110.

[4] Huber declares (p. 21) that in Rome they would like a Council to decree as a saving truth that it was allowable to use force to coerce con-sciences, and he appeals to prop. 24 and 25 of the Syllabus of 1864 in support of his assertion. Of these propositions, the first treats of eccle-siastical coercive authority in general, and the second even still more gene-rally. The infliction of censures also belongs to the 'potestas coactiva.'

§ 13.

The Catholic priesthood, who for centuries have recited, on the 29th April, the office of Peter Arbues, have taken no offence at his canonisation, as Professor Huber (p. 22) has done. It would indeed be a bold conclusion to infer the canonisation of the Inquisition, with all its acts, from the canonisation of an inquisitor. The infallibility of the teaching office of the Pope in morals does not involve the belief that in laws concerning the Inquisition the Pope always legislated in the best, most perfect, and most judicious manner possible, and in the punishments inflicted never outstepped the limits of true moderation.[1] The case of Peter Arbues was subject to as close a scrutiny as any other. The process of his canonisation began in 1490 ; it was resumed in 1537, after the application to that effect made by Charles V. to Paul III. Philip III. in 1614 applied to Paul V. for the same purpose, and in 1622 to Gregory XV. His beatification was pronounced by Alexander VII., on April 17, 1662.[2] After renewed investigations he was canonised by Pius IX. in 1867.

[1] M. Canus, de locis Theol. l. v. c. v.
[2] Bull. Rom. ed. Luxemb. t. vi. pp. 195, 196, Const. 139, Fortissimos.

§ 14.

Why should not a Spanish inquisitor have been a holy man ? Their bitterest enemies acknowledge the purity of intention and the blameless lives of the Spanish inquisitors. Llorente, the great historian of the Inquisition and its bitter enemy,[1] who had access to its private papers, and Buckle, who is certainly in this case above suspicion, attest the ' undeviating and incorruptible integrity' of the inquisitors.[2] Townsend, a Protestant clergyman and an Englishman, cannot accuse them ; on the contrary, when treating of the Inquisition at Barcelona, he acknowledges that *all* its members were men of worth, and most of them distinguished for humanity.[3] Why, indeed, should not a judge have been a holy man, who conscientiously acted according to the laws in force in his day, though not according to the ' refined morality' of the nineteenth century, which was unknown to his contemporaries ?

[1] Llorente, Histoire critique de l'Inquisition d'Espagne. Cf. Carnicero, La Inquisicion justamente restablecida, Madrid, 1816 ; Hefele, Cardinal Ximenes, 2d ed. p. 291 seq.
[2] Hist. of Civ. in Eng. by H. T. Buckle, vol. i. p. 187, London, 1867.
[3] Townsend, Journey through Spain in 1786 and 1787, i. 122, London, 1792, apud Buckle, l.c. p. 188.

§ 15.

The reformers of the sixteenth century were animated by principles identical with those which issued in the Inquisition. In 1531, Bucer said publicly in the pulpit at Strasburg of

Michael Servetus, that he deserved an ignominious death for his work against the Trinity. In fact, rather more than twenty years later (on the 27th October 1553) Calvin had him burnt at Geneva over a slow fire. Calvin justified the deed in a special work,[1] and his theory and practice were approved not merely by Theodore Beza,[2] the theologian of most repute in Switzerland, but also by Melanchthon, in a letter of the 14th October 1554, and in a special treatise.[3] The Calvinists in Switzerland and elsewhere firmly maintained the right of government to punish heretics with death.[4] The preacher Jacob Gruet was in 1547 tortured and beheaded by Calvin's order. Valentine Gentilis, who was beheaded at Berne on the 10th September 1566, in his theses for a theological disputation had decreed capital punishment for those who were heretical according to his doctrine.[5] Funk as an Ossiandrist, Sylvan as a Socinian, Grell as a Calvinist, Hennig Brabant[6] in the factions of the municipal governments, all fell victims to the dominant religious party. In the imperial city of Nuremberg many religious persecutions took place; and others, it is well known, were instituted against Cryptocalvinism in Saxony.[7] Martin Luther, indeed, several times expressed himself against severe measures,[8] but also in many ways approved of proceedings against heretics—for instance, of punishing Anabaptists with fire and sword—and he demanded the banishment of public sinners;[9] he persecuted fiercely his former friend Karlstadt for deviations in doctrine, and appealed to the civil government against the Zwinglians.[10] He held all measures to be lawful for the extirpation of the Papacy and its adherents,[11] and quietly allowed his partisans, according to the advice of the lawyers, to undertake to defend their religion by force of arms, and even revolt against emperor and empire.[12] It is true he disapproved the deposition of King Christian II. of Denmark, effected by the nation in 1523 on account of many grievances, amongst others the attempt to introduce a new and false religion; but he did this in his own interest, for the King of Denmark was his partisan. The Danish people were far at that time from a change of religion. Christian's successor, Frederick I., was obliged, on the 23d March 1523, to bind himself by oath not to permit any preachers of Luther's school, but to treat them as heretics :[13] the new king did not venture to confess that he was himself a Lutheran ; only after the religious conference held in 1529 at Copenhagen preparatory measures were taken for the introduction of the new doctrine, which was introduced by force in 1537 by Christian III.[1] Melanchthon, with increasing years, increased in severity towards members of other religious creeds,[15] especially towards strict Lutherans and the Schwenkfeldians, who had already been persecuted. Lutheranism was in general, especially in Germany, introduced by princely authority—for instance, into the duchy of Saxony after the death of Duke George, into Naumburg, and into Silesia.[16] Benedict Carpzov shows us the practice of the Saxon courts of justice, which punished blasphemy against God and Christ with death, and heresies with exile.[17] As late as 1636, John Adelgreiff was beheaded and burnt in Königsberg ; and in 1687, Gunther, for leaning towards Socinianism, was beheaded in Lübeck upon the judgment of the jurists of Kiel and of the Theological Faculty of Wittenberg.[18] In England, Henry VIII., both before and after his schism, allowed the execution of heretics ; Cranmer defended it on Scriptural grounds ;[19] and in the reign of Elizabeth, the celebrated jurist Edward Coke argued in favour of severe penalties for heresy, as a crime against the Majesty of God and a pestilential leprosy of the soul.[20] The cruelties perpetrated under Elizabeth against Catholics far exceed all the punishments of the Spanish Inquisition.[21] Ranke speaks of the High Commission as a species of Protestant Inquisition.[22] The greatest tyranny was exercised towards Nonconformists.[23] In Sweden, where Gustavus Wasa introduced the new doctrines by force, extreme cruelty was employed towards adherents of the ancient faith.[24] In the Netherlands, William Amesius (died 1634) urged the persecution of heretics ;[25] and Coster, in his apology against the Gomarists, mentions as a fact that Calvinists held it lawful to inflict the punishment of death upon Catholics, and executed it upon not a few.[26] Döllinger[27] was right, that ' nothing is historically more untrue than the assertion that the Reformation was a movement in favour of liberty of conscience ; it was quite the contrary.' Protestants demanded this liberty for themselves, but when they were the stronger party they never granted it to others.[28]

[1] Fidelis expositio errorum M. Serveti et brevis eorum refutatio, ubi docetur jure gladii coercendos esse haereticos, 1554, Calvini Opusc. p. 686 seq. Gibbon says : 'I am more deeply scandalised at the single execution of Servetus than at the hecatombs which have blazed in the auto da fés of Spain and Portugal. A Catholic inquisitor yields the same obedience which he requires, but Calvin proscribed in Servetus the guilt of his rebellion.' Hist. of the Decline and Fall, chap. liv. note.

[2] Beza, Tract. de haereticis a magistratu civili puniendis, 1554. Cf. Jean Barbeyrac, Préface au livre de Pufendorf, § 11 ; Schröckh, Kirch. Gesch. seit der Reform. vol. v. p. 189.

[3] Epistol. Calvini, n. 187. Consilia et Judicia theol. ed. Pezelius, ii. 204. Schröckh, l.c. p. 517.

[4] Confess. Helvet. ii. art. 26 ; i. c. xxx.; Belg. a. 36 ; Scot. a. 29. Hefele, Conc. vii. p. 215 seq. Guericke, Lehrb. d. Kirch. Gesch. iii. p. 434, 9th ed.

[5] Guericke, l.c. p. 435, nt. 2. Cf. Benedict Aretius, Hist. de Supplicio Valent. Gentilis.

[6] Menzel, Neuere Gesch. der Deutschen, iv. pp. 333, 404 ; v. pp. 217, 229-237. On the eve of the execution of Hennig Brabant, Pastor Wagner preached in St. Katharine's in Brunswick on the stoning of Achan ; he pointed out the proper attitude of Christian governments with regard to such criminals, and that pious Christians should assist at such executions.

[7] Besnard, Repertorium, 1842, p. 301. Menzel, iv. pp. 450-464 ; v. pp. 185-195, 205 seq.

[8] Luther, Epistol. a Joh. Aurifabro collect. t. ii. p. 381, Eisleb. 1665, 4. Schröckh, l.c. v. pp. 187, 188.

[9] Luther, Werke, v. 286 seq.; xx. 364, Altenb. ed.; xiii. 440-442, Hall. ed.

[10] Menzel, l.c. i. 273, 480. Riffel, K.G. der neuesten Zeit. vol. i. pp. 332, 403. Phillips, K.R. iii. § 139.

[11] Sleidan, l. i. c. xxv. Cf. M. Gerbert, op. cit. l. iii. c. viii. n. 2.

[12] Cf. 'Warnung an meine lieben Deutschen' (Admonition to my beloved Germans) against the decree of the Diet of 1530, Luther's Werke, xvi. pp. 1090-2062, Walch's ed. ; Menzel, l.c. pp. 422, 423 ; Rintel, l.c. pp. 49-51 ; Bossuet, Hist. des Variations, P. iii. l. i. ; Gerbert, l.c. n. 3.

[13] Mohler's K.G. by Gams, iii. p. 192. Dahlmann's Dänische Gesch. iii. pp. 356, 357.

[14] Pantopiddan, ii. p. 806.

[15] Döllinger, Die Reform. gives the proofs, i. p. 388 seq. Cf. p. 237 seq.

[16] Menzel, l.c. vol. ii. pp. 1, 145-150, 275-281.

[17] B. Carpzovii Practica criminalis, P. i. q. 44, de Crimine Haereseos ; q. 45, de Blasphemiae Poena.

[18] Arnold, Ketzerhistorie, ii. 643. Döllinger, Kirche und Kirchen, p. 81, nt. 2 ; Eng. trans. i. p. 37 seq.

[19] Schröckh, K.G. seit der Reformation, ii. 512, 588 seq.
[20] E. Coke, Instit. iii. 5.
[21] Spondan. a. 1581, n. 15.
[22] Ranke, Päpste, ii. p. 160; Eng. trans. b. v. p. 114.
[23] Chebus, Die Dissenters in England (Niedner's Zeitschrift f. Histor. Theol. 1848, i. pp. 87-96).
[24] Buckle, l.c. i. chap. v. p. 264, note 30.
[25] Schröckh, l.c. vol. v. pp. 163, 164.
[26] Joh. Gerard. de Magistr. polit. n. 316, p. 1046.
[27] Kirche und Kirchen, p. 68; Eng. trans. p. 65.
[28] The English Calvinists who in the reign of Queen Mary fled to Denmark not only received no welcome from the Lutherans there, but were even rejected by them in the harshest and most inhuman manner. Menzel, vol. v. p. 119.

§ 16.

To judge the Inquisition rightly, the principle must be distinguished from its application. It cannot be denied that in the latter there were grave and lamentable defects, although the question has been much obscured by falsehood. For example, confession of mere sins of thought, from which any confessor could absolve, was never extorted from an accused person, neither was an appeal refused.[1] Even men like Guizot,[2] Villemain,[3] and St.-Simon have acknowledged that the Inquisition kept the sincere conversion of the delinquent well in view. Abuses practised by individual inquisitors were always condemned, and the Inquisition itself is not responsible for them.[5]

The principle that formal heresy is the most grievous crime is a natural consequence of the acceptance of the Christian religion.[6] In every ordered commonwealth the first law is that which provides for the safety and welfare of all. In the Church, purity of faith and morals is regarded as an essential condition of salvation, and must therefore be provided for accordingly.[7] Christian society could not feel obliged to acquiesce in the external propagation and dissemination of false doctrines because those who held them might entertain a conviction of their truth; otherwise the adulterer, forger, or murderer should be unpunished if his ill-regulated conscience acquitted him of guilt. The Church holds that open formal heresy deserves punishment, and therefore when it has been punished this has been rightly done; the application of the penalty in individual instances may have been faulty, for this is an action not of the teaching office but of the judicial authority; it is regulated principally by the criminal laws of the age in question, and by the notions of the time with regard to the treatment of criminals, which the Church adopts *in foro externo.* In many countries the punishments for poaching, burglary, sodomy, and false coining were more severe than those of the Inquisition. The Inquisition is not 'a product of the Papal doctrine of faith and morals,'[8] but a form of applying a positive principle of law—an external means for the execution of the law.

[1] Devoti, Instit. Jur. Can. t. iv. tit. 8, § 14, pp. 116, 117, who refers to S. Thom. Sum. 1, 2, q. 91, a. 4, q. 100, a. 9 ; and Bened. XIV. Syn. Dioec. l. ix. c. iv. n. 4.

[2] Hist. de la Civil. leçon vi. p. 56.

[3] Cours de Littérat. Bruxelles, 1838, p. 27.

[4] Doctrine de St.-Simon, 1828, p. 313.

[5] Cf. Censura Facult. Theol. Paris. in Erasmum, tit. de Poenis Haeret. prop. 3, 8 ; Du Plessis d'Argentré, t. ii. P. i. pp. 70, 71.

[6] Cf. Beidtel, Das canonische Recht, pp. 563-569. Balmez, Protestantism and Catholicity, chaps. xxxiv. xxxvi. Cf. also c. 35, c. xxiii. q. 4: ' Neo omnino liberabis hominem, nisi eum persecutus fueris peccatorem.' Alan. ab Insulis, de Arte praedicat. c. xviii. (Migne, cxc. p. 148) : ' Reddat charitas compassionem homini, puniat aequitas enormitatem vitii.'

[7] Devoti, Jus Can. t. iv. l. iv. tit. 8, § 1, p. 102. Balmez, chap. xxxv.

[8] A. Z. June 19, 1870 ; Schulte, i. pp. 47-49. He makes a very confused collection of laws against heretics in proof of his twelfth proposition, ' The Pope can deprive excommunicated persons of all their social rights, and in particular can dissolve their marriages.' The proceedings of Urban V. against Barnabò Visconti of Milan are especially cited (p. 50) in proof of this. But the text of the Bull is not given ; we only find ourselves referred to the statement of H. Spondanus, ad a. 1363, n. 1. The text, apud Raynald. h.a. n. 2, has, on the contrary, nothing about the dissolution of the marriage bond. There is no sense in regarding a mere judicial sentence as *definitio ex cathedrá*, neither in bringing a definition of the Council of Trent to bear upon an event which occurred two hundred years before. Vide Fessler, Infallibility, Eng. trans. pp. 95 seq. 63 seq. ; Archiv f. Kath. Kirchenrecht, vol. xxv. p. 122, n. 10.

§ 17.

Inquisitors had to proceed not only against heretics, but against Catholics who apostatised to Judaism[1] or Mahometanism ;[2] the Councils also punished this apostasy like heresy.[3]

There were many Jews in Spain who feigned conversion and were baptised, and succeeded in attaining even to bishoprics.[4]

The Spanish Inquisition was directed especially against Jews and Moors,[5] and as a *purely State institution*[6] it sought to withdraw itself from Papal control, which opposed its severity.[7]

Sixtus IV. had in 1478 confirmed the institution, but as early as 1482 he had cause to complain of its practice ; and in 1483 appeals were accepted in Rome against the Spanish inquisitors, of whom, in 1519, some were even excommunicated. The grand inquisitors Thomas Torquemada (1483-1498) and Didacus Deza (1498-1506) relied chiefly upon the authority of the State, which was in continual danger from the ' new Christians.' The Inquisition was by no means unpopular, and the State found it an efficient safeguard.[8] The Holy See afforded protection to many victims of the persecution, and took measures for the maintenance of justice, especially by proceedings against false witnesses and false accusers.[9] Paul III. reorganised the Inquisition to meet the danger threatened by Protestantism ; it had been established in Portugal under Clement VII. in 1527,[10] and was intrusted to the charge of cardinals chosen for their fitness for the office, and invested with wide authority.[11] Paul IV., who, without regard for persons, even for cardinals, strictly maintained the purity of the Faith, was favourable to the Inquisition, which was approved in Italy. In 1551, Julius III. expressly ordained that, except bishops, no one beyond the persons bearing the commission of the Inquisition should interfere in its operations ; he wished to prevent the encroachments of State officials.[12] Pius IV. still further amended the existing regulations;[13] and Pius V., who had been an inquisitor, and as such had often incurred risk of his life,[14] insisted upon greater care in the proceedings of the tribunal.[15]

The Inquisition in Rome was, upon the whole, very lenient ;[16] far more so than the Spanish Inquisition, though this has been very often described with enormous exaggeration.[17] Not half as many Spanish subjects lost their lives by the Inquisition as in our century by civil wars, by wholesale political executions, by the massacres in Cuba and in the East Indies. It often happens that those who complain most loudly of the cruelty of bygone days are the last to notice the crimes of the age in which we live.

[1] Clem. IV. Const. 14, Turbato corde, 1267. Petra, t. iii. p. 248 seq. Boniface VIII. c. 13, Contra, v. 2, de Haer. in 6. Cf. Greg. X. Const. 3, a. 1273; Nicol. IV. Const. 4, a. 1288; Petra, l.c. pp. 253 seq. 266 seq.; Paul IV. 1566, ib. p. 251.

[2] Gregor. XI. Const. 2, Admodum, 3 August 1372. Petra, t. iv. p. 153.

[3] Council of Mainz, 1310, c. 125. Hefele, vi. p. 446.

[4] Conc. Tolet. xvii. 694, c. 8. Hefele, iii. p. 323.

[5] Balmez, l.c. chap. xxxvi.

[6] Leo, Weltgesch. ii. p. 431. Cf. also Ranke, Päpste, i. p. 242 seq.; Eng. trans. vol. ii. p. 14; Hefele, Ximenes, p. 241 seq.

[7] Menzel, l.c. iv. p. 197.

[8] Balmez, l.c.

[9] Leo X. Const. 32, Intelleximus, a. 1518, Bull. Rom. iii. p. 465.

[10] Phillips, K.R. vi. p. 586.

[11] Paul III. Const. Licet ab initio, 1542, Bull. Rom. vi. ed. Taur. vi. p. 344.

[12] Jul. III. Const. 11, Licet a diversis, Bull. ed. cit. p. 431. Phillips, l.c. § 322, p. 587.

[13] Phillips, l.c. p. 588.

[14] Gabutius, Vita Pii, v. l. i. c. ii. pp. 10-12.

[15] Phillips, l.c. p. 589. Huber, p. 49, considers him ' the embodiment of intolerance.'

[16] Bened. XIV. de Syn. Dioec. l. vi. c. xi. n. 8, 12. Phillips, l.c. p. 597 seq. When the Roman Republic under Mazzini, on Feb. 28, 1849, decreed the abolition of the S. Uffizio, they first of all caused skeletons, bones, and suchlike to be introduced into the building, and then incited the people to burn it down; but the Carabineers who were quartered there, and who knew of the deception, offered a firm resistance. La Rivoluzione Romana, Firenze, 1850, l. ii. c. xiv. p. 336.

[17] Such are to be found, for instance, in a work that appeared in 1811: La Inquisicion sin máscara, by Nathanael Jomtob. It is full of the most burning hatred against everything Spanish. Balmez, l.c. As the danger of the introduction of Protestantism into Spain diminished, and as the spirit of the criminal code became more lenient, in the same measure did the Inquisition lessen its severity. Ib.

§ 18.

The Inquisition is also charged with directing its operations towards mere delusions, viz. so-called magic, devil-worship, and witchcraft, and of increasing the number of trials for witchcraft after the introduction of torture. But at its commencement the Inquisition had very little to do with these. Alexander IV. forbade inquisitors to punish persons accused of witchcraft,[1] and John XXII. only permitted their interference when heresy was joined to witchcraft in the accusation.[2]

Sorcerers were in general sentenced by the Church only to excommunication;[3] but the civil power was far more severe.[4]

After the thirteenth century trials for witchcraft instituted by the State[5] became at last a sort of epidemic,[6] and a verdict of guilt was followed by the burning of the accused.[7] This penalty together with torture was also employed in the East at an earlier period.[8] There is no trace of popular superstitions being fostered by the mediæval Popes.[9] The Bull of Innocent VIII., called the Witchcraft Bull, was issued in the year 1484.[10] Its object was, by making sorcery a matter for spiritual jurisdiction alone, to put a stop to the panic and disorder created by the operations of the civil tribunals.[11] This object was accomplished for a certain period.

The belief in sorcery long prevailed, and was common to Catholics and Protestants. In 1560, John Wein of Grave-on-the-Maas, physician to the Duke of Cleves, wrote against the burning of witches. In 1565, the Protestant legal faculty of Marburg condemned his work, and the author barely escaped a severe persecution, such as overtook Cornelius Loos. Also the Jesuit Adam Tanner, Chancellor of the University of Prague, was most violently opposed in his endeavour to check the evil. Frederick von Spee, also a Jesuit, was the author of a work which marks an epoch in the struggle.[12] It shows the immense difficulties attending even so able a resistance of the predominant belief.[13] *No witches were burnt in Rome,* and an instruction[14] which issued thence in 1657 effected much towards bringing legal proceedings more into accord with justice and truth. It called in the aid not merely of theologians and canonists, but even more imperatively of lawyers and physicians. Time alone could afford a complete remedy. The last witch was burnt at Glarus in 1783,[15] not, as has been said, at Seville in 1781. It is very doubtful whether, as Huber says, Protestantism merely accepted the belief in witches as a legacy bequeathed to it by the Middle Ages. Carpzov's vehement opposition to Spee does not look like it; neither do the facts of the Protestant persecutions for witchcraft[16] nor Luther's expressions about the devil.[17] Certainly on this point Luther's judgment was not 'formed upon the example of St. Thomas Aquinas,' whom besides he hated bitterly.

¹ Alex. IV. c. 8, § 4, de Haer. v. 2 in 6.
² Joh. XXII. Const. 13, Super, 12 Aug. 1325. Petra, t. iv. p. 45 seq.
Eymeric, Direct. P. ii. q. 43, n. 9.
³ *E.g.* Synods of Grado, 1296, c. 23; of Salamanca, 1335, c. 15; of
Prague, 1349, c. 56 (Hefele, vi. pp. 335, 561, 598).
⁴ Friedberg (l.c. p. 93, No. 3, 5, 8, 9) quotes English codes of law and
the decrees of French parliaments. Görres (Mystik, iv. ii. p. 513 seq.)
gives other references. Charles V. reënacted the punishment of burning
for witches and sorcerers who bring evil upon others. Engel, Coll. Jur.
Can. 1. v. tit. 21, § 3, n. 17 fin. It is certain that in individual instances
many *crimes* were committed by witches and sorcerers. Monstrelet, Chron.
a. 1459, 1460; Du Plessis, t. i. P. ii. p. 418, c. 2.
⁵ Magic was held to be a crime *mixti fori*. Reiffenstuel, in l. v. Decret.
tit. 21, n. 18. Schmalzgrueber, in h.l. n. 51, with references to earlier
authors; also Van Espen, Jur. Eccl. Univ. P. iii. tit. 4, c. iii. n. 49-54.
⁶ Land-law of the Sachsenspiegel, b. ii. art. 13, § 7.
⁷ Phillips, Vermischte Schriften, iii. p. 193.
⁸ L. v-ix. Cod. ix. 18. Cf. Basil. 1. lx. c. xxxix. n. 21; Leo, Sap. Const.
65 (Migne, cvii. 565).
⁹ In the Decretals of Gregory IX. only three passages stand under the
title in question : the first belongs to the *penitentiale* of Theodore of Canterbury ; the second (of Alexander III.) refers to the *inspectio astrolabii*
for the discovery of theft ; the third (of Honorius III.) forbids the election
of bishops by lot (l. v. Decret. tit. 21, de Sortil.). Canonists treat of
these matters under this title.
¹⁰ Const. Summis desiderantes, Bull. Rom. iii. iii. p. 291.
¹¹ Phillips, Lehrbuch des K.R. § 204, p. 602, iii. Alexander VI. (c. nn.
de Malef. et Incant. v. 12 in Sept.), Leo X. (Const. Honestis petentinm,
1521, Bull. Rom. l.c. p. 499), and Hadrian VI. (ad Inquis. Com. 20 Juli
1522 ; Hard. Conc. ix. pp. 1907-1910) used their authority to repress the
evil of sorcerers, especially in Lombardy. 'The Popes,' says Görres (l.c.
p. 651 seq.) 'were bound to take cognisance of a matter so important, so
deeply rooted in the people, and in which the people believed, and therefore they sent out inquisitors. This Bull of Innocent was designed merely
for the protection within the limits of their jurisdiction of the courts
established in the Rhine lands, where the evil was freshly spreading ; it
confirmed their authority to arrest, punish, or reclaim from evil courses ;
permitting them especially for the better exercise of the latter duty to
expound the Word of God to the people in any parish church within their
jurisdiction as often as it should be necessary, and to have recourse to all
measures their opinion judged conducive to the instruction of the people.
Any sins they may through weakness have fallen into, by going too far or
not far enough, cannot be justified by the orders they received. Far rather
should this case be held as proof that the Popes' conduct was throughout
directed to moderate and soothe, and that whilst paying due regard to the
spirit of the time they always endeavoured to use the insight they had
acquired to introduce a better state of things.'
¹² Cautio criminalis s. de processibus contra sagas, Rintel, 1631, Francof.
1632. Dub. xxviii. shows how much strict judges mistrusted even confessors.

[13] Spee's chief opponent was the Protestant jurist Benedict Carpzov. This question is fully treated in the Historisch Polit. Blättern, vol. lxviii. H. 5, 6, to which we must here refer. The stanch Protestant M. Schröckh (K.G. seit der Reform. vol. vii. p. 326) observes with regard to Spee : ' It is an honour to Catholic Germany that even in the earlier years of this same seventeenth century, *that is, long before Protestants had begun to think of the reformation of this superstition*, a courageous friend of truth had entered the lists against it.' Schröckh takes note also of some later Italian writings to the same purport, as well as of the disputes which broke out in Bavaria in 1766.

[14] Vide also Görres, l.c. p. 652 seq.

[15] Histor. Polit. Bl. l.c.   Schröckh, l.c. p. 336, put it at 1780.

[16] Menzel, l.c. vol. v. p. 90; viii. p. 59 seq. Illgen's Zeitschr. für Histor. Theol. 1841, p. 181 seq. Döllinger, Die Reformation, ii. p. 418.

[17] The passages are given in the paper, Luther über das Zauberwesen, Histor. Polit. Bl. 1861 (vol. xlvii. pp. 890-918).

§ 19.

Huber tells us that the superstition of the Popes, the Inquisition, and the so-called Witchcraft Bull of Innocent VIII., raised trials for witchcraft to gigantic proportions. To disprove his statement we have but to glance at the German Synod of 799[1] against sorcerers and witches, at the massacre of witches in Germany in 1074, which Gregory VII. rebuked,[2] and at the schismatic Greeks, who also believed in sorcery and witchcraft. The treatise of Psellus[3] is anterior to all similar works in western countries on the same subject. The Greeks had an institution quite similar to the Inquisition of the Latins ; the *principle* was the same, although burning was not universally in use as the punishment. In the year 1338 a certain George Tzerentzes in Constantinople was accused of magic ; and when confession had been obtained, he was sentenced to severe ecclesiastical penance ; his relations were to keep strict watch over him, and if he relapsed, he was to be excommunicated and severely punished.[4]   The Patriarch John XIV. issued a pastoral to his clergy expressly against incantations and magic, which had again gained much ground ; and he gave orders that the clergy should go about in the town to make minute investigations after such sorcerers and seducers, and that every one should assist them in their search.[5]   He likewise ordered the civil authorities[6] to render assistance in this God-pleasing[7] work to the spiritual inquisitors, who in each quarter of the town should institute minute investigations after sorcerers,[8] that the guilty might be punished as they deserved. The Patriarch Kallistus published a charge to the people when a sorceress and soothsayer, Amarantine, who had long remained concealed, was converted of her own free will, and went to do penance in a convent; he admonished those whom she had corrupted to imitate her repentance, and insured to her a prebend from the emperor (1351).[9] The trial of two sorcerers was likewise undertaken.[10] In January 1365 a monk Isaias was dismissed for having given a fee to a sorcerer for the recovery of a sum of money lost by the monk Hilarion.[11] On the 12th May 1371 a synodal decree was published against sorcery.[12] A monk Phudules was accused of originating the disorder, especially of attracting women, who for love of him abandoned their husbands and children. He repented, and admitted having received books upon sorcery from a physician Syropulos.[13] Strict trials were instituted upon this monk, as well as upon Syropulos and a certain Gabrielopulos; they were banished from Constantinople and from the empire; a priest John Paradeisos, corrupted by Syropulos, a monk Joasaph, and a ' papas' James were deposed. In May 1371 three priests abjured sorcery with other errors.[14] On April 22, 1372, a priest Stylian Clidas was excommunicated for having used sorcery.[15] In May 1383 the monk Theodosius Phudules was made to promise before the Patriarch Nilus that he would never more employ magic.[16] It is certain that the superstition was not less strong amongst the Greeks than amongst the Latins, and was wider spread;[17] they were forced to be content with punishing its more glaring excesses. Balsamon frequently mentions punishments ordained by Synods for sorcerers and witches;[18] the belief in their existence and that they deserved punishment were the same as in the West: the proportion of the punishment was not always the same; all were not put to death as the magician Paulinus was in the sixth century.[19] I was justified therefore in inquiring: ' Were the Popes responsible for the introduction of witchcraft amongst the schismatic Greeks ?' when *Janus* asserted that all witchcraft was either directly or indirectly a product of the belief in the irrefragable authority of the Pope. This indictment concerning witchcraft is one of those which, as De Maistre[20] observes, must be fastened either upon the whole human race or upon no one at all. The Popes were not ahead of other men either in issuing penal decrees against sorcerers or witches, nor in sentencing individual delinquents. They were the children of their age, and acted accordingly. We know now how much is purely natural which even the most enlightened men of their age formerly accounted supernatural. In the Middle Ages the crime of magic occupied a large share of the attention of the learned.[21] No Christian can assert diabolic influences upon mankind to be absolutely impossible, nay that they are possible is shown by Scripture and tradition;[22] therefore the error was not one of principle; it existed only in the manner of treating particular manifestations, and for this subordinates only are responsible. Huber makes it a strong point that the patriarchs of the East laid no claim to be God's infallible vicegerents. We reply, that the question of the judicial persecution of witches has no connection with the infallibility of the teaching office; and Pichler shows that the Byzantine patriarchs undoubtedly did make this claim. The prerogative of infallibility is plainly asserted in an epistle of the Patriarch Isaias (1323–1333);[23] and we find the Byzantines claiming for their Church the prerogatives of the Church of Rome.[24] They call the Church of Constantinople 'the Mystical Sion, the Mother of all Churches, the New Jerusalem,'[25] 'the Author of Faith,'[26] 'the sublime resting-place, whence issue the fountains of pure doctrine that flow over the whole earth.'[27] Their patriarchs give themselves amongst other titles those of Universal Teacher of all Christians and Vicar of Christ.[28]

    There is sufficient proof that the Popes had very little to do with the persecution of witches, and did not instigate or excite them; but on the contrary, as Görres says, 'acted always with leniency and moderation.' Had they delighted in the opportunity, the codes of canon law would not have treated the subject so sparingly, and Papal decrees would have afforded a far richer prey to modern critics. Laws and their application are two widely different things in the administration of justice, whether civil or ecclesiastical.

[1] Others might be cited until the Synod of Magdeburg, 1390, c. 45 (Hefele, vi. p. 837), which decreed severe punishments against sorcerers. For examples of sorcery in the time of the Carolingians, vide Dümmler, Ostfränkische Geschichte, ii. p. 673, n. 79 ; i. 466, 329.

[2] Neander, Kirchengeschichte, ii. p. 380, n. 3 ; Greg. VII. Ep. 21. For passages from the Fathers, vide Gratian, c. xxvi. q. 5 ; also apud Görres, Mystik, iii. p. 44 seq. Cf. Greg. M. l. xi. Ep. 33 ; Jaffé, n. 1403, c. viii. c. et q. cit. As to Scripture, besides Levit. xx. 27, who has not heard of the history of the Witch of Endor, of the controversies concerning the *spiritus pythonicus*, and the possessed in the New Testament?

[3] Psellus, de Daemonum Energia (Migne, PP. gr. t. cxlv. p. 819 seq.), treats (c. vii.) of the appearances of demons amongst men ; c. xi. p. 844, of the possession of the latter by the former; c. xiii. p. 849, of the entering of demons into men and animals ; c. xv. p. 853, of a possessed person at Elason who prophesied many things, and whom he himself brought to Constantinople ; c. xix. p. 864, of the apparition of demons at births, &c. Cf. Blastare's Synt. Alphab. Lit. M. c. i. (Migne, l.c. p. 1 seq.).

[4] Acta Patriarchatus Cpl. ed. Müller et Miklosich, t. i. doc. 79, 80, pp. 180-182. Migne, PP. gr. t. clii. p. 1224 seq.

[5] Acta, t. i. doc. 85, pp. 184-187. Migne, l.c. p. 1228 seq.

[6] Acta, t. i. doc. 86, pp. 188-190. Migne, p. 1230.

[7] Cf. the prop. Migne, p. 1231 : Ποῖον γὰρ ἂν ἕτερον ἔργον ὑπὲρ τῆς δόξης εἴη κ.τ.λ.

[8] Migne, p. 1229 : ὥστε περιέναι αὐτοὺς καὶ ἀκριβῆ ζήτησιν ποιεῖσθαι ἐν ἑκάστῃ γειτονίᾳ τῆς βασιλευούσης ταύτης τῶν πόλεων. The inquisitors are ordered ζητῆσαι, the magicians καὶ εὑρεῖν καὶ εἰς μέσον ἑλκύσαι καὶ ταῖς πρεπούσαις ὑποβαλλεῖν κακώσεσι καὶ κολάσεσι, p. 1231 D.

[9] Acta, t. i. doc. 134, 137, pp. 301 seq. 317 seq. Migne, l.c. pp. 1303 seq. 1320.

[10] Acta, t. i. doc. 153, pp. 342, 344. Migne, p. 1338 seq. Unfortunately the important conclusion of the document is wanting.

[11] Acta, l.c. doc. 228, pp. 488, 489.

[12] Ib. doc. 292, pp. 541-550. Migne, l.c. p. 1431 seq.

[13] Chrys. hom. 38, in Act. mentions books of magic (Migne, Opp. Chrys. ix. p. 275).

[14] Acta, t. i. doc. 305, p. 560.

[15] Ib. doc. 331, pp. 594, 595.

[16] Ib. t. ii. doc. 377, pp. 84, 85.

[17] I adduced numerous proofs in my work on Photius, vol. i. pp. 605, 609 ; ii. pp. 261, 263 ; iii. pp. 133, 674, 837, 839 seq.

[18] Theodor. Balsam. in Can. Trull. 61, p. 720 seq. ; in Basil. can. 83, i. p. 720 seq. ; ii. p. 801.

[19] Theophyl. Simocatta, l. i. c. xi. pp. 56, 57.

[20] De Maistre, Lettres sur l'Inquisition Espagnole, lettre ii. p. 53.

[21] Raban. Maurus, de Praestigiis Magor. (cf. c. 5, c. xxvi. q. 5). Joh. Saresbur. Polycrat. l. i. c. ix. seq. p. 406 seq. ; l. ii. c. xxviii. p. 472 seq.

Gerson, de Errorib. circa art. Magic, i. p. 211, says : ' Philosophy makes it probable, and the Faith makes it certain, that there are demons ; a denial of their existence or power is an error against Holy Scripture ; those, therefore, should be corrected who would make sport of theologians for this belief.' Also (Collat. de Angel. iii. 1483) : ' Diabolic influences cannot be denied salva fidei integritate et rationis naturalis probabilitate' (vide Schwab, Gerson, pp. 711 seq. 718 seq.). Cf. also the Determinatio Fac. Theol. Paris, 1398; Du Plessis, Coll. Jud. t. i. P. ii. pp. 154-157.

[22] Cf. v. Schubert, Zaubersünden, Augs. Postzeitung, Suppl. 18 Jan. 1854; Civiltà Cattolica, 5 Maggio 1866, quad. 387, pp. 289-307.

[23] Acta Patr. Cpl. Vindob. 1860, t. i. doc. 71, p. 159.

[24] Pichler, Gesch. der kirchlichen Trennung, i. pp. 360, 361, § 45.

[25] Nicol. Methon. Orat. de Hierarchia, ed. Dimitracopul. i. p. 268. Cf. Phot. Orat. i. in Russorum Adventum, p. 209 seq. ed. Nauck.

[26] Nicetas Choniat. in Alex. Murzufl. n. 5.

[27] Thus Caerularius, in his Encyclica (Will, Acta et Scripta, p. 157), with the words of Photius. Cf. my work upon the latter, vol. i. p. 643, No. 11 ; vol. iii. p. 762, No. 7.

[28] Thus Nilus and Antony IV. in the Acta Patr. Cpl. t. ii. doc. 345, 347, 447. Similarly in the letters despatched to Russia in 1370, ib. t. i. doc. 264, 266. Cf. Photius, vol. iii. p. 806, No. 129, 130.

§ 20.

The case of Huss[1] is an example of the injustice of the charges brought against Popes for their manner of punishing heretics. His own confession and the decrees of the civil legislature show it, as also his condemnation at Constance by the reforming party, which was opposed to Papal rights. Unprejudiced minds are bound to confess ' that the moral horror awakened in us by the blazing pyres should not be directed entirely against the Popes and the Church in the Middle Ages, but against the ideas which governed the whole of mediæval society ;'[2] and why not also against Calvin and the ideas which governed society at the time of the Reformation? We should have then to pronounce sentence upon the whole human race before the nineteenth century, and to exalt and glorify this alone. But the nineteenth century, in spite of its boasted humanity, is stained with cruelty, though this cruelty is hidden under new forms ; and posterity may condemn our hypocritical concealment, as we condemn the unvarnished roughness of the past.

[1] Cf. Hefele, vii. p. 214 seq.

[2] Sigmund Riezler, on W. Berger's Johannes Hus und König Sigmund, Augsb. A. Z. Suppl. 21 April 1872.

ESSAY XVII.

THE CHURCH AND LIBERTY OF CONSCIENCE.

§ 1. Syllabus, prop. 16, 21, 77-79. § 2. What is toleration? § 3. Distinction between persons and principles. Syllabus, prop. 17. § 4. Truth and charity. § 5. Tolerance and intolerance in society. § 6. Demands upon the modern State. § 7. The State should not be without religion. § 8. The State must not allow absolute freedom to all forms of worship. § 9. Refusal and abolition of oaths. § 10. A State with no religion. § 11. Inconsistency of modern Liberalism. § 12, 13. Introduction of religious liberty, and respect for the equality of religions when once established. § 14-17. Religious liberty founded on untenable principles. Syllabus, prop. 15, 18. § 18. Liberty to err is liberty to do evil. § 19. The Church and the oath of allegiance to a constitution. § 20. Excommunication. § 21. Charge against Innocent XII. § 22. The massacre of St. Bartholomew. § 23. Complaints against the Bavarian Constitution. § 24. The French Charter of 1814. § 25. Consistency of the Catholic Church.

§ 1.

THE Catholic Church must, with St. Peter (2 ii. 1 seq.), condemn those who bring in sects of perdition (heretics), lying teachers, who bring upon themselves swift destruction. She claims, and must claim ever and everywhere as a necessity of her existence, that her doctrine is of God and of Christ. Wherefore she can admit no right to gainsay the divine revelation intrusted to her, nor even the right to remain indifferent towards it. The proposition once established that there is only one true Church, out of which there is no salvation, also the proposition that this Church can only be the Catholic Church, man's welfare demands that all attempts to withdraw him from the pale of this Church should be firmly resisted.

Hence we see the consistency of the condemnation of those propositions of the Syllabus : ' Men may in any religion find the

way of eternal salvation and obtain eternal salvation ;'[1] and
' The Church has not the power of defining dogmatically that the
religion of the Catholic Church is the only true religion.'[2] From
this point of view, too, it was quite necessary to condemn these
further propositions, that ' It is no longer necessary that the
Catholic religion should be held as the only religion of the
State, to the exclusion of all others ;[3] hence it has been wisely
provided by the law, in some countries called Catholic, that
persons coming to reside therein shall enjoy the free exercise of
their own worship ;[4] moreover, it is false that the civil liberty
of every mode of worship, and the full power given to all of
overtly and publicly manifesting their opinions and their ideas,
conduce more easily to corrupt the morals and minds of the
people, and to the propagation of the pest of indifferentism.'[5]

We must accurately distinguish the condition of the Catholic
State where unity of faith prevails from those States in which
this unity has long been absent.[6] We must distinguish the
question of preserving to Nonconformists in a State the rights
they have acquired from the question of what rights they are
to receive first of all. We must distinguish the principles on
which the Church acts from those on which modern governments
act. We must distinguish religious or dogmatic toleration from
civil and political toleration.[7]

[1] Syllab. a. 1864, n. 16 (Enc. of 9 Nov. 1846 and 17 March 1856. Alloc.
17 Dec. 1847).
[2] Syll. n. 21 ; Multiplices inter, 10 June 1851, against Vigil's book.
[3] Syll. n. 77 (Alloc. 26 July 1855, concerning Spain). Cf. Ketteler,
Deutschland nach dem Kriege v. 1866, Mainz, 1867, p. 136 seq.
[4] Syll. n. 78; Alloc. 27 Sept. 1852, on New Granada. Cf. Ketteler, l.c.
p. 138 seq.
[5] Syll. n. 79; Alloc. 15 Dec. 1856, on Mexico. Cf. Ketteler, l.c. p.
141 seq.
[6] Cf. Ketteler, in the reply to the Köln. Zeitung of 23 April (Mainzer
Journal, 2 May 1871).
[7] It is one of the ' ideals' of modern Liberalism that the State as such
shall be indifferent to all religious truth ; that it shall not merely tolerate
but protect every creed and every error ; that it shall further the multi-
plicity of forms of worship, and concede to every citizen an inalienable
right of unlimited liberty of belief, conscience, and worship. Locke has
greatly promoted this view. He acknowledged a letter, printed first in
Latin in 1698, and in French in 1710, in favour of universal toleration (Le

Clerc, Biblioth. Univers. t. xv. p. 403) in his will to be his work (Jean Barbograc, Notes sur le Droit de la Nature et des Gens du Baron de Pufendorf, l. vi. chap. iv. § 10. Cf. Noodt, dissert. de Religione ab Imperatorio Jure Libera, French ed. 1707). They were principally English and French free-thinkers and philosophers who upheld this view, in Germany in particular Teller, Semmler, Bahrt, Lessing. Many works were written on this subject in these countries down to Jules Simon's La Liberté de Conscience, Paris, 1857. On these various works on toleration see Döllinger, Kirche und Kirchen, p. 68, Eng. ed.

§ 2.

'Catholic intolerance' is a catchword of the Liberals, and one which stimulates the anger of modern Liberalism against the Church. What is toleration? The Spanish philosopher Balmez thus defines this misused word :[1] 'Strictly speaking it means the patience with which we suffer a thing we judge to be bad, but which we think it desirable not to punish. Thus some kinds of scandals are tolerated ; such and such abuses are tolerated ; the idea of toleration is always accompanied by the idea of evil. It would be absurd to speak of tolerating virtue or goodness. Toleration exercised in the order of ideas always presupposes an intellectual error or fault. No one will say that he tolerates the truth. We may *tolerate* opinions which appear to us manifestly erroneous ; but we can *respect* them only when we are not certain of their contradictory, when they are founded upon good arguments, as, for example, on hypotheses scientifically justifiable. To respect opinions also sometimes means to respect those who hold them for their good faith or for their good intentions.[2] A man is called *tolerant* when he is able to bear opinions contrary to his own without irritation or disturbance. Toleration or intolerance may be found in the sceptic and in the devout. St. Francis of Sales was tolerant ; Voltaire excessively intolerant.' 'The tolerance of a religious man arises not from want of faith ; it may coexist with a burning zeal for the spread and preservation of the truth ; it is born of two principles, charity and humility.'[3] Charity hopes all things from all men, and looks always on the best side ; it would always hope that those in error were not guilty of the error ; humility induces forbearance towards our neighbour.

[1] Protestantism and Catholicity compared, c. xxxiv. Eng. trans. London, 1849, p. 151. Professor Merkle (Die Toleranz nach Kathol. Principien, p. 4) justly says : ' There is scarcely any word used so foolishly and thoughtlessly as the word toleration. Things have been confused with persons, religious conviction with religious indifference and scepticism, the objective with the subjective, formal or voluntary error in matters of faith with material or involuntary error, and thus sin with evil or misfortune. The same rights have been claimed for error as for truth. Opposition·of principles has been said to be mere opposition of forms; a mere diversified manifestation of the same principle. To be indifferent in religious matters, to betray religious truth, to lull into false security, to recognise and favour what is known to be untrue, to be frivolous and superficial in religion, to be without principle and without conscience—all this has been called praiseworthy toleration.'

[2] Balmez, l.c. p. 151.
[3] Ibid.

§ 3.

The Church has always recognised that people might live in error of faith and yet be saved;[1] that they might be in unconscious spiritual communion with the true Church, although through invincible ignorance they were not in external communion with her ;[2] that condemnation regarded false *principles*, not the *persons* in error ;[3] that towards these all the duties of brotherly love were to be exercised, and that no Catholic had the smallest right to impute guilt to them.[4] Pius IX. teaches the same thing. In the Allocution of the 9th December 1854 (the same which condemns the proposition that there is *good* hope of the eternal salvation of *all* those who are not in the Church of Christ)[5] the Pope solemnly declares :[6] 'Far be it from us to dare to set bounds to the boundless mercy of God; far be it from us to desire to search into the depths of the hidden counsels and judgments of God, an abyss that the mind of man cannot explore. . . . We must hold as of faith that out of the Apostolic Roman Church there is no salvation ; that she is the only ark of safety, and whosoever is not in her perishes in the deluge ; we must also, on the other hand, recognise with certainty that those who are in invincible ignorance of the true religion are not guilty for this in the eye of the Lord. And who will presume to mark out the limits of this ignorance according to the character and diversity of peoples, countries, minds, and the rest? Doubtless when, divested of the bonds of our mortality, we see God as He is, we shall comprehend how beautiful and how close is the union between His justice and His mercy; but whilst we linger in our earthly abode, burdened by our bodies, let us hold firmly to the Catholic belief that there is one God, one faith, one baptism; and that to inquire further is not lawful. But as charity demands, let us be frequent in prayer that all nations may turn to Christ, and with all our strength let us labour for the salvation of all men; for the arm of the Lord is not shortened, and the gift of divine grace will never be refused to those who ask in all sincerity for its enlightenment.' In the same way the Encyclical to the Italian bishops, 10th August 1863, says:[7] 'It is known to us and to you that those who are in invincible ignorance of our most holy religion, but who observe carefully the natural law and the precepts graven by God upon the hearts of all men, and who being disposed to obey God lead an honest and upright life, may, aided by the light of divine grace, attain to eternal life; for God, who sees clearly, searches and knows the heart, the disposition, the thoughts and intentions of each, in His supreme mercy and goodness by no means permits that any one suffer eternal punishment who has not of his own free will fallen into sin.' Notwithstanding these words there are some who have ventured to describe the following as Papal doctrine: 'To whoever refuses submission [to the authority and government of priests] all his strivings after truth, all his moral conduct, all his fulfilment of the highest command of charity towards God and his neighbour, avail nothing; he is subject to the wrath of God and eternal damnation.'[8] Where has the Church taught that 'he who submits to the hierarchy, invokes their aid, lets them give him their spiritual treasures, although he troubles himself not at all to know the truth, and has broken or contemned all commands, divine or human, may rejoice in the certainty that by means of the Church he will attain salvation'? The doctrine of the Church is quite the contrary, and against the certainty of the Lutherans, deduced from their doctrine of *sola fides justificans* (justification by faith alone), the Church has always taught the uncertainty of salvation even for the faithful.[9]   Can, then, misrepresentation go further than this?

[1] Aug. Ep. 162, ad Glor. (c. 29, c. xxiv. q. 3) : ' Qui sententiam suam, quamvis falsam atque perversam, nulla pertinaci animositate defendunt, praesertim quam non audacia suae praesumptionis pepererunt, sed a seductis et in errorem lapsis parentibus accceperunt, quaerunt autem cauta sollicitudine veritatem, corrigi parati, cum invenerint, nequaquam sunt inter haereticos deputandi.' Cf. can. 31, ibid. ; Reiffenstuel, tract. 4, de Virt. Theol. q. 2, n. 17, 19 ; Sporer, Theol. Mor. Praec. i. Decal. c. iii. sect. 2, ass. 2, § 2 ; Devoti, Jus Can. t. iv. tit. 4, § 1, 2, p. 40.

[2] Aug. Brevicul. Coll. c. Donat. die iii.   Cf. Bellarm. de Eccl. Milit. l. iii. c. iii.; Suarez, de Fide, disput. 12, sect. 4, n. 22 ; Annot. in Schema de Eccl. c. iv. (Friedrich, Docum. ii. p. 119 seq.) ; Perrone, tract. de Ecclesia, P. i. sect. 1, c. ii. a. 4, prop. 2.

[3] Hettinger, Apologie des Christ. ii. 2, p. 93.   Merkle, l.c. p. 39 seq.

[4] Every Catholic readily admits that very often people out of the Church are better than the system to which they feel or imagine themselves bound ; just as *vice versâ* in the Church individuals are in theory and practice on the average lower than the system in which they live. Döllinger, Church and the Churches, Eng. trans. Introd. p. 17.

[5] Syllab. prop. 17.

[6] SS. Domini nostri Pii P. IX. Allocutio in Consistorio, 9 Decembris 1854, habita.   Recueil des Allocutions, &c. Paris, 1865, p. 340.

[7] Ib. p. 480.

[8] Augsb. A. Z. Sup. of 3d Dec. 1871.

[9] Conc. Trid. Sess. vi. de Justif. can. 12-15, cap. ix.

§ 4.

Charity may call for any sacrifice, but not for a denial of reason or logic. Catholic truth cannot be sacrificed to Catholic charity. Charity cannot require that what is highest—the truth of revelation—should be made subordinate ; neither can it regard truth and error with equal favour, nor accept error instead of truth.   We may regret the error of another, and excuse it as being held in good faith and ignorance ; but so far as he is in error we cannot allow him to hope for salvation ;[1] this would only strengthen him in his error and do him wrong ; it would be contrary to the precept of Christian charity.

[1] Pelisson à Mme. de Brinon, 1690 (Foucher de Careil, Œuvres de Leibnitz, i. p. 79) : ' Autre chose est excuser et plaindre quelqu'un et le regarder avec compassion, autre chose luy faire espérer le salut dans son erreur.'

§ 5.

Tolerance or intolerance may exist in governments and in society as in individuals, but this more as the effect of a habit than of a principle. Society is indebted for its prevailing spirit of toleration not to modern philosophers, who have had nothing new to say about it, but to the force of circumstances, the multitude of religious parties, to scepticism, to indifference, to the lassitude produced by wars, to greater gentleness in manners, to the improved means of travel and intercommunication amongst men, to the preponderance of material interests.[1] Philosophy upheld civil toleration; but its adherents went further. As Bossuet foresaw they desired ecclesiastical or dogmatic toleration, which is religious indifference.[2] Even if the former were conceded, the latter never could be from a Catholic point of view. For 'any ecclesiastical body conscious of being the depositary of absolute objective truth, and of holding the eternal destinies of the whole human race, must consider itself the only true Church, and all other creeds differing from its own as more or less in error. Therefore this Church must consider herself deputed to resist and refute all such creeds, and thereby to cause the true doctrine to prevail.'[3] This attitude, so natural and so necessary, which renders it impossible for the Church to come to terms with other religious opinions and parties, and renders her so dear and precious to her children, is precisely what causes the hatred felt for her by those without her pale.[4] So on this point as on many others, now as in her early days when the world was still heathen, her voice is raised in opposition to the spirit of the world. Religious intolerance, which the true Church firmly maintains, does not necessitate civil intolerance, which would permit no other religion to exist. However convinced any one may be of the truth of his own religion he may let others live in peace without belonging to it,[5] and fulfil towards them with joy and zeal all the duties of fraternal love expressly enjoined by the Catholic Church.[6]

[1] Balmez, p. 154.
[2] Bossuet, Hist. des Variations, Avertissement vi. sur les Lettres de

M. Jurieu, dern. part, n. 11, t. v. p. 165, ed. Paris, 1770 : ' Si on se decla-
rait ouvertement pour la *tolérance ecclésiastique,* c'est à dire qu'on recon-
nût tous les hérétiques pour vrais membres et vrais enfans de l'Eglise, on
marquerait trop évidemment l'indifférence des religions.   On fait donc
semblent de se renfermer dans *la tolérance civile* . . . . leur dessein véri-
table est de cacher l'indifférence des religions sous l'apparence miséricor-
dieuse de la tolérance civile.'
   ³ Walter, Naturrecht u. Politik, § 488, p. 479.
   ⁴ Bossuet, l.c. p. 155 : ' On voit clairement, que ce qui rend cette
Eglise si odieuse aux Protestans c'est principalment, et plus que tous les
autres dogmes, sa sainte et inflexible incompatibilité, si on peut parler de
cette sorte ; c'est qu'elle veut être seule, parcequ'elle se croit l'épouse—
titre que ne souffre point de partage. . . . Car c'est en effet ce qui la rend
si sévère, si insociable, et ensuite si odieuse à toutes les sectes séparées,
qui la plupart au commencement ne demandaient autre chose, si non
qu'elle voulût bien les tolérer, ou du moins ne le pas frapper de ses ana-
thèmes.   Mais la sainte sévérité et la sainte délicatesse de ses sentiments
ne lui permettait pas cette indulgence, ou plutôt cette mollesse ; et son in-
flexibilité, qui la fait haïr par les sectes schismatiques, la rend chère et
vénérable aux enfans de Dieu.'
   ⁵ Against J. Rousseau, vide Balmez, l.c. note 392.
   ⁶ Catechismus Rom. P. iv. c. v. § 1 seq.

§ 6.

   Civil authority or civil government must be guided by public opinion and accommodate itself to society, that the government may be the true expression of the dominant ideas and
feelings of the people.   Any government which professes a
definite religion, and pursues fixed principles is more or less
intolerant of those it does not profess.   Two demands have
been made upon the State to check this intolerance : (1) that the
State should have no religion ; (2) that it should grant perfect
liberty to all conceivable forms of worship.   Both these demands are in reality quite irrational.

§ 7.

   The result of a government without religion is a State without God, and this filled even heathens with horror.¹   No State
can exist without *law,* no law without *duty,* no duty without
God.   To acknowledge God is to grant the necessity of religion.
God cannot be an abstract, impersonal, veiled Deity with no
concern for the world.   As the very notion of God requires that
He should be a living, personal, perfect Godhead, so too reli-

gion cannot be indefinite, vague, and abstract, a conceit of man's
device. It must rest upon God's revelation, must be perfect,
concrete, and living ; to seek it when they have it not, to guard
it when possessed, is the duty of society and of individuals. It
is immoral to be without religion ; it is the same thing as to be
irreligious. To require the rulers of the State to be without
religion is to make the senseless demand that they should give
a pernicious example to the people ; it is also injurious to the
rights of the Christian people, who have a right to Christian
rulers. The State as such has duties towards God. A government that does not believe itself subject to God the Creator, and
holds itself absolved from all religious duties, can never win
the complete love and esteem of its subjects, neither can it have
a permanent existence.[2] Civil authority should conduct rational
beings by means of reason to goodness and truth, and to do
this it needs the help of religion. It can never fulfil its exalted
mission when it places truth and falsehood on a level, acknowledges no objective truth, no eternal divine law. Justice, which
should have the State as her protector and servant, is more in
truth than the mere repression of theft.[3]

[1] Cic. de Nat. Deor. l. i. : 'Pietate sublata fides etiam et societas humani generis et una excellentissima virtus justitia tollitur.' Or. pro Flacco :
'Sua cuique civitati religio est ; Deum quippe natura venerari novit nec
quisquam est homo, qui lege, quae haec praecipiat, careat.' De Legib. l. ii.
c. vi. vii. ; Plutarch, adv. Colotem. 31, p. 1125. Cf. also the speech of
the French privy-councillor Portalis on the Concordat of 1801, apud
Dupin, Manuel du Droit public ecclés. Français, Paris, 1847, p. 146 seq. ;
also Tüb. Theol. Quartalschr. 1832, p. 454 ; and Chilianeum, vol. vi. p.
191 seq.

[2] Liberatore, La Chiesa e lo Stato, c. ii. a. 3, p. 161 : 'The Prince is
either a delegate from God or from the people.'

[3] St. Augustine, de Civ. Dei, xix. 12, n. 1 : 'An qui fundum aufert ei,
a quo emtus est, et tradit ei,'qui nihil in eo habet juris, injustus est, et qui
se ipsum aufert dominanti Deo, a quo factus est, et malignis servit spiri-
tibus, justus est ?'

§ 8.

Reason teaches, and all wise and learned politicians and
jurists agree, that unlimited recognition or even toleration of
all forms of worship cannot be required of any State.[1] No State

can be required to permit what will endanger its own existence and destroy the foundations of all social order. Yet there are sects and religions which would do this. Supposing a sect were to arise desirous of restoring the sacrifice of human victims or the Phœnician and Babylonian worship of Astarte, or of renewing the principles of the Anabaptists of Münster; or supposing that the Mormons, who are too much even for the Free States of America, were to establish themselves in Europe; who would dream of requiring that these sects should be tolerated or recognised by the State, or deny that the State not only might but ought to resist them by all the means at its disposal? But if the State had guaranteed absolute liberty of conscience and worship, by what right could it exclude these sects and prevent their growth? How would it fare with the State and human society if political crimes could take their stand on a religious foundation, if Proudhon's dogma—'Property is theft'—were to spread and become practical, if no sins of error could be made amenable to civil penalties?[2] But where is the line to be drawn?[3] A general principle is that the State should regard the natural truths and foundations of religion, the *praeambula fidei*, as the foundation of its own authority, and should prohibit the exercise of any religion that does not conform to these natural truths,[4] as civil laws are based upon a certain number of moral principles, based in their turn upon a belief in God and immortality.[5] Any religious society, before obtaining State recognition, should be required to profess reverence for God, loyalty towards the State, and pure morality.[6] The positive law of most States makes a distinction between acknowledged religions and unacknowledged sects, and places some limits upon religious liberty with regard to their doctrines, forms of worship, and constitution.[7] No liberty is granted to doctrines hostile to property, morality, and personal freedom, which entail the denial of civil duties or aim at a complete subversion of social relations; nor again to forms of public worship which are immoral forms; nor finally to religious constitutions which threaten the constitution of the State and the observance of the civil laws.[8]

[1] Trendelenburg, Naturrecht, § 172, note; Dahlmann, Politik, § 292-294;

Walter, Naturrecht und Politik, § 491, 497. This is acknowledged also by the Liberals Tagliaferri, in the treatise Catholicity and Religious Freedom (Rivista Universale of Genoa, quaderno 58, p. 383), and Froschammer (A. Z. 23 Nov. 1867), although the latter holds that a belief in the existence of God cannot be required by the State as a condition of civil and political recognition, because interfering in this question would be to enter upon the domain of the transcendental, and to decide upon a question where nothing can be known with clearness and certainty.

[2] Cf. Balmez, c. liii.

[3] This question is a very difficult and almost impossible one to answer when Catholicism is disallowed. The purely Catholic State has a simple answer, for it possesses the divine authority of the Church, and can rely implicitly upon that. Therefore revolution must begin by overthrowing the Church.

[4] Histor. Polit. Blätter, 1859, vol. xliv. p. 224 seq.

[5] Walter, l.c. § 498, p. 493 seq., with references to Trendelenburg, Dahlmann, &c.

[6] Thus the land-law of Prussia, Th. ii. tit. 11, § 13.

[7] Kunstmann, Grundzüge des vergleichenden Kirchenrechts, Munich, 1867, § 36, p. 107 seq.

[8] Kunstmann, l.c. § 23. Even in the latest revision of the constitution of the Swiss Confederation it was thought advisable in the National Assembly at Berne to establish such limits to art. 41 and 48.

§ 9.

A case of recent occurrence in Italy is very instructive. A certain Professor G. B. Ceraulo, being called upon to give evidence before a police-court in Palermo, refused to take the usual oath prescribed by law, on the ground that he being an atheist and materialist could invoke no Deity contrary to the clear dictate of conscience. The court refused to grant the objection, and instituted further proceedings against him. On the other hand, a Cavaliere Vergara who also refused to take the oath, because he believed in no religion, was merely dismissed by the court of assizes, and his evidence was dispensed with. These proceedings gave rise to various newspaper articles and pamphlets, which discussed the bearings of the question whether the oath should be retained or abolished. Many of these were edited by Ceraulo with his comments thereon.[1] Some argued that liberty of conscience justified the refusal of an oath, for it included the right to profess no religion or form of worship;[2] that a man's evidence might be unexceptionable though it were not sworn to ; and that

as the law should be impartial, the best course would be entirely
to abolish the oath, at least where it was a question of hearing witnesses before a court of justice. But does not this reasoning apply
equally to the oaths taken by deputies,[3] electors, officials, and
soldiers, who therefore might equally require the abolition of the
oath? Others therefore demanded the entire abolition of the oath;
whilst others again contended that to abolish the oath in favour
of an atheistical minority would be an act of grave injustice towards the majority of the people, who regard the oath as the
chief security for the administration of law and justice. Besides,
they continued, it involves an absurdity. Theoretical atheism
is impossible to a reasonable man;[4] hence any one alleging this
as the ground of his refusal to take the oath should be dealt
with as a disturber of public order, especially as the first article
of the constitution still existing, though utterly broken through
and disregarded in the rest of the public law of the kingdom,
names the Catholic religion as the religion of the State; and
laws can never quite dispense with divine sanction. But there
is no doubt that in the new kingdom liberty of conscience has
always been understood to exempt any one from a compulsory
act of acknowledgment of God: consequently no one can be
punished for refusing any such act; even atheists are supposed
to act upon sincere conviction and in good faith; therefore in any
case the abolition of the oath would be a consistent measure,
especially nowadays when perjury is so frequent. Where God
is left out of legislation the oath loses its true significance.[5]
Paris in 1793 and 1871 has shown the world what happens
when the State professes atheism, and sound reason could have
taught us the lesson without these terrible experiences.[6] The
State without religion misses all the blessings and securities that
religion alone is able to impart. Walter's remarks are very
just.[7] He says: 'No State can exist without religion. Religion
tinctures every grade and rank of life with the spirit of duty.
Religion values and sanctifies every just claim, whether of the
high or of the low, of the strong or of the weak, and thus contains the true elements of the preservation of society. The religious oath consecrates the bonds of affection or of fidelity, by

which princes and peoples are mutually bound. Religion hand
in hand with power completes, modifies, and enlightens the acts
of government, or by earnest admonitions prevents abuses.
She elevates subjects to the virtue of voluntary obedience. She
stimulates mental activity, maintains nations in their youthful
vigour, and prevents that drying up of their spirit and heart which
would cause them to wither and decay. Religion is the foundation of the family, and of the discipline and reverence which the
family produces. She serves justice by the oath which is an indispensable auxiliary to the investigation of the truth. On the
battlefield she gives the soldier courage to die. She lessens the
distance between the rich and the poor, by inculcating upon the
former sympathy and active help, upon the latter gratitude
and hope ; she would soften and elevate all classes, and teach
all to become better through resignation. Religion is therefore
the true bond of the State, which keeps it together, fortifies it,
and preserves it from degeneration.'

¹ Il giuramento nella procedura e la libertà nella coscienza ; Tesi di
diritto pubblico, Palermo, 1871.

² Of this description is the Society dei Liberi Pensatori in Italy and
the Cogitanten in Germany. Civinini, one of their number, asserted in the
Chamber (1869) that atheists and materialists could be quite good citizens
(Atti uffiziali della Camera dei Deputati, p. 3644).

³ The Deputy Salvator Morelli had already demanded the abolition of
the deputy's oath.

⁴ Cicero tells how Cotta said of Epicurus : ' Nec quemquam vidi qui
magis ea, quae timenda esse negaret, timeret, mortem dico et Deos ;' and
Seneca says of the unbelieving: ' Mentiuntur, qui dicunt se non sentire
esse Deum, nam etsi tibi affirment interdiu, noctu tamen et soli dubi-
tant.' The same can be said of many ' bold thinkers' in modern times.

⁵ Cf. the observations of the Civiltà Cattolica, quad. 508 (19 Ag. 1871),
ser. viii. vol. iii. pp. 455-459.

⁶ Leibnitz, Ep. Censor. c. Pufendorf, § 6. Montesquieu, Esprit des
Lois, l. xxiv. c. vi. (against Bayle). Guizot, De la Démocratie en France,
1849, c. vii.

⁷ Walter, l.c. § 262.

§ 10.

Should, then, the State lightly and unnecessarily abandon
this bond by encouraging the formation of sects, and favouring
rebellion against religious authority ? Surely the authorisation

of every form of worship is a grave injustice in purely Catholic countries like Spain and South America—to which countries propositions 77, 78, and 79 of the Syllabus refer. The unity of the nation in faith is too great a benefit for the State to be sacrificed without necessity ;[1] and where only one religion exists the State has duties towards it, and should protect it, as far as possible, from attacks and divisions.[2] The reason alleged in New Granada, an increase of material prosperity, was on the one hand problematical, and on the other hand, even if realised, not to be preferred to the advantage of religious unity, which also would have turned to the advantage of the State.   General and unlimited freedom of worship is mischievous and objectionable, even from the point of view of the State interests.   As long as an ethical character is given to the State, as long as it is looked on as a something more than a mere instrument to material prosperity, it cannot put material goods above all others.   So long at least as the State believes in any first principles of reason and morality it must not surrender them without necessity; and so also where it believes in the Christian principles, and society rests on them, it must not without necessity sacrifice them. There is an old saying not easily gainsaid : *Regula operandi dependet a regula credendi.*   If the *regula credendi* allow full room for the caprice of each individual, nothing good, unless men are better than their principles, can be expected from the *regula operandi.*   How many crimes may be committed under the cloak of religion ![3]   What right has the State authority to punish them, having adopted the principle of complete religious liberty, and abandoned the right of punishing intellectual errors ?   We might ask the government : What right have you to punish a man, who, because he does not acknowledge that there is a God, cannot hold himself guilty in His sight, neither therefore in yours ?   You have laid down the law by which you punish him, but in the eyes of this man your law has no force, for you are only his equal, and he recognises the existence of no superior being who has conferred upon you the right of touching his freedom.   What right have you to punish this other, who is convinced that all his actions are only the effects of necessary causes,

and that free-will is a delusion; who believes, therefore, that he
was as unable to help committing the act which you call a crime
as the wild beast is unable to refrain from seizing the prey that
is before him, or attacking another beast with which he is infu-
riated? What right have you to punish one who maintains that
morality is a lie, that self-interest is the only true morality, that the
difference between good and evil is to understand or mistake your
own interest? If you punish him, still his conscience does not
tell him he is guilty, and he will take the punishment as having
befallen him because he was out in his reckoning, and had not
sufficiently calculated the chances of success. These are the
necessary and inevitable consequences of a doctrine which denies
to public authority the power of punishing crimes committed
through false opinions.[4] It may be said: This right of punishing exists only in regard to deeds; as far as doctrines are concerned the individual should be absolutely free. We reply:
That merely the internal workings of a man's mind, which no
earthly power can reach, are not doctrines;[5] doctrines are precepts openly taught and propagated amongst other men; that
the question is not one of inward liberty of conscience, but of
outward religious liberty; that every one is bound to *act* according to his own conscience and belief; and that the difficulty
remains of how a government that has granted absolute liberty
to conscience and subjective conviction can justly punish an act
commended or justified by the conscience of the perpetrator.

[1] Walter, Kirchenrecht, § 56; Naturrecht und Politik, § 496, p. 490
seq.
[2] Hugo Grotius, de Jure Belli et Pacis, l. ii. c. xx. n. 51. Domat, Droit
Public, l. i. tit. 19. Montesquieu, Esprit de Lois, l. xii. c. iv. v.; xxv. c. x.
Pey, De l'Autorité des deux Puissances, t. iv. P. iv. c. i. ii. Frayssinous,
Conférences sur les Principes religieux, t. i. et iii. Cf. Bellarm. de
Membr. Eccl. Milit. iii. 18; Suarez, de Fide, disp. 20, sect. 3; disp. 23,
sect. 1.
[3] When Charles I. of England was beheaded in 1649 as a ' rebel' proofs
were adduced from Scripture to show that monarchy was to be rejected,
and that the king was the beast of the Apocalypse; and when the parliament appeared dilatory to zealous Puritans in proceeding against the
' royal serpent,' the Bible preachers declared that bad representatives of
the people should be destroyed with rat's-bane. When it was desired to
extirpate the Irish with fire and sword, the Scriptural example of the Amale-

kites was ready to hand. Human passion, obstinacy, and folly have weapons always ready in men who have risen in rebellion against the truth.

⁴ Balmez, p. 158.

⁵ De internis non judicat praetor. Cogitationis poenam nemo patitur.

§ 11.

There is no inconsistency in the Catholic view of the question. The inconsistency is on the side of modern Liberalism. The latter declares all, or nearly all, errors of the intellect to be guiltless, and condones them with extraordinary indulgence. The former maintains that some errors of the intellect are crimes; that an error touching a truth of religion or morality is one of the gravest offences against God; that man's thought is free physically but not morally; and that it is his duty to seek, embrace, and retain divine truth under all circumstances and at whatever cost.[1]

The doctrine of unrestricted free thought involves the impossibility of committing sins of the intellect, and error must be henceforth excluded from the category of sins of which men may be guilty. But it is forgotten that to *will* we must *apprehend*, and that thus to will what is right we must apprehend what is true. If the source of so many evil affections of the heart lie in intellectual errors, it is man's duty to guard his intellect from error. But when every man is allowed absolute freedom of opinion, and may make choice of such opinions regarding faith or morals as recommend themselves to him,[2] then truth has lost its value, and very many hold themselves exonerated from the labour of seeking or attaining it. A lamentable delusion, one of the most terrible evils of modern society![3]

[1] Balmez, p. 158. He says further: 'The opponents of Catholicism have in the order of ideas confounded right with fact, declaring in this respect the uselessness and incompetency of all laws, divine and human. But this is the excess of folly. As though it were possible for that which is most noble and elevated in human nature to be exempt from all rule! As though it were possible for that which makes man the king of all creation to be an exception to the wonderful harmony of all parts of the universe with themselves and with God! As if this harmony could exist, or even be conceived in man, unless it were declared to be the first of human obligations to adhere constantly to truth!' Döllinger (Kirche und Kirchen, Eng. trans. Int. p. 8) refers to Niebuhr's words written on the 5th October

1830 : ' If God does not marvellously help, there is impending over us a destruction such as occurred to the Roman world in the middle of the third century—the annihilation of prosperity, freedom, civilisation, and literature.' Döllinger adds : ' And we have proceeded much further on the inclined plane since then. The Powers of Europe have overturned, or suffered to be overturned, the two main pillars of their edifice—the principles of legitimacy and public international law.' After a lapse of ten years have not these words an augmented force ? Have they not been terribly illustrated by the scenes in Paris during the spring of 1871 ? If in 1861 we had proceeded much further on the inclined plane, how do we stand in 1871 and 1872 ?

² This is exactly the signification of heresy, as Tertullian gives it, do Praescript. Haeret. c. vi. vii. According to Clem. Alex. Strom. ii. 11, opinion is the spiritual condition of heretics, ignorance of heathens, while certainty belongs to the Church alone. Cf. Hieron. in Gal. c. v. (c. 27, c. xxiv. q. 3).

³ Balmez, p. 161.

§ 12.

But the cry will be raised : Is all development to be checked? are the Middle Ages to be brought back on the plea of saving society ? Are all deserters to be ordered back into the one saving Church, and non-Catholics to be deprived of all their rights ? These are idle objections, for no Catholic, whether layman or ecclesiastic, ever demanded or said this. It is true that the Church considers the grant of religious liberty an occasion of danger for the salvation of the souls of Catholics; but when members of other religious communions are in possession of this religious liberty, or where they have equal rights with Catholics, she does not approve the violation of these rights, even though she should get momentary advantage thereby. In countries where religious liberty has been long ago introduced, it may rightly exist and should not be abolished.[1] The Pope's condemnation of the *introduction* of religious liberty into an empire like Austria² is not inconsistent with this. Where religious liberty has been inevitably produced by the force of circumstances, and has been established by treaties or legislation, it may be accepted and recognised ; but when it is needlessly proclaimed it looks like an invitation to sectarianism, and is perilous not merely to the salvation of souls but to the peace of the State.³

¹ Rintel, l.c. p. 124.
² As Huber asserted, p. 79.

³ Pignatelli, Consult. Can. t. i. Cons. 143, n. 24, p. 190, ed. Venet. : 'Necessitudo cum haereticis noxia et periculosa est, non modo quoad salutem animarum, sed etiam quoad pacem et tranquillitatem politicam, quae sine fidei unitate conservari nequit. Ubi enim est publica animorum dissensio, quam introducunt haeretici, ibi pax publica esse non potest. *Vix firma esse possunt pacis jura inter quos est fidei bellum,* ait Ambrosius, 1. iii. Offic. Hoc testatur ipsa veritas, cui exstant exempla, apud Becanum, de Fide, c. xv. n. 6 ; Legito, Justum Lipsium in libro contra Dialogistam de una religione ; et Joh. Saresb. Ep. Carnot. l. vi. Polycr.' Earlier this was the general view of Protestants.

§ 13.

There are two quite distinct questions to be considered. The first is : Can a Catholic ruler conscientiously concede equal rights to other forms of worship; can he introduce religious liberty[1] where it does not exist, and under what conditions ? The second : Is liberty of religion and worship once introduced to be respected and maintained, not merely by individual Catholics but by the Church ? No Catholic theologian adhering strictly to Papal decisions could reply decidedly in the negative to both these questions. The first question should be answered thus : Religious liberty may be introduced when it is required for the common good, to prevent greater evils, or when it has become a necessity.[2] Nature itself prompts us to accept a lesser evil to avoid a greater,[3] and civil wars and constant discord would imperil the true faith and even the life of the State.[4] Older theologians, from the circumstances of the age in which they lived, thought that such cases would be very rare and exceptional; but they admitted the possibility, nay the reality, of their occurrence, and even acknowledged that they might receive Papal ratification, which they in general considered to be a necessity,[5] when such concessions were made to guard the rights of Catholics and the safety of the Church. But since those days circumstances are much changed.

Taking the circumstances of the present day into consideration, we do not hesitate to say: 'Theologians teach that a Catholic sovereign may conscientiously grant religious liberty to members of other creeds in two cases for the welfare of the people. The first occurs when to refuse religious liberty would be more injurious than to grant it; the second 'when the grant would be accompanied with greater good than the refusal. These grounds are present in countries where Catholics and Protestants live mixed up together, holding constant intercourse with each other, for here religious liberty helps them to live together quietly and peaceably.'[6]

With regard to the second question, earlier Catholic authors,[7] as well as 'modern Ultramontanes,' teach that any liberties granted by law or treaty to other religious communions are always to be observed. As the *Civiltà Cattolica* says, this is not allowing that error as such has any just claim, 'but it means that those in error may have attained a legal right by constitutions sworn to, by express treaties, by long tradition, or customs that have acquired the force of law. When this has happened no one can doubt that Catholics as a body, and governments and all spiritual or civil authorities, are bound to respect this acquired right.'[8] The same reasons that warrant a Catholic ruler in tolerating other religions, and giving his sanction to liberty of worship, warrant him also in granting perfect equality in all civil relations. Of this equality the dissidents ought never again .to be deprived; the rights secured to them by charter and oath must be respected in every case; and the accusation that Catholic doctrine teaches that no faith is to be kept with heretics is totally unfounded. The Church holds the precepts of the primeval moral law quite as sacred and inviolable as her dogmas, and good faith is one of the foundation-stones of Christian society.

[1] Scientifically we should have had to distinguish between liberty of conscience and of worship; but as our opponents only treat fully of the latter, a detailed discussion on this distinction as on others would be out of place.

[2] Thus the theologians in the Commentaries on St. Thomas, Sum. 2, 2, q. 10, a. 11. Devoti, Instit. Jur. Can. t. iv. tit. 6, § 7, p. 77, ed. 1794. Laymann, Theol. Moral. ii. 3, 12. Schenkl, Syntagma Jur. Can. § 342. M. Becanus, Duell. de Primatu Regio, l. iii. c. x.; also quoted by Schrader, de Unit. Rom. Freib. 1862, i. p. 32, note. Merkle, l.c. p. 24. Riess, Staat und Kirche (Laacher, Stimmen über die Encyclica, xii. § 204 seq.).

[3] The official letter from Cardinal Pacca to La Mennais, of the 3d Feb. 1832, designates liberty of worship as 'minus malum' under some circumstances. Beidtel, Das Canonische Recht, p. 653.

⁴ Pelisson, l.c. says on this subject: ' Il faut bien tolérer la diversité des religions si l'Etat est perdu sans cela. Il faut bien de ne la pas tolérer s'il le peut sans perdre l'Etat, se souvenant toujours neanmoins de la charité, de l'humanité et que les supplices sont assez souvent des remèdes d'ignorant pour cette sorte de maux, et les irritent plutost qu'ils ne les guérissent.' Also in the report before the Parliament of Paris, of 26 Nov. 1610 (Du Plessis, t. ii, P. ii. p. 20), the edicts of Henry III. and Henry IV. were quoted in this sense : ' Edicts verifiez aux cours de parlement, qui tolèrent ceux de la religion prétendue réformée, parcequ'autrement on ne pourroit vivre sans troubles.'

⁵ Suarez, de Fide, disput. 20, sect. 3, n. 21. Card. de Lugo, de Fide, disp. 19, sect. 2, § 4, n. 124. Albitius, de Inconst. in Fide, c. xxvii. n. 33. Bellarm. de Laicis, iii. 18.

⁶ Merkle, l.c. p. 25.

⁷ Molanus, de Fide Hacret. Serv. i. 29. M. Becanus, l.c. Tanner, Theol. t. iii. disp. 1, de Fide, q. 9, dub. 4.

⁸ Civiltà Cattolica, 1864, ser. v. vol. x. p. 546 (in an article on the principles of 1789).

§ 14.

While statesmen of the present day estimate everything that comes before them from a political point of view,[1] the Catholic Church estimates and must estimate everything from a dogmatic point of view. This distinction is the source of innumerable misunderstandings and mistakes. The Catholic Church holds so fast to the purity of the faith, that she is forced to reprobate even an actual and established state of things if supported upon principles which are dogmatically false, or if it threaten to gain an entrance for an erroneous principle. The governments of the world, which have been more and more estranged from her, understand her language no longer, and being enchained by quite other and modern ideas are the less able to arrive at the logical consequences of her principles.

It is impossible for the Church to approve liberty of worship when the reason given for it is that every man has a natural and inalienable right to entertain and propagate any religious opinion.[2] Were this a true principle, the State would commit a grave injustice in imposing conditions upon or restricting liberty of worship or refusing it to any religious body ; and moreover we should have to deny the value of the whole of God's revelation, and to open the door to all extravagance in religious worship. The assertion must be condemned that every man is free to accept and confess the religion that appears to him true by the light of reason.[3] Such an assertion could only proceed from suppositions that are dogmatically false. Either there is no law at all to guide and regulate the consciences of men, or this law coincides with the subjective conviction of each individual conscience, or man has the right not to submit to such a law. All three assumptions are untenable and irrational from a Christian point of view. For we acknowledge a moral order, a law which directs consciences, an objective divine truth; moreover, this is independent of individual subjective conviction and superior to it, otherwise man becomes God, and we are led into pantheism; lastly, this law must be binding upon all, so that no true right can exist in opposition to this supreme rule. As man has no right to do evil, neither has he a right to think, teach, or spread evil, to defend or promote error;[4] otherwise why did Christ come into the world? How could He say, 'He that doth not believe is already judged'? (St. John iii. 18.) In the domain of religion and of ethics man has no right to contradict God, to accept or refuse His revelation. He may be physically free, but he is ethically bound. The denial of these propositions involves the denial of all supernatural revelation, of all the truths of Christianity, and the acceptance of the plainest rationalism. He who believes in the existence of God and in a divine revelation cannot reasonably hold that a creature may obey or disobey as he pleases the voice of his Creator. The rulers of our modern States proclaim loudly that the State should be founded upon moral principles, and as long as this is to be the case they cannot recognise this 'natural and inalienable right,' which must lead to the inevitable ruin of the State and of society.[5] In the sixteenth century the terrible consequences of this right were seen and estimated; there were as many opinions as individuals, the one as unreasonable as the other; and if any one may act according to his belief, he who is free to believe what he likes is also free to do what he likes.[6] Even if we disregard the corruption of human nature, which experience has made only too evident, and which results from original sin and also from bad education and habits, what would become not merely of religious faith but of civil life when every crime might take the form of religion?

[1] The character of the nineteenth century is rather political than religious.(Bluntschli, in Sybel's Zeitschr. p. 48). But, indeed, many political questions have always been closely connected with religious questions.

[2] Thus Binet (quoted by Bluntschli, St. R. b. ix. p. 513): 'La franche manifestation des convictions religieuses est un *droit* puisqu'elle est un *devoir*.'

[3] Syllab. prop. 15.

[4] M. Liberatore, La Chiesa e lo Stato, pp. 48, 55.

[5] Aug. de Civ. Dei, l. xix. c. xxi.: ' Ubi *homo Deo non servit,* quid in eo putandum est esse *justitiae?* Quandoquidem Deo non serviens nullo modo potest juste animus corpori, aut humana ratio vitiis imperare. Et si in homine tali non est ulla justitia, procul dubio nec in hominum coetu, qui ex hominibus talibus constat. Non est hic ergo juris ille consensus, qui hominum multitudinem populum facit, cujus res dicitur esse respublica.'

[6] Stanislaus Hosius, Ep. ad Martinum Sboroneschi, Palatinum Posnan. ap. Raynald. a. 1560, n. 8: ' Postquam hanc nonnulli sunt opinionem secuti, ut putarent *licere sibi credere, quidquid appareat in eorum conscientia,* quorsum res perlata sit, vidimus : nam et nostris temporibus eadem dicere licet, quae suo saeculo dixit Hilarius : *Periculosum admodum atque miserabile est, tot nunc fides existere, quot voluntates, et tot nobis doctrinas esse, quot mores, et tot causas blasphemiarum pullulare, quot vitia sunt, dum aut ita fides scribuntur ut volumus aut ita ut volumus intelliguntur, et cum secundum unum Deum et unum Dominum et unum baptisma etiam fides una sit, excidimus ab ea fide, quae sola est, et dum plures fiunt, ad id coeperunt esse ut nulla sit.* Dominatio vestra non procul abest a Pinczovia, ubi ante annos jam prope decem istud cacangelium potius quam evangelium cepit originem; nonne ipsi ejusdem illius scholae magistri se mutuo vocant haereticos? Certe Stancarum (cf. Schröckh, K.G. seit der Reform. iv. p. 584 seq.) parum abfuit, quin flammis traderent, qui tamen non major est haereticus, quam ii, qui diversum ab eo Pinczoviae sentiunt. . . . Sic fieri necesse est, quando *quisque sibi liberum esse vult,* non quod Ecclesia Cath. vult et docet, sed *quod sibi apparet in sua conscientia,* credere. Apparet uni in sua conscientia, quod non debeat esse neque sacerdotium neque sacrificium, qua ratione *Deus ipse quodammodo in ordinem cogi videtur.* Apparet alii falsum esse, quod Christus dixit: *Hoc est corpus meum,* sed significare tantum *corpus* esse figuram vel virtutem corporis. Apparet tertio, quandoquidem dixit Christus : *Qui crediderit et baptizatus fuerit, salvus erit,* propterea parvulorum baptismum nihil valere et eos dixit esse rebaptizandos. Apparet quarto, quandoquidem a propheta Scriptum est: *Audiam quid loquatur in me Deus* et rursus: *Beatus vir, quem tu erudieris, Domine* et ipse Christus docuerit : *Nolite plures fieri magistri, quoniam unus est magister vester in coelis,* non esse fidendum Scripturis, multo minus autem ferendum esse externum verbi s. praedicationis ministerium, sed de coelo revelationes exspectandas, ut ille nos

doceat, qui solus est verus magister. Sed quorsum attinet enumerare singula? Si liberum erit unicuique credere, quod apparet in illius conscientia, tot erunt fides, quot voluntates, *nec ulla est certior et celerior ad interitum via, quam ut quod vult, cuique credere, quod vult, facere cuique liberum sit;* ibi enim nullus jam videtur esse magistratus, nulla legitima potestas.'

§ 15.

Neither can the Church approve of religious liberty being conceded on the ground of religious indifference, one religion being held to be as good or as bad as the other.[1] That would be as unreasonable as immoral, whether in society or in individuals.[2] It annihilates the distinction between orthodoxy and heresy, sets aside all ecclesiastical tradition, and condemns entirely the ancient Church.[3] John Quintanus, professor of canon law, spoke in these terms to Charles IX.:[4] 'Suffer not, O most Christian king, that such injustice be done to the Fathers, to whom we owe Christendom, as that they should be called foolish and their ordinances foolishness; mingle not Christians and those who are not Christians; for the Fathers say[5] that heretics are not Christians, and Theodosius II. and Valentinian III. (in 437) forbade them to use the name of Christian.' The various Christian sects cannot be regarded as forms of one and the same Christianity, agreeing essentially in the fundamental articles of their creed. The question is one of principles, not merely of forms; for any one to take upon himself to decide what part or portion of positive Christianity is essential and what is not essential is to hold himself superior to revelation, superior to divine authority, and so essentially and decidedly to oppose Catholic principles that no accommodation with them is possible. Protestantism, in spite of the many remnants of Catholic truth which it has retained, cannot be regarded as a different form of the Christian religion, and one in which man may please God as well as in the Catholic Church.[6]

[1] 'He who begins by holding all religions equally good, ends by holding them all equally bad.' Vide Raumer (Nivelliren).

[2] 'Quod in singulis, id est in populis.' Cic. de Rep. iii. 18. Thom. de Reg. Princip. i. 15. Bellarm. de Laicis, i. 18, n. 1; de Rom. Pont. v. 7, n. 5.

[3] Cf. Merkle, l.c. pp. 20, 21.

[4] Ap. Raynald. a. 1561, n. 82. Concerning the petition of the Sorbonne of 1577, vide Du Plessis d'Argentré, t. ii. P. i. p. 449.

[5] Athan. Ep. ad Serapion, t. i. p. 266. Hilar. de Trin. l. ii. init. Ambros. in Luc. l. vii. c. xi. Aug. de Nupt. et Conc. ii. 31, c. Ep. Parmen. i. 7, de Util. Cred. c. xiv. n. 30. Enchir. ad Laur. c. v.

[6] Syllab. prop. 18, from the Encycl. of 8 Dec. 1849 to the Italian bishops, referring to the efforts to Protestantise Italy.

§ 16.

Again, the Church must condemn liberty of worship based on the ground that the best form of government, which all should aim at, requires the complete separation of Church and State. This separation has been often condemned by the Church;[1] it is contrary to the nature of things and the general welfare. And because in some unhappy circumstances it may exist as a necessity, it ought not to be proclaimed as an ideal; to dig up the roots which provide the State with life and vigour can scarcely be called the best form of government. Pius IX.[2] has expressly condemned the assertion, which contradicts both Scripture and the teaching of the Church that it is consonant with the best form of government and required by it, that human society should be constituted and governed without regard to religion, or at least without making any distinction between the true religion and false religions; that society is best off when the government recognises no duty of proceeding by penal laws against attacks upon the Catholic religion[3] except when public peace demands it. As Liberatore[4] observes, the Pope is not referring here to the *particular* hypothesis of this or that society which may, owing to long-established schism,[5] find it advisable to extend civil tolerance to all forms of worship, without any special protection to the true religion; but he lays down a general thesis concerning that form of State and of government most consonant with the divine idea and most conducive to the happiness of the people.

[1] Gregory XVI. Enc. 15 Aug. 1832. Pius IX. Alloc. 27 Sept. 1852; Syllab. prop. 55.

[2] Encyclical of 8 Dec. 1864.

[3] Officium coercendi sancitis poenis *violatores* Catholicae religionis.

⁴ L.c. c. i. a. 6, pp. 74, 75.

⁵ 'Atteso le divisioni religioso già in lei (nella società) *radicale.*' He also refers to the much-used parable of the wheat and cockle (Matt. xiii.). The lord of the field did not wish to deprive the cockle, which had already taken root, of growth, because the wheat would thus also have suffered. But this necessity, brought about by an enemy, he in no way declared to be the best condition. It was the lesser evil that served to prevent the greater.

§ 17.

It is wrong for a State that has been hitherto entirely Catholic to surrender its distinctively Catholic character, and no longer acknowledge the Catholic as the one State religion,[1] if this be done not to avoid a greater evil or attain a greater good, but because according to modern notions this is the right course to pursue. If this conduct were not wrong we should have to say that there is no harm in multiplying sects, and that religious unity is not a great good; that the State would not be bound to protect the well-won rights of the Catholic Church, nay, might abandon[2] her to attacks which the depravity of human nature and the arts employed to mislead it would easily render successful.[3] The Spanish diplomatist Castillo y Ayensa, on the subject of the often-projected changes in the constitution of his country, said:[4] 'The prohibition of other forms of worship is a natural and necessary consequence of the recognition of the Catholic religion as being the only true religion.[5] This can only be modified when circumstances not brought about by the legislator require the concession. In such a case it is lawful to respect and maintain the various forms of worship existing *de facto* in a country; but it would be a criminal act as well as an infatuation on the part of a legislator himself to destroy religious unity, to flood the country with a diversity of religious opinions, and exhibit to the people the sorry spectacle of his own entire want of religion. How strange it is that those should oppose religious unity who are so eager for all other kinds of unity—unity of constitution, of administration and commerce, of codes and tribunals, of coinage and weights and measures! They seek to build up new unities, but would destroy the unity that existed with the cradle of the monarchy, which sufficed and ever will suffice to weld our country into a compact and indestructible whole.' The transformation of a Catholic State into one professing religious equality is attended with the gravest evils. All religion gradually declines in a country whose government professes none. Although the zeal of some chosen souls, the piety of a dynasty, the firm adherence of the people to the faith of their fathers may arrest the complete downfall of the religious life; still the majority will yield to temptation, especially when it comes to them from persons in power, overlaid with deceit and fair seeming, encouraged by theatres, romances, newspapers, and public meetings, and supported by the passions that lie dormant in the heart. The atmosphere is gradually poisoned; Catholics become first tepid, then cold, and at last to be without religion and without God. Especially in southern lands, like Spain and Italy, opposition to the Church leads, not to Protestantism but to atheism; everything by degrees becomes unchristian—laws, government, courts of justice, public and domestic life. If man's moral imperfection and the doctrine of original sin be mistaken or denied, there is no limit to liberty of opinion. Anarchy in idea leads to anarchy in practice, which bayonets may restrain for a time, but cannot permanently suppress.

¹ Merkle, p. 22.
² Ibid.
³ Cf. Döllinger, Kirche und Kirchen, p. 81, trans.
⁴ Castillo y Ayensa, Historia critica de las negociaciones con Roma desde la muerte del Rey D. Fernando VII. Madrid, 1859, vol. ii. c. vi. pp. 94, 95.
⁵ Constitution of Cadiz, 1812, art. 12: ' La religion de la nacion Espagnola es y será perpetuamente la Cátolica, Apostólica, Romana, única verdadera. La nacion la proteje por leyes sabias y justas, y prohibe el ejercio de cualquiera otra.'

§ 18.

But it will be said that we should rely on the strength of truth, which, where there is free competition, will prevail over error. It will be asked: Is all confidence in truth gone, that truth, as the better commodity, will expel inferior ones from the market? But we can answer: Why, then, have you no confidence in virtue, which is a far better commodity than vice? Why does a wise man use such care in choosing his servants and friends, the teachers, surroundings, and books of his children? Why does he not leave them free, since virtue far outshines vice, and is sure of triumph in a struggle? Why, since justice being a nobler and better commodity than injustice must prevail over it, does the State require, for public order and safety, policemen and law-courts, soldiers and prisons, penal laws and measures of repression? Why not leave justice and injustice . free competition? The real truth in the matter is, that while we fully trust in virtue's own strength and the triumph of justice, we cannot trust to the individual man, whose understanding is often very weak, limited, and misled, and whose will is often still weaker, perverted, and evil. It is a mistake to compare the subjective with the objective, and to consider man, not as he is but as he might be. That the better commodity be chosen it must be recognised as better, and the cost not be thought too great. The understanding can easily find out amongst material things which is the best commodity, and the will immediately inclines to acquire it; but in the moral domain there are many difficulties to be overcome, for the judgment is easily corrupted and misled, as well as the will, which can be swayed and dominated by passions. This is especially the case in the domain of religion. Christianity needed miracles to overcome the Pagan world; but is the miraculous to become the ordinary course of nature, or is God continually to work miracles simply for the convenience of those who nowadays proclaim religious liberty? If so many errors and so many crimes are committed in spite of all that religion and the State can do for their prevention, what would not be the condition of things if the system of rationalism met with universal recognition?' In many Catholic countries the free competition of other religions might very possibly arouse and reanimate those Catholics who had become torpid and too easy-going. In many towns this would certainly be the case. Thus good *de consequenti* would arise. But we must follow the principle laid down by the Apostle: we must not do evil that good may come.

A government would be very unwise to promote evil with the ultimate object of some possible good. God may send or permit salutary trials, but man is not therefore authorised in countenancing evil. Liberty to err is liberty to do wrong; it is the death of the soul.[2]

[1] Liberatore, l.c. pp. 55-59.
[2] Aug. ap. Greg. XVI. Const. cit.

§ 19.

Thus we must reject all the views of religious liberty discussed in the preceding five sections. Our Lord willed that there should be one Faith, and forbade that it should be divided. He willed that there should be one Shepherd, one fold, one Church, one baptism : without unity of faith this could not be. He desired care and watchfulness against false prophets, who could not be absent if there were many religions. He willed a Church that should be one, and that should last for ever, against which the gates of hell should never prevail, and this is inconceivable without unity of faith.[1] We are told that if this view be true, ' it alone is enough to prevent any Catholic ever again swearing allegiance to any modern constitution without thereby violating his conscience.' We must here make a distinction. A constitution may declare religious liberty, either as a dogmatic principle to be held by all, or only as a fact existing in the positive law of the country. In the former case this oath, like any oath that required a denial of the Faith, would be inadmissible. In the latter case, when no claim was made over the religious convictions of the Catholic, the oath might be taken in any country where a number of denominations actually existed, and equal rights were conceded to them by law and treaty. The twelfth canon proposed to the Vatican Council ought not to be introduced here, for it belongs to another connection : ' If any one says that to this Church by Christ our Lord and Master was given only the power to lead by counsel and persuasion, and not to command by laws and restrain and compel the erring and obdurate by external courts of judgment and salutary punishment, let him be anathema.'[2]

Our opponent seems to be unaware that essentially the same thing was said in a dogmatic Bull of Pius VI.,[3] and that the Church at all times ascribed to herself a legislative, judicial, and executive authority and thereby a coercive authority. Has he read and disproved the proofs of this adduced by theologians and canonists?[4] In 1617 the Sorbonne declared the doctrine of the apostate Marcus Antonius de Dominus, in so far as it denied the true jurisdiction of the Church—that is, her coercive authority and right to external submission—to be heretical, subversive of the whole hierarchical order, and introducing a Babylonian confusion into the Church.[5]

[1] From this it follows that canon 6 of the projected Schema de Ecclesia Christi was completely justified, which condemned the propositions : ' The intolerance with which the Catholic Church proscribes and condemns all religious sects separated from her communion is not prescribed by the divine law;' and ' Man cannot have certainty but only opinion as to the truth of religions, and therefore all religious sects are to be tolerated by the Church.'

[2] Friedrich, Doc. ii. p. 103.

[3] Pius VI. Const. Auctorem fidei, 28 Aug. 1794, prop. 4, 5 (Denzinger, Enchir. p. 389, n. 1367 seq.) : ' Propositio affirmans, *abusum fore auctoritatis Ecclesiae, transferendo illam ultra limites doctrinae et morum et cam extendendo ad res exteriores et per vim exegendi id, quod pendet a persuasione et corde, tum etiam multo minus ad eam pertinere exigere per vim exteriorem subjectionem suis decretis;* quatenus indeterminatis illis verbis *extendendo ad res exteriores* notet velut abusum auctoritatis Ecclesiae usum ejus potestatis acceptae a Deo, qua usi sunt et ipsimet Apostoli in disciplina exteriore constituenda et sancienda, *haeretica ;* qua parte insinuat, Ecclesiam non habere auctoritatem subjectionis suis decretis exigendae aliter quam per media, quae pendent a persuasione, quatenus intendit, Ecclesiam non habere collatam sibi a Deo potestatem non solum *dirigendi per consilia et suasiones,* sed etiam *jubendi per leges ac devios contumacesque exteriore judicio ac salutaribus poenis coercendi atque cogendi* (precisely the terms of this 12th canon), ex Benedicto XIV. in Brevi Ad assiduas, 4 Mart. 1755, primatibus, archiepiscopis et episcopis regni Polon., *inducens in systema alias damnatum ut haereticum.*' Cf. Johannis XXII. 1327, Const. Licet, contra Marsilium Patav. (Denzinger, l.c. p. 178, n. 427). Thus the Encyclica of 8 Dec. 1864 also condemns the proposition : ' Ecclesiae jus non competere violatores legum suarum poenis temporalibus coercendi;' in which, in the term *violatores,* as Merkle (p. 21, No. 3) rightly remarks, only by a gross misrepresentation can all non-Catholics be included. Syllabus, prop. 24.

[4] Suarez, de Legibus, l. iii. c. i. seq. Petavius, de Eccles. Hierarch. l. iii. c. ix. x. (against Claude Saumaise). Bennettis, Privileg. S. Petri vind. Romae, 1761, t. vi. a. 6, p. 550 seq. Bianchi, t. iii. l. i. c. v. § 1, 2,

6. Gerdil, Apol. Compend. del Breve, Super soliditate, Opp. xiii. pp. 127-130.

⁵ Du Plessis d'Argentré, Collect. Judic. t. ii. P. ii. p. 105, prop. 2. Likewise the Faculty of Cologne, 1618 (ib. t. iii. P. ii. p. 193).

§ 20.

Huber, quoting the words of the Catholic theologian Kober,[1] exclaims against the terrible penalty of the anathema; but after having done so, he shows only too well that it had no terrors for him, any more than for non-Catholics. Whom does this anathema touch? Certainly not those non-Catholics who, without malice or obstinacy, remain in the errors transmitted to them from their parents. Excommunication is not, as Huber imagines, 'a delivering up to eternal perdition,' otherwise it could not be employed in the Church as *poena medicinalis.*[2] It is in itself the penalty of exclusion from the Church, which leads, if it lasts and be incurred guiltily, to exclusion from the Kingdom of God.[3] When St. Paul (Gal. i. 8), in the words the Pope now uses, says, 'Let him be anathema who preaches another gospel,' he certainly did not intend to consign to eternal perdition those men for whose salvation he was ready to sacrifice his life—nay, to be himself anathema from Christ (Rom. ix. 3); on the contrary, he wished to guard them from the danger. The Church, in using the same words in her condemnation of false doctrine, has the same intention as St. Paul. What the Apostle said at that time of seducers who spread false doctrine amongst the multitude applies now to such seducers. If they persist in their obstinacy, they forfeit their salvation.

---

¹ Huber, pp. 82, 83, quoting from Kober, Kirchenbann, p. 17. Hase, Handb. der Prot. Polemik, p. 48, 3d ed. says: 'This (*anathema sit*), as used by the Jews, meant anything destined for destruction on religious motives. In the ecclesiastical sense it is not merely an exclusion from the Church, nor yet a hopeless exclusion from eternal salvation.' Cf. ib. p. 52.

² Cf. c. 37, c. xxiv. q. 3. The early Fathers distinguished between *excommunicatio mortalis* and *medicinalis, e.g.* Aug. serm. 351, de Poenit. The following regard the ban as spiritual death: Cypr. Ep. 62, ad Pompon. c. iv.; Aug. tr. 50, in Joh. n. 11, in Deut. q. 39; Innoc. I. Ep. 29, ad Conc. Carth. n. 8. Cf. c. 13, Qui filii, iv. 19: '*Mori* praecipitur, i.e.

per excommunicationis sententiam velut mortuus a communiono fidelium separari.'

³ Huber appears to have known little of Kober's work beyond p. 17. At pp. 238 seq. 280 seq. 290 seq. he might have found further information; likewise apud Ad. Wuttke, Handb. der Christl. Sittenlehre, ii. p. 627. Cf. Merkle, pp. 45-49.

§ 21.

It is quite a false assertion that Innocent XII. declared that the children of non-Catholics[1] should be forcibly taken from their parents, that they might be educated as Catholics.[2] The only ground for the assertion is that the Congregation of the Inquisition, not the Pope himself, designated (1694) an edict of Duke Victor Amadeus II. of Savoy as scandalous, impious, and irreligious, for abolishing the laws published for the protection of Catholics, and ordering some children, many of whom had come to the age of reason, to be returned to the Waldenses, from whom they had been taken and educated in the Catholic faith.[3]

¹ Benedict XIV. Const. Postremum, 28 Feb. 1747. Const. Probe, 15 Dec. 1751, enjoined the prohibition with reference to the children of unbelievers. I treated the Mortara case in detail in the Katholik, 1859, p. 64 seq.

² A. Z. Suppl. 19 June 1870, No. 24.

³ Dom. Carutti, Storia del Regno di Vittorio Amadeo II. Torino, 1856, c. vi. pp. 82-90; c. vii. pp. 110, 111; c. x. pp. 138, 151; c. xii. pp. 117, 177-179.

§ 22.

Catholics have been upbraided times without number for the massacre of St. Bartholomew in 1572.[1] The reply has always been the same—that it was a political act, and had nothing to do with religious interests as such.[2] The Protestant theologians Andrea and Selneccius regard it in this light in their reports to Augustus Prince Elector of Saxony.[3]

The French Huguenots were, as a party, very dangerous to the court of France. They were a constant source of civil war, and it was their object to get the King Charles IX. into their power. Amongst other authors,[4] Buckle,[5] who has certainly no Catholic bias, states what is the undoubted fact—that the crimes of the French Protestants were 'as revolting as those of the Catholics, and quite as numerous relatively to the numbers and power of the two parties.' Gregory XIII., we are told,[6] was not under the delusion that the massacre of St. Bartholomew was merely the bloody quelling of a plot against the king, and the thanksgiving services and demonstrations of joy were for the destruction of the heretics.   Let us examine the events.

The first news of the death of Admiral Coligny and his followers was received in Rome on the 2d September, from a courier sent from Lyons by the secretary of the Governor Mandelot.[7] The Cardinal of Lorraine went to the Pope with the French ambassador to make him acquainted with the event, relating it, of course, from the point of view of the policy of France.   On the 5th September M. Beauville arrived from Paris, with credentials from the king and despatches from the nuncio.   The deed, as represented by the French court, was applauded in Rome, but it would, it was said, have been more praiseworthy had the king been able to proceed against the rebellious Huguenots in the proper judicial way.[8]   Only too much credence was given to the regal message : it was long held undoubted also in other courts, even in the court of England.[9]   Charles IX., whose object it was to represent the deed in the most favourable manner possible, had besought the nuncio not to despatch a courier until the royal message was prepared, and expressed the wish that his ambassador might be the first to bring the news to the Pope.   Beauville represented to the Pope the danger and audacity of the plot that had been so fortunately frustrated, as well as the necessity for vigorous measures, and his story was confirmed by a letter from the Duke of Montpensier.[10]   This was how the affair was understood in Rome.   On the 5th September a *Te Deum* was sung in the church of St. Mark, in thanksgiving for the preservation of the royal family and of the Catholic religion in France ; and on the 8th a solemn service was held in the church of the French nation.[11]

The service was not held in thanksgiving for the destruction of the heretics, but for the preservation of the king.   Muret's famous speech also shows this plainly.[12]   It is certainly false that the massacre of the Huguenots was a long-premeditated act, of which Pius V. had been given previous information,[13] and the events which followed place this beyond doubt.[14] Gregory XIII. grieved deeply over the blood that had been shed, and expressed his horror at the deed some time after to a nobleman, even with tears.[15]

The violent measures adopted by Louis XIV. against Protestants met with as little approval in Rome. Innocent XI. openly disapproved of them, and through his nuncio in London, D'Adda, besought James II. to intercede with Louis XIV. in favour of the oppressed Protestants.[16]

[1] Hase, Handbuch der Prot. Polemik, p. 47, No. 9. A. Z. 29 Dec. 1869.

[2] Rintel, pp. 43, 44.

[3] Hutter, Concord. c. ix. seq. 143-152. Menzel, N. Geschichte der Deutschen, v. p. 40.

[4] Sismondi, Hist. des Français, xviii. 516, 517. Capefigue, Hist. de la Réforme, ii. 173 ; vi. 54. Smedley, Hist. of the Reformed Religion in France, i. 199, 200, 237. Cf. Döllinger, Fortsetz. von Hortig's K.G. ii. p. 534 seq. ; Balmez, Catholicism, c. xxxvi.

[5] Buckle, Hist. of Civilisation in Eng. c. i. note 16.

[6] Huber, p. 54.

[7] Despatches of Vincent Parpaglia, ambassador from Savoy in Rome, d.d. 5 Sept. apud Cibrario, Archivio Storico Italiano, 1846, append. iii. p. 169.

[8] Parpaglia, l.c. Cf. Theiner, Annal. Eccl. cont. ad a. 1572, n. 36 seq. t. i. pp. 329-335.

[9] Coouper, Recenil des Depêches, Rapports, &c. Paris, 1840, t. v. pp. 120, 138, 161 seq. Theiner, l.c. n. 47, p. 46.

[10] Theiner, l.c. Mantissa, p. 336.

[11] Parpaglia, l.c. Maffei, Ann. di Greg. XIII. l. i. § 20.

[12] 'They' (the Huguenots), he said, 'hesitated not to plot against the head and the life of the king, from whom they had received, after so many grievous misdeeds, not merely pardon but a gracious and loving reception. But by God's providence, at the very time for its execution this conspiracy was discovered, and those things which these wicked men had designed for the king and the whole royal family were turned against themselves. O memorable night, which, by the death of some few rebels, freed the king from the peril of assassination and the kingdom from the ever-impending danger of civil war!' (Mureti, Orat. xxii. p. 177, ed. Ruhnkenii.) It should be noted that the first despatches of the Nuncio Salviati of the 24th and 27th August 1572 were not positively contrary to the French news, and Salviati only saw the matter more clearly in his later despatches of the 2d and 22d of Sept. Theiner, l.c.; Mantissa, pp. 328-331.

[13] Huber (p. 50), who refers to ' The Massacre of St. Bartholomew' in the North British Review, No. 101, Oct. 1869.

[14] Gandy (Revue des Questions historiques, 1866) has treated the subject in detail, and after him the Civiltà Cattolica (ser. vi. vol. viii. p. 679 seq.; vol. ix. pp. 267 seq. 662 seq.; vol. x. p. 268 seq.; vol. xi. p. 14 seq.), where the objections are duly considered.

[15] Brantôme (Vie de M. l'Amiral de Chastillon, Opp. viii. p. 190, ed. Haag, 1740) gives the words: ' Je pleure la façon dont le roy a usé, par trop illicite et defendue de Dieu, pour faire une telle punition, et je crains qu'il en tombera une sur luy, et ne la fera guères longue désormais.' Charles IX. died on 30 May 1574.

[16] Döllinger (Kirche und Kirchen, p. 72, Eng. ed.) cites Mazure, Hist. de la Révolution de 1688, Paris, 1825, ii. 126 ; Macaulay, ed. Tauchnitz, ii. 250. Cf. Ranke, Päpste, ii. p. 166 ; Raumer, Gesch. Europa's seit Ende des 16 Jahrh. vi. 206 ; Lingard, Hist. of England, xv. p. 89, Germ. ed.

§ 23.

Pius VII., in the Brief of January 19, 1819, to King Max Joseph of Bavaria, in which he expresses regret[1] at the retraction of the statement made by Cardinal Häffelin in the name of his sovereign on the 27th September 1818, distinctly declared that Catholics could not take unreservedly the constitutional oath without violation of their conscience.[2] The reasons of this were contained[3] in the *Fogli Dottrinali*, sent at the time to Munich. On this has been founded the assertion that Rome disliked to see all denominations on a legal equality, and disliked the equality of all classes before the law.[4] On the 10th November 1800 the right of settling in Bavaria, which had up till that time been a purely Catholic country, had, for the first time, been granted to Protestants. The parliament declared at that time, ' If unity and union is a fundamental law of the State, why should an exception exist in the case of religion? Bavaria enjoyed this unity in peace ; the introduction of divisions with the multiplying of religions can procure no superior advantages. The unreserved acceptance of members of strange sects is a source of perilous discord, and the great cause of the development and antagonism of parties. Unity of religion, on the other hand, is a sacred bond, which unites all citizens at the foot of the same altar, which points out to all in brotherly love the same duties ; which therefore, by identity of feelings and agreement in religious conduct, can more than any other means secure order and peace to the State."[5] This measure was at that time as little in favour with the people as with the Holy See, which stated its opinion on the subject in 1803 to the Elector of Bavaria.[6] The Prince Bishop of Trient, Count of Thun, complained that the toleration edict had extended toleration and equality to non-Catholics, even to those districts which had till then preserved themselves free from all heresy; so that if there were a sufficient number of misbelievers in those districts, they could have their pastors, service, churches, and schools, whence would arise great danger of the corruption of the Catholics; and thus it was desirable that the toleration edict should be revoked for purely Catholic districts; he said also that full toleration was not given to Catholics, and that their rights were violated.[7] In fact, as the bishops and vicars of the still existing dioceses said, in a remonstrance of 1816, liberty of conscience was actually restricted by the toleration edict, and especially the decree that no one under twenty-one years should change his religion was a wrong inflicted on every religion.[8] The *Fogli Dottrinali*[9] laid great stress upon this, as also did the later memorial of the bishops.[10]

In the mean time the circumstances of the Bavarian State were considerably changed, especially from the addition of new provinces, with populations partly of mixed religions and partly with a predominance of Protestants. The Holy See took note of these changes, and we find in the *Fogli Dottrinali* no protest against § 1 and 2 of the religious edict, which secure perfect religious liberty to all inhabitants, and forbid any constraint in matters of faith. We find complaints of the spirit of indifference pervading all the decrees in general of the religious edict; in particular of § 14, concerning the division of children of mixed marriages according to sex; of § 22, concerning the religion of foundlings; of § 18, concerning various cases of the change of religion of parents, &c.

[1] Vide the work Concordat und Constitutionseid der Katholiken in Bavaria, Augsb. 1847, appendix xi. pp. 241-243.
[2] Huber, p. 74.

[3] In the work cited, sup. xii. pp. 243-249.
[4] Janus, p. 39 seq.; see in answer Anti-Janus, pp. 25, 26.　Huber has not the least weakened my statement.
[5] Concordat und Constitutionseid, p. 6.
[6] Ib. sup. i. p. 177.
[7] Ib. p. 10.
[8] Ib. p. 41.
[9] Ib. p. 246.
[10] Freisinger, Memorial of October 1850.　On § 6 of the religious edict, cf. Silbernagl, Verfassung sämmtlicher Religionsgenossenschaften in Bayern, Landshut, 1870, p. 12, § 9, note 1.

§ 24.

The same scruples, occasioned by the religious edict of Bavaria, were earlier called forth by the French Charter of 1814, in which, although the Catholic religion was declared to be the religion of the State, equal liberty was granted to every one in his creed, and equal protection secured to all forms of worship.[1]　The point objected to in Rome was not the civil toleration of non-Catholic religious bodies,[2] 'but their being given the same liberty and the same protection as the Catholic Church.'　There was some apprehension lest Catholics by this constitutional oath should be forced to disregard divine and ecclesiastical laws, and that, as other religions were put upon an equal footing, naming the Catholic religion as the religion of the State was merely an illusion.[3]　But it is a fact that the Holy See declared itself satisfied when the ambassador Count Blacas d'Aulps, in the name of his sovereign Louis XVIII., on the 15th July 1817, made the solemn and written declaration,[4] that the king, after he had declared the Catholic religion to be the religion of the State, was obliged to guarantee the followers of other religions already established in France the free exercise of their religion, and even to incorporate this in the constitution and in the oath administered to the king ; but that this oath should do no injury either to the dogmas or the laws of the Church, since it referred only to those things which appertained to the civil authority, and that it would put no obligation upon his subjects that should be contrary to the law of God and of the Church.[5]　In the Allocution of July 26, 1817, Pius VII. spoke of this declaration as perfectly satisfactory.[6]　Pius VIII.

recalling this declaration sanctioned the Archbishop of Paris, on September 29, 1830, to take to Louis Philippe the formula of the oath of allegiance customary under Louis XVIII., and to say the prayers for him in the churches;[7] although the new constitution was in many ways more unfavourable to the Church than the old one,[8] and contained those grievances of the old one, which on the 4th of July 1824, Leo XII. had laid before Louis XVIII.,[9] especially in regard to the execution of former treaties, marriage laws, the *appel d'abus*, and other things. Neither also was the Belgian episcopate in the least kept back from recognising and observing the new constitution of Belgium.

[1] Charte, 1814, art. 5 : ' Chacun professe sa religion avec une égale liberté, et obtient pour son culte la même protection ;' art. 6 : ' Cependant la religion catholique, apostolique et romaine est la religion de l'Etat ;' art. 7 : ' Les ministres de la religion catholique, apostolique et romaine et ceux des autres cultes chrétiens recevront seuls les traitements du trésor royal.' The Charter of 1830 retained art. 5 unchanged, omitted art. 6, which, according to Dupin's declaration of 7 Aug. 1830, had been abused, and took art. 7 with the following alterations as art. 6 : (1) after the words *apostolique et romaine* was to be inserted, 'professée par la majorité des Français ;' (2) the last words were to be altered into ' reçoivent des traitements du trésor public.'

[2] Huber, pp. 73, 74.

[3] The Bishop of Troyes (Mgr. de Boulogne), whom Pius VII. on the 30th April 1814 from Cesena commissioned to inform the newly-restored Louis XVIII. of the grievances of the Church in France (Artaud, Vie de Pie VII. t. ii. ii. c. xxvi. p. 63 seq.) had his attention called to many other points.

[4] The Secretary of State had desired a satisfactory letter from the king, but acknowledged that an official note would do as well. Due de Richelieu to the ambassador, July 1, 1817. Artaud, l.c. t. ii. c. xxxvi. pp. 201, 202, Germ. ed.

[5] The same thing in French in Bullar. Rom. Cont. t. xiv. p. 377.

[6] Ib. pp. 362, 363, the chief contents are repeated by the Pope.

[7] Roscovány, Mon. ii. pp. 295-297, n. 335.

[8] Vide suprà, note 1. Louis Philippe swore on 9 Aug. 1830 before both Chambers : ' En présence de Dieu je jure d'observer fidèlement la Charte constitutionelle avec les modifications exprimées dans la déclaration, de ne gouverner que par les lois et selon les lois, de faire rendre bonne et exacte justice à chacun selon son droit, et d'agir en toutes choses dans la seule vue de l'intérêt, du bonheur et de la gloire du peuple Français.' Charles X. had sworn at Rheims on 25 May 1825 : ' En présence de Dieu je promets à mon peuple de maintenir et d'honorer notre sainte religion, comme il appartient au roi très chrétien et au fils ainé de l'Eglise, de rendre bonne justice à mes sujets, enfin de gouverner conformément aux

lois du royaume et à la Charte constitutionelle, que je jure d'observer fidèlement ; qu'ainsi Dieu me soit en aide.'

⁹ Cf. Scherer, Papst Leo XII. Schaffhausen, 1844, p. 136.

§ 25.

The Church has remained faithful to her old principles concerning religious liberty. She could not do otherwise; but States have changed theirs : some urged by pressing necessity have conceded to many religious denominations first toleration, then equal rights. The Church cannot condemn them for this proceeding. Others, however, have done the same thing without the necessity, and merely because they have adopted novel theories. In acting thus they have been wanting alike to their own interests and the doctrine of the Church, and have promoted the prevalent tendency towards the denial of all fixed principle.

The Church has guarded her dogmas without prejudice to any rights, and has condemned false principles without violating charity, which she proclaims and upholds, only not at the cost of truth. When the truth which she preaches arouses hatred against her she bears it with patience, throwing no veil over her doctrine, meeting reproaches with prayer, and enjoining her children to oppose Christian charity to the world's hatred. Thus too did Christ act with the Pharisees and Sadducees. He who was truth and charity gave His Church for all time a lasting example.[1]

[1] As to the censorship of books and publications, the Church from the earliest times (Acts xix. 19 seq.) has held it a sacred duty to condemn books dangerous to faith and morals. Vide Alphons. Liguori, Theol. Moral. t. i. l. i. append. iii. ed. Bassani, 1832, p. 154 seq. ; Zaccaria, Storia polemica della proibizione de' libri, 1777 ; Devoti, Instit. Jur. Can. t. iv. tit. 7, p. 78 seq., espec. § 6, not. 1, p. 88 seq. ; Fessler, Das Kirchliche Bücherverbot, Wien, 1858, pp. 27 seq. 39 ; Hausmann, Geschichte der päpstlichen Reservatfälle, p. 111 seq. ; Phillips, Kirchenrecht, vi. § 324, 325. That civil laws have changed in this matter is no reason for the Church to surrender her principles ; and just as she must reject unconditional liberty of religion and of thought, so also she must reject the unconditional liberty of the press, the alleged right of spreading publicly by word and writing every kind of opinion, and casting error in every form among the masses, whereby already many governments have been overthrown and indescribable disorder and disaster prepared. If our age thinks the poison a healing drug, the poison makes its deadly operation all the more evident. But here also Wisdom will be justified before her deluded children.

ESSAY XVIII.

CLAIMS OF THE POPES SINCE THE SIXTEENTH CENTURY.

§ 1.

WHEN a temporal monarch is tenacious of rights inherited from his ancestors, on any title whatsoever, even that of mere usurpation, conquest, and violence, far from being reviled he is esteemed for his firmness in maintaining the rights transmitted to him; while, on the other hand, he will meet with invariable censure should he through negligence, indolence, or cowardice suffer one of them to fall into disuse, or should he renounce any of them from scruple of conscience. Far different is the measure dealt out to the Pope. If he firmly maintains his rights, and refuses to suffer any diminution in the privileges of the Apostolic See, if he defends the rights exercised for many hundred years by his predecessors, whether founded upon the nature of the ecclesiastical primacy or on historical development, on solemn treaties or any other legitimate title, he is straightway accused of boundless ambition and pernicious sacerdotal arrogance, and every step taken by him towards this end is set down as an act

of pride and injustice ; and yet he cannot transmit his throne
either to his family or to his friends and favourites, and he, no
less than the civil ruler, is solemnly bound by oath to defend
his privileges to the utmost of his power ; and to complete the
injustice, those Popes who may in a moment of weakness have
neglected to defend their possessions receive the same blame as
civil rulers who have acted in a similar manner.

§ 2.

In times of transition, when the public law of the Middle
Ages, though frequently broken through, was not as yet in principle abolished, the charges brought against the Popes, as may
be seen especially in and since the time of Boniface VIII., were
chiefly occasioned by their refusal to surrender at once the prerogatives of their predecessors, which up to that time had been
universally acknowledged, and by their endeavour to maintain
them against the attacks of individual countries and sovereigns.
The Popes were blamed[1] when, instead of keeping to the strict
letter of the law, they, according to the principle upon which
Innocent III. laid such stress,[2] paid regard to considerations of
equity, and to distinctions between persons, things, and circumstances, times and places.[3]   Again, on the other hand, they
were blamed when they did not suffer such considerations to
prevail, but felt themselves bound to adhere to the letter of the
law.[4]   It was not possible for the Popes to satisfy censors who,
as occasion suited, blamed both courses of action, and by whom
even Christ Himself would not have been held blameless.   The
upholders of the modern State have been most severe towards
the Popes of the sixteenth and seventeenth centuries, who were
apparently under the delusion that what was possible and conceded to Innocent III. was likewise permitted to them.[5]

[1] L. viii. c. de Jud. iii. 1: ' In omnibus causis potior esse debet ratio
aequitatis, quam stricti juris.'   This aequitas is no mere subjective fairness, but the necessary regard to persons and circumstances partly ordered expressly by law (aequitas scripta), partly in virtue of the nature
and final end of all law (c. ii. d. 4 ; c. xiii. de Off. Jud. Deleg. i. 29).   Thus
Schulte, K.R. i. 195, 398.
[2] Cf. Döllinger, Kirche und Kirchen, pp. 544 seq. 616 seq.

¹ Innoc. III. l. vii. Ep. 119, p. 405 : ' Ad hoc Deus in Apostolica Sedo constituit *plenitudinem ecclesiasticae potestatis*, ut diligenter inspectis variis circumstantiis personarum et rerum, temporum et locorum, nunc rigorem exerceat, nunc mansuetudinem antepouat, interdum exsequatur justitiam, interdum gratiam largiatur, prout in causis diversis diverso modo viderit dispensandum.' Cf. l. viii. Ep. 137, p. 715; l. xvi. Ep. 74, p. 875.
⁴ Vide *e.g.* Alzog, Kirchengeschichte, ii. p. 58, 8th ed. on Bonifaco VIII. alone.
³ Huber, p. 46 and elsewhere.

§ 3.

A series of Papal Bulls of the sixteenth and seventeenth centuries is often cited, in which, in accordance with the ancient principles of law, sanction is given to penalties against various heretical princes; notably the Bull against Henry VIII. of England, against Elizabeth, and against Henry IV. of France. Let us more closely consider each one of these cases.

Henry VIII. of England, during his shameful attempt to obtain a divorce from Queen Katharine in order to marry Anne Boleyn, broke completely with the Apostolic See, forced the English Church by violence into schism, and subjected to the bitterest persecution all true Catholics who refused to renounce the head of the universal Church. Paul III. after long delay issued the Bull dated August 30, 1535 (first published December 17, 1538), in which he called upon the king, already quite separated from the Church, to submit to the Holy See; and in the event of his persistence in schism declared his kingdom forfeited, and his subjects freed from their oath of allegiance.[1] In the matter of the excommunication the Pope could appeal to the power of binding and loosing given to him by God ; but nowhere did he say that Henry's deposition followed directly in virtue of the divine law.[2] The feudal supremacy of the Roman See, so often acknowledged by the kings of England, gave a title by human law also, as being the public law of Christian States, at that time still in force. Henry VIII. himself still maintained the old laws against heresy and the whole mediæval principle of law,[3] with the single exception that he cast off the supremacy of the Pope, and in so far as concerned his own kingdom took the Papal office upon himself.

[1] Paul. III. Const. Ejus qui immobilis and Cum Redemptor, Bull. Rom. ed. Luxemb. 1742, i. pp. 707, 711 seq. Spondan. a. 1535, n. 15, a. 1538, n. 14.

[2] Gosselin, P. ii. c. iii. art. 1, § 2, p. 277, Germ. ed.

[3] Ranke, Englische Geschichte, i. p. 131.

§ 4.

It had ever been laid down by the public law of France that no heretic might possess the throne of the most Christian king. Accordingly Sixtus V., September 9, 1585, issued the Constitution 'Ab immensa aeterni Regis,'[1] intended, in the first place, publicly to denounce as heretics the two Princes Henry of Bourbon (King of Navarre) and Henry of Condé, who had relapsed into heresy. Thereupon, by the law then in force, followed loss of dignities and of the claim to the throne. In this Bull also the Pope appeals to the notorious character of the heresy, and to the forfeiture of the governing power and of dignity consequent upon it ; he moreover makes a judicial declaration on the censures incurred by the two princes in the old accustomed form, and on the ground of the existing law. The same principles were defended by the parliament,[2] the Sorbonne,[3] and the citizens of Paris,[4] while the counter-declaration was signed by only seven prelates.[5]

[1] Spondan. a. 1585, n. 17. Sentis, Clem. VIII. Decret. liber septimus, l. v. tit. 5, c. xxvii. p. 165. Goldast. Monarch. S.R.J. t. iii. p. 124. Scripta utriusque partis, Francof. 1580, 8.

[2] Spondan. a. 1585, n. 7.

[3] Spondan. a. 1589, n. 111 ; 1590, n. 3, 9. Crétineau-Joly, Hist. de la Comp. de Jésus, t. ii. p. 411 seq. The decree was afterwards declared to be ungenuine, extorted, and null and void. Du Plessis, t. ii. P. i. pp. 482 seq. 530 ; P. ii. p. 295 seq.

[4] Ep. ad Sixt. V. ap. Anon. de justa Henrici III. abdicatione, l. iv. p. 392, ed. 1591. On the League, see Schneemann in the Laacher Monatschrift, 1872, No. 6, p. 504 seq.

[5] Spondan. a. 1591, n. 8. Bianchi, l.c. n. 4, 5, pp. 591-594.

§ 5.

The Bull of Pius V. also, ' Regnans in excelsis,' is a grievous stumbling-block to Herr Huber.[1] Elizabeth of England was not merely a Protestant, but was in addition a persecutor of

Catholics.[2] In the eyes of the whole Catholic world she was moreover completely illegitimate, being the daughter of Henry VIII. and Anne Boleyn, born during the lifetime of the rightful Queen Katharine. The only rightful queen, as they considered, was Mary Stuart, Queen of Scotland,[3] descended from Margaret, sister of Henry VIII., who married James IV. of Scotland. Hard pressed by her rebellious subjects, in 1568 Mary sought refuge with her cousin Elizabeth, who, instead of giving her a hospitable reception, subjected her to severe imprisonment, and finally to the ignominious death of the scaffold.

In the Bull above mentioned of February 25, 1570, the Pope declares Elizabeth, who formerly under Mary (1553-1558) had hypocritically professed the Catholic faith, and had afterwards thrown aside the mask, to be a heretic, and as such to have fallen under censures, and to be separated from the unity of the Body of Christ.[4] It was the universal conviction, not alone of the Catholics of England but of all the Catholic nations of Europe, that she had thereby forfeited all claim upon the English crown, and that her subjects were no longer bound by the oaths taken to her.[5] The Pope necessarily took for granted the continuance of the ancient law, which had not been altered even by Henry VIII.[6] Catholic jurisprudence was in complete accordance with the Bull, which in no way went beyond former Bulls on similar subjects, and in which the same formula was used.[7]

---

[1] P. 50. The Bull stands in the Bullar. Rom. t. iv. P. iii. p. 98. Cf. Scutis, l.c. c. xxiv. p. 165.

[2] Raynald. a. 1559, n. 1-10.

[3] Cf. Joh. Leslaeus (Ep. Rossensis), De titulo et jure serenissimae principis Mariae Scotorum reginae, quo regni Angliae successionem sibi juste vindicat, Rhemis, 1581. On the author, vide Theiner, Annal. ad a. 1574, n. 10, c. iv.

[4] *Declaramus* praedictam Elisabeth, haereticam et haereticorum fautricem, eique adhaerentes in praedictis anathematis sententiam *incurrisse esseque* a Christi corporis unitate praecisos.

[5] Gosselin, ii. pp. 280 seq. 346 seq.

[6] Many contemporary writers took the same view as the Pope. W. Allen, Ad persecutores Anglos pro Catholicis vera responsio, 1584, c. iv. v. ; Exhortatio ad nobiles et populum Angliae, 1588 ; Dolemann, Conférence sur la Succession prochaine de la Couronne de l'Angleterre, 1593. (Persons) Elizabethae Angl. Reginae saevissimum in Catholicos sui regni

edictum cum responsioue per D. Andr. Philop. Lugd. 1593 : 'Hinc infert universa theologorum et jurisconsultorum schola, quemcumque principem Christianum, si a religione Catholica manifeste deflexerit et alios avocare voluerit, excidere *statim* omni potestate et dignitate *ex ipsa vi juris tum humani tum divini*, hocque *ante omnem sententiam* supremi pastoris ac judicis contra ipsum prolatam.'

⁷ It is said to have been drawn up by Peretti, afterwards Sixtus V. Crétineau-Joly, Hist. de la Compagnie de Jésus, t. ii. p. 241, ed. 1844.

§ 6.

But this is not all. Pius V., says Huber, 'in his fanaticism did not shrink even from the crime of hiring assassins to murder the queen.'[1] This is indeed a fearful charge to bring against a noble-minded[2] Pontiff, revered by all Catholics as a saint! How is it proved? From a letter of the Pope to Philip II., in which he commends to him an Italian, Roberto Ridolfi, 'who will impart to him weighty matters concerning not a little the honour of God and the well-being of Christendom;'[3] whom, therefore, the king might trust, and supply with means for carrying out his designs. What these designs were the letter does not say, nor is there any proof that assassination was one of the 'weighty matters.' Neither do we know whether Ridolfi said precisely the same to the Pope and to the King of Spain; whether to the Pope he may not have made known his plan more in general, and to the king in detail; nor how far and to what deeds he had been authorised by the Pope. But why does our narrator pass over in silence the matter first treated of—the release from captivity of the unfortunate Mary Stuart, the really legitimate queen, in the eyes not only of the Catholics of England but also of many Protestants?[4] Why does he omit to mention that there was at that time a considerable Catholic party in England, who, in November 1569, had set on foot a rising in the northern counties, and desired to place the Duke of Norfolk at their head? This party became afterwards so important that, in spite of executions and banishments, London still numbered 40,000 Catholics at Elizabeth's death.[5] Why does he conceal that in the life-and-death struggle between the two religions a rising of the English Catholics, aided by Spain, against Elizabeth's heavy yoke was, to say the very least, as justifiable as the rising of the Netherlands against the Spanish throne, which was continually supported by England, and was to Philip cause sufficient for a war against Elizabeth? Had not the Catholics of England at least as good cause for attempting rebellion against Elizabeth, by whose tyranny their most sacred interests were violated, as the Greeks for rising against the Turks, and the Poles against Russia?[6]

Roberto Ridolfi of Florence, who lived in England, was commissioned by the captive Mary Queen of Scots in 1571 to obtain her freedom from the Pope and the King of Spain.[7] Pius V., who had her freedom much at heart, was deeply interested in the envoy, who seemed, moreover, well acquainted with the state of things in England; the Pope gave him a letter to King Philip, in which he expressed the interest he felt;[8] he also earnestly commended the release of the Queen of Scots to the Catholic king through his nuncio the Archbishop of Rossano. But when and where did the Pope hire an assassin? Leaving out of the question the fact that Ridolfi's design of assassination has never been proved, there is not the smallest proof that the Pope, who was so deeply concerned for the Queen of Scots, in any way even favoured, far less instigated, such a plan, or that he desired means to be employed so wholly unsuited to the noble end of the release of the unhappy queen.[9] It is fortunate that the accusers of St. Pius are not judges in a criminal court; for by their mode of procedure, and with their idea of judicial proof, there would every day be imminent danger of judicial murder.

---

[1] Huber, p. 50. Also Döllinger, in the statement of March 13, 1872.

[2] Gachard, Correspondance de Philippe II. t. ii. p. lvi. seq., gives many evidences of the sanctity of Pius V. Cf. also Ranke, Hist. of Popes, i. 350-354; iii. 307-309 (Germ. ed.); and Falloux, Hist. de St. Pie V. Paris, 1843.

[3] Huber, p. 51.

[4] Ranke, Englische Gesch. Berlin, 1859, vol. i. p. 376.

[5] Ib. pp. 372, 375, 501.

[6] It is remarkable how severely the rising of Catholic nations in favour of their legitimate rulers has been condemned by the liberal enemies of the Church, who extolled the attempt made against Ferdinand II. of

Naples, the Duke of Parma and others, and the dethroning of the Italian princes since 1859; and who have ever sought to justify the revolutionary unification of Italy. The Spanish rising of 1868 against Isabella was justified by them, and they even placed a son of Victor Emmanuel on the throne of St. Ferdinand; but Carlist risings are in their eyes merely wicked rebellions.

[7] Gachard, Correspondance de Philippe II. t. ii. 180 seq.

[8] Mignet, Hist. de Marie Stuart, t. ii. App. p. 428.

[9] Vide Germ. ed. of F. A. Mignet's Hist. of Mary Stuart, Leipzig, 1851, c. ii. pp. 279-291.

§ 7.

The increasing persecution of Catholics in England under King James led in November 1605[1] to the notorious Gunpowder Plot, and upon its failure all Catholics, even those who had no share in it, suffered grievously for the guilt of a few. Father Garnet's trial[2] was evidently conducted so as to prove, cost what it might, the guilt of the Catholic priesthood, and in particular of the Jesuits. In his examination contradictory statements were recorded which he did not acknowledge as his own; the rack was freely employed to force the desired confession from him and from the other accused; no heed was paid to the binding nature of the seal of confession for a Catholic priest, nor to the self-possessed and conscientious behaviour of Father Garnet in his most difficult position.[3] Had other persons instead of Jesuits been concerned, this trial would have received a far different colouring from that in which men now endeavour to represent it. Jesuitical plots at that time, and long after, played a great part in England,[4] even when they were such arrant fabrications as the Titus Oates plot in 1678.[5] What effectual measures the Jesuits could have taken to hinder the Gunpowder Plot without breaking the seal of confession, which is binding on a Catholic priest under all circumstances, has as yet never been made known.

[1] The Calvinists of Antwerp had set the example by their attempt on the Duke of Parma. Crétineau-Joly, Hist. de la Comp. de Jésus, t. iii. c. ii. p. 78 seq.

[2] Huber, pp. 57-59. Cf. Döllinger, A. Z. March 15, 1872.

[3] Lingard's History of England, ix. p. 59 seq. Riffel, Die Aufhebung des Jesuitenordens, 2d ed. pp. 306-311, note. The condition of Catholics

under James I., Father Gerard's Narrative of the Gunpowder Plot, by John Morris, S.J., London, 1871. It appears from the documents made known by Crétineau-Joly, t. iii. p. 83 seq., that the conspirators most feared hindrances on the part of the Jesuits, and also the death of innocent Catholics, which could not be avoided if the catastrophe occurred; that they put their questions figuratively and ambiguously before Fr. Garnet; that even before the end of the trial the report was spread on the Continent that Fr. Garnet was the chief instigator of the plot, and the endeavour was being made to throw the blame altogether upon the Jesuits.

⁴ As early as the reign of Elizabeth many spies were kept, who searched the houses of Jesuits, even on the Continent, to find out pretended plots. De Thou, Hist. l. viii. a. 1580, p. 541 (French trans.).

⁵ Ranke, Engl. Gesch. vol. v. 1865, p. 76 seq. Nota in Defens. Cleri Gallic. l. iv. c. xxiii. p. 388.

§ 8.

The oath of allegiance imposed by parliament upon English Catholics in consequence of the Gunpowder Plot[1] was in spirit precisely analogous to the oath of supremacy. Besides designating the king as the highest ruler, which implied in this context that the Pope was a subordinate authority, Catholics taking this oath were forced expressly to acknowledge in words that the said oath, which treated of questions of faith, was demanded of them lawfully by a legitimate and plenary authority. This was nothing less than to acknowledge in a temporal prince authority to decide and guide the faithful in matters of faith.[2] Moreover, it is hurtful to faith and the welfare of souls to anticipate the judgment of the Church, and to condemn as impious and heretical an opinion which the Church has not thought good to condemn, which many pious and learned men hold in all good faith, and which has had many most distinguished defenders in the schools of theology. English Catholics in taking the oath of allegiance were guilty of sin; because in the oath the doctrine that the Church, in certain cases, especially for apostasy and heresy, can declare sovereigns to be deposed and their rights forfeited, was condemned as impious and heretical, and thus the Church was made guilty of tolerating heresy, and her very essence was attacked. The Catholics of England, like those of France at a later time, might indeed hold this doctrine to be doubtful, not in accordance with revelation, and even to be

false ;[3] but to condemn it as *impious* and *heretical* without
awaiting the judgment of the Church was a grievous wrong,
violating Christian love and every principle of the Church, and
appears even to Bossuet to be exaggerated and rash.[4] The oath
moreover attributed to the Roman Church, only in order to
make her hated, the doctrine that any private person might put
to death at will an excommunicated prince,[5] a doctrine which
was at that time rejected and stigmatised by almost all theologians. Impartial Protestant historians have fully acknowledged
that the Apostolic See had good ground for rejecting the form
of the oath. Thus Ranke says (will he next be called a Jesuit
in disguise ?) that had this oath been accepted the supremacy of
the king would have been in fact acknowledged, and the adherence of the English Catholics to the Papacy would have
come to an end.[6]

[1] Huber, p. 60.

[2] Gosselin, ii. pp. 282-288.

[3] Cardinal Barberini, in reply to a Scotchman, is said to have declared:
' *Francis* morem non esse, ut in hujusmodi quaestionibus *Romanos* consu-
lant; consultos vero *ab Anglis* hoc sine dubio resoluturos quod juri suo
magis congrueret, interim vero theologis *Britannis* fas esse sicut et
Francis, ut jus suum persequantur' (Remonstrantia Hibernorum a R. P.
Caron, P. i. c. iv. § 4, p. 8, ad Calcem. t. ii.; Tractatuum des droits et
libertés de l'Eglise Gallicane, t. ii. ed. 1731). The note to Bossuet, l. iv.
c. xxiii. p. 389, adds : ' Optime Barberinus et candide.'

[4] Defens. Decl. Cleri Gall. P. i. l. iv. c. xxiii. p. 387 : ' Et quidem ab
ea sententia abhorrere, prospectis melius rebus, uti nos Franci facimus,
erat licitum ac bonum ; damnare ut haereticam, absque Ecclesiae auctoritate, *nimium et temerarium* videbatur.'

[5] The words are : ' Je jure encore que j'abhorre de tout mon cœur
comme *impie et hérétique* cette *damnable* doctrine et assertion, que les
princes excommuniéz ou privéz de leurs états par le Pape peuvent être
déposéz *ou tuéz* par leurs sujets, ou par quelque autre personne que ce
soit' (Rapin Thoyras, Histoire de l'Angleterre, t. vii. l. xviii. a. 1606).

[6] Ranke, Engl. Geschichte, vol. i. pp. 544, 545.

§ 9.

Paul V. is charged with having sacrificed the reunion of
England with Rome to his own ambition for political power, and
reference is made to a diplomatic document of 22d July 1609 in
the National Library in Paris. But is the charge proved ?

The document does not treat of claims to political power, but of the setting aside of ecclesiastical rules in order to stigmatise a doctrinal opinion held in high esteem in the Church, and perhaps shared by the Pope himself. The French ambassador in Rome, M. de Brèves, announced that James had·desired to recognise the Pope as the first Bishop and Head of the Church, if only he would renounce the pretension that Popes have authority to depose kings; and that the Pope had declared himself unable to do so 'sans être taché d'hérésie.'[1] It may still be doubted whether the French diplomatist had got hold of the Pope's exact words; for diplomatists seldom enter into theological distinctions, and even at the present time in such circles the Syllabus of 1864 is spoken of as though all the propositions condemned therein *in globo* were to be considered as so many heresies. There was no formal declaration drawn up on the part of Paul V. Whoever defends an opinion approximate to heresy may be said to be 'stained by heresy,' and theologians of that day set down the denial of the indirect power as *proxima haeresi*. In any case, it went against the conscience of the Pope to suffer the condemnation of an opinion defended by the most renowned theologians and truest adherents of the Holy See, knowing the injurious consequences which would ensue from such a sentence; even had he not personally shared this opinion, he could not at that time have left it exposed to its enemies. This is shown by a glance at the theological literature of that day. Any one too who is acquainted with the condition of England under James I. must be aware that the king, even had he desired it, could never have brought about a reunion with Rome; the recognition of the Pope as first Bishop and Head of the Church[2] would have been altogether illusory, and somewhat like the later idea of Charles II., who desired a reunion with Rome, but without a complete restoration of the Pope's authority, and retaining as much independence as possible for his Anglican Church.[3] James I. was still further from the Roman See, and held to the maxim uttered on his accession to the throne : 'I make law and gospel as pleases me.'[4] Rome may have been unwilling openly to call in question either James's good intentions or the sufficiency of his power ; still there was good reason to doubt of both. But while James was dealing as severely as ever with Catholics, and was himself taking up the pen against their Church, Henry IV. of France was doing his best to mediate between him and the Pope, and in this matter De Brèves spared himself no pains. As to the words—'This pretended right of deposing kings was in the eyes of the Pope an article of faith,' &c.—they are not the words of De Brèves,[5] but of G. H. Gaillard, who gives his own account of the doings of De Brèves.

[1] Notices et Extraits, t. vii. p. 311. Döllinger, in the statement of March 13, 1872, already cited, puts forward the declaration of the Pope.
[2] Not as ' Lord of the Church,' as Huber says, p. 62.
[3] Ranke, Engl. Geschichte, vol. iv. p. 241 seq.
[4] Hist. Essays, by John Forster, London, 1858, i. 227.
[5] As is falsely said by Huber, p. 63.

§ 10.

A decision of Innocent X. in 1648, containing a fresh condemnation of this oath, is said to have been called forth by the Jesuits;[1] and yet it is precisely the Jesuits in England, many of whom with heroic courage suffered, like the early Christians, a martyr's death, who were defenders of the most indulgent principles. They it was who induced Gregory XIII. to supersede his predecessor's severe sentence against Elizabeth, and to declare obedience to her as a temporal sovereign to be lawful.[2] Facts and documents plainly show that they used their influence against revolt and violence,[3] of which they were incessantly accused, although perfect freedom might have been theirs had they consented to give up their faith.[4]

[1] Huber, p. 64.
[2] Camden. Annal. Regni Elisab. a. 1580. Crétineau-Joly, Hist. de la Comp. de Jésus, t. ii. c. v. pp. 257, 266.
[3] Hollingshead and Camden allow this of the time of Elizabeth. Crétineau-Joly, l.c. p. 301.
[4] Crétineau-Joly, l.c. pp. 297, 298.

§ 11.

The decision projected in the Congregation of 1648 was

never published either in Rome or in England. It is said to have declared that the Catholics of England were not at liberty to relinquish and condemn the following propositions: (*a*) The Pope can release any man from obedience to the existing government; (*b*) he can release from an oath taken to a heretic; (*c*) persons condemned by the Pope as heretics may, at his command or with his dispensation, be put to death or misused.[1] We have not the text of the decision in question.[2] It is certain the power of loosing from oaths cannot simply be denied to the Pope, whether they be taken to a Catholic or to a non-Catholic. Only in so far as the rejection of the three propositions involved a rejection of the rights of the Pope, by anticipating the decision of the Church and arbitrarily settling the controversies of the day, was it criminal and worthy of condemnation.[3]

[1] Al. Zeitung, June 19, 1870, A. Sup. No. 31.   Huber, p. 64.

[2] Huber refers to no original; the copy of the Al. Zeitung, after quoting the condemnation of the oath of allegiance by Paul V., gives the reference: Dodd, Church History of England, iii. 288 ; Tractatus Dogmat. et Schol. de Ecclesia, Romae, 1782, ii. 245. This last I have not seen. In the passage mentioned in Ch. Dodd (died 1745), who carried his work up to the year 1688, nothing relating to this matter is to be found, not at least in the edition brought out by Timey, 1784. On the other hand, three propositions are quoted by Caron (Remonst. Hibernorum, P. i. c. iv. § 3, p. 7), which are but slightly different from those given above : (1) ' Pontificem Romanum posse subditos regni Catholicos ab obedientia et fidelitate civili principum ac magistratuum Protestantium eximere ;' (2) ' Posse eosdem principes seu magistratus tamquam excommunicatos deponere vel occidere;' (3) 'Posse in juramentis ac contractibus Catholicorum quibuscunque cum Protestantibus dispensare.'

[3] This is proved by the words : ' (S. Congregatio) subscriptores (earum damnatarum propositionum) in poenas in sacris canonibus et constitutionibus apostolicis contra negantes potestatem Pontificiam in causis fidei incidisse declarat.'

§ 12.

When we learn that, in spite of the Papal decision, nine-and-fifty doctors of the Sorbonne[1] declared ' that the oath of allegiance might be taken with perfect security to a religious conscience,'[2] we must remember this was in exact accordance with the position adopted by this body, since 1663 more openly than ever before, towards the teaching of the Roman theologians, especially on the indirect power of the Church.[3] Other Theological Faculties, as, for instance, that of Lyons, did not agree in the vote passed by Paris.[4] The defenders of the 'Irish Remonstrance,' which was censured at Rome in 1662, pleaded in its favour that in it those propositions had been omitted which might have been found offensive in the oath of allegiance.[5] The Remonstrance contained eight articles, all designated as 'dogmas of religion,' though those signing it had no right to call them dogmas ; the mere slight mention of 'dependence on the Roman See,' the really insulting form of many of the articles towards the Holy See, the close analogy both in words and sense with the earlier oath of allegiance, the violent opposition to doctrines not yet condemned by the Church, necessarily gave the document a character dangerous to faith. It was a somewhat modified—in indifferent matters an extended—paraphrase of the oath of allegiance. The increasing persecution of Catholics and the establishment of the Test Oath in 1673,[6] by which even the denial of the dogma of Transubstantiation and the recognition of the king's ecclesiastical supremacy were required, showed plainly that declarations such as the Remonstrance availed nothing to those signing them, in spite of the sympathy of the king, in heart a Catholic.[7] A long list of penal laws against Catholics as such, with no mitigation towards those who adhered to Gallican doctrines, followed under William III., Anne, and George I.,[8] though no other dangerous conspiracies were alleged. It is acknowledged even by Protestants that Innocent XI. sought the restoration of the Catholic religion in England by evangelical means alone.[9]

---

[1] Du Plessis d'Argentré, Collect. Judic. t. iii. Paris, 1736, P. i. p. 139. Censures et Conclusions de la Faculté de Théologie de Paris touchant la souveraineté des Rois, Paris, 1720, iv. p. 393. Bossuet (l. iv. c. xxiii. p. 384) says that the judgment was put on the Index at Rome in 1683, which is however disputed by others.

[2] Huber, p. 62. The document says : ' Salva fide et tuta conscientia,' but still with the restriction ' si modo in propositione, quae est de depositione et caede principum, ut quae damnatur ut *haeretica*, deponi et occidi *conjunctim* accipiantur, imo etsi *divisim*, ita ut tamen propositio haeretica materialiter, id est verbo Dei contraria finiatur quatenus deponi

posse principes effert, formaliter vero etiam, quatenus et *occidi* posse super-
addit.' (Du Plessis, l.c.)

³ Bianchi, t. i. l. i. § 13, p. 113 seq.
⁴ Cf. Bossuet, l.c. p. 387; Gosselin, ii. p. 287, note.
⁵ Carou (l.c. c. iv. § 2, p. 6) points out the following distinctions between James' formula and that chosen in the Remonstrance: '(1) Quod
(formula Jacobi) non tantum *agnoscat*, ut nostra, sed et *juret* Deumque in
testem adducat, ea sic esse, prout exponit. ... (2) Quod illa declaratio
Jacobina *tamquam impiam haereticam et damnabilem* damnet opinionem
oppositam, quam Pontificiam vel Bellarminianam appellant. (3) Quod
illa *credat* Pontificem non posse in illo juramento vel ulla illius parte dispensare. *Quae omnia in nostra omittuntur.* ... Et nunc ex Em. D.D.
Cardinalibus ultramontanisque theologis quaero: Si in Remonstrantia
illa Jacobina multa contineantur per nos in nostra *omissa*, quomodo verum
erit, quod illi asserunt, Remonstrantiam nostram cum illa a Paulo V.
damnata convenire aut instar repullulantis hydrae continere propositiones
convenientes cum aliis a Sede Apostolica olim reprobatis?'

⁶ Cf. Ranke, Englische Geschichte, iv. pp. 422-424.
⁷ Ranke, ib. p. 363 seq.
⁸ Rintel, l.c. pp. 40, 41.
⁹ Ranke, l.c. v. p. 482.

§ 13.

Until long after the so-called 'Reformation' the ancient
principles of legislation were still maintained in the States of
Europe; and it is only by degrees, and by no means at the
same time in all countries, that these have undergone any complete change. Almost everywhere there was a State religion in
close union with the civil power. As in countries purely Catholic a ruler was strictly required to be of the Catholic faith,
which was constitutionally established,¹ so afterwards in Protestant States the Catholic faith was proscribed, and sovereigns
were required to be of the dominant religion. An act of the
English parliament of 1688, renewed in 1701, excluded all
Catholics and their wives from the throne;² and again in 1805
parliament enacted that an English king becoming a Catholic
should at once forfeit the crown.³ In Sweden, where the most
severe laws were passed against the Catholic religion,⁴ King
Sigismund, for being a Catholic, was dethroned in 1604 by
Charles IX. In 1720 this rule was actively enforced,⁵ and the
constitution of 1809 required the king and all State officials to
profess Lutheranism;⁶ the same public law was established by
the constitution of Norway in 1814,⁷ and this was also done in

Denmark and many German States. The Greek Church was in like manner maintained in Russia; and even to this day princesses coming into the country by marriage are required to enter the Greek Church.

[1] Cf. the stipulations of Philip II., May 6, 1598, on ceding Belgium to his daughter Isabella and her future husband Albrecht of Austria (J. Dumont, Corps Dipl. Univ. v. i. p. 574; Spondan. a. 1598, n. 15; Synopsis Monum. Eccl. Mechlin. t. iii. p. 1041); the Spanish constitution of 1808 (Dufau et Guadet, Collection des Constitutions, t. v. pp. 65, 86); that of Sicily (ib. iv. p. 464); that of Poland, 1697 and 1768 (l.c. 34, 35, Mémoires pour servir à l'Hist. ecclés. du 18 siècle, t. i. Introd. p. clx.; Lenglet-Dufresnoy, Méthode pour étudier l'Histoire, t. viii. p. 346); that of France, 1685 (Dufau et Guadet, t. i. p. 79).

[2] Dufau et Guadet, l.c. t. i. pp. 387 seq. 396.

[3] Parliamentary Debates, t. iv. Lond. 1805, p. 677. Cf. De Maistre, Du Pape, t. ii. concl. p. 251.

[4] Even the Edict of Gustavus III. of Jan. 24, 1781 (Theiner, Sammlung einiger Aktenstücke z. Gesch. der Emancipation der Kath. in Engl. Mainz, 1835, p. 77 seq.), shows extreme severity.

[5] Lenglet-Dufresnoy, l.c. pp. 220, 237, 260. Moréri, Diction. v. Suède et Sigismonde III., Ulrique, Eléonore, Frédéric de Hesse-Cassel.

[6] Dufau, l.c. t. iii. p. 306.

[7] Ib. t. iii. p. 322.

§ 14.

In Germany, at the opening of the sixteenth century, the relations of Church and State were, in their principles and chief characteristics, still thoroughly mediæval;[1] the temporal sword was to aid the spiritual, especially against heresy. The extermination of Protestantism was held to be a duty not by Popes Leo X., Hadrian VI., and Clement VII. alone,[2] but by all the Catholic princes, theologians, and jurists of Germany, in particular by Charles V. and many of his counsellors,[3] and by the Dukes of Bavaria;[4] negotiations or peace with sectaries, by which the rights of the Church were given up, were strongly reprobated.[5] Charles V. opposed with heart and soul the religious peace of Augsburg in 1555,[6] and before that the treaty of Passau in 1552, which wrought so great a change in Germany; but he was aware that his crippled power was insufficient to punish the wrongs done to himself and to the empire.

Paul IV. in protesting against the religious peace, regarding it as null, and being prepared to release any oath taken to

maintain it,[7] was expressing his own view of law, and his firm
conviction that as yet no necessity had arisen for any such de-
parture from the universal principles of law held both by himself and by the emperor; and there is therefore no ground[8] for
concluding it to have been a matter of indifference to him that
Germany was once more plunged into civil war and made the
prey of foreign lands. But setting entirely aside the fact that
numerous disputes arose over the interpretation of the Augsburg religious peace,[9] and that Germany lost blessings greater
than that of peace by the disunion of faith being completed,
was the treaty such as really to secure peace?[10] and was it
found capable of hindering incessant local battles, and at last
the Thirty Years' War? Was it not rather itself the cause of
that war?[11]

[1] Warnkönig, Die Staatsrechtl. stellung der Kath. Kirche in den Kath.
ländern des deutschen Reichs, Erlangen, 1855, p. 12.

[2] Huber, p. 40. Vide Letters from Campeggio to Clement VII. Nov.
13, 1530, and June 24, 1531; from Salviato to Campeggio, July 13, 1531
(Lämmer, Monum. Vaticana, pp. 64 seq. 73, 74). Campeggio's Memorial
of May 1530, in Maurenbrecher's Charles V. and the German Protestants,
Dusseldorf, 1865, Appendix, i. iii. p. 3 seq. Ranke, Popes, i. p. 111 seq. ·
Germ. ed.

[2] Letter to Clem. VII. Dec. 22, 1523. Lanz, i. 80. Maurenbrecher,
l.c. pp. 12, 25, 60, 344, Appendix, i. iii. p. 16 seq.

[4] The Bishop of Modena to Farnese, March 1541. Lämmer, l.c. p. 367;
Maurenbrecher, p. 51.

[5] Thus earlier Ferdinand and the Prince-Elector Joachim of Brandenburg. Seckendorf, Comment. Hist. Apol. de Luther, iii. 27. For Bavaria,
vide Pallavicini, Hist. Conc. Trid. l. iii. c. ix. n. 7; for Otto of Augsburg,
Buchholtz, vii. 178 seq.

[6] Maurenbrecher, l.c. pp. 308, 309, 311.

[7] Bzovius, Annal. Baron. Cont. t. xx. p. 306, ad a. 1555, n. 36, without
reference to sources. Cf. Fessler, Die wahre und die falsche Unfehlbarkeit, p. 65.

[8] Schulte, i. p. 51, note 2, and No. 44.

[9] Cf. Phillips, Kirchenrecht, iii. § 140, p. 442 seq.

[10] Schenkl, Syntagma Jur. Eccl. Salisb. 1786, § 184, p. 102.

[11] Onno Klopp (Kleindeutsche Geschichtsbaumeister, p. 131) calls the
Augsburg religious peace the fruit of the treachery of the Prince-Elector
Maurice, the seed which after long preparation grew up into the Thirty
Years' War.

§ 15.

The protest of the Pope against the peace of Westphalia, by which the Thirty Years' War was brought to a close, has given even greater offence. When the Bull of Innocent X. is justified as a protest against the immoral principle ' Cujus regio, illius religio' (He who rules the land settles its religion), it is objected that no such protest is to be found in the Bull.¹ It is true that no express condemnation of the principle appears in the Bull, but neither is it explicitly put forward in the treaty of peace; but like the religious peace of Augsburg, of which it was professedly the development, the whole treaty of Westphalia is based upon this principle.

The Pope's protest does not extend to the peace as such, nor to all parts of the treaty, but only to certain articles by which injury was done to the Church.² Moreover, he does not speak as ' sovereign of sovereigns,'³ but only as supreme Head of the Church, whose duty it is to guard the faith and the rights of the Church. The Pope lays especial stress on the following seven points in the treaty: (1) The Church property occupied by heretics was made over to them and theirs for ever.⁴ (2) The heretics of the so-called Augsburg Confession were permitted the free exercise of their heresy in numerous places;⁵ assignments of sites were promised for the building of suitable meeting-houses;⁶ and they, together with Catholics, were admitted to public posts and offices, to certain archbishoprics and other ecclesiastical dignities and benefices;⁷ also to a share in the privilege of the ' first petition' (jus primarum precum) granted by the Apostolic See to King Ferdinand on his election as emperor.⁸ (3) Annates, or firstfruits, the right of bestowing the pallium,⁹ confirmations, Papal months, and similar rights and reservations were removed from the Church goods of the said Augsburg Confession. (4) The confirmation of the election or postulation of the pretended archbishops, bishops, or prelates of the said Confession was given over to the civil power.¹⁰ (5) Several archbishoprics, bishoprics, convents, provostships, commendams, canonries, and other Church benefices

and properties—being no longer even called Church property—
were given to heretical princes and their heirs, as perpetual
fiefs, under the title of a civil dignity. (6) There was a special
provision that no law, canon or civil, universal or peculiar, no
decree of a Council, rule of an order, oath, Concordat with Popes,
or any other civil or ecclesiastical decree, dispensation, absolution, or other exemption, should be appealed to, listened to, or
admitted in contradiction to any single article of this peace.[11]
(7) The number of the prince-electors, which had been once
settled by apostolic authority,[12] was, without the consent of the
Pope and that of the Apostolic See, increased, and an eighth
elector appointed in favour of the heretical Count Palatine
Karl Ludwig and others, to the serious injury of the orthodox
religion, the Holy See, the Roman Church, and other Churches
dependent upon her.[13]

The Pope had without doubt the right of protesting, since
his own rights were wholly disregarded, Concordats strictly
observed by Rome were violated, and the rights of all Catholics
grievously injured. He could not have remained silent even
had he foreseen that his remonstrance would be in vain ;[14] had
he held his peace his tacit consent might have been inferred.[15]

¹ Huber, p. 66 seq.
² Fessler, Die wahre und die falsche Unfehlbarkeit, p. 56, note **.
³ The 'apostolical supremacy' to which Schulte (vol. i. p. 41, § 30)
refers applies solely to the domain of the Church.
⁴ No less ' stress' is laid on this provision, which is passed over by
Herr Huber, than upon that which follows, which he puts foremost.
Both by spiritual and by civil law, Church property could not be disposed
of without the authority of the Church, especially to her injury, and an
alienation of this sort was a grievous violation of law.
⁵ Huber (p. 67) speaks of perfect religious freedom, and the social
equality of the Protestants with the Catholics ; but perfect religious freedom was far from being given.
⁶ Coöperation in the spread of heresy was at all times subject to ecclesiastical penalties.
⁷ Nothing could be more absurd or more wounding to Catholics than
the Protestant bishops, who held these offices merely for the sake of the
temporalities, especially the alternate succession of Catholic and Protestant
bishops in Osnabrück.
⁸ Cf. J. A. Brand, diss. de Jur. Caesar. primar. precum, et Endres, diss.
de Insinuationis primarum precum necessitate, in Thesaur. Jur. Eccles. t. v.
n. 4, t. vii. n. 9, Lunig.; Spicil. Eccl. i. c. i. § 170 seq.; Friedberg, l.c.

pp. 180-183. Clement XI. still defended the Papal right in the Brief to the Chapter of Hildesheim, 1705, and in the Indult, Cum post factum, March 10, 1714:

⁹ 'Jura Palatii' in the Bullarium is a misprint; as appears from the decree in question, Instrum. Pac. Osnabr. art. 5, § 19.

¹⁰ Instr. Pac. Osnabr. art. 5, § 21.

¹¹ I. P. Osn. art. 17, § 3 ; Monast. c. xvi. § 113. By this clause the legislation and indeed all the rights of the Church and of ecclesiastics, especially of the Pope, were seriously and harmfully interfered with.

¹² This statement gives special offence to Huber, p. 68., But might not Innocent X. maintain what had been said more than three centuries before by the German King Albrecht in his document of July 17, 1303 ? Hefele (Conc. vi. p. 289, note 2) supposes Albrecht to have declared this earlier than the Popes. The tradition mentioned by the author of the work De Regimine Principum, iii. 10, that Gregory V. appointed the Electors, was received not alone by Hadrian VI. (Ep. ad Frideric. Saxon. 1522, Hard. ix. 1901), but also even by the Magdeburg Centuriators (Centur. x. c. xix). Friedberg (Diss. cit. p. 25, note 5) records many authors by whom the tradition is mentioned.

¹³ Ceteraque in dictis instrumentis contenta, quae Cath. religioni, divino cultui, animarum saluti, eidem Sedi Ap. Romanae et inferioribus ecclesiis . . . quomodolibet . . . praejudicium . . . afferunt.

¹⁴ Walter, Kirchenrecht, § 113, note 2. Phillips, Kirchenrecht, iii. § 141, p. 476. Fessler, l.c. pp. 56, 57.

¹⁵ Schenkl, Synt. Jur. Eccl. § 187, p. 105. The subject is treated well and in detail by Schmidt, Instit. Jur. Eccles. German. P. i. pp. 83-93.

§ 16.

The canonical, and in general the juridical, point of view is carefully to be distinguished from the political.¹ Looked at from the first, not the Pope alone but every Catholic had to pass judgment on the peace, as was acknowledged on almost all sides.² On political grounds only could it be defended. Rome accepted it as a momentous deed done, not as a just deed ; for injustice can never become justice, least of all when the Church is concerned. Apostasy from the one Church was indeed a violation of law, from which innumerable others ensued ; in so far, however, as the treaty, at least outwardly, restored peace and order to Germany it was beneficial, though scarcely in any other respect, for at the present day it is still a question with politicians whether this peace of Westphalia, in which the superior power and arrogance of France and Sweden dictated laws to the worn-out German Empire,³ was so great a blessing.⁴

Few acquainted with history would venture to reply to this question with an unconditional affirmative. Still less can it be considered as a blessing that, as has been most truly said by Döllinger,[5] it set a seal to the system of making sovereign princes the rulers over religion and conscience.

[1] Walter, l.c.

[2] Warnkönig, l.c. p. 21 : 'From the Catholic point of view the peace of Westphalia was indeed an act to be condemned in the Catholic princes of Germany, and necessarily drew an earnest protest from the Pope.' Martin Gerbert (op. cit. l. iii. c. viii. n. 13 seq. p. 566 seq.), in recording the provisions of the peace of Westphalia, and in stating the grounds for and against, makes his judgment plainly known, even though he does not venture to express it in words, having regard to I. P. Osn. a. 5, § 50; a. 17, § 2, 3.

[3] Onno Klopp, Kleindeutsche Geschichtsbaumeister, Freib. 1863, p. 3 seq.: 'The treaties of 1648 were the work of foreigners, of France and Sweden. They are not, as is well known, a development of our national life, but are to be considered as a maiming of it, and, moreover, a maiming by a foreign power.'

[4] Cf. Ludwig Bamberger (Gedanken zur Völkerpsychologie, ii. Allgemeine Zeitung, Sup. Jan. 24, 1871), in the sketch of the speech made by Thiers, March 14, 1867, in which he landed the peace of Westphalia as the happy cause of the peace of Europe up to 1866, and amongst other things said: 'Upon it (this great treaty) are founded the freedom of Europe, the independence of the smaller States of Germany, the glory of France ; thanks to this peace Europe has been set free, set free by France, and France itself is covered with glory.'

[5] Kirche und Kirchen, p. 58.

§ 17.

The numerous misinterpretations to which the Bull of Innocent X. had been exposed became known in Rome, and although the conduct of the Holy See for 160 years might have completely put an end to the uneasiness of princes, still the Pope gave a direct explanation. In the protest presented to the Congress of Vienna by Cardinal Consalvi[1] and confirmed by Pius VII. in a Consistory,[2] against all things done or not amended, to the injury of the Church in Germany, and against all things prejudicial to the salvation of souls resulting therefrom, the following statement was expressly made: That the Holy Father, in virtue of the charge of the flock of Christ laid upon him, and in virtue of the sacred oaths by which he was bound, could not keep silence amid so many violations of the rights of the Church,[3] lest it should appear as though he, by his forbearance, approved thereof; and also because, according to the example given by his predecessors, who had not failed frequently to raise their apostolic voice when the Church suffered injuries even far less serious, he was bound, so far as lay in his power, to maintain the interests and rights of the Church.[4] Amongst the examples of former Popes the accompanying note of Cardinal Consalvi cited the following: (1) that of Innocent X. in relation to the peace of Westphalia;[5] (2) that of Clement XI. in 1707 and 1714;[6] (3) that of Benedict XIV. in 1744.[7] This very comparison proves that the Bull of Innocent X. was understood only in the sense of an earnest protest. Still Herr Huber[8] cannot refrain from saying, 'The protestation of Cardinal Consalvi against the result of the Vienna Congress of June 14, 1814, is further proof that the rejection of the peace of Westphalia is insisted upon by Rome. Indeed since the time of Henry IV. it has been a tradition of Papal politics to raise civil war in Germany, and thus render the empire powerless.' Any person acquainted with the untold misery of the Catholic Church in Germany since the secularisation, and the state of things then introduced, is well able to estimate how idle it is thus to speak of so just a defence of rights.

[1] Bullar. Rom. Contin. t. xiii. pp. 403-407 (Italian). Klüber, Acten des Wiener Congresses, Erlangen, 1838, vol. vi. p. 442. Roscoványi, Monum. Cath. t. ii. pp. 96-99, n. 297. Also in French in the Monde, 3 Dec. 1863, n. 168, though not in full.

[2] Allocution of Sept. 4, 1815, Bull. Rom. Cont. l.c. p. 398.

[3] In the note accompanying the protest are the words: 'Il Santo Padre, responsabile a Dio, alla Chiesa ed ai fideli non potrebbe senza mancar ai suoi doveri, osservar il silenzio intorno a risoluzioni di questa sorta.'

[4] In the protest itself: 'Non solo non li può passare sotto silenzio, affinchè non sembri col tolerarli che Egli li approvi, ma sull' esempio ancora de suoi predecessori che contro pregiudizii di minore importanza fatti alla Chiesa non omisero di far sentire la loro apostolica voce, è costretto a difendere ed a conservare intatti *per quanto esso può* i diritti e le ragioni della Chiesa.'

[5] The protest itself mentions only the protest made at Münster by the Bishop of Nardo, Fabio Chigi, as a precedent for such a declaration on the part of the Papal legate ; and the Papal Allocution, § 8, simply says :

' Haec ab eo, qui nostram gerebat personam, agenda erant omnino, ut jura
Ecclesiae ponerentur in tuto.'
    ⁶ Supplem. ad Natal. Alex. H. E. t. ii. pp. 194, 306. Schröckh, Kirchen-
geschichte seit der Reform. vi. p. 383.
    ⁷ It appears that the protest against the treaty of Worms, Sept. 13,
1743, is meant. Cf. Gfrörer, Geschichte des 18 Jahrh. herausgegeben
von Weiss, vol. iii. p. 228 seq.; Carutti, Carlo Emanuele III. vol. i. c. ix.
pp. 237, 238.
    ⁸ Huber, p. 68.

§ 18.

To furnish grounds for the complaints against the protest
of Innocent X. history has been ransacked, and an attempt
made to get together a list of accusations. Rome and the Jesuits
have been charged with stirring up the war of religion,[1] and
Bunsen is declared to have been right in saying, 'The Thirty
Years' War was caused and perpetuated by the Jesuits' ![2] Are
we then to believe that France and Sweden and the Protestant
princes in general were guiltless, and that the Jesuits inspired
the all-powerful Richelieu and the princes leagued in defence
of the pure Gospel; and this, although Richelieu was exasperated against the Jesuits, while the princes fled from them as from
the plague? As a fact, the two works *Political Mysteries* and
the *Warning to the most Christian King*, published in 1625 by
the German Jesuit Keller, confessor to Duke Max of Bavaria,
irritated the king[3] even more than Santerelli's pamphlet somewhat later; moreover, the Jesuit Theophil Raynaud of Sos-
prello, in the territory of Nice, refused to place his able pen at
the disposal of Richelieu, and suffered many persecutions in
consequence; indeed many members of the Society were in
similar opposition to France.[4] Again, the edict of restitution,
we are to believe, was 'due to the pressure of the Curia and of
the Jesuits.' True, the emperor's confessor may alone have had
influence in this matter; but the four Catholic electors had spoken
in favour of the edict, as also the Papal nuncio.[5] It may indeed be doubted whether the edict was politically wise, but there
is no doubt that it was legally justified. 'From the strictly
legal point of view,' says K. A. Menzel,[6] 'it would be hard to
find fault with the edict of restitution.' But Urban VIII.,
we are told, 'looked with no friendly eye upon the victory of

the emperor, for he considered the independence of the Papacy
endangered by the ascendency of the House of Austria.' But
even supposing Urban VIII. to have thought too exclusively of
his position as a temporal prince,[7] what follows? Are Popes
never expected to make mistakes in politics? And was the independence of the Holy See an object which any Pope could
disregard? It is not correct that Urban VIII. refused all subsidies to the emperor. On July 19, 1631, the Pope declared
himself ready to give him all aid, and granted him, on the ex-
haustion of his own treasury, six full tithes of all the churches
of Italy.[8] Ferdinand desired not only large subsidies but also
that the war should be declared to be one of religion (1632).
Every one well read in history must concede that Urban VIII.
was right in refusing this ;[9] for it is shown by the whole course
of the contest. All the Catholic generals in Germany denied
that it was a war of religion, and even enrolled Protestant officers and soldiers under their banners ;[10] how then could the
Pope declare it to be such? However, after the death of Gustavus Adolphus[11] (November 6, 1632), Urban VIII. sent fresh
supplies[12] to Germany, for he perceived that the weightiest Catholic interests were at stake; later he renewed in the emperor's
favour the subsidy from Church property.[13] The letter of the
Secretary of State to the nuncio at Vienna, Archbishop Cyri-
acus Rocci of Patras, July 9, 1633, declared the Pope to be in
favour of a peace, but not on conditions such as to do lasting
injury to the Catholic cause.[14] At the same time Urban VIII.
endeavoured to induce Louis XIII. of France to assist the
emperor and the Catholic princes of Germany against the Swe-
dish generals, and to punish the lies of Ferdinand's adversaries,
who openly boasted of the aid of France.[15] But we are again
told that 'when in the year 1636 conferences were held at Cologne, having for their aim the pacification of Germany, they
were brought to naught by Urban VIII.'[16] That is to say, that
Urban sent thither his legate Ginetti, naturally with strict and
binding instructions.[17] It cannot be doubted that the Pope
was merely fulfilling his office in maintaining the rights of the
Catholic Church ; it was not his concern to obtain still further

powers for those 'who,' as K. A. Menzel says, 'looked upon it
as their charge to give the last blow to the Papacy;'[18] he would,
on the contrary, have laid himself open to severe and just censure had he blindly promoted or accepted any peace concluded
in any degree at the cost of Catholics. And even supposing the
' Roman policy' to have been to blame for the overthrow of the
Catholic cause in Germany, which has by no means been proved,
it was still from the Church's point of view a matter of conscience to refuse consent to stipulations positively dangerous to
the Church, which were never in the intention of the Pope,
which not only injured the ' interests of Rome' and its sovereign but primarily and directly those of the Church in Germany; stipulations which encroached in so many ways on the
domain of spiritual jurisdiction, and were the cause in the future
of evils so serious that they may well be considered irreparable.

¹ Huber, p. 65.
² Karl Josias von Bunsen, German edition of Nippold, iii. p. 409.
³ These works were condemned by the assembly of French clergy,
Dec. 13, 1625 (Du Plessis, t. iii. P. ii. pp. 231-238); also by the Sorbonne
(ib. t. ii. P. ii. pp. 190-198), and by the Paris parliament, Jan. 21, 1626
(ib. pp. 199, 200).
⁴ Crétineau-Joly, Hist. de la Compagnie de Jésus, vol. iii. pp. 422 seq.
433 seq.
⁵ Ranke's Popes, ii. pp. 517, 518, Germ. ed.
⁶ Neuere Geschichte der Deutschen, vol. vii. p. 182.
⁷ Ranke, l.c. ii. p. 537. Reumont, Geschichte der Stadt Rom. iii. ii.
p. 613.
⁸ Const. 160, Superna dispositione, xiv. Kal. Febr. 1631, Bullar. M. ed.
Luxemb. 1742, t. v. pp. 237-240.
⁹ Numerous proofs are given in J. Janssen's Schiller als Historiker,
Freiburg, 1863, pp. 97 seq. 110 seq.; Onno Klopp, Kleindeutsche Geschichtsbaumeister, pp. 25, 52, 302. Boguslav Chemnitz, or Hippolitus a
Lapide, as he called himself, wrote in 1640, de Ratione Status in Imperio
nostro, l'. iii. c. i. : ' Sileat ne cesset tandem vanus ille religionis praetex-
tus; non enim credimus *de religione* jam amplius principaliter, *sed de
regione* potius agi, ut aut liberi vivamus aut jugo domus Austriacae, his-
panico sanguine mixtae, colla nostra turpiter subdamus.'
¹⁰ Hurter, Zur Geschichte Wallensteins, p. 69. O. Klopp, Das Rest.
Edict im nordwestl. Deutschland, Göttingen, 1860, p. 84.
¹¹ The report of the Venetian ambassadors that the death of the King
of Sweden was displeasing to the Pope, and that he dreaded less the success of the Protestants than of the imperialists, cannot be taken as any
proof of the Pope's true mind.
¹² Artaud, Hist. des Souv. Pontifes, t. v. p. 369.

[13] Bullar. Magn. l.c. Const. 178, pp. 255-258.
[14] Cf. Lämmer, l.c. p. 39, No. 23 c.
[15] Cod. Vatic. 6929. Cf. Lämmer, l.c. p. 39, No. 23, lit. d.
[16] Huber, p. 66.
[17] Ranke, l.c. ii. 568, 569.
[18] K. A. Menzel, iii. 287.

§ 19.

The dispute between Paul V. and the Republic of Venice in 1606 has been at all times turned to account by the enemies of the Holy See.[1] Together with various differences as to their mutual borders at Ferrara, the tithes of the clergy, and the exemptions of benefices, a further dispute arose from the imprisonment by the Republic of two ecclesiastics, Scipio Seraceni, canon of Vicenza, and Brandolino Valmarino of Forli, abbot of Narvesa, in direct breach of the privilege of ecclesiastical immunity established, as elsewhere, within the territory of the Republic ; nor had any notice of the imprisonment been sent to the Holy See. The dispute was further occasioned by the maintenance by the Senate of two laws prejudicial to the Church, passed January 10, 1603, and March 26, 1605, by which laws the founding of new convents and hospitals, the building of churches, and the institution of new orders and confraternities were rendered difficult, the acquisition of property in land for the Church, as also the alienation of immovable property to her for more than two years without State approval, was forbidden.[2] These measures were to be the prelude to still further steps, to which the government was incessantly urged by the Protestant-minded Paul Sarpi.[3] As the Republic refused to make the slightest concession to the Pope's demands he at length excommunicated the Doge and the Senate, and laid Venice under an interdict.[4] The clergy were then forbidden by the Doge under pain of death to observe the sentence, and the greater number submitted to him ; only the Jesuits, the Capuchins, the Theatines, and the Minims obeyed the Pope, and these were forced to leave the Venetian territory. The cause of the Holy See was defended in writing by Bellarmine, the doctrinal theologian, by Baronius, the Church historian, and by Prosper Fagnanus, the learned canonist ;[5] while as champion for the

Venetian Republic stepped forth Paul Sarpi, who in this matter allowed free course to his bitter hatred against Rome.[6] It has been often asserted that he was for this cause in danger of falling 'a victim to an Ultramontane assassin.'[7] But the attempt in question was made on 5th October 1607, consequently when peace had been already restored with Rome: at that time a blow struck at Sarpi could only have been hurtful to the Papal interests instead of furthering them, for certain points of the peace desired by Rome were still under discussion. Moreover, the accounts in Siri, Thuanus, and in the relation of the Signoria to the ambassador in France do not in the least agree with the biography of Paul Sarpi, ascribed by many to P. Fulgenzio ; the place, persons, and circumstances of the conspiracy are everywhere differently given. The sentence passed by the 'Council of Ten,' October 10, 1607, on Ridolfo Poma, M. Viti, and accomplices, gives no ground for charging the Roman See or its supporters with complicity ; the evidence alleged will not bear the least investigation.[8] The Protestants took advantage of the dispute to promote their propaganda in Italy, distributing Geneva Bibles, and nourishing the opposition against the Holy See.[9] In the year following, however, absolution was given and the interdict removed upon the priests being released, the decree against the interdict retracted, and the rejected laws suspended.[10] Ranke observes : 'The points under dispute were not settled so entirely to the advantage of Venice as has been generally asserted.'[11] While the other banished religious orders were suffered to return, the Jesuits, so much dreaded by Sarpi's party, were only restored in 1657.[12]

[1] Huber, p. 56. Cf. Bluntschli, p. 68 seq.

[2] Cf. especially Muratori, Annali d' Italia, a. 1606, 1607 ; Novaës, Vitae Pontif. ix. pp. 92, 93 ; Artaud, Hist. des Souv. Pontifes, t. v. pp. 250-254 ; Natal. Alex. H. E. Cont. s. Supplem. t. ii. p. 9 seq. ; Moroni, Dizionario, v. Paolo V. t. li. p. 135 seq.

[3] Bossuet, Hist. des Variations, l. vii. n. 108, p. 447. Brunet, Vie de Guill. Bedell (chaplain to the English Embassy in Venice), pp. 9, 19, 20. Le Bret, Magazin, ii. p. 236.

[4] Bullar. t. x. p. 175. Roscovány, Monum. iii. pp. 87-90, n. 440. Goldast. t. iii. p. 282.

[5] Fagnanus, de Justitia et Validitate Censurarum Pauli V. in rempublicam Venetam, Romae, 1607.

[6] Ranke's Popes, iii. 281.   From Sarpi we have the Istoria particolare delle cose passate tra il Somno Pontefice Paolo V. e la serenissima Rep. di Venezia, Lione (Ginevra), 1624.   Vide also Lämmer, Zur Kirchengeschichte, p. 49.

[7] Huber, pp. 56, 57.   Hospinian, Lucius, and Stenius (De Facinore in M. Paulum Servitam perpetratro, Heidelb. 1608) said the same before him.

[8] Cf. Artaud, Hist. des Souverains Pontifes, t. v. Paris, 1847, p. 332, n. 2.

[9] Historisch Politische Blätter, 1852, vol. xxx. P. xii. p. 809 seq.

[10] Ranke's Popes, ii. Germ. ed. pp. 324 seq. 352.   Paul. Jov. Vita Pauli V. § 28. Bussières, Hist. de France, l. xxiii. n. 19.   Spondan. a. 1607, n. 2.   Bianchi, t. ii. l. vi. § 11, n. 1 seq. p. 610 seq.

[11] Ranke's Popes, p. 354, Germ. ed.

[12] Crétineau-Joly, l.c. pp. 141, 151.   Buss, Die Gesellschaft Jesu, pp. 973-976.

§ 20.

In the eighteenth century also 'monstrous pretensions' on the part of the Popes are alleged, and especially of Clement XI. 'When Philip V.,' says Huber, 'in order to join with Louis XIV. in a war against Austria, demanded subsidies in money from the Spanish clergy which they were quite willing to give, Clement XI. declared that the clergy might not accede to this demand without his permission.'[1]   But in this the Pope was merely standing up for a right of the Church, set forth in Decretals which had been longer in force and had a higher sanction than the claims of the Bourbon dynasty; moreover, the Pope, who was a neutral in the war of the Spanish succession, could make no such concessions to Philip V., whose possession of the throne was not then certain, without grave violation of his neutrality; as it was, Austria had vehemently attacked the Pope on the charge of partiality, and neither claimant had as yet been recognised as rightful king.[2]   . The king had already employed in the war against the emperor and his allies the Church tithes formerly granted, the revenues of the *Crociata* originally destined for the struggle against the Turks ;[3] how great would have been the scandal had the Father of Christendom, without regard to neutrality, given fresh grants of Church property for a purely political end! Until later times, the court of Madrid, according to the law then in force, recognised that the approval of the Pope was necessary to any extraordinary taxation of the clergy, already sufficiently burdened ; this may be seen in the Concordat of Sept. 26, 1737, art. 7 and 8,[4] and in the petition made and granted in 1740, for further contributions of Church property,[5] afterwards increased so as to be well-nigh intolerable.[6] It was in the reign of Charles III. (1759) that the Spanish government first claimed for itself alone the right of limiting and taxing Church property,[7] but it still for a long time continued to apply for Papal Indults for this.[8]

According to Huber,[9] the same Pope raised a tumult throughout Sicily for the sake of a few insignificant market dues, and endangered the salvation of the Sicilians for a basket of peas. Had Professor Huber read the monograph of Professor Sentis of Freiburg (the *Monarchia Sicula*),[10] were he acquainted with the discussions of the older canonists,[11] or even with the modern Piedmontese historians,[12] he would have known that though the occasion was trifling, a serious question of principle was involved, and that a crying abuse of the civil power was brought to light in this matter, of which Bauerband the jurist said : ' So ignominious a position of the Church towards the State, and one so completely incompatible with her constitution, could not long be tolerated.'[13] Our opponent must first refute the able monograph mentioned above before he can have any shadow of ground for his accusation.

[1] Huber, p. 69.

[2] Cf. the discussion in detail by the present author in the Archiv für Kath. Kirchenrecht, 1863, vol. x. p. 185 seq.

[3] Ibid. p. 188.

[4] Ibid. pp. 204-206.

[5] Moroni, Diz. v. Spagna, p. 148.

[6] Archiv, 1864, vol. xi. pp. 263, 380.

[7] Ibid. vol. xi. p. 368.

[8] Ibid. vol. xii. pp. 47, 52.

[9] Huber, p. 70.

[10] Die Monarchia Sicula. Eine historisch-canonistische Untersuchung von Dr. Fr. J. Sentis, Frieburg, 1869, especially p. 142 seq.

[11] Especially Pignatelli, Consultat. Can. t. vi. Cons. 22, n. 61 seq. p. 82 seq. Cf. t. ii. Cons. 34, n. 66 seq. p. 59 seq.

[12] Carutti, Storia del Regno di Vittorio Amadeo II. c. xix. p. 335 seq.
[13] Bonner, Theol. Literaturblatt, July 5, 1869, No. 14, p. 515 seq.
(review of Sentis); amongst other observations are the following: 'The writing of Sentis affords "proof" that in the contest raised (as to the pretended Monarchia Sicula), and in the most difficult circumstances, the Pope steadily adhered to the purely ecclesiastical view; while the Spanish and Bourbon kings, though for the most part behaving personally as pious Catholics, still had no scruple under pretext of inalienable crown privileges in making arbitrary encroachments of all sorts upon what was without question the purely spiritual domain.'

§ 21.

No mention is made of other Popes, especially of Benedict XIV., who was yielding in the extreme towards civil rulers,[1] and made great concessions in his Concordats;[2] of Clement XIV., who went still further, and even sacrificed his most faithful supporters the Jesuits to the Bourbon courts.[3] But still when it suits the purpose of our enemies the 'incontestable fact' is maintained, ' that in a decree of Clement XIV., as authentic as was ever published ex cathedrâ by any Pope, the Jesuits, nearly a hundred years ago, were suppressed and banished as a society generally pernicious.'[4] Whoever speaks thus has not read or not understood the Brief (not Bull) ' Dominus ac Redemptor ;'[5] it is so far from being a judgment ex cathedrâ, that it does not contain one judicial sentence as to the general perniciousness of the Society, while Clement XIII., in a solemn Bull, had expressed the contrary.[6] Only in order to restore the peace disturbed by the Bourbon courts, and convinced that the Society (already in fact suppressed in Portugal, France, Spain, Naples, &c.) could no longer be as useful as in former days, was it suppressed by Clement XIV. in a simple order, with a reference made to the suppression of the Templars by Clement V.[7] and to other examples, but without the slightest reference to any one of the charges brought against it by the courts. The enemies as well as the friends of the Church acknowledge that by this measure a grievous wound was inflicted upon her.

[1] Ranke's Popes, iii. p. 180, Germ. ed. Cf. Schröckh, Kirchengeschichte seit der Reform. vi. p. 436.
[2] For the convention with Sardinia, vide Carutti, Storia del Regno di

Carlo Emanuele III. Torino, 1859, vol. i. p. 151 seq., with the documents in the appendix ; on that with Spain, Archiv für Kath. Kirchenrecht, 1864, vol. xi. pp. 252, 253 ; on that with Portugal, Rigant, in Reg. ii. Canc. t. i. p. 227, n. a.; Schröckh, l.c. p. 437 seq.

³ By reëstablishing the Jesuits, Pius VII. in the Bull Sollicitudo, Aug. 7, 1814, made amends for the injustice extorted from his predecessor. But even this expiation has been put down by Huber (p. 74) in the category of Papal misdeeds. Yet the governments concerned had already, to a great extent, seen that in expelling the Jesuits they had been themselves the victims of intrigues. The Duke of Parma, as early as 1793, took steps towards the reintroduction of the Society (Crétineau-Joly, Hist. v. pp. 493-495). The Elector of Bavaria, and other Catholic princes of Germany, treated of the same matter in 1794 (Writings of the Nuncio della Genga to Pius VI. d.d. Augsburg, Nov. 9, 1794, in Boero, Osservazioni sopra l' istoria del Pontificato di Clem. XIV. Monza, 1854, vol. ii. pp. 263, 264). The ministers who brought about the suppression of the Jesuits were overthrown, and some, as Pombal (ib. pp. 223-225), were subjected to the most serious charges; in 1804, Ferdinand IV. had reëstablished the Society in Naples ; in 1815 the King of Spain did the same; in Prussia and Russia it had never been suppressed (Crétineau-Joly, l.c. pp. 509-511, 516 ; Boero, l.c. vol. i. p. 108; Theiner, Sammlung von Aktenstücken, pp. 23-27). But the injustice of the suppression is best shown by the documents published by Theiner (Histoire du Pontificat de Clément XIV.). Vide Historisch Polit. Blätter, 1854, vol. xxxiii. pp. 733-759 ; Clement XIV. Eine kritische Beleuchtung, Augsburg, 1854, p. 356.

⁴ Michelis, in the Munich September meeting, 1871 (Report, p. 216); Windthorst of Berlin, in the Reichstag, May 15, 1872 (Report, p. 392).

⁵ Bullar. Clem. XIV. pp. 607-618. Theiner, l.c. ii. pp. 358-379, t. iii. fin.

⁶ Const. Apostolicum pascendi munus, Jan. 7, 1765, Bull. Rom. Contin. t. iii. ed. Romae, 1838, p. 38 seq.

⁷ Text in the Tübingen Quartalschrift, 1866, i. pp. 56-84. Cf. Mansi, xxv. 389 seq.

§ 22.

The eighteenth century was a period of the deepest servitude and ignominy for the Catholic Church, and of indignities and insults to her Head, which reached their summit when Pius VI. was driven by force from Rome by the French Republic. The nineteenth century proved itself the heir of the eighteenth. An historian well versed in Bavarian affairs wrote in 1847 : 'If freedom of conscience is to apply to Catholics, it is impossible that this freedom should consist in their ceasing to be Catholics ; still less can it mean that they are to be Catholics in heart alone, while in their public profession, in education, in society, and in the State they are hampered, in spite of the assurances of government, by its usurpation of ecclesiastical power. Neither can it consist in a kindly acknowledgment of the power of the Church by the secular ruler and government in purely spiritual matters alone, which in fact can be no more controlled than thought, thus leaving her at best the invisible world as her field for action. But in truth liberty of conscience, which Protestants may understand to mean simply the legal interpretation of the phrase, consists for a Catholic in the enjoyment by the Church, and by himself within her, of that liberty of development which is her due from her divine foundation and from the canonical decrees, that is to say, that freedom which we (Bavarians) have one and all sworn to maintain to her.'[1] The old contest is not yet come to an end, but is ever reappearing under new conditions. The Church will content herself with what is indispensably and absolutely necessary ; but her freedom is to her above all earthly goods ; for it she will ever strive and do battle, and in this cause she will see gather round her Catholic nations in whom the spirit of freedom is still living and strong, who are not deceived by hollow phrases, who strive after the thing and not the name. 'The Church of God,' wrote St. Bernard[2] on one occasion to the German King Conrad III., 'has from the beginning been often oppressed and often set free. The arm of the Lord is not shortened, nor become powerless to save her. He will, without doubt, once again set free His Bride, whom He has redeemed with His blood, endowed with His Spirit, adorned with heavenly gifts, and moreover enriched with earthly gifts. He will set her free, I repeat He will set her free ; but if it is done by means of another hand, let the princes of the empire consider that this will be neither to the honour of the king nor to the benefit of the empire.'

[1] 'By § 1 of the last appendix but one of the constitution.' Concordat und Constitutionseid der Katholiken in Bayern, p. viii. seq.
[2] Bern. Ep. 244, c. ii. p. 441 seq.

§ 23.

The Catholic Church may perish, not indeed throughout the

whole earth but in individual lands, as happened in North Africa and in the East; the Kingdom of God may be taken from certain nations and bestowed upon others more worthy of it; but the Catholics of Germany have not as yet proved themselves an unworthy people; they are not yet enervated as were those nations; they may still hope for a better future. They feel and acknowledge that they are living in times of trial, that a gigantic war has been kindled against them, in which individuals may perish, suffer loss of earthly goods, and endure many sorts of martyrdom, but in which the Church, built upon the divine promise, can never be overcome. They do not conceal from themselves that, humanly speaking, they might almost envy the Roumanian Jews, upon whom so much tender care is bestowed by the great of this world and by diplomatists; but they know also that their firm trust is in a Divine Providence which will turn to good the very attempts of their enemies. What is now going on will not fail to have an influence and produce an impression upon our contemporaries, in whom faith is weak, and upon the noble-minded among non-Catholics. Many will admire the concord, the joyful self-devotion, and the constancy of their Catholic brethren, and when times are hardest they will see them uniting fidelity to God with fidelity to the king in the old Christian sense, maintaining openly and courageously the eternal and unchanging principles of justice and the holiest interests of mankind, but never bending the knee before the great Bel or Baal of the heathen. Such conduct will do more for the future union of Christendom than all the efforts for union based on Febronian and Jansenistic principles.

§ 24.

In that land in which the Catholic Church ceases to exist, the Christian State in these days ceases to exist also. If the Church is uprooted, all Christianity falls with her; for in her alone Christianity remains firm and undivided, a divine institution standing forth real and visible before the world. But let not those who destroy the Christian State think that with it they will destroy the Catholic Church. She will outlive their efforts, their sophistries, and their falsehoods ; and as once, when the civilisation of the ancient world was swept away by the barbarians, she gave a new life to Europe, so again, when Liberalism and Socialism, the unwelcome and disowned but most true son and heir of Liberalism, have done their evil work, she will awaken once more to life the Christian State, and bring back society from the Paganism to which it has sunk to the religion of the Cross. Then no longer will it be thought the highest wisdom to look on the State as a mere work of man resting on physical force alone, and to shut out religion as an hostile influence, till it be needed in some political extremity. Then at last the Catholic Church, so long despised, gainsaid, calumniated, while she has no cause to blush for the past, will be triumphantly justified in the present, and in the future a glorious field will be thrown open to her, when in her and through her the world is once more subdued by her Head and Defender as King of kings and Lord of lords. The Christian State, like other States, has only an earthly existence, and has no divine promise and pledge of endurance. But the Catholic Church, the work of God Incarnate, has a supernatural life, the fulness of the promises, and the most secure pledge of endurance even till the end of the world, when the state of struggle and pilgrimage shall be changed into the state of glory and triumph. And all that she knows and believes and hopes she can sum up in the words of her Spouse, who has said : ' Heaven and earth shall pass away, but My words shall not pass away.'

INDEX.

THE END.